THE COMPLETE WORKS OF ROBERT BROWNING, VOLUME XIV

Robert Browning photographed at home (19 Warwick Crescent, London) by Samuel Walker in the early 1880s. Private collection.

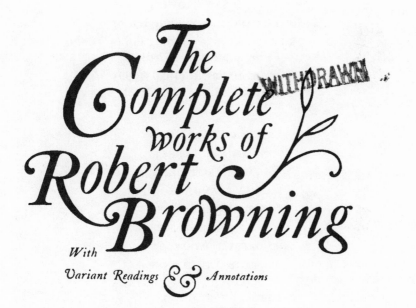

The Complete works of Robert Browning

With Variant Readings & Annotations

Volume XIV

EDITED BY

JOHN C. BERKEY
MICHAEL BRIGHT
DAVID EWBANK
PAUL D. L. TURNER

BAYLOR UNIVERSITY
WACO, TEXAS
OHIO UNIVERSITY PRESS
ATHENS, OHIO
2003

THE COMPLETE WORKS OF ROBERT BROWNING

Editorial Board

ALLAN C. DOOLEY, General Editor

SUSAN CROWL

PARK HONAN, Founding Editor

ROMA A. KING, Founding Editor
General Editor, 1967–1985

JACK W. HERRING (1925–1999)
General Editor, 1985–1999

Contributing Editors

JOHN C. BERKEY

MICHAEL BRIGHT

ASHBY BLAND CROWDER

SUSAN E. DOOLEY

DAVID EWBANK

RITA S. PATTESON

PAUL D.L. TURNER

Ohio University Press, Athens, Ohio 45701
© 2003 by Ohio University Press and Baylor University
Printed in the United States of America
All rights reserved

07 06 05 04 03   5 4 3 2 1

Ohio University Press books are printed on acid-free paper ∞ ™

Library of Congress Cataloging-in-Publication data
(Revised for vol. 14)

Browning, Robert, 1812–1889.
The complete works of Robert Browning, with variant readings & annotations.

Vol. 14 edited by John C. Berkey, Michael Bright,
David Ewbank, and Paul D. L. Turner
Includes bibliographical references and indexes.
I. King, Roma A., 1914–   , ed.
II. Title.
PR4201.K5 1969   821'.8   68-18389
ISBN 0-8214-1473-9 (v. 14)

CONTENTS

I CONTENTS

This edition of the works of Robert Browning is intended to be complete. It will comprise at least seventeen volumes and will contain:

1. The entire contents of the first editions of Browning's works, arranged in their chronological order of publication. (The poems included in *Dramatic Lyrics, Dramatic Romances and Lyrics,* and *Men and Women,* for example, appear in the order of their first publication rather than in the order in which Browning rearranged them for later publication.)

2. All prefaces and dedications which Browning is known to have written for his own works and for those of Elizabeth Barrett Browning.

3. The two prose essays that Browning is known to have published: the review of a book on Tasso, generally referred to as the "Essay on Chatterton," and the preface for a collection of letters supposed to have been written by Percy Bysshe Shelley, generally referred to as the "Essay on Shelley."

4. The front matter and the table of contents of each of the collected editions (1849, 1863, 1865, 1868 [70, 75], 1888-1889) which Browning himself saw through the press.

5. Poems published during Browning's lifetime but not collected by him.

6. Poems not published during Browning's lifetime which have come to light since his death.

7. John Forster's *Thomas Wentworth, Earl of Strafford,* to which Browning contributed significantly, though the precise extent of his contribution has not been determined.

8. Variants appearing in primary and secondary materials as defined in Section II below.

9. Textual emendations.

10. Informational and explanatory notes for each work.

II PRIMARY AND SECONDARY MATERIALS

Aside from a handful of uncollected short works, all of Browning's works but *Asolando* (1889) went through two or more editions during his lifetime. Except for *Pauline* (1833), *Strafford* (1837), and *Sordello*

(1840), all the works published before 1849 were revised and corrected for the 1849 collection. *Strafford* and *Sordello* were revised and corrected for the collection of 1863, as were all the other works in that edition. Though no further poems were added in the collection of 1865, all the works were once again corrected and revised. The 1868 collection added a revised *Pauline* and *Dramatis Personae* (1864) to the other works, which were themselves again revised and corrected. A new edition of this collection in 1870 contained further revisions, and Browning corrected his text again for an 1875 reimpression. The printing of the last edition of the *Poetical Works* over which Browning exercised control began in 1888, and the first eight volumes are dated thus on their title-pages. Volumes 9 through 16 of this first impression are dated 1889, and we have designated them 1889a to distinguish them from the second impression of all 16 volumes, which was begun and completed in 1889. Some of the earlier volumes of the first impression sold out almost immediately, and in preparation for a second impression, Browning revised and corrected the first ten volumes before he left for Italy in late August,1889. The second impression, in which all sixteen volumes bear the date 1889 on their title-pages, consisted of a revised and corrected second impression of volumes 1-10, plus a second impression of volumes 11-16 altered by Browning in one instance. This impression we term 1889 (see section III below).

Existing manuscripts and editions are classified as either primary or secondary material. The primary materials include the following:

1. The manuscript of a work when such is known to exist.

2. Proof sheets, when known to exist, that contain authorial corrections and revisions.

3. The first and subsequent editions of a work that preserve evidence of Browning's intentions and were under his control.

4. The collected editions over which Browning exercised control:

1849—*Poems.* Two Volumes. London: Chapman and Hall.

1863—*The Poetical Works.* Three Volumes. London: Chapman and Hall.

1865—*The Poetical Works.* Three Volumes. London: Chapman and Hall.

1868—*The Poetical Works.* Six Volumes. London: Smith, Elder and Company.

1870—*The Poetical Works.* Six Volumes. London: Smith, Elder and Company. This resetting constituted a new edition, which was stereotyped and reimpressed several times; the 1875 impression contains revisions by Browning.

1888-1889—*The Poetical Works.* Sixteen Volumes. London: Smith,

Elder and Company. Exists in numerous stereotype impressions, of which two are primary material:

1888-1889a—The first impression, in which volumes 1-8 are dated 1888 and volumes 9-16 are dated 1889.

1889—The corrected second impression of volumes 1-10 and a second impression of volumes 11-16 altered by Browning only as stated in section III below; all dated 1889 on the title pages.

5. The corrections in Browning's hand in the Dykes Campbell copy of 1888-1889a, and the manuscript list of corrections to that impression in the Brown University Library (see section III below).

Other materials (including some in the poet's handwriting) that affected the text are secondary. Examples are: the copy of the first edition of *Pauline* which contains annotations by Browning and John Stuart Mill; the copies of the first edition of *Paracelsus* which contain corrections in Browning's hand; a very early manuscript of *A Blot in the 'Scutcheon* which Browning presented to William Macready, but not the one from which the first edition was printed; informal lists of corrections that Browning included in letters to friends, such as the corrections to *Men and Women* he sent to D. G. Rossetti; verbal and punctuational changes Browning essayed in presentation copies of his works or in his own copies, if not used by his printers; Elizabeth Barrett's suggestions for revisions in *A Soul's Tragedy* and certain poems in *Dramatic Romances and Lyrics;* and the edition of *Strafford* by Emily Hickey for which Browning made suggestions.

The text and variant readings of this edition derive from collation of primary materials as defined above. Secondary materials are occasionally discussed in the notes and sometimes play a part when emendation is required.

III COPY-TEXT

The copy-text for this edition is Browning's final text: the first ten volumes of 1889 and the last six volumes of 1888-1889a, as described above. For this choice we offer the following explanation.

Manuscripts used as printer's copy for twenty of Browning's thirty-four book publications are known to exist; others may yet become available. These manuscripts, or, in their absence, the first editions of the works, might be considered as the most desirable copy-text. And this would be the case for an author who exercised little control over his text after the manuscript or first edition stage, or whose text clearly became corrupted in a succession of editions. To preserve the intention of such an author, one would have to choose an early text and emend it as evidence and judgment demanded.

With Browning, however, the situation is different, and our copy-text choice results from that difference. Throughout his life Browning continually revised his poetry. He did more than correct printer's errors and clarify previously intended meanings; his texts themselves remained fluid, subject to continuous alteration. As the manuscript which he submitted to his publisher was no doubt already a product of revision, so each subsequent edition under his control reflects the results of an ongoing process of creating, revising, and correcting. If we were to choose the manuscript (where extant) or first edition as copy-text, preserving Browning's intention would require extensive emendation to capture the additions, revisions, and alterations which Browning demonstrably made in later editions. By selecting Browning's final corrected text as our copy-text, emending it only to eliminate errors and the consequences of changing house-styling, we present his works in the form closest to that which he intended after years of revision and polishing.

But this is true only if Browning in fact exercised extensive control over the printing of his various editions. That he intended and attempted to do so is apparent in his comments and his practice. In 1855, demanding accuracy from the printers, he pointed out to his publisher Chapman, "I attach importance to the mere stops . . ." (DeVane and Knickerbocker, p. 83). There is evidence of his desire to control the details of his text as early as 1835, in the case of *Paracelsus*. The *Paracelsus* manuscript, now in the Forster and Dyce collection in the Victoria and Albert Museum Library, demonstrates a highly unconventional system of punctuation. Of particular note is Browning's unrestrained use of dashes, often in strings of two or three, instead of more precise or orthodox punctuation marks. It appears that this was done for its rhetorical effect. One sheet of Part 1 of the manuscript and all but the first and last sheets of Part 3 have had punctuation revised in pencil by someone other than Browning, perhaps J. Riggs, whose name appears three times in the margins of Part 3. In addition to these revisions, there are analogous punctuation revisions (in both pencil and ink) which appear to be in Browning's hand, and a few verbal alterations obviously in the poet's script.

A collation of the first edition (1835) with the manuscript reveals that a major restyling of punctuation was carried out before *Paracelsus* was published. However, the revisions incorporated into the first edition by no means slavishly follow the example set by the pencilled revisions of Parts 1 and 3 of the manuscript. Apparently the surviving manuscript was not used as printer's copy for the first edition. Browning may have submitted a second manuscript, or he may have revised extensively in proof. The printers may have carried out the revisions to punctuation, with or without the poet's point by point involvement. With the present evidence, we cannot be conclusive about the extent of Browning's control over the first edition of *Paracelsus*. It can be stated, however, in the light of the incompleteness of the pencilled revisions and the frequent lack or correspondence between the pencilled revisions and the lines as printed in 1835, that Browning himself may have been responsible for the punctuation of the first edition of *Paracelsus*. Certainly he was responsible for the frequent instances in the first and subsequent editions where the punctuation defies conventional rules, as in the following examples:

> What though
> It be so?—if indeed the strong desire
> Eclipse the aim in me—if splendour break
> (Part I, ll. 329-331)

> I surely loved them—that last night, at least,
> When we . . . gone! gone! the better: I am saved
> (Part II, ll. 132-133)

> Of the body, even,)—what God is, what we are,
> (Part V, l. 642, 1849 reading)

The manuscripts of *Colombe's Birthday* (1844) and *Christmas-Eve and Easter-Day* (1850) were followed very carefully in the printing of the first editions. There are slight indications of minor house-styling, such as the spellings *colour* and *honour* for the manuscripts' *color* and *honor*. But the unorthodox punctuation, used to indicate elocutionary and rhetorical subtleties as well as syntactical relationships, is carried over almost unaltered from the manuscripts to the first editions. Similar evidence of Browning's painstaking attention to the smallest details in the printing of his poems can be seen in the manuscript and proof sheets of *The Ring and the Book* (1868-69). These materials reveal an interesting and significant pattern. It appears that Browning wrote swiftly, giving primary attention to wording and less to punctuation, being satisfied to use dashes to indicate almost any break in thought, syntax, or rhythm. Later, in the proof sheets for Books 1-6 of the poem and in the manuscript itself for Books 7-12, he changed the dashes to more specific and purposeful punctuation marks. The revised punctuation is what was printed, for the most part, in the first edition of *The Ring and the Book*; what further revisions there are conform to Browning's practice, though hardly to standard rules. Clearly Browning was in control of nearly every aspect of the published form of his works, even to the "mere stops."

Of still greater importance in our choice of copy-text is the substantial evidence that Browning took similar care with his collected editions. Though he characterized his changes for later editions as trivial and few in number, collations reveal thousands of revisions and corrections in each successive text. *Paracelsus,* for example, was extensively revised for the 1849 *Poems;* it was again reworked for the *Poetical Works* of 1863. *Sordello,* omitted in 1849, reappeared in 1863 with 181 new lines and short marginal glosses; Browning admitted only that it was "corrected *throughout*" (DeVane and Knickerbocker, p. 157). The poems of *Men and Women* (1855) were altered in numerous small but meaningful ways for both the 1863 and 1865 editions of the *Poetical Works* (see Allan C. Dooley, "The Textual Significance of Robert Browning's 1865 *Poetical Works,*" *PBSA* 71 [1977], 212-18). Michael Hancher cites evidence of the poet's close supervision of the 1868 collected edition ("Browning and the *Poetical Works* of 1888-1889," *Browning Newsletter,* Spring, 1971, 25-27), and Michael Meredith has traced Browning's attentions to his text in the 1870 edition and an 1875 reimpression of it ("Learning's Crabbed Text," *SBHC* 13 [1985], 97-107); another perspective is offered in Allan C. Dooley's *Author and Printer in Victorian England* (1992), Ch. 4-5. Mrs. Orr, writing of the same period in Browning's life, reports his resentment of those who garbled his text by misplacing his stops (*Life,* pp. 357-58).

There is plentiful and irrefutable evidence that Browning controlled, in the same meticulous way, the text of his last collected edition, that which we term 1888-1889. Hancher has summarized the relevant information:

> The evidence is clear that Browning undertook the 1888-1889 edition of his *Poetical Works* intent on controlling even the smallest minutiae of the text. Though he at one time considered supplying biographical and explanatory notes to the poems, he finally decided against such a scheme, concluding, in his letter to Smith of 12 November 1887, "I am correcting them carefully, and *that* must suffice." On 13 January 1888, he wrote, regarding the six-volume edition of his collected works published in 1868 which was to serve as the printer's copy for the final edition: "I have thoroughly corrected the six volumes of the Works, and can let you have them at once." . . . Browning evidently kept a sharp eye on the production of all sixteen of the volumes, including those later volumes. . . . Browning returned proof for Volume 3 on 6 May 1888, commenting, "I have had, as usual, to congratulate myself on

the scrupulous accuracy of the Printers"; on 31 December he returned proofs of Volume 11, "corrected carefully"; and he returned "the corrected Proofs of Vol. XV" on 1 May 1889.

Throughout his long career, then, Browning continuously revised and corrected his works. Furthermore, his publishers took care to follow his directions exactly, accepting his changes and incorporating them into each successive edition. This is not to say that no one else had any effect whatsoever on Browning's text: Elizabeth Barrett made suggestions for revisions to *A Soul's Tragedy* and *Dramatic Romances and Lyrics*. Browning accepted some suggestions and rejected others, and those which he accepted we regard as his own. Mrs. Orr reports that Browning sent proof sheets to Joseph Milsand, a friend in France, for corrections (*Life*, p. 183), and that Browning accepted suggestions from friends and readers for the corrections of errors in his printed works. In some of the editions, there are slight evidences of minor house-styling in capitalization and the indication of quotations. But the evidence of Browning's own careful attention to revisions and corrections in both his manuscripts and proof sheets assures us that other persons played only a very minor role in the development of his text. We conclude that the vast majority of the alterations in the texts listed above as Primary Materials are Browning's own, and that only Browning's final corrected text, the result of years of careful work by the poet himself, reflects his full intentions.

The first impression of Browning's final collected edition (i.e., 1888-1889a) is not in and of itself the poet's final corrected text. By the spring of 1889 some of the early volumes of the first impression were already sold out, and by mid-August it was evident that a new one would be required. About this time James Dykes Campbell, Honorary Secretary of the London Browning Society, was informed by Browning that he was making further corrections to be incorporated into the new impression. According to Dykes Campbell, Browning had corrected the first ten volumes and offered to transcribe the corrections into Dykes Campbell's copy of 1888-1889a before leaving for Italy. The volumes altered in Browning's hand are now in the British Library and contain on the flyleaf of Volume I Dykes Campbell's note explaining precisely what happened. Of course, Dykes Campbell's copy was not the one used by the printer for the second impression. Nevertheless, these changes are indisputably Browning's and are those which, according to his own statement, he proposed to make in the new impression. This set of corrections carries, therefore, great authority.

Equally authoritative is a second set of corrections, also in Browning's hand, for part of 1888-1889a. In the poet's possession at the time of his death, this handwritten list was included in lot 179 of Sotheby, Wilkinson, and Hodge's auction of Browning materials in 1913; it is today located in the Brown University Library. The list contains corrections only to Volumes 4-10 of 1888-1889a. We know that Browning, on 26 July 1889, had completed and sent to Smith "the corrections for Vol. III in readiness for whenever you need them." By the latter part of August, according to Dykes Campbell, the poet had finished corrections for Volumes 1-10. Browning left for Italy on 29 August. The condition of the Brown University list does not indicate that it was ever used by the printer. Thus we surmise that the Brown list (completing the corrections through volume 10) may be the poet's copy of another list sent to his publisher. Whatever the case, the actual documents used by the printers—a set of marked volumes or handwritten lists—are not known to exist. A possible exception is a marked copy of *Red Cotton Night-Cap Country* (now in the Berg Collection of the New York Public Library) which seems to have been used by printers. Further materials used in preparing Browning's final edition may yet appear.

The matter is complicated further because neither set of corrections of 1888-1889a corresponds exactly to each other nor to the 1889 second impression. Each set contains corrections the other omits, and in a few cases the sets present alternative corrections of the same error. Our study of the Dykes Campbell copy of 1888-1889a reveals fifteen discrepancies between its corrections and the 1889 second impression. The Brown University list, which contains far fewer corrections, varies from the second impression in thirteen instances. Though neither of these sets of corrections was used by the printers, both are authoritative; we consider them legitimate textual variants, and record them as such. The lists are, of course, useful when emendation of the copy-text is required.

The value of the Dykes Campbell copy of 1888-1889a and the Brown University list is not that they render Browning's text perfect. The corrections to 1888-1889a must have existed in at least one other, still more authoritative form: the documents which Browning sent to his publisher. That this is so is indicated by the presence of required corrections in the second impression which neither the Dykes Campbell copy nor the Brown University list calls for. The significance of the existing sets of corrections is that they clearly indicate two important points: Browning's direct and active interest in the preparation of a corrected second impression of his final collected edition; and, given the high degree of correspondence between the two sets of corrections and the affected lines of the second impression, the concern of the printers to follow the poet's directives.

The second impression of 1888-1889 incorporated most of Browning's corrections to the first ten volumes of the first impression. There is no evidence whatever that any corrections beyond those which Browning sent to his publisher in the summer of 1889 were ever made. We choose, therefore, the 1889 corrected second impression of volumes 1-10 as copy-text for the works in those volumes. Corrections to the first impression were achieved by cutting the affected letters or punctuation out of the stereotype plates and pressing or soldering in the correct pieces of type. The corrected plates were then used for many copies, without changing the date on the title pages (except, of course, in volumes 17 [*Asolando*] and 18 [*New Poems*], added to the set by the publishers in 1894 and 1914 respectively). External evidence from publishers' catalogues and the advertisements bound into some volumes of 1889 indicate that copies of this impression were produced as late as 1913, although the dates on the title pages of volumes 1-16 remained 1889. Extensive plate deterioration is characteristic of the later copies, and use of the Hinman collator on early and late examples of 1889 reveals that the inserted corrections were somewhat fragile, some of them having decayed or disappeared entirely as the plates aged. (See Allan C. Dooley, "Browning's *Poetical Works* of 1888-1889," *SBHC* 7:1 [1978], 43-69.)

We do not use as copy-text volumes 11-16 of 1889, because there is no present evidence indicating that Browning exercised substantial control over this part of the second impression of 1888-1889. We do know that he made one correction, which he requested in a letter to Smith quoted by Hancher:

> I have just had pointed out to [me] that an error, I supposed corrected, still is to be found in the 13th Volume—(Aristophanes' Apology) page 143, line 9, where the word should be Opora—without an i. I should like it altered, if that may be possible.

This correction was indeed made in the second impression. Our collations of copies of volumes 11-16 of 1889a and 1889 show no other intentional changes. The later copies do show, however, extensive type batter, numerous scratches, and irregular inking. Therefore our copy-text for the works in the last six volumes of 1888-1889 is volumes 11-16 of 1888-1889a.

IV VARIANTS

In this edition we record, with a very few exceptions discussed below, all variants from the copy-text appearing in the manuscripts and in the editions under Browning's control. Our purpose in doing this is two-fold.

1. We enable the reader to reconstruct the text of a work as it stood at the various stages of its development.

2. We provide the materials necessary to an understanding of how Browning's growth and development as an artist are reflected in his successive revisions to his works.

As a consequence of this policy our variant listings inevitably contain some variants that were not created by Browning; printer's errors and readings that may result from house-styling will appear occasionally. But the evidence that Browning assumed responsibility for what was printed, and that he considered and used unorthodox punctuation as part of his meaning, is so persuasive that we must record even the smallest and oddest variants. The following examples, characteristic of Browning's revisions, illustrate the point:

> *Pauline*, l. 700:
> 1833: I am prepared—I have made life my own—
> 1868: I am prepared: I have made life my own.
> "Evelyn Hope," l. 41:
> 1855: I have lived, I shall say, so much since then,
> 1865: I have lived (I shall say) so much since then,
> "Bishop Blougram's Apology," l. 267:
> 1855: That's the first cabin-comfort I secure—
> 1865: That's the first-cabin comfort I secure:
> *The Ring and the Book*, Book 11 ("Guido"), l. 1064:
> 1869: What if you give up boys' and girls' fools'-play
> 1872: What if you give up boy and girl fools'-play
> 1889a: What if you give up boy-and-girl-fools' play

We have concluded that Browning himself is nearly always responsible for such changes. But even if he only accepted these changes (rather than originating them), their effect on syntax, rhythm, and meaning is so significant that they must be recorded in our variant listings.

The only variants we do not record are those which strongly appear to result from systematic house-styling. For example, Browning nowhere indicated that he wished to use typography to influence meaning, and our inference is that any changes in line-spacing, depth of paragraph indentation, and the like, were the responsibility of the printers of the various editions, not the poet himself. House-styling was also very probably the cause of certain variants in the apparatus of Browning's plays, including variants in stage directions which involve a change only in manner of statement, such as *Enter Hampden* instead of

Hampden enters; variants in the printing of stage directions, such as *Aside* instead of *aside,* or [*Aside.*] instead of [*Aside*], or [*Strafford.*] instead of [*Strafford*]; variants in character designations, such as *Lady Carlisle* instead of *Car* or *Carlisle.* Browning also accepted current convention for indicating quotations (see section V below). Neither do we list changes in type face (except when used for emphasis), nor the presence or absence of a period at the end of the title of a work.

V ALTERATIONS TO THE COPY-TEXT

We have rearranged the sequence of works in the copy-text, so that they appear in the order of their first publication. This process involves the restoration to the original order of the poems included in *Dramatic Lyrics, Dramatic Romances and Lyrics,* and *Men and Women.* We realize, of course, that Browning himself was responsible for the rearrangement of these poems in the various collected editions; in his prefatory note for the 1888-1889 edition, however, he indicates that he desired a chronological presentation:

> The poems that follow are again, as before, printed in chronological order; but only so far as proves compatible with the prescribed size of each volume, which necessitates an occasional change in the distribution of its contents.

We would like both to indicate Browning's stated intentions about the placement of his poems and to present the poems in the order which suggests Browning's development as a poet. We have chosen, therefore, to present the poems in order of their first publication, with an indication in the notes as to their respective subsequent placement. We also include the tables of contents of the editions listed as Primary Materials above.

We have regularized or modernized the copy-text in the following minor ways:

1. We do not place a period at the end of the title of a work, though the copy-text does.

2. In some of Browning's editions, including the copy-text, the first word of each work is printed in capital letters. We have used the modern practice of capitalizing only the first letter.

3. The inconsistent use of both an ampersand and the word *and* has been regularized to the use of *and.*

4. We have eliminated the space between the two parts of a contraction; thus the copy-text's *it 's* is printed as *it's,* for example.

5. We uniformly place periods and commas within closing quotation marks.

6. We have employed throughout the modern practice of indicating quoted passages with quotation marks only at the beginning and end of the quotation. Throughout Browning's career, no matter which publisher or printer was handling his works, this matter was treated very inconsistently. In some of the poet's manuscripts and in most of his first editions, quotations are indicated by quotation marks only at the beginning and end. In the collected editions of 1863 and 1865, issued by Chapman and Hall, some quoted passages have quotation marks at the beginning of each line of the quotation, while others follow modern practice. In Smith, Elder's collected editions of 1868 and 1888-1889, quotation marks usually appear at the beginning of each line of a quotation. We have regularized and modernized what seems a matter of house-styling in both copy-text and variants.

The remaining way in which the copy-text is altered is by emendation. Our policy is to emend the copy-text to eliminate apparent errors of either Browning or his printers. It is evident that Browning did make errors and overlook mistakes, as shown by the following example from "One Word More," the last poem in *Men and Women*. Stanza sixteen of the copy-text opens with the following lines:

> What, there's nothing in the moon noteworthy?
> Nay: for if that moon could love a mortal,
> Use, to charm him (so to fit a fancy,
> All her magic ('tis the old sweet mythos)
> She . . .

Clearly the end punctuation in the third line is incorrect. A study of the various texts is illuminating. Following are the readings of the line in each of the editions for which Browning was responsible:

MS:	fancy)	1855:	fancy)	1865:	fancy)	1888:	fancy
P:	fancy)	1863:	fancy)	1868:	fancy)	1889:	fancy,

The omission of one parenthesis in 1888 was almost certainly a printer's error. Browning, in the Dykes Campbell copy corrections to 1888-1889a, missed or ignored the error. However, in the Brown University list of corrections, he indicated that *fancy* should be followed by a comma. This is the way the line appears in the corrected second impression of Volume 4, but the correction at best satisfies the demands of syntax only partially. Browning might have written the line:

> Use, to charm him, so to fit a fancy,

or, to maintain parallelism between the third and fourth lines:

> Use, to charm him (so to fit a fancy),

or he might simply have restored the earlier reading. Oversights of this nature demand emendation, and our choice would be to restore the punctuation of the manuscript through 1868. All of our emendations will be based, as far as possible, on the historical collation of the passage involved, the grammatical demands of the passage in context, and the poet's treatment of other similar passages. Fortunately, the multiple editions of most of the works provide the editor with ample textual evidence to make an informed and useful emendation.

All emendations to the copy-text are listed at the beginning of the Editorial Notes for each work. The variant listings for the copy-text also incorporate the emendations, which are preceded and followed there by the symbol indicating an editor's note.

VI APPARATUS

1. *Variants.* In presenting the variants from the copy-text, we list at the bottom of each page readings from the known manuscripts, proof sheets of the editions when we have located them, and the first and subsequent editions.

A variant is generally preceded and followed by a pickup and a drop word (example a). No note terminates with a punctuation mark unless the punctuation mark comes at the end of the line; if a variant drops or adds a punctuation mark, the next word is added (example b). If the normal pickup word has appeared previously in the same line, the note begins with the word preceding it. If the normal drop word appears subsequently in the line, the next word is added (example c). If a capitalized pickup word occurs within the line, it is accompanied by the preceding word (example d). No pickup or drop words, however, are used for any variant consisting of an internal change, for example a hyphen in a compounded word, an apostrophe, a tense change or a spelling change (example e). A change in capitalization within a line of poetry will be preceded by a pickup word, for which, within an entry containing other variants, the < > is suitable (example f). No drop word is used when the variant comes at the end of a line (example g).

a. ⁶¹¹| *1840*:but that appeared   *1863*:but this appeared
b. variant at end of line: ¹⁰⁹| *1840*:intrigue:"   *1863*:intrigue.
   variant within line: ⁸²| *1840*:forests like   *1863*:forests, like
c. ¹³²| *1840*:too sleeps; but   *1863*:too sleeps: but   ⁷⁷| *1840*:that night
   by   *1863*:that, night by night,   *1888*:by night
d. ²⁹⁵| *1840*:at Padua to repulse the   *1863*:at Padua who repulsed the
e. ²⁸⁴| *1840*:are   *1863*:were
   ³⁴⁴| *1840*:dying-day,   *1863*:dying day,
f. capitalization change with no other variants: ⁷⁴¹| *1840*:
   retaining Will,   *1863*:will,
   with other variants: ⁸⁴³| *1840*:Was < > Him back! Why   *1863*:Is
   < > back!" Why   *1865*:him
g. ⁴²⁷| *1840*:dregs: *1863*:dregs.

Each recorded variant will be assumed to be incorporated in the next edition if there is no indication otherwise. This rule applies even in cases where the only change occurs in 1888-1889, although it means that the variant note duplicates the copy-text. A variant listing, then, traces the history of a line and brings it forward to the point where it matches the copy-text.

With regard to manuscript readings, our emphasis is on the textual development and sequence of revisions; visual details of the manuscripts are kept to a minimum. For economy of space, we use formulae such as §crossed out and replaced above by§, but these often cannot report fine details such as whether, when two words were crossed out, the accompanying punctuation was precisely cancelled also. Our MS entries provide enough information to reconstruct with reasonable accuracy B's initial and revised manuscript readings, but they cannot substitute for direct scrutiny of the documents themselves.

It should be noted that we omit drop words in manuscript entries where the final reading is identical to the printed editions—thus

MS:Silence, and all that ghastly §crossed out and replaced above by§ tinted pageant, base
Printed editions: Silence, and all that tinted pageant, base

is entered as

MS:that ghastly §crossed out and replaced above by§ tinted

in our variant listings.

An editor's note always refers to the single word or mark of punctuation immediately preceding or following the comment, unless otherwise specified.

In Browning's plays, all character designations which happen to occur in variant listings are standardized to the copy-text reading. In listing variants in the plays, we ignore character designations unless the designation comes within a numbered line. In such a case, the character designation is treated as any other word, and can be used as a pickup or drop word. When a character designation is used as a pickup word, however, the rule excluding capitalized pickup words (except at the beginning of a line) does not apply, and we do not revert to the next earliest uncapitalized pickup word.

2. *Line numbers*. Poetic lines are numbered in the traditional manner, taking one complete poetic line as one unit of counting. In prose passages the unit of counting is the type line of this edition.

3. *Table of signs in variant listings*. We have avoided all symbols and signs used by Browning himself. The following is a table of the signs used in the variant notes:

§ . . . §	Editor's note
< >	Words omitted
/	Line break
/ / , / / / , . . .	Line break plus one or more lines without internal variants

4 *Annotations*. In general principle, we have annotated proper names, phrases that function as proper names, and words or groups of words the full meaning of which requires factual, historical, or literary background. Thus we have attempted to hold interpretation to a minimum, although we realize that the act of selection itself is to some extent interpretive.

Notes, particularly on historical figures and events, tend to fullness and even to the tangential and unessential. As a result, some of the information provided may seem unnecessary to the scholar. On the other hand, it is not possible to assume that all who use this edition are fully equipped to assimilate unaided all of Browning's copious literary, historical, and mythological allusions. Thus we have directed our efforts toward a diverse audience.

TABLES

1. *Manuscripts*. We have located manuscripts for the following of Browning's works; the list is chronological.

Paracelsus
    Forster and Dyce Collection,
    Victoria and Albert Museum, London
Colombe's Birthday
    New York Public Library
Christmas-Eve and Easter-Day
    Forster and Dyce Collection,
    Victoria and Albert Museum, London
"Love Among the Ruins"
    Lowell Collection,
    Houghton Library, Harvard University
"The Twins"
    Pierpont Morgan Library, New York
"One Word More"
    Pierpont Morgan Library, New York
"James Lee's Wife," ll. 244-69
    Armstrong Browning Library, Baylor University
"May and Death"
    Armstrong Browning Library, Baylor University
"A Face"
    Armstrong Browning Library, Baylor University
Dramatis Personae
    Pierpont Morgan Library, New York
The Ring and the Book
    British Library, London
Balaustion's Adventure
    Balliol College Library, Oxford
Prince Hohenstiel-Schwangau
    Balliol College Library, Oxford
Fifine at the Fair
    Balliol College Library, Oxford
Red Cotton Night-Cap Country
    Balliol College Library, Oxford
Aristophanes' Apology
    Balliol College Library, Oxford
The Inn Album
    Balliol College Library, Oxford
Of Pacchiarotto, and How He Worked in Distemper
    Balliol College Library, Oxford
"Hervé Riel"
    Pierpont Morgan Library, New York

The Agamemnon of Aeschylus
    Balliol College Library, Oxford
La Saisiaz and The Two Poets of Croisic
    Balliol College Library, Oxford
Dramatic Idylls
    Balliol College Library, Oxford
Dramatic Idylls, Second Series
    Balliol College Library, Oxford
Jocoseria
    Balliol College Library, Oxford
Ferishtah's Fancies
    Balliol College Library, Oxford
Parleyings With Certain People of Importance in Their Day
    Balliol College Library, Oxford
Asolando
    Pierpont Morgan Library, New York

We have been unable to locate manuscripts for the following works, and request that persons with information about any of them communicate with us.

Pauline   *The Return of the Druses*
Strafford   *A Blot in the 'Scutcheon*
Sordello   *Dramatic Romances and Lyrics*
Pippa Passes   *Luria*
King Victor and King Charles   *A Soul's Tragedy*
"Essay on Chatterton"   "Essay on Shelley"
Dramatic Lyrics   *Men and Women*

2. *Editions referred to in Volume XIV.* The following editions have been used in preparing the text and variants presented in this volume. The dates given below are used as symbols in the variant listings at the foot of each page.

1877   *The Agamemnon of Æschylus.*
            London: Smith, Elder and Company.

1878   *La Saisiaz* and *The Two Poets of Croisic.*
            London: Smith, Elder and Company.

1879   *Dramatic Idyls.*
            First Edition. London: Smith, Elder and Company.

1882   *Dramatic Idyls, First Series.*
          Second Edition. London: Smith, Elder and Company.

1889a   *The Poetical Works.*
          Volumes 9-16. London: Smith, Elder and Company.

   3. *Short titles and abbreviations.* The following short forms of reference have been used in the Editorial Notes:

ABL	Armstrong Browning Library, Baylor University, Waco, TX
ADP	*Aeschylus: Agamemnon,* ed. J. D. Denniston and Denys Page. Oxford, 1957.
AEP	F. A. Paley. *Aeschylus Translated into English Prose.* Cambridge, 1864.
AF	*Aeschylus: Agamemnon,* ed. Eduard Fraenkel. 3 Vols. Oxford, 1950.
AL	*Agamemnon,* in *Aeschylus,* Vol. 3 (Loeb Classical Library), ed. and tr. H. W. Smyth. Cambridge, MA and London, 1926.
AP	*Agamemnon,* in *Tragedies of Aeschylus, Re-edited by F. A. Paley,* 3rd ed. London, 1870.
AW	*Agamemnon,* in *Aeschyli Tragoediae Recensuit C. H. Weise.* Leipsig, 1843.
B	Browning
Broughton	L. N. Broughton, C. S. Northup, and R. Pearsall. *Robert Browning: A Bibliography, 1830-1950.* Ithaca, NY, 1953.
BSN	*Browning Society Notes*
Bunyan	*The Pilgrim's Progress.* London, 1987.
DeVane and Knickerbocker	*New Letters of Robert Browning,* ed. W. C. DeVane and K. L. Knickerbocker. New Haven, CT, 1950.
Correspondence	*The Brownings' Correspondence,* ed. P. Kelley and R. Hudson. Winfield, KS, 1984-.
DeVane, *Hbk.*	W. C. DeVane. *A Browning Handbook,* 2nd ed. New York, 1955.
EBB	Elizabeth Barrett Browning
Hood	*Letters of Robert Browning Collected by Thomas J. Wise,* ed. T. L.Hood. New Haven, CT, 1933.
Irvine and Honan	W. Irvine and P. Honan. *The Book, the Ring, and the Poet.* New York, 1974.

Liddell and Scott, 1871	*A Lexicon , Abridged from Liddell and Scott's Greek-English* 1871 *Lexicon,* comp. H. G. Liddell and R. Scott, et al. Oxford, 1871.
Liddell and Scott, 1996	*A Greek-English Lexicon,* comp. H. G. Liddell and R. Scott, rev. 1996 Sir H. S. Jones. Oxford, 1996.
McAleer	*Learned Lady: Letters from Robert Browning to Mrs. Thomas FitzGerald 1876-1889,* ed. Edward C. McAleer. Cambridge, MA, 1966.
OED	*The Oxford English Dictionary,* 2nd ed. Oxford, 1989.
Orr, *Hbk.*	Mrs. Sutherland Orr. *A Handbook to the Works of Robert Browning.* 6th ed. London, 1892.
Orr, *Life*	Mrs. Sutherland Orr. *Life and Letters of Robert Browning.* 2nd ed. London, 1891.
Reconstruction	*The Browning Collections, a Reconstruction, with Other Memorabilia,* comp. P. Kelley and B. A. Coley. Waco, TX; New York; Winfield, KS, and London, 1984.
Scholia	*Scholia in Agamemnon,* in *Aeschyli Tragoediea Quae Supersunt, Recensuit C. G. Schütz.* Halae, 1821.

Citations and quotations from the Bible refer to the King James Version unless otherwise specified.

Citations and quotations from Shakespeare refer to T*he Riverside Shakespeare,* 2nd ed., ed. G. B. Evans, et al., Boston, 1997.

ACKNOWLEDGMENTS

For providing services and money which have made it possible
for us to prepare this volume, the following institutions have our grat-
itude: Baylor University; the Director and staff of the Armstrong
Browning Library; the Kent State University Research Council, De-
partment of English, and Institute for Bibliography and Editing; and
the Ohio University Press.

For making available to us materials under their care we thank
the Armstrong Browning Library, Baylor University; the Balliol Col-
lege Library, the Bodleian Library, the English Faculty Library, and
Sackler Library, all of Oxford University; the Victoria and Albert Mu-
seum Library; the London Library; Penelope Bulloch, Librarian of
Balliol; Cl. Ch. Hémon, Musées Départementaux de Loire-Atlantique
Musée Dobrée, Nantes.

For scholarly assistance in preparing this volume, we particularly
thank the following: Nancy Birk, Philip Kelley, Liza Picard, S. W. Reid,
Alan Tadiello.

THE AGAMEMNON OF ÆSCHYLUS

Text edited by John C. Berkey
Annotations by Paul D. L. Turner

LA SAISIAZ and THE TWO POETS OF CROISIC

Edited by Michael Bright

DRAMATIC IDYLS, FIRST SERIES

Edited by David Ewbank

THE AGAMEMNON OF ÆSCHYLUS

Text edited by John C. Berkey
Annotations by Paul D. L. Turner

THE AGAMEMNON OF ÆSCHYLUS

Title| MS:Agamemnon translated by Robert Browning   *CP1877:* THE AGAMEMNON
of ÆSCHYLUS / TRANSCRIBED BY ROBERT BROWNING   *1889a:* THE
AGAMEMNON OF ÆSCHYLUS

May I be permitted to chat a little, by way of recreation, at the end of a somewhat toilsome and perhaps fruitless adventure?

If, because of the immense fame of the following Tragedy, I wished to acquaint myself with it, and could only do so by the help of a translator, I should require him to be literal at every cost save that of absolute violence to our language. The use of certain allowable constructions which, happening to be out of daily favour, are all the more appropriate to archaic workmanship, is no violence: but I would be tolerant for once,—in the case of so immensely famous an original,—of even a clumsy attempt to furnish me with the very turn of each phrase in as Greek a fashion as English will bear: while, with respect to amplifications and embellishments,—anything rather than, with the good farmer, experience that most signal of mortifications, "to gape for Æschylus and get Theognis." I should especially decline,—what may appear to brighten up a passage,—the employment of a new word for some old one—πόνος, or μέγας, or τέλος, with its congeners, recurring four times in three lines: for though such substitution may be in itself perfectly justifiable, yet this exercise of ingenuity ought to be within the competence of the unaided English reader if he likes to show himself ingenious. Learning Greek teaches Greek, and nothing else: certainly not common sense, if that have failed to precede the teaching. Further,—if I obtained a mere strict bald version of thing by thing, or at least word pregnant with thing, I should hardly look for an impossible transmission of the reputed magniloquence and sonority of the

---

§MS in Balliol College Library, *P1877, CP1877, 1877, 1889a*. For description of texts see Editorial Notes and Table of Editions§
[1]| MS:recreation at   *P1877*:recreation, at   [5]| MS:at all §crossed out and replaced above by§ every   [8]| MS:appropriate in §crossed out and replaced above by§ to
[13]| MS:mortifications—"to   *P1877*:mortifications, "to   [14]| MS:Theognis!" Esp §crossed out§ I   *P1877*:Theognis." I   [16]| one—πόνος or < > τέλος < > congeners recurring   *P1877*:one—πόνος, or < > τέλος, < > congeners, recurring   [20]| MS:teaches Greek and   *P1877*:teaches Greek, and   [21]| MS:commonsense   *P1877*:common sense

25 Greek; and this with the less regret, inasmuch as there is abundant musicality elsewhere, but nowhere else than in his poem the ideas of the poet. And lastly, when presented with these ideas, I should expect the result to prove very hard reading indeed if it were meant to resemble Æschylus, ξυμβαλεῖν οὐ ῥᾴδιος, "not easy to understand," in the opin-
30 ion of his stoutest advocate among the ancients; while, I suppose, even modern scholarship sympathizes with that early declaration of the redoubtable Salmasius, when, looking about for an example of the truly obscure for the benefit of those who found obscurity in the sacred books, he protested that this particular play leaves them all behind in
35 this respect, with their "Hebraisms, Syriasms, Hellenisms, and the whole of such bag and baggage."[1] For, over and above the purposed ambiguity of the Chorus, the text is sadly corrupt, probably interpolated, and certainly mutilated; and no unlearned person enjoys the scholar's privilege of trying his fancy upon each obstacle whenever he
40 comes to a stoppage, and effectually clearing the way by suppressing what seems to lie in it.

All I can say for the present performance is, that I have done as I would be done by, if need were. Should anybody, without need, honour my translation by a comparison with the original, I beg him to ob-
45 serve that, following no editor exclusively, I keep to the earlier readings so long as sense can be made out of them, but disregard, I hope, little of importance in recent criticism so far as I have fallen in with it. Fortunately, the poorest translation, provided only it be faithful,—

---

[1] "Quis Æschylum possit affirmare Græce nunc scienti magis patere explicabilem quam Evangelia aut Epistolas Apostolicas? Unus ejus Agamemnon obscuritate superat quantum est librorum sacrorum cum suis Hebraismis et Syriasmis et tota Hellenisticæ supellectili vel farragine."

SALMASIUS *de Hellenistica*, Epist. Dedic.

25| MS:Greek, and that §crossed out and replaced above by§ this < > MS:regret §word crossed out§ inasmuch < > abundance §altered to§ abundant of §crossed out§ *P1877:*Greek; and < > regret, inasmuch 29| MS:ξυμβαλεῖν"hard §crossed out and replaced above by§ not easy *1889a:*ξυμβαλειν §emended to§ ξυμβαλεῖν §see Editorial Notes§ 30| MS:ancients: while I suppose, that §crossed out and replaced in margin by§ even *P1877:*ancients; while 33| MS:Sacred *P1877:*sacred 34| MS:Books, he protested §last two words inserted above§ *P1877:*books, 35| MS:respect, "Hebraisms *P1877:*respect, with their "Hebraisms 38| MS:mutilated: and what unlearned *P1877:*mutilated; and no unlearned 39| MS:upon the §crossed out and replaced above by§ each 40-41| MS:and effectually §inserted above§ < > suppressing it? *P1877:*suppressing what seems to lie in it. 47| MS:have obs §crossed out§ fallen

Footnote MS:Quis < > farragine. *P1877:*"Quis < > farragine. *1889a:*farragine."

though it reproduce all the artistic confusion of tenses, moods, and persons, with which the original teems,—will not only suffice to display what an eloquent friend maintains to be the all-in-all of poetry—"the action of the piece"—but may help to illustrate his assurance that "the Greeks are the highest models of expression, the unapproached masters of the grand style: their expression is so excellent because it is so admirably kept in its right degree of prominence, because it is so simple and so well subordinated, because it draws its force directly from the pregnancy of the matter which it conveys . . . not a word wasted, not a sentiment capriciously thrown in, stroke on stroke!"[1] So may all happen!

Just a word more on the subject of my spelling—in a transcript from the Greek and there exclusively—Greek names and places precisely as does the Greek author. I began this practice, with great innocency of intention, some six-and-thirty years ago. Leigh Hunt, I remember, was accustomed to speak of his gratitude, when ignorant of Greek, to those writers (like Goldsmith) who had obliged him by using English characters, so that he might relish, for instance, the smooth quality of such a phrase as "hapalunetai galené;" he said also that Shelley was indignant at "Firenze" having displaced the Dantesque "Fiorenza," and would contemptuously English the intruder "Firence." I supposed I was doing a simple thing enough: but there has been till lately much astonishment at *os* and *us*, *ai* and *oi*, representing the same letters in Greek. Of a sudden, however, whether in translation or out of it, everybody seems committing the offence, although the adoption of *u* for *v* still presents such difficulty that it is a wonder how we have hitherto escaped "Eyripides." But there existed a sturdy Briton who,

---

[1] *Poems by Matthew Arnold*, Preface.

49| MS:though it §last two words inserted above§ reproduces it in §*s* and last two words crossed out§ all   51| MS:what my admirable §last two words crossed out and replaced above by two words§ an eloquent friend Matthew Arnold §last two words crossed out§ maintains   55| MS:prominence; because   *P1877:*prominence, because   56| MS:subordinated; because   *P1877:*subordinated, because   58| MS:in,—stroke   *P1877:*in, stroke   63| MS:some six and §last two words inserted above§ thirty   *P1877:* some six-and-thirty   65| MS:writers like Goldsmith who   *P1877:*writers (like Goldsmith) who   70-71| MS:been lately < > *oi*, do §crossed out§ representing   *1889a:*been till lately   73| MS:offence: although   *P1877:*offence, although   74| MS:such §inserted above§   75| MS:there was once §last two words crossed out§ existed §inserted above§

Ben Jonson informs us, wrote "The Life of the Emperor Anthony Pie"—whom we now acquiesce in as Antoninus Pius: for "with time and patience the mulberry leaf becomes satin." Yet there is, on all sides, much profession of respect for what Keats called "vowelled Greek"—

80 "consonanted," one would expect; and, in a criticism upon a late admirable translation of something of my own, it was deplored that, in a certain verse corresponding in measure to the fourteenth of the sixth Pythian Ode, "neither Professor Jebb in his Greek, nor Mr. Browning in his English, could emulate that matchlessly musical γόνον ἰδὼν

85 κάλλιστον ἀνδρῶν." Now, undoubtedly, "Seeing her son the fairest of men" has more sense than sound to boast of: but then, would not an Italian roll us out "Rimirando il figliuolo bellissimo degli uomini!" whereat Pindar, no less than Professor Jebb and Mr. Browning, τριακτῆρος οἴχεται τυχών.

90 It is recorded in the annals of Art[1] that there was once upon a time, practising so far north as Stockholm, a painter and picture-cleaner—sire of a less unhappy son—Old Muytens: and the annalist, Baron de Tessé, has not concealed his profound dissatisfaction at Old Muytens' conceit "to have himself had something to do with

95 the work of whatever master of eminence might pass through his hands." Whence it was,—the Baron goes on to deplore,—that much detriment was done to that excellent piece "The Recognition of Achilles," by Rubens, through the perversity of Old Muytens, "who must needs take on him to beautify every nymph of the twenty by the

100 bestowment of a widened eye and an enlarged mouth." I, at least, have left eyes and mouths everywhere as I found them, and this conser-

---

[1] *Lettres à un jeune Prince*, traduites du Suédois.

77| MS:Pie" whom <> Pius: and   *P1877*:Pie"—whom Pius: for   78| MS:mulberry-leaf <> on all sides, §last three words and comma inserted above and circled§   *P1877*:mulberry leaf
80| MS:expect—and   *P1877*:expect; and   82| MS:the 14th <> 6th   *P1877*:the fourteenth <> sixth   84| MS:his English could <> musical "γδνον   *P1877*:his English, could <> musical γδνον   87| MS:uomini?"—whereat   *P1877*:uomini!" whereat
92-93| MS:the Annalist, Baron §inserted above§   *P1877*:annalist   94| MS:have himself §inserted above§   96| MS:was, the <> deplore, that   *P1877*:was,—the <> deplore,— that   100| MS:of an enlarged mouth and a widened eye." I have   *P1877*:of a widened eye and an enlarged mouth." I, at least, have   101| MS:as §two illegible letters crossed out§ I

vatism is all that claims praise for—what is, after all, ἀκέλευστος ἄμισθος ἀοιδά. No, neither "uncommanded" nor "unrewarded:" since it was commanded of me by my venerated friend Thomas Carlyle, and rewarded will it indeed become if I am permitted to dignify it by the [105] prefatory insertion of his dear and noble name.

R. B.

LONDON: *October 1st, 1877.*

---

¹⁰³| MS:αοιδα? No <> "unrewarded." For §crossed out§ Since §in margin§ *P1877:* αοιδα.
No <> "unrewarded:" since   ¹⁰⁴| MS:commanded of §inserted above§
me <> Carlyle: and *P1877:*of m e by <> Carlyle, and   *CP1877:*me
¹⁰⁵| MS:become, if   *1889a:*become if   ¹⁰⁶| MS:the insertion   *P1877:*the prefatory
insertion   *Date*| MS:London, May,'77. R.B.   *1877:*LONDON: *October* 1ˢᵗ, 1877. R.B.

PERSONS

Warder
Choros of Old Men
KLUTAIMNESTRA
TALTHUBIOS, *Herald*
AGAMEMNON
KASSANDRA
AIGISTHOS

THE AGAMEMNON OF ÆSCHYLUS

1877

WARDER

The gods I ask deliverance from these labours,
Watch of a year's length whereby, slumbering through it
On the Atreidai's roofs on elbow,—dog-like—
I know of nightly star-groups the assemblage,
5   And those that bring to men winter and summer
Bright dynasts, as they pride them in the æther
—Stars, when they wither, and the uprisings of them.
And now on ward I wait the torch's token,
The glow of fire, shall bring from Troia message
10   And word of capture: so prevails audacious
The man's-way-planning hoping heart of woman.
But when I, driven from night-rest, dew-drenched, hold to
This couch of mine—not looked upon by visions,
Since fear instead of sleep still stands beside me,
15   So as that fast I fix in sleep no eyelids—
And when to sing or chirp a tune I fancy,
For slumber such song-remedy infusing,
I wail then, for this House's fortune groaning,
Not, as of old, after the best ways governed.
20   Now, lucky be deliverance from these labours,
At good news—the appearing dusky fire!
O hail, thou lamp of night, a day-long lightness
Revealing, and of dances the ordainment!

---

²| MS:length which I, slumbering through   *P1877:*length whereby, slumbering through it
³| MS:elbow—dog-like—   *P1877:*elbow,—dog-like—   ⁴| MS:Know   *P1877:*I know
⁵| MS:summer,   *1889a:*summer   ⁶| MS:Bright potentates, as in the air they pride
them   *P1877:*Bright dynasts, as they pride them in the æther
⁸| MS:on guard I   *P1877:*on ward I   ¹⁰| MS:capture—so   *P1877:*capture: so
¹²| MS:dew-drenched, hold   *1889a:*dew-drenched hold §emended to§ dew-drenched, hold
§see Editorial Notes§   ¹⁴| MS:of slumber stands   *P1877:*of sleep still stands
¹⁵| MS:So that I fix no eyelids fast in slumber—   *P1877:*So as that fast I fix in sleep no
eyelids—   ¹⁸| MS:groaning   *P1877:*groaning,   ²⁰| MS:Now, happy §crossed out
and replaced above by§ lucky be   ²²| MS:night—a   *P1877:*night, a

13

Halloo, halloo!
25 To Agamemnon's wife I show, by shouting,
That, from bed starting up at once, i' the household
Joyous acclaim, good-omened to this torch-blaze,
She send aloft, if haply Ilion's city
Be taken, as the beacon boasts announcing.
30 Ay, and, for me, myself will dance a prelude,
For, that my masters' dice drop right, I'll reckon:
Since thrice-six has it thrown to me, this signal.
Well, may it hap that, as he comes, the loved hand
O' the household's lord I may sustain with this hand!
35 As for the rest, I'm mute: on tongue a big ox
Has trodden. Yet this House, if voice it take should,
Most plain would speak. So, willing I myself speak
To those who know: to who know not—I'm blankness.

CHOROS

The tenth year this, since Priamos' great match,
40 King Menelaos, Agamemnon King,
—The strenuous yoke-pair of the Atreidai's honour
Two-throned, two-sceptred, whereof Zeus was donor—
Did from this land the aid, the armament despatch,
The thousand-sailored force of Argives clamouring
45 "Ares" from out the indignant breast, as fling
Passion forth vultures which, because of grief
Away,—as are their young ones,—with the thief,
Lofty above their brood-nests wheel in ring,
Row round and round with oar of either wing,
50 Lament the bedded chicks, lost labour that was love:
Which hearing, one above
—Whether Apollon, Pan or Zeus—that wail,
Sharp-piercing bird-shriek of the guests who fare

25| MS:show by shouting *P1877*:Show, by shouting, 26| MS:That from bed §last two words insertedabove§ 29| MS:taken as *P1877*:taken, as 30| MS:prelude *P1877*:prelude, 31| MS:For that <> dice fall right, I reckon: *P1877*:For, that <> dice drop right, I'll reckon: 32| MS:this beacon. §crossed out and replaced by§ signal. 38| MS:not—I blank am. *P1877*:not—I'm blankness. 44| MS:Argives thundering *P1877*:Argives clamouring 49| MS:oars §last letter crossed out§ 50| MS:chicks, the §crossed out and replaced by§ lost 53| guests th §last two letters crossed out§ who

Housemates with gods in air—
55 Suchanone sends, against who these assail,
What, late-sent, shall not fail
Of punishing—Erinus. Here as there,
The Guardian of the Guest, Zeus, the excelling one,
Sends against Alexandros either son
60 Of Atreus: for that wife, the many-husbanded,
Appointing many a tug that tries the limb,
While the knee plays the prop in dust, while, shred
To morsels, lies the spear-shaft; in those grim
Marriage-prolusions when their Fury wed
65 Danaoi and Troes, both alike. All's said:
Things are where things are, and, as fate has willed,
So shall they be fulfilled.
Not gently-grieving, not just doling out
The drops of expiation—no, nor tears distilled—
70 Shall he we know of bring the hard about
To soft—that intense ire
At those mock rites unsanctified by fire.
But we pay nought here: through our flesh, age-weighed,
Left out from who gave aid
75 In that day,—we remain,
Staying on staves a strength
The equal of a child's at length.
For when young marrow in the breast doth reign,
That's the old man's match,—Ares out of place
80 In either: but in oldest age's case,
Foliage a-fading, why, he wends his way
On three feet, and, no stronger than a child,
Wanders about gone wild,
A dream in day.

60| MS:Atreus,—for <> many husbanded, *P1877:*Atreus: for <> many-husbanded,
61| MS:limb— *P1877:*limb, 63| MS:spear-shaft,—in *P1877:*spear-shaft; in
65| MS:said— *P1877:*said: 68| MS:gently-grieving—not *P1877:*gently-grieving, not
70| MS:Shall—He <> of—bring *P1877:*Shall he <> of bring 71| MS:To softness—
that stretched ire *P1877:*To soft that intense ire 73| MS:here; through <> flesh age-
weighted, *P1877:*here: through <> flesh, age-weighted, 75| MS:remain—
*P1877:*remain, 77| MS:length; *P1877:*length. 82| MS:feet and *P1877:*feet, and
83| MS:Wanders about gone wild, §line added between 82 and 84§

15

⁸⁵ But thou, Tundareus' daughter, Klutaimnestra queen,
What need? What new? What having heard or seen,
By what announcement's tidings, everywhere
Settest thou, round about, the sacrifice a-flare?
For, of all gods the city-swaying,
⁹⁰ Those supernal, those infernal,
Those of the fields', those of the mart's obeying,—
The altars blaze with gifts;
And here and there, heaven-high the torch uplifts
Flame—medicated with persuasions mild,
⁹⁵ With foul admixture unbeguiled—
Of holy unguent, from the clotted chrism
Brought from the palace, safe in its abysm.
Of these things, speaking what may be indeed
Both possible and lawful to concede,
¹⁰⁰ Healer do thou become!—of this solicitude
Which, now, stands plainly forth of evil mood,
And, then . . . but from oblations, hope, to-day
Gracious appearing, wards away
From soul the insatiate care,
¹⁰⁵ The sorrow at my breast, devouring there!

Empowered am I to sing
The omens, what their force which, journeying,
Rejoiced the potentates:

---

^{89|} MS:gods our city-swaying *P1877:*gods the city-swaying, ^{90|} MS:God supernal, God
§over illegible erasure§ infernal, *P1877:*Those supernal, those infernal,
^{91|} MS:Gods <> fields' Gods <> marts' *P1877:*Those <> fields', those <> marts'
^{92|} MS:gifts— *P1877:*gifts; ^{93|} MS:heaven high *P1877:*heaven-high
^{95|} MS:With And §crossed out§ foul admixture §last two words inserted above§ unbeguiled,
*P1877:*unbeguiled— ^{96|} MS:unguent, from the §last two words inserted above§
^{97|} MS:the Palace *P1877:*palace ^{98|} MS:things speaking *P1877:*things, speaking
^{100|} MS:Become those §crossed out; last two words circled§ Healer of this same §crossed out§
*P1877:*Healer do thou become!—of ^{101|} MS:Which, one while §last two words crossed
out and replaced by§ now, stands forth plainly of §altered to§ stands plainly forth of
^{102|} MS:And, §now and illegible word crossed out§ then . . but from oblations, §last word and
comma inserted above three illegible words crossed out§ hope today *P1877:*then . . . but <>
oblations, hope, today ^{103|} MS:wards from out §last two words crossed out§
^{104|} MS:soul, the <> care *P1877:*soul the <> care, ^{105|} MS:my heart §crossed out
and replaced above by§ breast ^{107|} MS:omens, what §two illegible words inserted above
and crossed out§ ^{108|} MS:potentates— *P1877:*potentates:

16

(For still, from God, inflates
110   My breast song-suasion: age,
Born to the business, still such war can wage)
—How the fierce bird against the Teukris land
Despatched, with spear and executing hand,
The Achaian's two-throned empery—o'er Hellas' youth
115   Two rulers with one mind:
The birds' king to these kings of ships, on high,
—The black sort, and the sort that's white behind,—
Appearing by the palace, on the spear-throw side,
In right sky-regions, visible far and wide,—
120   Devouring a hare-creature, great with young,
Baulked of more racings they, as she from whom they sprung!
Ah, Linos, say—ah, Linos, song of wail!
But may the good prevail!

The prudent army-prophet seeing two
125   The Atreidai, two their tempers, knew
Those feasting on the hare
The armament-conductors were;
And thus he spoke, explaining signs in view.
"In time, this outset takes the town of Priamos:
130   But all before its towers,—the people's wealth that was,
Of flocks and herds,—as sure, shall booty-sharing thence
Drain to the dregs away, by battle violence.
Only, have care lest grudge of any god disturb
With cloud the unsullied shine of that great force, the curb

110| MS:song-suasion,—age *P1877:*song-suasion: age   113| MS:Despatched—with < >
hand— *P1877:*Despatched, with < > hand,   114| MS:two-throned force §crossed out
and replaced above by§ empery   115| MS:mind— *P1877:*mind:
121| MS:§illegible word crossed out and replaced above by§ Baulked of further §crossed out
and replaced above by§ more   122| MS:say—ah, Linos,—song *P1877:*Linos, song
123| MS:§four illegible words crossed out§ But   124| MS:seeing-two, *P1877:*seeing two
126| MS:hare— *P1877:*hare   127| MS:The foremost §crossed out§ armament §two
letters crossed out§ —conductors were; an *P1877:*were;
128| MS:this expedition §crossed out and replaced by§ outset
130| MS:Of Priamos/: §last two words and punctuation crossed out§ But   131| MS:herds,
as sure, §last two words and comma inserted above§   133| MS:Only have < > lest any
§crossed out§ *P1877:*Only, have   134| MS:than §crossed out and replaced by§ the
§next five words crossed out and replaced by§ unsullied shine of that great force, the

135 Of Troia, struck with damp
Beforehand in the camp!
For envyingly is
The virgin Artemis
Toward—her father's flying hounds—this House—
140 The sacrificers of the piteous
And cowering beast,
Brood and all, ere the birth: she hates the eagles' feast.
Ah, Linos, say—ah, Linos, song of wail!
But may the good prevail!

145 "Thus ready is the beauteous one with help
To those small dewdrop-things fierce lions whelp,
And udder-loving litter of each brute
That roams the mead; and therefore makes she suit,
The fair one, for fulfilment to the end
150 Of things these signs portend—
Which partly smile, indeed, but partly scowl—
The phantasms of the fowl.
I call Ieïos Paian to avert
She work the Danaoi hurt
155 By any thwarting waftures, long and fast
Holdings from sail of ships:

135| MS:Of Troia—struck with §before and illegible word inserted above and crossed out§ some §crossed out§ damp *P1877:*Troia, struck ¹³⁶|camp. *P1877:*camp!
139| MS:Toward,— §dash and next four words followed by comma and dash circled and inserted above§ an father's flying hounds,—this House—those hounds with wings, his loves; §last six words and punctuation crossed out§ §illegible word crossed out§ *P1877:*Toward— <> hounds—this 140| MS:sacrificers of §inserted above§ the §illegible word crossed out§ piteous §over erasure§ §illegible word crossed out§, *P1877:*piteous
141| MS:cowering §illegible word above crossed out§ beast— *P1877:*beast,
142| MS:Together both her §last three words crossed out§ all ere <> feast, *P1877:*all, ere <> feast." *CP1877:*feast. 143| MS:say—Ah, Linos,—song *P1877:*say—ah, Linos, song
144| MS:§four illegible words crossed out§ But 145| MS:Thus kind of heart, §last three words and comma crossed out§ ready is §inserted above§ <> one, is the §last two words crossed out§ with *P1877:*one with *1889a:*"Thus 146| MS:dew-drop-things *P1877:*dew-drop things *1889a:*dew-drop-things 148| MS:Which §crossed out§ That <> mead,—and *P1877:*mead; and 151| MS:That <> scowl. *P1877:*Which <> scowl— 153| MS:But §crossed out§ I invoke §crossed out and replaced above by§ call
154| MS:Lest §crossed out§ She work §two illegible words inserted above and crossed out§ the
155| MS:By thwarting winds, that §last three words and comma crossed out and altered to§ any thwarting waftures, long 156| MS:Holdings §written over erasure§ from sail

And sacrifice, another than the last,
She for herself precipitate—
Something unlawful, feast for no man's lips,
160 Builder of quarrels, with the House cognate—
Having in awe no husband: for remains
A frightful, backward-darting in the path,
Wily house-keeping chronicler of wrath,
That has to punish that old children's fate!"
165 Such things did Kalchas,—with abundant gains
As well,—vociferate,
Predictions from the birds, in journeying,
Above the abode of either king.
With these, symphonious, sing—
170 Ah, Linos, say—ah, Linos, song of wail!
But may the good prevail!

Zeus, whosoe'er he be,—if that express
Aught dear to him on whom I call—
So do I him address.
175 I cannot liken out, by all
Admeasurement of powers,
Any but Zeus for refuge at such hours,
If veritably needs I must
From off my soul its vague care-burthen thrust.

180 Not—whosoever was the great of yore,
Bursting to bloom with bravery all round—
Is in our mouths: he was, but is no more.

---

§inserted above§ of ships—in harbour §last two words crossed out§ *P1877:*ships:
157| MS:sacrifice—another <> last— *P1877:*sacrifice, another <> last,
158| MS:precipitate *P1877:*precipitate— 163| MS:Crafty §crossed out and altered to§
Wily house- §ruler, and illegible word crossed out and replaced above by§ keeping chronicler
167| MS:birds, which §crossed out§ in the §crossed out§ 168| MS:the §two illegible
words crossed out§ abode §inserted above§ of either §crossed out and then restored§ king
§illegible word crossed out§ . 169| MS:sing *P1877:*sing— 170| MS:say, ah,
Linos—song *P1877:*say—ah, Linos, song 171| MS:Woe is the word §four words
crossed out§ But 173| MS:him I *P1877:*him on whom I 177| MS:Zeus §illegible
word crossed out§ for <> hours *P1877:*hours, 180| MS:Not he, who once was §last
three words crossed out and replaced above by§ —whosoever was the *P1877:*Not—
whosoever 182| MS:mouths: now §word crossed out and replaced above by§ he

And who it was that after came to be,
Met the thrice-throwing wrestler,—he
185 Is also gone to ground.
But "Zeus"—if any, heart and soul, that name—
Shouting the triumph-praise—proclaim,
Complete in judgment shall that man be found.
Zeus, who leads onward mortals to be wise,
190 Appoints that suffering masterfully teach.
In sleep, before the heart of each,
A woe-remembering travail sheds in dew
Discretion,—ay, and melts the unwilling too
By what, perchance, may be a graciousness
195 Of gods, enforced no less,—
As they, commanders of the crew,
Assume the awful seat.

And then the old leader of the Achaian fleet,
Disparaging no seer—
200 With bated breath to suit misfortune's inrush here
—(What time it laboured, that Achaian host,
By stay from sailing,—every pulse at length
Emptied of vital strength,—
Hard over Kalchis shore-bound, current-crost
205 In Aulis station,—while the winds which post
From Strumon, ill-delayers, famine-fraught,
Tempters of man to sail where harbourage is naught,

183| MS:And—who *P1877:*And who   185| MS:Is gone *P1877:*Is also gone
186| MS:soul, prod §word crossed out§ that   187| MS:Showing §illegible word above
crossed out and replaced by§ the triumphant-praise §altered to§ triumph-praise
188| MS:that §over erasure§ <> found: *P1877:*found.   189| MS:Zeus who <> wise—
*P1877:*Zeus, who <> wise,   190| MS:Appoints that §over illegible word§
192| MS:The woe-remembering weight §last three letters of hyphenated word and next word
crossed out and replaced above by§ and travail *P1877:*A woe-remembering travail
193| MS:unwilling §word crossed out and restored§ too: *P1877:*too   195| MS:gods,
§three illegible words crossed out and replaced by§ forced *P1877:*gods, enforced
196| MS:As they §illegible word above and first two words crossed out§ Commanders of §last
three letters of first word and next crossed out and then restored§   197| MS:§illegible
word crossed out§ Testing the awful §word circled and inserted above§ seat. *P1877:*Assume
the   198| MS:the old §inserted above§ leader   199| MS:The elder, §last two words
and comma crossed out§   200| MS:here— *P1877:*here   201| MS:What *P1877:*—
(What   202| MS:pulse §over erasure§   204| MS:current-crossed *P1877:*current-crost

Spendthrifts of ships and cables, turning time
To twice the length,—these carded, by delay,
210   To less and less away
The Argeians' flowery prime:
And when a remedy more grave and grand
Than aught before,—yea, for the storm and dearth,—
The prophet to the foremost in command
215   Shrieked forth, as cause of this
Adducing Artemis,
So that the Atreidai striking staves on earth
Could not withhold the tear)—
Then did the king, the elder, speak this clear.

220   "Heavy the fate, indeed,—to disobey!
Yet heavy if my child I slay,
The adornment of my household: with the tide
Of virgin-slaughter, at the altar-side,
A father's hands defiling: which the way
225   Without its evils, say?
How shall I turn fleet-fugitive,
Failing of duty to allies?
Since for a wind-abating sacrifice
And virgin blood,—'tis right they strive,
230   Nay, madden with desire.
Well may it work them—this that they require!"

But when he underwent necessity's
Yoke-trace,—from soul blowing unhallowed change
Unclean, abominable,—thence—another man—

211| MS:prime,— *P1877*:prime: 212| MS:more grave and §last two words inserted above§   213| MS:Than all §crossed out and altered to§ ought before < > for that bitter §last two words crossed out§ storm   215| MS:forth—as   *P1877*:forth, as
218| MS:tear—   *P1877*:tear)—   219| MS:speak §over illegible word§
225| MS:fleet-fugitive, he left §last two words crossed out §   227| MS:Alone of my confederates through §last five words and illegible word inserted above crossed out§ Failing of duty §two words inserted above§ to   228| MS:for of §crossed out§ a wind-abating §inserted above§ sacrifice that wind abated §last two words crossed out§
229| MS:By §crossed out and altered to§ And < > 'tis §illegible word crossed out§ , < > strive *P1877*:strive,   230| MS:desire! *P1877*:desire.   233| MS:change, *P1877*:change
234| MS:abominable, thence   *P1877*:abominable,—thence

235 The audacious mind of him began
    Its wildest range.
    For this it is gives mortals hardihood—
    Some vice-devising miserable mood
    Of madness, and first woe of all the brood.
240 The sacrificer of his daughter—strange!—
    He dared become, to expedite
    Woman-avenging warfare,—anchors weighed
    With such prelusive rite!

    Prayings and callings "Father"—naught they made
245 Of these, and of the virgin-age,—
    Captains heart-set on war to wage!
    His ministrants, vows done, the father bade—
    Kid-like, above the altar, swathed in pall,
    Take her—lift high, and have no fear at all,
250 Head-downward, and the fair mouth's guard
    And frontage hold,—press hard
    From utterance a curse against the House
    By dint of bit—violence bridling speech.
    And as to ground her saffron-vest she shed,
255 She smote the sacrificers all and each
    With arrow sweet and piteous,
    From the eye only sped,—
    Significant of will to use a word,
    Just as in pictures: since, full many a time,
260 In her sire's guest-hall, by the well-heaped board
    Had she made music,—lovingly with chime
    Of her chaste voice, that unpolluted thing,

235| MS:mind began   *P1877:*mind of him began   236| MS:range: *P1877:*range.
238| MS:A vice-devising   *P1877:*Some vice-devising   239| MS:madness, some first
*P1877:*madness and first   241| MS:become—to *P1877:*become, to
247| MS:Vows done, §two words and comma circled and inserted after ministrants,§
249| MS:Take and §word crossed out and replaced by§ her—   250| MS:Head-
downwards, and *P1877:*Head-downward, and   252| MS:the House— *P1877:*the
House   254| MS:§¶indicated in margin§   *1889a:*§no¶indicated§
258| MS:word— *P1877:*word,   259| MS:pictures—since *P1877:*pictures: since
261| MS:music, lovingly *P1877:*music, —lovingly   262| MS:of her §inserted above§
voice, that unpolluted girl, §word and comma crossed out§ thing,

Honoured the third libation,—paian that should bring
Good fortune to the sire she loved so well.

265 What followed—those things I nor saw nor tell.
But Kalchas' arts,—whate'er they indicate,—
Miss of fulfilment never: it is fate.
True, justice makes, in sufferers, a desire
To know the future woe preponderate.
270 But—hear before is need?
To that, farewell and welcome! 'tis the same, indeed,
As grief beforehand: clearly, part for part,
Conformably to Kalchas'art,
Shall come the event.
275 But be they as they may, things subsequent,—
What is to do, prosperity betide
E'en as we wish it!—we, the next allied,
Sole guarding barrier of the Apian land.

I am come, reverencing power in thee,
280 O Klutaimnestra! For 'tis just we bow
To the ruler's wife,—the male-seat man-bereaved.
But if thou, having heard good news,—or none,—
For good news' hope dost sacrifice thus wide,
I would hear gladly: art thou mute,—no grudge!

263| MS:third out pouring §last two words crossed out§ libation 266| MS:indicate,
P1877:indicate,— 267| MS:shall fulfil §last two words crossed out§ Miss §illegible word
crossed out and replaced above by§ of 268| MS:justice bid §crossed out§ makes,
preponderates §crossed out and replaced by two words§ in sufferers 271| MS:Farewell
P1877:To that, farewell 272| MS:part with §crossed out and replaced by§ for
274| MS:event: *P1877*:event. 275| MS:§line revised from latter part of l. 274§ But
however §word crossed out§ be they as they may, §last four words and comma inserted above§
things 276| MS:May §crossed out§ What is now §last two words crossed out§ is < >
betide §written over illegible word§ 277| MS:it,—we *P1877*:it!—we
281| MS:To the chief §word crossed out§ < > wife,—ruler §word crossed out and replaced
above by§ the male-seat man-bereaved. of man §last two words crossed out§
282| MS:But thou, §last word and comma circled and placed after§ if < > none, *P1877*:none,—
283| MS:For good news §last two words crossed out and replaced above by two illegible words
crossed out§ hope,—dost < > wide— *P1877*:For good news' hope < > wide,

KLUTAIMNESTRA

285   Good-news-announcer, may—as is the by-word—
Morn become, truly,—news from Night his mother!
But thou shalt learn joy past all hope of hearing.
Priamos' city have the Argeioi taken.

CHOROS

How sayest? The word, from want of faith, escaped me.

KLUTAIMNESTRA

290   Troia the Achaioi hold: do I speak plainly?

CHOROS

Joy overcreeps me, calling forth the tear-drop.

KLUTAIMNESTRA

Right! for, that glad thou art, thine eye convicts thee.

CHOROS

For—what to thee, of all this, trusty token?

KLUTAIMNESTRA

What's here! how else? unless the god have cheated.

CHOROS

295   Haply thou flattering shows of dreams respectest?

KLUTAIMNESTRA

No fancy would I take of soul sleep-burthened.

285| MS:the §illegible word crossed out and replaced above by§ by-word—
288-89| MS:§in margin, "Print the names separately above"§   289| MS:word—from <>
faith—escaped   *P1877:*word, from <> faith, escaped   290| MS:hold—do *P1877:*hold: do
291| MS:me—calling <> tear-drop!   *P1877:*me, calling <> tear-drop.
292| MS:for that <> art thine   *P1877:*for, that <> art, thine   294| MS:What's I have
§last two words crossed out and replaced by§ here : how   *P1877:*here! how

CHOROS

But has there puffed thee up some unwinged omen?

KLUTAIMNESTRA

As a young maid's my mind thou mockest grossly.

CHOROS

Well, at what time was—even sacked, the city?

KLUTAIMNESTRA

300 Of this same mother Night—the dawn, I tell thee.

CHOROS

And who of messengers could reach this swiftness?

KLUTAIMNESTRA

Hephaistos—sending a bright blaze from Ide.
Beacon did beacon send, from fire the poster,
Hitherward: Ide to the rock Hermaian
305 Of Lemnos: and a third great torch o' the island
Zeus' seat received in turn, the Athoan summit.
And,—so upsoaring as to stride sea over,
The strong lamp-voyager, and all for joyance—
Did the gold-glorious splendour, any sun like,
310 Pass on—the pine-tree—to Makistos' watch-place;
Who, did not,—tardy,—caught, no wits about him,
By sleep,—decline his portion of the missive.

297| MS:But—has *P1877:*But has   300| MS:mother night—the dawn—I tell you!
*P1877:*mother Night—the dawn, I tell thee.   302| MS:from Idé. *1889a:*from Ide.
303| MS:Beacon that §word crossed out and replaced above by§ did
304| MS:Hitherward—Idé from §crossed out and replaced above by§ to   *1889a:*Ide
306| MS:Received in turn Zeus' seat, the   *P1877:*Zeus' seat received in turn, the
307| MS:And, so *P1877:*And,—so   308| MS:lamp-voyager—and
*P1877:*lamp-voyager, and   309| MS:splendor—any < > like— *P1877:*splendor, any < >
like, *1889a:*splendour   310| MS:to Makistos watch-place.
*P1877:*to Makistos' watch-place;   311| MS:And §crossed out§ Who did §inserted above§
caught §over erasure of first three letters§   312| MS:sleep §over illegible word§ < > the
missive. §inserted above crossed out word, possibly *envoy*§

And far the beacon's light, on stream Euripos
Arriving, made aware Messapios' warders,
315 And up they lit in turn, played herald onwards,
Kindling with flame a heap of grey old heather.
And, strengthening still, the lamp, decaying nowise,
Springing o'er Plain Asopos,—full-moon-fashion
Effulgent,—toward the crag of Mount Kithairon,
320 Roused a new rendering-up of fire the escort—
And light, far escort, lacked no recognition
O' the guard—as burning more than burnings told you.
And over Lake Gorgopis light went leaping,
And, at Mount Aigiplanktos safe arriving,
325 Enforced the law—"to never stint the fire-stuff."
And they send, lighting up with ungrudged vigour,
Of flame a huge beard, ay, the very foreland
So as to strike above, in burning onward,
The look-out which commands the Strait Saronic.
330 Then did it dart until it reached the outpost
Mount Arachnaios here, the city's neighbour;
And then darts to this roof of the Atreidai
This light of Ide's fire not unforefathered!
Such are the rules prescribed the flambeau-bearers:
335 He beats that's first and also last in running.
Such is the proof and token I declare thee,
My husband having sent me news from Troia.

CHOROS

The gods, indeed, anon will I pray, woman!
But now, these words to hear, and sate my wonder

313| MS:the beacons' §circled and inserted above§ light 316| MS:heather:
*P1877:*heather. 317| MS:strengthening, the *P1877:*strengthening still, the
318| MS:full-moon-fashion, *1889a:*full-moon-fashion 319| MS:towards
*P1877:*toward 321| MS:And §over illegible word§ light, from §word crossed out§ far
escorting, §altered to§ escort lacked 331| MS:Mount Arachnaios, here, the §last two
words inserted above two illegible words crossed out§ <> neighbour— *P1877:*Mount
Arachnaios here, the <> neighbour; 332| MS:the Atreidai, *P1877:*the Atreidai
333| MS:light—of *P1877:*light of 334| MS:flambeau-bearers— *P1877:*flambeau-
bearers: 336| MS:thee *P1877:*thee, 338| MS:pray, Lady! *P1877:*pray, woman!
339| MS:now these *P1877:*now, these

340 Thoroughly, I am fain—if twice thou tell them.

KLUTAIMNESTRA

Troia do the Achaioi hold, this same day.
I think a noise—no mixture—reigns i' the city.
Sour wine and unguent pour thou in one vessel—
Standers-apart, not lovers, wouldst thou style them:
345 And so, of captives and of conquerors, partwise
The voices are to hear, of fortune diverse.
For those, indeed, upon the bodies prostrate
Of husbands, brothers, children upon parents
—The old men, from a throat that's free no longer,
350 Shriekingly wail the death-doom of their dearest:
While these—the after-battle hungry labour,
Which prompts night-faring, marshals them to breakfast
On the town's store, according to no billet
Of sharing, but as each drew lot of fortune.
355 In the spear-captured Troic habitations
House they already: from the frosts upæthral
And dews delivered, will they, luckless creatures,
Without a watch to keep, slumber all night through.
And if they fear the gods, the city-guarders,
360 And the gods' structures of the conquered country,
They may not—capturers—soon in turn be captive.
But see no prior lust befall the army
To sack things sacred—by gain-cravings vanquished!
For there needs homeward the return's salvation,
365 To round the new limb back o' the double race-course.
And guilty to the gods if came the army,

344| MS:Standers-apart—not lovers—wouldst   P1877:Standers-apart, not lovers, wouldst
345| MS:so of P1877:so, of   346| MS:diverse— P1877:diverse.   347| MS:those
indeed upon P1877:those, indeed, upon   348| MS:brothers §over erasure§
349| MS:men,—from P1877:men, from   351| MS:labour P1877:labour,
353| MS:On §over erasure§ <> store—according P1877:store, according
356| MS:already; from <> upaithral P1877:already: from <> upæthral
358| MS:keep—slumber P1877:keep, slumber   363| MS:sacred— §illegible word
crossed out§ greed §crossed out and replaced by§ by gain-cravings vanquished—
P1877:vanquished!   364| MS:salvation— P1877:salvation,   365| MS:limb of
§crossed out and replaced by two words§ back o' the   366| MS:came §over erasure§

Awakened up the sorrow of those slaughtered
Might be—should no outbursting evils happen.
But may good beat—no turn to see i' the balance!
370   For, many benefits I want the gain of.

CHOROS

Woman, like prudent man thou kindly speakest.
And I, thus having heard thy trusty tokens,
The gods to rightly hail forthwith prepare me;
For, grace that must be paid has crowned our labours.

375   O Zeus the king, and friendly Night
Of these brave boons bestower—
Thou who didst fling on Troia's every tower
The o'er-roofing snare, that neither great thing might,
Nor any of the young ones, overpass
380   Captivity's great sweep-net—one and all
Of Ate held in thrall!
Ay, Zeus I fear—the guest's friend great—who was
The doer of this, and long since bent
The bow on Alexandros with intent
385   That neither wide o' the white
Nor o'er the stars the foolish dart should light.
The stroke of Zeus—they have it, as men say!
This, at least, from the source track forth we may!
As he ordained, so has he done.

367| MS:Awakened-up may be §last two words crossed out§ the   *P1877:*Awakened up the
370| MS:many are those good things §last four words crossed out and replaced by§ benefits
371| MS:Lady, like   *P1877:*Woman, like   373| MS:me,   *P1877:*me;
374| MS:For grace, that <> have payment, §last two words and comma crossed out and
replaced above by§ be paid, has §over erasure§   *P1877:*For, grace <> paid has
377| MS:on Troia's tower   *P1877:*on Troia's every tower
378| MS:neither great thing §last two words inserted above§ might   *P1877:*might,
379| MS:any §crossed out then restored§ <> ones overpass   *P1877:*ones, overpass
380| MS:one and all §written on 381 and moved to 380§   381| MS:held in thrall!
§written on 380 and moved to 381§   382| MS:Great §crossed out and replaced above by§
Ay, <> the Hospitable, §word and comma crossed out and replaced above by three words and
dash§ guest's friend great—   387| MS:The blow of   *P1877:*The stroke of
389| MS:§line missing§   *P1877:*As he ordained, so has he done.

390 "No"—said someone—
"The gods think fit to care
Nowise for mortals, such
As those by whom the good and fair
Of things denied their touch
395 Is trampled!" but he was profane.
That they do care, has been made plain
To offspring of the over-bold,
Outbreathing "Ares" greater than is just—
Houses that spill with more than they can hold,
400 More than is best for man. Be man's what must
Keep harm off, so that in himself he find
Sufficiency—the well-endowed of mind!
For there's no bulwark in man's wealth to him
Who, through a surfeit, kicks—into the dim
405 And disappearing—Right's great altar.

                              Yes—
It urges him, the sad persuasiveness,
Ate's insufferable child that schemes
Treason beforehand: and all cure is vain.
It is not hidden: out it glares again,
410 A light dread-lamping-mischief, just as gleams
The badness of the bronze;
Through rubbing, puttings to the touch,
Black-clotted is he, judged at once.

390-91| MS:Someone said—Gods think fit to have no §last two words crossed out§ care
P1877: "No"—said someone—/"The gods think fit to care   392| MS:Of §crossed out and
replaced above by two words§ Nowise for mortals, those §word crossed out and replaced
above by§ such   393| MS:the good-and-fair   *P1877:* the good and fair
394| MS:touch,   *P1877:* touch   395| MS:trampled: but   *P1877:* trampled!" but
396| MS:That certainly §word crossed out§ they do §inserted above§   397| MS:the
insufferably §word crossed out§   399| MS:that spill §word crossed out and then
restored§ overflow §word inserted above then crossed out§ with what §word crossed out and
replaced above by two words§ more than they cannot §altered to§ can   400| MS:man: be
P1877: man. Be   401| MS:off—so   *P1877:* off, so   402| MS:mind.   *P1877:* mind!
406| MS:him, §illegible word crossed out and replaced above by§ the   410| MS:light
dismally §word crossed out and replaced above by§ dread-   411| MS:bronze   *P1877:* bronze;
412| MS:rubbing—puttings <> touch—   *P1877:* rubbing puttings <> touch,
CP1877: rubbing, puttings   413| MS:Black-clotted—is   *P1877:* Black-clotted is

He seeks—the boy—a flying bird to clutch,
415   The insufferable brand
Setting upon the city of his land
Whereof not any god hears prayer;
While him who brought about such evils there,
That unjust man, the god in grapple throws.
420   Such an one, Paris goes
Within the Atreidai's house—
Shamed the guest's board by robbery of the spouse.

And, leaving to her townsmen throngs a-spread
With shields, and spear-thrusts of sea-armament,
425   And bringing Ilion, in a dowry's stead,
Destruction—swiftly through the gates she went,
Daring the undareable. But many a groan outbroke
From prophets of the House as thus they spoke.
"Woe, woe the House, the House and Rulers,—woe
430   The marriage-bed and dints
A husband's love imprints!
There she stands silent! meets no honour—no
Shame—sweetest still to see of things gone long ago!
And, through desire of one across the main,
435   A ghost will seem within the house to reign:
And hateful to the husband is the grace
Of well-shaped statues: from—in place of eyes
Those blanks—all Aphrodite dies.

"But dream-appearing mournful fantasies—
440   There they stand, bringing grace that's vain.

414| MS:§line missing§ *P1877:*He seeks—the boy—a flying bird to clutch,
418| MS:there *P1877:*there, 422-23| MS:§no ¶§ 422| MS:And leaving citizens—
the throngs *P1877:*And, leaving to her townsmen throngs 428| MS:the house as
*P1877:*the House as 430-31| MS:§lines indented; B. writes in margin, "All begin in a
line."§ 432| MS:honor *1889a:*honour 433| MS:Reproach §crossed out and
replaced above by§ Shame—sweetest 434| MS:And through <> main *P1877:*And,
through <> main, 437| MS:statues: with those blanks §last three words crossed out and
replaced above by§ from—in <> eyes, *1889a:*eyes 438| MS:of eyes, §last two words
and comma crossed out and replaced above by two words and dash§ Those blanks—all
Aprodite temps in vain! §last three words and punctuation crossed out and replaced above by§
dies. *P1877:*Aphrodite 439| MS:But *P1877:*"But 440| MS:vain *P1877:*vain.

For vain 'tis, when brave things one seems to view;
The fantasy has floated off, hands through;
Gone, that appearance,—nowise left to creep,—
On wings, the servants in the paths of sleep!"
445 Woes, then, in household and on hearth, are such
As these—and woes surpassing these by much.
But not these only: everywhere—
For those who from the land
Of Hellas issued in a band,
450 Sorrow, the heart must bear,
Sits in the home of each, conspicuous there.
Many a circumstance, at least,
Touches the very breast.
For those
455 Whom any sent away,—he knows:
And in the live man's stead,
Armour and ashes reach
The house of each.

For Ares, gold-exchanger for the dead,
460 And balance-holder in the fight o' the spear,
Due-weight from Ilion sends—
What moves the tear on tear—
A charred scrap to the friends:
Filling with well-packed ashes every urn,
465 For man—that was—the sole return.
And they groan—praising much, the while,
Now this man as experienced in the strife,
Now that, fallen nobly on a slaughtered pile,
Because of—not his own—another's wife.

441| MS:view— *P1877*:view;   444| MS:On §over illegible word§ <> sleep. *P1877*:sleep."
451| MS:the house §altered to§ home   455| MS:knows— *P1877*:knows:
459| MS:Ares, the §crossed out§ gold-exchanging §word altered to§ gold-exchanger
460| MS:balance-holding §altered to§ balance-holder   461| MS:sends *P1877*:sends—
463| MS:friends— *P1877*:friends: 464| MS:Bewept with and bitter is the tear!— §line crossed out and replaced by§ Filling with well-packed §illegible word crossed out and altered to§ ashes every urn *P1877*:urn,   465| MS:man that was the   *1889a*:man—that was—the
467| MS:the fight; §word and punctuation crossed out and replaced by§ strife,
469| MS:own,—but §word crossed out and replaced by§ another's *P1877*:own—another's

31

470 But things there be, one barks,
When no man harks:
A surreptitious grief that's grudge
Against the Atreidai who first sought the judge.
But some there, round the rampart, have
475 In Ilian earth, each one his grave:
All fair-formed as at birth,
It hid them—what they have and hold—the hostile earth.

And big with anger goes the city's word,
And pays a debt by public curse incurred.
480 And ever with me—as about to hear
A something night-involved—remains my fear:
Since of the many-slayers—not
Unwatching are the gods.
The black Erinues, at due periods—
485 Whoever gains the lot
Of fortune with no right—
Him, by life's strain and stress
Back-again-beaten from success,
They strike blind: and among the out-of-sight
490 For who has got to be, avails no might.
The being praised outrageously
Is grave, for at the eyes of such an one
Is launched, from Zeus, the thunder-stone.
Therefore do I decide
495 For so much and no more prosperity
Than of his envy passes unespied.

470| MS:be, which, under breath §last three words and comma crossed out and replaced
above by§ which here and there §last four words crossed out§ one growls— §last word and
dash crossed out and replaced above by§ barks—   *P1877:*barks,   471| MS:harks—
*P1877:*harks: 472| MS:Ay, and A §first two words and comma crossed out§
473| MS:the Atreidai, that §word crossed out and replaced above by§ who   *1889a:*Atreidai who
475| MS:grave—   *P1877:*grave: 476| MS:birth   *P1877:*birth,   477| MS:It hides
§altered to§ hid   478| MS:And grave with wrath, of citizens the §last four words and
comma crossed out and replaced above by§ anger goes the city's   *1889a:*And big with
479| MS:public §over illegible word§ curse incurred—   *P1877:*incurred.   483| MS:gods:
*P1877:*gods.   485| MS:Whoever §over illegible word§   489| MS:By life's §two words
crossed out§ They   490| MS:be, §new line indicated§ Avails no might.   *P1877:*be, avails
§recorded on same line§   493| MS:thunder-stone—   *P1877:*thunder-stone.

Neither a city-sacker would I be,
Nor life, myself by others captive, see.
A swift report has gone our city through,
500 From fire, the good-news messenger: if true,
Who knows? Or is it not a god-sent lie?
Who is so childish and deprived of sense
That, having, at announcements of the flame
Thus novel, felt his own heart fired thereby,
505 He then shall at a change of evidence,
Be worsted just the same?
It is conspicuous in a woman's nature,
Before its view to take a grace for granted:
Too trustful,—on her boundary, usurpature
510 Is swiftly made;
But swiftly, too, decayed,
The glory perishes by woman vaunted.

KLUTAIMNESTRA

Soon shall we know—of these light-bearing torches,
And beacons and exchanges, fire with fire—
515 If they are true, indeed, or if, dream-fashion,
This gladsome light came and deceived our judgment.
Yon herald from the shore I see, o'ershadowed
With boughs of olive: dust, mud's thirsty brother,
Close neighbours on his garb, thus testify me
520 That neither voiceless, nor yet kindling for thee
Mountain-wood-flame, shall he explain by fire-smoke:
But either tell out more the joyance, speaking. . . .
Word contrary to which, I aught but love it!
For may good be—to good that's known—appendage!

497| MS:be *P1877*:be,   501| MS:knows? Or if §crossed out and altered to§ is it not a §last two words over illegible words§   505| MS:Shall then, at just a §last two words crossed out§ change *P1877*:He then shall at a change   508| MS:Ere 'tis in view *P1877*:Be its view   510| MS:made, *P1877*:made;   514| MS:with fire, *P1877*:with fire—   517| MS:see—o'ershadowed *P1877*:see, o'ershadowed   519| MS:thus bear me witness *P1877*:thus testify me   521| MS:flame shall <> fire-smoke, *P1877*:flame, shall <> fire-smoke: 522| MS:speaking . . . *1889a*:speaking . . . .

CHOROS

525 Whoever prays for aught else to this city
—May he himself reap fruit of his mind's error!

HERALD

Ha, my forefathers' soil of earth Argeian!
Thee, in this year's tenth light, am I returned to—
Of many broken hopes, on one hope chancing;
530 For never prayed I, in this earth Argeian
Dying, to share my part in tomb the dearest.
Now, hail thou earth, and hail thou also, sunlight,
And Zeus, the country's lord, and king the Puthian
From bow no longer urging at us arrows!
535 Enough, beside Skamandros, cam'st thou adverse:
Now, contrary, be saviour thou and healer,
O king Apollon! And gods conquest-granting,
All—I invoke too, and my tutelary
Hermes, dear herald, heralds' veneration,—
540 And Heroes our forthsenders,—friendly, once more
The army to receive, the war-spear's leavings!
Ha, mansions of my monarchs, roofs beloved,
And awful seats, and deities sun-fronting—
Receive with pomp your monarch, long time absent!
545 For he comes bringing light in night-time to you,
In common with all these—king Agamemnon.
But kindly greet him—for clear shows your duty—
Who has dug under Troia with the mattock
Of Zeus the Avenger, whereby plains are out-ploughed,

526| MS:—May himself reap the fruit of judgment's §illegible word above crossed out§ error!
P1877:—May he himself reap fruit of his mind's error!   527| MS:Ha, soil of my
forefathers, earth   *P1877:*Ha, my forefather's soil of earth   529| MS:chancing.
*P1877:*chancing;   531| MS:Dying to   *P1877:*Dying, to   533| MS:lord,—and King
the   *P1877:*lord, and king the   534| MS:longer urging §inserted above§< > arrows!
§illegible word crossed out§   544| MS:your King, this §two words and comma crossed
out and replaced above by§ monarch, long   545| MS:comes to you, §word above crossed
out§ light in night time bringing   *P1877:*comes bringing light in night-time to you,
546| MS:these—King Agamemnon! §altered to§ . *P1877:*these—king   547| MS:for plain
stands §two words crossed out and replaced above by§ clear shows   549| MS:whereby
plain is out- §inserted above§ ploughed—   *P1877:*whereby plains are out-ploughed,

550   Altars unrecognizable, and gods' shrines,
    And the whole land's seed thoroughly has perished.
    And such a yoke-strap having cast round Troia,
    The elder king Atreides, happy man—he
    Comes to be honoured, worthiest of what mortals
555   Now are. Nor Paris nor the accomplice-city
    Outvaunts their deed as more than they are done-by:
    For, in a suit for rape and theft found guilty,
    He missed of plunder and, in one destruction,
    Fatherland, house and home has mowed to atoms:
560   Debts the Priamidai have paid twice over.

CHOROS

Hail, herald from the army of Achaians!

HERALD

I hail:—to die, will gainsay gods no longer!

CHOROS

Love of this fatherland did exercise thee?

HERALD

So that I weep, at least, with joy, my eyes full.

550| MS:and the §inserted above§ gods' fane's,—   *P1877:*and gods' shrines,
551| MS:And §illegible word above crossed out§ the < > perished: *P1877:*perished.
552| MS:round Troia   *P1877:*Troia,   553| MS:king Atreides, high in §last two words and illegible word crossed out and replaced above by§ happy man—he
554| MS:A man §two words crossed out§ Comes to be §word inserted above§ < > of what §inserted above§   555| MS:That Now are: §three words crossed out but last two restored§ nor   *P1877:*are. Nor   557| MS:For cast § word crossed out§ in a §inserted above§ suit   *P1877:*For, in   558| MS:and in < > destruction   *P1877:*and, in < > destruction,   560| MS:§illegible word crossed out and replaced above by§ Debts the
561| MS:Hail, Herald of §word crossed out and replaced above by§ from
562| MS:I take the §two words and illegible word crossed out and replaced above by§ hail:—to die,—will   *P1877:*die, will   563| MS:of the fatherland here exercised   *P1877:*of this fatherland did exercise   564| MS:joy my   *P1877:*joy, my

CHOROS

565 What, of this gracious sickness were ye gainers?

HERALD

How now? instructed, I this speech shall master.

CHOROS

For those who loved you back, with longing stricken.

HERALD

This land yearned for the yearning army, say'st thou?

CHOROS

So as to set me oft, from dark mind, groaning.

HERALD

570 Whence came this ill mind—hatred to the army?

CHOROS

Of old, I use, for mischief's physic, silence.

HERALD

And how, the chiefs away, did you fear any?

CHOROS

So that now,—late thy word,—much joy were—dying!

HERALD

For well have things been worked out: these,—in much time,

565| MS:this sweet disease were ye infected?   *P1877:*this gracious sickness were ye gainers?
566| MS:How so? instructed   *P1877:*How now? instructed   567| MS:those you §word crossed out§ who < > with §illegible word crossed out and replaced above by§ longing
569| MS:from hearts depth, groaning.   *P1877:*from dark mind, groaning.
573| MS:that now,—late §last two words and punctuation inserted above§ your word, just now— §last two words crossed out§ great joy.   *P1877:*late thy word,—much joy.
574| MS:these,—this long time,   *P1877:*these,—in much time,

575 Some of them, one might say, had luck in falling,
While some were faulty: since who, gods excepted,
Goes, through the whole time of his life, ungrieving?
For labours should I tell of, and bad lodgments,
Narrow deckways ill-strewn, too,—what the day's woe
580 We did not groan at getting for our portion?
As for land-things, again, on went more hatred!
Since beds were ours hard by the foemen's ramparts,
And, out of heaven and from the earth, the meadow
Dews kept a-sprinkle, an abiding damage
585 Of vestures, making hair a wild-beast matting.
Winter, too, if one told of it—bird-slaying—
Such as, unbearable, Idaian snow brought—
Or heat, when waveless, on its noontide couches
Without a wind, the sea would slumber falling
590 —Why must one mourn these? O'er and gone is labour:
O'er and gone is it, even to those dead ones,
So that no more again they mind uprising.
Why must we tell in numbers those deprived ones,
And the live man be vexed with fate's fresh outbreak?
595 Rather, I bid full farewell to misfortunes!
For us, the left from out the Argeian army,
The gain beats, nor does sorrow counterbalance.
So that 'tis fitly boasted of, this sunlight,
By us, o'er sea and land the aery flyers,

576| MS:faulty: for who *1889a:*faulty: since who 577| MS:Is, through *P1877:*Goes, through 578| MS:and sad lodgments, *P1877:*and bad lodgments,
579| MS:And §crossed out§ Narrow §inserted above§ deckways ill strewn, §last two words and comma written above§ *P1877:*ill-strewn, 581| MS:land-things again—on *P1877:*land-things, again, on 582| MS:ramparts: *P1877:*ramparts, 583| MS:For, out *P1877:*And, out 584| MS:abiding mischief §word crossed out§ damage 586| MS:Winter too if *P1877:*Winter, too, if 589| MS:falling— *P1877:*falling 590| MS:labour— *P1877:*labour: 591| MS:it—even §circled at end of line and transposed§ to <> ones *P1877:*it, even to <> ones, 592| MS:that they never §last two words crossed out and replaced above by§ no 593| MS:we §over illegible word§ say in <> ones *P1877:*we tell in <> ones, 594| MS:And vex the live man with fate fresh outbreaking? *P1877:*And the live man be vexed with fate's fresh outbreak? 595| MS:Rather, full farewell to these fortunes, bid I! *P1877:*Rather, I bid full farewell to misfortunes! 597| MS:beats—nor *P1877:*beats, nor 598| MS:'tis fit to boast of, this same sunlight, *P1877:*'tis fitly boasted of, this sunlight, 599| MS:land, the *P1877:*land the

600   "Troia at last taking, the band of Argives
      Hang up such trophies to the gods of Hellas
      Within their domes—new glory to grow ancient!"
      Such things men having heard must praise the city
      And army-leaders: and the grace which wrought them—
605   Of Zeus, shall honoured be. Thou hast my whole word.

CHOROS

      O'ercome by words, their sense I do not gainsay.
      For, aye this breeds youth in the old—"to learn well."
      But these things most the house and Klutaimnestra
      Concern, 'tis likely: while they make me rich, too.

KLUTAIMNESTRA

610   I shouted long ago, indeed, for joyance,
      When came that first night-messenger of fire
      Proclaiming Ilion's capture and dispersion.
      And someone, girding me, said, "Through fire-bearers
      Persuaded—Troia to be sacked now, thinkest?
615   Truly, the woman's way,—high to lift heart up!"
      By such words I was made seem wit-bewildered:
      Yet still I sacrificed; and,—female-song with,—
      A shout one man and other, through the city,
      Set up, congratulating in the gods' seats,
620   Soothing the incense-eating flame right fragrant.

600| MS:taking—the   *P1877:*taking, the   601| MS:Hang up §inserted above§ such
602| MS:domes—a glory to be ancient!"   *P1877:*domes—new glory to grow ancient!"
603| MS:things those having   *P1877:*things men having   604| MS:army leaders: and
the §inserted above§ grace which §inserted below§ outwrought §altered to wrought§ these—
*P1877:*army-leaders <> wrought them—   605| MS:Of Zeus shall <> word!
*P1877:*Zeus, shall <> word.   606| MS:words—their sense §inserted above illegible word
crossed out§   607| MS:For, over §crossed out and replaced by two words§ aye this <>
old—to <> well.   *P1877:*old—"to <> well."   608| MS:But that these things the <>
Klutaimnestra,   *P1877:*But these things most the <> Klutaimnestra
609| MS:'Tis like, concern most—while   *P1877:*Concern, 'tis likely: while
610| MS:longago   *P1877:*long ago   612| MS:dispertion.   *P1877:*dispersion.
613| MS:said— <> fire-senders §word after hyphen crossed out and replaced by§ bearers
616| MS:wit-bewildered—   *P1877:*wit-bewildered: 617| MS:sacrificed: and, <> with,
*P1877:*sacrificed; and,— <> with,—   618| MS:shout, one   *P1877:*shout one
619| MS:seats—   *P1877:*seats,   620| MS:right-fragrant.   *P1877:*right fragrant.

And now, what's more, indeed, why need'st thou tell me?
I of the king himself shall learn the whole word:
And,—as may best be,—I my revered husband
Shall hasten, as he comes back, to receive: for—
625   What's to a wife sweeter to see than this light
(Her husband, by the god saved, back from warfare)
So as to open gates? This tell my husband—
To come at soonest to his loving city.
A faithful wife at home may he find, coming!
630   Such an one as he left—the dog o' the household—
Trusty to him, adverse to the ill-minded,
And, in all else, the same: no signet-impress
Having done harm to, in that time's duration.
I know nor pleasure, nor blameworthy converse
635   With any other man more than—bronze-dippings!

HERALD

Such boast as this—brimful of the veracious—
Is, for a high-born dame, not bad to send forth!

CHOROS

Ay, she spoke thus to thee—that hast a knowledge
From clear interpreters—a speech most seemly.
640   But speak thou, herald! Meneleos I ask of:

621| MS:needst *P1877:*need'st   623| MS:And,—as may §two words crossed out and then restored§ for the §inserted above then crossed out§ best be,— §word and punctuation inserted above§ I shall §word crossed out§ my   624| MS:hasten—as he comes back §circled and transposed to§ —to *P1877:*hasten, as he comes back, to 626| MS:god preserved §word crossed out and replaced above by§ saved   627| MS:come, at soonest, to *P1877:*come at soonest to   629| MS:find coming *CP1877:*find, coming 630| MS:Such truly §word crossed out and replaced above by two words§ an one   631| MS:him, hostile §word crossed out and replaced above by§ adverse < > ill-minded *P1877:*ill-minded,   632| MS:same—no *P1877:*same: no   634| MS:pleasure—nor *P1877:*pleasure, nor   635| MS:bronze drippings! *P1877:*bronze-drippings! 636| MS:this—of the veracious brimful— *P1877:*this—brimful of the veracious— 637| MS:Is not bad, for a high born dame, to *P1877:*bad for a high-born dame   *1889a:*Is, for a high-born dame, not bad to   638| MS:thee,—that *P1877:*thee—that 639| MS:interpreters,—a < > seemly! *P1877:*interpreters—a   *1889a:*seemly. 640| MS:But thou, speak, Herald! < > of— *P1877:*But speak thou, herald! < > of:

If he, returning, back in safety also
Will come with you—this land's beloved chieftain?

HERALD

There's no way I might say things false and pleasant
For friends to reap the fruits of through a long time.

CHOROS

645   How then if, speaking good, things true thou chance on?

HERALD

For not well-hidden things become they, sundered.
The man has vanished from the Achaic army,
He and his ship too. I announce no falsehood.

CHOROS

Whether forth-putting openly from Ilion,
650   Or did storm—wide woe—snatch him from the army?

HERALD

Like topping bowman, thou hast touched the target,
And a long sorrow hast succinctly spoken.

CHOROS

Whether, then, of him, as a live or dead man
Was the report by other sailors bruited?

HERALD

655   Nobody knows so as to tell out clearly
Excepting Helios who sustains earth's nature.

645| MS:good—things   *P1877:*good, things   646| MS:For, sundered, not well-hidden
things become they.   *1889a:*For not well-hidden things become they, sundered.
647| MS:army— *P1877:*army,   649| MS:from Ilion—   *P1877:*from Ilion,
651| MS:Thou hast, like topping bowman, touched   *1889a:*Like topping bowman, thou hast
touched   656| MS:Excepting Helios that sustains   *P1877:*Helios who sustains

CHOROS

How say'st thou then, did storm the naval army
Attack and end, by the celestials' anger?

HERALD

It suits not to defile a day auspicious
660   With ill-announcing speech: distinct each god's due:
And when a messenger with gloomy visage
To a city bears a fall'n host's woes—God ward off!—
One popular wound that happens to the city,
And many sacrificed from many households—
665   Men, scourged by that two-thonged whip Ares loves so,
Double spear-headed curse, bloody yoke-couple,—
Of woes like these, doubtless, whoe'er comes weighted,
Him does it suit to sing the Erinues' paian.
But who, of matters saved a glad-news-bringer,
670   Comes to a city in good estate rejoicing. . . .
How shall I mix good things with evil, telling
Of storm against the Achaioi, urged by gods' wrath?
For they swore league, being arch-foes before that,
Fire and the sea: and plighted troth approved they,
675   Destroying the unhappy Argeian army.
At night began the bad-wave-outbreak evils;
For, ships against each other Threkian breezes
Shattered: and these, butted at in a fury
By storm and typhoon, with surge rain-resounding,—

657| MS:then did   *P1877:*then, did   659| MS:A day auspicious to defile it suits not
*P1877:*It suits not to defile a day auspicious   660| MS:distinct the §word crossed out and
replaced above by§ each   662| MS:fallen hosts woes   *P1877:*fallen host's woes
*CP1877:*fall'n   664| MS:And §crossed out and then restored§   665| MS:Men—by
the two thonged whip of §word crossed out and replaced above by§ which Ares < > so,—
*P1877:*Men, scourged by that two-thonged whip Ares < > so,   669| MS:who of < >
bringer   *P1877:*who, of < > bringer,   670| MS:rejoicing...   *P1877:*rejoicing....
671| MS:I §illegible word crossed out and replaced above by two words§ mix good things with
ill, mix §last two words and comma crossed out and replaced above by§ evil, telling §word
crossed out and then restored§   674| MS:sea, and < > they   *P1877:*sea: and < > they,
676| MS:evils—   *P1877:*evils;   677| MS:For ships   *P1877:*For, ships
678| MS:Shattered—and   *P1877:*Shattered: and
679| MS:storm, and < > resounding   *P1877:*storm < > resounding,—

41

680　Off they went, vanished, thro' a bad herd's whirling.
　　And, when returned the brilliant light of Helios,
　　We view the Aigaian sea on flower with corpses
　　Of men Achaian and with naval ravage.
　　But us indeed, and ship, unhurt i' the hull too,
685　Either someone outstole us or outprayed us—
　　Some god—no man it was the tiller touching.
　　And Fortune, saviour, willing on our ship sat.
　　So as it neither had in harbour wave-surge
　　Nor ran aground against a shore all rocky.
690　And then, the water-Haides having fled from
　　In the white day, not trusting to our fortune,
　　We chewed the cud in thoughts—this novel sorrow
　　O' the army labouring and badly pounded.
　　And now—if anyone of them is breathing—
695　They talk of us as having perished: why not?
　　And we—that they the same fate have, imagine.
　　May it be for the best! Meneleos, then,
　　Foremost and specially to come, expect thou!
　　If (that is) any ray o' the sun reports him
700　Living and seeing too—by Zeus' contrivings,
　　Not yet disposed to quite destroy the lineage—
　　Some hope is he shall come again to household.
　　Having heard such things, know, thou truth art hearing!

CHOROS

　　Who may he have been that named thus wholly with exactitude—
705　(Was he someone whom we see not, by forecastings of the future

---

681| MS:And when <> Helios   P1877:And, when <> Helios,   683| MS:men Achaian,
and   P1877:Achaian and   684| MS:ship too, §word crossed out§
685| MS:some one out stole <> out-prayed us—   P1877:out-stole   1889a:someone outstole
<> outprayed us—   687| MS:And Fortune, Saviour, <> sat   P1877:And Fortune,
saviour, <> sat.   688| MS:as she neither   P1877:as it neither   689| MS:a landing
§word crossed out and replaced above by two words§ shore all   690| MS:water Hades
P1877:water-Hades   1889a:water-Haides   694| MS:now—of them if anyone is
1889a:now—if anyone of them is   696| MS:imagine—   P1877:imagine.
698| MS:specially to come, §last two words and comma inserted above§   699| MS:If—
that is—any   P1877:If (that is) any   704| MS:exactitude   P1877:exactitude—
705| MS:§parenthesis crossed out§ —Was <> future,   P1877:(Was <> future

Guiding tongue in happy mood?)
—Her with battle for a bridegroom, on all sides contention-wooed,
Helena? Since—mark the suture!—
Ship's-Hell, Man's-Hell, City's-Hell,
710   From the delicately-pompous curtains that pavilion well,
Forth, by favour of the gale
Of earth-born Zephuros did she sail.
Many shield-bearers, leaders of the pack,
Sailed too upon their track,
715   Theirs who had directed oar,
Then visible no more,
To Simois' leaf-luxuriant shore—
For sake of strife all gore!

To Ilion Wrath, fulfilling her intent,
720   This marriage-care—the rightly named so—sent:
In after-time, for the tables' abuse
And that of the hearth-partaker Zeus,
Bringing to punishment
Those who honoured with noisy throat
725   The honour of the bride, the hymenæal note
Which did the kinsfolk then to singing urge.
But, learning a new hymn for that which was,
The ancient city of Priamos
Groans probably a great and general dirge,
730   Denominating Paris
"The man that miserably marries:"—
She who, all the while before,

706| MS:mood?—) §parenthesis crossed out§ *P1877*:mood?)
707| MS:Her *P1877*:—Her 712| MS:Of earth-born §hyphenated word circled and transposed to§ Zephuros the §word crossed out§ did 713| MS:Many §over illegible word§ 714| MS:track— *P1877*:track, 715| MS:Who had *P1877*:Theirs who had 718| MS:strife, all *P1877*:strife all 719| MS:To Ilion, Wrath, fulfilling its intent, *P1877*:To Ilion Wrath, fulfilling her intent, 720| MS:marriage-care,— <> so,—sent: *P1877*:marriage-care— <> so—sent: 721| MS:At after time *P1877*:In after-time 724| MS:honoured then §word crossed out§ with 725| MS:hymeneal note— *P1877*:hymenoeal note *CP1877*:hymenæal 726| MS:That §over illegible word§ which the <> to sing did urge. *P1877*:Which did the <> to singing urge. 727| MS:But learning <> was *P1877*:But, learning <> was, 729| MS:and universal §word crossed out and replaced above by§ general dirge. *P1877*:dirge,

A life, that was a general dirge
For citizens' unhappy slaughter, bore.

735 And thus a man, by no milk's help,
Within his household reared a lion's whelp
That loved the teat
In life's first festal stage:
Gentle as yet,
740 A true child-lover, and, to men of age,
A thing whereat pride warms;
And oft he had it in his arms
Like any new-born babe, bright-faced, to hand
Wagging its tail, at belly's strict command.

745 But in due time upgrown,
The custom of progenitors was shown:
For—thanks for sustenance repaying
With ravage of sheep slaughtered—
It made unbidden feast;
750 With blood the house was watered,
To household came a woe there was no staying:
Great mischief many-slaying!
From God it was—some priest

733| MS:life that   *P1877:*life, that   734| MS:citizens—"unhappy slaughter!" bore.
*P1877:*citizens' unhappy slaughter, bore.   735| MS:thus, §two illegible words and
comma crossed out and replaced above by two words and comma§ a man, by no milk's help,
§last four words and comma crossed out and then restored§ §four illegible words inserted
above crossed out§   *P1877:*thus a   736| MS:household by no milk's help §last four
words crossed out and replaced above by three words§ reared a lion's whelp
737-38| MS:teat In life's first festal stage, §last five words and comma circled and new line
indicated§   738| *P1877:*stage: 740| MS:and to <> age   *P1877:*and, to <> age,
741| MS:warms: *P1877:*warms;   743| MS:bright faced   *P1877:*bright-faced
745| MS:But, up with §last two words crossed out and replaced above by§ in due   *P1877:*But in
746| MS:shown—   *P1877:*shown: 747| MS:repaying,—   *P1877:*repaying
748| MS:slaughtered,   *P1877:*slaughtered—   749-50| MS:feast,   *P1877:*feast; With blood
the house was watered: §last six words and punctuation circled and new line indicated§
750| *P1877:*watered,   751| MS:household—woe   *1889a:*household came a woe
752-76| MS:§twenty-four lines are indented; in margin B. writes, "Make all lines begin from
same place—"§   753| MS:From §over illegible word§ <> was, some §two illegible words
inserted above and crossed out§   *P1877:*was—some

Of Até, in the house, by nurture thus increased.

755 At first, then, to the city of Ilion went
A soul, as I might say, of windless calm—
Wealth's quiet ornament,
An eyes'-dart bearing balm,
Love's spirit-biting flower.
760 But—from the true course bending—
She brought about, of marriage, bitter ending:
Ill-resident, ill-mate, in power
Passing to the Priamidai—by sending
Of Hospitable Zeus—
765 Erinus for a bride,—to make brides mourn, her dower.

Spoken long ago
Was the ancient saying
Still among mortals staying:
"Man's great prosperity at height of rise
770 Engenders offspring nor unchilded dies;
And, from good fortune, to such families,
Buds forth insatiate woe."
Whereas, distinct from any,
Of my own mind I am:
775 For 'tis the unholy deed begets the many,
Resembling each its dam.

754| MS:Of Ate in the house §illegible word§ greatness §last five words crossed out and replaced above by seven words circled with punctuation§ in the house, by nature thus increased! *P1877:*Of Até, in <> increased. 754-55| MS:§¶§ *1889a:*§no¶; emended to restore ¶; see Editorial Notes§ 755| MS:went §over illegible word§
757| MS:Of wealth the quiet *P1877:*Wealth's quiet 760| MS:But she accomplished §last two words crossed out§ 761| MS:She brought to pass, §last four words and comma added to beginning of line§ Of *P1877:*brought about, of 762| MS:An a §last two words crossed out§ Ill resident, §illegible word crossed out§ ill mate, §illegible word crossed out§ in *P1877:*Ill-resident, ill-mate, in 763| MS:Passing §over erasure§ <> by power §word crossed out and replaced above by§ sending 764| MS:Zeus. *P1877:*Zeus—
765| MS:a §illegible word above crossed out§ bride 766| MS:ago, *P1877:*ago
768| MS:staying— *P1877:*staying: 770| MS:Rears §crossed out and replaced above by§ Engenders offspring forth §crossed out§ nor un §inserted above§ childless §altered to§ unchilded dies: *P1877:*dies; 773| MS:Whereas, §in margin§ Distinct *P1877:*distinct
774| MS:Of my §inserted above§ 775| MS:For 'tis §inserted above§

Of households that correctly estimate,
Ever a beauteous child is born of Fate.

But ancient Arrogance delights to generate
780   Arrogance, young and strong mid mortals' sorrow,
Or now, or then, when comes the appointed morrow.
And she bears young Satiety;
And, fiend with whom nor fight nor war can be,
Unholy Daring—twin black Curses
785   Within the household, children like their nurses.

But Justice shines in smoke-grimed habitations,
And honours the well-omened life;
While,—gold-besprinkled stations
Where the hands' filth is rife,
790   With backward-turning eyes
Leaving,—to holy seats she hies,
Not worshipping the power of wealth
Stamped with applause by stealth:
And to its end directs each thing begun.

795   Approach then, my monarch, of Troia the sacker, of Atreus the son!
How ought I address thee, how ought I revere thee,—nor yet overhitting
Nor yet underbending the grace that is fitting?
Many of mortals hasten to honour the seeming-to-be—
Passing by justice: and, with the ill-faring, to groan as he groans all are
        free.

777| MS:estimate   *P1877:*estimate,   778| MS:—A < > is ever Fate.   *P1877:*Ever a < > is
born of Fate.   778-79| MS:§¶§   *1889a:*§no¶§;   emended to restore ¶; see Editorial Notes§
781| MS:At this time, or at this §last six words and comma crossed out and replaced by four
words and comma§ Or now, or then—when   *P1877:*then, when
782| MS:she, the new, brings forth §last four words and comma crossed out and replaced
above by two words§ bears young   783| MS:Dæmon with   *P1877:*And, fiend with
784| MS:Unholy Enterprise— §last word and dash crossed out and replaced above by two
words and dash§ Daring—twin black   785| MS:like §over illegible word§
787| MS:honors   *1889a:*honours   791| MS:Leaving, to   *P1877:*Leaving,—to
794| MS:And everything §word crossed out§ to its set term §last two words crossed out and
replaced above by§ end   794-95| MS:§no¶§   *P1877:*§¶§   797| MS:The mark, Not
§first two words and comma crossed out§   798| MS:honor   *1889a:*honour
799| MS:Passing-by < > and with   *P1877:*Passing by < > and, with

⁸⁰⁰ But no bite of the sorrow their liver has reached to:
They joy with the joyful,—one outside on each, too,
As they force to a smile smileless faces.
But whoever is good at distinguishing races
In sheep of his flock—it is not for the eyes
⁸⁰⁵ Of a man to escape such a shepherd's surprise,
As they seem, from a well-wishing mind,
In watery friendship to fawn and be kind.
Thou to me, then, indeed, sending an army for Helena's sake,
(I will not conceal it) wast—oh, by no help of the Muses!—depicted
⁸¹⁰ Not well of thy midriff the rudder directing,—convicted
Of bringing a boldness they did not desire to the men with existence
    at stake.
But now—from no outside of mind, nor unlovingly—gracious thou art
To those who have ended the labour, fulfilling their part;
And in time shalt thou know, by inquiry instructed,
⁸¹⁵ Who of citizens justly, and who not to purpose, the city conducted.

AGAMEMNON

First, indeed, Argos, and the gods, the local,
'Tis right addressing—those with me the partners

---

^{800|} MS:But the grief §last two words crossed out and replaced above by§ no <> their inwards
§word crossed out and replaced above by§ lives <> to—*P1877:*to: ^{801|} MS:Such also
rejoice §last three words crossed out and replaced above by two words§ They joy with the
joyful, one   *P1877:*They say with the joyful,—one §emended to§ They joy with §see Editorial
Notes§   ^{802|} MS:smile—smileless   *P1877:*smile smileless   ^{805|} MS:escape
§illegible word crossed out§ surprise—   *P1877:*escape such a shepherd's surprise,
^{806|} MS:well wishing   *P1877:*well-wishing   ^{807|} MS:In watered §inserted above§
friendship half water, §last two words and comma crossed out§ to §illegible word crossed out§
fawn   ^{808|} MS:sending a host forth §last three words crossed out and replaced above by
two words§ an army   ^{809|} MS:depicted—   *P1877:*depicted   ^{810|} MS:directing,—
of bringing,—convicted,—   *P1877:*directing,—convicted   ^{811|} MS:A holdup apart
from §last two words crossed out and replaced above by three words§ they did not desire to
§illegible word crossed out§ whose lives were §last three words crossed out and replaced above
by four words§ the men with existence at stake: *P1877:*Of bringing a boldness they <>
stake.   ^{812|} MS:unlovingly, gracious   *P1877:*unlovingly—gracious
^{813|} MS:have brought to an end the labor, <> part.   *P1877:*have ended the labour, <> part;
^{814|} MS:know, bring §word crossed out§ by <> instructed   *P1877:*instructed   ^{815|}
^{815|} MS:Both §word crossed out§ Who of citizens §last two words inserted above§ justly and <>
purpose the   *P1877:*justly, and <> purpose, the   ^{816|} MS:gods—the local—
*P1877:*gods, the local,   ^{817|} MS:those with §word crossed out and then
restored§ me the §last two words circled and inserted above§ partners

In this return and right things done the city
Of Priamos: gods who, from no tongue hearing

820   The rights o' the cause, for Ilion's fate man-slaught'rous
Into the bloody vase, not oscillating,
Put the vote-pebbles, while, o' the rival vessel,
Hope rose up to the lip-edge: filled it was not.
By smoke the captured city is still conspicuous:

825   Até's burnt offerings live: and, dying with them,
The ash sends forth the fulsome blasts of riches.
Of these things, to the gods grace many-mindful
'Tis right I render, since both nets outrageous
We built them round with, and, for sake of woman,

830   It did the city to dust—the Argeian monster,
The horse's nestling, the shield-bearing people
That made a leap, at setting of the Pleiads,
And, vaulting o'er the tower, the raw-flesh-feeding
Lion licked up his fill of blood tyrannic.

835   I to the gods indeed prolonged this preface;
But—as for *thy* thought, I remember hearing—
I say the same, and thou co-pleader hast me.
Since few of men this faculty is born with—
To honour, without grudge, their friend, successful.

840   For moody, on the heart, a poison seated
Its burthen doubles to who gained the sickness:
By his own griefs he is himself made heavy,
And out-of-door prosperity seeing groans at.

818| MS:return, and §word circled and inserted above§ right things §illegible word crossed out§ done   *P1877:*return and   819| MS:Of Priamos: since §word crossed out and replaced above by two words and comma§ gods who, from   820| MS:o' the case, for *P1877:*o' the cause, for   821| MS:oscillating   *P1877:*oscillating,   822| MS:vote-pebbles—while on §altered to§ o' the other §word crossed out and replaced above by§ rival vessel   *P1877:*vessel,   829| MS:We found §word crossed out and replaced above by§ built < > and—for < > woman—   *P1877:*and, for < > woman,   830| MS:It did §last two words added to beginning of line§ The city did §crossed out§   *P1877:*did the city   831| MS:The Horse's   *P1877:*horse's   833| MS:And vaulting   *P1877:*And, vaulting   834| MS:licked §over erasure§   835| MS:preface—   *P1877:*preface;   836| MS:thought—I   *P1877:*thought, I   838| MS:this quality §word crossed out and replaced above by§ faculty   839| MS:Their friend, successful, without grudge to honor. *1889a:*To honour, without grudge, their friend, successful.   842| MS:heavy—   *P1877:*heavy,   843| MS:out-of-door wealth §word crossed out§

Knowing, I'd call (for well have I experienced)
845 "Fellowship's mirror," "phantom of a shadow,"
Those seeming to be mighty gracious to me:
While just Odusseus—he who sailed not willing—
When joined on, was to me the ready trace-horse.
This of him, whether dead or whether living,
850 I say. For other city-and-gods' concernment—
Appointing common courts, in full assemblage
We will consult. And as for what holds seemly—
How it may lasting stay well, must be counselled:
While what has need of medicines Paionian
855 We, either burning or else cutting kindly,
Will make endeavour to turn pain from sickness.
And now into the domes and homes by altar
Going, I to the gods first raise the right-hand—
They who, far sending, back again have brought me.
860 And Victory, since she followed, fixed remain she!

KLUTAIMNESTRA

Men, citizens, Argeians here, my worships!
I shall not shame me, consort-loving manners
To tell before you: for in time there dies off
The diffidence from people. Not from others
865 Learning, I of myself will tell the hard life
I bore so long as this man was 'neath Ilion.
First: for a woman, from the male divided,
To sit at home alone, is monstrous evil—
Hearing the many rumours back-revenging:

845| MS:shadow"— *P1877:*shadow," 847| MS:just Odusseus,—he < > willing,—
*P1877:*just Odusseus—he < > willing— 850| MS:say. For §over erasure§
851| MS:Appointing public §word crossed out and replaced above by§ common
852| MS:consult. And—what indeed is §word crossed out and replaced above by§ proves
seemly— *P1877:*And as for what holds seemly— 853| MS:counseled:
*1889a:*counselled: 854| MS:medicines Paionian, *P1877:*Paionian
860| MS:she follows, fixed *P1877:*she followed, fixed 862| MS:shame my §word
crossed out and replaced above by one word and comma§ me, 863| MS:To speak of to
§last three words crossed out and replaced above by two words§ tell before you—for
*P1877:*you: for 866| MS:was at Ilion. *P1877:*was 'neath Ilion.
867| MS:First—for *P1877:*First: for 868| MS:alone—is *P1877:*alone, is

870 And for now This to come, now That bring after
Woe, and still worse woe, bawling in the household!
And truly, if so many wounds had chanced on
My husband here, as homeward used to dribble
Report, he's pierced more than a net to speak of!
875 While, were he dying (as the words abounded)
A triple-bodied Geruon the Second,
Plenty above—for loads below I count not—
Of earth a three-share cloak he'd boast of taking,
Once only dying in each several figure!
880 Because of suchlike rumours back-revenging,
Many the halters from my neck, above head,
Others than *I* loosed—loosed from neck by main force!
From this cause, sure, the boy stands not beside me—
Possessor of our troth-plights, thine and mine too—
885 As ought Orestes: be not thou astonished!
For, him brings up our well-disposed guest-captive
Strophios the Phokian—ills that told on both sides
To me predicting—both of thee 'neath Ilion
The danger, and if anarchy's mob-uproar
890 Should overthrow thy council; since 'tis born with
Mortals,—whoe'er has fallen, the more to kick him.
Such an excuse, I think, no cunning carries!
As for myself—why, of my wails the rushing
Fountains are dried up: not in them a drop more!
895 And in my late-to-bed eyes I have damage,

872| MS:She and another §last three words crossed out and replaced above by three words
and comma§ Woe, and still worse woe, noising in   *P1877:*woe, bawling in
873| MS:The man §last two words crossed out and replaced above by§ My husband
874| MS:of.   *P1877:*of!   875| MS:dying—as < > abounded—   *P1877:*dying (as < >
abounded)   876| MS:triple bodied < > second,   *P1877:*triple-bodied < > Second,
877| MS:§Parenthesis crossed out§ Plenty Of earth §last two words inserted above then crossed
out§ above   878| MS:Of earth §restored from l. 877§ —a < > taking—   *P1877:*earth a < >
taking,   879| MS:figure.   *P1877:*figure!   880| MS:back-revenging   *P1877:*back-
revenging,   881| MS:neck—above head—   *P1877:*neck, above head,
882| MS:loosed—loosed it was by   *P1877:*loosed from neck by   883| MS:cause—sure—
the   *P1877:*cause, sure, the   884| MS:troth plights   *P1877:*troth-plights
885| MS:ought Orestes: do not be astonished!   *P1877:*Orestes: be not thou astonished!
886| MS:For him   *P1877:*For, him   890| MS:Thy council should o'erthrow; since it is
*1889a:*Should overthrow thy council; since 'tis   894| MS:up—not   *P1877:*up: not
895| MS:eyes damage have I   *1889a:*eyes I have damage,

50

Bewailing what concerned thee, those torch-holdings
For ever unattended to. In dreams—why,
Beneath the light wing-beats o' the gnat, I woke up
As he went buzzing—sorrows that concerned thee
900   Seeing, that filled more than their fellow-sleep-time.
Now, all this having suffered, from soul grief-free
I would style this man here the dog o' the stables,
The saviour forestay of the ship, the high roof's
Ground-prop, son sole-begotten to his father,
905   —Ay, land appearing to the sailors past hope,
Loveliest day to see after a tempest,
To the wayfaring-one athirst a well-spring,
—The joy, in short, of 'scaping all that's—fatal!
I judge him worth addresses such as these are
910   —Envy stand off!—for many those old evils
We underwent. And now, to me—dear headship!
Dismount thou from this car, not earthward setting
The foot of thine, O king, that's Ilion's spoiler!
Slave-maids, why tarry?—whose the task allotted
915   To strew the soil o' the road with carpet-spreadings.
Immediately be purple-strewn the pathway,
So that to home unhoped may lead him—Justice!
As for the rest, care shall—by no sleep conquered—
Dispose things—justly (gods to aid!) appointed.

AGAMEMNON

920   Offspring of Leda, of my household warder,

896| MS:thee—those   *P1877:*thee, those   898| MS:up, *P1877:*up
901| MS:suffered—from   *P1877:*suffered, from   902| MS:this my husband—dog
*P1877:*this man here the dog   905| MS:hope—   *P1877:*hope,   907| MS:way faring
one athirst—a   *P1877:*wayfaring-one athirst a   908| MS:of scaping <> fatal.
*P1877:*fatal!   *1889a:*of 'scaping   909| MS:are—   *P1877:*are   910| MS:—Envy be
off   *P1877:*—Envy stand off   912| MS:car—not   *P1877:*car, not   914| MS:tarry?—
to §dash and last word inserted above§ whom the task's app §altered to§ allotted   *P1877:*tarry?—
whose the task allotted   915| MS:The soil o' the road to strew with   *1889a:*To strew the
soil o' the road with   917| MS:That—to a home unhoped—may   *P1877:*So that to home
unhoped may   918| MS:rest, my §word crossed out and replaced above by§ care
919| MS:justly, gods to aid, appointed!   *P1877:*justly (god's to aid!) appointed.
920| MS:of Leda, guardian of my household,   *P1877:*of Leda, of my household warder,

Suitably to my absence hast thou spoken,
For long the speech thou didst outstretch! But aptly
To praise—from others ought to go this favour.
And for the rest,—not me, in woman's fashion,
925   Mollify, nor—as mode of barbarous man is—
To me gape forth a groundward-falling clamour!
Nor, strewing it with garments, make my passage
Envied! Gods, sure, with these behoves we honour:
But, for a mortal on these varied beauties
930   To walk—to me, indeed, is nowise fear-free.
I say—as man, not god, to me do homage!
Apart from foot-mats both and varied vestures,
Renown is loud, and—not to lose one's senses,
God's greatest gift. Behoves we him call happy
935   Who has brought life to end in loved well-being.
If all things I might manage thus—brave man, I!

KLUTAIMNESTRA

Come now, this say, nor feign a feeling to me!

AGAMEMNON

With feeling, know indeed, I do not tamper!

KLUTAIMNESTRA

Vowed'st thou to the gods, in fear, to act thus?

922| MS:didst §over erasure§   923| MS:So praise §circled and inserted above crossed out illegible word§ < > others §illegible word crossed out and replaced above by§ ought
928| MS:behoves us honor—   *P1877:*honor: *1889a:*behoves we honour:
932| MS:foot-mats both §word inserted above§ and < > vestures,— *P1877:*vestures,
933| MS:Renown cries §word crossed and replaced above by two words and comma§ is loud,
< > not praised, §word and comma crossed out§ to   934| MS:Behoves us him
*1889a:*Behoves we him   935| MS:Who life has brought to *1889a:*Who has brought life
to   937| MS:now,—this say—to me—nor feign a feeling! *P1877:*now, this say, nor feign
a feeling to me!   938| MS:With §over illegible word§ feeling, §comma crossed out and
then restored§ be sure, §last two words and comma crossed out and replaced above by
illegible word crossed out then two words and comma§, know indeed, I

AGAMEMNON

⁹⁴⁰ If any, *I* well knew resolve I outspoke.

KLUTAIMNESTRA

What think'st thou Priamos had done, thus victor?

AGAMEMNON

On varied vests—I do think—he had passaged.

KLUTAIMNESTRA

Then, do not, struck with awe at human censure. . . .

AGAMEMNON

Well, popular mob-outcry much avails too.

KLUTAIMNESTRA

⁹⁴⁵ Ay, but the unenvied is not the much valued.

AGAMEMNON

Sure, 'tis no woman's part to long for battle.

KLUTAIMNESTRA

Why, to the prosperous, even suits a beating.

AGAMEMNON

What? thou this beating us in war dost prize too?

---

^{940|} MS:any, §illegible word crossed out and replaced above by two words and comma crossed out§ I <> knew §illegible word crossed out§ resolve   *P1877:*any, *I*
^{941|} MS:How think'st   *P1877:*What think'st   ^{942|} MS:On §illegible word and dash crossed out and replaced above by two words and dash§ varied vests—that § word crossed out§ I
^{943|} MS:censure...   *1889a:*censure....   ^{945|} MS:unenvied one §word crossed out§ , is not the much valued! §last three words and punctuation inserted above§ *P1877:*unenvied is <> valued.   ^{946|} MS:battle!   *1889a:*battle.
^{947|} MS:beating!   *1889a:*beating.   ^{948|} MS:What? §word and punctuation crossed out and replaced above by illegible word and punctuation crossed out§ What? §inserted above§ you, too, prize §last two words and comma crossed out§ this beating one in warfare prize too?   *P1877:*What? thou this beating us in war dost prize too?

KLUTAIMNESTRA

Persuade thee! power, for once, grant *me*—and willing!

AGAMEMNON

950 But if this seem so to thee—shoes, let someone
Loose under, quick—foot's serviceable carriage!
And me, on these sea-products walking, may no
Grudge from a distance, from the god's eye, strike at!
For great shame were my strewment-spoiling—riches
955 Spoiling with feet, and silver-purchased textures!
Of these things, thus then. But this female-stranger
Tenderly take inside! Who conquers mildly
God, from afar, benignantly regardeth.
For, willing, no one wears a yoke that's servile:
960 And she, of many valuables, outpicked
The flower, the army's gift, myself has followed.
So,—since to hear thee, I am brought about thus,—
I go into the palace—purples treading.

KLUTAIMNESTRA

There is the sea—and what man shall exhaust it?—
965 Feeding much purple's worth-its-weight-in-silver
Dye, ever fresh and fresh, our garments' tincture;
At home, such wealth, king, we begin—by gods' help—
With having, and to lack, the household knows not.
Of many garments had I vowed a treading

949| MS:thee! Power *P1877:*thee! power   950| MS:some one *P1877:*someone
951| MS:serviceable walking §crossed out and replaced above by§ carriage— *P1877:*carriage!
952| MS:me, upon §crossed out§ these sea-works §last word of compound crossed out and
replaced above by§ products   953| MS:from afar, §last word and comma crossed out and
replaced above by two words and comma§ a distance, from < > strike me! *P1877:*strike at!
956| MS:then! But *P1877:*then. But   960| MS:outpicked— *P1877:*outpicked
965| MS:Feeding §illegible word crossed out§ much   966| MS:and fresh, the §crossed out
and replaced above by§ our < > tincture— *P1877:*tincture;
967| MS:such matters §crossed out and replaced above by two words and punctuation§ wealth,
king, we begin— §last two words and dash crossed out and restored§ by
968| MS:having, monarch §crossed out and replaced above by two words§ and to
969| MS:vowed the §crossed out and replaced above by § a

54

970 (In oracles if fore-enjoined the household)
   Of this dear soul the safe-return-price scheming!
   For, root existing, foliage goes up houses,
   O'erspreading shadow against Seirios dog-star;
   And, thou returning to the hearth domestic,
975 Warmth, yea, in winter dost thou show returning.
   And when, too, Zeus works, from the green-grape acrid,
   Wine—then, already, cool in houses cometh—
   The perfect man his home perambulating!
   Zeus, Zeus Perfecter, these my prayers perfect thou!
980 Thy care be—yea—of things thou mayst make perfect!

CHOROS

   Wherefore to me, this fear—
   Groundedly stationed here
   Fronting my heart, the portent-watcher—flits she?
   Wherefore should prophet-play
985 The uncalled and unpaid lay,
   Nor—having spat forth fear, like bad dreams—sits she
   On the mind's throne beloved—well-suasive Boldness?
   For time, since, by a throw of all the hands,
   The boat's stern-cables touched the sands,
990 Has past from youth to oldness,—

971| MS:safe-return- §third word of compound illegibly crossed out and replaced above by§
price scheming. *P1877:*scheming!   972| MS:existing §written over erasure§
973| MS:o'erspreading a Shadow §first word circled and placed after *Shadow*, second word
crossed out§   *1889a:*O'erspreading shadow   975| MS:Warmth, yes, in   *P1877:*Warmth,
yea, in   976| MS:works from <> acrid   *P1877:*works, from <> acrid,
977| MS:then already cool is §crossed out§ in the §crossed out§
980| MS:Thine care §inserted above§ be §illegible word crossed out§   —yea <> may'st
*P1877:*Thy care   *1889a:*mayst   981-83| MS:§lines indented;   B. states in margin, "Begin
from the same place."§   981| MS:fear,—   *P1877:*fear—   983| MS:Fronting
§written over illegible word§ <> watcher,—flits   *P1877:*watcher—flits
984| MS:Why §last letter crossed out§ erefore §inserted above§ prophet— §circled and placed
after *should*§ play,   *P1877:*play   985| MS:uncalled unpaid for §crossed out§ lay,
§illegible word crossed out§   *1889a:*uncalled and unpaid   986| MS:Nor §written over
erasure§   988| MS:by a throw of §last three words crossed out and restored§ all
989| MS:The throw of §last three words crossed out and replaced above by two words circled§
The boat's stern §illegible word crossed out and replaced above by§ —cables §two illegible
words crossed out and replaced above by two words§ touched the
990| MS:ship-borne §written over illegible words§ bands: *P1877:*bands.

55

When under Ilion rushed the ship-borne bands.

And from my eyes I learn—
Being myself my witness—their return.
Yet, all the same, without a lyre, my soul,
995　Itself its teacher too, chants from within
Erinus' dirge, not having now the whole
Of Hope's dear boldness : nor my inwards sin—
The heart that's rolled in whirls against the mind
Justly presageful of a fate behind.
1000　But I pray—things false, from my hope, may fall
Into the fate that's not-fulfilled-at-all!

Especially at least, of health that's great
The term's insatiable: for, its weight
—A neighbour, with a common wall between—
1005　Ever will sickness lean;
And destiny, her course pursuing straight,
Has struck man's ship against a reef unseen.
Now, when a portion, rather than the treasure,
Fear casts from sling, with peril in right measure,
1010　It has not sunk—the universal freight,
(With misery freighted over-full)
Nor has fear whelmed the hull.

996| MS:This dirge o'the Fury—having not the   *P1877*:Erinus' dirge, not having now the
998| MS:two illegible words crossed out and replaced above by§ The <> rolled in whirls §last
two words circled and inserted above line§ against   999| MS:In whirls §last two words
crossed out§ Justly   1000| MS:false, and fear §last two words crossed out§ from my
§inserted above§ hope   1001| MS:the fate that's §last two words inserted above§
1002| MS:Aparently, at §first word and comma crossed out and replaced above by§ Especially
at   1003| MS:for, §illegible word crossed out§ its weight,   *P1877*:weight
1004| MS:§two illegible words crossed out§ —A neighbour, with §written over erasure§ a
§illegible word crossed out and replaced above by§ common   1006| MS:destiny §illegible
word written above and crossed out §   1007| MS:struck §written over erasure§ a §word
crossed out§   man's §parenthesis crossed out§ ship §illegible letter crossed out§
1008| MS:portion— <> treasure—   *P1877*:portion, <> treasure,   1009| MS:Fear §written
above illegible word crossed out§ forth §crossed out then circled and placed after next word§
casting §word altered to§ cast from sling, with need §word crossed out and replaced above by§
peril in right §inserted above§ measure,—   *P1877*:Fear casts from <> measure,
1010| MS:sunk §written over erasure§ <> freight,— §dash crossed out§   1012| MS:Nor
did fear whelm in wave §last two words written above§ the   *P1877*:Nor has fear whelmed the

Then too the gift of Zeus,
Two-handedly profuse,
1015   Even from the furrows' yield for yearly use
Has done away with famine, the disease;
But blood of man to earth once falling—deadly, black—
In times ere these,—
Who may, by singing spells, call back?
1020   Zeus had not else stopped one who rightly knew
The way to bring the dead again.
But, did not an appointed Fate constrain
The Fate from gods, to bear no more than due,
My heart, outstripping what tongue utters,
1025   Would have all out: which now, in darkness, mutters
Moodily grieved, nor ever hopes to find
How she a word in season may unwind
From out the enkindling mind.

KLUTAIMNESTRA

Take thyself in, thou too—I say, Kassandra!
1030   Since Zeus—not angrily—in household placed thee
Partaker of hand-sprinklings, with the many
Slaves stationed, his the Owner's altar close to.
Descend from out this car, nor be high-minded!
And truly they do say Alkmené's child once
1035   Bore being sold, slaves' barley-bread his living.
If, then, necessity of this lot o'erbalance,
Much is the favour of old-wealthy masters:
For those who, never hoping, made fine harvest
Are harsh to slaves in all things, beyond measure.

1013| MS:§several lines are indented; B. writes in margin, "In a line"§
1013| MS:Then too §inserted above§ the great §word crossed out§ gift of Zeus   *P1877*:of
Zeus,   1014| MS:profuse   *P1877*:profuse,   1017| MS:man to earth §last two words
inserted above§ once falling,— < > black,—   *1889a:*falling— < > black—
1022| MS:But did   *P1877*:But, did   1024| MS:heart, anticipating §crossed out and
replaced above by§ outstripping   1026| MS:grieved—nor   *P1877*:grieved, nor
1027| MS:A word in season §last four words marked for transposition to follow *she*§ how
§altered to§ How   1028| MS:enkindling §first two letters inserted above§
1031| MS:hand sprinklings—with   *P1877*:hand-sprinklings, with   1035| MS:slaves'
§written over erasure§   1036| MS:If then necessity   *P1877*:If, then, necessity

1040   Thou hast—with us—such usage as law warrants.

CHOROS

To thee it was, she paused plain speech from speaking.
Being inside the fatal nets—obeying,
Thou mayst obey: but thou mayst disobey too!

KLUTAIMNESTRA

Why, if she is not, in the swallow's fashion,
1045   Possessed of voice that's unknown and barbaric,
I, with speech—speaking in mind's scope—persuade her.

CHOROS

Follow! The best—as things now stand—she speaks of.
Obey thou, leaving this thy car-enthronement!

KLUTAIMNESTRA

Well, with this thing at door, for me no leisure
1050   To waste time: as concerns the hearth mid-navelled,
Already stand the sheep for fireside slaying
By those who never hoped to have such favour.
If thou, then, aught of this wilt do, delay not!
But if thou, being witless, tak'st no word in,
1055   Speak thou, instead of voice, with hand as Kars do!

1040| MS:such §illegible word crossed out and replaced above by§ usage
1041| MS:she stopped §crossed out and replaced above by§ paused from saying. §last two
words circled and inserted after§ plain speech.   *P1877:*from speaking,   1043| MS:Thou
may'st < > may'st   *1889a:*Thou mayst < > mayst   1045| MS:An unknown and §inserted
above§ voice §circled and inserted after§ barbaric possessed of,   *1889a:*Possessed of voice
that's unknown and barbaric   1046| MS:with word—speaking in mind's reach—persuade
*P1877:*with speech—speaking in mind's scope—persuade   1048| MS:she bids thee.
*P1877:*she speaks of   1049| MS:Certes, with   *P1877:*Well, with   1051| MS:fireside
slaughter   *1889a:*fireside slaying   1053| MS:those, §written over illegible word§ then, if
§crossed out§ aught < > wilt §written over erasure§   1054| MS:if thou— §last word and
dash inserted above§ < > witless—tak'st   *P1877:*thou, being witless, tak'st
1055| MS:Instead of voice, speak thou with   *P1877:*Speak thou, instead of voice, with

CHOROS

She seems a plain interpreter in need of,
The stranger! and her way—a beast's new-captured!

KLUTAIMNESTRA

Why, she is mad, sure,—hears her own bad senses,—
Who, while she comes, leaving a town new-captured,
1060 Yet knows not how to bear the bit o' the bridle
Before she has out-frothed her bloody fierceness.
Not I—throwing away more words—will shamed be!

CHOROS

But I,—for I compassionate,—will chafe not.
Come, O unhappy one, this car vacating,
1065 Yielding to this necessity, prove yoke's use!

KASSANDRA

Otototoi, Gods, Earth,—
Apollon, Apollon!

CHOROS

Why didst thou "ototoi" concerning Loxias?
Since he is none such as to suit a mourner.

KASSANDRA

1070 Otototoi, Gods, Earth,—
Apollon, Apollon!

CHOROS

Ill-boding here again the god invokes she
—Nowise empowered in woes to stand by helpful.

1056| MS:plain §written over illegible word§   1057| MS:new captured!   *P1877*:new-captured!   1059| MS:new captured,   *P1877*:new-captured,   1061| MS:out frothed *P1877*:out-frothed   1062| MS:words—shall shamed   *P1877*:words—will shamed
1066| MS:Earth—   *1889a:*Earth,—   1072| MS:Here she again the god invokes, ill-boding!   *P1877*:Ill-boding here again the god invokes she

KASSANDRA

Apollon, Apollon,
1075 Guard of the ways, my destroyer!
For thou hast quite, this second time, destroyed me.

CHOROS

To prophesy she seems of her own evils:
Remains the god-gift to the slave-soul present.

KASSANDRA

Apollon, Apollon,
1080 Guard of the ways, my destroyer!
Ha, whither hast thou led me? to what roof now?

CHOROS

To the Atreidai's roof: if this thou know'st not,
I tell it thee, nor this wilt thou call falsehood.

KASSANDRA

How! How!
1085 God-hated, then! Of many a crime it knew—
Self-slaying evils, halters too:
Man's-shambles, blood-besprinkler of the ground!

CHOROS

She seems to be good-nosed, the stranger: dog-like,
She snuffs indeed the victims she will find there.

1076| MS:quite—this <> time—destroyed   *P1877:*quite, this time <> time, destroyed
1081| MS:me—to   *P1877:*me? to   1083| MS:thee—nor   *P1877:*thee, nor
1085| MS:then—of   *P1877:*then! Of   1086| MS:too,   *P1877:*too:
1087| MS:shambles—blood-besprinkler   *P1877:*shambles, blood-besprinkler
1088| MS:seems to be §last two words inserted above§ good nosed, the stranger—
§hyphenated word inserted above§ dog-like hound— §crossed out§
*P1877:*good-nosed, the stranger: dog-like,   1089| MS:Is he: scents §last three words and
punctuation crossed out and replaced above by two words§ She snuffs

KASSANDRA

1090 How! How!
By the witnesses here I am certain now!
These children bewailing their slaughters— flesh dressed in the fire
And devoured by their sire!

CHOROS

Ay, we have heard of thy soothsaying glory,
1095 Doubtless: but prophets none are we in scent of!

KASSANDRA

Ah, gods, what ever does she meditate?
What this new anguish great?
Great in the house here she meditates ill
Such as friends cannot bear, cannot cure it: and still
1100 Off stands all Resistance
Afar in the distance!

CHOROS

Of these I witless am—these prophesyings.
But those I knew: for the whole city bruits them.

KASSANDRA

Ah, unhappy one, this thou consummatest?
1105 Thy husband, thy bed's common guest,
In the bath having brightened. . . How shall I declare
Consummation? It soon will be there:
For hand after hand she outstretches,
At life as she reaches!

1091| MS:now— *P1877:*now! 1092| MS:Bewailing—these children—their *P1877:*
These children bewailing their 1099| MS:cure, and *P1877:*cure it: and
1100| MS:stands Resistance *P1877:*stands all Resistance 1102| MS:prophesyings
*P1877:*prophesyings. 1103| MS:knew—for < > whole town noises. *P1877:*knew: for < >
whole city bruits them. 1107| MS:Consummation?—It soon shall be there! *P1877:*
Consummation? It soon will be there: 1108| MS:outstretches— *P1877:*outstretches,

CHOROS

1110 Nor yet I've gone with thee! for—after riddles—
Now, in blind oracles, I feel resourceless.

KASSANDRA

Eh, eh, papai, papai,
What this, I espy?
Some net of Haides undoubtedly
1115 Nay, rather, the snare
Is she who has share
In his bed, who takes part in the murder there!
But may a revolt—
Unceasing assault—
1120 On the Race, raise a shout
Sacrificial, about
A victim—by stoning—
For murder atoning!

CHOROS

What this Erinus which i' the house thou callest
1125 To raise her cry? Not me thy word enlightens!
To my heart has run
A drop of the crocus-dye:
Which makes for those
On earth by the spear that lie,
1130 A common close
With life's descending sun.

1110| MS:yet I go with   *P1877:*yet I've gone with   1114| MS:of Hades   *1889a:*of Haides
1115| MS:Nay, but §crossed out and replaced above by§ rather, the
1119| MS:assault   *P1877:*assault—   1120| MS:the Race—raise   *P1877:*the Race, raise
1121| MS:Sacrificial about   *P1877:*Sacrificial, about
1122| MS:A sacrifice worthy of §last three words crossed out and replaced above by two words
and punctuation§ victim—by stoning,—   *P1877:*stoning—   1124| MS:What kind of
Fury, call'st §crossed out and replaced above by illegibly crossed out word; replaced by one
word and comma§ this, in house   *P1877:*What this Erinus which i'the house
1127| MS:crocus-dye   *P1877:*crocus-dye: 1128| MS:Which, §word inserted above§ makes
1129| MS:who §crossed out§ On < > that §written over erasure§
1130| MS:Makes §crossed out§ A common end §crossed out and replaced above by§ close
1131| MS:life's sinking §crossed out and replaced above by§ descending

Swift is the curse begun!

KASSANDRA

How! How!
See—see quick!
¹¹³⁵ Keep the bull from the cow!
In the vesture she catching him, strikes him now
With the black-horned trick,
And he falls in the watery vase!
Of the craft-killing cauldron I tell thee the case!

CHOROS

¹¹⁴⁰ I would not boast to be a topping critic
Of oracles: but to some sort of evil
I liken these. From oracles, what good speech
To mortals, beside, is sent?
It comes of their evils: these arts word-abounding that sing the event
¹¹⁴⁵ Bring the fear 'tis their office to teach.

KASSANDRA

Ah me, ah me—
Of me unhappy, evil-destined fortunes!
For I bewail my proper woe
As, mine with his, all into one I throw.
¹¹⁵⁰ Why hast thou hither me unhappy brought ?
—Unless that I should die with him—for nought!
What else was sought?

CHOROS

Thou art some mind-mazed creature, god-possessed:
And all about thyself dost wail
¹¹⁵⁵ A lay—no lay!

---

^{1132|} MS:Swift is §crossed out and restored§ the curse §illegible word crossed out§
^{1136|} MS:the §illegible word§ she <> him strikes *P1877:*the vesture she <> him, strikes
^{1144|} MS:Because of <> evils these <> event, *P1877:*It comes of <> evils: these <> event
^{1145|} MS:teach! *P1877:*teach. ^{1149|} MS:As mine *P1877:*As, mine
^{1153|} MS:god-possessed— *P1877:*god-possessed:

Like some brown nightingale
Insatiable of noise, who—well-away!—
From her unhappy breast
Keeps moaning Itus, Itus, and his life
1160 With evils, flourishing on each side, rife.

KASSANDRA

Ah me, ah me,
The fate o' the nightingale, the clear resounder!
For a body wing-borne have the gods cast round her,
And sweet existence, from misfortunes free:
1165 But for myself remains a sundering
With spear, the two-edged thing!

CHOROS

Whence hast thou this on-rushing god-involving pain
And spasms in vain?
For, things that terrify,
1170 With changing unintelligible cry
Thou strikest up in tune, yet all the while
After that Orthian style!
Whence hast thou limits to the oracular road,
That evils bode?

KASSANDRA

1175 Ah me, the nuptials, the nuptials of Paris, the deadly to friends!
Ah me, of Skamandros the draught

1157| MS:noise—who,— §over illegible word§ *P1877*:noise, who—
1162| MS:nightingale—the *P1877*:nightingale, the   1163| MS:a wing-borne body have
§inserted above§ *P1877*:a body wing-borne have   1164| MS:from §illegible word
crossed out and replaced above by§ misfortune free— *P1877*:free:
1165| MS:remains the sundering *P1877*:remains a sundering
1166| MS:With the spear *P1877*:With spear   1168| MS:—And all the spasms
P1877:And spasms   1169| MS:For §word written over And§ things *P1877*:For, things
1170| MS:changing §last three letters inserted above§ ill-boding §last two words crossed our
and replaced above by§ unintelligible   1171| MS:tune—yet *P1877*:tune, yet
1173| MS:thou limits §crossed out and replaced above by§ limits   1174| MS:—That
P1877:That   1175| MS:me! the *P1877*:me, the   1176| MS:the water §crossed out
and replaced above by§ draught §crossed out and replaced below by§ draught

Paternal! There once, to these ends,
On thy banks was I brought,
The unhappy ! And now, by Kokutos and Acheron's shore
¹¹⁸⁰ I shall soon be, it seems, these my oracles singing once more!

CHOROS

Why this word, plain too much,
Hast thou uttered? A babe might learn of such!
I am struck with a bloody bite—here under—
At the fate woe-wreaking
¹¹⁸⁵ Of thee shrill shrieking:
To me who hear—a wonder!

KASSANDRA

Ah me, the toils—the toils of the city
The wholly destroyed: ah, pity,
Of the sacrificings my father made
¹¹⁹⁰ In the ramparts' aid—
Much slaughter of grass-fed flocks—that afforded no cure
That the city should not, as it does now, the burthen endure!
But I, with the soul on fire,
Soon to the earth shall cast me and expire.

CHOROS

¹¹⁹⁵ To things, on the former consequent,
Again hast thou given vent:
And 'tis some evil-meaning fiend doth move thee,
Heavily falling from above thee,
To melodize thy sorrows—else, in singing,
¹²⁰⁰ Calamitous, death-bringing!

---

^{1178|} MS:On thy §over illegible word§ <> brought *P1877*:brought,
^{1179|} MS:shore, *P1877*:shore ^{1180|} MS:be—it seems—these *P1877*:be, it seems,
these ^{1186|} MS:hear—what §crossed out and replaced above by§ a
^{1187|} MS:me—the *P1877*:me, the ^{1188|} MS:pity— *P1877*:pity,
^{1192|} MS:not—as <> now—the *P1877*:not, as <> now, the ^{1193|} MS:fire—,
P1877:fire, ^{1194|} MS:expire! *1889a:*expire. ^{1197|} MS:And 'tis §crossed out and
replaced above by§ 'tis <> evil wounded §crossed out and replaced above by§ -meaning
demon §crossed out§ fiend §inserted above and marked to follow *meaning*§

And of all this the end
I am without resource to apprehend.

KASSANDRA

Well then, the oracle from veils no longer
Shall be outlooking, like a bride new-married:
1205 But bright it seems, against the sun's uprisings
Breathing, to penetrate thee: so as, wave-like,
To wash against the rays a woe much greater
Than this. I will no longer teach by riddles.
And witness, running with me, that of evils
1210 Done long ago, I nosing track the footstep!
For, this same roof here—never quits a Choros
One-voiced, not well-tuned since no "well" it utters:
And truly having drunk, to get more courage,
Man's blood—the Komos keeps within the household
1215 —Hard to be sent outside—of sister Furies:
They hymn their hymn—within the house close sitting—
The first beginning curse: in turn spit forth at
The Brother's bed, to him who spurned it hostile.
Have I missed aught, or hit I like a bowman?
1220 False prophet am I,—knock at doors, a babbler?
Henceforward witness, swearing now, I know not
By other's word the old sins of this household!

CHOROS

And how should oath, bond honourably binding,
Become thy cure? No less I wonder at thee
1225 —That thou, beyond sea reared, a strange-tongued city

1202| MS:apprehend.   *1889a:*apprehend §emended to§ apprehend. §see Editorial Notes§
1204| MS:new-married—   *P1877:*new-married: 1206| MS:thee—so   *P1877:*thee: so
1208| MS:this: §colon crossed out and period in margin inserted§ I
1212| MS:well-tuned—for no <> utters.   *P1877:*well-tuned since no <> utters:
1214| MS:household— §dash crossed out§   1216| MS:And §word crossed out and replaced
above by§ They   1218| MS:bed—to   *P1877:*bed, to   1221| MS:witness—swearing
now—I   *P1877:*witness, swearing now, I   1223| MS:oath—bond honorably binding—
*P1877:*oath, bond <> binding,   *1889a:*honourably   1224| MS:Become §illegible word
crossed out and replaced above by two words and punctuation§ thy cure?   No less, §last two
words and comma inserted above§ I <> thee— §dash   crossed out§   *P1877:*less I

66

Shouldst hit in speaking, just as if thou stood'st by!

KASSANDRA

Prophet Apollon put me in this office.

CHOROS

What, even though a god, with longing smitten?

KASSANDRA

At first, indeed, shame was to me to say this.

CHOROS

1230   For, more relaxed grows everyone who fares well.

KASSANDRA

But he was athlete to me—huge grace breathing!

CHOROS

Well, to the work of children, went ye law's way?

KASSANDRA

Having consented, I played false to Loxias.

CHOROS

Already when the wits inspired possessed of?

KASSANDRA

1235   Already townsmen all their woes I foretold.

1226| MS:Shouldst <> speaking—just   *P1877:*Should'st <> speaking, just   *1889a:*Shouldst
1227| MS:Prophet Apollo put   *P1877:*Apollon   1230| MS:For more <>every one
*P1877:*For, more <> everyone   1233| MS:consented—Loxias I played false to.
*P1877:*consented, Loxias   *1889a:*consented, I played false to Loxias.
1235| MS:Already townsmen §inserted above§   all

CHOROS

How wast thou then unhurt by Loxias' anger?

KASSANDRA

I no one aught persuaded, when I sinned thus.

CHOROS

To us, at least, now sooth to say thou seemest.

KASSANDRA

Halloo, halloo, ah, evils!
1240 Again, straightforward foresight's fearful labour
Whirls me, distracting with prelusive last-lays!
Behold ye those there, in the household seated,—
Young ones,—of dreams approaching to the figures?
Children, as if they died by their beloveds—
1245 Hands they have filled with flesh, the meal domestic—
Entrails and vitals both, most piteous burthen,
Plain they are holding!—which their father tasted!
For this, I say, plans punishment a certain
Lion ignoble, on the bed that wallows,
1250 House-guard (ah, me!) to the returning master
—Mine, since to bear the slavish yoke behoves me!
The ship's commander, Ilion's desolator,
Knows not what things the tongue of the lewd she-dog
Speaking, outspreading, shiny-souled, in fashion
1255 Of Até hid, will reach to, by ill fortune!
Such things she dares—the female, the male's slayer!
She is . . . how calling her the hateful bite-beast

1237| MS:I none §crossed out and replaced above by two words§ no one persuaded aught
§marked for insertion after *no one*§   1238| MS:now, sooth   *P1877:*now sooth
1240| MS:straight-forward   *P1877:*straightforward   1244| MS:Children—as < > by hand
of dear or §last four words crossed out and replaced above by one word§ their beloveds,—
*P1877:*beloveds—   1245| MS:the house §crossed out and replaced above by§ meal
domestic,—   *P1877:*domestic—   1246| MS:burthen,—   *P1877:*burthen,
1248| MS:this, I say, §last two words and comma inserted above§ plans
1249| MS:ignoble—on   *P1877:*ignoble, on   1251| MS:—Mine—since   *P1877:*—Mine,
since   1252| MS:Ilion's Desolator,   *P1877:*desolator,   1255| MS:to—by   *P1877:*to, by

May I hit the mark? Some amphisbaina,—Skulla
Housing in rocks, of mariners the mischief,
1260 Revelling Haides' mother,—curse, no truce with,
Breathing at friends! How piously she shouted,
The all-courageous, as at turn of battle!
She seems to joy at the back-bringing safety!
Of this, too, if I nought persuade, all's one! Why?
1265 What is to be will come. And soon thou, present,
"True prophet all too much" wilt pitying style me.

CHOROS

Thuestes' feast, indeed, on flesh of children,
I went with, and I shuddered. Fear too holds me
Listing what's true as life, nowise out-imaged.

KASSANDRA

1270 I say, thou Agamemnon's fate shalt look on.

CHOROS

Speak good words, O unhappy! Set mouth sleeping!

KASSANDRA

But Paian stands in no stead to the speech here.

CHOROS

Nay, if the thing be near: but never be it!

KASSANDRA

Thou, indeed, prayest: they to kill are busy.

1258| MS:amphisbæna—Skulla *P1877*:amphisbaina   *1889a*:amphisbaina,—Skulla
1260| MS:curse—no <> with *P1877*:curse, no <> with,
1261| MS:Breathing against! §crossed out and replaced above by two words§ at friends
1265| MS:present, §written over erasure§   1267| MS:feast §written over erasure§ <>
children— *P1877*:children,   1269| MS:life—nowise *P1877*:life, nowise
1270| MS:on! *1889a*:on.   1271| MS:words, O §inserted above§
1273| MS:near! But *P1877*:near: but   1274| MS:busy! *1889a*:busy.

CHOROS

1275 Of what man is it ministered, this sorrow?

KASSANDRA

There again, wide thou look'st of my foretellings.

CHOROS

For, the fulfiller's scheme I have not gone with.

KASSANDRA

And yet too well I know the speech Hellenic.

CHOROS

For Puthian oracles, thy speech, and hard too.

KASSANDRA

1280 Papai: what fire this! and it comes upon me!
Ototoi, Lukeion Apollon, ah me—me!
She, the two-footed lioness that sleeps with
The wolf, in absence of the generous lion,
Kills me the unhappy one: and as a poison
1285 Brewing, to put my price too in the anger,
She vows, against her mate this weapon whetting
To pay him back the bringing me, with slaughter.
Why keep I then these things to make me laughed at,
Both wands and, round my neck, oracular fillets?
1290 Thee, at least, ere my own fate will I ruin:
Go, to perdition falling! Boons exchange we—
Some other Até in my stead make wealthy!
See there—himself, Apollon stripping from me
The oracular garment! having looked upon me

1276| MS:again—wide <> foretellings! *P1877*:again, wide <> foretellings
1889a:foretellings.   1279| MS:speech—and <> too! *P1877*:speech, and   *1889a*:too.
1284| MS:me, the <> one, and   *P1877*:me the <> one: and
1285| MS:anger   *P1877*:anger,   1287| MS:She's bringing me, to pay again with slaughter.
P1877:To pay him back the bringing me, with slaughter.   1290| MS:exchange I—
P1877:exchange we—   1294| MS:garment—having   *P1877*:garment! Having

1295 —Even in these adornments, laughed by friends at,
As good as foes, i' the balance weighed: and vainly—
For, called crazed stroller,—as I had been gipsy,
Beggar, unhappy, starved to death,—I bore it.
And now the Prophet—prophet me undoing,
1300 Has led away to these so deadly fortunes!
Instead of my sire's altar, waits the hack-block
She struck with first warm bloody sacrificing!
Yet nowise unavenged of gods will death be:
For there shall come another, our avenger,
1305 The mother-slaying scion, father's doomsman:
Fugitive, wanderer, from this land an exile,
Back shall he come,—for friends, copestone these curses!
For there is sworn a great oath from the gods that
Him shall bring hither his fallen sire's prostration.
1310 Why make I then, like an indweller, moaning?
Since at the first I foresaw Ilion's city
Suffering as it has suffered: and who took it,
Thus by the judgment of the gods are faring.
I go, will suffer, will submit to dying!
1315 But, Haides' gates—these same I call, I speak to,
And pray that on an opportune blow chancing,
Without a struggle,—blood the calm death bringing
In easy outflow,—I this eye may close up!

CHOROS

O much unhappy, but, again, much learned
1320 Woman, long hast thou outstretched! But if truly

1295| MS:at *P1877:*at,   1297| MS:stroller—as *P1877:*stroller,—as   1299| MS:me,
undoing *P1877:*me undoing   1301| MS:altar—waits the hack block *P1877:*altar, waits
the hack-block   1302| MS:with the §crossed out and replaced above by§ first
1303| MS:gods shall death be! *P1877:*gods will death be: 1305| MS:scion, the father's
§over illegible erasure§ *P1877:*scion, father's   1307| MS:curses. *P1877:*curses!
1312| MS:Suffering—as it did §crossed out and replaced above by§ has suffered; and, who
*P1877:*Ssuffering as < > suffered: and who   1314| MS:suffer—will *P1877:*suffer, will
1315| MS:these same §inserted above§ I call—I speak to— *P1877:*call, I speak to,
1317| MS:§Four illegible words and comma crossed out and replaced above with three words
and punctuation§ Without a struggle,—blood < > bringing §last three letters crossed out and
restored§   1318| MS:In easy §inserted above§

71

Thou knowest thine own fate, how comes that, like to
A god-led steer, to altar bold thou treadest?

KASSANDRA

There's no avoidance,—strangers, no! Some time more!

CHOROS

He last is, anyhow, by time advantaged.

KASSANDRA

1325 It comes, the day: I shall by flight gain little.

CHOROS

But know thou patient art from thy brave spirit!

KASSANDRA

Such things hears no one of the happy-fortuned.

CHOROS

But gloriously to die—for man is grace, sure.

KASSANDRA

Ah, sire, for thee and for thy noble children!

CHOROS

1330 But what thing is it? What fear turns thee backwards?

KASSANDRA

Alas, alas!

1321| MS:fate—how *P1877:*fate, how   1322| MS:treadest? §stepped written above then
crossed out§   1323| MS:no! Some *1889a:*avodiance <> no some §emended to§
avodiance <> no! Some §see Editorial Notes§   1324| MS:§illegible word crossed out and
replaced above by§ He   1327| MS:No one hears Such things §last five words
repositioned§ Such things hears no one <> happy fortuned. *P1877:*happy-fortuned.
1328| MS:sure! *1889a:*sure.   1329| MS:Ah, father, §crossed out and replaced above by§

CHOROS

Why this "Alas!" if 'tis no spirit's loathing?

KASSANDRA

Slaughter blood-dripping does the household smell of!

CHOROS

How else? This scent is of hearth-sacrifices.

KASSANDRA

1335 Such kind of steam as from a tomb is proper!

CHOROS

No Surian honour to the House thou speak'st of!

KASSANDRA

But I will go,—even in the household wailing
My fate and Agamemnon's. Life suffice me!
Ah, strangers!
1340 I cry not "ah"—as bird at bush—through terror
Idly! to me, the dead this much bear witness:
When, for me—woman, there shall die a woman,
And, for a man ill-wived, a man shall perish!
This hospitality I ask as dying.

CHOROS

1345 O sufferer, thee—thy foretold fate I pity.

---

sire < > and for §inserted below§   1332| MS:loathing—   *P1877*:loathing....   *1889a:*
loathing?   1333| MS:blood dripping   *P1877*:blood-dripping   1335| MS:tomb
comes §crossed out§ is   1336| MS:honor < > house   *P1877*:honour < > House
1341| MS:me the dead bear witness this much—   *P1877*:me, the dead, bear < > much:
*1889a:*dead this much bear witness: 1343| MS:perish.   *P1877*:perish!
1344| MS:ask you— §last word and punctuation crossed out and replaced above by§ as
1345| MS:sufferer—thy fate foretold §last two words repositioned§ I   *P1877*:sufferer, thee—thy

KASSANDRA

Yet once for all, to speak a speech, I fain am:
No dirge, mine for myself! The sun I pray to,
Fronting his last light!—to my own avengers—
That from my hateful slayers they exact too
1350 Pay for the dead slave—easy-managed hand's work!

CHOROS

Alas for mortal matters! Happy-fortuned,—
Why, any shade would turn them: if unhappy,
By throws the wetting sponge has spoiled the picture!
And more by much in mortals this I pity.
1355 The being well-to-do—
Insatiate a desire of this
Born with all mortals is,
Nor any is there who
Well-being forces off, aroints
1360 From roofs whereat a finger points,
"No more come in!" exclaiming. This man, too,
To take the city of Priamos did the celestials give,
And, honoured by the god, he homeward comes;
But now if, of the former, he shall pay

---

¹³⁴⁶| MS:all, I fain would speak §last three words crossed out and replaced above by two words, the second of which is crossed out§ to speak §crossed out and restored§ durge at, §last two words and comma crossed out and replaced above by three words and period§ I fain am. *P1877:*am: ¹³⁴⁷| MS:No dirge— §last two words and dash inserted at beginning of line§ <> to—   *P1877:*dirge, <> to,   ¹³⁴⁸| MS:avengers *P1877:*avengers—
¹³⁴⁹| MS:from the foes §last two words crossed out§ my hateful §inserted above§ slayers
¹³⁵¹| MS:fortuned, *P1877:*fortuned,—   ¹³⁵³| MS:throws the wetting §inserted above§ sponge   ¹³⁵⁶| MS:Insatiate the §crossed out and replaced above by§ a
¹³⁵⁷| MS:Was §word crossed out§ Born <> all men §crossed out and replaced above by two words and comma§ mortals is,   ¹³⁵⁸| MS:Nor §crossed out§ any, who §two illegible words written above then crossed out§ *P1877:*any is there who
¹³⁵⁹| MS:off—aroints *P1877:*off, aroints   ¹³⁶¹| MS:§seven illegible words crossed out and replaced above by four words and punctuation§ "No more come in!" exclaiming. §illegible word crossed out and replaced above by two words§ This man   ¹³⁶²| MS:And to this personage §last four words crossed out and replaced by§ To take the city of Priamos did the celestials give, §last six words circled and inserted above§   ¹³⁶⁴| MS:former, over the blood §last three words crossed out and replaced above by three words§ he shall pay

¹³⁶⁵ The blood back, and, for those who ceased to live,
Dying, for deaths in turn new punishment he dooms—
Who, being mortal, would not pray
With an unmischievous
Daimon to have been born—who would not, hearing thus?

AGAMEMNON

¹³⁷⁰ Ah me! I am struck—a right-aimed stroke within me!

CHOROS

Silence! Who is it shouts "stroke"—"right-aimedly" a wounded one?

AGAMEMNON

Ah me! indeed again,—a second, struck by!

CHOROS

This work seems to me completed by this "Ah me" of the king's;
But we somehow may together share in solid counsellings.

CHOROS 1

¹³⁷⁵ I, in the first place, my opinion tell you:
—To cite the townsmen, by help-cry, to house here.

CHOROS 2

To me, it seems we ought to fall upon them
At quickest—prove the fact by sword fresh-flowing!

---

^{1365|} MS:§Four illegible words crossed out and replaced above by three words and comma§
The blood back, and, for those §inserted above§ ^{1366|} MS:deaths new *P1877:*deaths
in turn new ^{1367|} MS:Who, being mortal, §last two words and commas inserted above§
would ^{1369|} MS:born—who would not, §last three words and comma inserted above§
hearing ^{1373|} MS:work appears to *P1877:*work seems to ^{1374|} MS:we somehow
§inserted above§ may common §crossed out and replaced above by§ together
^{1376|} MS:the citizens, for §crossed out and replaced above by§ by help-cry, §hyphen and last
word inserted above§ to *P1877:*the townsmen, by

CHOROS 3

And I, of such opinion the partaker,
1380 Vote—to do something: not to wait—the main point!

CHOROS 4

'Tis plain to see: for they prelude as though of
A tyranny the signs they gave the city.

CHOROS 5

For we waste time; while they,—this waiting's glory
Treading to ground,—allow the hand no slumber.

CHOROS 6

1385 I know not—chancing on some plan—to tell it:
'Tis for the doer to plan of the deed also.

CHOROS 7

And I am such another: since I'm schemeless
How to raise up again by words—a dead man!

CHOROS 8

What, and, protracting life, shall we give way thus
1390 To the disgracers of our home, these rulers?

CHOROS 9

Why, 'tis unbearable: but to die is better:
For death than tyranny is the riper finish!

CHOROS 10

What, by the testifying "Ah me" of him,
Shall we prognosticate the man as perished?

1387| MS:another—since *P1877:*another: since   1391| *P1877:*isbetter: *CP1877:*is
better: 1392| MS:finish §written over erasure§

CHOROS 11

1395 We must quite know ere speak these things concerning:
For to conjecture and "quite know" are two things.

CHOROS 12

This same to praise I from all sides abound in—
Clearly to know—Atreides, what he's doing!

KLUTAIMNESTRA

Much having been before to purpose spoken,
1400 The opposite to say I shall not shamed be:
For how should one, to enemies,—in semblance,
Friends,—enmity proposing,—sorrow's net-frame
Enclose, a height superior to outleaping?
To me, indeed, this struggle of old—not mindless
1405 Of an old victory—came: with time, I grant you!
I stand where I have struck, things once accomplished:
And so have done,—and this deny I shall not,—
As that his fate was nor to fly nor ward off.
A wrap-round with no outlet, as for fishes,
1410 I fence about him—the rich woe of the garment:
I strike him twice, and in a double "Ah-me!"
He let his limbs go—*there!* And to him, fallen,
The third blow add I, giving—of Below-ground
Zeus, guardian of the dead—the votive favour.
1415 Thus in the mind of him he rages, falling,
And blowing forth a brisk blood-spatter, strikes me

1397| MS:praise—I   *P1877:*praise I   1403| MS:Impale §word crossed out and replaced
above by§ Enclose   1405| MS:came—with   *P1877:*came: with
1406| MS:I have stood §last two words crossed out and replaced above by§ stand < > have
§inserted above§ struck—things < > accomplished,   *P1877:*struck, things < > accomplished:
1407| MS:Thus did I, §last three words and comma crossed out and replaced by four words
and punctuation§ And so have done,—and this thing, §last word and comma crossed out§ deny
1408| MS:fate he could §last three words crossed out and replaced above by§ was nor to
§inserted above§   1409| MS:outlet—as < > fishes—   *P1877:*outlet, as < > fishes,
1410| MS:I strike §crossed out and replaced above by§ hit him twice—and
*P1877:*I strike him twice, and   1413| MS:blow I add, giving—of below-ground
*P1877:*blow add I, giving—of Below-ground

With the dark drop of slaughterous dew—rejoicing
No less than, at the god-given dewy-comfort,
The sown-stuff in its birth-throes from the calyx.
1420 Since so these things are,—Argives, my revered here,—
Ye may rejoice—if ye rejoice: but I—boast!
If it were fit on corpse to pour libation,
That would be right—right over and above, too!
The cup of evils in the house he, having
1425 Filled with such curses, himself coming drinks of.

CHOROS

We wonder at thy tongue: since bold-mouthed truly
Is she who in such speech boasts o'er her husband!

KLUTAIMNESTRA

Ye test me as I were a witless woman:
But I—with heart intrepid—to you knowers
1430 Say (and thou—if thou wilt or praise or blame me,
Comes to the same)—this man is Agamemnon,
My husband, dead, the work of the right hand here,
Ay, of a just artificer: so things are.

CHOROS

What evil, O woman, food or drink, earth-bred
1435 Or sent from the flowing sea,

1418| MS:than at the God §two illegible words crossed out and replaced above by three words
and comma§ given dewy-comfort, *P1877:*than at the god-given   1420| MS:Since so
§inserted above§   1421| MS:ye rejoice, but *P1877:*ye rejoice: but   1422| MS:were
seemly §crossed out and replaced above by§ fit < > libation *P1877:*libation,
1424| MS:of evils in §last two words crossed out and replaced above by word illegibly crossed
out; original words restored§ the house, the man here §last three words crossed out and
replaced above by two words and comma§ he, having *P1877:*house he
1425| MS:curses—himself, coming, drinks *P1877:*curses, himself coming drinks
1426| MS:tongue,—since *P1877:*tongue: since   1427| MS:who in §inserted above§ such
1429| MS:knowing §last three letters crossed out and replaced above by three letters§ ers—
*P1877:*knowers   1430| MS:and thou, if *P1877:*and thou—if
1434| MS:evil, or woman, food Earth-bred §last three words crossed out§ food
*P1877:*evil, O woman   1435| MS:Or drink, spring out of §last five words and comma
crossed out and replaced by three words§ Or sent from

Of such having fed
Didst thou set on thee
This sacrifice
And popular cries
1440 Of a curse on thy head?
Off thou hast thrown him, off hast cut
The man from the city: but—
Off from the city thyself shalt be
Cut—to the citizens
1445 A hate immense!

KLUTAIMNESTRA

Now, indeed, thou adjudgest exile to me,
And citizens' hate, and to have popular curses:
Nothing of this against the man here bringing,
Who, no more awe-checked than as 'twere a beast's fate,—
1450 With sheep abundant in the well-fleeced graze-flocks,—
Sacrificed *his* child,—dearest fruit of travail
To me,—as song-spell against Threkian blowings.
Not *him* did it behove thee hence to banish
—Pollution's penalty? But hearing *my* deeds
1455 Justicer rough thou art! Now, this I tell thee:
To threaten thus—me, one prepared to have thee
(On like conditions, thy hand conquering) o'er me
Rule: but if God the opposite ordain us,
Thou shalt learn—late taught, certes—to be modest.

1436| MS:Of this having *P1877:*Of such having   1437| MS:thou place this sacrifice §last three words crossed out and replaced by one word§ set   1439| MS:And this §crossed out§
1440| MS:Of a §inserted above§   14 41| MS:him, §inserted above§ off hast §inserted above§   1444| MS:the townsmen §crossed out§ citizens   1445| MS:A hatred immense! *P1877:*A hate immense!   1447| MS:curses *P1877:*curses:
1448| MS:—Nothing *P1877:*Nothing   1449| MS:awe checked *P1877:*awe-checked
1451| MS:child, dearest *P1877:*child,—dearest   1453| MS:behove you < > banish—
*P1877:*behove thee < > banish   1454| MS:penalty §over erasure§
1455| MS:thee, *P1877:*thee: 1456|MS:me,—one *P1877:*me, one
1457| MS:conditions, by §inserted above then crossed out§
1459| MS:modest §illegible word above crossed out§

CHOROS

1460 Greatly-intending thou art:
Much-mindful, too, hast thou cried
(Since thy mind, with its slaughter-outpouring part,
Is frantic) that over the eyes, a patch
Of blood—with blood to match—
1465 Is plain for a pride!
Yet still, bereft of friends, thy fate
Is—blow with blow to expiate!

KLUTAIMNESTRA

And this thou hearest—of my oaths, just warrant!
By who fulfilled things for my daughter, Justice,
1470 Ate, Erinus,—by whose help I slew him,—
Not mine the fancy—Fear will tread my palace
So long as on my hearth there burns a fire
Aigisthos, as before well-caring for me;
Since he to me is shield, no small, of boldness.
1475 Here does he lie—outrager of this female,
Dainty of all the Chruseids under Ilion;
And she—the captive, the soothsayer also
And couchmate of this man, oracle-speaker,
Faithful bed-fellow,—ay, the sailors' benches
1480 They wore in common, nor unpunished did so,
Since he is—thus! While, as for her,—swan-fashion,
Her latest having chanted,—dying wailing

1460| MS:art— *P1877*:art: 1461| MS:hast cried §crossed out§5 thou uttered in §last three words written above and crossed out§ thou 1463| MS:Is §illegible word crossed out and replaced above by§ frantic) that plain §illegible word§ last two words crossed out§ over thine §altered to§ the 1464| MS:blood—of §crossed out and replaced above by§ with blood the §crossed out and replaced above by§ to 1466| MS:Yet §crossed out and restored§ <> friends, his §crossed out§ thy 1467| MS:blow §over erasure§ 1468| MS:just §over illegible word crossed out§ 1469| MS:By Justice §crossed out§ the fulfilled one of my daughter, Justice— *P1877*:By who fulfilled things for my <> Justice, 1470| MS:Vengeance, the Fury,—by *P1877*:Ate, Erinus,—by 1471| MS:Not to me looks as Fear *P1877*:Not mine the fancy—Fear 1472| MS:there lights the §last two words crossed out and replaced above by two words§ burns a fire *P1877*:fire, §emended to§ fire §see Editorial Notes§ 1473| MS:Aigisthos, as <> me. *P1877*:Aigisthos as <> me; §emended to§ Aigisthos, as §see Editorial Notes§ 1478| MS:oracle-teller §altered to§ oracle-speaker *P1877*:oracle-speaker, 1480| MS:common—nor <> so! *P1877*:common, nor <> so,

She lies,—to him, a sweetheart: me she brought to—
My bed's by-nicety—the whet of dalliance.

CHOROS

1485 Alas, that some
Fate would come
Upon us in quickness—
Neither much sickness
Neither bed-keeping—
1490 And bear unended sleeping,
Now that subdued
Is our keeper, the kindest of mood!
Having borne, for a woman's sake, much strife—
By a woman he withered from life!
1495 Ah me!
Law-breaking Helena who, one,
Hast many, so many souls undone
'Neath Troia! and now the consummated
Much-memorable curse
1500 Hast thou made flower-forth, red
With the blood no rains disperse,
That which was then in the House—
Strife all-subduing, the woe of a spouse.

KLUTAIMNESTRA

Nowise, of death the fate—
1505 Burdened by these things—supplicate!
Nor on Helena turn thy wrath
As the man-destroyer, as "she who hath,
Being but one,
Many and many a soul undone

1483| MS:brought to   *1889a:*to—   1484| MS:beds' §illegible word crossed out and
replaced by§ by-nicety, the   *CP1877:*bed's   *1889a:*by-nicety—the
1489| MS:bed-keeping,—   *P1877:*bed-keeping—
1490| MS:And Bringing §altered to§   Bring unended   *P1877:*And bear unended
1496| MS:who—one—   *P1877:*who, one,   1498| MS:'Neath Troia! Host undone §last two
words crossed out§ and now the §inserted above§   1501| §ddisperse—   *P1877:*disperse,
1502| MS:house—   *P1877:*House—   1504| MS:death thy §altered to§ the

81

1510 Of the men, the Danaoi"—
And wrought immense annoy!

CHOROS

Daimon, who fallest
Upon this household and the double-raced
Tantalidai, a rule, minded like theirs displaced,
1515 Thou rulest me with, now,
Whose heart thou gallest!
And on the body, like a hateful crow,
Stationed, all out of tune, his chant to chant
Doth Something vaunt!

KLUTAIMNESTRA

1520 Now, of a truth, hast thou set upright
Thy mouth's opinion,—
Naming the Sprite,
The triply gross,
O'er the race that has dominion:
1525 For through him it is that Eros
The carnage-licker
In the belly is bred: ere ended quite
Is the elder throe—new ichor!

CHOROS

Certainly, great of might
1530 And heavy of wrath, the Sprite

1510| MS:men, the §inserted above§ Danaoi,"— *P1877:*Danaoi"—
1511-12| MS:KLUTAIMNESTRA. *1889a:*CHOROS. 1514| MS:Tantalidai—a
*P1877:*Tantalidai, a 1515| MS:now— §written above crossed out illegible word§
*P1877:*now, 1516| MS:gallest! *P1877:*gallest: *CP1877:*gallest! 1516| MS:body
like < > crow *P1877:*body, like < > crow, 1518| MS:his chant, to *CP1877:*his chant to
1519| MS:§illegible word crossed out§ Doth vaunt— §last two words and dash crossed out§
Doth vaunt! *CP1877:*Doth something vaunt! 1522| MS:The triply-gross, *P1877:*
Naming the Sprite, 1523| MS:O'er the case that has dominion, *P1877:*The triply —
gross, 1524| MS:Naming the Sprite: *P1877:*O'er the race that has dominion:
1525| MS:For of §last word crossed out and replaced above by§ through him, §comma
crossed out§ is §inserted above§ Eros *P1877:*him it is that Eros
1527| MS:belly is §crossed out§ bred *P1877:*belly is bred

82

Thou tellest of, in the palace
(Woe, woe!)
—An evil tale of a fate
By Até's malice
1535 Rendered insatiate!
Oh, oh,—
King, king, how shall I beweep thee?
From friendly soul whatever say?
Thou liest where webs of the spider o'ersweep thee
1540 In impious death, life breathing away.
O me—me!
This couch, not free!
By a slavish death subdued thou art,
From the hand, by the two-edged dart.

KLUTAIMNESTRA

1545 Thou boastest this deed to be mine:
But leave off styling me
"The Agamemnonian wife!"
For, showing himself in sign
Of the spouse of the corpse thou dost see,
1550 Did the ancient bitter avenging-ghost
Of Atreus, savage host,
Pay the man here as price—
A full-grown for the young ones' sacrifice.

CHOROS

That no cause, indeed, of this killing art thou,
1555 Who shall be witness-bearer?
How shall he bear it—how?
But the sire's avenging-ghost might be in the deed a sharer.

1531| MS:palace, *P1877:*palace   1533| MS:—And §altered to§ —An
1535| MS:Insatiate! §altered to§   Rendered insatiate!   1537| MS:From the friendly <>
what ever   *P1877:*From friendly <> whatever   1539| MS:thee; *1889a:*thee
1542| MS:free— *P1877:*free! *1889a:*free. §emended to§ free! §see Editorial Notes§
1543| MS:art— *P1877:*art,   1544| MS:dart! *P1877:*dart.   1546| MS:leave desire
§illegible word§ §last two words crossed out§ off   1547| MS:wife": *P1877:*wife!"
1553| MS:ones' *P1877-1889a:*one's §emended to§ ones' §see Editorial Notes§

He is forced on and on
By the kin-born flowing of blood,
1560 —Black Ares: to where, having gone,
He shall leave off, flowing done,
At the frozen-child's-flesh food.
King, king, how shall I beweep thee?
From friendly soul whatever say?
1565 Thou liest where webs of the spider o'ersweep thee
In impious death, life breathing away.
O me—me!
This couch, not free!
By a slavish death subdued thou art,
1570 From the hand, by the two-edged dart.

KLUTAIMNESTRA

No death "unfit for the free"
Do I think this man's to be:
For did not himself a slavish curse
To his household decree?
1575 But the scion of him, myself did nurse—
That much-bewailed Iphigeneia, he
Having done well by,—and as well, nor worse,
Been done to,—let him not in Haides loudly
Bear himself proudly!
1580 Being by sword-destroying death amerced
For that sword's punishment himself inflicted first.

CHOROS

I at a loss am left—

1558| MS:forced on his way §last two words crossed out and replaced by§ and on
*P1877:*forced on   1559| MS:By the kindred-spring §altered to§ kin-born §two illegible
words crossed out and replaced above by§ flowing   1563| MS:thee! *1889a:*thee?
1564| MS:what ever *1889a:*whatever   1565| MS:thee, *1889a:*thee
1567-68| MS:Oh, me, me—this couch not free! §one line in MS:§   *P1877:*Oh, me—me! This
couch not *1889a:*couch, not   1569| MS:art,— *P1877:*art,   1572| MS:be: §over
erasure§   1578| MS:in Hades loud §altered to§ loudly   1579| MS:Boast §altered to§
Bear himself proud §altered to§   proudly!— *P1877:*proudly!   1580| MS:Being §over
illegible word crossed out§   with   §crossed out and replaced above by§ by

Of a feasible scheme of mind bereft—
Where I may turn: for the house is falling:
1585 I fear the bloody crash of the rain
That ruins the roof as it bursts amain:
The warning-drop
Has come to a stop.
Destiny doth Justice whet
1590 For other deed of hurt, on other whetstones yet.
Woe, earth, earth—would thou hadst taken *me*
Ere I saw the roan I see,
On the pallet-bed
Of the silver-sided bath-vase, dead!
1595 Who is it shall bury him, who
Sing his dirge? Can it be true
That *thou* wilt dare this same to do—
Having slain thy husband, thine own,
To make his funeral moan:
1600 And for the soul of him, in place
Of his mighty deeds, a graceless grace
To wickedly institute? By whom
Shall the tale of praise o'er the tomb
At the god-like man be sent—
1605 From the truth of his mind as he toils intent?

KLUTAIMNESTRA

It belongs not to thee to declare
This object of care!
By us did he fall—down there!
Did he die—down there! and down, no less,
1610 We will bury him there, and not beneath
The wails of the household over his death:
But Iphigeneia,—with kindliness,—

1584| MS:falling. *P1877:*falling: 1586| MS:bursts §over illegible word crossed out§
1592| MS:see *P1877:*see, 1597| MS:do? *P1877:*7do—
1599| MS:moan,— *P1877:*moan:
1605| MS:he §two illegible words crossed out and replaced above by§ toils intent?
1610| MS:There will we bury him § altered to§ We will bury him there—and *P1877:*there, and

His daughter,—as the case requires,
Facing him full, at the rapid-flowing
1615 Passage of Groans shall—both hands throwing
Around him—kiss that kindest of sires!

CHOROS

This blame comes in the place of blame:
Hard battle it is to judge each claim.
"He is borne away who bears away:
1620 And the killer has all to pay."
And this remains while Zeus is remaining,
"The doer shall suffer in time"—for, such his ordaining.
Who may cast out of the House its cursed brood?
The race is to Até glued!

KLUTAIMNESTRA

1625 Thou hast gone into this oracle
With a true result. For me, then,—I will
—To the Daimon of the Pleisthenidai
Making an oath—with all these things comply
Hard as they are to bear. For the rest—
1630 Going from out this House, a guest,
May he wear some other family
To nought, with the deaths of kin by kin!
And,—keeping a little part of my goods,—
Wholly am I contented in
1635 Having expelled from the royal House
These frenzied moods
The mutually-murderous.

1613| MS:daughter, shall— §crossed out§ as <> requires—   *P1877:*requires,   1614| MS:full,
§written above§ at   1617| MS:This §written above§ blame   1621| MS:this §over
illegible word§ remains—while   *P1877:*remains while   1622| MS:for such the §crossed
out and replaced by§ his   *P1877:*for, such   1624| MS:house   *P1877:*House
1630| MS:house, a guest   *P1877:*House, a guest,   1632| MS:To nought, §written above§
with   1633| MS:And,—keeping §written above§ a   1635| MS:Retaining,—to §last
two words and punctuation crossed out§ Having expelled these words §last two words crossed
out and replaced above by four words§ from the royal house   *P1877:*royal House
1636| MS:These mad fits §last two words crossed out and replaced above by§ frenzied moods

AIGISTHOS

O light propitious of day justice-bringing!
I may say truly, now, that men's avengers,
¹⁶⁴⁰ The gods from high, of earth behold the sorrows—
Seeing, as I have, i' the spun robes of the Erinues,
This man here lying,—sight to me how pleasant!—
His father's hands' contrivances repaying.
For Atreus, this land's lord, of this man father,
¹⁶⁴⁵ Thuestes, my own father—to speak clearly—
His brother too,—being i' the rule contested,—
Drove forth to exile from both town and household:
And, coming back, to the hearth turned, a suppliant,
Wretched Thuestes found the fate assured him
¹⁶⁵⁰ —Not to die, bloodying his paternal threshold
Just there: but host-wise this man's impious father
Atreus, soul-keenly more than kindly,—seeming
To joyous hold a flesh-day,—to my father
Served up a meal, the flesh of his own children.
¹⁶⁵⁵ The feet indeed and the hands' top divisions
He hid, high up and isolated sitting:
But, their unshowing parts in ignorance taking,
He forthwith eats food—as thou seest—perdition
To the race: and then, 'ware of the deed ill-omened,
¹⁶⁶⁰ He shrieked O!—falls back, vomiting, from the carnage,
And fate on the Pelopidai past bearing
He prays down—putting in his curse together
The kicking down o' the feast—that so might perish
The race of Pleisthenes entire: and thence is
¹⁶⁶⁵ That it is given thee to see this man prostrate.

---

^{1639|} MS:truly now   *P1877:*truly, now   ^{1641|} MS:the Furies   *P1877:*the Erinues,
^{1644|} MS:land's ruler §crossed out and replaced above by§ lord   ^{1645|} MS:Did §crossed
out§ Thuestes   ^{1651|} MS:O'the spot §last three words crossed out and replaced above by
three words§ Then and there §first two words crossed out and replaced by§ Just
^{1652|} MS:Atreus, did §crossed out and replaced above by§ soul-keenly   ^{1653|}   MS:To hold
a joyous §marked for transposition to follow *To*§   ^{1654|}   MS:meal—the   *P1877:*meal, the
^{1656|}   MS:hid—high   *P1877:*hid, high   ^{1657|}   MS:But their   *P1877:*But, their
^{1658|}   MS:see'st—perdition §illegible word written above and crossed out§   *P1877:*seest
^{1663|}   MS:the supper §crossed out and replaced above by§ feast
^{1665|}   MS:to behold §crossed out and replaced above by§ see

And I was rightly of this slaughter stitch-man:
Since me,—being third from ten,—with my poor father
He drives out—being then a babe in swathe-bands:
But, grown up, back again has justice brought me:

1670 And of this man I got hold—being without-doors—
Fitting together the whole scheme of ill-will.
So, sweet, in fine, even to die were to me,
Seeing, as I have, this man i' the toils of justice!

CHOROS

Aigisthos, arrogance in ills I love not.

1675 Dost thou say—willing, thou didst kill the man here,
And, alone, plot this lamentable slaughter?
I say—thy head in justice will escape not
The people's throwing—know that!—stones and curses!

AIGISTHOS

Thou such things soundest—seated at the lower

1680 Oarage to those who rule at the ship's mid-bench?
Thou shalt know, being old, how heavy is teaching
To one of the like age—bidden be modest!
But chains and old age and the pangs of fasting
Stand out before all else in teaching,—prophets

1685 At souls'-cure! Dost not, seeing aught, see this too?
Against goads kick not, lest tript-up thou suffer!

CHOROS

Woman, thou,—of him coming new from battle
Houseguard—thy husband's bed the while disgracing,—
For the Army-leader didst thou plan this fate too?

1670| MS:hold—though §crossed out and replaced above by being   1672| MS:sweet—in
fine—even   *P1877:*sweet, in fine, even   1673| MS:Seeing—as I have—this
*P1877:*Seeing, as I have, this   1682| MS:age—told to be   *CP1877:*age—bidden be
1683| MS:chains, and old age, and   *P1877:*chains and old age and
1688| MS:The §crossed out§ Houseguard
1689| MS:this slaughter? §crossed out and replaced above by§ fate too?

AIGISTHOS

1690 These words too are of groans the prime-begetters!
Truly a tongue opposed to Orpheus hast thou:
For he led all things by his voice's grace-charm,
But thou, upstirring them by these wild yelpings,
Wilt lead them! Forced, thou wilt appear the tamer!

CHOROS

1695 So—thou shalt be my king then of the Argeians—
Who, not when for this man his fate thou plannedst,
Daredst to do this deed—thyself the slayer!

AIGISTHOS

For, to deceive him was the wife's part, certes:
I was looked after—foe, ay, old-begotten!
1700 But out of this man's wealth will I endeavour
To rule the citizens: and the no-man-minder
—Him will I heavily yoke—by no means trace-horse,
A corned-up colt! but that bad friend in darkness,
Famine its housemate, shall behold him gentle.

CHOROS

1705 Why then, this man here, from a coward spirit,
Didst not thou slay thyself? But,—helped,—a woman,
The country's pest, and that of gods o' the country,
Killed him! Orestes, where may he see light now?
That coming hither back, with gracious fortune,
1710 Of both these he may be the all-conquering slayer?

1691| MS:thou— *P1877:*thou: 1694| MS:them!! Forced, though §altered to§ thou
1695| MS:then—of *P1877:*then of   1696| MS:plannedst *P1877:*plannedst,
1698| MS:Ay §crossed out§ For, to trick §crossed out and replaced above by§ deceive
1699| MS:foe,—ay *P1877:*foe, ay   1701| MS:rule the townsmen §crossed out and
replaced above by word and punctuation§ citizens: 1702| MS:I heavily §inserted above§
yoke with— §crossed out§ by < > trace horse, *P1877:*trace-horse,
1703| MS:colt: but *P1877:*colt! But   1706| MS:Did not < > woman *P1877:*Didst not
< > woman,   1707| MS:pest—and < > god's o'the §apostrophe and last word inserted
above§ country, *P1877:*pest, and < > gods < > country,

AIGISTHOS

But since this to do thou thinkest—and not talk—thou soon shalt know!
Up then, comrades dear! the proper thing to do—not distant this!

CHOROS

Up then! hilt in hold, his sword let everyone aright dispose!

AIGISTHOS

Ay, but I myself too, hilt in hold, do not refuse to die.

CHOROS

1715   Thou wilt die, thou say'st, to who accept it. We the chance demand.

KLUTAIMNESTRA

Nowise, O belovedest of men, may we do other ills!
To have reaped away these, even, is a harvest much to me.
Go, both thou and these the old men, to the homes appointed each,
Ere ye suffer! It behoved one do these things just as we did:
1720   And if of these troubles there should be enough—we may assent
—By the Daimon's heavy heel unfortunately stricken ones!
So a woman's counsel hath it—if one judge it learning-worth.

AIGISTHOS

But to think that these at me the idle tongue should thus o'er-bloom,
And throw out such words—the Daimon's power experimenting on—
1725   And, of modest knowledge missing,—me, the ruler, . . .

1712| MS:dear,—the business to be done §last four words crossed out and replaced above by
four words§ proper thing to do— §5not   *P1877:*dear! The   1715| MS:sayst
*P1877:*say'st   1717| MS:reaped away §inserted above§ these < > me!   *1889a:*me.
1719| MS:behoved us §crossed out and replaced above by§ one < > did.   *P1877:*did:
1720| MS:And §over illegible erasure§ if of §inserted above§ these < > enough—assent we may
§last three words marked for transposition to *we may assent*§   1721| MS:heel—
unfortunately   *P1877:*heel unfortunately   1722| MS:learning- §circled and inserted
above§ worth.   1723| MS:But to think §last two words circled and inserted above§ These
< > o'er-bloom—   *P1877:*o'er-bloom,   *1889a:*o'erbloom, §emended to§ o'er-bloom, §see
Editorial Notes§   1725| MS:ruler, . . §illegible word crossed out over ellipsis§   *P1877:*ruler,...

90

CHOROS

Ne'er may this befall Argeians—wicked man to fawn before!

AIGISTHOS

Anyhow, in after days, will I, yes, I, be at thee yet!

CHOROS

Not if hither should the Daimon make Orestes straightway come!

AIGISTHOS

O, I know, myself, that fugitives on hopes are pasture-fed!

CHOROS

1730   Do thy deed, get fat, defiling justice, since the power is thine!

AIGISTHOS

Know that thou shalt give me satisfaction for this folly's sake!

CHOROS

Boast on, bearing thee audacious, like a cock his females by!

KLUTAIMNESTRA

Have not thou respect for these same idle yelpings! I and thou
Will arrange it, o'er this household ruling excellently well.

---

¹⁷²⁶| MS:befall Argeians— §two illegible words crossed out§ wicked   ¹⁷²⁷| MS:Wilt
§crossed out and replaced above by§ Anyhow, in <> yes, I,—be   *P1877:*yes, I, be
¹⁷²⁹| MS:know—myself—that   *P1877:*know, myself, that   ¹⁷³⁰| MS:justice—since
*P1877:*justice, since   ¹⁷³²| MS:on, bearing thee §last three words and comma inserted
above§ audacious   ¹⁷³³| MS:yelpings: I   *P1877:*yelpings! I   ¹⁷³⁴| MS:arrange
things, ruling §inserted above§ o'er this household excellently   *P1877:* arrange it, ruling
*1889a:*it, o'er <> household ruling excellently   ¹⁷³⁴| MS: §below last line of verse§
Apr.23, '77. L. D. I. E.

LA SAISIAZ and THE TWO POETS OF CROISIC

Edited by Michael Bright

DEDICATED

TO

MRS. SUTHERLAND ORR

LA SAISIAZ

I

Good, to forgive;
　　Best, to forget!
　　Living, we fret;
Dying, we live.
⁵ Fretless and free,
　　Soul, clap thy pinion!
　　Earth have dominion,
Body, o'er thee!

II

Wander at will,
¹⁰ 　　Day after day,—
　　Wander away,
Wandering still—
Soul that canst soar!
　　Body may slumber:
¹⁵ 　　Body shall cumber
Soul-flight no more.

III

Waft of soul's wing!
　　What lies above?
　　Sunshine and Love,
²⁰ Skyblue and Spring!
Body hides—where?
　　Ferns of all feather,
　　Mosses and heather,
Yours be the care!

---

§MS in Balliol College Library.　Ed. P1878, CP1878, 1878, 1889a.　See Editorial Notes§
GOOD, TO FORGIVE　　¹| 　MS:forgive　*P1878:*forgive;　　³| 　MS:fret:　*P1878:*fret;
¹³| 　MS:cans't　*P1878:*canst　　¹⁴| 　MS:slumber　*P1878:*slumber:　　²⁰| 　MS:Sky blue
*P1878:*Skyblue

LA SAISIAZ

1878

A. E. S. September 14, 1877

Dared and done: at last I stand upon the summit, Dear and True!
Singly dared and done; the climbing both of us were bound to do.
Petty feat and yet prodigious: every side my glance was bent
O'er the grandeur and the beauty lavished through the whole ascent.
5   Ledge by ledge, out broke new marvels, now minute and now immense:
Earth's most exquisite disclosure, heaven's own God in evidence!
And no berry in its hiding, no blue space in its outspread,
Pleaded to escape my footstep, challenged my emerging head,
(As I climbed or paused from climbing, now o'erbranched by shrub
        and tree,
10   Now built round by rock and boulder, now at just a turn set free,
Stationed face to face with—Nature? rather with Infinitude)
—No revealment of them all, as singly I my path pursued,
But a bitter touched its sweetness, for the thought stung "Even so
Both of us had loved and wondered just the same, five days ago!"
15   Five short days, sufficient hardly to entice, from out its den
Splintered in the slab, this pink perfection of the cyclamen;
Scarce enough to heal and coat with amber gum the sloe-tree's gash,
Bronze the clustered wilding apple, redden ripe the mountain-ash:
Yet of might to place between us—Oh the barrier! Yon Profound
20   Shrinks beside it, proves a pin-point: barrier this, without a bound!
Boundless though it be, I reach you: somehow seem to have you here
—Who are there. Yes, there you dwell now, plain the four low walls
        appear;

LA SAISIAZ   ²⏐ MS:done, *P1878:*done;   ³⏐ MS:bent, *P1878:*bent
⁴⏐ MS:For the *P1878:*O'er the   ⁸⏐ MS:head *P1878:*head,   ¹²⏐ MS:my upward
§crossed out§   ¹⁶⏐ MS:cyclamen,— *P1878:*cyclamen;   ¹⁸⏐ MS:mountain-ash,—
*P1878:*mountain-ash: ¹⁹⏐ MS:Oh, the *P1878:*Oh the   ²¹⏐ MS:§¶ called for in
margin§ you—somehow *P1878:*you: somehow   ²²⏐ MS:there: yes *P1878:*there. Yes

Those are vineyards they enclose from; and the little spire which
    points
—That's Collonge, henceforth your dwelling. All the same, howe'er
    disjoints

25 Past from present, no less certain you are here, not there: have dared,
Done the feat of mountain-climbing,—five days since, we both
    prepared
Daring, doing, arm in arm, if other help should haply fail.
For you asked, as forth we sallied to see sunset from the vale,
"Why not try for once the mountain,—take a foretaste, snatch by
    stealth

30 Sight and sound, some unconsidered fragment of the hoarded
    wealth?
Six weeks at its base, yet never once have we together won
Sight or sound by honest climbing: let us two have dared and done
Just so much of twilight journey as may prove tomorrow's jaunt
Not the only mode of wayfare—wheeled to reach the eagle's haunt!"

35 So, we turned from the low grass-path you were pleased to call "your
    own,"
Set our faces to the rose-bloom o'er the summit's front of stone
Where Salève obtains, from Jura and the sunken sun she hides,
Due return of blushing "Good Night," rosy as a borne-off bride's,
For his masculine "Good Morrow" when, with sunrise still in hold,

40 Gay he hails her, and, magnific, thrilled her black length burns to
    gold.
Up and up we went, how careless—nay, how joyous! All was new,
All was strange. "Call progress toilsome? that were just insulting you!
How the trees must temper noontide! Ah, the thicket's sudden break!
What will be the morning glory, when at dusk thus gleams the lake?

45 Light by light puts forth Geneva: what a land—and, of the land,
Can there be a lovelier station than this spot where now we stand?
Is it late, and wrong to linger? True, to-morrow makes amends.
Toilsome progress? child's play, call it—specially when one descends!

23| MS:vineyards they <> from, and   *P1878:*vineyards, they from; and   *1889a:*vineyards
they   24| MS:Collonges §last letter crossed out forming *Collonge*§ <> dwelling! All <>
same, what e'er disjoints   *P1878:*same, howe'er disjoints   *1889a:*dwelling. All
25| MS:there—have dared   *P1878:*there: have dared,   35| MS:And we   *P1878:*So, we
37| MS:obtains from <> hides   *P1878:*obtains, from <> hides,

There, the dread descent is over—hardly our adventure, though!
50 Take the vale where late we left it, pace the grass-path, 'mine,' you
    know!
Proud completion of achievement!" And we paced it, praising still
That soft tread on velvet verdure as it wound through hill and hill;
And at very end there met us, coming from Collonge, the pair
—All our people of the Chalet—two, enough and none to spare.
55 So, we made for home together, and we reached it as the stars
One by one came lamping—chiefly that prepotency of Mars—
And your last word was "I owe you this enjoyment!"—met with "Nay:
With yourself it rests to have a month of morrows like to-day!"
Then the meal, with talk and laughter, and the news of that rare nook
60 Yet untroubled by the tourist, touched on by no travel-book,
All the same—though latent—patent, hybrid birth of land and sea,
And (our travelled friend assured you)—if such miracle might be—
Comparable for completeness of both blessings—all around
Nature, and, inside her circle, safety from world's sight and sound—
65 Comparable to our Saisiaz. "Hold it fast and guard it well!
Go and see and vouch for certain, then come back and never tell
Living soul but us; and haply, prove our sky from cloud as clear,
There may we four meet, praise fortune just as now, another year!"

Thus you charged him on departure: not without the final charge
70 "Mind to-morrow's early meeting! We must leave our journey marge
Ample for the wayside wonders: there's the stoppage at the inn
Three-parts up the mountain, where the hardships of the track begin;
There's the convent worth a visit; but, the triumph crowning all—
There's Salève's own platform facing glory which strikes greatness
    small,
75 —Blanc, supreme above his earth-brood, needles red and white and
    green,

52| MS:hill, *P1878:*hill;   53| MS:Collonges §last letter crossed out forming *Collonge*§
55| MS:So we   *P1878:*So, we   56| MS:prepotency §first three letters over illegible
erasure§   57| MS:enjoyment"—met *P1878:*enjoyment!"—met   62| MS:And—our
<> you,—if <> be,—   *P1878:*And (our <> you)—if <> be—   64| MS:inside that
circle *P1878:*inside her circle   67| MS:us: and *P1878:*us; and   69| MS:§no ¶§
—So you *P1878:*Thus you *1889a:*§¶§   72| MS:Three parts <> begin: *P1878:*Three-
parts <> begin;   73| MS:visit: but *P1878:*visit; but   74| MS:small *P1878:*small,
75| MS:earth-brood,—needles *P1878:*earth-brood, needles

Horns of silver, fangs of crystal set on edge in his demesne.
So, some three weeks since, we saw them: so, to-morrow we intend
You shall see them likewise; therefore Good Night till to-morrow,
    friend!"
Last, the nothings that extinguish embers of a vivid day:
80   "What might be the Marshal's next move, what Gambetta's
    counter-play?"
Till the landing on the staircase saw escape the latest spark :
"Sleep you well!" "Sleep but as well, you!"—lazy love quenched, all was
    dark.

Nothing dark next day at sundawn! Up I rose and forth I fared:
Took my plunge within the bath-pool, pacified the watch-dog scared,
85   Saw proceed the transmutation—Jura's black to one gold glow,
Trod your level path that let me drink the morning deep and slow,
Reached the little quarry—ravage recompensed by shrub and fern—
Till the overflowing ardours told me time was for return.
So, return I did, and gaily. But, for once, from no far mound
90   Waved salute a tall white figure. "Has her sleep been so profound?
Foresight, rather, prudent saving strength for day's expenditure!
Ay, the chamber-window's open: out and on the terrace, sure!"

No, the terrace showed no figure, tall, white, leaning through the
    wreaths,
Tangle-twine of leaf and bloom that intercept the air one breathes,
95   Interpose between one's love and Nature's loving, hill and dale
Down to where the blue lake's wrinkle marks the river's inrush pale
—Mazy Arve: whereon no vessel but goes sliding white and plain,
Not a steamboat pants from harbour but one hears pulsate amain,

---

⁷⁶| MS:demesne,— *P1878:*demesne.   ⁷⁸| MS:likewise: therefore *P1878:*likewise;
therefore   ⁷⁹| MS:day, *P1878:*day: ⁸⁰| MS:what Gambetta needs must §last two
words crossed out and replaced above by two words§ next might say" *CP1878:*Gambetta
§altered to§ Gambetta's next might say" §last three words crossed out and replaced above by§
counter-play   *1878:*what Gambetta's counter-play" *1889a:*counter-play?"
⁸¹| MS:spark *P1878:*spark: ⁸³| MS:§¶ called for in margin§   ⁸⁸| MS:ardors
*P1878:*ardours   ⁹²| MS:terrace sure!" *P1878:*terrace, sure!"   ⁹³| MS:§no ¶§
1889a:§¶§   ⁹⁴| MS:breathes *P1878:*breathes,   ⁹⁵| MS:loving hill *P1878:*loving,
hill   ⁹⁸| MS:steam-boat <> amain,— *P1878:*amain, *1889a:*steamboat

Past the city's congregated peace of homes and pomp of spires
100 —Man's mild protest that there's something more than Nature, man
  requires,
And that, useful as is Nature to attract the tourist's foot,
Quiet slow sure money-making proves the matter's very root,—
Need for body,—while the spirit also needs a comfort reached
By no help of lake or mountain, but the texts whence Calvin
  preached.
105 "Here's the veil withdrawn from landscape: up to Jura and beyond,
All awaits us ranged and ready; yet she violates the bond,
Neither leans nor looks nor listens: why is this?" A turn of eye
Took the whole sole answer, gave the undisputed reason "why!"

This dread way you had your summons! No premonitory touch,
110 As you talked and laughed ('tis told me) scarce a minute ere the
  clutch
Captured you in cold forever. Cold? nay, warm you were as life
When I raised you, while the others used, in passionate poor strife,
All the means that seemed to promise any aid, and all in vain.
Gone you were, and I shall never see that earnest face again
115 Grow transparent, grow transfigured with the sudden light that leapt,
At the first word's provocation, from the heart-deeps where it slept.

Therefore, paying piteous duty, what seemed You have we consigned
Peacefully to—what I think were, of all earth-beds, to your mind
Most the choice for quiet, yonder: low walls stop the vines' approach,
120 Lovingly Salève protects you; village-sports will ne'er encroach
On the stranger lady's silence, whom friends bore so kind and well
Thither "just for love's sake,"—such their own word was: and who can
  tell?

99| MS:And the *P1878:*Past the   102| MS:root, *P1878:*root,—
105| MS:landscape up <> beyond *P1878:*landscape: up <> beyond,
106| MS:ready: yet *P1878:*ready; yet   109| MS:§¶ called for in margin§ touch—
*P1878:*touch,   112| MS:strife *P1878:*strife,   113| MS:vain: *P1878:*vain.
117| MS:§no ¶§ Therefore, once the piteous duty done, and—what seemed you—consigned
*P1878:*Therefore, paying piteous duty, what seemed you have we consigned *1889a:*§¶§
seemed You   118| MS:earth-beds §last four letters over illegible erasure§
119| MS:Most your choice <> yonder,—low *P1878:*Most the choice <> yonder: low
120| MS:Lovingly Saleve <> you,—village-sports *P1878:*Lovingly Salève <> you; village-sports

You supposed that few or none had known and loved you in the
    world:
May be! flower that's full-blown tempts the butterfly, not flower that's
    furled.
¹²⁵ But more learned sense unlocked you, loosed the sheath and let
    expand
Bud to bell and outspread flower-shape at the least warm touch of
    hand
—Maybe, throb of heart, beneath which,—quickening farther than it
    knew,—
Treasure oft was disembosomed, scent all strange and unguessed hue.
Disembosomed, re-embosomed,—must one memory suffice,
¹³⁰ Prove I knew an Alpine-rose which all beside named Edelweiss?

Rare thing, red or white, you rest now: two days slumbered through;
    and since
One day more will see me rid of this same scene whereat I wince,
Tetchy at all sights and sounds and pettish at each idle charm
Proffered me who pace now singly where we two went arm in arm,—
¹³⁵ I have turned upon my weakness: asked "And what, forsooth, prevents
That, this latest day allowed me, I fulfil of her intents
One she had the most at heart—that we should thus again survey
From Salève Mont Blanc together?" Therefore,—dared and done
    to-day
Climbing,—here I stand: but you—where?

                If a spirit of the place
¹⁴⁰ Broke the silence, bade me question, promised answer,—what disgrace
Did I stipulate "Provided answer suit my hopes, not fears!"
Would I shrink to learn my life-time's limit—days, weeks, months or
    years?

---

^{124|} MS:be: flower *P1878:*be! flower   ^{126|} MS:hand. *P1878:*hand   ^{127|} MS:May
be *1889a:*Maybe   ^{128|} MS:Was not treasure disembosomed *P1878:*Treasure of was
disembosomed *CP1878:*of §altered to§ oft *1878:*oft   ^{129|} MS:Disembosomed, re-
interred now,—must *P1878:*Disembosomed, re-embosomed,—must   ^{130|} MS:Alpine
rose *P1878:*Alpine-rose   ^{131|} MS:§¶ called for in margin§ through: and
*P1878:*through; and   ^{135|} MS:weakness, asked *P1878:*weakness: asked
^{139|} MS:where? §¶ called for in margin§   ^{141|} MS:hopes—not *P1878:*hopes, not

Would I shirk assurance on each point whereat I can but guess—
"Does the soul survive the body? Is there God's self, no or yes?"
145 If I know my mood, 'twere constant—come in whatsoe'er uncouth
Shape it should, nay, formidable—so the answer were but truth.

Well, and wherefore shall it daunt me, when 'tis I myself am tasked,
When, by weakness weakness questioned, weakly answers—weakly
    asked?
Weakness never needs be falseness: truth is truth in each degree
150 —Thunderpealed by God to Nature, whispered by my soul to me.
Nay, the weakness turns to strength and triumphs in a truth beyond:
"Mine is but man's truest answer—how were it did God respond?"
I shall no more dare to mimic such response in futile speech,
Pass off human lisp as echo of the sphere-song out of reach,
155 Than,—because it well may happen yonder, where the far snows
    blanch
Mute Mont Blanc, that who stands near them sees and hears an
    avalanche,—
I shall pick a clod and throw,—cry "Such the sight and such the sound!
What though I nor see nor hear them? Others do, the proofs abound!"
Can I make my eye an eagle's, sharpen ear to recognize
160 Sound o'er league and league of silence? Can I know, who but surmise?
If I dared no self-deception when, a week since, I and you
Walked and talked along the grass-path, passing lightly in review
What seemed hits and what seemed misses in a certain fence-play,—
    strife
Sundry minds of mark engaged in "On the Soul and Future Life,"—
165 If I ventured estimating what was come of parried thrust,
Subtle stroke, and, rightly, wrongly, estimating could be just
—Just, though life so seemed abundant in the form which moved by
    mine,
I might well have played at feigning, fooling,—laughed "What need
    opine
Pleasure must succeed to pleasure, else past pleasure turns to pain,

---

147| MS:§¶ called for in margin§   150| MS:nature   *P1878:* to Nature
152| MS:answer: how   *P1878:* answer—how   166| MS:stroke and   *P1878:* stroke, and
169| MS:to pleasure else   *1889a:* to pleasure, else

170 And this first life claims a second, else I count its good no gain?"—
Much less have I heart to palter when the matter to decide
Now becomes "Was ending ending once and always, when you died?"
Did the face, the form I lifted as it lay, reveal the loss
Not alone of life but soul? A tribute to yon flowers and moss,
175 What of you remains beside? A memory! Easy to attest
"Certainly from out the world that one believes who knew her best
Such was good in her, such fair, which fair and good were great
    perchance
Had but fortune favoured, bidden each shy faculty advance;
After all—who knows another? Only as I know, I speak."
180 So much of you lives within me while I live my year or week.
Then my fellow takes the tale up, not unwilling to aver
Duly in his turn "I knew him best of all, as he knew her:
Such he was, and such he was not, and such other might have been
But that somehow every actor, somewhere in this earthly scene,
185 Fails." And so both memories dwindle, yours and mine together
    linked,
Till there is but left for comfort, when the last spark proves extinct,
This—that somewhere new existence led by men and women new
Possibly attains perfection coveted by me and you;
While ourselves, the only witness to what work our life evolved,
190 Only to ourselves proposing problems proper to be solved
By ourselves alone,—who working ne'er shall know if work bear fruit
Others reap and garner, heedless how produced by stalk and root,—
We who, darkling, timed the day's birth,—struggling, testified to
    peace,—
Earned, by dint of failure, triumph,—we, creative thought, must cease
195 In created word, thought's echo, due to impulse long since sped!
Why repine? There's ever someone lives although ourselves be dead!

170| MS:This <> life requires a <> gain,"— *P1878:*And this <> life claims a <> gain?"—
172| MS:ending once and always ending, when <> died? *P1878:*ending ending once and
always, when <> died?"   176| MS:believes §over illegible erasure§
178| MS:favored *1889a:*favoured   180| MS:week: *P1878:*week.   186| MS:the
latest spark's extinct, *P1878:*the last spark proves extinct,   187| MS:That already new
*P1878:*This—that somewhere new   191| MS:alone,—whom wanting, what if work of ours
bear *P1878:*alone,—who working, ne'er shall know if work bear *CP1878:*working, §comma
crossed out§ ne'er *1878:* working ne'er   192| MS:root?— *P1878:*root,—
195| MS:word its echo *P1878:*word, thought's echo   196| MS:dead. *P1878:*dead!

Well, what signifies repugnance? Truth is truth howe'er it strike.
Fair or foul the lot apportioned life on earth, we bear alike.
Stalwart body idly yoked to stunted spirit, powers, that fain
200   Else would soar, condemned to grovel, groundlings through the
        fleshly chain,—
Help that hinders, hindrance proved but help disguised when all too
        late,—
Hindrance is the fact acknowledged, howsoe'er explained as Fate,
Fortune, Providence: we bear, own life a burthen more or less.
Life thus owned unhappy, is there supplemental happiness
205   Possible and probable in life to come? or must we count
Life a curse and not a blessing, summed-up in its whole amount,
Help and hindrance, joy and sorrow?

                  Why should I want courage here?
I will ask and have an answer,—with no favour, with no fear,—
From myself. How much, how little, do I inwardly believe
210   True that controverted doctrine? Is it fact to which I cleave,
Is it fancy I but cherish, when I take upon my lips
Phrase the solemn Tuscan fashioned, and declare the soul's eclipse
Not the soul's extinction? take his "I believe and I declare—
Certain am I—from this life I pass into a better, there
215   Where that lady lives of whom enamoured was my soul"—where this
Other lady, my companion dear and true, she also is?

I have questioned and am answered. Question, answer presuppose
Two points: that the thing itself which questions, answers,—*is*, it
        knows;
As it also knows the thing perceived outside itself,—a force

197| MS:§¶ called for in margin§   198| MS:we §over illegible erasure§ <> alike:
*P1878:*alike.   200| MS:chain, *P1878:*chain,—   201| MS:Helps <> hinder
*P1878:*Help <> hinders   203| MS:Fortune, Providence,—we <> less: *P1878:*Fortune,
Providence: we <> less.   205| MS:come, or *P1878:*come? or   206| MS:blessing
summing up <> amount *P1878:*blessing, summed-up <> amount,   207| MS:sorrow?
§no ¶§ *P1878:*sorrow? §¶§   208| MS:favor *P1878:*favour   209| MS:myself: how
*P1878:*myself. How   210| MS:Of that *P1878:*True that   211| MS:cherish when
*P1878:*cherish, when   213| MS:extinction? solemn "I *P1878:*extinction? take his "I
217| MS:§¶ called for in margin§   218| MS:thing which <> is itself, it knows:
*P1878:*thing itself which <> is, it knows; *1889a:is*   219| MS:it knows too that the thing
which proves §last two words crossed out and replaced above by§ perceived *P1878:*it also

107

220 Actual ere its own beginning, operative through its course,
Unaffected by its end,—that this thing likewise needs must be;
Call this—God, then, call that—soul, and both—the only facts for me.
Prove them facts? that they o'erpass my power of proving, proves
     them such:
Fact it is I know I know not something which is fact as much.

225 What before caused all the causes, what effect of all effects
Haply follows,—these are fancy. Ask the rush if it suspects
Whence and how the stream which floats it had a rise, and where and
     how
Falls or flows on still! What answer makes the rush except that now
Certainly it floats and is, and, no less certain than itself,

230 *Is* the everyway external stream that now through shoal and shelf
Floats it onward, leaves it—may be—wrecked at last, or lands on shore
There to root again and grow and flourish stable evermore.
—May be! mere surmise not knowledge: much conjecture styled
     belief,
What the rush conceives the stream means through the voyage blind
     and brief.

235 Why, because I doubtless am, shall I as doubtless be? "Because
God seems good and wise." Yet under this our life's apparent laws
Reigns a wrong which, righted once, would give quite other laws to
     life.
"He seems potent." Potent here, then: why are right and wrong at
     strife ?
Has in life the wrong the better? Happily life ends so soon!

240 Right predominates in life? Then why two lives and double boon?
"Anyhow, we want it: wherefore want?" Because, without the want,
Life, now human, would be brutish: just that hope, however scant,
Makes the actual life worth leading; take the hope therein away,
All we have to do is surely not endure another day.

245 This life has its hopes for this life, hopes that promise joy: life done—
Out of all the hopes, how many had complete fulfilment? none.

---

knows the   221| MS:be: *P1878:*be;   230| MS:every way   *P1878:*everyway
232| MS:evermore   *P1878:*evermore.   233| MS:belief: *P1878:*belief,
234| MS:conceived <> meant   *P1878:*conceives <> means   241| MS:it: why the want?"
Because without   *P1878:*it:wherefore want?"   Because, without   242| MS:human, so
were brutish   *P1878:*human, would be brutish   243| MS:leading: take   *P1878:*leading;
take   244| MS:day   *P1878:*day.   246| MS:fulfilment? None.   *P1878:*none.

"But the soul is not the body:" and the breath is not the flute;
Both together make the music: either marred and all is mute.
Truce to such old sad contention whence, according as we shape
250 Most of hope or most of fear, we issue in a half-escape:
"We believe" is sighed. I take the cup of comfort proffered thus,
Taste and try each soft ingredient, sweet infusion, and discuss
What their blending may accomplish for the cure of doubt, till—slow,
Sorrowful, but how decided! needs must I o'erturn it—so!
255 Cause before, effect behind me—blanks! The midway point I am,
Caused, itself—itself efficient: in that narrow space must cram
All experience—out of which there crowds conjecture manifold,
But, as knowledge, this comes only—things may be as I behold,
Or may not be, but, without me and above me, things there are;
260 I myself am what I know not—ignorance which proves no bar
To the knowledge that I am, and, since I am, can recognize
What to me is pain and pleasure: this is sure, the rest—surmise.
If my fellows are or are not, what may please them and what pain,—
Mere surmise: my own experience—that is knowledge, once again!

265 I have lived, then, done and suffered, loved and hated, learnt and
taught
This—there is no reconciling wisdom with a world distraught,
Goodness with triumphant evil, power with failure in the aim,
If—(to my own sense, remember! though none other feel the same!)—
If you bar me from assuming earth to be a pupil's place,
270 And life, time,—with all their chances, changes,—just probation-space,
Mine, for me. But those apparent other mortals—theirs, for them?
Knowledge stands on my experience: all outside its narrow hem,
Free surmise may sport and welcome! Pleasures, pains affect mankind
Just as they affect myself? Why, here's my neighbour colour-blind,
275 Eyes like mine to all appearance: "green as grass" do I affirm?

254| MS:Sorrowful,—but < > decided!—needs   *P1878:*Sorrowful, but < > decided! needs
257| MS:experience out   *P1878:*experience—out   258| MS:only—Things   *P1878:*things
259| MS:are: *P1878:*are;   263| MS:pain,   *P1878:*pain,—
265| MS:§no ¶§   *P1878:*§¶§   266| MS:reconciling Wisdom   *P1878:*wisdom
267| MS:evil, Power   *P1878:*power   269| MS:I am hindered from   *P1878:*If you bar me
from   271| MS:mortals,—theirs   *P1878:*mortals—theirs   272| MS:hem   *P1878:*hem,

"Red as grass" he contradicts me: which employs the proper term?
Were we two the earth's sole tenants, with no third for referee,
How should I distinguish? Just so, God must judge 'twixt man and me.
To each mortal peradventure earth becomes a new machine,
280   Pain and pleasure no more tally in our sense than red and green;
Still, without what seems such mortal's pleasure, pain, my life were lost
—Life, my whole sole chance to prove—although at man's apparent
    cost—
What is beauteous and what ugly, right to strive for, right to shun,
Fit to help and fit to hinder,—prove my forces everyone,
285   Good and evil,—learn life's lesson, hate of evil, love of good,
As 'tis set me, understand so much as may be understood—
Solve the problem: "From thine apprehended scheme of things, deduce
Praise or blame of its contriver, shown a niggard or profuse
In each good or evil issue! nor miscalculate alike
290   Counting one the other in the final balance, which to strike,
Soul was born and life allotted: ay, the show of things unfurled
For thy summing-up and judgment,—thine, no other mortal's world!"
What though fancy scarce may grapple with the complex and immense
—"His own world for every mortal?" Postulate omnipotence!
295   Limit power, and simple grows the complex: shrunk to atom size,
That which loomed immense to fancy low before my reason lies,—
I survey it and pronounce it work like other work: success

276| MS:me:which   *P1878*:me—which   *1889a*:me:which   277| MS:referee   *P1878*:referee,
278| MS:twixt men   *P1878*:'twixt man   279| MS:Peradventure to each mortal earth
P1878:To each mortal peradventure earth   280| MS:Pains <> pleasures <> green:
P1878:Pain <> pleasure <> green;   282| MS:chance of learning—at mankind's
apparent   *P1878*:chance to prove—although at man's apparent   283| MS:ugly, what to
strive for, what to   *P1878*:ugly, right to strive for, right to   284| MS:What to help and
what to   *P1878*:Fit to help and fit to   286| MS:understanding what is to be
understood,—   *P1878*:understand so much as may be understood—   287| MS:Solve
this problem: "From the apprehended   *P1878*:Solve the problem: "From thine apprehended
288| MS:contriver shown   *P1878*:contriver, shown   289| MS:issue,—nor   *P1878*:issue!
nor   290| MS:balance which, to   *P1878*:balance, which to   291| MS:born, and <>
allotted, and the   *P1878*:born and <> allotted: ay, the   292| MS:thy solitary summing-
up <> no other's world!"   *P1878*:thy summing-up <> no other mortal's world!"
294| MS:—His <> mortal?   Postulate   *P1878*:"His <> mortal?"   Postulate
295| MS:complex, shrunk to pin-point size   *P1878*:complex: shrunk to atom size,
296| MS:lies   *P1878*:lies,—   297| MS:work, success   *P1878*:work: success

Here and there, the workman's glory,—here and there, his shame no
    less,
Failure as conspicuous. Taunt not "Human work ape work divine?"
300 As the power, expect performance! God's be God's as mine is mine!
God whose power made man and made man's wants, and made, to
    meet those wants,
Heaven and earth which, through the body, prove the spirit's
    ministrants,
Excellently all,—did He lack power or was the will in fault
When He let blue heaven be shrouded o'er by vapours of the vault,
305 Gay earth drop her garlands shrivelled at the first infecting breath
Of the serpent pains which herald, swarming in, the dragon death?
What, no way but this that man may learn and lay to heart how rife
Life were with delights would only death allow their taste to life?
Must the rose sigh "Pluck—I perish!" must the eve weep "Gaze—I fade!"
310 —Every sweet warn "'Ware my bitter!" every shine bid "Wait my
    shade"?
Can we love but on condition, that the thing we love must die?
Needs there groan a world in anguish just to teach us sympathy—
Multitudinously wretched that we, wretched too, may guess
What a preferable state were universal happiness?
315 Hardly do I so conceive the outcome of that power which went
To the making of the worm there in yon clod its tenement,
Any more than I distinguish aught of that which, wise and good,
Framed the leaf, its plain of pasture, dropped the dew, its fineless food.
Nay, were fancy fact, were earth and all it holds illusion mere,
320 Only a machine for teaching love and hate and hope and fear
To myself, the sole existence, single truth mid falsehood,—well!
If the harsh throes of the prelude die not off into the swell

---

²⁹⁸| MS:there, a workman's <> there, his shame   *P1878:*there, the workman's <> here and
there, shame   *CP1878:*here and there, his §in margin§ shame   *1878:*here and there, his
shame   ²⁹⁹| MS:apes <> divine!"   *P1878:*ape <> divine?"   ³⁰⁰| MS:performance!
God's is God's <> mine.   *P1878:*performance! God's be God's <> mine!
³⁰³| MS:he   *1889a:*did He   ³⁰⁴| MS:he   *1889a:*When He   ³⁰⁵| MS:garland
*P1878:*garlands   ³⁰⁶| MS:pains that §crossed out and replaced above by§ which
³¹⁰| MS:shade!"   *P1878:*shade?"   *1889a:*shade"?   ³¹¹| MS:condition that
*P1878:*condition, that   ³¹¹⁻¹²| MS:§lines are reversed, with marginal notes that they be
transposed§   ³¹⁸| MS:its place of <> its atom-food.   *P1878:*its plain of <> its fineless
food.   *CP1878:*fienless §altered to§ fineless   *1878:*fineless   ³²¹| MS:well   *P1878:*well!

Of that perfect piece they sting me to become a-strain for,—if
Roughness of the long rock-clamber lead not to the last of cliff,
325 First of level country where is sward my pilgrim-foot can prize,—
Plainlier! if this life's conception new life fail to realize,—
Though earth burst and proved a bubble glassing hues of hell, one huge
Reflex of the devil's doings—God's work by no subterfuge—
(So death's kindly touch informed me as it broke the glamour, gave
330 Soul and body both release from life's long nightmare in the grave)
Still,—with no more Nature, no more Man as riddle to be read,
Only my own joys and sorrows now to reckon real instead,—
I must say—or choke in silence—"Howsoever came my fate,
Sorrow did and joy did nowise,—life well weighed,—preponderate."
335 By necessity ordained thus? I shall bear as best I can;
By a cause all-good, all-wise, all-potent? No, as I am man!
Such were God: and was it goodness that the good within my range
Or had evil in admixture or grew evil's self by change?
Wisdom—that becoming wise meant making slow and sure advance
340 From a knowledge proved in error to acknowledged ignorance?
Power? 'tis just the main assumption reason most revolts at! power
Unavailing for bestowment on its creature of an hour,
Man, of so much proper action rightly aimed and reaching aim,
So much passion,—no defect there, no excess, but still the same,—
345 As what constitutes existence, pure perfection bright as brief
For yon worm, man's fellow-creature, on yon happier world—its leaf!
No, as I am man, I mourn the poverty I must impute:
Goodness, wisdom, power, all bounded, each a human attribute!

But, O world outspread beneath me! only for myself I speak,

328| MS:doings, God's <> subterfuge,   *P1878:*doings—God's <> subterfuge—
333| MS:say or <> silence "Howsoever   *P1878:*say—or <> silence—"Howsoever
334| MS:Sorrows <> joys did never,—life   *P1878:*Sorrow <> joy did nowise,—life
335| MS:By Necessity <> can: *P1878:*necessity <> can;   336| MS:a Cause all-wise, all-good §transposed to§ Cause all-good, all-wise   *P1878:*cause   341| MS:Power—'tis
*P1878:*Power? 'tis   343| MS:Man, that medium §last two words crossed out§ of so much proper §last three words inserted above§   344| MS:So much §two words added in margin§ Passion §altered to§passion§ , no <> same,   *P1878:*passion,—no <> same-,
CP1878: same-, §dash and comma transposed to§ same,—   *1878:*same,—
346| MS:world—a leaf!   *P1878:*world—its leaf!   347| MS:mourn the poverty §last two words over illegible erasure§ <> must needs §crossed out§ impute—   *P1878:*impute:
348| MS:attribute. *P1878:*attribute!   349| MS:§¶ called for in margin§

³⁵⁰ Nowise dare to play the spokesman for my brothers strong and weak,
Full and empty, wise and foolish, good and bad, in every age,
Every clime, I turn my eyes from, as in one or other stage
Of a torture writhe they, Job-like couched on dung and crazed with
    blains
—Wherefore? whereto? ask the whirlwind what the dread voice thence
    explains!
³⁵⁵ I shall "vindicate no way of God's to man," nor stand apart,
"Laugh, be candid!" while I watch it traversing the human heart.
Traversed heart must tell its story uncommented on: no less
Mine results in "Only grant a second life, I acquiesce
In this present life as failure, count misfortune's worst assaults
³⁶⁰ Triumph, not defeat, assured that loss so much the more exalts
Gain about to be. For at what moment did I so advance
Near to knowledge as when frustrate of escape from ignorance?
Did not beauty prove most precious when its opposite obtained
Rule, and truth seem more than ever potent because falsehood
    reigned?
³⁶⁵ While for love—Oh how but, losing love, does whoso loves succeed
By the death-pang to the birth-throe—learning what is love indeed?
Only grant my soul may carry high through death her cup unspilled,
Brimming though it be with knowledge, life's loss drop by drop
    distilled,
I shall boast it mine—the balsam, bless each kindly wrench that wrung
³⁷⁰ From life's tree its inmost virtue, tapped the root whence pleasure
    sprung,
Barked the bole, and broke the bough, and bruised the berry, left all
    grace
Ashes in death's stern alembic, loosed elixir in its place!

Witness, Dear and True, how little I was 'ware of—not your worth
—That I knew, my heart assures me—but of what a shade on earth
³⁷⁵ Would the passage from my presence of the tall white figure throw

---

³⁵³| MS:they Job-like   *P1878:*they, Job-like   ³⁵⁶| MS:candid," while <> heart!   *1*
*889a:*candid!" while <> heart.   ³⁶¹| MS:be: for   *P1878:*be. For
³⁶⁴| MS:truth not more   *P1878:*truth seem more   ³⁷²| MS:in Death's   *P1878:*death's
³⁷³| MS:§no ¶§ <> ware   *P1878:*§¶§ <> 'ware   ³⁷⁴| MS:me! but   *P1878:*me—but

O'er the ways we walked together! Somewhat narrow, somewhat slow
Used to seem the ways, the walking: narrow ways are well to tread
When there's moss beneath the footstep, honeysuckle overhead:
Walking slow to beating bosom surest solace soonest gives,
380 Liberates the brain o'erloaded—best of all restoratives.
Nay, do I forget the open vast where soon or late converged
Ways though winding?—world-wide heaven-high sea where music
    slept or surged
As the angel had ascendant, and Beethoven's Titan mace
Smote the immense to storm Mozart would by a finger's lifting chase?
385 Yes, I knew—but not with knowledge such as thrills me while I view
Yonder precinct which henceforward holds and hides the Dear and
    True.
Grant me (once again) assurance we shall each meet each some day,
Walk—but with how bold a footstep! on a way—but what a way!
—Worst were best, defeat were triumph, utter loss were utmost gain.
390 Can it be, and must, and will it?

                  Silence! Out of fact's domain,
Just surmise prepared to mutter hope, and also fear—dispute
Fact's inexorable ruling "Outside fact, surmise be mute!"
Well!
      Ay, well and best, if fact's self I may force the answer from!
'Tis surmise I stop the mouth of. Not above in yonder dome
395 All a rapture with its rose-glow,—not around, where pile and peak
Strainingly await the sun's fall,—not beneath, where crickets creak,
Birds assemble for their bed-time, soft the tree-top swell subsides,—
No, nor yet within my deepest sentient self the knowledge hides.
Aspiration, reminiscence, plausibilities of trust

376| MS:together: somewhat <> slow, *P1878:*together! Somewhat <> slow
384| MS:Smote to storm §last two words crossed out§ <> storm, Mozart *1889a:*storm Mozart
385| MS:knew: but *P1878:*knew—but   387| MS:me—once again—assurance
*P1878:*me (once again) assurance   389| MS:gain! *P1878:*gain.
390| MS:it? §no ¶§ *P1878:*it? §¶§   391| MS:hope: and fear as well, dispute
*P1878:*hope, and also fear—dispute   393| MS:Well! §¶ called for in margin§ <> from,
*P1878:*from!   394| MS:No surmise <> of! Not *P1878:*'Tis surmise *1889a:*of. Not
396| MS:Straining fix upon the <> beneath where *P1878:*Strainingly await the <> beneath,
where   398| MS:hides! *1889a:*hides.

400 —Now the ready "Man were wronged else," now the rash "and God
  unjust"—
None of these I need. Take thou, my soul, thy solitary stand,
Umpire to the champions Fancy, Reason, as on either hand
Amicable war they wage and play the foe in thy behoof!
Fancy thrust and Reason parry! Thine the prize who stand aloof.

FANCY

405 I concede the thing refused: henceforth no certainty more plain
Than this mere surmise that after body dies soul lives again.
Two, the only facts acknowledged late, are now increased to three—
God is, and the soul is, and, as certain, after death shall be.
Put this third to use in life, the time for using fact!

REASON

  I do:
410 Find it promises advantage, coupled with, the other two.
Life to come will be improvement on the life that's now; destroy
Body's thwartings, there's no longer screen betwixt soul and soul's joy.
Why should we expect new hindrance, novel tether? In this first
Life, I see the good of evil, why our world began at worst:
415 Since time means amelioration, tardily enough displayed,
Yet a mainly onward moving, never wholly retrograde.
We know more though we know little, we grow stronger though still
  weak,
Partly see though all too purblind, stammer though we cannot speak.
There is no such grudge in God as scared the ancient Greek, no fresh
420 Substitute of trap for dragnet, once a breakage in the mesh.
Dragons were, and serpents are, and blindworms will be: ne'er emerged

---

401| MS:need! Take *1889a:*need. Take   403| MS:they waging, play *P1878:*they
wage and play   404| MS:aloof! *1889a:*aloof.   406| MS:after body §over illegible
erasure§ < > again *P1878:*again.   407| MS:three: *P1878:*three—
410| MS:advantage, judging by the *P1878:*advantage, coupled with the   411| MS:now:
destroy *P1878:*now; destroy   412| MS:joy *P1878:*joy.   415| MS:displayed
*P1878:*displayed,   416| MS:Yet no less in one direction moving, never retrograde.
*P1878:*Yet a mainly onward moving, never wholly retrograde.   417| MS:little: we
*P1878:*little, we   418| MS:stammer if we < > speak: *P1878:*stammer though we < >
speak.   420| MS:dragnet once < > mesh: *P1878:*dragnet, once < > mesh.
421| MS:are, and earthworms will *P1878:*are, and blindworms will

Any new-created python for man's plague since earth was purged.
Failing proof, then, of invented trouble to replace the old,
O'er this life the next presents advantage much and manifold:
425 Which advantage—in the absence of a fourth and farther fact
Now conceivably surmised, of harm to follow from the act—
I pronounce for man's obtaining at this moment. Why delay?
Is he happy? happiness will change: anticipate the day!
Is he sad? there's ready refuge: of all sadness death's prompt cure!
430 Is he both, in mingled measure? cease a burthen to endure!
Pains with sorry compensations, pleasures stinted in the dole,
Power that sinks and pettiness that soars, all halved and nothing whole,
Idle hopes that lure man onward, forced back by as idle fears—
What a load he stumbles under through his glad sad seventy years,
435 When a touch sets right the turmoil, lifts his spirit where, flesh-freed,
Knowledge shall be rightly named so, all that seems be truth indeed!
Grant his forces no accession, nay, no faculty's increase,
Only let what now exists continue, let him prove in peace
Power whereof the interrupted unperfected play enticed
440 Man through darkness, which to lighten any spark of hope sufficed,—
What shall then deter his dying out of darkness into light?
Death itself perchance, brief pain that's pang, condensed and
    infinite?
But at worst, he needs must brave it one day, while, at best, he laughs—
Drops a drop within his chalice, sleep not death his science quaffs!
445 Any moment claims more courage when, by crossing cold and gloom,
Manfully man quits discomfort, makes for the provided room
Where the old friends want their fellow, where the new acquaintance
    wait,
Probably for talk assembled, possibly to sup in state!
I affirm and re-affirm it therefore: only make as plain
450 As that man now lives, that, after dying, man will live again,—
Make as plain the absence, also, of a law to contravene

422| MS:new-created Python *P1878:*python   429| MS:he sad? there's §last two words
and question mark over illegible erasure§   430| MS:measure?   What a
*P1878:*measure? cease   436| MS:be truly knowledge, all   *P1878:*be rightly named so, all
441| MS:What is to deter   *P1878:*What shall then deter   443| MS:day: while   *P1878:*day,
while   450| MS:that after §inserted above§ dying man   *1889a:*that, after dying, man

Voluntary passage from this life to that by change of scene,—
And I bid him—at suspicion of first cloud athwart his sky,
Flower's departure, frost's arrival—never hesitate, but die!

FANCY

455 Then I double my concession: grant, along with new life sure,
This same law found lacking now: ordain that, whether rich or poor
Present life is judged in aught man counts advantage—be it hope,
Be it fear that brightens, blackens most or least his horoscope,—
He, by absolute compulsion such as made him live at all,
460 Go on living to the fated end of life whate'er befall.
What though, as on earth he darkling grovels, man descry the sphere,
Next life's—call it, heaven of freedom, close above and crystal-clear?
He shall find—say, hell to punish who in aught curtails the term,
Fain would act the butterfly before he has played out the worm.
465 God, soul, earth, heaven, hell,—five facts now: what is to desiderate?

REASON

Nothing! Henceforth man's existence bows to the monition "Wait!
Take the joys and bear the sorrows—neither with extreme concern!
Living here means nescience simply: 'tis next life that helps to learn.
Shut those eyes, next life will open,—stop those ears, next life will teach
470 Hearing's office,—close those lips, next life will give the power of speech!
Or, if action more amuse thee than the passive attitude,
Bravely bustle through thy being, busy thee for ill or good,
Reap this life's success or failure! Soon shall things be unperplexed
And the right and wrong, now tangled, lie unravelled in the next."

FANCY

475 Not so fast! Still more concession! not alone do I declare
Life must needs be borne,—I also will that man become aware

452| MS:scene, *P1878:*scene,—   456| MS:poor *P1878:*poor, *CP1878:*poor, §comma crossed out§ *1878:*poor   457| MS:advantage,—be *P1878:*advantage—be
464| MS:worm! *P1878:*worm.   467| MS:concern: *P1878:*concern!   468| MS:simply, 'tis <> learn *P1878:*simply: 'tis <> learn.   476| MS:I also §over illegible erasure§

Life has worth incalculable, every moment that he spends
So much gain or loss for that next life which on this life depends.
Good, done here, be there rewarded,—evil, worked here, there
    amerced!
480   Six facts now, and all established, plain to man the last as first.

REASON

There was good and evil, then, defined to man by this decree?
Was—for at its promulgation both alike have ceased to be.
Prior to this last announcement "Certainly as God exists,
As He made man's soul, as soul is quenchless by the deathly mists,
485   Yet is, all the same, forbidden premature escape from time
To eternity's provided purer air and brighter clime,—
Just so certainly depends it on the use to which man turns
Earth, the good or evil done there, whether after death he earns
Life eternal,—heaven, the phrase be, or eternal death,—say, hell.
490   As his deeds, so proves his portion, doing ill or doing well!"
—Prior to this last announcement, earth was man's probation-place:
Liberty of doing evil gave his doing good a grace;
Once lay down the law, with Nature's simple "Such effects succeed
Causes such, and heaven or hell depends upon man's earthly deed
495   Just as surely as depends the straight or else the crooked line
On his making point meet point or with or else without incline,"—
Thenceforth neither good nor evil does man, doing what he must.
Lay but down that law as stringent "Wouldst thou live again, be just!"
As this other "Wouldst thou live now, regularly draw thy breath!
500   For, suspend the operation, straight law's breach results in death—"
And (provided always, man, addressed this mode, be sound and sane)
Prompt and absolute obedience, never doubt, will law obtain!

477| MS:incalculable, every   *1889a:*incalculable. every §emended to§ incalculable, every §see Editorial Notes§   478| MS:life which §over illegible erasure§   479| MS:God, done <> evil worked   *P1878:*Good, done <> evil, worked   484| MS:he *P1878:*As He
488| MS:Earth, does good there or does evil, whether   *P1878:*Earth, the good or evil done there, whether   490| MS:well!"   *1889a:*well" §emended to § well!" §see Editorial Notes§
492| MS:grace: *P1878:*grace;   493| MS:nature's   *P1878:*with Nature's
498| MS:"Would'st <> again? Be *P1878:*again, be   *1889a:*"Wouldst
499| MS:"Would'st <> now? Regularly *P1878:*now, regularly   *1889a:*"Wouldst
500| MS:operation and law's   *P1878:*operation, straight law's

Tell not me "Look round us! nothing each side but acknowledged law,
Now styled God's—now, Nature's edict!" Where's obedience without
   flaw
505 Paid to either? What's the adage rife in man's mouth? Why, "The best
I both see and praise, the worst I follow"—which, despite professed
Seeing, praising, all the same he follows, since he disbelieves
In the heart of him that edict which for truth his head receives.
There's evading and persuading and much making law amends
510 Somehow, there's the nice distinction 'twixt fast foes and faulty friends,
—Any consequence except inevitable death when "Die,
Whoso breaks our law!" they publish, God and Nature equally.
Law that's kept or broken—subject to man's will and pleasure! Whence?
How comes law to bear eluding? Not because of impotence:
515 Certain laws exist already which to hear means to obey;
Therefore not without a purpose these man must, while those man may
Keep and, for the keeping, haply gain approval and reward.
Break through this last superstructure, all is empty air—no sward
Firm like my first fact to stand on "God there is, and soul there is,"
520 And soul's earthly life-allotment: wherein, by hypothesis,
Soul is bound to pass probation, prove its powers, and exercise
Sense and thought on fact, and then, from fact educing fit surmise,
Ask itself, and of itself have solely answer, "Does the scope
Earth affords of fact to judge by warrant future fear or hope?"

525 Thus have we come back full circle: fancy's footsteps one by one
Go their round conducting reason to the point where they begun,
Left where we were left so lately, Dear and True! When, half a week
Since, we walked and talked and thus I told you, how suffused a cheek
You had turned me had I sudden brought the blush into the smile
530 By some word like "Idly argued! you know better all the while!"
Now, from me—Oh not a blush but, how much more, a joyous glow,

---

503| MS:round you! nothing   *P1878:*round us! nothing   504| MS:edict: where's <>
flaw?   *P1878:*edict!   Where's <> flaw   507| MS:follows since   *P1878:*follows, since
512| MS:nature equally   *P1878:*and Nature equally.   513| MS:—Subject to man's will
and pleasure, law that's kept or broken!   Whence?   *P1878:*Law that's kept or broken—
subject to man's will and pleasure!   Whence?   514| MS:illuding   *P1878:*eluding
516| MS:must while   *P1878:*must, while   519| MS:soul there is,   *P1878:*soul there is,"
523| MS:answer, "If the   *P1878:*answer, "Does the   527| MS:when, not a   *P1878:*and
True!   When, half a   531| MS:Now—from me—Oh, not   *P1878:*Now, from me—Oh not

Laugh triumphant, would it strike did your "Yes, better I do know"
Break, my warrant for assurance! which assurance may not be
If, supplanting hope, assurance needs must change this life to me.
535 So, I hope—no more than hope, but hope—no less than hope, because
I can fathom, by no plumb-line sunk in life's apparent laws,
How I may in any instance fix where change should meetly fall
Nor involve, by one revisal, abrogation of them all:
—Which again involves as utter change in life thus law-released,
540 Whence the good of goodness vanished when the ill of evil ceased.
Whereas, life and laws apparent re-instated,—all we know,
All we know not,—o'er our heaven again cloud closes, until, lo—
Hope the arrowy, just as constant, comes to pierce its gloom, compelled
By a power and by a purpose which, if no one else beheld,
545 I behold in life, so—hope!

Sad summing-up of all to say!
Athanasius contra mundum, why should he hope more than they?
So are men made notwithstanding, such magnetic virtue darts
From each head their fancy haloes to their unresisting hearts!

Here I stand, methinks a stone's throw from yon village I this morn
550 Traversed for the sake of looking one last look at its forlorn
Tenement's ignoble fortune: through a crevice, plain its floor
Piled with provender for cattle, while a dung-heap blocked the door.
In that squalid Bossex, under that obscene red roof, arose,
Like a fiery flying serpent from its egg, a soul—Rousseau's.
555 Turn thence! Is it Diodati joins the glimmer of the lake?
There I plucked a leaf, one week since,—ivy, plucked for Byron's sake.
Famed unfortunates! And yet, because of that phosphoric fame
Swathing blackness' self with brightness till putridity looked flame,
All the world was witched: and wherefore? what could lie beneath,
allure

535| MS:than hope: but   *P1878:*than hope, but   538| MS:all   *1889a:*all:
545| MS:hope! §¶ called for in margin§ <> summing up   *P1878:*summing-up
549| MS:§no ¶§   *P1878:*§¶§   551| MS:fortune, through <> crevice eyed its
*P1878:*fortune: through <> crevice, plain its   553| MS:roof, there rose,   *P1878:*roof,
arose,   557| MS:Famous wretched pair! And   *P1878:*Famed unfortunates! And

560 Heart of man to let corruption serve man's head as cynosure?
Was the magic in the dictum "All that's good is gone and past;
Bad and worse still grows the present, and the worst of all comes last:
Which believe—for I believe it?" So preached one his gospel-news;
While melodious moaned the other "Dying day with dolphin-hues!
565 Storm, for loveliness and darkness like a woman's eye! Ye mounts
Where I climb to 'scape my fellow, and thou sea wherein he counts
Not one inch of vile dominion! What were your especial worth
Failed ye to enforce the maxim 'Of all objects found on earth
Man is meanest, much too honoured when compared with—what by odds
570 Beats him—any dog: so, let him go a-howling to his gods!'
Which believe—for I believe it!" such the comfort man received
Sadly since perforce he must: for why? the famous bard believed!

Fame! Then, give me fame, a moment! As I gather at a glance
Human glory after glory vivifying yon expanse,
575 Let me grasp them all together, hold on high and brandish well
Beacon-like above the rapt world ready, whether heaven or hell
Send the dazzling summons earthward, to submit itself the same,
Take on trust the hope or else despair flashed full on face by—Fame!
Thanks, thou pine-tree of Makistos, wide thy giant torch I wave!
580 Know ye whence I plucked the pillar, late with sky for architrave?
This the trunk, the central solid Knowledge, kindled core, began
Tugging earth-deeps, trying heaven-heights, rooted yonder at
  Lausanne.
This which flits and spits, the aspic,—sparkles in and out the boughs
Now, and now condensed, the python, coiling round and round allows
585 Scarce the bole its due effulgence, dulled by flake on flake of Wit—
Laughter so bejewels Learning,—what but Ferney nourished it?

560| MS:serve his head *P1878:*serve man's head 561| MS:past *P1878:*past;
563| MS:it!" so *P1878:*it?" So 566| MS:scape *P1878:*'scape
567| MS:dominion!—what *P1878:*dominion! What 569| MS:honored *1889a:*honoured
573| MS:§no ¶§ then *P1878:*§¶§ Fame! Then 577| MS:summons downward, to
*1889a:*summons earthward, to 581| MS:knowledge *P1878:*solid Knowledge
582| MS:Tugging earth and trying < > Lausanne: *P1878:*Tugging earth-deeps, trying < >
Lausanne. 585| MS:effulgence dulled *P1878:*effulgence, dulled
586| MS:be-jewels < > but §inserted above§ *P1878:*bejewels

121

Nay, nor fear—since every resin feeds the flame—that I dispense
With yon Bossex terebinth-tree's all-explosive Eloquence:
No, be sure! nor, any more than thy resplendency, Jean-Jacques,
590   Dare I want thine, Diodati! What though monkeys and macaques
Gibber "Byron"? Byron's ivy rears a branch beyond the crew,
Green for ever, no deciduous trash macaques and monkeys chew!
As Rousseau, then, eloquent, as Byron prime in poet's power,—
Detonations, fulgurations, smiles—the rainbow, tears—the shower,—
595   Lo, I lift the coruscating marvel—Fame! and, famed, declare
—Learned for the nonce as Gibbon, witty as wit's self Voltaire . . .
O the sorriest of conclusions to whatever man of sense
Mid the millions stands the unit, takes no flare for evidence!
Yet the millions have their portion, live their calm or troublous day,
600   Find significance in fireworks: so, by help of mine, they may
Confidently lay to heart and lock in head their life long—this:
"He there with the brand flamboyant, broad o'er night's forlorn abyss,
Crowned by prose and verse; and wielding, with Wit's bauble,
       Learning's rod . . .
Well? Why, he at least believed in Soul, was very sure of God."

---

605   So the poor smile played, that evening: pallid smile long since extinct
Here in London's mid-November! Not so loosely thoughts were linked,
Six weeks since as I, descending in the sunset from Salève,
Found the chain, I seemed to forge there, flawless till it reached your
       grave,—

587-94| MS:§these eight lines inserted on verso§   588| MS:eloquence: *P1878:*all-explosive
Eloquence: 589| MS:nor any   *P1878:*nor, any   591| *P1878:*Gibber "Byron?"
Byron's   *1889a:*Gibber "Byron"? Byron's   592| MS:deciduous leaves macaques
*P1878:*deciduous trash macaques   595| MS:corruscating marvel—Fame, and
*P1878:*marvel—Fame! and   *1889a:*coruscating   596| MS:self Voltaire—   *P1878:*self
Voltaire . . .   600| MS:so by < > mine they   *P1878:*so, by < > mine, they
602| MS:the brow flamboyant   *P1878:*the brand flamboyant   603| MS:Crowned with
prose < > verse and wielding with < > bauble Learning's rod—   *P1878:*Crowned by prose
< > verse; and wielding, with < > bauble, Learning's rod . . .   604| MS:why < > soul < >
God! *P1878:*Well? Why < > Soul   *1889a:*God. §emended to§ God." §see Editorial Notes§
606| MS:mid-November: not < > linked,—   *P1878:*mid-November! Not < > linked,
607| MS:I descended in < > from Salève   *P1878:*I, descending in < > from Salève,
608| MS:With the chain I   *P1878:*Found the chain, I

Not so filmy was the texture, but I bore it in my breast
610 Safe thus far. And since I found a something in me would not rest
Till I, link by link, unravelled any tangle of the chain,
—Here it lies, for much or little! I have lived all o'er again
That last pregnant hour: I saved it, just as I could save a root
Disinterred for re-interment when the time best helps to shoot.
615 Life is stocked with germs of torpid life; but may I never wake
Those of mine whose resurrection could not be without earthquake!
Rest all such, unraised forever! Be this, sad yet sweet, the sole
Memory evoked from slumber! Least part this: then what the whole?

610| MS:far; and *P1878*:far. And   613| MS:it just *P1878*:it, just
615| MS:life: but *P1878*:life; but   617| MS:such unraised forever; be *P1878*:such,
unraised forever! Be   618| MS:Least part §over illegible erasure§ this, then
P1878:this: then   MS:§below last line of verse and flush right§ L. D. I. E.   Nov. 9. '77.
RB.   *P1878*:§below last line of verse and flush left§ *November* 9, 1877.

THE TWO POETS OF CROISIC

Such a starved bank of moss
  Till that May-morn,
Blue ran the flash across:
  Violets were born!

II

5   Sky—what a scowl of cloud
  Till, near and far,
Ray on ray split the shroud
  Splendid, a star!

III

World—how it walled about
10 Life with disgrace
Till God's own smile came out:
  That was thy face!

---

§MS in Balliol College Library. Ed. P1878, CP1878, 1878, 1889a. See Editorial Notes§
SUCH A STARVED BANK   ²| MS:Till, that   *1889a:*Till that
³| MS:across—   *P1878:*across: ⁷| MS:shroud: *1889a:*shroud
⁹| MS:it §word above illegibly crossed out§   ¹²| MS:That was §last two words crossed
out, replaced above by illegibly crossed out words, and then restored§

THE TWO POETS OF CROISIC

1878

I

"Fame!" Yes, I said it and you read it. First,
　　Praise the good log-fire! Winter howls without.
Crowd closer, let us! Ha, the secret nursed
　　Inside yon hollow, crusted roundabout
5　With copper where the clamp was,—how the burst
　　Vindicates flame the stealthy feeder! Spout
Thy splendidest—a minute and no more?
So soon again all sobered as before?

II

Nay, for I need to see your face! One stroke
10　　Adroitly dealt, and lo, the pomp revealed!
Fire in his pandemonium, heart of oak
　　Palatial, where he wrought the works concealed
Beneath the solid-seeming roof I broke,
　　As redly up and out and off they reeled
15　Like disconcerted imps, those thousand sparks
From fire's slow tunnelling of vaults and arcs!

III

Up, out, and off, see! Were you never used,—
　　You now, in childish days or rather nights,—
As I was, to watch sparks fly? not amused
20　　By that old nurse-taught game which gave the sprites

THE TWO POETS OF CROISIC　　　¹| MS:First—　*P1878:*First,
²| MS:At §crossed out and replaced above by§ Praise　　　⁴| MS:Inside the §crossed out
and replaced above by§ yon hollow crusted round about　*P1878:*hollow, crusted roundabout
⁷| MS:Your §crossed out and replaced above by§ Thy　　　⁹| MS:face! §colon altered to
exclamation point§ one stroke §inserted above illegibly crossed out word§　*P1878:*face!
One　　　¹³| *P1878:*solid seeming　*1889a:*solid-seeming
¹⁴| MS:And §crossed out and replaced above by§ As　　　¹⁶| MS:From fire's §over illegible
erasure§ long §crossed out and replaced above by§ slow < > arcs.　*P1878:*arcs!

Each one his title and career,—confused
  Belief 'twas all long over with the flights
From earth to heaven of hero, sage and bard,
And bade them once more strive for Fame's award?

IV

²⁵ New long bright life! and happy chance befell—
  That I know—when some prematurely lost
Child of disaster bore away the bell
  From some too-pampered son of fortune, crossed
Never before my chimney broke the spell!
³⁰   Octogenarian Keats gave up the ghost,
While—never mind Who was it cumbered earth—
Sank stifled, span-long brightness, in the birth.

V

Well, try a variation of the game!
  Our log is old ship-timber, broken bulk.
³⁵ There's sea-brine spirits up the brimstone flame,
  That crimson-curly spiral proves the hulk
Was saturate with—ask the chloride's name
  From somebody who knows! I shall not sulk
If yonder greenish tonguelet licked from brass
⁴⁰ Its life, I thought was fed on copperas.

---

²¹| MS:career,— §comma inserted above§ refused *P1878:*career,—confused
²⁵| MS:The §crossed out and replaced above by§ New < > life! and §over illegible erasure§
²⁸| MS:fortune—crossed *P1878:*fortune, crossed   ²⁹| MS:spell; *P1878:*spell!
³¹| MS:mind what §altered to§ who was it §last two words inserted above§ cumbered of
§crossed out§ earth *P1878:*mind Who < > earth—   ³²| MS:Sank §inserted above
illegibly crossed out word§ strangled §crossed out and replaced above by§ stifled—span-long
brightness—in *P1878:*stifled, span-long brightness, in   ³³| MS:Well, but §crossed out
and replaced above by§ try   ³⁴| MS:This log < > bulk; *P1878:*Our log < > bulk.
³⁵| MS:the greenish §crossed out, replaced above by illegibly crossed out word, perhaps
yellow, and then replaced by§ brimstone flame— *P1878:*flame,   ³⁶| MS:crimson—
curling §altered to§ crimson-curly§ tonguelet §crossed out and replaced above by§ spiral
³⁷| MS:with oozing §crossed out and replaced above by two ellipsis points and two words§ . .
ask the chloride's §over illegible erasure§ *P1878:*with—ask   ³⁹| MS:yonder brimstone
§crossed out and replaced above by§ greenish spirit §inserted above illegibly crossed out
word, then crossed out and replaced above by§ tonguelet licked §over illegible word§

130

VI

Anyhow, there they flutter! What may be
    The style and prowess of that purple one?
Who is the hero other eyes shall see
    Than yours and mine? That yellow, deep to dun—
45 Conjecture how the sage glows, whom not we
    But those unborn are to get warmth by! Son
O' the coal,—as Job and Hebrew name a spark,—
    What bard, in thy red soaring, scares the dark?

VII

Oh and the lesser lights, the dearer still
50   That they elude a vulgar eye, give ours
The glimpse repaying astronomic skill
    Which searched sky deeper, passed those patent powers
Constellate proudly,—swords, scrolls, harps, that fill
    The vulgar eye to surfeit,—found best flowers
55 Hid deepest in the dark,—named unplucked grace
    Of soul, ungathered beauty, form or face!

41| MS:flutter! What shall §crossed out and replaced above by§ may
45| MS:Conjecture whose §crossed out and replaced above by§ how < > sage shall §crossed out§ glow §altered to§ glows,whom §comma and word inserted above§   46| MS:unborn shall §crossed out and replaced above by three words§ are to get   49| MS:lights, the §inserted above illegibly crossed out word§ dearer §crossed out, replaced above by illegibly crossed out word, and then restored§   50| MS:elude the §crossed out and followed by illegible erasure§ a vulgar §inserted above§   51| MS:glimpse that §crossed out§ repays §altered to§ repaying the §crossed out§   52| MS:That §crossed out and replaced above by§ Which searching §altered to§ searched heaven §inserted above, then crossed out and replaced above by§ sky deeper, than swords, lyres, and §last four words crossed out and replaced above by four words§ passed those patent powers   53| MS:Constellate proudly,— §last word, comma, and dash inserted above illegibly crossed out word§ < > scrolls, lyres §crossed out and replaced above by§ harps   54| MS:The unlearned §crossed out and replaced above by§ vulgar eye with §crossed out and replaced above by§ to surfeit,— §word, comma, and dash inserted above illegibly crossed out word§
55| MS:the heaven,—named §dash and last word inserted above illegibly crossed out word§
56| MS:soul, §next word illegibly crossed out§ < > face? *P1878:*face!

VIII

Up with thee, mouldering ash men never knew,
    But I know! flash thou forth, and figure bold,
Calm and columnar as yon flame I view!
    Oh and I bid thee,—to whom fortune doled
Scantly all other gifts out—bicker blue,
    Beauty for all to see, zinc's uncontrolled
Flake-brilliance! Not my fault if these were shown,
Grandeur and beauty both, to me alone.

IX

No! as the first was boy's play, this proves mere
    Stripling's amusement: manhood's sport be grave!
Choose rather sparkles quenched in mid career,
    Their boldness and their brightness could not save
(In some old night of time on some lone drear
    Sea-coast, monopolized by crag or cave)
—Save from ignoble exit into smoke,
Silence, oblivion, all death-damps that choke!

---

[57] MS:thee, noble heart §last two words crossed out, replaced above by illegibly crossed out word, and then replaced above by§ mouldering mind §crossed out and replaced by§ ash <> knew; *P1878:*knew,   [58] MS:figure calm §crossed out and replaced by§ bold *P1878:*bold, [59] MS:Golden §crossed out and replaced above by§ Calm <> flame we §crossed out and replaced above by§ I   [60] MS:and I give §crossed out and replaced above by§ bid [61] MS:Scantly all other gifts out—bicker §last six words inserted above illegibly crossed out words§ blue *P1878:*blue,   [62] MS:Beauty, §word and comma inserted above§ For <> see, and like yonder §last three words crossed out and replaced above by§ zinc's *P1878:*Beauty   [63] MS:Flake-brilliance! Why were §last two words crossed out and replaced above by§ Not my   [65] MS:Lo—will it be,—for why? It so had been, §last ten words and comma crossed out and replaced above by ten words§ No §over illegible word§ ! as the first was §last four words inserted above illegibly crossed out words§ boy's play, this were §crossed out and replaced above by§ proves mere   [66] MS:Everywhere §crossed and replaced above by§ Stripling's   [67] MS:Which is the §last three words crossed out and replaced above by three words§ Name we §next word illegibly crossed out and replaced by§ a sparkle *P1878:*Choose rather sparkles   [68] MS:Its boldness and its brightness <> save— §comma altered to dash§ *P1878:*True boldness and true brightness <> save *1889a:*Their boldness and their brightness   [69] MS:time; §next word illegibly crossed out§ on *P1878:*time on   [70] MS:Sea-coast monopolized by crag or cave) §last five words inserted above illegibly crossed out words§   [71] MS:Save §inserted in margin§ From §altered to§ from ignominious §altered to§ ignoble *P1878:*—Save [72] MS:all the §crossed out and replaced above by word and hyphen§ death-

X

Launched by our ship-wood, float we, once adrift
  In fancy to that land-strip waters wash,
75 We both know well! Where uncouth tribes made shift
  Long since to just keep life in, billows dash
Nigh over folk who shudder at each lift
  Of the old tyrant tempest's whirlwind-lash
Though they have built the serviceable town
80 Tempests but tease now, billows drench, not drown.

XI

Croisic, the spit of sandy rock which juts
  Spitefully northward, bears nor tree nor shrub
To tempt the ocean, show what Guérande shuts
  Behind her, past wild Batz whose Saxons grub
85 The ground for crystals grown where ocean gluts
  Their promontory's breadth with salt: all stub

---

⁷³| MS:You see §last two words crossed out and replaced above by two words§ Launched by
< > ship-wood float we, §last two words and comma inserted above illegibly crossed out word§
once voyaging §crossed out and replaced above by word and comma§ adrift,   *1889a:*adrift
⁷⁴| to that §crossed out and then restored above§ far §crossed and replaced below by§ old
§crossed out§   land-strip §hyphen and last five letters inserted above§ ocean §crossed out
and replaced above by §waters washed §altered to§ wash   ⁷⁵| MS:We both know well!
§last four words and exclamation point inserted above illegibly crossed out words§ where
§altered to§ Where uncouth folk made   *P1878:*uncouth tribes made   ⁷⁶| MS:Hardly
§crossed out and replaced above by§ Somehow to keep in life §last two words transposed to§
life in that §crossed out and replaced above by§ which billows dashed §altered to§ dash
*P1878:*Long since < > keep the life in billows   *1889a:*to just keep life in, billows
⁷⁷| MS:Right over, all a-shudder at   *P1878:*over; still they shudder at   *1889a:*Nigh over folk
who shudder   ⁷⁸| MS:Of tempests, §comma crossed out§ this old tyrant §transposed to§
this old tyrant tempest's whirlwind-lash,   *P1878:*Of the old   CP:1878:whirlwind-lash,
§comma crossed out§   *1878:*whirlwind-lash   ⁷⁹| MS:Long ere they built < > town,
*P1878:*Though they have built < > town,   C*P1878:*town, §comma crossed out§   *1878:*town
⁸⁰| MS:Tempests now spare, and §last three words crossed out and replaced above by three
words and comma§ but teaze now,   *1889a:*tease   ⁸¹| MS:rock that juts   *P1878:*rock
which juts   ⁸²| MS:northward, §first five letters over illegible letters and dash altered to
comma§ bears nor single §crossed out§   ⁸³| MS:To tempt §inserted above illegibly
crossed out word§ < > ocean, show §inserted above§ what §next word illegibly crossed out§
Guerande   *P1878:*Guérande   ⁸⁴| MS:her, from §crossed out and replaced above by§
past   ⁸⁵| MS:crystal §altered to§ crystals salt that §last two words crossed out§ grows
§altered to§ grown   ⁸⁶| MS:The promontory's   *P1878:*Their promontory's

Of rock and stretch of sand, the land's last strife
To rescue a poor remnant for dear life.

XII

And what life! Here was, from the world to choose,
90 The Druids' chosen chief of homes: they reared
—Only their women,—mid the slush and ooze
Of yon low islet,—to their sun, revered
In strange stone guise,—a temple. May-dawn dews
  Saw the old structure levelled; when there peered
95 May's earliest eve-star, high and wide once more
Up towered the new pile perfect as before:

XIII

Seeing that priestesses—and all were such—
  Unbuilt and then rebuilt it every May,
Each alike helping—well, if not too much!
100 For, mid their eagerness to outstrip day
And get work done, if any loosed her clutch
  And let a single stone drop, straight a prey
Herself fell, torn to pieces, limb from limb,
By sisters in full chorus glad and grim.

88| MS:rescue just a remnant for dear §inserted above illegibly crossed out word§ life. §dash altered to period *1889a:*rescue a poor remnant   89| MS:was, out of §last two words crossed out and replaced above by§ from the §next word illegibly crossed out§ < > choose,— *P1878:*choose,   90| MS:The Druids' chief of chosen §last three words transposed to§ chosen chief of < > they built §crossed out§   92| MS:sun,—revered *P1878:*sun, revered   93| MS:strange stone §inserted above§ < > temple; May-dawn *P1878:*temple. May-dawn   94| MS:levelled: where there §inserted above illegibly crossed out word§ *P1878:*levelled; where   95| MS:May's earliest §inserted above§
96| MS:Here stood §last two word crossed out and replaced above by two words§ Up towered the new pile §last two words over illegible erasure§ < > before. *P1878:*before:
98| MS:Unbuilt it §crossed out§ < > it every May, §last two words and comma inserted above illegibly crossed out words§   99| MS:§first two words illegibly crossed out, replaced above by illegibly crossed out words, and then replaced in margin by two words§ All alike helping §inserted above§ *P1878:*Each alike   102| MS:let our single stone fall §crossed out and replaced above by word and comma§ drop, *P1878:*let a single

XIV

105 And still so much remains of that grey cult,
    That even now, of nights, do women steal
To the sole Menhir standing, and insult
    The antagonistic church-spire by appeal
To power discrowned in vain, since each adult
110   Believes the gruesome thing she clasps may heal
Whatever plague no priestly help can cure:
Kiss but the cold stone, the event is sure!

XV

Nay more: on May-morns, that primeval rite
    Of temple-building, with its punishment
115 For rash precipitation, lingers, spite
    Of all remonstrance; vainly are they shent,
Those girls who form a ring and, dressed in white,
    Dance round it, till some sister's strength be spent:
Touch but the Menhir, straight the rest turn roughs
120 From gentles, fall on her with fisticuffs.

105| MS:cult *P1878:*cult,   106| MS:nights, the §crossed out and replaced above by§ do
109| MS:vain, that §crossed out and replaced above by§ since   110| MS:Believes
§inserted above illegibly crossed out words§ < > clasps to §crossed out and replaced above by§
may   111| MS:Whatever §inserted above illegibly crossed out words§ plague not §last
letter crossed out forming *no*§   113| MS:on May days §crossed out and replaced above by
hyphen and word§ -morns   115| MS:precipitation, holds, §last word and comma crossed
out and replaced above by§ keeps §crossed out and replaced above by word and comma§
lingers, despite §first two letters crossed out forming *spite*§   116| MS:Of all §last two
words crossed out and then restored§ priest's §inserted above illegibly crossed out word and
then crossed out§ remonstrance; §last word and semicolon inserted above§
117| MS:and, all §crossed out and replaced above by§ dressed   118| MS:round the
menhir §last two words crossed out and replaced above by word and comma§ it, till their
§crossed out and replaced above by two words§ some sister's < > spent,— *P1878:*spent:
119| MS:§first word illegibly crossed out and replaced in margin by§ Touch but §inserted
above illegibly crossed out word§ against §inserted above and then crossed out§ the Menhir,
§last word and comma inserted above illegibly crossed out word§ straight §inserted above§

XVI

Oh and, for their part, boys from door to door
    Sing unintelligible words to tunes
As obsolete: "scraps of Druidic lore,"
    Sigh scholars, as each pale man importunes
125 Vainly the mumbling to speak plain once more.
    Enough of this old worship, rounds and runes!
They serve my purpose, which is but to show
Croisic to-day and Croisic long ago.

XVII

What have we sailed to see, then, wafted there
130   By fancy from the log that ends its days
Of much adventure 'neath skies foul or fair,
    On waters rough or smooth, in this good blaze
We two crouch round so closely, bidding care
    Keep outside with the snow-storm? Something says
135 "Fit time for story-telling!" I begin—
Why not at Croisic, port we first put in?

XVIII

Anywhere serves: for point me out the place
    Wherever man has made himself a home,

121| MS:and, the boys, §last two words and comma crossed out§ < > part, §next word illegibly crossed out§ from door §over illegible word§ to door §over illegible word§
122| MS:§first word illegibly crossed out§ sing §altered to§ Sing §next word illegibly crossed out§   123| MS:lore,—"   *P1878:*lore,"   124| MS:Sighs §last letter crossed out forming *Sigh*§ < > as some pale   *P1878:*as each pale   126| MS:purpose which is just to *P1878:*purpose, which   *1889a:*is but to   128| MS:Croisic—to-day   *P1878:*Croisic to-day
129| MS:What are we there to see then   *P1878:*What have we sailed to see, then
131| MS:Of rough §crossed out and replaced above by§ much   133| MS:We crowd about so closely, bidding §crossed out and then restored§   *P1878:*We two crouch round so
134| MS:something says—   *P1878:*snow-storm? Something says   135| MS:"The time   *P1878:*"Fit time   137| MS:Any where < > for: all things §last two words crossed out§ point to §crossed out and replaced above by three words§ me out the   *P1878:*Anywhere < > for point   138| MS:Where man has ever §transposed to§ Wherever man has

And there I find the story of our race
140　　In little, just at Croisic as at Rome.
What matters the degree? the kind I trace.
Druids their temple, Christians have their dome:
So with mankind; and Croisic, I'll engage,
With Rome yields sort for sort, in age for age.

XIX

145　No doubt, men vastly differ: and we need
　　Some strange exceptional benevolence
Of nature's sunshine to develop seed
　　So well, in the less-favoured clime, that thence
We may discern how shrub means tree indeed
150　　Though dwarfed till scarcely shrub in evidence.
Man in the ice-house or the hot-house ranks
With beasts or gods: stove-forced, give warmth the thanks!

XX

While, is there any ice-checked? Such shall learn
　　I am thankworthy, who propose to slake
155　His thirst for tasting how it feels to turn
　　Cedar from hyssop-on-the-wall. I wake

139|　MS:All of §last two words crossed out and replaced by three words§ And there I <> the history of the race　　*P1878:*the story of our race　　140|　MS:little, §dash altered to comma§ <> at Rome:　*P1878:*at Rome.　　141|　MS:kind we §crossed out and replaced above by§ I trace: §dash altered to colon§　*P1878:*trace.　　144|　MS:Corresponds §crossed out and replaced above by three words§ With Rome yields　　145|　MS:doubt, so vast they differ §next word illegibly crossed out§ that we　*P1878:*doubt, men vastly differ: and we　　149|　MS:discern the §crossed out, replaced above by illegibly crossed out word, and then replaced by§ how shrub who §crossed out and replaced above by§ meant §altered to§ means　150|　MS:dwarfed until §altered to§ till scarce a shrub　*P1878:*till scarcely shrub　151|　MS:ice-house and the　*1889a:*ice-house or the　　152|　MS:With god §crossed out§　153|　MS:While, ice-checked is there any?　§last four words transposed to§ is there any ice-checked?　　154|　MS:Who is §last two words crossed out and replaced above by two words§ I am thank-worthy, who propose to §last three words inserted above illegibly crossed out words§　*P1878:*thankworthy　　155|　MS:for growing §crossed out and replaced above by§ tasting what §crossed out and replaced above by§ how it is §crossed out and replaced above by§ feels　156|　MS:hyssop on the wall　*P1878:*hyssop-on-the-wall

No memories of what is harsh and stern
    In ancient Croisic-nature, much less rake
The ashes of her last warmth till out leaps
160   Live Hervé Riel, the single spark she keeps.

XXI

Take these two, see, each outbreak,—spirt and spirt
    Of fire from our brave billet's either edge
Which—call maternal Croisic ocean-girt!
    These two shall thoroughly redeem my pledge.
165   One flames fierce gules, its feebler rival—vert,
    Heralds would tell you: heroes, I allege,
They both were: soldiers, sailors, statesmen, priests,
    Lawyers, physicians—guess what gods or beasts!

XXII

None of them all, but—poets, if you please!
170   "What, even there, endowed with knack of rhyme,

158| MS:And cold §last two words crossed out§ in §altered to§ In ancient §inserted above§
Croisic-nature—much   *P1878:*Croisic-nature, much   159| MS:of its warmer annals—
§last two words and dash crossed out and replaced above by two words§ last warmth till I find
§last two words crossed out and replaced by two words§ out leaps   *P1878:*of her last
160| MS:Live §inserted above illegibly crossed out word§ <> single soul I mind— §last three
words and dash crossed out and replaced above by three words and period§ spark it keeps.
*P1878:*spark she keeps   161| MS:Now, §last word and comma crossed out and replaced
above by§ Take <> see, that outbreak   *P1878:*see, each outbreak
162| MS:fire from §inserted above illegibly crossed out words§ our fresh §inserted above§
billet's breadth length §last two words crossed out and replaced above by two words§ either
edge   *P1878:*our brave billet's   163| MS:(That's §crossed out and replaced above by two
words§ Call it §next word illegibly crossed out§ maternal §inserted above§ <> ocean-girt)
*P1878:*Which call maternal <> ocean-girt!—   *1889a:*Which—call <> ocean-girt!
164| MS:§line added in margin§   165| MS:One is fierce ruby §crossed out and replaced
above by§ gules, the other §last two words crossed out and replaced above by two words§ its
feebler <> vert, §dash altered to comma§   *P1878:*One flames fierce
166| MS:With touch of §next word illegibly crossed out§ to increase its strength—
§last eight words and dash crossed out and replaced below by eight words and comma§ In
§crossed out§ herald's §altered to§ Heralds language §crossed out and replaced above by§
blazon §crossed out and replaced above by three words and colon§ would tell you:
is §crossed out§ heroes, I allege,   170| MS:What, even there, §last two words and comma
inserted above illegibly crossed out word and crossed out comma§

138

Did two among the aborigines
    Of that rough region pass the ungracious time
Suiting, to rumble-tumble of the sea's,
    The songs forbidden a serener clime?
175 Or had they universal audience—that's
To say, the folk of Croisic, ay and Batz?"

XXIII

Open your ears! Each poet in his day
    Had such a mighty moment of success
As pinnacled him straight, in full display,
180   For the whole world to worship—nothing less!
Was not the whole polite world Paris, pray?
    And did not Paris, for one moment—yes,
Worship these poet-flames, our red and green,
One at a time, a century between?

XXIV

185 And yet you never heard their names! Assist,
    Clio, Historic Muse, while I record
Great deeds! Let fact, not fancy, break the mist
    And bid each sun emerge, in turn play lord

171| MS:Did two §last two words inserted above illegibly crossed out words§
172| MS:region, pass the ungracious §inserted above illegibly crossed out word§
*P1878:*region pass   173| MS:Suiting §over illegible erasure§   175| MS:Or had
§inserted above illegibly crossed out word§   176| MS:ay, and *P1878:*ay and
177| MS:Erect §crossed out and replaced above by§ Open   178| MS:such glorious
§crossed out and replaced above by two words§ a splendid < > of renown §crossed out and
replaced above by§ success   179| MS:As pinnacled him straight, in full display, §last six
words and comma inserted above illegibly crossed out words§   180| MS:worship—could
it less? *P1878:*worship—nothing less!   181| MS:§first word illegibly crossed out§ was
§altered to§ Was not Paris the whole §inserted above§ polite world §last five words transposed
to§ the whole polite world Paris   182| MS:not Paris, §dash altered to comma§
185| MS:names! Assist *P1878:*names! Assist,   186| MS:historic *P1878:*Clio,
Historic   187| MS:And §crossed out, replaced above by illegibly crossed out word, and
then replaced in margin by two words and exclamation point§ Great deeds! for truth §last
two words crossed out and replaced above by two words§ Let fact
188| MS:bid the §crossed out and replaced above by§ each < > emerge, and §crossed out and
replaced above by two words§ in turn play heaven's §crossed out§ lord, *P1878:*lord

Of day, one moment! Hear the annalist
190   Tell a strange story, true to the least word!
At Croisic, sixteen hundred years and ten
Since Christ, forth flamed yon liquid ruby, then.

XXV

Know him henceforth as René Gentilhomme
      —Appropriate appellation! noble birth
195   And knightly blazon, the device wherefrom
      Was "Better do than say"! In Croisic's dearth
Why prison his career while Christendom
      Lay open to reward acknowledged worth?
He therefore left it at the proper age
200   And got to be the Prince of Condé's page.

XXVI

Which Prince of Condé, whom men called "The Duke,"
      —Failing the king, his cousin, of an heir,
(As one might hold would hap, without rebuke,
      Since Anne of Austria, all the world was 'ware,
205   Twenty-three years long sterile, scarce could look
      For issue)—failing Louis of so rare
A godsend, it was natural the Prince
Should hear men call him "Next King" too, nor wince.

189| MS:For §crossed out and replaced above by two words and comma§ Of heaven, one brief
§crossed out§ moment.   Thus §crossed out and replaced above by§ Hear <> annalist!
*P1878:*Of day, one moment! Hear <> annalist   190| MS:Begins, then. §last two words
and period crossed out and replaced above by four words§ Takes up this tale §last four words
crossed out and replaced above by three words and comma§ A simple story,   *P1878:*Tell a
strange story   192| MS:Since Christ, was born my first §last four words crossed out and
replaced above by four words§ forth flamed yon liquid ruby, §word and comma inserted above
illegibly crossed out word§   194| MS:The lucky §last two words crossed out and replaced
above by dash and word§ —Appropriate <> birth §over illegible erasure§   196| MS:say"!
In §over illegible erasure§   197| MS:Why prison his §last three words inserted above
illegibly crossed out words§   201| MS:of Condé, whom men §last two words crossed out,
replaced above by illegibly crossed out words, and then restored§   202| MS:—Failing the
king, §last two words and comma inserted above§ his brother, Louis §crossed out§ of
*CP1878:*his cousin §crossed out and replaced in margin by§ cousin, of   *1878:*his cousin, of
204| MS:ware,   *P1878:*'ware,   205| MS:years'   *P1878:*years   208| MS:men style
§crossed out and replaced above by§ call him future §crossed out and replaced above by

140

XXVII

Now, as this reasonable hope, by growth
210   Of years, nay, tens of years, looked plump almost
To bursting,—would the brothers, childless both,
     Louis and Gaston, give but up the ghost—
Condé, called "Duke" and "Next King," nothing loth
     Awaited his appointment to the post,
215 And wiled away the time, as best he might,
Till Providence should settle things aright.

XXVIII

So, at a certain pleasure-house, withdrawn
     From cities where a whisper breeds offence,
He sat him down to watch the streak of dawn
220   Testify to first stir of Providence;
And, since dull country life makes courtiers yawn,
     There wanted not a poet to dispense
Song's remedy for spleen-fits all and some,
Which poet was Page René Gentilhomme.

---

quotation marks and word§ "Next King too" §last word and quotation marks inserted above§
nor   *P1878:*him "Next King" too, nor   210| MS:of years, was §crossed out and replaced
above by§ looked   211| MS:To perfect certainty §last two words crossed out and replaced
above by§ bursting,—would the brothers, childless §last four words inserted above illegibly
crossed out words§   213| MS:and "Next King", nothing loth   *P1878:*and "Next King,"
nothing loth   216| MS:providence   *P1878:*Till Providence   217| MS:pleasure-
house, reserved §crossed out and replaced by§ withdrawn   218| MS:From town, §word
and comma crossed out and replaced above by§ cities make §crossed out and replaced above
by§ which §crossed out§   where a whisper breeds §last four words inserted above illegibly
crossed out words§   219| MS:sat him down §last two words inserted above§ < > of early
§crossed out§   220| MS:Testify to first §last two words inserted above illegibly crossed out
words§ work §crossed out and replaced above by§ stir of §over illegible word§ providence:
*P1878:*providence;   *1889a:*of Providence;   221| MS:And, seeing §crossed out and
replaced above by§ since dull §inserted above§   222| MS:not the people who §last three
words crossed out and replaced above by three words§ a poet to
223| MS:Song's §inserted avove illegibly crossed out word§ antidote to
§last two words crossed out and replaced above by two words§ remedy for

141

XXIX

225 A poet born and bred, his very sire
    A poet also, author of a piece
    Printed and published, "Ladies—their attire":
      Therefore the son, just born at his decease,
      Was bound to keep alive the sacred fire,
230   And kept it, yielding moderate increase
    Of songs and sonnets, madrigals, and much
    Rhyming thought poetry and praised as such.

XXX

    Rubbish unutterable (bear in mind!)
      Rubbish not wholly without value, though,
235 Being to compliment the Duke designed
      And bring the complimenter credit so,—
    Pleasure with profit happily combined.
      Thus René Gentilhomme rhymed, rhymed till—lo,
    This happened, as he sat in an alcove
240 Elaborating rhyme for "love"—*not* "dove."

225| MS:Because in him they had a poet missed §last eight words crossed out and replaced above by eight words§ A poet born and bred—his very sire *P1878:*bred, his
226| MS:also; author *P1878:*also, author   227| MS:published "Ladies *P1878:*published, "Ladies   228| MS:son—just < > decease— *P1878:*son, just < > decease,
230| MS:And did so, yielding *P1878:*And kept it, yielding   231| MS:Of songs and sonnets, §last three words and comma inserted above§   232| MS:Rhyming §next word illegibly crossed out§ thought verse §crossed out and replaced above by§ poetry
233| MS:unutterable—bear < > mind— *P1878:*unutterable (bear < > mind!)
234| MS:Yet §crossed out and replaced above by§ Rubbish not wholly §inserted above§ without is purpose, worth or no— §last five words and comma§ value, though, §crossed out and replaced above by two words and comma§ value, though,   236| MS:so, *P1878:*so,—
237| MS:Pleasure and §crossed out and replaced above by§ with < > combined: *P1878:*combined.   238| MS:So §crossed out and replaced above by§ And René *P1878:*Thus René   239| MS:This strange thing §last two words crossed out§
240| MS:Enquiring after §last two words inserted above illegibly crossed out word§ rhyme §next letter illegibly crossed out§ for love—*not* *P1878:*Elaborating rhyme for "love"—*not*

XXXI

He was alone: silence and solitude
　　Befit the votary of the Muse. Around,
Nature—not our new picturesque and rude,
　　But trim tree-cinctured stately garden-ground—
245　Breathed polish and politeness. All-imbued
　　With these, he sat absorbed in one profound
Excogitation "Were it best to hint
　　Or boldly boast 'She loves me,—Araminte'?"

XXXII

When suddenly flashed lightning, searing sight
250　Almost, so close to eyes; then, quick on flash,
Followed the thunder, splitting earth downright
　　Where René sat a-rhyming: with huge crash
Of marble into atoms infinite—
　　Marble which, stately, dared the world to dash
255　The stone-thing proud, high-pillared, from its place:
　　One flash, and dust was all that lay at base.

---

[241] MS:alone: buried in §colon added and last two words crossed out§ <> solitude, §dash altered to comma§　*P1878:*solitude　　[242] MS:Befit §over illegible word§ should one §last two words crossed out and replaced above by three words§ the votary of the Muse; §dash altered to semicolon§ around　*P1878:*the Muse. Around,　　[243] MS:Nature,—not modern picturesque <> rude—　*P1878:*Nature—not our new picturesque <> rude,　　[244] MS:trim and §crossed out and replaced above by§ tree-cinctured <> garden-ground: *P1878:*garden-ground—　　[245] MS:All §crossed out and replaced above by§ Breathed <> politeness; all imbued　*P1878:*politeness. All-imbued　　[247] MS:Enquiry,—should one §last three words crossed out and replaced above by three words§ Excogitation—were it *P1878:*Excogitation "Were　　[248] MS:boast "She <> Araminte."　*P1878:*boast 'She <> Araminte?'"　*1889a:*me,—Araminte'?"　　[249] MS:lightning,—searing §first three letters inserted above illegible erasure§ *P1878:*lightning, searing　　[250] MS:close his eyes; then followed such a §last three words crossed out and replaced above by two words§ quick on flash *P1878:*then, quick <> flash,　*1889a:*close to eyes　　[251] MS:The thunder followed splitting §transposed and altered to§ Followed the thunder splitting　*P1878:*thunder, splitting　　[252] MS:Just §crossed out§ where §altered to§ Where he §crossed out and replaced above by§ René sat §inserted above illegibly crossed out word§ his fourteenth line §last three words crossed out and replaced above by word and colon§ a-rhyming: with huge §inserted above　　[253] MS:Of something §crossed out and replaced above by§ marble　　[254] MS:Marble §in margin§ which §over illegible word§ ,stately, §next word illegibly crossed out and replaced above by illegibly crossed out word§　　[255] MS:The ornament §crossed out and replaced above by two words and comma§ stone-thing proud,

XXXIII

So, when the horrible confusion loosed
    Its wrappage round his senses, and, with breath,
Seeing and hearing by degrees induced
260   Conviction what he felt was life, not death—
His fluttered faculties came back to roost
    One after one, as fowls do: ay, beneath,
About his very feet there, lay in dust
Earthly presumption paid by heaven's disgust.

XXXIV

265 For, what might be the thunder-smitten thing
    But, pillared high and proud, in marble guise,
A ducal crown—which meant "Now Duke: Next, King"?
    Since such the Prince was, not in his own eyes
Alone, but all the world's. Pebble from sling
270   Prostrates a giant; so can pulverize
Marble pretension—how much more, make moult
A peacock-prince his plume—God's thunderbolt.

XXXV

That was enough for René, that first fact
    Thus flashed into him. Up he looked: all blue

258| MS:Its wrap §altered to§ wrappage around §altered to§ round
260| MS:A confidence that §last three words crossed out and replaced above by four words§
Conviction what he felt   262| MS:fowls would: ay, beneath—   *P1878:*fowls do: ay,
beneath,   263| MS:there lay   *P1878:*there, lay   264| MS:The thing heaven's
thunderbolt §last four words crossed out and replaced above by five words§ Earthly
presumption paid by heaven's   267| MS:A §over illegible word§ ducal §over illegible
word§ crown . . which meant "now §altered to§ Now Duke; next §altered to§ Next, King?"
§dash altered to question mark§   *P1878:*crown—which meant "Now Duke: Next   *1889a:*meant
"Now Duke: Next, King"?   269| MS:world's. Pebble §inserted above illegibly crossed
out words§ from a §crossed out§   270| MS:§first word illegibly crossed out and replaced
above by illegibly crossed out word§ prostrate §altered to§ Prostrates the §crossed out and
replaced above by§ a giant's §apostrophe and last letter crossed out forming *giant*§ , so
*P1878:*giant; so   271| MS:Earthly §crossed out and replaced above by§ Marble pretension
§over illegible word§   272| MS:A peacock-prince his plume §transposed and altered to§
His plume a peacock-prince—God's thunderbolt?   *P1878:*plume, a < > thunderbolt!   *1889a:*A
peacock-prince his plume—God's thunderbolt.   274| MS:Thus §in margin§ Flashed
§altered to§ flashed into René §crossed out and replaced above by§ him: up   *P1878:*him. Up

²⁷⁵ And bright the sky above; earth firm, compact
    Beneath his footing, lay apparent too;
Opposite stood the pillar: nothing lacked
    There, but the Duke's crown: see, its fragments strew
The earth,—about his feet lie atoms fine
²⁸⁰ Where he sat nursing late his fourteenth line!

XXXVI

So, for the moment, all the universe
    Being abolished, all 'twixt God and him,—
Earth's praise or blame, its blessing or its curse,
    Of one and the same value,—to the brim
²⁸⁵ Flooded with truth for better or for worse,—
    He pounces on the writing-paper, prim,
Keeping its place on table: not a dint
    Nor speck had damaged "Ode to Araminte."

XXXVII

And over the neat crowquill calligraph
²⁹⁰   His pen goes blotting, blurring, as an ox
Tramples a flower-bed in a garden,—laugh
    You may!—so does not he, whose quick heart knocks
Audibly at his breast: an epitaph
    On earth's break-up, amid the falling rocks,

---

^{275|} MS:above, §dash altered to comma§ all §crossed out and replaced above by§ earth
*P1878:*above; earth   ^{276|} MS:footing, earth §crossed out and replaced above by§ lay < >
too: *P1878:*too;   ^{277|} MS:pillar—nothing *P1878:*pillar: nothing   ^{279|} MS:earth
§over illegible erasure§ < > feet, the §crossed out and replaced above by§ lie *P1878:*feet lie
^{282|} MS:abolished, all §over illegible word§ 'twixt §over illegible word§   ^{283|} MS:And
§crossed out and replaced in margin by§ Earth's < > blame, its §inserted above illegibly
crossed out word§   ^{284|} MS:value,—mid that swim §last three words crossed out and
replaced above by three words§ to the brim   ^{286|} MS:He pounced §altered to§ pounces
upon §first two letters crossed out forming *on*§ the writing- §last word and hyphen inserted above§
paper, §dash altered to comma§ prim *1889a:*prim,   ^{288|} MS:speck had §over illegible
word§ damaged his "To *P1878:*damaged "Ode to   ^{289|} MS:the fine §crossed out and
replaced above by§ neat crow-quill character §crossed out and replaced above by§ calligraph
*P1878:*crowquill   ^{290|} MS:As §crossed out§ his §altered to§ His pen goes §crossed out,
replaced above by illegibly crossed out word, and then restored§   ^{291|} MS:laugh,
*P1878:*laugh   ^{292|} MS:may,—so does §over illegible erasure, perhaps *did*§ < > he, whose
§inserted above illegibly crossed out word, perhaps *his*§ *P1878:*may!—so   ^{293|} MS:breast:
§dash altered to colon§   ^{294|} MS:amid its §crossed out and replaced above by§ the

295   He might be penning in a wild dismay,
      Caught with his work half-done on Judgment Day.

XXXVIII

     And what is it so terribly he pens,
        Ruining "Cupid, Venus, wile and smile,
       Hearts, darts," and all his day's *divinior mens*
300   Judged necessary to a perfect style?
     Little recks René, with a breast to cleanse,
      Of Rhadamanthine law that reigned erewhile:
      Brimful of truth, truth's outburst will convince
      (Style or no style) who bears truth's brunt—the Prince.

XXXIX

305 "Condé, called 'Duke,' be called just 'Duke,' not more
      To life's end! 'Next King' thou forsooth wilt be?
     Ay, when this bauble, as it decked before
       Thy pillar, shall again, for France to see,
       Take its proud station there! Let France adore
310   No longer an illusive mock-sun—thee—
      But keep her homage for Sol's self, about
      To rise and put pretenders to the rout!

296| MS:Caught §inserted above illegibly crossed out words§ with his §inserted above§ work unfinished §crossed out and replaced above by§ half-done   298| MS:Ruining Cupid, Venus, wiled §last letter crossed out forming *wile*§ and smiled §last letter crossed out forming *smile*§ *P1878:*Ruining "Cupid   299| MS:Arts, darts, and all that day's *P1878:*Hearts, darts," and all his day's   301| MS:recks §over illegible word§ , §comma crossed out§   302| MS:Of That §altered to§ that was Rhadamanthine law, §last four words transposed to§ Rhadamanthine law, that was erewhile: §colon over illegible punctuation mark, perhaps a dash§ *P1878:*law that reigned erewhile: 303| MS:Brimful §over illegible word§ < > truth,—its outburst *P1878:*truth, truth's outburst   304| MS:bears the §crossed out and replaced above by§ truth's   305| MS:Prince §crossed out and replaced above by§ Condé styled §altered to§ called "Duke," be called just §inserted above§ "Duke," and §crossed out§ no more, *P1878:*'Condé' called 'Duke,' be < > just 'Duke,' not more, C*P1878:*'Condé' §altered to§ "Condé, called *1878:*"Condé, called *1889a:*more   306| MS:end! "Next §quotation marks and last word inserted above§ King" most §crossed out and replaced above by§ thou forsooth §inserted above illegibly crossed out word§ would §crossed out and replaced above by§ wilt *P1878:*end! 'Next King' thou   307| MS:when this §over illegible word§   308| MS:for men §crossed out and replaced above by§ France   309| MS:Shall §crossed out§ take §crossed out, restored, and altered to§ Take its proud §inserted above§   312| MS:To rise and §last two words inserted above§ < > pretenders §next word illegibly crossed out and replaced above by illegibly crossed out word§ to the §inserted above§

XL

"What? France so God-abandoned that her root
 Regal, though many a Spring it gave no sign,
³¹⁵ Lacks power to make the bole, now branchless, shoot
  Greenly as ever? Nature, though benign,
 Thwarts ever the ambitious and astute.
  In store for such is punishment condign:
 Sure as thy Duke's crown to the earth was hurled,
³²⁰ So sure, next year, a Dauphin glads the world!"

XLI

Which penned—some forty lines to this effect—
 Our René folds his paper, marches brave
Back to the mansion, luminous, erect,
 Triumphant, an emancipated slave.
³²⁵ There stands the Prince. "How now? My Duke's crown wrecked?
  What may this mean?" The answer René gave
Was—handing him the verses, with the due
 Incline of body: "Sir, God's word to you!"

---

³¹³| MS:"What? France so §over illegible word§ far §crossed out and replaced above by word and hyphen§ God-abandoned, that the §crossed out and replaced above by§ her *P1878:*so God-abandoned that ³¹⁴| MS:Regal, so §crossed out and replaced above by§ though many years without a §last three words crossed out and replaced above by five words§ a spring it gave no sign, *P1878:*a Spring ³¹⁵| MS:Of §crossed out and replaced above by§ Lacks < > bole, long §crossed out and replaced above by§ now ³¹⁶| MS:as §first letter of next word illegibly crossed out§ ever? Nature, is §crossed out and replaced above by§ though ³¹⁷| MS:Confuses the ambitious §inserted above illegibly crossed out word§ and astute: §last two words crossed out and then restored§ *P1878:*astute. *1889a:*Thwarts ever the ³¹⁸| MS:§line added§ ³¹⁹| MS:Briefly so §last two words crossed out§ sure §altered to§ Sure ³²²| MS:marches brave §over illegible erasure§ ³²³| MS:erect *P1878:*erect, ³²⁴| MS:Past fear for §last three words crossed out and replaced above by word and comma§ Triumphant, < > slave: *P1878:*slave. ³²⁵| MS:the Prince: "How now? My Duke's-crown *P1878:*the Prince. "How *1889a:*now? My Duke's crown ³²⁶| MS:mean?" The §over illegible erasure§ ³²⁷| MS:him the §last letter over illegible letter§ paper §crossed out and replaced above by§ verses with the §over illegible word, perhaps *a*§ bow— §word and dash crossed out and replaced above by§ due *P1878:*verses, with ³²⁸| MS:body: "Prince §crossed out and replaced above by word and comma§ Sir,

XLII

The Prince read, paled, was silent; all around,
330   The courtier-company, to whom he passed
The paper, read, in equal silence bound.
    René grew also by degrees aghast
At his own fit of courage—palely found
    Way of retreat from that pale presence: classed
335 Once more among the cony-kind. "Oh, son,
It is a feeble folk!" saith Solomon.

XLIII

Vainly he apprehended evil: since,
    When, at the year's end, even as foretold,
Forth came the Dauphin who discrowned the Prince
340   Of that long-craved mere visionary gold,
'Twas no fit time for envy to evince
    Malice, be sure! The timidest grew bold:
Of all that courtier-company not one
But left the semblance for the actual sun.

329| MS:read, paled, §word and comma inserted above illegibly crossed out word§ <> silent: all *P1878:*silent; all   330| MS:The company of courtiers §last three words transposed and altered to§ courtier-company, to §inserted above§   331| MS:paper to §crossed out§ 332| MS:By degrees René also grew aghast *1889a:*René grew also by degrees aghast 333| MS:his late §crossed out and replaced above by§ own <> courage,—palely *P1878:*courage—palely   335| MS:the human §inserted above and then crossed out§ conies §altered to§ cony, §comma crossed out§ every on §last two words crossed out and replaced by§ whereon §crossed out and replaced above by hyphen, three words, comma, and quotation marks§ -kind: "Oh, son," *P1878:*cony-kind. "Oh, son,   336| MS:folk!" says §altered to§ saith   337| MS:And all in vain his apprehension, §last six words and comma crossed out and replaced above by four words and colon§ Vainly he apprehended evil: 338| MS:end, just §crossed out and replaced above by§ even as §next word illegibly crossed out§ 339| MS:the wondrous§crossed out§ Dauphin, and §crossed out and replaced above by§ who *P1878:*the Dauphin who   340| MS:Of the long-cherished §hyphen and word crossed out and replaced above by hyphen and two words§ -hoped for visionary *P1878:*Of that long-craved mere visionary   341| MS: 'T §letter over illegible erasure, perhaps *It*§ <> no fit §inserted above§ *P1878:*'Twas   343| MS:courtier-company, not *P1878:*courtier-company not   344| MS:for the very sun. *P1878:*for the actual sun.

XLIV

³⁴⁵ And all sorts and conditions that stood by
　　At René's burning moment, bright escape
Of soul, bore witness to the prophecy.
　　Which witness took the customary shape
Of verse; a score of poets in full cry
³⁵⁰ 　　Hailed the inspired one. Nantes and Tours agape,
Soon Paris caught the infection; gaining strength,
How could it fail to reach the Court at length?

XLV

"O poet!" smiled King Louis, "and besides,
　　O prophet! Sure, by miracle announced,
³⁵⁵ My babe will prove a prodigy. Who chides
　　Henceforth the unchilded monarch shall be trounced
For irreligion: since the fool derides
　　Plain miracle by which this prophet pounced
Exactly on the moment I should lift

---

³⁴⁶| MS:At René's splendid §inserted below illegible erasure§ moment—brief escape
*P1878:*At René's burning moment, bright escape ³⁴⁷| MS:soul, §comma crossed out
and replaced by dash§ bore <> prophecy. §colon altered to period§ *P1878:*soul, bore
³⁴⁸| MS:Which §over illegible erasure§ <> took in many cases §last three words crossed out
and replaced above by two words§ the customary ³⁴⁹| MS:verse; §dash altered to
semicolon§ ³⁵⁰| MS:one. §comma altered to period§ ³⁵¹| MS:infection;
§followed by illegible erasure§ gaining strength §last two words in margin§ *P1878:*strength,
³⁵²| MS:§first words illegibly crossed out§ it but arrive at §last three words crossed out and
replaced above by four words§ fail to reach the ³⁵³| MS:"O §over illegible erasure§
poet," quoth the §crossed out§ King Louis §inserted above§ "and prophet too? §last two
words crossed out and replaced above by word and comma§ besides *P1878:*poet!" smiled
*1889a:*smiled King Louis, "and ³⁵⁴| MS:My babe will be a prodigy §last six words
crossed out and replaced above by five words§ O §over illegible erasure§ prophet! §question
mark altered to exclamation point§ Sure, by miracle ³⁵⁵| MS:By miracle delayed so
long because he bides §last eight words crossed out and replaced above by eight words§ My
babe will prove a prodigy! Who chides *P1878:*prodigy. Who ³⁵⁶| MS:His time §last
two words crossed out and replaced above by§ Henceforth §crossed out§ the §altered to§
The unchilded §first two letters inserted above§ monarch §first letter over illegible word,
perhaps *is*§ now §crossed out and replaced above by§ henceforth shall be §last two words
inserted above illegibly crossed out word§ *P1878:*Henceforth the <> monarch shall
³⁵⁷| MS:irreligion,—since the fool §last three words inserted above illegibly crossed out
word§ *P1878:*irreligion: since ³⁵⁸| MS:The §crossed out and replaced above by§ Plain
§crossed out and replaced in margin by§ The miracle *P1878:*Plain miracle

360   Like Simeon, in my arms, a babe, 'God's gift!'

XLVI

"So call the boy! and call this bard and seer
      By a new title! him I raise to rank
Of 'Royal Poet:' poet without peer!
      Whose fellows only have themselves to thank
365 If humbly they must follow in the rear
      My René. He's the master: they must clank
Their chains of song, confessed his slaves; for why?
      They poetize, while he can prophesy!"

XLVII

So said, so done; our René rose august,
370   "The Royal Poet;" straightway put in type
His poem-prophecy, and (fair and just
      Procedure) added,—now that time was ripe
For proving friends did well his word to trust,—
      Those attestations, tuned to lyre or pipe,
375 Which friends broke out with when he dared foretell
The Dauphin's birth: friends trusted, and did well.

XLVIII

Moreover he got painted by Du Pré,
      Engraved by Daret also, and prefixed
The portrait to his book: a crown of bay
380   Circled his brows, with rose and myrtle mixed;

360| MS:babe, 'God's gift'! §single quotation marks over double quotation marks§ *P1878:*gift!'
363| MS:Of 'Royal Poet' §next punctuation mark illegibly erased and replaced by comma§ ,
poet *P1878:*Of 'Royal Poet:' poet   364| MS:His §crossed out and replaced in margin
by§ Whose   366| MS:My René; he's the Master, §comma crossed out§ they *P1878:*My
René. He's < > master: they   367| MS:of song §over illegible erasure§ confessed < >
slaves: for *P1878:*song, confessed < > slaves; for   368| MS:poetized < > he could
prophesy!" *P1878:*poetize < > he can prophesy!"   369| MS:done; great René
*P1878:*done; our René   370| MS:"The Royal Poet;" and he put
P1878:"The Royal Poet;" straightway put   371| MS:and—fair *P1878:*and (fair
372| MS:Procedure—added *P1878:*Procedure) added   376| MS:well! *1889a:*well.
378| MS:also; and *1889a:*also, and   379| MS:book,—a < > bay, *P1878:*book: a < > bay
380| MS:About his *P1878:*Circled his

And Latin verses, lovely in their way,
    Described him as "the biforked hill betwixt:
Since he hath scaled Parnassus at one jump,
Joining the Delphic quill and Getic trump."

XLIX

385   Whereof came . . . What, it lasts, our spirt, thus long
    —The red fire? That's the reason must excuse
My letting flicker René's prophet-song
    No longer; for its pertinacious hues
Must fade before its fellow joins the throng
390   Of sparks departed up the chimney, dues
To dark oblivion. At the word, it winks,
Rallies, relapses, dwindles, deathward sinks!

L

So does our poet. All this burst of fame,
    Fury of favour, Royal Poetship,
395   Prophetship, book, verse, picture—thereof came
    —Nothing! That's why I would not let outstrip
Red his green rival flamelet: just the same
Ending in smoke waits both! In vain we rip

381| MS:verses lovely < > way   *P1878:*verses, lovely < > way,   382| MS:betwixt—
*P1878:*betwixt: 383| MS:jump   *P1878:*jump,   384| MS:the Getic quill and Delphic
§last four words transposed to§ the Delphic quill and Getic   385| MS:what   *P1878:*came
. . . What   387| MS:My making flicker   *P1878:*My letting flicker   388| MS:So
pertinaciously before you §last two words crossed out and replaced above by two words§ for
fear its hues   *P1878:*No longer; for its pertinacious hues   389| MS:Should fade before
yon §crossed out and replaced above by§ its fellow joins §altered to§ joined   *P1878:*Must fade
< > joins   390| MS:chimney—dues   *P1878:*chimney, dues   391| MS:To darkness
§last four letters crossed out forming *dark*§ and §crossed out§ < > winks, §dash altered to
comma§   392| MS:Rallies, relapses, §last word and comma inserted above illegibly
crossed out word§ dwindles, dwindles §crossed out and replaced above by two words§ down
and §last two words crossed out and replaced below by§ dwindling sinks!   *P1878:*dwindles,
dwindles, sinks!   *1889a:*dwindles, deathward sinks!   393| MS:poet. All   *P1878:*poet.
All   394| MS:favor   *P1878:*favour   396| MS:—Nothing! §dash altered to
exclamation point§ that's §altered to§ That's   397| MS:Ruby, §last word and comma
crossed out and replaced above by§ Strontian < > rival, §comma crossed out§ René—just
*P1878:*Red his green rival flamelet: just   398| MS:smoke to both   *P1878:*smoke waits both

The past, no further faintest trace remains
400   Of René to reward our pious pains.

LI

Somebody saw a portrait framed and glazed
        At Croisic. "Who may be this glorified
Mortal unheard-of hitherto?" amazed
        That person asked the owner by his side,
405   Who proved as ignorant. The question raised
        Provoked inquiry; key by key was tried
On Croisic's portrait-puzzle, till back flew
The wards at one key's touch, which key was—Who?

LII

The other famous poet! Wait thy turn,
410   Thou green, our red's competitor! Enough
Just now to note 'twas he that itched to learn
        (A hundred years ago) how fate could puff
Heaven-high (a hundred years before) then spurn
To suds so big a bubble in some huff:

399| MS:The past's §apostrophe and last letter crossed out forming *past*§ black §crossed out§ shroud §crossed out and replaced above by § coverlet §crossed out§ ; nor further faintest §inserted above§ *P1878:*past, no   401| MS:saw this §crossed out and replaced above by§ a   403| MS:unheard of hitherto?" §last word, question mark, and quotation marks inserted above§ he enquired §last two words crossed out§ *P1878:*unheard-of 404| MS:Of §crossed out§ Enquired he of the *P1878:*That person asked the 406| MS:enquiry *1889a:*inquiry   407| MS:On Croisic's portrait- §last word and hyphen inserted above§ puzzle vainly §crossed out§   408| MS:key's entrance, that was—Who? *P1878:*key's touch, which key was—Who *1889a:*was—Who?   409| MS:other famous §inserted above§ poet! §exclamation point over illegibly erased punctuation mark§ but of him anon §last four words crossed out and replaced above by three words§ Croisic's famous son §last three words crossed out and replaced by three words and comma§ wait §altered to§ Wait your turn, *P1878:*poet! Wait thy turn,   410| MS:You §over illegible erasure§ , the green flame—competitor §last half of hyphenated word over illegible erasure§ *P1878:*Thou green, our red's competitor   411| MS:now to note §last two words inserted above§ that §crossed out§ he too §crossed out§ had an itch to *P1878:*note 'twas he that itched to 412| MS:years before §crossed out and replaced above by§ ago   413| MS:So high §last two words in margin§ (a §inserted above illegibly crossed out word§ <> before) §parenthesis over dash§ so high, §last two words and comma inserted above and then crossed out§ *P1878:*Hoaven-high C*P1878:*Hoaven-high §altered to§ Heaven-high *1878:*Heaven-high 414| MS:To naught so <> huff: §dash altered to colon§ *P1878:*To suds so

152

⁴¹⁵ Since green too found red's portrait,—having heard
 Hitherto of red's rare self not one word.

LIII

And he with zeal addressed him to the task
 Of hunting out, by all and any means,
 —Who might the brilliant bard be, born to bask
⁴²⁰ Butterfly-like in shine which kings and queens
 And baby-dauphins shed? Much need to ask!
 Is fame so fickle that what perks and preens
 The eyed wing, one imperial minute, dips
 Next sudden moment into blind eclipse?

LIV

⁴²⁵ After a vast expenditure of pains,
 Our second poet found the prize he sought:
 Urged in his search by something that restrains
 From undue triumph famed ones who have fought,

---

⁴¹⁵| MS:Since he too had §crossed out and replaced above by§ found the portrait, and had §last two words crossed out and replaced above by dash and word§ —having *P1878:*Since green too found red's portrait ⁴¹⁶| MS:of its subject not < > word,— *P1878:*of red's rare self not < > word. ⁴¹⁷| MS:So he §last two words crossed out and replaced above by§ Therefore addressed him to the task with zeal §last seven words transposed to§ with zeal addressed him to the task *P1878:*And he with ⁴¹⁸| MS:Of finding §crossed out and replaced above by§ hunting out, what §crossed out§ ⁴¹⁹| MS:the brilliant §inserted above§ < > born §next word illegibly crossed out§ ⁴²⁰| MS:in sunshine, §dash altered to comma§ Kings and Queens *P1878:*in shine which kings < > queens ⁴²¹| MS:baby-Dauphins shed? §dash altered to question mark§ No §crossed out and replaced above by§ Much *P1878:*baby-dauphins ⁴²²| MS:If France §last two words crossed out and replaced above by three words§ Did loyal serf §last three words crossed out and replaced in margin by five words§ Is fame so fickle that what §inserted above§ ⁴²³| MS:This §crossed out and replaced above by§ The wings §last letter crossed out forming *wing*§ there, §last word and comma inserted above§ one imperial minute, §last three words and comma inserted above illegibly crossed out words§ *P1878:*The eyed wing ⁴²⁴| MS:All of §last two words crossed out and then restored§ a §crossed out, replaced above by crossed out *As,* and then restored§ suddenly §last two letters crossed out forming *sudden*§ into §next word inserted above and illegibly crossed out§ *P1878:*Next sudden moment into ⁴²⁵| MS:After §first letter of next incomplete word illegibly crossed out§ < > pains, §dash altered to comma§ ⁴²⁶| MS:poet, §comma crossed out§ ⁴²⁷| MS:Pushed §crossed out and replaced above by§ Urged ⁴²⁸| MS:undue triumph §crossed out, replaced above by illegibly crossed out word, and then restored§ people who *P1878:*triumph famed ones who

Or simply, poetizing, taxed their brains:
430   Something that tells such—dear is triumph bought
If it means only basking in the midst
Of fame's brief sunshine, as thou, René, didst.

LV

For, what did searching find at last but this?
    Quoth somebody "I somehow somewhere seem
435   To think I heard one old De Chevaye is
Or was possessed of René's works!" which gleam
Of light from out the dark proved not amiss
    To track, by correspondence on the theme;
And soon the twilight broadened into day,
440   For thus to question answered De Chevaye.

LVI

"True it is, I did once possess the works
    You want account of—works—to call them so,—
Comprised in one small book: the volume lurks
    (Some fifty leaves in *duodecimo*)

430| MS:Which §crossed out and replaced above by§ Telling §crossed out and replaced in margin by three words§ Something that tells them—triumph has been §last two words crossed out§ dearly §last two letters crossed out forming *dear*§ is §inserted above; last three words transposed to§ dear is triumph *P1878:* tells such—dear 431| MS:it meant §altered to§ means merely §crossed out and replaced above by§ only 432| MS:Of man's applause §last two words crossed out and replaced above by three words and comma§ fame's brief sunshine, < > thou, §next word illegibly crossed out§ < > didst! *1889a:* didst.
433| MS:And §crossed out, replaced above by crossed out *For,* and then restored§ what did searching find at last §last five words inserted above illegibly crossed out words§ *P1878:* For, what 434| MS:What §crossed out and replaced above by§ Quoth somebody had §crossed out and replaced above by quotation marks and word§ "I < > somewhere seemed §last two letters crossed out forming *seem*§ 435| MS:think he §crossed out and replaced above by§ I < > that one §altered to§ old *P1878:* heard one old 438| MS:§line added§ track by < > theme: *P1878:* track, by < > theme; 439| MS:§first words illegibly crossed out§ And soon the twilight §last three words inserted below; next word illegibly crossed out§
440| MS:When §crossed out and replaced above by§ For 441| MS:is, that §crossed out§ I did §inserted above§ once possessed §last two letters crossed out forming *possess*§
442| MS:of,—works,— §dash inserted above§ come §crossed out§ to *P1878:* of—works—to 443| MS:All §crossed out and replaced above by § Comprised in §over illegible word§ one little §crossed out and replaced above by§ small volume; which still §last two words crossed out and replaced above by two words§ but it lurks *P1878:* small book: the volume lurks

⁴⁴⁵ 'Neath certain ashes which my soul it irks
    Still to remember, because long ago
That and my other rare shelf-occupants
    Perished by burning of my house at Nantes.

LVII

    "Yet of that book one strange particular
⁴⁵⁰   Still stays in mind with me"—and thereupon
Followed the story. "Few the poems are;
    The book was two-thirds filled up with this one,
And sundry witnesses from near and far
    That here at least was prophesying done
⁴⁵⁵ By prophet, so as to preclude all doubt,
    Before the thing he prophesied about."

LVIII

That's all he knew, and all the poet learned,
    And all that you and I are like to hear
Of René; since not only book is burned
⁴⁶⁰   But memory extinguished,—nay, I fear,
Portrait is gone too: nowhere I discerned
    A trace of it at Croisic. "Must a tear

---

^{445|} MS:'Neath §over illegible word§   ^{446|} MS:Yet §crossed out and replaced above by§ Still < > remember, though tis §last two words crossed out and replaced above by§ because ^{447|} MS:Since §crossed out§ that §altered to§ That book §inserted above§ and other books §crossed out and replace above by§ rare   *P1878:*That and my other ^{449|} MS:"But §crossed out and replace above by§ Yet < > book, one   *P1878:*book one   ^{450|} MS:Yet stays < > mind with me"— §last two words, quotation marks, and dash inserted above§   *P1878:*Still stays   ^{451|} MS:story. "Few §quotation marks and last word inserted above illegibly crossed out word§ the §over illegible word§   ^{452|} MS:The book was §last three words inserted above§ two-third's   *P1878:*two-thirds   ^{453|} MS:And all §crossed out and replaced above by§ with the witnesses   *P1878:*And sundry witnesses ^{454|} MS:least was §inserted above illegibly crossed out word§   ^{455|} MS:Before the §last two words crossed out and replaced above by two words and comma§ by prophet, so as §last two words inserted above illegibly crossed out word§ ^{457|} MS:learnt §altered to§ learned   ^{459|} MS:since the §crossed out and replaced above by two words§ not only < > burnt §altered to§ burned   ^{461|} MS:The §crossed out§ portrait §altered to§ Portrait < > too: §colon over dash§   ^{462|} MS:at Croisic. "Must a §last two words inserted above illegibly crossed out words, perhaps *There's no*§

155

Needs fall for that?" you smile. "How fortune fares
With such a mediocrity, who cares?"

LIX

465 Well, I care—intimately care to have
          Experience how a human creature felt
In after-life, who bore the burden grave
          Of certainly believing God had dealt
For once directly with him: did not rave
470   —A maniac, did not find his reason melt
—An idiot, but went on, in peace or strife,
The world's way, lived an ordinary life.

LX

How many problems that one fact would solve!
          An ordinary soul, no more, no less,
475 About whose life earth's common sights revolve,
          On whom is brought to bear, by thunder-stress,
This fact—God tasks him, and will not absolve
          Task's negligent performer! Can you guess
How such a soul,—the task performed to point,—
480 Goes back to life nor finds things out of joint?

463| MS:that? §question mark over dash§ <> smile: "How *P1878:*smile. "How
465| MS:Well, . . . I care . . . §ellipsis points crossed out and replaced by dash§ intimately §first
two letters over illegible letters§ *P1878:*Well, I   466| MS:after life *P1878:*after-life
467| MS:Of certainly §first three letters removed by water drop§ <> dealt §second and third
letters over illegible letters§   469| MS:For once §inserted above§ Directly §altered to§
directly <> rave, §comma erased§   470| MS:melt, §comma erased§   472| MS:way,
living §last three letters crossed out and replaced above by *ed*§ an §inserted above§
477| MS:Actual or figurative §last three words crossed out, replaced above by illegibly crossed
out words, and then replaced above by five words and comma§ This fact—God tasks him, <>
will not §crossed out, replaced below by illegibly crossed out word, and then restored§
478| MS:The §crossed out and replaced above by§ Task's negligent performer §inserted above
illegibly crossed out word§   480| MS:finds all §crossed out and replaced above by§ things

LXI

Does he stand stock-like henceforth? or proceed
    Dizzily, yet with course straightforward still,
Down-trampling vulgar hindrance?—as the reed
    Is crushed beneath its tramp when that blind will
485 Hatched in some old-world beast's brain bids it speed
    Where the sun wants brute-presence to fulfil
Life's purpose in a new far zone, ere ice
Enwomb the pasture-tract its fortalice.

LXII

I think no such direct plain truth consists
490   With actual sense and thought and what they take
To be the solid walls of life: mere mists—
    How such would, at that truth's first piercing, break
Into the nullity they are!—slight lists
    Wherein the puppet-champions wage, for sake
495 Of some mock-mistress, mimic war: laid low
At trumpet-blast, there's shown the world, one foe!

481| MS:stand still §crossed out and replaced above by§ stock-like   482| MS:Dizzily yet §inserted above§ with course §inserted above§ straight-forward purpose §crossed out§ *P1878:*Dizzily, yet *1889a:*straightforward   483| MS:hindrance? §question mark over comma§ as *P1878:*hindrance?—as   484| MS:beneath the §crossed out and replaced above by§ its §crossed out and replaced below by§ his tread, of §crossed out and replaced above by§ when that blind §inserted above illegibly crossed out word§ *P1878:*beneath its tramp when   485| MS:Born §crossed out and replaced above by§ Hatched <> bids him speed *P1878:*bids it speed   486| MS:Where §over illegible word§ <> sun §next letter illegibly crossed out§ broken §crossed out and replaced above by§ wants his presence §crossed out and then restored§ *P1878:*wants brute-presence *CP1878:*brure-presence §altered to§ brute-presence *1878:*brute-presence   487| MS:His §crossed out and replaced above by§ Life's <> in new §crossed out and replaced above by§ a   488| MS:Enwomb the §over *this*§ will §crossed out and replaced above by§ ancient world his §last three words transposed to§ world his ancient fortalice.. *P1878:*the world its pasture-tract fortalice. *CP1878:*the world §crossed out§ its pasture-tract fortilice. §transposed to§ the pasture-tract its fortilice. *1878:*the pasture-tract its fortilice. *1889a:*fortalice §emended to§ fortalice. §see Editorial Notes§   489| MS:direct and §crossed out and replaced above by§ plain   491| MS:solid things §crossed out and replaced above by§ walls   492| MS:How they §crossed out and replaced above by§ such   494| MS:puppet-champions waged §last letter crossed out forming *wage*§   496| MS:Showing the outside §last three words crossed out and replaced above by five words§ At trumpet-blast, there's shown the world, and §crossed out§

LXIII

No, we must play the pageant out, observe
    The tourney-regulations, and regard
Success—to meet the blunted spear nor swerve,
500   Failure—to break no bones yet fall on sward;
Must prove we have—not courage? well then,—nerve!
    And, at the day's end, boast the crown's award—
Be warranted as promising to wield
Weapons, no sham, in a true battle-field.

LXIV

505 Meantime, our simulated thunderclaps
    Which tell us counterfeited truths—these same
Are—sound, when music storms the soul, perhaps?
    —Sight, beauty, every dart of every aim
That touches just, then seems, by strange relapse,
510   To fall effectless from the soul it came
As if to fix its own, but simply smote
And startled to vague beauty more remote?

497| MS:No, we §over illegible word§   498| MS:The tourneys §last letter crossed out
forming *tourney*§ and §crossed out and replaced above by hyphen and two words§ -regulations,
and   499| MS:Glory §crossed out and replaced above by word and dash§ Success—
500| MS:Did g §word and first letter of incomplete word crossed out and replaced above by§
Failure <> bones by fall *P1878:*bones yet fall   501| MS:Give proof §last two words
crossed out and replaced above by two words§ Must prove <> have— §dash over illegible
letter§   503| MS:warranted as §crossed out, replaced above by illegibly crossed out word,
and then restored§   504| MS:in very §crossed out and replaced above by two words§ a
true   505| MS:our simulated §last two letters over illegible letters§   506| MS:That
§crossed out and replaced above by§ Which <> counterfeited of §crossed out§
507| MS:Are—sound, when §dash and last two words inserted above§ music's §altered to§
music message to §last two words crossed out and replaced above by two words§ storming
§altered to§ storms through§ crossed out   508| MS:—Lights, §dash, word, and comma
inserted above§ Beauty §altered to§ beauty, of §crossed out§ *P1878:*—Sight, beauty
509| MS:touches it §crossed out and replaced above by§ just   510| MS:fall back §crossed
out, replaced above by illegibly crossed out word, and then replaced above by§ effectless <>
soul §next two words illegibly crossed out§   511| MS:own, §dash altered to comma§
512| MS:To frighten it §last two words crossed out and replaced above by§ startle towards
vague §inserted above§ <> remote? §question mark over dash§   *P1878:*And startled to
towards vague *CP1878:*to towards §crossed out§ vague *1878:*to vague

LXV

So do we gain enough—yet not too much—
    Acquaintance with that outer element
515 Wherein there's operation (call it such!)
    Quite of another kind than we the pent
On earth are proper to receive. Our hutch
    Lights up at the least chink: let roof be rent—
How inmates huddle, blinded at first spasm,
520 Cognizant of the sun's self through the chasm!

LXVI

Therefore, who knows if this our René's quick
    Subsidence from as sudden noise and glare
Into oblivion was impolitic?
    No doubt his soul became at once aware
525 That, after prophecy, the rhyming-trick
    Is poor employment: human praises scare
Rather than soothe ears all a-tingle yet
With tones few hear and live, but none forget.

513| MS:enough—yet §over *and*§   515| MS:operation,— §dash crossed out and replaced by parenthesis over comma§ <> such!— §dash crossed out and replaced by parenthesis 516| MS:By §crossed out and replaced above by two words§ Quite of another means §crossed out and replaced by§ kind than play §crossed out and replaced above by word and comma§ we, the   *P1878:*we the   517| MS:receive: our   *P1878:*receive. Our 519| MS:The weak-eyed §last two words crossed out and replaced above by§ How <> huddle, from §crossed out and replaced above by§ blinded it §altered to§ at   520| MS:Struck blind by §last three words crossed out and replaced above by two words§ Cognizant of <> sun's appearance §crossed out and replaced above by§ self   521| MS:§first words illegibly crossed out, replaced above by illegibly crossed out words, then replaced below by illegibly crossed out words, and finally replaced in margin by eight words§ Therefore, who knows if this subsidence quick §last two words crossed out and replaced above by three words§ our René's quick   522| MS:§first words illegibly crossed out and replaced in margin by§ Subsidence from as sudden §last two words inserted above illegibly crossed out word§ <> glare to quiet and the §last four words crossed out and next word illegibly crossed out§ 523| MS:To silence and §last three words crossed out, replaced above by illegibly crossed out words, and then replaced below by two words§ Into oblivion was impolitic §first two letters of last word over illegible letters§   524| MS:doubt his §over illegible erasure§ 526| MS:employment: while men's praises   *P1878:*employment: human praises 527| MS:than tickle §crossed out and replaced above by§ sooth ears all §inserted above§ *P1878:*soothe   528| MS:live but   *P1878:*live, but

LXVII

There's our first famous poet. Step thou forth
530   Second consummate songster! See, the tongue
Of fire that typifies thee, owns thy worth
     In yellow, purple mixed its green among,
No pure and simple resin from the North,
     But composite with virtues that belong
535 To Southern culture! Love not more than hate
Helped to a blaze . . . But I anticipate.

LXVIII

Prepare to witness a combustion rich
     And riotously splendid, far beyond
Poor René's lambent little streamer which
540   Only played candle to a Court gown fond
By baby-birth: this soared to such a pitch,
     Alternately such colours doffed and donned,
That when I say it dazzled Paris—please
Know that it brought Voltaire upon his knees!

LXIX

545 Who did it, was a dapper gentleman,
     Paul Desforges Maillard, Croisickese by birth,

529| MS:There's your first <> poet! Step *P1878:*There's our first *1889a:*poet. Step
530| MS:songster! See the *P1878:*songster! See, the   532| MS:yellows, purples
mixed thy §crossed out and replaced above by§ its greens *P1878:*yellow, purple <> green
533| MS:No pure §second letter of last word over illegible letter§
534| MS:But composite §inserted above§ with a §crossed out§ virtues §inserted above illegibly
crossed out word§ of §crossed out§   535| MS:culture! §exclamation point over colon§
love §altered to§ Love   536| MS:Helps <> blaze: §dash altered to colon§ but
*P1878:*Helped <> blaze . . .but *1889a:*blaze . . . But   538| MS:riotously splendid
§inserted above illegibly crossed out word§ far *P1878:*splendid, far   539| MS:lambent
little §inserted above§ streamer, §comma crossed out§   540| MS:Played candle only
§transposed and altered to§ Only played candle   542| MS:§line added§ Alternately
§next word illegibly crossed out§   544| MS:that I mean §last two words crossed out and
replaced above by two words§ it sent Voltaire *P1878:*it brought Voltaire
545| MS:There §crossed out and replaced above by three words and comma§ Who did it, <>
a dapper §inserted above illegibly crossed out word§   546| MS:birth,— *P1878:*birth,

Whose birth that century ended which began
    By similar bestowment on our earth
Of the aforesaid René. Cease to scan
    The ways of Providence! See Croisic's dearth—
Not Paris in its plenitude—suffice
To furnish France with her best poet twice!

550

LXX

Till he was thirty years of age, the vein
    Poetic yielded rhyme by drops and spirts:
In verses of society had lain
    His talent chiefly; but the Muse asserts
Privilege most by treating with disdain
    Epics the bard mouths out, or odes he blurts
Spasmodically forth. Have people time
And patience nowadays for thought in rhyme?

555

560

LXXI

So, his achievements were the quatrain's inch
    Of homage, or at most the sonnet's ell

547| MS:§first words illegibly crossed out and replaced above by four words §In that same century §last four words crossed out and replaced above by five words§ At end of this same §last five words crossed out and replaced in margin by two words§ Birth which that century ended which §last four words inserted below§ *P1878:*Whose birth that
548| MS:By similar bestowment §last two words inserted above illegibly crossed out words§ on §inserted above§ <> earth— *P1878:*earth   549| MS:Of the aforesaid §last two words inserted above§ René. §period added§ Gentilhomme §crossed out§ Cease to §last two words inserted above illegibly crossed out word§   550| MS:of Providence! See §inserted above illegibly crossed out word§ <> dearth, *P1878:*dearth—   551| MS:in her plenitude, §last word and comma inserted above§ suffice §inserted above illegibly crossed out words§ *P1878:*in its plenitude—suffice   552| MS:To furnish §last two words inserted below illegibly crossed out words§ France with her best poet twice! §last five words and exclamation point inserted below illegibly crossed out words§   554| MS:yielded rhyme §over illegible word§ <> spirts; *P1878:*spirts: 556| MS:chiefly; §dash altered to semicolon§   557| MS:Privilege §crossed out, replaced in margin by illegibly crossed out word, and then restored§ most §inserted above§ by treating §over illegible word§
558| MS:Epics and odes,—and all that bards mouth §last seven words crossed out and replaced above by seven words§ the bard mouths out or odes he
559| MS:Magniloquently §crossed out and replaced above by§ Spasmodically forth; who builds this §last three words crossed out§ have *P1878:*forth. Have
560| MS:patience for §crossed out and replaced above by three words§ now a days *P1878:*now-a-days   *1889a:*nowadays   562| MS:or at most §last two words inserted above§

Of admiration: welded lines with clinch
   Of ending word and word, to every belle
565 In Croisic's bounds; these, brisk as any finch,
   He twittered till his fame had reached as well
Guérande as Batz; but there fame stopped, for—curse
   On fortune—outside lay the universe!

LXXII

That's Paris. Well,—why not break bounds, and send
570   Song onward till it echo at the gates
Of Paris whither all ambitions tend,
   And end too, seeing that success there sates
The soul which hungers most for fame? Why spend
   A minute in deciding, while, by Fate's
575 Decree, there happens to be just the prize
Proposed there, suiting souls that poetize?

LXXIII

A prize indeed, the Academy's own self
   Proposes to what bard shall best indite

563| MS:admiration: §colon over illegible punctuation mark§ welded by the §last two words
crossed out and replaced above by two words§ lines with   564| MS:Of ending §inserted
above§ <> to every §inserted above illegibly crossed out words§   565| MS:This, that,
§last two words and comma crossed out and replaced above by two words§ In Croisic's
bounds; and, §last two words and comma inserted above two illegibly crossed out words,
perhaps *tried other*§ brisk   *P1878:*bounds; these, brisk   567| MS:as Batz: but there they
stopped   *P1878:*as Batz; but there fame stopped   568| MS:On fortune's §apostrophe
and last letter crossed out forming *fortune*§ —outside was the   *P1878:*outside lay the
569| MS:That's Paris. Well, §last three words and comma inserted above§ why not §next
word illegibly crossed out§ breaking §inserted above illegibly crossed out word and altered to§
break bounds, and §crossed out, replaced above by *to,* and then restored§   *P1878:*That's
Paris. Well,—why   570| MS:Song onwards §last letter crossed out forming *onward*§
571| MS:all ambitions §inserted above illegibly crossed out word, crossed out, and then
restored§   573| MS:soul that §crossed out and replaced above by§ which
574| MS:A moment §crossed out and replaced above by§ minute <> while by   *P1878:*while,
by   576| MS:Proposed at Paris §last two words crossed out and replaced above by§ there
§next two words illegibly crossed out and replaced above by four words§ for the folks that
*P1878:*there, suiting souls that   577| MS:"What is this prize the Academy's own §inserted
above§ itself §first two letters crossed out forming *self*§   *P1878:*A prize indeed, the
578| MS:to the man who §last two words crossed out and replaced above by two words§ bard
shall <> indites §last letter crossed out forming *indite*§   *P1878:*to what bard

A piece describing how, through shoal and shelf,
580   The Art of Navigation, steered aright,
Has, in our last king's reign,—the lucky elf,—
Reached, one may say, Perfection's haven quite,
And there cast anchor. At a glance one sees
The subject's crowd of capabilities!

LXXIV

585   Neptune and Amphitrité! Thetis, who
Is either Tethys or as good—both tag!
Triton can shove along a vessel too:
It's Virgil! Then the winds that blow or lag,—
De Maille, Vendôme, Vermandois! Toulouse blew
590   Longest, we reckon: he must puff the flag
To fullest outflare; while our lacking nymph
Be Anne of Austria, Regent o'er the lymph!

LXXV

Promised, performed! Since *irritabilis gens*
Holds of the feverish impotence that strives

579| MS:piece describing §first three letters of last word over illegible letters§
580| MS:of Navigation steering right,   *P1878:*of Navigation, steered aright,
581| MS:During §crossed out and replaced above by two words§ Has, in our Monarch's §crossed out and replaced above by two words§ last king's   583| MS:anchor? §colon altered to question mark§ At   *P1878:*anchor. At   585| MS:"Neptune and Amphitrité! Thetis, §comma over erased parenthesis§   *P1878:*Neptune   586| MS:both rhyme! §last word crossed out and replaced above by§ tag! §exclamation point over erased parenthesis§
587| MS:along a §over illegible letter§   588| MS:It's Virgil,— §comma and dash altered to exclamation point§ then §altered to§ Then   590| MS:Longest I reckon: §colon over a dash§   *P1878:*Longest, we reckon   591| MS:lacking Nymph   *P1878:*nymph
592| MS:Is Anne of Austria, Regent of §crossed out and replaced above by§ o'er <> lymph!" *P1878:*Be Anne <> lymph!   *1889a:*lymph §emended to§ lymph! §see Editorial Notes§
593| MS:So said §last two words crossed out and replaced above by§ Promised §next two words illegibly crossed out and replaced above by dash and word§ —performance §altered to§ performed! Since §inserted above illegibly crossed out word§ *irritabilis* §first and last letters over illegible letters§   *P1878:*Promised, performed   594| MS:Holds of the feverish impotence §last five words inserted above illegibly crossed out words§ that §crossed out, replaced above by illegibly crossed out word, and then restored§ strives §over illegible word§

595   To stay an itch by prompt resource to pen's
       Scratching itself on paper; placid lives,
    Leisurely works mark the *divinior mens*:
       Bees brood above the honey in their hives;
       Gnats are the busy bustlers. Splash and scrawl,—
600   Completed lay thy piece, swift penman Paul!

LXXVI

To Paris with the product! This despatched,
       One had to wait the Forty's slow and sure
Verdict, as best one might. Our penman scratched
       Away perforce the itch that knows no cure
605   But daily paper-friction: more than matched
       His first feat by a second—tribute pure
And heartfelt to the Forty when their voice
       Should peal with one accord "Be Paul our choice!"

LXXVII

Scratch, scratch went much laudation of that sane
610   And sound Tribunal, delegates august
Of Phœbus and the Muses' sacred train—
       Whom every poetaster tries to thrust

595| MS:To §over illegible word§ stay §over illegible word§ an itch §last two words inserted above§ <> prompt recourse to §next word illegibly crossed out§   *P1878:*resource
596| MS:Rubbing §crossed out and replaced above by two words§ Scratching itself <> paper; quiet §crossed out and replaced above by§ placid   597| MS:Leisurely works §last letter over illegible erasure§ mark the §last two words inserted above illegibly crossed out word§ <> *mens*;   *P1878:* mens.   598| MS:Bees slowly mass §last two words crossed out and replaced above by two words§ brood above   600| MS:Soon perfect §last two words crossed out, replaced above by illegibly crossed out word, and then replaced above by§ Completed <> piece, of §crossed out and replaced above by§ swift   601| MS:the product §crossed out, replaced above by *poem,* and then restored§   603| MS:might: our   *P1878:*might. Our 604| MS:Away perforce §in margin§ the §crossed out and then restored § writer's §crossed out§   605| MS:Besides the §last two words inserted above illegibly crossed out words, then crossed out and replaced   above by§ But daily §crossed out and then restored§ paper-§word and hyphen inserted above§ friction: more than §last two words inserted above§ 606| MS:This first   *P1878:*His first   609| MS:So there was §last three words crossed out and replaced above by three words§ Scratch, scratch went much laudation §last two words inserted above illegibly crossed out words§   611| MS:Of Phiebus <> the Muses' §inserted above§ sacred train— §last word over illegible erasure§   *P1878:*Of Phoebus 612| MS:poetaster tries §over illegible erasure§

From where, high-throned, they dominate the Seine:
Fruitless endeavour,—fail it shall and must!
615 Whereof in witness have not one and all
The Forty voices pealed "Our Choice be Paul"?

LXXVIII

Thus Paul discounted his applause. Alack
For human expectation! Scarcely ink
Was dry when, lo, the perfect piece came back
620 Rejected, shamed! Some other poet's clink
"Thetis and Tethys" had seduced the pack
Of pedants to declare perfection's pink
A singularly poor production. "Whew!
The Forty are stark fools, I always knew."

LXXIX

625 First fury over (for Paul's race—to-wit,
Brain-vibrios—wriggle clear of protoplasm
Into minute life that's one fury-fit),
"These fools shall find a bard's enthusiasm

614| MS:endeavour,—failing §last three letters crossed out forming *fai*§ it shall §inserted over
illegibly crossed out word§ needs §crossed out and replaced above by§ and the §inserted
above and then crossed out§   615| MS:All such— §last two words and dash crossed out§
whereof §altered to§ Whereof < > witness, have not §last two words inserted above§
*P1878:*witness have   616| MS:forty just §crossed out and replaced above by§ voices §next
word illegibly crossed out§ < > choice < > Paul?" *P1878:*The Forty *1889a:*pealed "Our
Choice < > Paul"?   617| MS:So Paul *P1878:*Thus Paul   620| MS:shamed. §period
crossed out and replaced by colon§ Some §altered to§ some *P1878:*shamed!   Some
621| MS:Of "Thetis, Tethys," had < > the §over illegible erasure§ *P1878:*"Thetis and Tethys"
had   622| MS:pedants, dotards, §comma, last word, and comma crossed out and
replaced above by two words§ to declare   623| MS:His §crossed out and replaced above
by § A < > production: phew! §altered to§ "Whew! *P1878:*production. "Whew!
624| MS:fools, we §crossed out and replaced above by§ I < > knew!" *1889a:*knew."
625| MS:First §next word illegibly crossed out§ < > over,—all the §last two words crossed out
and replaced above by two words§ for Paul's §next word illegibly crossed out§ *P1878:*over (for
626| MS:Brain- §word and hyphen inserted above illegibly crossed out word§ vibrios, §next
words illegibly crossed out, replaced above by illegibly crossed out words, and then replaced
above by three words§ wriggle clear of *P1878:*Brain-vibrios—wriggle
627| MS:§first word illegibly crossed out§ Into a §crossed out and replaced above by§ minute
< > that's one §inserted above illegibly crossed out words§ fury-fit,— *P1878:*fury-fit),

Comports with what should counterbalance it—
630   Some knowledge of the world! No doubt, orgasm
Effects the birth of verse which, born, demands
Prosaic ministration, swaddling-bands!

LXXX

"Verse must be cared for at this early stage,
    Handled, nay dandled even. I should play
635 Their game indeed if, till it grew of age,
    I meekly let these dotards frown away
My bantling from the rightful heritage
    Of smiles and kisses! Let the public say
If it be worthy praises or rebukes,
640 My poem, from these Forty old perukes!"

LXXXI

So, by a friend, who boasts himself in grace
    With no less than the Chevalier La Roque,—
Eminent in those days for pride of place,
    Seeing he had it in his power to block
645 The way or smooth the road to all the race
    Of literators trudging up to knock

630| MS:Some §over illegible erasure§   631| MS:Effects a poem's §last two words crossed
out and replaced above by§ the <> verse prosaic hands §last two words crossed out and
replaced above by three words§ which, born, demands   632| MS:swaddling bands!
P1878: swaddling-bands!   634| MS:Handled, and §crossed out and replaced above by§
nay <> even: I   *P1878:* even. I   635| MS:This §altered to§ Their dotard §crossed out§
game indeed §inserted above, transposed to beginning of line, and then restored§
636| MS:I calmly §crossed out and replaced above by§ meekly   637| MS:from his rightful
P1878: from the rightful   638| MS:kisses! Let §inserted above illegibly crossed out
word§ <> public pay §crossed out and replaced above by§ say   639| MS:The bard his
proper homage— §last five words and dash crossed out and replaced above by two words§ My
poem §last two words crossed out and replaced above by six words§ If it be worthy praises or
640| MS:forty   *P1878:* these Forty   641| MS:himself a friend §last two words crossed out
and replaced by two words§ in grace   642| MS:With §next word illegibly crossed out§
643| MS:In those days eminent §transposed and altered to§ Eminent in those days
644| MS:he had §last letter over illegible letter, perhaps s§   645| MS:smoothe the road
§over illegible erasure§   *P1878:* smooth   646| MS:trudging on to   *P1878:* trudging up to

166

At Fame's exalted temple-door—for why?
He edited the Paris "Mercury":—

LXXXII

By this friend's help the Chevalier receives
650   Paul's poem, prefaced by the due appeal
To Cæsar from the Jews. As duly heaves
     A sigh the Chevalier, about to deal
With case so customary—turns the leaves,
     Finds nothing there to borrow, beg or steal—
655   Then brightens up the critic's brow deep-lined.
"The thing may be so cleverly declined!"

LXXXIII

Down to desk, out with paper, up with quill,
     Dip and indite! "Sir, gratitude immense
For this true draught from the Pierian rill!
660   Our Academic clodpoles must be dense
Indeed to stand unirrigated still.
     No less, we critics dare not give offence
To grandees like the Forty: while we mock
We grin and bear. So, here's your piece! La Roque."

---

[647]| MS:At Fame's exalted §inserted above illegibly crossed out word, perhaps *high*§ temple-
§word and hyphen crossed out and then restored§ door—§dash altered to colon§ for
P1878: temple-door—for   [648]| MS:edited the §last letter over illegible letter§ Journal,
§word and comma crossed out and replaced above by§ Paris "Mercury":—   *P1878:* the Paris
"Mercury:"—   *1889a:* the Paris "Mercury":—   [650]| MS:The §crossed out and replaced
above by§ Paul's   [651]| MS:the Jews; as   *P1878:* the Jews.   As
[653]| MS:customary— §dash altered to colon§ turns   *P1878:* customary—turns
[654]| MS:steal,—   *P1878:* steal—   [659]| MS:this deep §crossed out and replaced above
by§ true   [660]| MS:The §crossed out and replaced above by§ Our Academic brain
§crossed out and replaced above by§ clodpoles <> be §next word illegibly crossed out§
[661]| MS:to stand §over illegible word§ <> still: *P1878:* still.   [662]| MS:All the same,
§last three words and comma crossed out and replaced above by three words§ No less, we
[663]| MS:To grandees §crossed out, replaced above by illegibly crossed out word, and then
replaced above by§ grandees <> mock,—   *P1878:* mock,   *1889a:* mock
[664]| MS:We grin, and bear. §last four words and period inserted above illegibly crossed out
words§ So, §word and comma inserted above§ here's §first letter over illegible letter§ piece
again §inserted above and then crossed out§ !   La Roque."   *P1878:* grin and
1889a: piece!   La Roque. §emended to§ piece!   La Roque." §see Editorial Notes§

LXXXIV

665   "There now!" cries Paul: "the fellow can't avoid
       Confessing that my piece deserves the palm;
     And yet he dares not grant me space enjoyed
       By every scribbler he permits embalm
     His crambo in the Journal's corner! Cloyed
670   With stuff like theirs, no wonder if a qualm
     Be caused by verse like mine: though that's no cause
     For his defrauding me of just applause.

LXXXV

     "Aha, he fears the Forty, this poltroon?
       First let him fear *me*! Change smooth speech to rough!
675   I'll speak my mind out, show the fellow soon
       Who is the foe to dread: insist enough
     On my own merits till, as clear as noon,
       He sees I am no man to take rebuff
     As patiently as scribblers may and must!
680   Quick to the onslaught, out sword, cut and thrust!"

665| MS:the fellow §inserted above illegibly crossed out word§ can't but help §last two words crossed out and replaced above by§ avoid   666| MS:deserved §altered to§ deserves < > palm, *P1878:*palm;   667| MS:me what's §crossed out and replaced above by§ space 668| MS:scribbler whom §crossed out§ he bids §crossed out and replaced above by§ permits 669| MS:His rubbish §crossed out and replaced above by§ crambo   670| MS:With verse §crossed out and replaced above by§ stuff < > their's < > wonder if §inserted above illegibly crossed out word, perhaps *there's*§ *P1878:*theirs   671| MS:§first word illegibly crossed out, perhaps *When*§ verse §crossed out and replaced above by four words§ Is caused by verse < > mine: though §inserted above illegibly crossed out word§ that's §crossed out and then restored§ *P1878:*Be caused 672| MS:For this defrauding *P1878:*For his defrauding   673| MS:Aha, §word and comma in margin above illegibly crossed out word§ He *P1878:*he   674| MS:Well, §first word and comma crossed out, replaced above by illegibly crossed out word, and then replaced in margin by§ First < > *me*! He shall soon §last three words crossed out and replaced above by two words§ Change smooth speech §inserted above illegibly crossed out word§ for *gruff:* §last two words and colon crossed out and replaced above by two words and exclamation point§ to rough!   675| MS:the fellow §replaced above by illegibly erased word and then restored§   676| MS:dread: insist enough§last two words crossed out and then restored§ 677| MS:till as < > noon *P1878:*till, as < > noon,   679| MS:As §over *So*§ 680| MS:onslaught, swords out, cut *P1878:*onslaught, out sword, cut

LXXXVI

And thereupon a fierce epistle flings
    Its challenge in the critic's face. Alack!
Our bard mistakes his man! The gauntlet rings
    On brazen visor proof against attack.
685   Prompt from his editorial throne up springs
    The insulted magnate, and his mace falls, thwack,
On Paul's devoted brainpan,—quite away
From common courtesies of fencing-play!

LXXXVII

"Sir, will you have the truth? This piece of yours
690   Is simply execrable past belief.
I shrank from saying so; but, since nought cures
    Conceit but truth, truth's at your service! Brief,
Just so long as 'The Mercury' endures,
    So long are you excluded by its Chief
695   From corner, nay, from cranny! Play the cock
O' the roost, henceforth, at Croisic!" wrote La Roque.

LXXXVIII

Paul yellowed, whitened, as his wrath from red
    Waxed incandescent. Now, this man of rhyme

682| MS:Its challenge §inserted above illegibly crossed out word, perhaps *glove*§ in §next word illegibly crossed out§   683| MS:man! §colon altered to exclamation point§ the §altered to§ The   684| MS:On §inserted above illegibly crossed out word§ <> attack: *P1878:*attack.   685| MS:Up §crossed out and replaced above by§ Prompt
686| MS:La Roque §last two words crossed out and replaced above by two words§ The insulted <> falls, thwack, §last two words and comma added in margin§   687| MS:On §in margin§ Thwack §crossed out and replaced above by§ Paul's devoted §inserted above illegibly crossed out word§   688| MS:From common §first two letters of last word over illegible letters§   690| MS:belief: *P1878:*belief.   691| MS:so: but *P1878:*so; but
692| MS:Conceit but §over illegible word§ truth, truth's §inserted above illegibly crossed out word§   693| MS:as "the §altered to§ The Mercury" endures, *P1878:*as 'The Mercury' endures,   696| MS:the roost, §last word and comma inserted above illegible erasure§ <> at Croisic!" quoth La *P1878:*at Croisic!" wrote La   697| MS:Paul sickened, and turned white §last four words crossed out and replaced above by two words and comma§ yellowed, whitened, as anger §crossed out and replaced above by two words§ his wrath
698| MS:Grew §crossed out and replaced above by§ Waxed incandescent. Now §crossed out and replaced above by§ Well §crossed out and replaced by word and comma§ Now,

Was merely foolish, faulty in the head
700   Not heart of him: conceit's a venial crime.
"Oh by no means malicious!" cousins said:
       Fussily feeble,—harmless all the time,
Piddling at so-called satire—well-advised,
He held in most awe whom he satirized.

LXXXIX

705   Accordingly his kith and kin—removed
       From emulation of the poet's gift
By power and will—these rather liked, nay, loved
       The man who gave his family a lift
Out of the Croisic level; "disapproved
710   Satire so trenchant." Thus our poet sniffed
Home-incense, though too churlish to unlock
"The Mercury's" box of ointment was La Roque.

699| MS:foolish,—faulty <> the heart §altered to§ head   *P1878:*foolish, faulty
700| MS:heart,— §next words illegibly crossed out§ conceit's §slash mark between last two
letters§ a §crossed out, replaced above by illegibly crossed out word, and then restored§
merely §inserted above§ venial §crossed out, replaced above by illegibly crossed out word, and
then restored§   *P1878:*heart of him: conceit 's a venial   *1889a:*conceit's
701| MS:"Oh, by <> means malicious!" §last word, exclamation point, and quotation marks
inserted above illegibly crossed out words§ people said,   *P1878:*"Oh by <> malicious!"
cousins said: 703| MS:He did his little §last four words crossed out and replaced above
by three words§ Piddling at so-called satire §last letter crossed out forming *satire*§ —well-
advised   *1889a:*well-advised,   704| MS:awe those §crossed out and replaced above by§
whom   706| MS:gift,   *P1878:*gift   707| MS:Be power and §last two words inserted
above§ will §next word illegibly crossed out§ —they §altered to§ these <> liked—nay
*P1878:*By power <> liked, nay   708| MS:gave this §crossed out and replaced above by§
his   709| MS:Out §over illegible erasure§ <> level: §dash altered to colon§ disapproved
*P1878:*level; disapproved   *1889a:*level; "disapproved   710| MS:Be well assured §last
three words crossed out and replaced above by three words and semicolon§ Satire so fierce;—
but still §last two words inserted over illegibly crossed out words§ our   *P1878:*so trenchant,—
still   *1889a:*so trenchant." Thus our   711| MS:Home-incense,—though too §next
word illegibly crossed out§ churlish to §last two words inserted above illegibly crossed out
word§   *1889a:*Home-incense, though   712| MS:Its §crossed out and replaced above by
four words§ His box of precious ointment, proved §inserted above illegibly crossed out word§
La   *P1878:*"The Mercury's" box of ointment proved La   *1889a:*ointment was La

XC

But when Paul's visage grew from red to white,
    And from his lips a sort of mumbling fell
715 Of who was to be kicked,—"And serve him right"—
    A gay voice interposed—"did kicking well
Answer the purpose! Only—if I might
    Suggest as much—a far more potent spell
Lies in another kind of treatment. Oh,
720 Women are ready at resource, you know!

XCI

"Talent should minister to genius! Good:
    The proper and superior smile returns.
Hear me with patience! Have you understood
    The only method whereby genius earns
725 Fit guerdon nowadays? In knightly mood
    You entered lists with visor up; one learns
Too late that, had you mounted Roland's crest,
'Room!' they had roared—La Roque with all the rest!

XCII

"Why did you first of all transmit your piece
730   To those same priggish Forty unprepared

---

^{713|} MS:Accordingly §crossed out and replaced above by§ So when Paul's face §crossed out
and replaced above by§ visage < > from red to §last two words inserted above§ white
*P1878:*But when < > white,   ^{714|} MS:Yellow, §word and comma crossed out§ so §altered
to§ And < > his mouth §crossed out and replaced above by§ lips a sort of §last two words
inserted above§   ^{715|} MS:kicked,—" And §crossed out and replaced above by§ Why
§crossed out and replaced below by§ And < > right!"—   *P1878:*right!"   *1889a:*right"—
^{716|} MS:A soft voice interposed—"did §over I§   *P1878:*interposed "did   *1889a:*A gay voice
interposed—"did   ^{717|} MS:Answered §last two letters crossed out forming *Answer*§ < >
purpose! §colon altered to exclamation point§   Only §first letter of last word over illegible
letter, probably *o*§   ^{719|} MS:treatment,—Oh,   *P1878:*treatment. Oh,
^{721|} MS:genius: §dash altered to colon§ good!   *P1878:*genius! good: *1889a:*genius! Good:
^{722|} MS:returns!   *P1878:*returns.   ^{724|} MS:The only §inserted above§   ^{725|} MS:His
§over *This*§ guerdon now-a-days   *P1878:*Fit guerdon nowadays   ^{726|} MS:up; and
§crossed out and replaced above by§ one   ^{728|} MS:§first word illegibly erased§ 'Room!'
had they roared §last three words transposed to§ they had roared   ^{729|} MS:§first word
illegibly crossed out and replaced above by illegibly crossed out word§ Why did §last two words
inserted above§   ^{730|} MS:priggish Forty unprepared §over illegible erasure§

Whether to rank you with the swans or geese
　　By friendly intervention? If they dared
Count you a cackler,—wonders never cease!
　　I think it still more wondrous that you bared
735　Your brow (my earlier image) as if praise
　　Were gained by simple fighting nowadays!

XCIII

"Your next step showed a touch of the true means
　　Whereby desert is crowned: not force but wile
Came to the rescue. 'Get behind the scenes!'
740　　Your friend advised: he writes, sets forth your style
And title, to such purpose intervenes
　　That you get velvet-compliment three-pile;
And, though 'The Mercury' said 'nay,' nor stock
Nor stone did his refusal prove La Roque.

XCIV

745　"Why must you needs revert to the high hand,
　　Imperative procedure—what you call

731| MS:By frie §word and partial word crossed out and replaced above by§ Whether
732| MS:intervention? §exclamation point altered to question mark§ If §first letter over
illegible letter§　　733| MS:Count §inserted above illegibly crossed out word, perhaps *Call*§
< > a goose §crossed out and replaced above by§ cackler　　734| MS:§first words illegibly
crossed out§ I §inserted above§ think most §crossed out and replaced above by three words§ it
still more　　735| MS:brow (my earlier image) §parentheses over dashes§
736| MS:now-a-days! *1889a:*nowadays!　　737| MS:next step §inserted above illegibly
crossed out word§ < > of the §inserted above§　　738| MS:crowned: a little craft §last
three words crossed out and replaced by four words§ not force but wile
739| MS:rescue. "Peep §crossed out and replaced above by§ Get < > scenes"!　*P1878:*'Get
< > scenes!'　　740| MS:friend advised: he writes, §last three words and comma inserted
above illegibly crossed out words§　　741| MS:title, §next word illegibly crossed out§
742| MS:§line added in margin§ That you get §last two words inserted above illegibly crossed
out words§ < > three-pile,　*P1878:*three-pile;　　743| MS:And §over illegible erasure§ ,
though he §altered to§ the needs must §last two words crossed out and replaced above by
word and quotation marks§ "Mercury" say §altered to§ said you §crossed out§ "nay," yet
§crossed out and replaced above by§ nor　*P1878:*though 'The Mercury' said 'nay,' nor
744| MS:did that §crossed out and replaced above by§ his　　745| MS:"Then §crossed out,
replaced above by illegibly crossed out word, and then replaced above by§ Why you must
needs §last three words transposed to§ must you needs revert §first letter of last word over
illegible letter§　　746| MS:Insistance, threats, §last two words and comma crossed out and
replaced above by two words and dash§ Imperative procedure—

'Taking on merit your exclusive stand'?
    Stand, with a vengeance! Soon you went to wall,
You and your merit! Only fools command
750   When folk are free to disobey them, Paul!
You've learnt your lesson, found out what's o'clock,
By this uncivil answer of La Roque.

XCV

"Now let me counsel! Lay this piece on shelf
    —Masterpiece though it be! From out your desk
755 Hand me some lighter sample, verse the elf
    Cupid inspired you with, no god grotesque
Presiding o'er the Navy! I myself
    Hand-write what's legible yet picturesque;
I'll copy fair and femininely frock
760 Your poem masculine that courts La Roque!

XCVI

"Deïdamia he—Achilles thou!
    Ha, ha, these ancient stories come so apt!
My sex, my youth, my rank I next avow
    In a neat prayer for kind perusal. Sapped

747| MS:stand?' §colon altered to question mark§ *1889a:*stand'?   749| MS:merit!
Foolish to §last two words crossed out and replaced above by two words§ Only fools command,
*P1878:*command   750| MS:folks <> disobey you §crossed out and replaced above by§
them *1889a:*folk   751| MS:You §altered to§ You've learnt §over illegible erasure§ <>
lesson, find §altered to§ found   752| MS:this incivil §inserted above illegibly crossed out
word§ *P1878:*uncivil   753| MS:"Now, let <> counsel! §colon altered to exclamation
point§ put §crossed out and replaced above by§ Lay this piece §inserted above§ on the
§crossed out§ *P1878:*"Now let   754| MS:be! §colon altered to exclamation point§ and
§crossed out and replaced above by§ from §altered to§ From out of §crossed out and replaced
above by§ your   755| MS:some pretty little piece, §last three words and comma crossed
out and replaced above by three words§ lighter sample, verse the §last letter over illegible
letter§   756| MS:no such §crossed out and replaced above by§ god   757| MS:That
glorifies §last two words crossed out and replaced above by two words§ Presiding o'er <> navy
§altered to§ Navy   758| MS:Will §crossed out and replaced above by word and hyphen§
Hand-   759| MS:§first word illegibly crossed out and replaced in margin by§ I'll copy
fairly §last two letters crossed out forming *fair*§ and §inserted above§   760| MS:Your
§over illegible word, perhaps *The*§   761| MS:"Teïdamia *P1878:*Deïdamia
763| MS:rank, I *P1878:*rank I   764| MS:In a §over illegible erasure§

173

765   I see the walls which stand so stoutly now!
     I see the toils about the game entrapped
     By honest cunning! Chains of lady's-smock,
     Not thorn and thistle, tether fast La Roque!"

XCVII

     Now, who might be the speaker sweet and arch
770   That laughed above Paul's shoulder as it heaved
     With the indignant heart?—bade steal a march
     And not continue charging? Who conceived
     This plan which set our Paul, like pea you parch
     On fire-shovel, skipping, of a load relieved,
775   From arm-chair moodiness to escritoire
     Sacred to Phœbus and the tuneful choir?

XCVIII

     Who but Paul's sister! named of course like him
     "Desforges'; but, mark you, in those days a queer
     Custom obtained,—who knows whence grew the whim?—
780   That people could not read their title clear
     To reverence till their own true names, made dim
     By daily mouthing, pleased to disappear,

766| MS:game §followed by illegible erasure§   767| MS:of lady's—§apostrophe apparently added, last letter over illegible letter, and dash apparently added§   768| MS:thistle tether   *P1878:*thistle, tether   770| MS:Who laughed *P1878:*That laughed   772| MS:charging §followed by illegible erasure§   774| MS:On fire- §word and hyphen inserted above§ <> skipping, from §crossed out and replaced above by§ with a *P1878:*skipping, of a   777| MS:but his §crossed out and replaced above by§ Paul's sister? §comma altered to question mark§ Demoiselle Desforges §last two words crossed out and replaced by five words§ named of course like him *P1878:*sister! named   778| MS:That was her name, of course, §last six words and comma crossed out and replaced above by three words, colon, and quotation marks§ Like him, §last two words and comma inserted above§ "Desforges:" but, mark you, §comma, last two words, and comma inserted above§ <> a queer §over illegible erasure *P1878:*"Desforges"; but   779| MS:Custom there was, §last two words and comma crossed out and replaced above by word and comma§ obtained, 780| MS:That §first letter over illegible erasure§ people never §crossed out and replaced above by two words§ should not *P1878:*people could not   781| MS:To §next word illegibly crossed out and replaced above by illegibly crossed out word§ reverence §crossed out and then restored§ <> their own true §last two words inserted above§ names, grown §crossed out and replaced above by§ made   782| MS:mouthing, pleased §over illegible word§ <> disappear *CP1878:*disappear, §comma inserted§ *1878:*disappear,

Replaced by brand-new bright ones: Arouet,
For instance, grew Voltaire; Desforges—Malcrais.

XCIX

785   "Demoiselle Malcrais de la Vigne"—because
      The family possessed at Brederac
   A vineyard,—few grapes, many hips-and-haws,—
      Still a nice Breton name. As breast and back
   Of this vivacious beauty gleamed through gauze,
790   So did her sprightly nature nowise lack
   Lustre when draped, the fashionable way,
   In "Malcrais de la Vigne"—more short, "Malcrais."

C

   Out from Paul's escritoire behold escape
      The hoarded treasure! verse falls thick and fast,
795   Sonnets and songs of every size and shape.
      The lady ponders on her prize; at last
   Selects one which—Oh angel and yet ape!—
      Her malice thinks is probably surpassed

783| MS:Replaced §first letter of next incomplete word illegibly crossed out§ by §inserted
above§ new and bright ones: §dash altered to colon§   *P1878:*by brand-new bright
784| MS:instance, by §crossed out and replaced above by§ grew Voltaire, Desforges §first three
letters of last word over illegible letters§   *1889a:*grew Voltaire; Desforges   785|
MS:Demoiselle <> la Vigne—because   *P1878:*"Demoiselle <> la Vigne"—because
786| MS:The Family   *P1878:*family   787| MS:vineyard—few <> hips and haws—
*P1878:*vineyard,—few <> haws,—   *1889a:*hips-and-haws   788| MS:a good §crossed out
and replaced above by§ nice <> name: with much applause §last three words crossed out and
replaced above by four words§ as breast and back   *P1878:*name. As   789| MS:this
vivacious §crossed out and then restored§ beauty §inserted above illegibly crossed out word,
perhaps *lady*§ gleamed §inserted above illegibly crossed out word§   791| MS:§first word
illegibly crossed out§ Lustre when §inserted above§   792| MS:In Malcrais <> la Vigne—
more short, Malcrais.   *P1878:*"In Malcrais <> la Vigne"—more short, "Malcrais."
CP1878:"In Malcrais §altered to§ In "Malcrais   *1878:*In "Malcrais
793| MS:behold §next words illegibly crossed out, replaced above by illegibly crossed out
words, and then replaced in margin by§ escape   794| MS:Of §crossed out and replaced
above by illegibly crossed out word§ The §crossed out and then restored§ <> treasures! §last
letter over illegible letter, perhaps *d*; comma altered to exclamation point§
*P1878:*treasure   795| MS:shape;   *P1878:*shape.   796| MS:prize: §dash altered to
colon§ at   *P1878:*prize; at   797| MS:Selects the §crossed out§ one which— §last word
and dash inserted above§ Oh, angel   *P1878:*which—Oh angel
798| MS:He §crossed out and replaced above by two words§ Her malice

In badness by no fellow of the flock,
800 Copies it fair, and "Now for my La Roque!"

CI

So, to him goes, with the neat manuscript,
    The soft petitionary letter. "Grant
A fledgeling novice that with wing unclipt
    She soar her little circuit, habitant
805 Of an old manor; buried in which crypt,
    How can the youthful châtelaine but pant
For disemprisonment by one *ad hoc*
Appointed 'Mercury's' Editor, La Roque?"

CII

'Twas an epistle that might move the Turk!
810   More certainly it moved our middle-aged
Pen-driver drudging at his weary work,
    Raked the old ashes up and disengaged
The sparks of gallantry which always lurk
    Somehow in literary breasts, assuaged
815 In no degree by compliments on style;
Are Forty wagging beards worth one girl's smile?

799| MS:By none §last two words crossed out and replaced above by two words§ In badness
800| MS:Copies §first three letters over illegible erasure§   801| MS:So to <> the fine
§crossed out and replaced above by§ neat *P1878:*So, to   802| MS:letter: §dash altered
to colon§ "Grant *P1878:*letter. "Grant   803| MS:The §crossed out and replaced above
by§ A   804| MS:little flight §crossed out and replaced above by§ circuit
805| MS:Of the §crossed out and replaced above by§ an <> crypt,— *P1878:*crypt,
806| MS:chatelaine *P1878:*châtelaine   808| MS:Appointed "Mercury's"Editor
*P1878:*Appointed 'Mercury's' Editor   809| MS:that had §crossed out and replaced above
by§ might moved §last letter of last word crossed out forming *move*§   810| MS:Don't you
see how it had §last six words crossed out and replaced above by two words§ More certainly
812| MS:Raked the §over illegible erasure§ <> ashes §illegibly crossed out word inserted
above§   813| MS:gallantry that §crossed out and replaced above by§ which
814| MS:Somewhere §altered to§ Somehow   815| MS:Little §crossed out and replaced
above by three words§ In no degree <> style: *P1878:*style;
816| MS:Are Forty wags of beard, worth *P1878:*Are Forty wagging beards worth

CIII

In trips the lady's poem, takes its place
    Of honour in the gratified Gazette,
With due acknowledgment of power and grace;
820   Prognostication, too, that higher yet
The Breton Muse will soar: fresh youth, high race,
    Beauty and wealth have amicably met
That Demoiselle Malcrais may fill the chair
Left vacant by the loss of Deshoulières.

CIV

825 "There!" cried the lively lady. "Who was right—
    You in the dumps, or I the merry maid
Who know a trick or two can baffle spite
    Tenfold the force of this old fool's? Afraid
Of Editor La Roque? But come! next flight
830   Shall outsoar—Deshoulières alone? My blade,
Sappho herself shall you confess outstript!
    Quick, Paul, another dose of manuscript!"

CV

And so, once well a-foot, advanced the game:
    More and more verses, corresponding gush
835 On gush of praise, till everywhere acclaim
    Rose to the pitch of uproar. "Sappho? Tush!

817| MS:In goes §crossed out and replaced above by§ trips   818| MS:honor
*1889a:*honour   819| MS:acknowledgement *P1878:*acknowledgment
820| MS:Prognostications *P1878:*Prognostication   821| MS:The Breton Muse may soar
*P1878:*The Breton Muse will soar   822| MS:had *P1878:*have   823| MS:That
Demoiselle Malcrais might fill *P1878:*That Demoiselle Malcrais may fill   825| MS:the
little §crossed out and replaced above by§ lively lady "Who *1889a:*lady. "Who
827| MS:two could §crossed out and replaced above by§ can   828| MS:fools? §colon
altered to question mark§ afraid §altered to§ Afraid   830| MS:outsoar—Deshoulières?
§question mark crossed out§ Nay, Sappho's self? §last three words and question mark crossed
out and replaced above by three words and comma§ alone? My blade,   832| MS:Come, Paul, another dose §over illegible erasure§ *P1878:*Quick, Paul
833| MS:well a-foot §first letter of last word over illegible erasure§ , went on §last two words
crossed out and replaced above by§ advanced   835| MS:till up §crossed out and replaced
above by§every   836| MS:Of §crossed out§ Rose to the §last three words crossed out and
then restored§ < > uproar: "Sappho *P1878:*uproar. "Sappho

Sure 'Malcrais on her Parrot' puts to shame
    Deshoulières' pastoral, clay not worth a rush
Beside this find of treasure, gold in crock,
840   Unearthed in Brittany,—nay, ask La Roque!"

CVI

Such was the Paris tribute. "Yes," you sneer,
    "Ninnies stock Noodledom, but folk more sage
Resist contagious folly, never fear!"
    Do they? Permit me to detach one page
845   From the huge Album which from far and near
    Poetic praises blackened in a rage
Of rapture! and that page shall be—who stares
Confounded now, I ask you?—just Voltaire's!

CVII

Ay, sharpest shrewdest steel that ever stabbed
850   To death Imposture through the armour-joints!
How did it happen that gross Humbug grabbed
    Thy weapons, gouged thine eyes out? Fate appoints

837| MS:Read §crossed out and replaced in margin by§ Sure this, "to §altered to§ To Sylvia's parrot" §last word crossed out, replaced above by illegibly crossed out word, and then restored§ puts §first letter over illegible erasure§ *P1878:*Sure 'Malcrais on her Parrot' puts 838| MS:pastorals, not *P1878:*pastorals, clay not *1889a:*pastoral 839| MS:Beside §next words illegibly crossed out, replaced above by illegibly crossed out words, and then replaced above by four words§ this find of treasure 840| MS:Unearthed §inserted above illegibly crossed out word§ in Brittany §sixth and seventh letters of last word over illegible letters§ <> ask La §first letter of last word over illegible letter§ 841| MS:Paris §crossed out and replaced above by§ Such <> tribute: "yes," §altered to§ "Yes," <> sneer *P1878:*tribute. "Yes," <> sneer, 842| MS:"Ninnies are never wanting; but the §last two words crossed out and replaced above by two words§ folks more *P1878:*"Ninnies stock Noodledom, but folks *1889a:*folk 843| MS:inglorious follies §altered to§ folly, never §first two letters of last word over illegible letters§ 844| MS:huge Album blacker §crossed out and replaced above by§ which 845| MS:§first word illegibly crossed out, replaced above by illegibly crossed out words, and then replaced above by two words§ Poetic praises <> in her praise §last two words crossed out and replaced above by two words§ a rage 848| MS:now, I wonder?—just *P1878:*now, I ask you?—just 850| MS:Armoured §crossed out and replaced above by two words§ To death imposture §altered to§ Imposture <> armour-joints— *P1878:*armour-joints! 851| MS:did it §inserted above§ happen that §inserted above§ grossest §last three letters crossed out forming *gross*§ 852| MS:weapons, nay thine eyesight! Fate *P1878:*weapons, gouged thine eyes out? Fate

That pride shall have a fall, or I had blabbed
    Hardly that Humbug, whom thy soul aroints,
855 Could thus cross-buttock thee caught unawares,
    And dismalest of tumbles proved—Voltaire's!

CVIII

See his epistle extant yet, wherewith
    "Henri" in verse and "Charles" in prose he sent
To do her suit and service! Here's the pith
860   Of half a dozen stanzas—stones which went
To build that simulated monolith—
    Sham love in due degree with homage blent
As sham—which in the vast of volumes scares
The traveller still: "That stucco-heap—Voltaire's?"

CIX

865 "Oh thou, whose clarion-voice has overflown
    The wilds to startle Paris that's one ear!
Thou who such strange capacity hast shown
    For joining all that's grand with all that's dear,

854| MS:Never §crossed out and replaced above by§ Hardly that thou wast caught thus §last four words crossed out and replaced above by four words§ Humbug §next word illegibly crossed out§ felled thee §last two words crossed out and replaced above by four words§ whom thy soul aroints *P1878:*that Humbug, whom < > aroints,   855| MS:§line added in margin§ Can §over illegible word§ thus < > caught unawares— §word and dash inserted above§ *P1878:*Could thus < > unawares,   856| MS:Tremendousest of tumbles—just §last four words crossed out, replaced above by illegibly crossed out words, and then replaced by five words, the first above and the others below§ And dismalest of tumbles proved Voltaire's. *P1878:*proved—Voltaire's!   857| MS:See §first letter over illegible letter§ < > wherewith he sent §last two words crossed out§   858| MS:"Henri" in §crossed out, replaced above by illegibly crossed out word, and then restored§ < > and "Charles" in §crossed out, replaced above by illegibly crossed out word, and then restored§
859| MS:service: here's *P1878:*service! Here's   860| MS:Of that epistolary monolith §last four words crossed out and replaced above by eight words§ Of half a dozen stanzas— stones which went   861| MS:that memorable §crossed out and replaced below by§ simulated   862| MS:Of §crossed out and replaced in margin by§ Sham
863| MS:the hundred volumes *P1878:*the vast of volumes   864| MS:still—"That monument— §last word and dash crossed out and replaced above by two words and dash§ folly was— Voltaire's?" *P1878:*still: "That stucco-heap—Voltaire's?"   865| MS:whose brilliant voice has *P1878:*whose clarion-voice has   866| MS:to per §three letters of incomplete word crossed out§ < > Paris, that's all §crossed out and replaced above by§ one *P1878:*Paris that's
868| MS:that's high §crossed out and replaced above by§ grand < > thats *P1878:*that's

Knowledge with power to please—Deshoulières grown
870   Learned as Dacier in thy person! mere
Weak fruit of idle hours, these crabs of mine
I dare lay at thy feet, O Muse divine!

CX

"Charles was my taskwork only; Henri trod
My hero erst; and now, my heroine—she
875   Shall be thyself! True—is it true, great God?
Certainly love henceforward must not be!
Yet all the crowd of Fine Arts fail—how odd!—
Tried turn by turn, to fill a void in me!
There's no replacing love with these, alas!
880   Yet all I can I do to prove no ass.

CXI

"I labour to amuse my freedom; but
Should any sweet young creature slavery preach,
And—borrowing thy vivacious charm, the slut!—
Make me, in thy engaging words, a speech,

869| MS:—Knowledge §dash in margin§ <> please—Deshoulière *P1878:*Knowledge <> please—Deshoulières 870| MS:as Dacier—let thy Muse §dash and last three words crossed out and replaced above by three words and exclamation point§ in thy person! mere §over illegible erasure§ 871| MS:Her feet §last two words crossed out and replaced by word and comma§ Trifles, §word and comma crossed out§ weak §altered to§ Weak <> these things of *P1878:*these crabs of 872| MS:feet, §dash altered to comma§
873| MS:was the offspring of hard §last four words crossed out and replaced above by four words and quotation marks§ my task-work only: §word and colon inserted above§ "Henri" dawned §crossed out and replaced above by§ trod *P1878:*only; Henri trod *1889a:*taskwork
874| MS:hero forth, §word and comma inserted above illegibly crossed out letter of incomplete word§ and, the §crossed out and replaced above by two words§ for my heroine,— she *P1878:*and now, my heroine—she *1889a:*hero erst; and 875| MS:thyself! And, §comma crossed out§ is §over illegible erasure§ <> true, Great *P1878:*thyself! True—is <> great 876| MS:love henceforward §inserted above§ must §next word illegibly crossed out§ no §altered to§ not more on me: §last three words crossed out and replaced above by word and exclamation point§ be! 878| MS:Tried turn by turn, §last four words and comma inserted above§ To §altered to§ to fill the void *P1878:*fill a void
880| MS:Yet §next word illegibly crossed out and replaced above by illegibly crossed out word§ <> I can §over illegible erasure§ I do §last two words inserted above
881| MS:freedom: §dash altered to colon§ but *P1878:*freedom; but 883| MS:And join to §last two words crossed out and replaced above by dash and word§ —borrowing <> charm, §dash altered to comma§ <> slut!— §comma altered to exclamation point§

180

885   Soon should I see myself in prison shut
        With all imaginable pleasure." Reach
    The washhand-basin for admirers! There's
    A stomach-moving tribute—and Voltaire's!

CXII

    Suppose it a fantastic billet-doux,
890   Adulatory flourish, not worth frown!
    What say you to the Fathers of Trévoux?
       These in their Dictionary have her down
    Under the heading "Author": "Malcrais, too,
       Is 'Author' of much verse that claims renown."
895   While Jean-Baptiste Rousseau . . . but why proceed?
    Enough of this—something too much, indeed!

CXIII

    At last La Roque, unwilling to be left
       Behindhand in the rivalry, broke bounds
    Of figurative passion; hilt and heft,
900   Plunged his huge downright love through what surrounds
    The literary female bosom; reft
       Away its veil of coy reserve with "Zounds!
    I love thee, Breton Beauty! All's no use!
    Body and soul I love,—the big word's loose!"

885| MS:Soon I should see   *P1878:*Soon should I see   886| MS:pleasure." There's §crossed out and replaced by§ Reach   887| MS:A washhand basin   *P1878:*The washhand-basin   888| MS:tribute—just §crossed out and replaced above by§ and 890| MS:frown: *P1878:*frown!   891| MS:of Trevoux? *P1878:*of Trévoux? 892| MS:Who §crossed out and replaced above by§ These   893| MS:heading "Author": §dash altered to colon§   894| MS:verse that claims §last two words inserted above illegibly crossed out word§   895| MS:While Jean Baptiste Rousseau . . but *P1878:*While Jean-Baptiste Rousseau . . . but   896| MS:this—and something more, indeed! *P1878:*this—something too much, indeed!   897| MS:last, La §first letter of last word over illegible letter§   899| MS:Of figurative §over illegible erasure§ passion: §colon over illegible punctuation mark§ hilt *P1878:*passion; hilt   900| MS:his prose §crossed out and replaced above by§ whole §crossed out and replaced above by§ huge   901| MS:bosom, §semicolon altered to comma§ reft *P1878:*bosom; reft   902| MS:its veil §inserted above§ soft §crossed out and replaced above by§ of < > "Zounds! §dash altered to exclamation point§ 903| MS:thee, Breton Beauty! §colon altered to exclamation point§ all's < > use: *P1878:*thee, Breton Beauty! All's < > use!   904| MS:love—the *P1878:*love,—the

CXIV

905   *He's greatest now and to de-struc-ti-on*
      Nearest. Attend the solemn word I quote,
O Paul! *There's no pause at per-fec-ti-on.*
      Thus knolls thy knell the Doctor's bronzed throat!
Greatness a period hath, no sta- ti-on!
910   Better and truer verse none ever wrote
(Despite the antique outstretched *a-i-on*)
Than thou, revered and magisterial Donne!

CXV

Flat on his face, La Roque, and,—pressed to heart
      His dexter hand,—Voltaire with bended knee!
915 Paul sat and sucked-in triumph; just apart
      Leaned over him his sister. "Well!" smirks he,
And "Well?" she answers, smiling—woman's art
      To let a man's own mouth, not hers, decree
What shall be next move which decides the game:
920 Success? She said so. Failure? His the blame.

905| MS:*to destruction* §crossed out and replaced by§ *de-struc-ti-on*   906| MS:*Nearest.* §next word illegibly crossed out, replaced by illegibly crossed out word, and then replaced above by§ Attend the solemn §crossed out and then restored§ word §crossed out, replaced above by illegibly crossed out word, and then restored§   907| MS:§first words illegibly crossed out, replaced above by illegibly crossed out words, and then replaced below by two words and exclamation point§ Oh Paul!   908| MS:Solemnly peals §last two words crossed out and replaced above by four words§ Thy knell thus knolls the Doctor's §crossed out, replaced above by *bronzed* and then restored§   *1889a:*Thus knolls thy knell the
909| MS:*no sta-tion!* §word and exclamation point crossed out and replaced by word and exclamation point§ *sta-ti-on!*   910| MS:truer verse §inserted above§ never poet §last two words crossed out and replaced above by two words§ none ever   911| MS:(Despite the §last letter over illegible erasure§ antique §inserted above§ outstretched §next word illegibly crossed out§ *i* §altered to§ *a-i* §over illegible letter§   912| MS:thou, §next words illegibly crossed out and replaced above by illegibly crossed out words§ revered and magisterial §last three words inserted above§   914| MS:hand, Voltaire §inserted above§   *P1878:*hand,— Voltaire   916| MS:sister. "Well?" asks §crossed out and replaced above by§ smirks he; *P1878:*he,   *1889a:*sister. "Well!" smirks   917| MS:answers with the §last two words crossed out and replaced above by word and dash§ smiling—   *P1878:*answers, smiling
919| MS:move that §crossed out and replaced above by§ which

CXVI

"Well!" this time forth affirmatively comes
   With smack of lip, and long-drawn sigh through teeth
Close clenched o'er satisfaction, as the gums
   Were tickled by a sweetmeat teased beneath
925 Palate by lubricating tongue: "Well! crumbs
   Of comfort these, undoubtedly! no death
Likely from famine at Fame's feast! 't is clear
I may put claim in for my pittance, Dear!

CXVII

"La Roque, Voltaire, my lovers! Then disguise
930   Has served its turn, grows idle; let it drop!
I shall to Paris, flaunt there in men's eyes
   My proper manly garb and mount a-top
The pedestal that waits me, take the prize
   Awarded Hercules. He threw a sop
935 To Cerberus who let him pass, you know,
   Then, following, licked his heels: exactly so!

921| MS:"Well!" this time forth §last four words transposed and then restored§
923| MS:That shut in §last three words crossed out and replaced above by three words§ Close clenched o'er 924| MS:Their slow §last two words crossed out and replaced above by three words§ Were tickled by a §inserted above illegibly crossed out word§ sweetmeat rolled §crossed out and replaced above by§ teazed *1889a:*teased 925| MS:by lubricating §inserted above§ tongue: "Well! Crums *P1878:*crums *1889a:*crumbs 926| MS:If comfort these, no doubt: but meal-time's §last four words crossed out and replaced above by three words§ undoubtedly! no death §inserted above illegibly crossed out word§ *P1878:*Of comfort 927| MS:§line added§ Threaten with §last two words crossed out and replaced in margin by two words§ Likely from 928| MS:I may put claim in for §last six words inserted above illegibly crossed out words§ the loaf, my dear! *P1878:*for my pittance, Dear! 929| MS:Voltaire would love me if he dared,— §last seven words, comma, and dash crossed out and replaced above by quotation marks and seven words§ "La Roque, Voltaire, my §crossed out, replaced above by illegibly crossed out word, and then restored§ lovers? Then disguise §question mark and last two words inserted above illegibly crossed out words§ *1889a:*lovers! Then 930| MS:idle: let *P1878:*idle; let 932| MS:garb, and *P1878:*garb and 934| MS:Awarded Hercules! He §over illegible erasure§ threw the §crossed out and replaced above by§ a *1889a:*Awarded Hercules. He 935| MS:To Cerberus—who *P1878:*To Cerberus who 936| MS:Then §over illegible erasure§ , following, at §crossed out and replaced above by§ licked

CXVIII

"I like the prospect—their astonishment,
　　Confusion: wounded vanity, no doubt,
　　Mixed motives; how I see the brows quick bent!
940　　'What, sir, yourself, none other, brought about
　　This change of estimation? Phœbus sent
　　　　His shafts as from Diana?' Critic pout
Turns courtier smile: 'Lo, him we took for her!
Pleasant mistake! You bear no malice, sir?'

CXIX

945　"Eh, my Diana?" But Diana kept
　　Smilingly silent with fixed needle-sharp
　　Much-meaning eyes that seemed to intercept
　　　　Paul's very thoughts ere they had time to warp
　　From earnest into sport the words they leapt
950　　　　To life with—changed as when maltreated harp
Renders in tinkle what some player-prig
Means for a grave tune though it proves a jig.

CXX

"What, Paul, and are my pains thus thrown away,
　　My lessons end in loss?" at length fall slow

937|　MS:prospect—that astonishment,　*P1878:*prospect—their astonishment,
938|　MS:Confusion; wounded <> doubt:　*P1878:*Confusion: wounded <> doubt,
939|　MS:motives; there's no question §last three words crossed out and replaced above by four words§ how I see the　　942|　MS:His arrows in §last two words crossed out and replaced above by three words§ shafts as from Diana's §altered to§ Diana?' §question mark over illegible punctuation mark§ the §crossed out§ critics' §altered to§ Critics'　*P1878:*from Diana? Critic　*1889a:*from Diana?' Critic　943|　MS:Turns §last letter over illegible erasure§ to a smile: "Lo, him you §crossed out and replaced above by§ we　*P1878:*Turns courtier smile: 'Lo　944|　MS:Pleasant mistake!　You §last three words inserted above illegibly crossed out words§ <> malice, Sir?'　*P1878:*sir?'　945|　MS:"Eh §inserted above illegibly crossed out word§　949|　MS:Aside §crossed out§ from §altered to§ From　950|　MS:when maltreated §inserted above illegibly crossed out words§　951|　MS:Gives you §last two words crossed out and replaced above by§ Renders　952|　MS:Means for §last two words inserted above illegibly crossed out word § <> tune turns into §last two words crossed out and replaced by five words§ would make for as to §last five words crossed out and replaced below by three words§　though it proves　953|　MS:and is the teaching §last three words crossed out and replaced above by four words§ are my pains thus　954|　MS:The §crossed out and replaced above by§ My lessons perfect loss　*1889a:*lessons end in loss

955　The pitying syllables, her lips allay
　　　　The satire of by keeping in full flow,
　　Above their coral reef, bright smiles at play:
　　　　"Can it be, Paul thus fails to rightly know
　　And altogether estimate applause
960　As just so many asinine hee-haws?

CXXI

　　"I thought to show you" . . . "Show me," Paul in-broke
　　　　"My poetry is rubbish, and the world
　　That rings with my renown a sorry joke!
　　　　What fairer test of worth than that, form furled,
965　I entered the arena? Yet you croak
　　　　Just as if Phœbé and not Phœbus hurled
　　The dart and struck the Python! What, he crawls
　　Humbly in dust before your feet, not Paul's?

CXXII

　　"Nay, 'tis no laughing matter though absurd
970　　　If there's an end of honesty on earth!

956| MS:The §crossed out and then restored§　　957| MS:The smiles above their coral-reef
§transposed and altered to§ Above their coral-reef, the smiles　*P1878:*coral reef, bright smiles
958| MS:be Paul has §altered to§ thus not attained §last two words crossed out and replaced
above by§ fails §last letter over illegible letters, perhaps *ed*§ to rightly §inserted above§
*P1878:*be, Paul　　959| MS:By this experiment popular §last four words crossed out and
replaced above by three words§ And altogether §inserted above§ estimate §next word illegibly
crossed out§　　960| MS:he-haws? *1889a:*hee-haws?　　961| MS:you" . . . "show
*P1878:*you" . . . "Show　　962| MS:is worthless, and　*P1878:*is rubbish, and
963| MS:with its §crossed out and replaced above by§ my renown is §crossed out, replaced
above by *does*, and then restored§ all a §crossed out, replaced above by illegibly crossed out
word, and then restored§ joke!　*P1878:*renown a sorry joke!　　964| MS:that, face furled,
*P1878:*that, form furled,　　966| MS:if Phoebus—full his play—had hurled
*P1878:*if Phoebus' fan, not bow, had　hurled　*CP1878:*if Phoebus' §altered to§ Phoebé fan,
not bow, had §last four words crossed out and replaced in margin by three words§ and not
Phoebus hurled　*1878:*if Phoebé and not Phoebus hurled　967| MS:His darts and struck
§over illegible word§ no Python—though §crossed out, replaced above by illegibly crossed out
word, and then replaced above by word and comma§ what,　*P1878:*The dart <> struck the
Python! What　　968| MS:before §followed by illegible erasure§
969| MS:absurd! §comma altered to exclamation point§　　970| MS:If §crossed out and
replaced in margin by word and comma§ So, there's　*P1878:*If there's

La Roque sends letters, lying every word!
   Voltaire makes verse, and of himself makes mirth
To the remotest age! Rousseau's the third
   Who, driven to despair amid such dearth
975 Of people that want praising, finds no one
More fit to praise than Paul the simpleton!

CXXIII

"Somebody says—if a man writes at all
   It is to show the writer's kith and kin
He was unjustly thought a natural;
980   And truly, sister, I have yet to win
Your favourable word, it seems, for Paul
   Whose poetry you count not worth a pin
Though well enough esteemed by these Voltaires,
Rousseaus and suchlike: let them quack, who cares?"

CXXIV

985 "—To Paris with you, Paul! Not one word's waste
   Further: my scrupulosity was vain!

971| MS:La Roque writes §crossed out and replaced above by§ sends   972| MS:makes verses §last letter crossed out forming *verse*§ —and §dash and word crossed out and replaced above by comma and two words§ , and of   973| MS:age! §colon altered to exclamation point§   974| MS:Simpleton that §last two words crossed out and replaced above by three words§ Who, driven to despairs §last letter crossed out forming *despair*§   975| MS:Of people that want §last three words crossed out, replaced above by *folks repaying folks that need his,* and then restored§ praising, of §crossed out§ finding §last three letters crossed out and replaced above by *s*§ no §inserted above§   976| MS:fit §next word illegibly crossed out and replaced above by illegibly crossed out word§ to §inserted above§ praise than §inserted above§ Paul the §last two words crossed out, replaced above by illegibly crossed out word, and then restored§   977| MS:says—the use of writing books §last five words crossed out and replaced above by five words§ if people §crossed out and replaced above by two words§ a man writes at all   978| MS:It's §altered to§ It is just §inserted above and then crossed out§ <> writers' *P1878*:writer's   979| MS:was not §crossed out§ <> natural: *P1878*:natural;   981| MS:word it seems for *P1878*:word, it seems, for 982| MS:Whose §last letter over illegible letter§   983| MS:enough esteemed §first letter of last word over *i*§   984| MS:Rousseaus §inserted above§ And such like: rabble rout §last two words crossed out and replaced above by three words and comma§ let them quack, *P1878:* and suchlike   985| MS:you, Paul! §comma altered to exclamation point§ not §altered to§ Not   986| MS:Further! §colon altered to exclamation point§ <> my scrupulosity was §over illegible erasure§ *P1878*:Further: my

Go triumph! Be my foolish fears effaced
From memory's record! Go, to come again
With glory crowned,—by sister re-embraced,
990　　Cured of that strange delusion of her brain
Which led her to suspect that Paris gloats
On male limbs mostly when in petticoats!"

CXXV

So laughed her last word, with the little touch
Of malice proper to the outraged pride
995　　Of any artist in a work too much
Shorn of its merits. "By all means be tried
The opposite procedure! Cast your crutch
Away, no longer crippled, nor divide
The credit of your march to the World's Fair
1000　　With sister Cherry-cheeks who helped you there!"

CXXVI

Crippled, forsooth! what courser sprightlier pranced
Paris-ward than did Paul? Nay, dreams lent wings:
He flew, or seemed to fly, by dreams entranced.
Dreams? wide-awake realities: no things

---

⁹⁸⁷| MS:Go to your §last two words crossed out§ triumph! §comma altered to exclamation point§ and all §last two words crossed out and replaced above by think §crossed out and replaced above by§ Be my foolish §inserted above§ ⁹⁸⁸| MS:record! Go, and come *P1878:*record! Go, to come _, ⁹⁸⁹| MS:re-embraced *P1878:*re-embraced, ⁹⁹¹| MS:That §crossed out and replaced above by§ Which led her §crossed out and then restored§ to §next word illegibly crossed out and replaced above by words§ the belief §last two words crossed out and replaced above by§ suspect that Paris §inserted above§ ⁹⁹²| MS:Only §crossed out§ on §altered to§ On <> limbs masked by §last two words crossed out and replaced above by three words§ only when in *P1878:*limbs mostly when ⁹⁹³| MS:laughed the §crossed out and replaced above by§ her ⁹⁹⁶| MS:merits. §colon altered to period§ "by §altered to§ By <> means, be *1889a:*means be ⁹⁹⁸| MS:Away, by all means, §last three words and comma crossed out and replaced above by two words§ no longer ⁹⁹⁹| MS:your marching to the Fair *P1878:*your march to the World's Fair ¹⁰⁰⁰| MS:there! *P1878:*there!" ¹⁰⁰¹| MS:forsooth—what *P1878:*forsooth! what ¹⁰⁰²| MS:did Paul? §question mark over illegible punctuation marks, perhaps comma and dash§ nay §altered to§ Nay <> wings: §colon over punctuation marks, perhaps comma and dash§ ¹⁰⁰³| MS:entranced— *P1878:*entranced. ¹⁰⁰⁴| MS:Dreams? §first three letters over illegible letters; last three letters and question mark inserted above§

1005　Dreamed merely were the missives that advanced
　　　　The claim of Malcrais to consort with kings
　　　　Crowned by Apollo—not to say with queens
　　　　Cinctured by Venus for Idalian scenes.

CXXVII

　　　　Soon he arrives, forthwith is found before
1010　　The outer gate of glory. Bold tic-toc
　　　　Announces there's a giant at the door.
　　　　"Ay, sir, here dwells the Chevalier La Roque."
　　　　"Lackey! Malcrais,—mind, no word less nor more!—
　　　　Desires his presence. I've unearthed the brock:
1015　Now, to transfix him!" There stands Paul erect,
　　　　Inched out his uttermost, for more effect.

CXXVIII

　　　　A bustling entrance: "Idol of my flame!
　　　　Can it be that my heart attains at last
　　　　Its longing? that you stand, the very same
1020　　As in my visions? . . . Ha! hey, how?" aghast
　　　　Stops short the rapture. "Oh, my boy's to blame!
　　　　You merely are the messenger! Too fast
　　　　My fancy rushed to a conclusion. Pooh!
　　　　Well, sir, the lady's substitute is—who?"

1009| MS:So he §two words inserted above§ Arrived §last letter crossed out and replaced above
by *s*§ at §crossed out§　*P1878:*Soon he arrives　　1010| MS:glory: bold　*P1878:*glory.
Bold　　　　1012| MS:the Chevalier La Roque"!　*P1878:*the Chevalier La Roque."
1013| MS:Tell him §last two words crossed out and replaced above by quotation marks, word,
and exclamation point§ "Lackey! <> more,—　*P1878:*more!—　　　1014| MS:presence!"
"I've <> brock,　*P1878:*presence. I've <> brock:　　　1015| MS:him!" There §inserted
above illegibly crossed out word§ Paul stands §transposed to§ stands Paul
1016| MS:out, his §over illegible word§　*P1878:*out his　　　1017| MS:entrance: "Idol of my
flame! §quotation marks, last four words, and exclamation point inserted above five illegibly
crossed out words, perhaps *a blank stop and stand*§　　　1018| MS:And stare §last two words
crossed out and replaced above by three words§ And §crossed out§ can §altered to§ Can it be
that §inserted above§　　　1019| MS:longing? §colon altered to question mark§ that §altered
to§ That　　　1020| MS:visions? §colon altered to question mark§ . . Ha, hey, how?" §ellipsis
points, three words, question mark, and quotation marks inserted above illegibly crossed out
words§ . . . aghast . . .　*P1878:*visions? . . . Ha! <> how?" aghast
1021| MS:rapture: §dash altered to colon§ Shake hands! §exclamation point over illegible
punctuation mark, perhaps a comma§　*P1878:*inordinate. "Shake

CXXIX

1025   Then Paul's smirk grows inordinate. "Shake hands!
       Friendship not love awaits you, master mine,
    Though nor Malcrais nor any mistress stands
       To meet your ardour! So, you don't divine
    Who wrote the verses wherewith ring the land's
1030   Whole length and breadth? Just he whereof no line
    Had ever leave to blot your Journal—eh?
    Paul Desforges Maillard—otherwise Malcrais!"

CXXX

    And there the two stood, stare confronting smirk,
       Awhile uncertain which should yield the *pas*.
1035   In vain the Chevalier beat brain for quirk
       To help in this conjuncture; at length "Bah!
    Boh! Since I've made myself a fool, why shirk
       The punishment of folly? Ha, ha, ha,
    Let me return your handshake!" Comic sock
1040   For tragic buskin prompt thus changed La Roque.

CXXXI

    "I'm nobody—a wren-like journalist;
       You've flown at higher game and winged your bird,

1025| MS:inordinate: §dash altered to colon§ <> hands! §comma altered to exclamation point§   1030| MS:breadth? Just §first letter of last word over illegible letter§ he, whereof *P1878:*he whereof   1031| MS:Had §first letter over illegible letter§ ever leave §inserted above§ to disgrace§crossed out and replaced above by§ blot your Journal's §apostrophe and last letter partially erased forming *Journal*§ page §crossed out and replaced above by dash, word, and question mark§ —eh?   1032| MS:otherwise, Malcrais!" *P1878:*otherwise Malcrais!' *1889a:*otherwise Malcrais!"   1033| MS:smirk; *P1878:*smirk,   1034| MS:should yield §over illegible erasure§ <> *pas*: *P1878:pas.*
1035| MS:In vain §last two words inserted above§ The *P1878:*the
1036| MS:conjuncture: at <> "Bah, *P1878:*conjuncture; at <> "Bah!
1037| MS:Bah,—since his §crossed out and replaced above by§ I've *P1878:*Bah! Since
1039| MS:Shake hands, Sir. §last three words and period crossed out and replaced above by five words, exclamation point, and quotations marks§ Let me return your hand-shake!" *P1878:*handshake   1040| MS:buskin prompt §inserted above§ thus could §crossed out§
1041| MS:"But, Sir, I'm nobody,—a Journalist; *P1878:*"I'm nobody—a wren-like journalist;

The golden eagle! That's the grand acquist!
Voltaire's sly Muse, the tiger-cat, has purred
1045   Prettily round your feet; but if she missed
Priority of stroking, soon were stirred
The dormant spit-fire. To Voltaire! away,
Paul Desforges Maillard, otherwise Malcrais!

CXXXII

Whereupon, arm in arm, and head in air,
1050   The two begin their journey. Need I say,
La Roque had felt the talon of Voltaire,
Had a long-standing little debt to pay,
And pounced, you may depend, on such a rare
Occasion for its due discharge? So, gay
1055   And grenadier-like, marching to assault,
They reach the enemy's abode, there halt.

CXXXIII

"I'll be announcer!" quoth La Roque: "I know,
Better than you, perhaps, my Breton bard,
How to procure an audience! He's not slow
1060   To smell a rat, this scamp Voltaire! Discard
The petticoats too soon,—you'll never show
Your *haut-de-chausses* and all they've made or marred
In your true person. Here's his servant. Pray,
Will the great man see Demoiselle Malcrais?

1044| MS:Voltaire §altered to§ Voltaire's—whose §dash and word crossed out and replaced above by§ sly muse *P1878:*sly Muse   1045| MS:feet: and if you §crossed out and replaced above by§ she *P1878:*feet; but if   1046| MS:Priority of stroking, §last three words and comma inserted above illegibly crossed out words§   1047| MS:The sleeping §crossed out and replaced above by§ dormant spit-fire. To Voltaire's §apostrophe and last letter crossed out forming *Voltaire*§ ! I say,— *P1878:*spit-fire. To Voltaire! away,   1049| MS:heads *P1878:*head   1050| MS:their march §altered to§ marching. §period inserted below§ what §crossed out§ need §altered to§ Need I §over illegible letter§ *P1878:*their journey. Need   1052| MS:long standing *P1878:*long-standing   1054| MS:discharge? §colon altered to question mark§ so §altered to§ So   1059| MS:audience. §colon altered to period§ he's §altered to§ He's *P1878:*audience! He's   1060| MS:this same Voltaire *P1878:*this scamp Voltaire   1061| MS:petticoat < > soon,—I doubt §last two words crossed out§ you'll never §apostrophe, two letters, and word inserted above§   1063| MS:servant! Pray, *P1878:*servant. Pray

CXXXIV

1065 Now, the great man was also, no whit less,
    The man of self-respect,—more great man he!
And bowed to social usage, dressed the dress,
    And decorated to the fit degree
His person; 'twas enough to bear the stress
1070   Of battle in the field, without, when free
From outside foes, inviting friends' attack
By—sword in hand? No,—ill-made coat on back!

CXXXV

And, since the announcement of his visitor
    Surprised him at his toilet,—never glass
1075 Had such solicitation! "Black, now—or
    Brown be the killing wig to wear? Alas,
Where's the rouge gone, this cheek were better for
    A tender touch of? Melted to a mass,
All my pomatum! There's at all events
1080 A devil—for he's got among my scents!"

1065| MS:also, no §illegibly crossed out word above§   1066| MS:of much observance §last three words crossed out§ of §crossed out and replaced above by word and hyphen§ self- < > he,— *P1878:*he!   1067| MS:§first word illegibly crossed out and replaced above by three words§ And bound by §last three words crossed out and replaced in margin by§ And bowed to §last two words inserted above§ < > usage, pink of courtliness,— §last three words, comma, and dash crossed out and replaced above by three words and comma§ dressed the dress,   1068| MS:And looked §crossed out§   1069| MS:person; quite §crossed out and replaced above by§ 'twas   1071| MS:foes, the tempting §last two words crossed out and replaced above by§ inviting   1072| MS:hand? No, ill-made §inserted above illegibly crossed out word§ < > back. *P1878:*hand? No,—ill-made < > back!
1074| MS:never glass §over illegible erasure§   1075| MS:such devout consulting §last two words crossed out, replaced above by illegibly crossed out word, and then replaced above by word and exclamation point§ solicitation! §colon altered to exclamation point§ "this §crossed out and replaced above by§ "Black   1076| MS:That §crossed out and replaced above by§ Brown were §crossed out and replaced above by§ proves §crossed out and replaced above by§ be < > wig to §first letter of last word over illegible letter, perhaps *F*§
1078| MS:A tender §inserted above§   1079| MS:pomatum! There's at §last letter over illegible letter§ all events §inserted above illegibly crossed out word§
1080| MS:for he's §over illegible erasure§ got §second letter over illegible letter§

CXXXVI

So, "barbered ten times o'er," as Antony
Paced to his Cleopatra, did at last
Voltaire proceed to the fair presence: high
In colour, proud in port, as if a blast
1085   Of trumpet bade the world "Take note! draws nigh
To Beauty, Power! Behold the Iconoclast,
The Poet, the Philosopher, the Rod
Of iron for imposture! Ah my God!"

CXXXVII

For there stands smirking Paul, and—what lights fierce
1090   The situation as with sulphur flash—
There grinning stands La Roque! No carte and tierce
Observes the grinning fencer, but, full dash
From breast to shoulderblade, the thrusts transpierce
That armour against which so idly clash
1095   The swords of priests and pedants! Victors there,
Two smirk and grin who have befooled—Voltaire!

1081| MS:oer *P1878:*o'er   1082| MS:at length §crossed out and replaced by§ last
1083| MS:proceed in §crossed out and replaced by§ to the fair §inserted above§ presence,—
high *P1878:*presence: high   1085| MS:trumpet bade §last two letters over illegible
letters§ <> world "take §altered to§ Take   1086| MS:To Beauty now §crossed out and
replaced above by dash§ —Power! §colon altered to exclamation point§ behold §altered to§
Behold *P1878:*To Beauty, Power   1088| MS:imposture!—Ah, my *P1878:*imposture!
Ah my   1089| MS:smirking Paul, §dash altered to comma§ <> what explains §crossed
out and replaced above by two words§ lights fierce   1090| MS:The dreadful §crossed out§
<> with sulphur §inserted above§   1091| MS:Of lightning §last two words crossed out
and replaced above by three words§ There grinning stands La §over illegible word§
1092| MS:Observes §over illegible erasure§ from §crossed out§ that §crossed out and then
restored§ savage fencer, §dash altered to comma§ *P1878:*Observes the grinning fencer
1093| MS:to shoulderblade §first two letters of last word over illegible letters§
1095| MS:pedants! Tis Voltaire §last two words crossed out and replaced in margin by two
words§ Victors, there *P1878:*pedants! Victors there *CP1878:*there, §comma inserted§
*1878:*there,   1096| MS:They smirk <> grin, and have *P1878:*Two smirk <> grin who have

CXXXVIII

A moment's horror; then quick turn-about
  On high-heeled shoe,—flurry of ruffles, flounce
Of wig-ties and of coat-tails,—and so out
1100 Of door banged wrathfully behind, goes—bounce—
Voltaire in tragic exit! vows, no doubt,
  Vengeance upon the couple. Did he trounce
Either, in point of fact ? His anger's flash
Subsided if a culprit craved his cash.

CXXXIX

1105 As for La Roque, he having laughed his laugh
  To heart's content,—the joke defunct at once,
Dead in the birth, you see,—its epitaph
  Was sober earnest. "Well, sir, for the nonce,
You've gained the laurel; never hope to graff
1110 A second sprig of triumph there! Ensconce
Yourself again at Croisic: let it be
Enough you mastered both Voltaire and—me!

CXL

"Don't linger here in Paris to parade
  Your victory, and have the very boys

1097| MS:horror: then a §crossed out and replaced above by§ quick *P1878:*horror; then
1098| MS:shoe,—flurry §first letter of last word over illegible erasure§ < > ruffles, §dash altered to comma§   1100| MS:Of door §followed by illegible erasure§ behind, goes §over illegible erasure§   1101| MS:There's Oedipus his §last three words crossed out and replaced above by three words§ Voltaire in tragic exit! §colon altered to exclamation point§ did §altered to§ Did he trounce *P1878:*exit! vows, no doubt,   1102| MS:La Roque as soundly as he vowed? I doubt *P1878:*Vengeance upon the couple. Did he trounce
1103| MS:He ever long §inserted above§ bore malice: anger's *P1878:*Either, in point of fact? His anger's   1105| MS:for the culprit, §last two words and comma crossed out and replaced above by three words and comma§ La Roque, he, having *P1878:*he having
1106| MS:joke defunct§inserted above§   1108| MS:earnest. "Well, Sir *P1878:*sir
1109| MS:You've §over illegible erasure§ masters of the field §last four words crossed out and replaced above by four words§ gained the laurel: never *P1878:*laurel; never
1113| MS:"Dont *P1878:*"Don't

1115 Point at you! 'There's the little mouse which made
        Believe those two big lions that its noise,
        Nibbling away behind the hedge, conveyed
        Intelligence that—portent which destroys
        All courage in the lion's heart, with horn
1120 That's fable—there lay couched the unicorn!'

CXLI

"Beware us, now we've found who fooled us! Quick
        To cover! 'In proportion to men's fright,
        Expect their fright's revenge!' quoth politic
        Old Macchiavelli. As for me,—all's right:
1125 I'm but a journalist. But no pin's prick
        The tooth leaves when Voltaire is roused to bite!
        So, keep your counsel, I advise! Adieu!
        Good journey! Ha, ha, ha, Malcrais was—you!"

1115| MS:you—' §double quotation marks altered to single mark; next word illegibly crossed
out, replaced above by illegibly crossed out words, and then replaced below by§ There's < >
mouse that §crossed out and replaced above by§ which   *P1878:*you! 'There's
1116| MS:that its §first two letters of last word over illegible letters§ noise §third letter over
illegible letter§   1117| MS:Nibbling away §last two words inserted above§ Behind
§altered to§ behind < > hedge, intelligence §crossed out§   1118| MS:Intelligence,
§comma crossed out§ that,—portent   *P1878:*that—portent   1119| MS:the kingly
§crossed out and replaced above by§ lion's   1120| MS:That's a mere fable,—comes the
*P1878:*That's fable—there lay couched the   1121| MS:now we find   *P1878:*now we've
found   1122| MS:cover! §comma and dash altered to exclamation point§ more the §last
two words crossed out and replaced above by three words§ for as the §last three words crossed
out§ fright §crossed out§ recovered from §last two words crossed out and replaced above by
three words§ has been extreme §last three words crossed out and replaced in margin by five
words and comma§ In proportion to men's fright,   *P1878:*cover! 'In
1123| MS:More cruel the revenge,—quoth politic §last six words crossed out and replaced
above by eight words and first letter of incomplete word§ Has been excessive so be assured
once recovered f §last eight words and letter crossed out and replaced in margin by six words§
Expect that fright's revenge, quoth politic   *P1878:*Expect their fright's revenge!' quoth
1124| MS:Old Macchiavelli §last two words crossed out and then restored§ . §colon or
semicolon altered to period§ as §altered to§ As < > right: §semicolon or comma altered to
colon§   1125| MS:journalist,—but   *P1878:*journalist. But   1126| MS:tooth leaves
§over illegible erasure; illegibly crossed out word below§ when Voltaire is §over illegible
erasure§ round to   *P1878:*is roused to   1127| MS:advise. Adieu!   *P1878:*advise!
Adieu!   1128| MS:ha, so §inserted above§ Malcrais   *P1878:*ha, ha, Malcrais

194

CXLII

"—Yes, I'm Malcrais, and somebody beside,
1130   You snickering monkey!" thus winds up the tale
Our hero, safe at home, to that black-eyed
      Cherry-cheeked sister, as she soothes the pale
Mortified poet. "Let their worst be tried,
      I'm their match henceforth—very man and male!
1135 Don't talk to me of knocking-under! man
And male must end what petticoats began!

CXLIII

"How woman-like it is to apprehend
      The world will eat its words! why, words transfixed
To stone, they stare at you in print,—at end,
1140   Each writer's style and title! Choose betwixt
Fool and knave for his name, who should intend
      To perpetrate a baseness so unmixed
With prospect of advantage! What is writ
Is writ: they've praised me, there's an end of it.

1129| MS:—"Yes §dash in margin§ <> and Paul Desforges, §last two words and comma crossed out and replaced above by§ somebody beside,— *P1878:* "—Yes <> beside,
1130| MS:monkey!" So §crossed out and replaced above by§ Thus winds up the §last three words crossed out, replaced above by *concludes his,* and then restored§ Tale, *P1878:*thus <> tale   1131| MS:safe at §first letter of last word over illegible letter§   1132| MS:sister, who would §last two words crossed out and replaced above by two words§ as she soothed §altered to§ soothes   1134| MS:match henceforth §sixth, seventh, and eighth letters of last word over illegible erasure§   1136| MS:what petticoats §first four letters of last word over illegible letters§ <> began. §question mark erased and replaced by period§
1138| MS:That §crossed out and replaced by§ The <> words! §colon altered to exclamation point§ why, there they §crossed out§ transfixed *P1878:*why, words transfixed
1140| MS:title! §colon altered to exclamation point§ choose §altered to§ Choose
1141| MS:knave, for <> name who §over illegible word§ *P1878:*knave for <> name, who
1142| MS:baseness that §crossed out§   1143| MS:advantage! §question mark altered to exclamation point§ <> writ, *P1878:*writ   1144| MS:writ: §comma altered to colon§ <> praised and §crossed out, replaced above by illegible erasure, and then restored§ there's <> it! *P1878:*praised me, there's *1889a:*it.

CXLIV

1145 "No, Dear, allow me! I shall print these same
    Pieces, with no omitted line, as Paul's.
    Malcrais no longer, let me see folk blame
      What they—praised simply?—placed on pedestals,
    Each piece a statue in the House of Fame!
1150   Fast will they stand there, though their presence galls
    The envious crew: such show their teeth, perhaps
    And snarl, but never bite! I know the chaps!"

CXLV

    Oh Paul, oh piteously deluded! Pace
      Thy sad sterility of Croisic flats,
1155 Watch, from their southern edge, the foamy race
    Of high-tide as it heaves the drowning mats
    Of yellow-berried web-growth from their place,
      The rock-ridge, when, rolling as far as Batz,
    One broadside crashes on it, and the crags,
1160 That needle under, stream with weedy rags!

1145| MS:"No, sweet, allow   *P1878:*"No, Dear, allow   1146| MS:no omission §altered to§
omitted of §crossed out and replaced below by§ line, as Paul's—   *P1878:*as Paul's.
1147| MS:Malcrais' < > longer: let < > see them §crossed out and replaced above by§ folks
*P1878:*Malcrais < > longer, let   *1889a:*folk   1148| MS:praised simply §crossed out,
replaced above and below by illegibly crossed out words, and then restored§
1149| MS:Each favoured §inserted above and then crossed out§ piece §over illegible erasure§
poetic, §word and comma crossed out and replaced below by two words§ a statue < > the
house §altered to§ House   1150| MS:Fast shall they stand there, §word and comma
inserted above illegibly crossed out word§   *P1878:*Fast will they   1151| MS:crew: they'll
show < > perhaps,   *P1878:*crew: such show   *1889a:*perhaps   1152| MS:And grin, but
*P1878:*And snarl, but   1153| MS:Oh, Paul   *P1878:*Oh Paul   1155| MS:Watch from
< > edge §over illegible erasure§ the   *P1878:*Watch, from < > edge, the   1156| MS:heaves
the §crossed out§ seaweed §crossed out and replaced above by§ drowning   *P1878:*heaves the
drowning   1157| MS:Of §crossed out and then restored§ yellow-berried sea §crossed out
and replaced above by word and hyphen§ web-   1158| MS:rock ridge §over illegible
erasure§ < > rolling from here to Batz,   *P1878:*rock-ridge < > rolling as far as Batz,
1159| MS:broadside breaks thereon, §two words and comma crossed out and replaced above
by three words and comma§ crashes on it, and all §crossed out§ < > crags   *P1878:*crags,

CXLVI

Or, if thou wilt, at inland Bergerac,
  Rude heritage but recognized domain,
Do as two here are doing: make hearth crack
  With logs until thy chimney roar again
1165 Jolly with fire-glow! Let its angle lack
  No grace of Cherry-cheeks thy sister, fain
To do a sister's office and laugh smooth
  Thy corrugated brow—that scowls forsooth!

CXLVII

Wherefore? Who does not know how these La Roques,
1170 Voltaires, can say and unsay, praise and blame,
Prove black white, white black, play at paradox
  And, when they seem to lose it, win the game?
Care not thou what this badger, and that fox,
  His fellow in rascality, call "fame!"
1175 Fiddlepin's end! Thou hadst it,—quack, quack, quack!
Have quietude from geese at Bergerac!

---

¹¹⁶¹| MS:Or, qu §first two letters of incomplete word crossed out§   ¹¹⁶²| MS:Thine
§crossed out and replaced above by§ Rude heritage and §crossed out and replaced above by§
but   ¹¹⁶³| MS:as we §crossed out§ two here §inserted above§ < > doing,—pile with
wrack §last three words crossed out and replaced in margin by three words§ make hearth
crack   *P1878*:doing: make   ¹¹⁶⁴| MS:Thy hearth §last two words crossed out and
replaced above by two words§ With logs until the §crossed out and replaced above by illegible
word, perhaps *its*§ chimney roars   *P1878:*until thy chimney roar
¹¹⁶⁵| MS:With jolly §transposed and altered to§ Jolly with fire-flame §second half of
hyphenated word crossed out and replaced above by§ glow: let its corner §crossed out and
replaced above by§ angle   *P1878:*fire-glow! Let   ¹¹⁶⁶| MS:of cherry-cheeks §altered
to§ Cherry-cheeks   ¹¹⁶⁸| MS:brow—that's sad forsooth!   *P1878:*brow—that scowls
forsooth!   ¹¹⁶⁹| MS:how these §last three letters over illegible letters§ Laroques
*P1878:*these La Roques,   ¹¹⁷¹| MS:Prove one the other, play   *P1878:*Prove black white,
white black, play   ¹¹⁷²| MS:And when   *P1878:*And, when   ¹¹⁷³| MS:thou what
§over illegible erasure§ this wild-cat and §over illegible erasure§ < > fox   *P1878:*this badger.
and < > fox,   *CP1878:*badger, §period altered to comma§ and   *1878:*badger, and
¹¹⁷⁴| MS:fellow in §inserted above§ rascal §altered to§ rascality both §crossed out§ call
"fame"—   *P1878:*rascality, call "fame!"   ¹¹⁷⁵| MS:Fiddlestick's §altered to§ Fiddlepin's
< > it,—quack, quack, quack!— §comma altered to exclamation point§   *P1878:*it,—quack,
quack, quack!   *1889a:*it,—quack, quack quack! §emended to§ it,—quack, quack, quack! §see
Editorial Notes§   ¹¹⁷⁶| MS:Then §crossed out and replaced in margin by§ Have < >
from geese §third letter of last word over illegible letter§

CXLVIII

Quietude! For, be very sure of this!
    A twelvemonth hence, and men shall know or care
As much for what to-day they clap or hiss
1180   As for the fashion of the wigs they wear,
Then wonder at. There's fame which, bale or bliss,—
    Got by no gracious word of great Voltaire
Or not-so-great La Roque,—is taken back
By neither, any more than Bergerac!

CXLIX

1185 Too true! or rather, true as ought to be!
    No more of Paul the man, Malcrais the maid,
Thenceforth for ever! One or two, I see,
    Stuck by their poet: who the longest stayed
Was Jean-Baptiste Rousseau, and even he
1190   Seemingly saddened as perforce he paid
A rhyming tribute "After death, survive—
    He hoped he should; and died while yet alive!"

1177| MS:Quietude! For of this §last two words inserted above§ be very sure: §last five words transposed to§ be very sure of this: *P1878:*Quietude! For, be < > this!   1178| MS:A year §crossed out and replaced above by two words§ twelve month   *P1878:*twelvemonth
1179| MS:as much §inserted above§ For what they praise and §last three words crossed out and replaced above by two words§ today they < > or blame and §last two words crossed out§   *P1878:*As < > for < > to-day   1180| MS:To-day, §word and comma crossed out§ as §altered to§ As for the §first letter of last word over illegible letter§ money thou didst §last three words crossed out and replaced above by four words§ fashion of the wigs < > wear   *P1878:*wear,
1181| MS:at. There's true fame,—bale   *P1878:*at. There's fame which, bale
1182| MS:That's got another way §last two words crossed out and replaced above by three words§ by no good word §first letter of last word over comma and dash§   *P1878:*Got < > no gracious word   1183| MS:not-so-great La Roque,—that's §crossed out and replaced above by word and comma§ fame, taken   *P1878:*not-so-great La Roque,—is taken   1184| MS:neither any   *P1878:*neither, any   1185| MS:true—or   *P1878:*true! or   1186| MS:of Paul, the §inserted above illegibly crossed out word, perhaps *as*§ man, or §crossed out and replaced above by two words§ Malcrais the maid, thenceforth, §word and comma crossed out§   *P1878:*of Paul the   1187| MS:Thenceforth, §word and comma in margin§ For §altered to§ for ever! §colon altered to exclamation point§ one §altered to§ One < > two, §dash altered to comma§ I seem to §last two words crossed out§ see—   *P1878:*see,   1189| MS:Was Jean-Baptiste-Rousseau   *P1878:*Was Jean-Baptiste Rousseau   1191| MS:His rhyming tribute: "After death, §comma over illegible punctuation mark§ survive— §dash over illegible punctuation mark§   *P1878:*A rhyming tribute "After   1192| MS:hoped—and ye §last two words crossed out and replaced above by three words§ he should: and   *1889a:*should; and

CL

No, he hoped nothing of the kind, or held
    His peace and died in silent good old age.
1195 Him it was, curiosity impelled
    To seek if there were extant still some page
Of his great predecessor, rat who belled
    The cat once, and would never deign engage
In after-combat with mere mice,—saved from
1200 More sonnetteering,—René Gentilhomme.

CLI

Paul's story furnished forth that famous play
    Of Piron's "Métromanie": there you'll find
He's Francaleu, while Demoiselle Malcrais
    Is Demoiselle No-end-of-names-behind!
1205 As for Voltaire, he's Damis. Good and gay
    The plot and dialogue, and all's designed
To spite Voltaire: at "Something" such the laugh
    Of simply "Nothing!" (see his epitaph).

1193| MS:No, he §first letter of last word over illegible letter§ hopes <> kind: §dash altered to colon§ so, kept §crossed out and replaced above by§ held *P1878:*hoped <> kind, or held
1194| MS:age. §period over illegible erasure§   1196| MS:there remained §crossed out and replaced above by two words§ were extant   1197| MS:predecessor, he who *P1878:*predecessor, rat who   1198| MS:once, §dash altered to comma§
1199| MS:Thenceforth §in margin and then crossed out§ In after §inserted above§ combat with the §crossed out and replaced above by§ mere rats and §last two words crossed out§ *P1878:*after-combat   1200| MS:sonnetteering,—René Gentilhomme! *P1878:*sonnetteering,—René Gentilhomme.   1201| MS:Paul's makes a figure in §last four words crossed out and replaced above by three words§ story furnished forth
1202| MS:Of Piron's, §dash altered to comma§ "Metromanie" *P1878:*Of Piron's "Métromanie"   1204| MS:Is Demoiselle §next word illegibly crossed out§ No-end-of-names-behind: *P1878:*Is Demoiselle No-end-of-names-behind!   1205| MS:he's Damis: good *P1878:*he's Damis. Good   1207| MS:spite the Sage of Ferney— §last four words and dash crossed out and replaced above by three words and comma§ Voltaire: at Something, such *P1878:*at "Something" such   1208| MS:Of No—not §last two words crossed out and replaced above by§ simply "Nothing"! §dash altered to exclamation point§ <> epitaph.) §period over erased exclamation point§ *P1878:*simply "Nothing!" *1889a:*epitaph).

199

CLII

But truth, truth, that's the gold! and all the good
1210   I find in fancy is, it serves to set
Gold's inmost glint free, gold which comes up rude
     And rayless from the mine. All fume and fret
Of artistry beyond this point pursued
     Brings out another sort of burnish: yet
1215   Always the ingot has its very own
Value, a sparkle struck from truth alone.

CLIII

Now, take this sparkle and the other spirt
     Of fitful flame,—twin births of our grey brand
That's sinking fast to ashes! I assert,
1220   As sparkles want but fuel to expand
Into a conflagration no mere squirt
     Will quench too quickly, so might Croisic strand,
Had Fortune pleased posterity to chowse,
Boast of her brace of beacons luminous.

1209| MS:gold! §semicolon altered to exclamation point§   1211| MS:§first word illegibly crossed out, perhaps *That*§ inmost glint of §crossed out§ gold §altered to§ Gold's §transposed to§ Gold's inmost glint free §first letter of last word over illegible letter§, gold §inserted above§   1212| MS:mine: all *P1878:*mine. All   1213| MS:point pursued §last two letters over illegible erasure§   1214| MS:out an §altered to§ another sort of §last two words inserted above illegibly crossed out word§ burnish: §comma altered to colon§   1215| MS:had *P1878:*has   1216| MS:Value, the sparkle *P1878:*Value, a sparkle   1217| MS:So §crossed out and replaced in margin by word and comma§ Now, Take §altered to§ take   1218| MS:of this §crossed out and replaced above by§ our < > brand, *P1878:*brand   1219| MS:sinking fast §inserted above§ < > ashes! §colon altered to exclamation point§   1220| MS:That just §last two words crossed out§ as §altered to§ As sparks §altered to§ sparkles want but §replaced above by *only* and then restored§ fuels §last letter crossed out forming *fuel*§   1221| MS:Into such §crossed out and replaced above by§ a conflagration, which §comma and last word crossed out§ no mere §inserted above§   1222| MS:Will §over *Would*§ < > quickly,— §colon altered to comma and dash§ so < > strand— *P1878:*quickly, so < > strand,   1223| MS:Had §first two letters over illegible letters§ only §crossed out§ < > chowse— *P1878:*chowse,   1224| MS:Boasted *P1878:*Boast

CLIV

1225 Did earlier Agamemnons lack their bard?
　　　But later bards lacked Agamemnon too!
　　　How often frustrate they of fame's award
　　　Just because Fortune, as she listed, blew
　　　Some slight bark's sails to bellying, mauled and marred
1230 　　And forced to put about the First-rate! True,
　　　Such tacks but for a time: still—small-craft ride
　　　At anchor, rot while Beddoes breasts the tide!

CLV

　　　Dear, shall I tell you? There's a simple test
　　　Would serve, when people take on them to weigh
1235 The worth of poets, "Who was better, best,
　　　This, that, the other bard?" (bards none gainsay
　　　As good, observe! no matter for the rest)
　　　"What quality preponderating may
　　　Turn the scale as it trembles?" End the strife
1240 By asking "Which one led a happy life?"

1225| MS:"Did §quotation marks crossed out and word over illegible erasure§ earlier
Agamemnon lack §over illegible word§ <> bard?" §dash altered to question mark§ P1878:bard?
1226| MS:But §crossed out and replaced above by§ The later <> too, P1878:But later <>
too! 1227| MS:Frustrate §in margin§ How often §transposed and altered to§ How often
frustrate of the lucky breath debarred §last four words crossed out and replaced by two words§
fame's award P1878:frustrate they of 1228| MS:Which §crossed out and replaced
above by two words§ Just because Fortune, §dash altered to comma§ blowing §crossed out§
1229| MS:A §crossed out and replaced in margin by§ Some slight bark's §last two words
inserted above illegibly crossed out word§ 1230| MS:first-rate! §colon altered to
exclamation point§ true §altered to§ True, §comma over illegible punctuation mark§
P1878:the First-rate 1231| MS:Baffled §crossed out and replaced above by§ Tacking but
§first letter of last word over illegible letter§ <> time: still— §last word and dash inserted
above illegibly crossed out word§ cockles §crossed out and replaced above by two words§ small
craft P1878:Such tacks but <> small-craft 1232| MS:anchor, rot §inserted above§
while §next word illegibly crossed out, perhaps big§ 1234| MS:Would §in margin§ Serves
§altered to§ serve me §crossed out§ <> people make comparis §last word and partial word
crossed out and replaced above by four words§ take on them to 1235| MS:poets, §dash
erased and replaced by comma§ who §altered to§ Who <> best P1878:poets, "Who <> best,
1236| MS:bard,—(whom §crossed out and replaced above by§ bards P1878:bard?" (bards
1237| MS:observe!— §comma altered to exclamation point§ no <> rest)— §parenthesis over
exclamation point§ P1878:observe! no <> rest) 1238| MS:Which quality P1878:What
quality CP:"What §quotation marks in margin§ 1878:"What 1239| MS:trembles;
end P1878:trembles?" End 1240| MS:asking "Did he §last two words crossed out,
replaced above by who most had, and then restored§ lead P1878:asking "Which one led

CLVI

If one did, over his antagonist
    That yelled or shrieked or sobbed or wept or wailed
Or simply had the dumps,—dispute who list,—
    I count him victor. Where his fellow failed,
1245   Mastered by his own means of might,—acquist
    Of necessary sorrows,—he prevailed,
A strong since joyful man who stood distinct
Above slave-sorrows to his chariot linked.

CLVIII

Was not his lot to feel more? What meant "feel"
1250   Unless to suffer! Not, to see more? Sight—
What helped it but to watch the drunken reel
    Of vice and folly round him, left and right,
One dance of rogues and idiots! Not, to deal
    More with things lovely? What provoked the spite
1255   Of filth incarnate, like the poet's need
Of other nutriment than strife and greed!

1241| MS:If he did—over   *P1878:*If one did, over   1242| MS:Who §crossed out and
replaced above by§ That yelled, or shrieked, or sobbed, or wept, and §crossed out and
replaced above by§ or wailed,   *P1878:*yelled or shrieked or sobbed or wept or wailed
1244| MS:I place that poet §last three words crossed out and replaced above by three words§
count him victor: where   *P1878:*victor. Where   1245| MS:might,— §colon altered to
comma and dash§   1246| MS:he prevails, §altered to§ prevailed,   1247| MS:The
proud §last two words crossed out and replaced above by two words§ A strong and joyful man,
and stood   *P1878:*strong since joyful man who stood   1248| MS:Above slow §crossed out
and replaced above by word and hyphen§ slave-   1249| MS:his lot §over illegible erasure§
< > more?   What means—§word and dash inserted above illegibly crossed out word§ feel
*P1878:*meant "feel"   1250| MS:If not §last two words crossed out and replaced above by§
Unless < > suffer! §question mark altered to exclamation point§ Not to < > more?   Sight
§first letter of last word over illegible letter§   *P1878:*suffer! Not, to < > more?   Sight—
1251| MS:What helps §over illegible word, perhaps *is*§   *P1878:*helped   1252| MS:Of sin
§crossed out and replaced above by§ vice < > him, §colon altered to comma§ < > right
*P1878:*right,   1253| MS:of imps and idiots! Not to   *P1878:*idiots! Not, to   *1889a:*of
rogues and   1254| MS:provokes   *P1878:*provoked   1255| MS:Of ugliness §crossed
out and replaced above by§ filth < > the poet's §inserted above§   1256| MS:Of other §first
letter of last word over illegible letter§ < > greed! §question mark altered to exclamation point§

CLVIII

Who knows most, doubts most; entertaining hope,
　　Means recognizing fear; the keener sense
Of all comprised within our actual scope
1260　　Recoils from aught beyond earth's dim and dense.
Who, grown familiar with the sky, will grope
　　Henceforward among groundlings? That's offence
Just as indubitably: stars abound
O'erhead, but then—what flowers make glad the ground!

CLIX

1265　So, force is sorrow, and each sorrow, force:
　　What then? since Swiftness gives the charioteer
The palm, his hope be in the vivid horse,
　　Whose neck God clothed with thunder, not the steer
Sluggish and safe! Yoke Hatred, Crime, Remorse,
1270　　Despair: but ever mid the whirling fear,
Let, through the tumult, break the poet's face
Radiant, assured his wild slaves win the race!

1258| MS:Is §crossed out and replaced above by§ Means　　1259| MS:scope,　*P1878:*scope
1260| MS:Hinders our flight §last three words crossed out and replaced above by three words§ Recoils from aught beyond the §crossed out and replaced above by§ earth's <> dense; *P1878:*dense　　1262| MS:Henceforward with §crossed out and replaced by§ among
1264| MS:Overhead §altered to§ O'erhead, but then— §word and dash inserted above§
1265| MS:Well, force <> sorrow then §crossed out§ , and each §inserted above§ sorrow force—　*P1878:*So, force <> each sorrow, force: §comma altered to question mark§ 'tis §crossed out and replaced above by§ since swiftness wins §crossed out and replaced above by§ plucks the　*P1878:*since Swiftness gives the　　1267| MS:His §crossed out and replaced above by§ The palm, §letter at the end of the word illegibly crossed out; comma crossed out and replaced below by dash§ awards §crossed out§ his hope §inserted above illegibly crossed out word, perhaps *yokes*§ be §inserted above illegibly crossed out word§ <> the vivid §inserted above§ horse,　*P1878:*palm, his <> horse　　1268| MS:thunder— not　*P1878:*thunder, not　　1269| MS:safe! §colon altered to exclamation point§ yoke §altered to§ Yoke hatred §altered to§ Hatred, crime §altered to§ Crime, remorse §altered to§ Remorse　*P1878:*safe! Yoke Hatred, Crime, Remorse,　　1270| MS:Despair, but　*P1878:*Despair: but　　1271| MS:the smother §crossed out and replaced above by§ storm-cloud §crossed out and replaced below by§ tumult, break on me a face　*P1878:*break the poet's face　　1272| MS:assured it wild　*P1878:*assured his wild

CLX

Therefore I say . . . no, shall not say, but think,
    And save my breath for better purpose. White
1275 From grey our log has burned to: just one blink
    That quivers, loth to leave it, as a sprite
    The outworn body. Ere your eyelids' wink
    Punish who sealed so deep into the night
Your mouth up, for two poets dead so long,—
1280 Here pleads a live pretender: right your wrong!

I

What a pretty tale you told me
    Once upon a time
—Said you found it somewhere (scold me!)
    Was it prose or was it rhyme,
5 Greek or Latin? Greek, you said,
While your shoulder propped my head.

1273| MS:So shall §last two words crossed out and replaced above by§ Therefore <> say . . no
<> not say, but §over illegible word§ think §first three letters over illegible erasure§
*P1878:*say . . . no <> think,   1274| MS:And §over *Out*§ save §over illegible word§
1275| MS:grey the §crossed out and replaced above by§ our <> has got §crossed out and
replaced above by§ burned to—just *P1878:*to: just   1276| MS:That §first two letters
over illegible letters§ quivers §next word illegibly crossed out§   1277| MS:body. §colon
altered to period§ Ere §first letter over illegible letter§ your §over illegible word§ <> wink,
§comma crossed out§   1278| MS:Convict me, that so §last two words crossed out and
replaced above by§ sealing deep *P1878:*Punish who sealed so deep   1279| MS:I
§crossed out§ tired §crossed out and replaced above by§ sealed §crossed out§ you §altered to§
Your with §crossed out and replaced above by§ mouth up,—for <> long— *P1878:*up, for
<> long,—   1280|. MS:Here is a live one opes it: §last two words and colon inserted
above illegibly crossed out word§ right *P1878:*Here pleads a live pretender: right
MS:§two spaces below last line and to the right§ (L. D. I. E. Begun Saturday Nov. 10. ended
Dec. 8. '77. RB)

WHAT A PRETTY TALE YOU TOLD ME   *Titl*e| MS:Eunomos of Locri §last three words
crossed out§   1| MS:a funny §crossed out and replaced above by§ pretty
4| MS:rhyme *P1878:*rhyme,

II

Anyhow there's no forgetting
    This much if no more,
That a poet (pray, no petting!)
    Yes, a bard, sir, famed of yore,
Went where suchlike used to go,
Singing for a prize, you know.

III

Well, he had to sing, nor merely
    Sing but play the lyre;
Playing was important clearly
    Quite as singing: I desire,
Sir, you keep the fact in mind
For a purpose that's behind.

IV

There stood he, while deep attention
    Held the judges round,
—Judges able, I should mention,
    To detect the slightest sound
Sung or played amiss: such cars
Had old judges, it appears!

V

None the less he sang out boldly,
    Played in time and tune,
Till the judges, weighing coldly
    Each note's worth, seemed, late or soon,

---

⁷| MS:Anyhow I'm scarce §last two words crossed out and replaced above by two words§ there's no   ¹⁰| MS:a famous §crossed out§ bard, sir, famed §last two words inserted above§   ¹¹| MS:such like *P1878:*suchlike   ¹⁴| MS:lyre: *P1878:*lyre;   ¹⁶| MS:as singing §second and third letters of last word over illegible erasure§ < > desire *P1878:*desire,   ¹⁷| MS:That §in margin§ You, Sir, §comma, last word, and comma crossed out§ *P1878:*Sir, you   ²⁸| MS:worth were §crossed out and replaced above by§ seemed *P1878:*worth, seemed

Sure to smile "In vain one tries
30   Picking faults out: take the prize!

VI

When, a mischief! Were they seven
          Strings the lyre possessed?
Oh, and afterwards eleven,
          Thank you! Well, sir,—who had guessed
35   Such ill luck in store?—it happed
One of those same seven strings snapped.

VII

All was lost, then! No! a cricket
          (What "cicada"? Pooh!)
—Some mad thing that left its thicket
40   For mere love of music—flew
With its little heart on fire,
Lighted on the crippled lyre.

VIII

So that when (ah joy!) our singer
          For his truant string
45   Feels with disconcerted finger,
          What does cricket else but fling
Fiery heart forth, sound the note
Wanted by the throbbing throat?

IX

Ay and, ever to the ending,
50   Cricket chirps at need,
Executes the hand's intending,
          Promptly, perfectly,—indeed

30| MS:Picking §first four letters over illegible erasure§ <> prize!   *P1878*:prize!"
34| MS:you! Well, Sir   *P1878*:sir   36| MS:same seven §crossed out§
40| MS:music, flew   *P1878*:music-flew   43| MS:when (Ah, joy   *P1878*:when (Ah joy
1889a:ah   49| MS:Ay, and <> ending   *P1878*:Ay and <> ending,
51| MS:Executes §last letter over illegible letter§

Saves the singer from defeat
With her chirrup low and sweet.

X

⁵⁵ Till, at ending, all the judges
    Cry with one assent
"Take the prize—a prize who grudges
    Such a voice and instrument?
Why, we took your lyre for harp,
⁶⁰ So it shrilled us forth F sharp!"

XI

Did the conqueror spurn the creature,
    Once its service done?
That's no such uncommon feature
    In the case when Music's son
⁶⁵ Finds his Lotte's power too spent
For aiding soul-development.

XII

No! This other, on returning
    Homeward, prize in hand,
Satisfied his bosom's yearning:
⁷⁰   (Sir, I hope you understand!)
—Said "Some record there must be
Of this cricket's help to me!"

XIII

So, he made himself a statue:
    Marble stood, life-size;
⁷⁵ On the lyre, he pointed at you
    Perched his partner in the prize;

---

^{53|} MS:defeat, C*P1878:*defeat, §comma crossed out§ *1878:*defeat   ^{56|} MS:Cried §altered to§ Cry   ^{58|} MS:instrument *P1878:*instrument?   ^{59|} MS:—Why *P1878:*Why   ^{60|} MS:So §over illegible word§   ^{61|} MS:conqueror crush §crossed out and replaced above by§ spurn <> creature *P1878:*creature,   ^{73|} MS:statue, *P1878:*statue: ^{75|} MS:lyre he <> you *P1878:*lyre, he <> you, *1889a:*you

Never more apart you found
Her, he throned, from him, she crowned.

XIV

That's the tale: its application?
80   Somebody I know
Hopes one day for reputation
    Through his poetry that's—Oh,
All so learned and so wise
And deserving of a prize!

XV

85 If he gains one, will some ticket,
    When his statue's built,
Tell the gazer "'T was a cricket
    Helped my crippled lyre, whose lilt
Sweet and low, when strength usurped
90 Softness' place i' the scale, she chirped?

XVI

"For as victory was nighest,
    While I sang and played,—
With my lyre at lowest, highest,
    Right alike,—one string that made
95 'Love' sound soft was snapt in twain,
Never to be heard again,—

XVII

"Had not a kind cricket fluttered,
    Perched upon the place

81| MS:Seeks §crossed out and replaced above by§ Hopes <> day some §crossed out and replaced above by§ for   83| MS:so rational §crossed out and replaced above by§ learned and so §inserted above§   84| MS:And deserving §crossed out and replaced above by two words§ so certain of   *P1878:*And deserving of   85| MS:ticket;   *P1878:*ticket,   87| MS:Teach §crossed out and replaced above by§ Tell   92| MS:played   *P1878:*played–   *CP1878:*played,— §comma inserted§   *1878:*played,—   94| MS:alike, one   *P1878:*alike,—one   95| MS:"Love" sound   *P1878:*'Love' sound   97| MS:Had   *P1878:*"Had   98| MS:Perching §last three letters crossed out and

Vacant left, and duly uttered
100   'Love, Love, Love,' whene'er the bass
Asked the treble to atone
For its somewhat sombre drone."

XVIII

But you don't know music! Wherefore
    Keep on casting pearls
105 To a—poet? All I care for
    Is—to tell him that a girl's
"Love" comes aptly in when gruff
Grows his singing. (There, enough!)

---

replaced above by *ed*§ < > the §followed by illegibly crossed out letter§   100| MS:"Love,
Love, Love" whene'er   *P1878:*'Love, Love, Love,' whene'er   102| MS:drone.
*P1878:*drone."   105| MS:To—my §crossed out and replaced above by§ a §transposed to§
To a—   106| MS:tell you §crossed out and replaced above by§ him
108| MS:Grows the §crossed out and replaced above by§ his   MS:§in right margin below
last line of verse§ L. D. I. E. Jan. 15. '78.   *P1878:*§below and flush left§ January 15, 1878.

DRAMATIC IDYLS, FIRST SERIES

Edited by David Ewbank

DRAMATIC IDYLS, FIRST SERIES

DRAMATIC IDYLS, FIRST SERIES

1879

MARTIN RELPH

My grandfather says he remembers he saw, when a youngster long ago,
On a bright May day, a strange old man, with a beard as white as snow,
Stand on the hill outside our town like a monument of woe,
And, striking his bare bald head the while, sob out the reason—so!

5   If I last as long as Methuselah I shall never forgive myself:
But—God forgive me, that I pray, unhappy Martin Relph,
As coward, coward I call him—him, yes, him! Away from me!
Get you behind the man I am now, you man that I used to be!

What can have sewed my mouth up, set me a-stare, all eyes, no
    tongue?
10   People have urged "You visit a scare too hard on a lad so young!
You were taken aback, poor boy," they urge, "no time to regain your
    wits:
Besides it had maybe cost you life." Ay, there is the cap which fits!

So, cap me, the coward,—thus! No fear! A cuff on the brow does good:
The feel of it hinders a worm inside which bores at the brain for food.
15   See now, there certainly seems excuse: for a moment, I trust, dear
    friends,
The fault was but folly, no fault of mine, or if mine, I have made
    amends!

For, every day that is first of May, on the hill-top, here stand I,
Martin Relph, and I strike my brow, and publish the reason why,

DRAMATIC IDYLS, FIRST SERIES §MS in Balliol College Library. Ed. 1879, 1882, 1889a. See
Editorial Notes§
MARTIN RELPH   ¹⁻⁴| MS:§italics called for in margin§
³| MS:town, like   *1879:* town like   ¹⁰| MS:a scare §last two words inserted above§

When there gathers a crowd to mock the fool. No fool, friends, since
    the bite
20 Of a worm inside is worse to bear: pray God I have baulked him quite!

I'll tell you. Certainly much excuse! It came of the way they cooped
Us peasantry up in a ring just here, close huddling because tight-hooped
By the red-coats round us villagers all: they meant we should see the
    sight
And take the example,—see, not speak, for speech was the Captain's
    right.

25 "You clowns on the slope, beware!" cried he: "This woman about to die
Gives by her fate fair warning to such acquaintance as play the spy.
Henceforth who meddle with matters of state above them perhaps will
    learn
That peasants should stick to their plough-tail, leave to the King the
    King's concern.

"Here's a quarrel that sets the land on fire, between King George and
    his foes:
30 What call has a man of your kind—much less, a woman—to interpose?
Yet you needs must be meddling, folk like you, not foes—so much the
    worse!
The many and loyal should keep themselves unmixed with the few
    perverse.

"Is the counsel hard to follow? I gave it you plainly a month ago,
And where was the good? The rebels have learned just all that they
    need to know.
35 Not a month since in we quietly marched: a week, and they had the
    news,
From a list complete of our rank and file to a note of our caps and
    shoes.

"All about all we did and all we were doing and like to do!
Only, I catch a letter by luck, and capture who wrote it, too.
Some of you men look black enough, but the milk-white face demure
40 Betokens the finger foul with ink: 'tis a woman who writes, be sure!

"Is it 'Dearie, how much I miss your mouth!'—good natural stuff, she
    pens?
Some sprinkle of that, for a blind, of course: with talk about cocks and
    hens,
How 'robin, has built on the apple-tree, and our creeper which came
    to grief
Through the frost, we feared, is twining afresh round casement in
    famous leaf.'

45   "But all for a blind! She soon glides frank into 'Horrid the place is
    grown
With Officers here and Privates there, no nook we may call our own:
And Farmer Giles has a tribe to house, and lodging will be to seek
For the second Company sure to come ('tis whispered) on Monday
    week.'

"And so to the end of the chapter! There! The murder, you see, was
    out:
50   Easy to guess how the change of mind in the rebels was brought
    about!
Safe in the trap would they now lie snug, had treachery made no sign:
But treachery meets a just reward, no matter if fools malign!

"That traitors had played us false, was proved—sent news which fell so
    pat:
And the murder was out—this letter of love, the sender of this sent
    that!
55   'Tis an ugly job, though, all the same—a hateful, to have to deal
With a case of the kind, when a woman's in fault: we soldiers need
    nerves of steel!

"So, I gave her a chance, despatched post-haste a message to Vincent
    Parkes
Whom she wrote to; easy to find he was, since one of the King's own
    clerks,

41| MS:mouth!"—good   *1879:*mouth!"—good   45| MS:But   *1879:*"But
49| MS:And   *1879:*"And   53| MS:That   *1879:*"That   57| MS:So   *1879:*"So

Ay, kept by the King's own gold in the town close by where the rebels
    camp:
60 A sort of a lawyer, just the man to betray our sort—the scamp!

"'If her writing is simple and honest and only the loverlike stuff it
    looks,
And if you yourself are a loyalist, nor down in the rebels' books,
Come quick,' said I, 'and in person prove you are each of you clear of
    crime,
Or martial law must take its course: this day next week's the time!'

65 "Next week is now: does he come? Not he! Clean gone, our clerk, in a
    trice!
He has left his sweetheart here in the lurch: no need of a warning
    twice!
His own neck free, but his partner's fast in the noose still, here she
    stands
To pay for her fault. 'Tis an ugly job: but soldiers obey commands.

"And hearken wherefore I make a speech! Should any acquaintance
    share
70 The folly that led to the fault that is now to be punished, let fools
    beware!
Look black, if you please, but keep hands white: and, above all else,
    keep wives—
Or sweethearts or what they may be—from ink! Not a word now, on
    your lives!"

Black? but the Pit's own pitch was white to the Captain's face—the
    brute
With the bloated cheeks and the bulgy nose and the bloodshot eyes to
    suit!
75 He was muddled with wine, they say: more like, he was out of his wits
    with fear;
He had but a handful of men, that's true,—a riot might cost him dear.

61| MS:looks.,   *1879:*looks,   69| MS:harken   *1879:*hearken   71| MS:wives
*1879:*wives—   72| MS:—Or *1879:*Or   74| MS:blood-shot *1889a:*bloodshot

And all that time stood Rosamund Page, with pinioned arms and face
Bandaged about, on the turf marked out for the party's firing-place.
I hope she was wholly with God: I hope 'twas His angel stretched a
hand
80 To steady her so, like the shape of stone you see in our church-aisle
stand.

I hope there was no vain fancy pierced the bandage to vex her eyes,
No face within which she missed without, no questions and no
replies—
"Why did you leave me to die?"—"Because . . ." Oh, fiends, too soon
you grin
At merely a moment of hell, like that—such heaven as hell ended in!

85 Let mine end too! He gave the word, up went the guns in a line.
Those heaped on the hill were blind as dumb,—for, of all eyes, only
mine
Looked over the heads of the foremost rank. Some fell on their knees
in prayer,
Some sank to the earth, but all shut eyes, with a sole exception there.

That was myself, who had stolen up last, had sidled behind the group:
90 I am highest of all on the hill-top, there stand fixed while the others
stoop!
From head to foot in a serpent's twine am I tightened: *I* touch ground?
No more than a gibbet's rigid corpse which the fetters rust around!

Can I speak, can I breathe, can I burst—aught else but see, see, only
see?
And see I do—for there comes in sight—a man, it sure must be!—
95 Who staggeringly, stumblingly rises, falls, rises, at random flings his
weight
On and on, anyhow onward—a man that's mad he arrives too late!

83| MS:"How could §last two words crossed out and replaced above by two words§ Why did
85| MS:line: *1882:*line. 90| *1882:*stoop *1889a:*stoop! 92| MS:gibbet's
fettered §crossed out and replaced above by§ rigid 94| MS:do: §altered to§ do—for

Else why does he wave a something white high-flourished above his
    head?
Why does not he call, cry,—curse the fool!—why throw up his arms
    instead?
O take this fist in your own face, fool! Why does not yourself shout
    "Stay!
100   Here's a man comes rushing, might and main, with something he's
    mad to say"?

And a minute, only a moment, to have hell-fire boil up in your brain,
And ere you can judge things right, choose heaven,—time's over,
    repentance vain!
They level: a volley, a smoke and the clearing of smoke: I see no more
Of the man smoke hid, nor his frantic arms, nor the something white
    he bore.

105   But stretched on the field, some half-mile off, is an object. Surely
    dumb,
Deaf, blind were we struck, that nobody heard, not one of us saw him
    come!
Has he fainted through fright? One may well believe! What is it he
    holds so fast?
Turn him over, examine the face! Heyday! What, Vincent Parkes at
    last?

Dead! dead as she, by the self-same shot: one bullet has ended both,
110   Her in the body and him in the soul. They laugh at our plighted
    troth.
"Till death us do part?" Till death us do join past parting—that
    sounds like
Betrothal indeed! O Vincent Parkes, what need has my fist to strike?

I helped you: thus were you dead and wed: one bound, and your soul
    reached hers!

---

¹⁰⁰| *1879:*say?"   *1889a:*say"?   ¹⁰⁵| MS:dumb   *1879:*dumb,
¹⁰⁷| *1882:*fright One < > fast   *1889a:*fright? One < > fast?
¹¹¹| MS:"'Till death us do part?" 'Till   *1879:*"Till death us do part?" Till

There is clenched in your hand the thing, signed, sealed, the paper
    which plain avers

115 She is innocent, innocent, plain as print, with the King's Arms broad
    engraved:

No one can hear, but if anyone high on the hill can see, she's saved!

And torn his garb and bloody his lips with heart-break—plain it grew

How the week's delay had been brought about: each guess at the end
    proved true.

It was hard to get at the folk in power: such waste of time! and then

120 Such pleading and praying, with, all the while, his lamb in the lions'
    den!

And at length when he wrung their pardon out, no end to the stupid
    forms—

The licence and leave: I make no doubt—what wonder if passion
    warms

The pulse in a man if you play with his heart?—he was something
    hasty in speech;

Anyhow, none would quicken the work: he had to beseech, beseech!

125 And the thing once signed, sealed, safe in his grasp,—what followed
    but fresh delays?

For the floods were out, he was forced to take such a roundabout of
    ways!

And 'twas "Halt there!" at every turn of the road, since he had to cross
    the thick

Of the red-coats: what did they care for him and his "Quick, for God's
    sake, quick!"

Horse? but he had one: had it how long? till the first knave smirked
    "You brag

130 Yourself a friend of the King's? then lend to a King's friend here your
    nag!"

117| MS:bloody his mouth §crossed out and replaced above by§ lips
119| MS:folks   *1889a:*folk   120| MS:lion's   *1889a:*lions'
130| MS:to a King's-friend   *1879:*to a King's friend

Money to buy another? Why, piece by piece they plundered him still,
With their "Wait you must,—no help: if aught can help you, a guinea
    will!"

And a borough there was—I forget the name—whose Mayor must
    have the bench
Of Justices ranged to clear a doubt: for "Vincent," thinks he, sounds
    French!
135   It well may have driven him daft, God knows! all man can certainly
    know
Is—rushing and falling and rising, at last he arrived in a horror—so!

When a word, cry, gasp, would have rescued both! Ay bite me! The
    worm begins
At his work once more. Had cowardice proved—that only—my sin of
    sins!
Friends, look you here! Suppose . . . suppose . . . But mad I am, needs
    must be!
140   Judas the Damned would never have dared such a sin as I dream! For,
    see!

Suppose I had sneakingly loved her myself, my wretched self, and
    dreamed
In the heart of me "She were better dead than happy and his!"—while
    gleamed
A light from hell as I spied the pair in a perfectest embrace,
He the saviour and she the saved,—bliss born of the very
    murder-place!

145   No! Say I was scared, friends! Call me fool and coward, but nothing
    worse!
Jeer at the fool and gibe at the coward! 'Twas ever the coward's curse
That fear breeds fancies in such: such take their shadow for substance
    still,
—A fiend at their back. I liked poor Parkes,—loved Vincent, if you
    will!

131| MS:still   *1889a:*still,   137| MS:gasp would   *1879:*gasp, would   139| MS:here!
suppose . . suppose . . But   *1879:*here! suppose . . . suppose . . . But

And her—why, I said "Good morrow" to her, "Good even," and
nothing more:
150 The neighbourly way! She was just to me as fifty had been before.
So, coward it is and coward shall be! There's a friend, now! Thanks! A
drink
Of water I wanted: and now I can walk, get home by myself, I think.

PHEIDIPPIDES

Χαίρετε, νικῶμεν

First I salute this soil of the blessed, river and rock!
Gods of my birthplace, dæmons and heroes, honour to all!
Then I name thee, claim thee for our patron, co-equal in praise
—Ay, with Zeus the Defender, with Her of the ægis and spear!
5   Also, ye of the bow and the buskin, praised be your peer,
Now, henceforth and forever,—O latest to whom I upraise
Hand and heart and voice! For Athens, leave pasture and flock!
Present to help, potent to save, Pan—patron I call!

Archons of Athens, topped by the tettix, see, I return!
10   See, 'tis myself here standing alive, no spectre that speaks!
Crowned with the myrtle, did you command me, Athens and you,
"Run, Pheidippides, run and race, reach Sparta for aid!
Persia has come, we are here, where is She?" Your command I obeyed,
Ran and raced: like stubble, some field which a fire runs through,
15   Was the space between city and city: two days, two nights did I burn
Over the hills, under the dales, down pits and up peaks.

Into their midst I broke: breath served but for "Persia has come!
Persia bids Athens proffer slaves'-tribute, water and earth;
Razed to the ground is Eretria—but Athens, shall Athens sink,
20   Drop into dust and die—the flower of Hellas utterly die,
Die, with the wide world spitting at Sparta, the stupid, the stander-by?
Answer me quick, what help, what hand do you stretch o'er
    destruction's brink?
How,—when? No care for my limbs!—there's lightning in all and
    some,—

PHEIDIPPIDES   ²| MS:honor   *1879:*demons   *1889a:*dæmons <> honour
⁶| MS:whom we §crossed out and replaced above by§ I   ¹⁴| MS:fire goes §crossed out
and replaced above by§ runs   ¹⁸| MS:bids Athens pay her §last two words crossed out
and replaced above by§ proffer   ²¹| MS:Die, leave §crossed out and replaced above by§
with   ²³| MS:How, and §crossed out and replaced above by dash§ —when? o care for
§last three words inserted above§ My <> and in §crossed out§   *1879:*my

Fresh and fit your message to bear, once lips give it birth!"

25 O my Athens—Sparta love thee? Did Sparta respond?
Every face of her leered in a furrow of envy, mistrust,
Malice,—each eye of her gave me its glitter of gratified hate!
Gravely they turned to take counsel, to cast for excuses. I stood
Quivering,—the limbs of me fretting as fire frets, an inch from dry
    wood:
30 "Persia has come, Athens asks aid, and still they debate?
Thunder, thou Zeus! Athene, are Spartans a quarry beyond
Swing of thy spear? Phoibos and Artemis, clang them 'Ye must'!"

No bolt launched from Olumpos! Lo, their answer at last!
"Has Persia come,—does Athens ask aid,—may Sparta befriend?
35 Nowise precipitate judgment—too weighty the issue at stake!
Count we no time lost time which lags through respect to the Gods!
Ponder that precept of old, 'No warfare, whatever the odds
In your favour, so long as the moon, half-orbed, is unable to take
Full-circle her state in the sky!' Already she rounds to it fast:
40 Athens must wait, patient as we—who judgment suspend."

Athens,—except for that sparkle,—thy name, I had mouldered to ash!
That sent a blaze through my blood; off, off and away was I back,
—Not one word to waste, one look to lose on the false and the vile!
Yet "O Gods of my land!" I cried, as each hillock and plain,
45 Wood and stream, I knew, I named, rushing past them again,
"Have ye kept faith, proved mindful of honours we paid you erewhile?

24| MS:bear when §crossed out and replaced above by§ once   27| MS:of her §last two words inserted above§   28| MS:excuses: I *1879:*excuses. I   34| MS:come,—asks §crossed out and replaced above by§ does <> for §crossed out and replaced above by§ ask <> shall §crossed out and replaced above by§ may   37| MS:old, Ware fighting §last two words crossed out and replaced above by quotation mark and two words§ 'No warfare <> seem §crossed out and replaced above by§ the   40| MS:must needs be §last two words crossed out and replaced above by one word and comma§ wait, <> answer §crossed out and replaced above by§ promise §crossed out and replaced below by§ judgment
41| MS:that §last two letters crossed out and replaced above by an illegible letter, crossed out and original reading restored§ <> from §crossed out and replaced above by comma and dash§ ,—thy <> smouldered §first letter crossed out§   42| MS:blood; and §crossed out and replaced above by one word and comma§ off,   43| MS:false and the §last three words inserted above§   44| MS:land," I <> each §inserted above§ *1879:*land!" I
45| MS:knew and I §crossed out§ *1879:*knew, I   46| MS:honors *1889a:*honours

Vain was the filleted victim, the fulsome libation! Too rash
Love in its choice, paid you so largely service so slack!

"Oak and olive and bay,—I bid you cease to enwreathe
50 Brows made bold by your leaf! Fade at the Persian's foot,
You that, our patrons were pledged, should never adorn a slave!
Rather I hail thee, Parnes,—trust to thy wild waste tract!
Treeless, herbless, lifeless mountain! What matter if slacked
My speed may hardly be, for homage to crag and to cave
55 No deity deigns to drape with verdure? at least I can breathe,
Fear in thee no fraud from the blind, no lie from the mute!"

Such my cry as, rapid, I ran over Parnes' ridge;
Gully and gap I clambered and cleared till, sudden, a bar
Jutted, a stoppage of stone against me, blocking the way.
60 Right! for I minded the hollow to traverse, the fissure across:
"Where I could enter, there I depart by! Night in the fosse?
[Athens to aid? Though the dive were through Erebos, thus I obey—]
Out of the day dive, into the day as bravely arise! No bridge
Better!"—when—ha! what was it I came on, of wonders that are?

65 There, in the cool of a cleft, sat he—majestical Pan!
Ivy drooped wanton, kissed his head, moss cushioned his hoof:
All the great God was good in the eyes grave-kindly—the curl
Carved on the bearded cheek, amused at a mortal's awe,

48| MS:dearly §first four letters crossed out and replaced above by five letters§ large
50| MS:leafage §last three letters crossed out§   51| MS:that our <> pledged should
*1879:*that, our <> pledged, should   52| MS:thee, wild waste §last two words crossed
out§ <> to §inserted above§   thy wild waste §last two words inserted above§
53| MS:mountain §last three letters added below§   54| MS:be for <> and to §inserted
above§   *1879:*be, for   55| MS:verdure,—at <> can §inserted above§   *1889a:*verdure?
at   56| MS:Fearing §last three letters crossed out§   57| MS:as rapid I   *1879:*as,
rapid, I   58| MS:gap, I   *1889a:*gap I   61| MS:there I §crossed out§   *1879:*there I
61-63| *1889a:*fosse? / Out §emended to§ fosse? / Athens to aid? though the dive were through
Erebos, thus I obey— / Out §see Editorial Notes§   63| MS:into the day arise! Bravely!
§altered to§ bravely! §word circled and transposed to§ bravely arise!! No   *1879:*into the day
as bravely arise! No   64| MS:when what came §crossed out and replaced above by two
words§ was it I right out §last two words crossed out and replaced above by§ came
*1879:*when—ha! what   66| MS:kissing §altered to§ kissed   67| MS:was grand
§crossed out and replaced above by§ good   68| MS:Carved upon bearded §inserted
above§ cheek and mouth amused   *1879:*Carved on the bearded cheek, amused

As, under the human trunk, the goat-thighs grand I saw.
70 "Halt, Pheidippides!"—halt I did, my brain of a whirl:
"Hither to me! Why pale in my presence?" he gracious began:
"How is it,—Athens, only in Hellas, holds me aloof?

"Athens, she only, rears me no fane, makes me no feast!
Wherefore? Than I what godship to Athens more helpful of old?
75 Ay, and still, and forever her friend! Test Pan, trust me!
Go, bid Athens take heart, laugh Persia to scorn, have faith
In the temples and tombs! Go, say to Athens, 'The Goat-God saith:
When Persia—so much as strews not the soil—is cast in the sea,
Then praise Pan who fought in the ranks with your most and least,
80 Goat-thigh to greaved-thigh, made one cause with the free and the
    bold!'

"Say Pan saith: 'Let this, foreshowing the place, be the pledge!'"
(Gay, the liberal hand held out this herbage I bear
—Fennel—I grasped it a-tremble with dew—whatever it bode)
"While, as for thee . . . " But enough! He was gone. If I ran hitherto—
85 Be sure that, the rest of my journey, I ran no longer, but flew.
Parnes to Athens—earth no more, the air was my road:
Here am I back. Praise Pan, we stand no more on the razor's edge!
Pan for Athens, Pan for me! I too have a guerdon rare!

---

⁶⁹| MS:As under <> trunk the <> huge §crossed out and replaced above by§ grand
*1879:*As, under <> trunk, the   ⁷¹| MS:began, *1879:*began: ⁷²| MS:"Why
§crossed out and replaced above by§ How is it, Athens *1879:*it,—Athens
⁷⁵| MS:friend! Put Pan to the test! *1882:*friend! Test Pan, trust me!   ⁷⁷| MS:say that
§crossed out and replaced above by§ this §crossed out§ to Athens — §last two words and dash
inserted above§ the <> saith— *1879:*to Athens, 'The <> saith: ⁷⁸| MS:'When <>
plain §crossed out and replaced above by§ soil <> sea *1879:*When <> sea,
⁷⁹| MS:and your §crossed out§   ⁸¹| MS:saith 'Let *1879:*saith: 'Let   ⁸²| MS:(Gay,
out held the <> hand this herb that I §marked for rearrangement to§ (Gay, the <> hand
held out this *1879:*this herbage I   ⁸³| MS:—Fennel, whatever it bode—which §crossed
out§ I grasped it §inserted above§ a-tremble with dew) *1882:*—Fennel—I <> dew—
whatever it bode)   ⁸⁴| MS:"And §word crossed out and replaced above by§ While
⁸⁵| MS:that the <> journey I *1879:*that, the <> journey, I   ⁸⁵⁻⁸⁷| MS:flew. / Here
*1882:*flew. / Parnes to Athens—earth no more, the air was my road: / Here
⁸⁸| MS:me—myself have a guerdon too! *1879:*me! myself *1882:*me! I too have <> rare!

Then spoke Miltiades. "And thee, best runner of Greece,
90 Whose limbs did duty indeed,—what gift is promised thyself?
Tell it us straightway,—Athens the mother demands of her son!"
Rosily blushed the youth: he paused: but, lifting at length
His eyes from the ground, it seemed as he gathered the rest of his
    strength
Into the utterance—"Pan spoke thus: 'For what thou hast done
95 Count on a worthy reward ! Henceforth be allowed thee release
From the racer's toil, no vulgar reward in praise or in pelf!'

"I am bold to believe, Pan means reward the most to my mind!
Fight I shall, with our foremost, wherever this fennel may grow,—
Pound—Pan helping us—Persia to dust, and, under the deep,
100 Whelm her away for ever; and then,—no Athens to save,—
Marry a certain maid, I know keeps faith to the brave,—
Hie to my house and home: and, when my children shall creep
Close to my knees,—recount how the God was awful yet kind,
Promised their sire reward to the full—rewarding him—so!"

105 Unforeseeing one! Yes, he fought on the Marathon day:
So, when Persia was dust, all cried "To Akropolis!
Run, Pheidippides, one race more! the meed is thy due!
'Athens is saved, thank Pan,' go shout!" He flung down his shield,
Ran like fire once more: and the space 'twixt the Fennel-field
110 And Athens was stubble again, a field which a fire runs through,
Till in he broke: "Rejoice, we conquer!" Like wine through clay,
Joy in his blood bursting his heart, he died—the bliss!
So, to this day, when friend meets friend, the word of salute
Is still "Rejoice!"—his word which brought rejoicing indeed.

89| MS:thee, prime §crossed out and replaced above by§ best   93| MS:gathered the
whole §crossed out and replaced above by§ rest   94| MS:utterance "Pan
*1879:*utterance—"Pan   95| MS:be conceded §crossed out and replaced above by two
words§ allowed thee   97| MS:means the payment §last two words crossed out and
replaced above by§ reward   102| MS:when my boys §crossed out and replaced above by§
children   103| MS:repeat §last four letters crossed out and replaced above by five
letters§ count < > grand §crossed out and replaced above by§ awful yet kind *1879:*kind,
104| MS:their father §crossed out and replaced above by§ sire < > his mind §last two words
crossed out and replaced by two words§ the full   114| MS:indeed! *1879:*indeed.

115 So is Pheidippides happy for ever,—the noble strong man
   Who could race like a God, bear the face of a God, whom a God loved
       so well;
   He saw the land saved he had helped to save, and was suffered to tell
   Such tidings, yet never decline, but, gloriously as he began,
   So to end gloriously—once to shout, thereafter be mute:
120 "Athens is saved!"—Pheidippides dies in the shout for his meed.

115| MS:forever   *1879:*for ever   118| MS:tidings yet <> decline but gloriously <>
began   *1879:*tidings, yet <> decline, but, gloriously <> began,   119| MS:mute,   *1879:*
mute: 120| MS:saved"—Pheidippides   *1879:*saved!"—Pheidippides

HALBERT AND HOB

Here is a thing that happened. Like wild beasts whelped, for den,
In a wild part of North England, there lived once two wild men
Inhabiting one homestead, neither a hovel nor hut,
Time out of mind their birthright: father and son, these—but—
⁵ Such a son, such a father! Most wildness by degrees
Softens away: yet, last of their line, the wildest and worst were these.

Criminals, then? Why, no: they did not murder and rob;
But, give them a word, they returned a blow—old Halbert as young
    Hob:
Harsh and fierce of word, rough and savage of deed,
¹⁰ Hated or feared the more—who knows?—the genuine wild-beast
    breed.

Thus were they found by the few sparse folk of the country-side;
But how fared each with other? E'en beasts couch, hide by hide,
In a growling, grudged agreement: so, father and son lay curled
The closelier up in their den because the last of their kind in the
    world.

¹⁵ Still, beast irks beast on occasion. One Christmas night of snow,
Came father and son to words—such words! more cruel because the
    blow
To crown each word was wanting, while taunt matched gibe, and curse
Competed with oath in wager, like pastime in hell,—nay, worse:
For pastime turned to earnest, as up there sprang at last
²⁰ The son at the throat of the father, seized him and held him fast.

"Out of this house you go!"—(there followed a hideous oath)—
"This oven where now we bake, too hot to hold us both!
If there's snow outside, there's coolness: out with you, bide a spell

---

HALBERT AND HOB   ²| MS:north *1879:*of North
⁷| MS:murder or rob; *1879:*murder and rob;   ¹³| MS:son lay curled *1882:*son ay
curled *1889a:*son aye curled §emended to§ son lay curled §see Editorial Notes§
¹⁴| MS:closier *1879:*closelier   ²²| MS:were *1879:*where

In the drift and save the sexton the charge of a parish shell!"

25 Now, the old trunk was tough, was solid as stump of oak
Untouched at the core by a thousand years: much less had its seventy
broke
One whipcord nerve in the muscly mass from neck to shoulder-blade
Of the mountainous man, whereon his child's rash hand like a feather
weighed.

Nevertheless at once did the mammoth shut his eyes,
30 Drop chin to breast, drop hands to sides, stand stiffened—arms and
thighs
All of a piece—struck mute, much as a sentry stands,
Patient to take the enemy's fire: his captain so commands.

Whereat the son's wrath flew to fury at such sheer scorn
Of his puny strength by the giant eld thus acting the babe new-born:
35 And "Neither will this turn serve!" yelled he. "Out with you! Trundle,
log!
If you cannot tramp and trudge like a man, try all-fours like a dog!"

Still the old man stood mute. So, logwise,—down to floor
Pulled from his fireside place, dragged on from hearth to door,—
Was he pushed, a very log, staircase along, until
40 A certain turn in the steps was reached, a yard from the
house-door-sill.

Then the father opened eyes—each spark of their rage extinct,—
Temples, late black, dead-blanched,—right-hand with left-hand
linked,—
He faced his son submissive; when slow the accents came,
They were strangely mild though his son's rash hand on his neck lay
all the same.

27| MS:muscly from   *1879:*muscly mass from   28| *1879:*weighed   *1889a:*weighed.
30| MS:stiffened §inserted above§   37| MS:log-wise   *1879:*logwise
38| MS:fire-side   *1879:*fireside   41| MS:opened his eyes   *1882:*opened eyes

45 "Hob, on just such a night of a Christmas long ago,
For such a cause, with such a gesture, did I drag—so—
My father down thus far: but, softening here, I heard
A voice in my heart, and stopped: you wait for an outer word.

"For your own sake, not mine, soften you too! Untrod
50 Leave this last step we reach, nor brave the finger of God!
I dared not pass its lifting: I did well. I nor blame
Nor praise you. I stopped here: and, Hob, do you the same!"

Straightway the son relaxed his hold of the father's throat.
They mounted, side by side, to the room again: no note
55 Took either of each, no sign made each to either: last
As first, in absolute silence, their Christmas-night they passed.

At dawn, the father sate on, dead, in the self-same place,
With an outburst blackening still the old bad fighting-face:
But the son crouched all a-tremble like any lamb new-yeaned.

60 When he went to the burial, someone's staff he borrowed—tottered
and leaned.
But his lips were loose, not locked,—kept muttering, mumbling.
"There!
At his cursing and swearing!" the youngsters cried: but the elders
thought "In prayer."
A boy threw stones: he picked them up and stored them in his vest.

So tottered, muttered, mumbled he, till he died, perhaps found rest.
65 "Is there a reason in nature for these hard hearts?" O Lear,
That a reason out of nature must turn them soft, seems clear!

---

^{45|} MS:Halbert, on such   *1882:*Hob, on just such   ^{52|} MS:here: Halbert, do
*1882:*here: and, Hob, do   ^{56|} MS:silence their   *1879:*silence, their
^{57|} MS:place   *1879:*place,   ^{60|} MS:borrowed,—tottered   *1889a:*borrowed—tottered
^{63-64|} MS:vest. / §no ¶§ So   *1879:*vest. / §¶§ So   ^{64-65|} MS:rest. / §¶§ "Is   *1879:*rest. /
§no ¶§ "Is   ^{66|} MS:clear.   *1879:*clear!

IVÀN IVÀNOVITCH

"They tell me, your carpenters," quoth I to my friend the Russ,
"Make a simple hatchet serve as a tool-box serves with us.
Arm but each man with his axe, 'tis a hammer and saw and plane
And chisel, and—what know I else? We should imitate in vain
5   The mastery wherewithal, by a flourish of just the adze,
He cleaves, clamps, dovetails in,—no need of our nails and brads,—
The manageable pine: 'tis said he could shave himself
With the axe,—so all adroit, now a giant and now an elf,
Does he work and play at once!"

                Quoth my friend the Russ to me,
10   "Ay, that and more beside on occasion! It scarce may be
You never heard tell a tale told children, time out of mind,
By father and mother and nurse, for a moral that's behind,
Which children quickly seize. If the incident happened at all,
We place it in Peter's time when hearts were great not small,
15   Germanized, Frenchified. I wager 'tis old to you
As the story of Adam and Eve, and possibly quite as true."

In the deep of our land, 'tis said, a village from out the woods
Emerged on the great main-road 'twixt two great solitudes.
Through forestry right and left, black verst and verst of pine,
20   From village to village runs the road's long wide bare line.
Clearance and clearance break the else-unconquered growth
Of pine and all that breeds and broods there, leaving loth
Man's inch of masterdom,—spot of life, spirt of fire,—
To star the dark and dread, lest right and rule expire
25   Throughout the monstrous wild, a-hungered to resume

IVÀN IVÀNOVITCH   ¹| MS:carpenters" quoth < > Russ   *1879:*carpenters," quoth < >
Russ,   ⁴| MS:and what   *1879:*and—what   ⁹| MS:me   *1879:*me,
¹³| MS:all   *1879:*all,   ¹⁶| MS:true.   *1879:*true."   ¹⁶⁻¹⁷| MS:true. / §no¶§ In
*1879:*true." / §¶§ In   ¹⁸| MS:solitudes;   *1879:*solitudes.   ¹⁹| MS:forestry §last two
letters possibly added when following word was crossed out§ on §crossed out§
²⁰| MS:line: *1879:*line.   ²⁴| MS:dread lest   *1879:*dread, lest
²⁵| MS:monstruous   *1879:*monstrous

Its ancient sway, suck back the world into its womb:
Defrauded by man's craft which clove from North to South
This highway broad and straight e'en from the Neva's mouth
To Moscow's gates of gold. So, spot of life and spirt
30   Of fire aforesaid, burn, each village death-begirt
By wall and wall of pine—unprobed undreamed abyss.

Early one winter morn, in such a village as this,
Snow-whitened everywhere except the middle road
Ice-roughed by track of sledge, there worked by his abode
35   Ivàn Ivànovitch, the carpenter, employed
On a huge shipmast trunk; his axe now trimmed and toyed
With branch and twig, and now some chop athwart the bole
Changed bole to billets, bared at once the sap and soul.
About him, watched the work his neighbours sheepskin-clad;
40   Each bearded mouth puffed steam, each grey eye twinkled glad
To see the sturdy arm which, never stopping play,
Proved strong man's blood still boils, freeze winter as he may.
Sudden, a burst of bells. Out of the road, on edge
Of the hamlet—horse's hoofs galloping. "How, a sledge?
45   What's here?" cried all as—in, up to the open space,
Workyard and market-ground, folk's common meeting-place,—
Stumbled on, till he fell, in one last bound for life,
A horse: and, at his heels, a sledge held—"Dmìtri's wife!
Back without Dmìtri too! and children—where are they?
50   Only a frozen corpse!"

                    They drew it forth: then—"Nay,
Not dead, though like to die! Gone hence a month ago:
Home again, this rough jaunt—alone through night and snow—
What can the cause be? Hark—Droug, old horse, how he groans:
His day's done! Chafe away, keep chafing, for she moans:
55   She's coming to! Give here: see, motherkin, your friends!
Cheer up, all safe at home! Warm inside makes amends
For outside cold,—sup quick! Don't look as we were bears!

26| MS:womb   *1879:*womb: 29| MS:To Moskow's   *1879:*To Moscow's
35| MS:Iván Ivánovitch   *1879:*Ivàn Ivànovitch   42| MS:strong-man's   *1879:*strong
man's   53| MS:groans!   *1879:*groans: 54| MS:moans!   *1879:*moans:

What is it startles you? What strange adventure stares
Up at us in your face? You know friends—which is which?
60   I'm Vàssili, he's Sergeì, Ivàn Ivànovitch . . ."

At the word, the woman's eyes, slow-wandering till they neared
The blue eyes o'er the bush of honey-coloured beard,
Took in full light and sense and—torn to rags, some dream
Which hid the naked truth—O loud and long the scream
65   She gave, as if all power of voice within her throat
Poured itself wild away to waste in one dread note!
Then followed gasps and sobs, and then the steady flow
Of kindly tears: the brain was saved, a man might know.
Down fell her face upon the good friend's propping knee;
70   His broad hands smoothed her head, as fain to brush it free
From fancies, swarms that stung like bees unhived. He soothed—
"Loukèria, Loùscha!"—still he, fondling, smoothed and smoothed.
At last her lips formed speech.

                "Ivàn, dear—you indeed!
You, just the same dear you! While I . . . O intercede,
75   Sweet Mother, with thy Son Almighty—let his might
Bring yesterday once more, undo all done last night!
But this time yesterday, Ivàn, I sat like you,
A child on either knee, and, dearer than the two,
A babe inside my arms, close to my heart—that's lost
80   In morsels o'er the snow! Father, Son, Holy Ghost,
Cannot you bring again my blessed yesterday?"

When no more tears would flow, she told her tale: this way.

"Maybe a month ago,—was it not?—news came here,
They wanted, deeper down, good workmen fit to rear
85   A church and roof it in. 'We'll go,' my husband said:
'None understands like me to melt and mould their lead.'

68| MS:tears—the   *1879:*tears: the   72| MS:"Loukèria, Loùscha!" still
1879:"Loukèria, Loùscha!"—still   74| MS:dear You! <> I . . O   *1879:*you! <> I . . . O
81| MS:blessed Yesterday?"   *1879:*yesterday?"
82-83| MS:way / §no¶§ "Maybe   *1889a:*way / §¶§ "Maybe

So, friends here helped us off—Ivàn, dear, you the first!
How gay we jingled forth, all five—(my heart will burst)—
While Dmìtri shook the reins, urged Droug upon his track!

90   "Well, soon the month ran out, we just were coming back,
When yesterday—behold, the village was on fire!
Fire ran from house to house. What help, as, nigh and nigher,
The flames came furious? 'Haste,' cried Dmìtri, 'men must do
The little good man may: to sledge and in with you,
95   You and our three! We check the fire by laying flat
Each building in its path,—I needs must stay for that,—
But you . . . no time for talk! Wrap round you every rug,
Cover the couple close,—you'll have the babe to hug.
No care to guide old Droug, he knows his way, by guess,
100   Once start him on the road: but chirrup, none the less!
The snow lies glib as glass and hard as steel, and soon
You'll have rise, fine and full, a marvel of a moon.
Hold straight up, all the same, this lighted twist of pitch!
Once home and with our friend Ivàn Ivànovitch,
105   All's safe: I have my pay in pouch, all's right with me,
So I but find as safe you and our precious three!
Off, Droug!'—because the flames had reached us, and the men
Shouted 'But lend a hand, Dmìtri—as good as ten!'

"So, in we bundled—I, and those God gave me once;
110   Old Droug, that's stiff at first, seemed youthful for the nonce:
He understood the case, galloping straight ahead.
Out came the moon: my twist soon dwindled, feebly red
In that unnatural day—yes, daylight, bred between
Moon-light and snow-light, lamped those grotto-depths which screen
115   Such devils from God's eye. Ah, pines, how straight you grow
Nor bend one pitying branch, true breed of brutal snow!
Some undergrowth had served to keep the devils blind

90| MS:Well *1879:*"Well   94| MS:little that man *1879:*little good man
97| MS:you . . no *1879:*you . . . no   102| MS:moon: *1879:*moon.
110| MS:first grew §crossed out and replaced above by§ seemed *1879:*first, seemed
114| MS:Moonlight *1879:*Moon-light

While we escaped outside their border!

"Was that—wind?
Anyhow, Droug starts, stops, back go his ears, he snuffs,
¹²⁰ Snorts,—never such a snort! then plunges, knows the sough's
Only the wind: yet, no—our breath goes up too straight!
Still the low sound,—less low, loud, louder, at a rate
There's no mistaking more! Shall I lean out—look—learn
The truth whatever it be? Pad, pad! At last, I turn—

¹²⁵ " 'Tis the regular pad of the wolves in pursuit of the life in the sledge!
An army they are: close-packed they press like the thrust of a wedge:
They increase as they hunt: for I see, through the pine-trunks ranged
    each side,
Slip forth new fiend and fiend, make wider and still more wide
The four-footed steady advance. The foremost—none may pass!
¹³⁰ They are elders and lead the line, eye and eye—green-glowing brass!
But a long way distant still. Droug, save us! He does his best:
Yet they gain on us, gain, till they reach,—one reaches . . . How utter
    the rest?
O that Satan-faced first of the band! How he lolls out the length of his
    tongue,
How he laughs and lets gleam his white teeth! He is on me, his paws
    pry among
¹³⁵ The wraps and the rugs! O my pair, my twin-pigeons, lie still and seem
    dead!
Stepàn, he shall never have you for a meal,—here's your mother
    instead!
No, he will not be counselled—must cry, poor Stiòpka, so foolish!
    though first
Of my boy-brood, he was not the best: nay, neighbours have called
    him the worst:
He was puny, an undersized slip,—a darling to me, all the same!
¹⁴⁰ But little there was to be praised in the boy, and a plenty to blame.

---

^{118|} MS:border! §¶§ Was   *1879:*border! §¶§ "Was   ^{127|} MS:hunt, for   *1879:*hunt: for
^{132|} MS:reaches . . How   *1879:*reaches . . . How   ^{133|} MS:of the throng §crossed out
and replaced above by§ band   ^{136|} MS:meal,—there's your   *1879:*meal,—here's your
^{139|} MS:undersized thing §crossed out and replaced above by§ slip

I loved him with heart and soul, yes—but, deal him a blow for a fault,
He would sulk for whole days. 'Foolish boy! lie still or the villain will
    vault,
Will snatch you from over my head!' No use! he cries, screams,—who
    can hold
Fast a boy in a frenzy of fear! It follows—as I foretold!
145   The Satan-face snatched and snapped: I tugged, I tore—and then
His brother too needs must shriek! If one must go, 'tis men
The Tsar needs, so we hear, not ailing boys! Perhaps
My hands relaxed their grasp, got tangled in the wraps:
God, he was gone! I looked: there tumbled the cursed crew,
150   Each fighting for a share: too busy to pursue!
That's so far gain at least: Droug, gallop another verst
Or two, or three—God sends we beat them, arrive the first!
A mother who boasts two boys was ever accounted rich:
Some have not a boy: some have, but lose him,—God knows which
155   Is worse: how pitiful to see your weakling pine
And pale and pass away! Strong brats, this pair of mine!
"O misery! for while I settle to what near seems
Content, I am 'ware again of the tramp, and again there gleams—
Point and point—the line, eyes, levelled green brassy fire!
160   So soon is resumed your chase? Will nothing appease, nought tire
The furies? And yet I think—I am certain the race is slack,
And the numbers are nothing like. Not a quarter of the pack!
Feasters and those full-fed are staying behind . . . Ah why?
We'll sorrow for that too soon! Now,—gallop, reach home, and die,
165   Nor ever again leave house, to trust our life in the trap
For life—we call a sledge! Terióscha, in my lap!
Yes, I'll lie down upon you, tight-tie you with the strings
Here—of my heart! No fear, this time, your mother flings . . .

142| MS:days. "Foolish   *1879:*days. 'Foolish   143| MS:head!" No use: he <> screams—
who   *1879:*head!' No use! he <> screams,—who   145| MS:and §over illegible word§
snap §altered to§ snapped—I tugged   *1879:*snapped: I tugged
146| MS:shriek—If   *1879:*shriek! If   147| MS:hear, no ailing   *1879:*hear, not ailing
150| MS:pursue—   *1879:*pursue!   151| MS:least! Droug   *1879:*least: Droug
154| MS:him, and God   *1879:*him,—God   158| MS:ware   *1879:*'ware
160| MS:will §altered to§ chase? ill   163| MS:behind . . . Ah, why?   *1879:*behind . . . Ah
why?   164| MS:die   *1879:*die,   168| MS:Here,—of my very §crossed out§ <> flings
. . . *1879:*Here—of   *1889a:*flings . . §emended to§ flings. . .   §see Editorial Notes§

Flings? I flung? Never! But think!—a woman, after all,
170 Contending with a wolf! Save you I must and shall,
Terentiì!

"How now? What, you still head the race,
Your eyes and tongue and teeth crave fresh food, Satan-face?
There and there! Plain I struck green fire out! Flash again?
All a poor fist can do to damage eyes proves vain!
175 My fist—why not crunch that? He is wanton for . . . O God,
Why give this wolf his taste? Common wolves scrape and prod
The earth till out they scratch some corpse—mere putrid flesh!
Why must this glutton leave the faded, choose the fresh?
Terentiì—God, feel!—his neck keeps fast thy bag
180 Of holy things, saints' bones, this Satan-face will drag
Forth, and devour along with him, our Pope declared
The relics were to save from danger!

"Spurned, not spared!
'Twas through my arms, crossed arms, he—nuzzling now with snout,
Now ripping, tooth and claw—plucked, pulled Terentiì out,
185 A prize indeed! I saw—how could I else but see?—
My precious one—I bit to hold back—pulled from me!
Up came the others, fell to dancing—did the imps!—
Skipped as they scampered round. There's one is grey, and limps:
Who knows but old bad Màrpha,—she always owed me spite
190 And envied me my births,—skulks out of doors at night
And turns into a wolf, and joins the sisterhood,
And laps the youthful life, then slinks from out the wood,
Squats down at door by dawn, spins there demure as erst
—No strength, old crone,—not she!—to crawl forth half a verst!

195 "Well, I escaped with one: 'twixt one and none there lies

---

169| MS:all,   *1889a:*all §emended to§ all, §see Editorial Notes§   171| MS:Terentiì! §¶§
How   *1879:*Terentiì!   §¶§ "How   175| MS:for . . O   *1879:*for . . . O
179| MS:feel,—his   *1879:*feel!—his   181| MS:Forth. and < > him our pope
*1879:*Forth, and < > Pope   *1889a:*him, our   182| MS:danger! §¶§ Spurned
*1879:*danger! §¶§ "Spurned   183| MS:arms—crossed arms—he,—nuzzling
*1879:*arms, crossed arms, he—nuzzling   184| MS:Now, ripping < > claw, he pulled
*1879:*Now ripping < > claw—plucked, pulled   189| MS:bad Màrpha that §crossed out
and replaced above by§ she   193| MS:erst,   *1879:*erst

The space 'twixt heaven and hell. And see, a rose-light dyes
The endmost snow: 'tis dawn, 'tis day, 'tis safe at home!
We have outwitted you! Ay, monsters, snarl and foam,
Fight each the other fiend, disputing for a share,—
200   Forgetful, in your greed, our finest off we bear,
Tough Droug and I,—my babe, my boy that shall be man,
My man that shall be more, do all a hunter can
To trace and follow and find and catch and crucify
Wolves, wolfkins, all your crew! A thousand deaths shall die
205   The whimperingest cub that ever squeezed the teat!
'Take that!' we'll stab you with,—'the tenderness we met
When, wretches, you danced round—not this, thank God—not this!
Hellhounds, we baulk you!'

           "But—Ah, God above!—Bliss, bliss—
Not the band, no! And yet—yes, for Droug knows him! One—
210   This only of them all has said 'She saves a son!
His fellows disbelieve such luck: but he believes,
He lets them pick the bones, laugh at him in their sleeves:
He's off and after us,—one speck, one spot, one ball
Grows bigger, bound on bound,—one wolf as good as all!
215   Oh but I know the trick! Have at the snaky tongue!
That's the right way with wolves! Go, tell your mates I wrung
The panting morsel out, left you to howl your worst!
Now for it—now! Ah me! I know him—thrice-accurst
Satan-face,—him to the end my foe!

           "All fight's in vain:
220   This time the green brass points pierce to my very brain.
I fall—fall as I ought—quite on the babe I guard:

197| MS:snow—'tis   *1879:* snow: 'tis   200| MS:bear   *1882:* bear,
204| MS:crew—a   *1879:* crew!   206| MS:"Take that!—" we'll <> with,—"the
1879: 'Take that!' we'll <> with,—'the   208| MS:you"! §¶§ But   *1879:* you!' §¶§ "But
210| MS:Of them all, only this has said "She <> son!"   *1879:* said 'She <> son!'
1889a: This only of them all has   211| MS:luck—but   *1879:* luck: but
212| MS:bones,—laughs §altered to§ laugh <> sleeves,—   *1879:* bones, laugh <> sleeves:
216| MS:wolves! Go. tell <> mates—<u>who</u> §next word illegibly crossed out§ wrung
1879: wolves! Go, tell <> mates I wrung   219| MS:foe! §¶§ All   *1879:* foe! §¶§ "All
220| MS:brain,   *1879:* brain.   221| MS:fall—but §crossed out§ <> guard—   *1879:* guard:

I overspread with flesh the whole of him. Too hard
To die this way, torn piecemeal? Move hence? Not I—one inch!
Gnaw through me, through and through: flat thus I lie nor flinch!
225   O God, the feel of the fang furrowing my shoulder!—see!
It grinds—it grates the bone. O Kìrill under me,
Could I do more? Besides he knew wolf's way to win:
I clung, closed round like wax: yet in he wedged and in,
Past my neck, past my breasts, my heart, until . . . how feels
230   The onion-bulb your knife parts, pushing through its peels,
Till out you scoop its clove wherein lie stalk and leaf
And bloom and seed unborn?

              "That slew me: yes, in brief,
I died then, dead I lay doubtlessly till Droug stopped
Here, I suppose. I come to life, I find me propped
235   Thus—how or when or why,—I know not. Tell me, friends,
All was a dream: laugh quick and say the nightmare ends!
Soon I shall find my house: 'tis over there: in proof,
Save for that chimney heaped with snow, you'd see the roof
Which holds my three—my two—my one—not one?

                          "Life's mixed
240   With misery, yet we live—must live. The Satan fixed
His face on mine so fast, I took its print as pitch
Takes what it cools beneath. Ivàn Ivànovitch,

222| MS:him: not §crossed out and replaced above by§ too   *1879:*him. Too
223| MS:piecemeal?—Move   *1879:*piecemeal? Move   224| MS:and through, flat
*1879:*and through: flat   225| MS:O God the < > fang right past my < > see—
*1879:*O God, the < > fang furrowing my < > see!   227| MS:more? Besides
*1889a:*more? Beside §emended to§ more? Besides §see Editorial Notes§
229| MS:until . . what feels   *1879:*until . . . how feels   230| MS:parts—pushing
*1879:*parts, pushing   232| MS:unborn? §¶§ That   *1879:*unborn? §¶§ "That
233| MS:lay: no §crossed out§ doubt §altered to§ doubtlessly—untill §altered to§ till
*1879:*lay doubtlessly till   234| MS:suppose,—To come to life and find   *1879:*suppose. I
come to life, I find   236| MS:dream,—laugh < > prove §crossed out and replaced above
by§ say   *1879:*dream: laugh   238| MS:that chimney-screen snow-piled, you'd
*1879:*that chimney heaped with snow, you'd   239| MS:That holds < > not one? §¶§ Life's
*1879:*Which holds < > not one? §¶§ "Life's   240| MS:must live. If I blasphemed §last
three words crossed out and replaced above by three words§ The Satan fixed
241| MS:Lay it not all on me. Twas only while I dreamed, §last eleven words and comma crossed
out and replaced above by twelve words§ His face on mine so fast, I took its print as pitch

'Tis you unharden me, you thaw, disperse the thing!
Only keep looking kind, the horror will not cling.
245   Your face smooths fast away each print of Satan. Tears
—What good they do! Life's sweet, and all its after-years,
Iван Iванovitch, I owe you! Yours am I!
May God reward you, dear!"

                              Down she sank. Solemnly
Iван rose, raised his axe,—for fitly, as she knelt,
250   Her head lay: well-apart, each side, her arms hung,—dealt
Lightning-swift thunder-strong one blow—no need of more!
Headless she knelt on still: that pine was sound at core
(Neighbours were used to say)—cast-iron-kernelled—which
Taxed for a second stroke Iван Iванovitch.

255   The man was scant of words as strokes. "It had to be:
I could no other: God it was bade 'Act for me!'"
Then stooping, peering round—what is it now he lacks?
A proper strip of bark wherewith to wipe his axe.
Which done, he turns, goes in, closes the door behind.
260   The others mute remain, watching the blood-snake wind
Into a hiding-place among the splinter-heaps.

At length, still mute, all move: one lifts,—from where it steeps
Redder each ruddy rag of pine,—the head: two more
Take up the dripping body: then, mute still as before,

243| MS:I well-nigh grew myself a devil, Satan §last seven words crossed out and replaced
above by seven words§ 'Tis you unharden me, you thaw, disperse   244| MS:cling,
*1879:*cling.   245| MS:fast §over illegible word§   247| MS:am I!" §quotation marks
scraped off§   248| MS:dear"! §altered to§ dear!' §¶§ Down she sank. Then §crossed out§
solemnly §first letter altered to upper case§ Solemnly   *1879:*dear!" §¶§ Down
249| MS:fitly as she knelt   *1879:*fitly, as she knelt,   250| MS:lay, well-apart < > side her
< > lay §illegible word, possibly *full*§ ,— §two words, comma and dash crossed out and
replaced above by one word, comma and dash§ hung,—dealt   *1879:*lay: well-apart < > side,
her   253| MS:cast-iron-kerneled   *1889a:*cast-iron-kernelled
258| MS:axe;   *1879:*axe.   259| MS:Then he turns slow, goes in, shuts soft §last two
words crossed out and replaced above by§ closes   *1879:*Which done, he turns, goes
263| MS:Redder the §crossed out and replaced above by§ each < > rags §last letter crossed
out§   264| MS:dripping corpse §crossed out and replaced above by§ body < > mutely
§last two letters crossed out and replaced above by§ still

242

265 Move in a sort of march, march on till marching ends
Opposite to the church; where halting,—who suspends,
By its long hair, the thing, deposits in its place
The piteous head: once more the body shows no trace
Of harm done: there lies whole the Loùscha, maid and wife
270 And mother, loved until this latest of her life.
Then all sit on the bank of snow which bounds a space
Kept free before the porch for judgment: just the place!

Presently all the souls, man, woman, child, which make
The village up, are found assembling for the sake
275 Of what is to be done. The very Jews are there:
A Gipsy troop, though bound with horses for the Fair,
Squats with the rest. Each heart with its conception seethes
And simmers, but no tongue speaks: one may say,—none breathes.

Anon from out the church totters the Pope—the priest—
280 Hardly alive, so old, a hundred years at least.
With him, the Commune's head, a hoary senior too,
Stàrosta, that's his style,—like Equity Judge with you,—
Natural Jurisconsult: then, fenced about with furs,
Pomeschìk,—Lord of the Land, who wields—and none demurs—
285 A power of life and death. They stoop, survey the corpse.

Then, straightened on his staff, the Stàrosta—the thorpe's
Sagaciousest old man—hears what you just have heard,
From Droug's first inrush, all, up to Ivàn's last word
"God bade me act for him: I dared not disobey!"

266| MS:the Church gates §crossed out§ ; there §altered to§ where, §comma scraped off§
halting   *1879:*church   267| MS:thing §over *head*§   268| MS:piteous thing §crossed
out and replaced above by§ head   269| MS:the Loùsha   *1879:*the Loùscha
271| MS:snow around a   *1879:*snow which bounds a   272-73| MS:place! / §no¶§ Presently
*1879:*place! / §¶§ Presently   274| MS:up are   *1879:*up, are   276| MS:A Gypsy-
troop *1879:*A Gipsy-troop   278-79| MS:breathes. / §no¶§ Presently from the Church <>
Pope,—the priest,—   *1879:*breathes. / §¶§ Anon from out the church <> Pope—the priest—
282| MS:Starosta §illegible accent marks over the first a and the o crossed out§   *1879:*Stàrosta
*1889a:*Starosta §emended to§ Stàrosta §see Editorial Notes§   284| MS:The §crossed out§
285-86| MS:A §over *The*§ <> corpse: / §no¶§ Then *1879:*corpse. / §¶§ Then
287| MS:man,—hears   *1879:*man—hears   288| MS:From Droug's wild §crossed out and
replaced above by§ first <> all, §word and comma inserted above§

243

290 Silence—the Pomeschìk broke with "A wild wrong way
Of righting wrong—if wrong there were, such wrath to rouse!
Why was not law observed? What article allows
Whoso may please to play the judge, and, judgment dealt,
Play executioner, as promptly as we pelt
295 To death, without appeal, the vermin whose sole fault
Has been—it dared to leave the darkness of its vault,
Intrude upon our day! Too sudden and too rash!
What was this woman's crime ? Suppose the church should crash
Down where I stand, your lord: bound are my serfs to dare
300 Their utmost that I 'scape: yet, if the crashing scare
My children,—as you are,—if sons fly, one and all,
Leave father to his fate,—poor cowards though I call
The runaways, I pause before I claim their life
Because they prized it more than mine. I would each wife
305 Died for her husband's sake, each son to save his sire:
'Tis glory, I applaud—scarce duty, I require.
Ivàn Ivànovitch has done a deed that's named
Murder by law and me: who doubts, may speak unblamed!"

All turned to the old Pope. "Ay, children, I am old—
310 How old, myself have got to know no longer. Rolled
Quite round, my orb of life, from infancy to age,
Seems passing back again to youth. A certain stage
At least I reach, or dream I reach, where I discern
Truer truths, laws behold more lawlike than we learn
315 When first we set our foot to tread the course I trod
With man to guide my steps: who leads me now is God.
'Your young men shall see visions:' and in my youth I saw
And paid obedience to man's visionary law:
'Your old men shall dream dreams:' and, in my age, a hand

293| MS:the Judge *1879:*judge   298| MS:the §over illegible word, probably *our*§
301| MS:are,—and sons *1879:*are,—if sons   302| MS:—Leave *1879:*Leave
305| MS:sake,—each *1879:*sake, each   306| MS:That's §crossed out and replaced in
margin by§ 'Tis glory I < > duty I *1879:*glory, I < > duty, I   307| MS:done the §crossed
out and replaced above by§ a   310| MS:old—myself, I get §last three words transposed
to§ I get myself, to   *1879:*old, I get myself to *1882:*old, myself have got to
312| MS:youth: a *1879:*youth. A   317| MS:visions:" and *1879:*visions:' and

244

³²⁰ Conducts me through the cloud round law to where I stand
Firm on its base,—know cause, who, before, knew effect.

"The world lies under me: and nowhere I detect
So great a gift as this—God's own—of human life.
'Shall the dead praise thee?' No! 'The whole live world is rife,
³²⁵ God, with thy glory,' rather! Life then, God's best of gifts,
For what shall man exchange? For life—when so he shifts
The weight and turns the scale, lets life for life restore
God's balance, sacrifice the less to gain the more,
Substitute—for low life, another's or his own—
³³⁰ Life large and liker God's who gave it: thus alone
May life extinguish life that life may trulier be!
How low this law descends on earth, is not for me
To trace: complexed becomes the simple, intricate
The plain, when I pursue law's winding. 'Tis the straight
³³⁵ Outflow of law I know and name: to law, the fount
Fresh from God's footstool, friends, follow while I remount.

"A mother bears a child: perfection is complete
So far in such a birth. Enabled to repeat
The miracle of life,—herself was born so just
³⁴⁰ A type of womankind, that God sees fit to trust
Her with the holy task of giving life in turn.
Crowned by this crowning pride,—how say you, should she spurn
Regality—discrowned, unchilded, by her choice
Of barrenness exchanged for fruit which made rejoice
³⁴⁵ Creation, though life's self were lost in giving birth
To life more fresh and fit to glorify God's earth?

---

^{322|} MS:The   *1879:*"The   ^{323|} MS:this—God §altered to§ God's gives §crossed out and
replaced above by§ own   ^{324|} MS:"Shall <> thee?" No   *1879:*'Shall <> thee?' No
^{325|} MS:glory," rather   *1879:*glory,' rather   ^{327|} MS:let   *1879:*lets
^{332|} MS:How far §inserted above, crossed out and replaced by§ low <> extends §first three
letters crossed out and replaced above by four letters§ disc <> earth is   *1879:*descends on
earth, is   ^{333|} MS:trace—complexed   *1879:*trace: complexed   ^{334|} MS:plain
when <> winding: 'tis   *1879:*plain, when <> winding. 'Tis   ^{335|} MS:fount,
*1879:*fount   ^{336|} MS:footstool,—friends   *1879:*footstool, friends   ^{337|} MS:A <>
child? perfection   *1879:*"A <> child: perfection   ^{340|} MS:womankind that God saw
*1879:*womankind, that God sees   ^{345|} MS:Creation though   *1879:*Creation, though

How say you, should the hand God trusted with life's torch
Kindled to light the world—aware of sparks that scorch,
Let fall the same? Forsooth, her flesh a fire-flake stings:
350 The mother drops the child! Among what monstrous things
Shall she be classed? Because of motherhood, each male
Yields to his partner place, sinks proudly in the scale:
His strength owned weakness, wit—folly, and courage—fear,
Beside the female proved male's mistress—only here.
355 The fox-dam, hunger-pined, will slay the felon sire
Who dares assault her whelp: the beaver, stretched on fire,
Will die without a groan: no pang avails to wrest
Her young from where they hide—her sanctuary breast.
What's here then? Answer me, thou dead one, as, I trow,
360 Standing at God's own bar, he bids thee answer now!
Thrice crowned wast thou—each crown of pride, a child—thy charge!
Where are they? Lost? Enough: no need that thou enlarge
On how or why the loss: life left to utter 'lost'
Condemns itself beyond appeal. The soldier's post
365 Guards from the foe's attack the camp he sentinels:
That he no traitor proved, this and this only tells—
Over the corpse of him trod foe to foe's success.
Yet—one by one thy crowns torn from thee—thou no less
To scare the world, shame God,—livedst! I hold He saw
370 The unexampled sin, ordained the novel law,
Whereof first instrument was first intelligence
Found loyal here. I hold that, failing human sense,
The very earth had oped, sky fallen, to efface
Humanity's new wrong, motherhood's first disgrace.
375 Earth oped not, neither fell the sky, for prompt was found

---

348| MS:world,—because of   *1879:*world—aware of   349| MS:stings—   *1879:*stings:
*1889a:*stings §emended to§ stings: §see Editorial Notes§   351| MS:motherhood, the
§crossed out and replaced above by§ each   353| MS:weak, his §comma and last word
crossed out and replaced above by four letters and comma§ ness, < > fear   *1879:*fear,
354| MS:proved his mistress   *1879:*proved male's mistress   357| MS:groan—no
*1879:*groan: no   362| MS:they? Lost! Enough   *1879:*they? Lost? Enough
366| MS:proves   *1879:*proved   369| MS:he   *1889a:*hold He   370| MS:The §over
illegible word, possibly *Her*§   372| MS:worthy §crossed out and replaced above by§ loyal
here: I   *1879:*here. I   373| MS:oped—sky fallen—to   *1879:*oped, sky fallen, to
374| MS:wrong,—motherhood's   *1879:*wrong, motherhood's

A man and man enough, head-sober and heart-sound,
Ready to hear God's voice, resolute to obey,
Ivàn Ivànovitch, I hold, has done, this day,
No otherwise than did, in ages long ago,
380 Moses when he made known the purport of that flow
Of fire athwart the law's twain-tables! I proclaim
Ivàn Ivànovitch God's servant!"

                      At which name
Uprose that creepy whisper from out the crowd, is wont
To swell and surge and sink when fellow-men confront
385 A punishment that falls on fellow flesh and blood,
Appallingly beheld—shudderingly understood,
No less, to be the right, the just, the merciful.
"God's servant!" hissed the crowd.

                    When that Amen grew dull
And died away and left acquittal plain adjudged,
390 "Amen!" last sighed the lord. "There's none shall say I grudged
Escape from punishment in such a novel case.
Deferring to old age and holy life,—be grace
Granted! say I. No less, scruples might shake a sense
Firmer than I boast mine. Law's law, and evidence
395 Of breach therein lies plain,—blood-red-bright,—all may see!
Yet all absolve the deed: absolved the deed must be!

"And next—as mercy rules the hour—methinks 'twere well
You signify forthwith its sentence, and dispel
The doubts and fears, I judge, which busy now the head
400 Law puts a halter round—a halo—you, instead!
Ivàn Ivànovitch—what think you he expects
Will follow from his feat? Go, tell him—law protects

376| MS:enough—head-sober   *1879:*enough, head-sober   378| MS:day   *1879:*day,
381| MS:the Law's   *1879:*law's   382| MS:Ivàn Ivanovitch   *1879:*Ivàn Ivànovitch
383| *1882:*wont,   *1889a:*wont   388| MS:'God's servant' hissed the crowd when < >
'Amen' grew   *1879:*"God's servant!" hissed the crowd.   §¶§ When < > Amen grew
389-90| MS:adjudged. / §¶§ "Amen," last < > lord: "there's   *1879:*adjudged, / §no¶§
"Amen!" last < > lord.   "There's   391| MS:case—   *1879:*case.
396-97| MS:be! / §no¶§ And   *1879:*be! / §¶§ "And   399| MS:fears, I guess, which
*1879:*fears, I judge, which   400| MS:halo, §comma altered to dash§ halo—you

Murder, for once: no need he longer keep behind
The Sacred Pictures—where skulks Innocence enshrined,
405 Or I missay! Go, some! You others, haste and hide
The dismal object there: get done, whate'er betide!"

So, while the youngers raised the corpse, the elders trooped
Silently to the house: where halting, someone stooped,
Listened beside the door; all there was silent too.
410 Then they held counsel; then pushed door and, passing through,
Stood in the murderer's presence.
                                       Ivàn Ivànovitch
Knelt, building on the floor that Kremlin rare and rich
He deftly cut and carved on lazy winter nights.
Some five young faces watched, breathlessly, as, to rights,
415 Piece upon piece, he reared the fabric nigh complete.
Stèscha, Ivàn's old mother, sat spinning by the heat
Of the oven where his wife Kàtia stood baking bread.
Ivàn's self, as he turned his honey-coloured head,
Was just in act to drop, 'twixt fir-cones,—each a dome,—
420 The scooped-out yellow gourd presumably the home
Of Kolokol the Big: the bell, therein to hitch,
—An acorn-cup—was ready: Ivàn Ivànovitch
Turned with it in his mouth.

                        They told him he was free
As air to walk abroad. "How otherwise?" asked he.

403| MS:longer crouch §crossed out and replaced above by§ keep   406| MS:there—get
1879:there: get   408| MS:house; where <> stooped   1879:house: where <> stooped,
409| MS:door; but §crossed out§ all there §inserted above§ <> too;   1879:too.
410| MS:counsel,—then   1879:counsel; then   411| MS:presence.   §mark indicating
new paragraph§ Ivàn Ivanovitch   1879:presence. §¶§ Ivàn Ivànovitch
412| MS:Sate §crossed out and replaced above by§ Knelt building   1879:Knelt, building
413| MS:nights: 1879:nights.   414| MS:breathlessly, §comma scraped off§ as, to-rights
1879:breathlessly, as, to rights   415| MS:piece he   1879:piece, he
416| MS:Ivàn's old mother, Stèsha, §transposed to§ Stèsha, Ivàn's old mother, sat   1879:Stèscha
417| MS:bread: 1879:bread.   421| MS:the Big— §altered to§ the Big: which bell
1879:the Big: the bell   423| MS:mouth. §mark indicating new paragraph§ They

TRAY

Sing me a hero! Quench my thirst
Of soul, ye bards!
            Quoth Bard the first:
"Sir Olaf, the good knight, did don
His helm and eke his habergeon . . ."
5   Sir Olaf and his bard—!

"That sin-scathed brow" (quoth Bard the second)
"That eye wide ope as though Fate beckoned
My hero to some steep, beneath
Which precipice smiled tempting death . . ."
10   You too without your host have reckoned!

"A beggar-child" (let's hear this third!)
"Sat on a quay's edge: like a bird
Sang to herself at careless play,
And fell into the stream. 'Dismay!
15   Help, you the standers-by!' None stirred.

"Bystanders reason, think of wives
And children ere they risk their lives.
Over the balustrade has bounced
A mere instinctive dog, and pounced
20   Plumb on the prize. 'How well he dives!

"'Up he comes with the child, see, tight
In mouth, alive too, clutched from quite
A depth of ten feet—twelve, I bet!

TRAY   ²| MS:first *1879:*first: ⁶| MS:That <> brow (quoth   *1879:*"That <>
brow" (quoth   ⁷| MS:That *1879:*"That   ⁹| MS:tempting Death . . .   *1882:*death
. . . " *1889a:*death . . §emended to§ death . . . " §see Editorial Notes§
¹¹| MS:A beggar-child (let's *1879:*"A beggar-child" (let's   ¹²| MS:Sat *1879:*"Sat
¹⁴| MS:stream. "Dismay! *1879:*stream. 'Dismay!   ¹⁵| MS:standers by!" None
*1879:*standers-by!' None   ¹⁶| MS:Bystanders *1879:*"Bystanders
²⁰| MS:prize. "How *1879:*prize. 'How   ²¹| MS:"Up *1879:*"'Up

Good dog! What, off again? There's yet
25   Another child to save? All right!

"'How strange we saw no other fall!
It's instinct in the animal.
Good dog! But he's a long while under:
If he got drowned I should not wonder—
30   Strong current, that against the wall!

"'Here he comes, holds in mouth this time
—What may the thing be? Well, that's prime!
Now, did you ever? Reason reigns
In man alone, since all Tray's pains
35   Have fished—the child's doll from the slime!'

"And so, amid the laughter gay,
Trotted my hero off,—old Tray,—
Till somebody, prerogatived
With reason, reasoned: 'Why he dived,
40   His brain would show us, I should say.

"'John, go and catch—or, if needs be,
Purchase—that animal for me!
By vivisection, at expense
Of half-an-hour and eighteenpence,
45   How brain secretes dog's soul, we'll see!'"

26| MS:"How   *1879:*"'How   31| MS:"Here   *1879:*"'Here   34| MS:In Man
*1879:*man   35| MS:slime!"   *1879:*slime!'   36| MS:And   *1879:*"And
39| MS:reasoned: "Why   *1879:*reasoned: 'Why   41| MS:"John   *1879:*"'John
42| MS:Purchase that   *1889a:*Purchase—that
44| MS:eighteen pence,   *1882:*eighteenpence,   45| MS:see!"   *1879:*see!'"

NED BRATTS

'Twas Bedford Special Assize, one daft Midsummer's Day:
A broiling blasting June,—was never its like, men say.
Corn stood sheaf-ripe already, and trees looked yellow as that;
Ponds drained dust-dry, the cattle lay foaming around each flat.
5   Inside town, dogs went mad, and folk kept bibbing beer
While the parsons prayed for rain. 'Twas horrible, yes—but queer:
Queer—for the sun laughed gay, yet nobody moved a hand
To work one stroke at his trade: as given to understand
That all was come to a stop, work and such worldly ways,
10   And the world's old self about to end in a merry blaze.
Midsummer's Day moreover was the first of Bedford Fair,
With Bedford Town's tag-rag and bobtail a-bowsing there.

But the Court House, Quality crammed: through doors ope, windows
    wide,
High on the Bench you saw sit Lordships side by side.
15   There frowned Chief Justice Jukes, fumed learned Brother Small, ·
And fretted their fellow Judge: like threshers, one and all,
Of a reek with laying down the law in a furnace. Why?
Because their lungs breathed flame—the regular crowd forbye—
From gentry pouring in—quite a nosegay, to be sure!
20   How else could they pass the time, six mortal hours endure
Till night should extinguish day, when matters might haply mend?
Meanwhile no bad resource was—watching begin and end
Some trial for life and death, in a brisk five minutes' space,
And betting which knave would 'scape, which hang, from his sort of
    face.

NED BRATTS   ⁴| MS:round *1879:*around   ⁵| MS:folks *1889a:*folk
¹¹| MS:Moreover Midsummer Day §transposed to§ Midsummer Day Moreover < > of Bedford
Fair; *1879:*moreover *1889a:*of Bedford Fair,   ¹²| MS:So, Bedford < > there
*1879:*there. *1889a:*With Bedford   ¹⁴| MS:by side; *1879:*by side.
¹⁵| MS:frowned Chief Justice Jukes, and fumed Our Brother *1879:*frowned Chief Justice
Jukes, fumed learned Brother   ¹⁹| MS:sure! §exclamation mark over punctuation mark
illegibly crossed out§   ²⁰| MS:time? how six long hours *1879:*time, six mortal hours
²⁴| MS:scape < > for §crossed out and replaced above by§ from *1879:*'scape

25   So, their Lordships toiled and moiled, and a deal of work was done
      (I warrant) to justify the mirth of the crazy sun
      As this and 't other lout, struck dumb at the sudden show
      Of red robes and white wigs, boggled nor answered "Boh!"
      When asked why he, Tom Styles, should not—because Jack Nokes
30   Had stolen the horse—be hanged: for Judges must have their jokes,
      And louts must make allowance—let's say, for some blue fly
      Which punctured a dewy scalp where the frizzles stuck awry—
      Else Tom had fleered scot-free, so nearly over and done
      Was the main of the job. Full-measure, the gentles enjoyed their fun,
35   As a twenty-five were tried, rank puritans caught at prayer
      In a cow-house and laid by the heels,—have at 'em, devil may care!—
      And ten were prescribed the whip, and ten a brand on the cheek,
      And five a slit of the nose—just leaving enough to tweak.
      Well, things at jolly high-tide, amusement steeped in fire,
40   While noon smote fierce the roof's red tiles to heart's desire,
      The Court a-simmer with smoke, one ferment of oozy flesh,
      One spirituous humming musk mount-mounting until its mesh
      Entoiled all heads in a fluster, and Serjeant Postlethwayte
      —Dashing the wig oblique as he mopped his oily pate—
45   Cried "Silence, or I grow grease! No loophole lets in air?
      Jurymen,—Guilty, Death! Gainsay me if you dare!"
      —Things at this pitch, I say,—what hubbub without the doors?
      What laughs, shrieks, hoots and yells, what rudest of uproars?

      Bounce through the barrier throng a bulk comes rolling vast!
50   Thumps, kicks,—no manner of use!—spite of them rolls at last
      Into the midst a ball which, bursting, brings to view
      Publican Black Ned Bratts and Tabby his big wife too:
      Both in a muck-sweat, both . . . were never such eyes uplift
      At the sight of yawning hell, such nostrils—snouts that sniffed
55   Sulphur, such mouths a-gape ready to swallow flame!
      Horrified, hideous, frank fiend-faces! yet, all the same,
      Mixed with a certain . . . eh? how shall I dare style—mirth

²⁶| MS:sun, *1889a:*sun   ⁴⁶| MS:Jurymen, guilty, death   *1879:*Jurymen,—Guilty, Death
⁴⁸| MS:yells, the rudest   *1879:*yells, what rudest   ⁴⁹| MS:barrier-throng   *1882:*barrier
throng   ⁵⁰| MS:no sort of use,—spite   *1879:*no manner of use!—spite
⁵³| MS:both . . were   *1879:*both . . . were   ⁵⁷| MS:certain . . eh   *1879:*certain . . . eh

The desperate grin of the guess that, could they break from earth,
Heaven was above, and hell might rage in impotence
60 Below the saved, the saved!

"Confound you! (no offence!)
Out of our way,—push, wife! Yonder their Worships be!"
Ned Bratts has reached the bar, and "Hey, my Lords," roars he,
"A Jury of life and death, Judges the prime of the land,
Constables, javelineers,—all met, if I understand,
65 To decide so knotty a point as whether 'twas Jack or Joan
Robbed the henroost, pinched the pig, hit the King's Arms with a
        stone,
Dropped the baby down the well, left the tithesman in the lurch,
Or, three whole Sundays running, not once attended church!
What a pother—do these deserve the parish-stocks or whip,
70 More or less brow to brand, much or little nose to snip,—
When, in our Public, plain stand we—that's we stand here,
I and my Tab, brass-bold, brick-built of beef and beer,
—Do not we, slut? Step forth and show your beauty, jade!
Wife of my bosom—that's the word now! What a trade
75 We drove! None said us nay: nobody loved his life
So little as wag a tongue against us,—did they, wife?
Yet they knew us all the while, in their hearts, for what we are
—Worst couple, rogue and quean, unhanged—search near and far!
Eh, Tab? The pedlar, now—o'er his noggin—who warned a mate
80 To cut and run, nor risk his pack where its loss of weight
Was the least to dread,—aha, how we two laughed a-good
As, stealing round the midden, he came on where I stood
With billet poised and raised,—you, ready with the rope,—
Ah, but that's past, that's sin repented of, we hope!
85 Men knew us for that same, yet safe and sound stood we!
The lily-livered knaves knew too (I've baulked a d——)
Our keeping the 'Pied Bull' was just a mere pretence:

---

⁵⁸| MS:grin o' §altered to§ of the §over a§   ⁶¹| MS:the Judges §crossed out and
replaced above by§ their Worships   ⁶²| MS:he *1879:*he,   ⁶⁶| MS:hen-roost
*1879:*henroost   ⁷²| MS:brick built *1879:*brick-built   ⁸¹| MS:dread,—Aha
*1879:*aha   ⁸⁴| MS:sin §next word, probably was, crossed out§   ⁸⁶| MS:lily-livered
fools §crossed out and replaced above by§ knaves   ⁸⁷| MS:the "Pied Bull" was < > a
pure pretence: *1879:*the 'Pied Bull' was < > a mere pretence:

Too slow the pounds make food, drink, lodging, from out the pence!
There's not a stoppage to travel has chanced, this ten long year,
90   No break into hall or grange, no lifting of nag or steer,
Not a single roguery, from the clipping of a purse
To the cutting of a throat, but paid us toll. Od's curse!
When Gipsy Smouch made bold to cheat us of our due,
—Eh, Tab? the Squire's strong-box we helped the rascal to—
95   I think he pulled a face, next Sessions' swinging-time!
He danced the jig that needs no floor,—and, here's the prime,
'Twas Scroggs that houghed the mare! Ay, those were busy days!

"Well, there we flourished brave, like scripture-trees called bays,
Faring high, drinking hard, in money up to head
100   —Not to say, boots and shoes, when . . . Zounds, I nearly said—
Lord, to unlearn one's language! How shall we labour, wife?
Have you, fast hold, the Book? Grasp, grip it, for your life!
See, sirs, here's life, salvation! Here's—hold but out my breath—
When did I speak so long without once swearing? 'Sdeath,
105   No, nor unhelped by ale since man and boy! And yet
All yesterday I had to keep my whistle wet
While reading Tab this Book: book? don't say 'book'—they're plays,
Songs, ballads and the like: here's no such strawy blaze,
But sky wide ope, sun, moon, and seven stars out full-flare!
110   Tab, help and tell! I'm hoarse. A mug! or—no, a prayer!
Dip for one out of the Book! Who wrote it in the Jail
—He plied his pen unhelped by beer, sirs, I'll be bail!

"I've got my second wind. In trundles she—that's Tab.
'Why, Gammer, what's come now, that—bobbing like a crab

---

⁸⁸| MS:slow make <> lodging, the pounds from   *1889a:*slow the pounds make <> lodging,
from   ⁸⁹| MS:stoppage has chanced to travel, this   *1882:*stoppage to travel has
chanced, this   ⁹¹| MS:of a throat §crossed out and replaced above by§ purse
⁹²| MS:throat but   *1879:*throat, but   ⁹³| MS:When Gipsy   *1879:*When Gipsy
⁹⁸| MS:Well   *1879:*"Well   ¹⁰⁰| MS:when . . Zounds   *1879:*when . . . Zounds
¹⁰¹| MS:unlearn the §crossed out and replaced above by§ one's   ¹⁰²| MS:book §altered
to§ the Book   ¹⁰³| MS:See, Sirs   *1879:*sirs   ¹⁰⁷| MS:say "book"—they're
*1879:*say 'book'—they're   ¹⁰⁸| MS:blaze   *1879:*blaze,   ¹⁰⁹| MS:But Heaven
§crossed out and replaced above by§ sky   ¹¹¹| MS:book §altered to§ the Book
¹¹²| MS:beer, Sirs   *1879:*sirs   ¹¹³| MS:I've   *1879:*"I've

¹¹⁵ On Yule-tide bowl—your head's a-work and both your eyes
Break loose? Afeard, you fool? As if the dead can rise!
Say—Bagman Dick was found last May with fuddling-cap
Stuffed in his mouth: to choke's a natural mishap!'
'Gaffer, be—blessed,' cries she, 'and Bagman Dick as well!
¹²⁰ I, you, and he are damned: this Public is our hell:
We live in fire: live coals don't feel!—once quenched, they learn—
Cinders do, to what dust they moulder while they burn!'

"'If you don't speak straight out,' says I—belike I swore—
'A knobstick, well you know the taste of, shall, once more,
¹²⁵ Teach you to talk, my maid!' She ups with such a face,
Heart sunk inside me. 'Well, pad on, my prate-apace!'

"'I've been about those laces we need for . . . never mind!
If henceforth they tie hands, 't is mine they'll have to bind.
You know who makes them best—the Tinker in our cage,
¹³⁰ Pulled-up for gospelling, twelve years ago: no age
To try another trade,—yet, so he scorned to take
Money he did not earn, he taught himself the make
Of laces, tagged and tough—Dick Bagman found them so!
Good customers were we! Well, last week, you must know,
¹³⁵ His girl,—the blind young chit, who hawks about his wares,—
She takes it in her head to come no more—such airs
These hussies have! Yet, since we need a stoutish lace,—
"I'll to the jail-bird father, abuse her to his face!"
So, first I filled a jug to give me heart, and then,
¹⁴⁰ Primed to the proper pitch, I posted to their den—

---

¹¹⁶| MS:Broke   *1879:*Break   ¹¹⁸| MS:drink's §first five letters crossed out and replaced
above by five letters§ choke   ¹¹⁹| MS:"Gaffer <> blessed," cries she "and   *1879:*'Gaffer
<> blessed,' cries she, 'and   ¹²⁰| MS:hell,   *1879:*hell: ¹²²| MS:We §crossed out§
<> what §added above§ <> they §over we§ <> they §over we§ burn!   *1879:*burn!'
¹²³| MS:'If   *1879:*"'If   ¹²⁴| MS:knobstick, that you <> more   *1879:*knobstick, well
you <> more,   ¹²⁵| MS:my girl!' She   *1879:*my maid!' She   ¹²⁶| MS:me. 'Well,
go §crossed out and replaced above by§ pad   ¹²⁷| MS:"I've <> for . . never   *1879:*"'I've
<> for . . . never   ¹²⁹| MS:cage   *1879:*cage,   ¹³³| MS:so,—   *1879:*so!
¹³⁴| MS:know,   *1889a:*know §emended to§ know, §see Editorial Notes§   ¹³⁷| MS:a good
§crossed out§ stout §altered to§ stoutish   ¹³⁸| MS:'I'll <> face'!   *1879:*"'I'll <> face!"

Patmore—they style their prison! I tip the turnkey, catch
My heart up, fix my face, and fearless lift the latch—
Both arms a-kimbo, in bounce with a good round oath
Ready for rapping out: no "Lawks" nor "By my troth!"

145 "'There sat my man, the father. He looked up: what one feels
When heart that leapt to mouth drops down again to heels!
He raised his hand . . . Hast seen, when drinking out the night,
And in, the day, earth grow another something quite
Under the sun's first stare? I stood a very stone.

150 "'"Woman!" (a fiery tear he put in every tone),
"How should my child frequent your house where lust is sport,
Violence—trade? Too true! I trust no vague report.
Her angel's hand, which stops the sight of sin, leaves clear
The other gate of sense, lets outrage through the ear.
155 What has she heard!—which, heard shall never be again.
Better lack food than feast, a Dives in the—wain
Or reign or train—of Charles!" (His language was not ours:
'Tis my belief, God spoke: no tinker has such powers).
"Bread, only bread they bring—my laces: if we broke
160 Your lump of leavened sin, the loafs first crumb would choke!"
"'Down on my marrow-bones! Then all at once rose he:
His brown hair burst a-spread, his eyes were suns to see
Up went his hands: "Through flesh, I reach, I read thy soul!
So may some stricken tree look blasted, bough and bole,
165 Champed by the fire-tooth, charred without, and yet, thrice-bound
With dreriment about, within may life be found,
A prisoned power to branch and blossom as before,
Could but the gardener cleave the cloister, reach the core,

143| MS:a jolly §crossed out and replaced above by two words§ good round
145| MS:There *1879:*"'There   147| MS:hand—Hast <> night *1879:*hand . . . Hast
<> night,   148| MS:in—the *1879:*in, the   150| MS:'Woman!' (as if he put a tear
in <> tone) *1879:*"'"Woman!" (a fiery tear he put in <> tone),   151| MS:'How
1879:"How   152| MS:report: *1879:*report.   156| MS:lack §first two letters over
illegible letters§   157| MS:of Charles!' (His *1879:*of Charles!" (His
158| MS:powers) *1879:*powers).   159| MS:'Bread *1879:*"Bread
160| MS:choke!' *1879:*choke!"   161| MS:Down *1879:*"'Down
163| MS:hands: 'Through *1879:*hands: "Through

Loosen the vital sap: yet where shall help be found?
170 Who says 'How save it?'—nor 'Why cumbers it the ground?'
Woman, that tree art thou! All sloughed about with scurf,
Thy stag-horns fright the sky, thy snake-roots sting the turf!
Drunkenness, wantonness, theft, murder gnash and gnarl
Thine outward, case thy soul with coating like the marle
175 Satan stamps flat upon each head beneath his hoof!
And how deliver such? The strong men keep aloof,
Lover and friend stand far, the mocking ones pass by,
Tophet gapes wide for prey: lost soul, despair and die!
What then? 'Look unto me and be ye saved!' saith God:
180 'I strike the rock, outstreats the life-stream at my rod!
Be your sins scarlet, wool shall they seem like,—although
As crimson red, yet turn white as the driven snow!' "

"'There, there, there! All I seem to somehow understand
Is—that, if I reached home, 'twas through the guiding hand
185 Of his blind girl which led and led me through the streets
And out of town and up to door again. What greets
First thing my eye, as limbs recover from their swoon?
A book—this Book she gave at parting. "Father's boon—
The Book he wrote: it reads as if he spoke, himself:
190 He cannot preach in bonds, so,—take it down from shelf
When you want counsel,—think you hear his very voice!"

"'Wicked dear Husband, first despair and then rejoice!
Dear wicked Husband, waste no tick of moment more,
Be saved like me, bald trunk! There's greenness yet at core,
195 Sap under slough! Read, read!'

"Let me take breath, my lords!
I'd like to know, are these—hers, mine, or Bunyan's words?

170| MS:says "How <> it?"—nor "Why <> ground?"   *1879:*says 'How <> it?'—nor 'Why <>
ground?'   179| MS:then?   "Look <> saved"! saith   *1879:*then?   'Look <> saved!'
saith   180| MS:"I   *1879:*'I   182| MS:snow!"   *1879:*snow!' "   183| MS:There,
there, there! All that §crossed out§   *1879:* "'There, there, there   188| MS:book
*1879:*this Book   189| MS:book   *1879:*The Book   192| MS:Wicked   *1879:* "'Wicked
195| MS:read!" §¶§ Let   *1879:*read!' §¶§ "Let   197| MS:alone   *1879:*alone!

I'm 'wildered—scarce with drink,—nowise with drink alone!
You'll say, with heat: but heat's no stuff to split a stone
Like this black boulder—this flint heart of mine: the Book—
200   That dealt the crashing blow! Sirs, here's the fist that shook
His beard till Wrestler Jem howled like a just-lugged bear!
You had brained me with a feather: at once I grew aware
Christmas was meant for me. A burden at your back,
Good Master Christmas? Nay,—yours was that Joseph's sack,
205   —Or whose it was,—which held the cup,—compared with mine!
Robbery loads my loins, perjury cracks my chine,
Adultery . . . nay, Tab, you pitched me as I flung!
One word, I'll up with fist . . . No, sweet spouse, hold your tongue!

"I'm hasting to the end. The Book, sirs—take and read!
210   You have my history in a nutshell,—ay, indeed!
It must off, my burden! See,—slack straps and into pit,
Roll, reach the bottom, rest, rot there—a plague on it!
For a mountain's sure to fall and bury Bedford Town,
'Destruction'—that's the name, and fire shall burn it down!
215   O 'scape the wrath in time! Time's now, if not too late.
How can I pilgrimage up to the wicket-gate?
Next comes Despond the slough: not that I fear to pull
Through mud, and dry my clothes at brave House Beautiful—
But it's late in the day, I reckon: had I left years ago
220   Town, wife, and children dear . . . Well, Christmas did, you know!—
Soon I had met in the valley and tried my cudgel's strength
On the enemy horned and winged, a-straddle across its length!
Have at his horns, thwick—thwack: they snap, see! Hoof and hoof—
Bang, break the fetlock-bones! For love's sake, keep aloof
225   Angels! I'm man and match,—this cudgel for my flail,—

198| MS:say, the heat   *1879:*say, with heat   199| MS:book §altered to§ the Book
207| MS:Adultery . . nay, old §crossed out§   *1879:*Adultery . . . nay   208| MS:fist . . No
*1879:*fist . . . No   209| MS:I'm   *1879:* "I'm   213| MS:bury Bedford Town
*1879:*bury Bedford Town,   214| MS: "Destruction"—that's the name, for fire
1879:'Destruction'—that's the name, and fire   215| MS:scape   *1879:* 'scape
217| MS:slough—not   *1879:*slough: not   218| MS:mud and   *1879:*mud, and
220| MS:dear . . Well   *1879:*dear . . . Well   221| MS:the Valley   *1879:*valley
222| MS:winged a-straddle   *1879:*winged, a-straddle   223| MS:thwack—they <> hoof,
*1879:*thwack: they <> hoof—   224| MS:aloof,   *1879:*aloof

To thresh him, hoofs and horns, bat's wing and serpent's tail!
A chance gone by! But then, what else does Hopeful ding
Into the deafest ear except—hope, hope's the thing?
Too late i' the day for me to thrid the windings: but
230 There's still a way to win the race by death's short cut!
Did Master Faithful need climb the Delightful Mounts?
No, straight to Vanity Fair,—a fair, by all accounts,
Such as is held outside,—lords, ladies, grand and gay,—
Says he in the face of them, just what you hear me say.
235 And the Judges brought him in guilty, and brought him out
To die in the market-place—St. Peter's Green's about
The same thing: there they flogged, flayed, buffeted, lanced with
          knives,
Pricked him with swords,—I'll swear, he'd full a cat's nine lives,—
So to his end at last came Faithful,—ha, ha, he!
240 Who holds the highest card? for there stands hid, you see,
Behind the rabble-rout, a chariot, pair and all:
He's in, he's off, he's up, through clouds, at trumpet-call,
Carried the nearest way to Heaven-gate! Odds my life—
Has nobody a sword to spare? not even a knife?
245 Then hang me, draw and quarter! Tab—do the same by her!
O Master Worldly-Wiseman . . . that's Master Interpreter,
Take the will, not the deed! Our gibbet's handy close:
Forestall Last Judgment-Day! Be kindly, not morose!
There wants no earthly judge-and-jurying: here we stand—
250 Sentence our guilty selves: so, hang us out of hand!
Make haste for pity's sake! A single moment's loss
Means—Satan's lord once more: his whisper shoots across

228| MS:ear but hope, hope, hope's   *1879:*ear except—hope, hope's
229| MS:to travel §crossed out and replaced above by two words§ thrid the windings—but
*1879:*windings: but   232| MS:to Vanity Fair, a   *1879:*to Vanity Fair,—a
233| MS:outside, lords   *1879:*outside,—lords   234| MS:say: *1879:*say.
236| MS:market-place—Saint   *1879:*market-place—St.   237| MS:thing—there they
§inserted above§   *1879:*thing: there   238| MS:And pricked with   *1879:*Pricked him
with   241| MS:all—   *1879:*all: 245| MS:quarter,—Tab   *1879:*quarter! Tab
246| MS:O Master Worldly-Wiseman . . that's   *1879:*O Master Worldly-Wiseman . . . that's
247| MS:handy, close—   *1879:*close: *1882:*hand close: *1889a:*handy close:
248| MS:Forestall our §crossed out and replaced above by§ the   *1879:*Forestall Last Judgment-Day
250| MS:hand,—   *1879:*hand!   252| MS:lord again: his   *1879:*lord once more: his

All singing in my heart, all praying in my brain,
'It comes of heat and beer!'—hark how he guffaws plain!
255 'To-morrow you'll wake bright, and, in a safe skin, hug
Your sound selves, Tab and you, over a foaming jug!
You've had such qualms before, time out of mind!' He's right!
Did not we kick and cuff and curse away, that night
When home we blindly reeled, and left poor humpback Joe
260 I' the lurch to pay for what . . . somebody did, you know!
Both of us maundered then 'Lame humpback,—never more
Will he come limping, drain his tankard at our door!
He'll swing, while—somebody . . . ' Says Tab, 'No, for I'll peach!'
'I'm for you, Tab,' cries I, 'there's rope enough for each!'
265 So blubbered we, and bussed, and went to bed upon
The grace of Tab's good thought: by morning, all was gone!
We laughed—'What's life to him, a cripple of no account?'
Oh, waves increase around—I feel them mount and mount!
Hang us! To-morrow brings Tom Bearward with his bears:
270 One new black-muzzled brute beats Sackerson, he swears:
(Sackerson, for my money!) And, baiting o'er, the Brawl
They lead on Turner's Patch,—lads, lasses, up tails all,—
I'm i' the thick o' the throng! That means the Iron Cage,
—Means the Lost Man inside! Where's hope for such as wage
275 War against light? Light's left, light's here, I hold light still,
So does Tab—make but haste to hang us both! You will?"

I promise, when he stopped you might have heard a mouse
Squeak, such a death-like hush sealed up the old Mote House.

253| MS:my ears, all *1879:*my heart, all   254| MS:" §altered to§ 'It <> beer!'" §altered
to§ beer!'—hark   258| MS:away that *1879:*away, that   259| MS:hump-back
*1879:*humpback   263| MS:somebody! . . "says §altered to§ somebody! . . Says Tab,—
"No,— for <> peach!" *1879:*somebody . . .' Says Tab, 'No, for <> peach!'
265| MS:we and bussed and went §over illegible erasure§ *1879:*we, and bussed, and
267| MS:him,—cripple *1879:*him, a cripple   268| MS:Black §crossed out and replaced
above by one word and comma§ Oh, waves   269| MS:brings Jack §crossed out and
replaced above by§ Tom bearward *1879:*brings Tom Bearward
273| MS:throng!—that *1879:*throng! hat   274| MS:lost man *1879:*the Lost Man
275| MS:here, I §over possibly we§ hold it §crossed out and replaced by§ light
276| MS:us, both! You will?' *1879:*us both! You will?"   278| MS:the Sessions §crossed
out and replaced above by two words§ Old Mote House: *1879:*the Old Mote House.

But when the mass of man sank meek upon his knees,
280 While Tab, alongside, wheezed a hoarse "Do hang us, please!"
Why, then the waters rose, no eye but ran with tears,
Hearts heaved, heads thumped, until, paying all past arrears
Of pity and sorrow, at last a regular scream outbroke
Of triumph, joy and praise.

My Lord Chief justice spoke,
285 First mopping brow and cheek, where still, for one that budged,
Another bead broke fresh: "What Judge, that ever judged
Since first the world began, judged such a case as this?
Why, Master Bratts, long since, folk smelt you out, I wis!
I had my doubts, i' faith, each time you played the fox
290 Convicting geese of crime in yonder witness-box—
Yea, much did I misdoubt, the thief that stole her eggs
Was hardly goosey's self at Reynard's game, i' feggs!
Yet thus much was to praise—you spoke to point, direct—
Swore you heard, saw the theft: no jury could suspect—
295 Dared to suspect,—I'll say,—a spot in white so clear:
Goosey was throttled, true: but thereof godly fear
Came of example set, much as our laws intend;
And though a fox confessed, you proved the Judge's friend.
What if I had my doubts? Suppose I gave them breath,
300 Brought you to bar: what work to do, ere 'Guilty, Death,'—
Had paid our pains! What heaps of witnesses to drag
From holes and corners, paid from out the County's bag!
Trial three dog-days long! *Amicus Curiæ*—that's
Your title, no dispute—truth-telling Master Bratts!
305 Thank you, too, Mistress Tab! Why doubt one word you say?
Hanging you both deserve, hanged both shall be this day!
The tinker needs must be a proper man. I've heard

279| MS:the bulky §crossed out and replaced above by two words§ mass of <> down §crossed out and replaced above by§ meek   280| MS:hoarse 'Do <> please!'   *1879:*hoarse "Do <> please!"   284| MS:praise. §¶; no line space§ My   *1889a:*praise. §¶; line space added§ My   285| MS:cheek where   *1879:*cheek, where
286| MS:fresh: What   *1879:*fresh: "What   294| MS:suspect   *1879:*suspect—
297| MS:intend,   *1879:*intend;   298| MS:And though   *1879:*And, though
300| MS:ere 'Guilty, Death'   *1889a:*ere 'Guilty, Death,'—   307| MS:Not that, by any means, §illegible words§ as you §line crossed out and replaced above by§ This Tinker needs must be a proper man: I've heard   *1879:*The tinker <> man. I've

261

He lies in Jail long since: if Quality's good word
Warrants me letting loose,—some householder, I mean—
310   Freeholder, better still,—I don't say but—between
Now and next Sessions . . . Well! Consider of his case,
I promise to, at least: we owe him so much grace.
Not that—no, God forbid!—I lean to think, as you,
The grace that such repent is any jail-bird's due:
315   I rather see the fruit of twelve years' pious reign—
Astræa Redux, Charles restored his rights again!
—Of which, another time! I somehow feel a peace
Stealing across the world. May deeds like this increase!
So, Master Sheriff, stay that sentence I pronounced
320   On those two dozen odd: deserving to be trounced
Soundly, and yet . . . well, well, at all events despatch
This pair of—shall I say, sinner-saints?—ere we catch
Their jail-distemper too. Stop tears, or I'll indite
All weeping Bedfordshire for turning Bunyanite!"

325   So, forms were galloped through. If Justice, on the spur,
Proved somewhat expeditious, would Quality demur?
And happily hanged were they,—why lengthen out my tale?—
Where Bunyan's Statue stands facing where stood his Jail.

311| MS:next Sessions . . Well *1879:*next Sessions . . . Well   312| MS:promise that, at
<> grace *1879:*promise to, at <> grace.   313| MS:that,—No *1879:*that—no
314| MS:that you repent *1879:*that such repent   319| MS:So, Master Sheriff,—stay
*1879:*So, Master Sheriff, stay   320| MS:odd—deserving *1879:*odd: deserving
321| MS:yet,—well, well <> dispatch *1879:*despatch *1882:*yet . . . well, well
322| MS:pair of §circled and inserted above§   323| MS:too,—Stop *1879:*too. Stop
324-27| MS:turning Bunyanite! / §¶§ So, happily hanged they were,—why *1879:*turning
Bunyanite!" / §¶§ <> hanged were they,—why *1882:*turning Bunyanite!" / §¶§ So, forms
were galloped through. If Justice, on the spur, / Proved somewhat expeditious, would quality
demur? / And happily *1889a:*would Quality   328| MS:stood the §crossed out and
replaced above by§ his

THE AGAMEMNON OF ÆSCHYLUS

Emendations to the Text

The following emendations have been made to the 1889a copy-text:

Introductory Note, l. 29: In his MS, B placed a tilde (rather than the more customary circumflex) over the iota in the first Greek word in this line; he was probably following the practice of Weise's 1843 edition of Aeschylus (see *The Agamemnon of Aeschylus, Sources*, below), which regularly printed its circumflexes as small tildes. P1877 and 1877 printed a tilde here, but 1889a lacks the required mark above the iota. A very small inked fragment remains visible only in some copies of the Large Paper issue of 1889a. A parallel example involves the omega in l. 85 of the *Introductory Note*. B placed a tilde over the omega in his MS, and P1877-1877 printed it; 1889a provides a correct circumflex. For consistency, we have emended l. 29 by placing a circumflex over the iota.

l. 12: MS-1877 have a comma after *dew-drenched* to establish parallelism with the preceding adjectival phrase; 1889a omits the comma. The MS-1877 punctuation is restored.

ll. 754-55: A line-space marking this new paragraph, present in MS-1877, fell at the bottom of a page in the copy-text, obscuring the break in the discourse; the paragraph is restored.

ll. 778-79: A line-space marking this new paragraph, present in MS-1877, fell at the bottom of a page in the copy-text, obscuring the break in the discourse; the paragraph is restored.

l. 801: The compositors in 1877 misread MS *joy* as *say*; the error remained uncorrected. The MS reading is restored.

l. 1202: The necessary period at the end of this line, present in MS-1877, is absent from 1889a; the period is restored.

l. 1323: The copy-text misspells *avoidance*, while MS-1877 have the word correctly spelled; further, 1889a garbles the sense of the line by printing *no some* where MS-1877 read *no! Some*. The MS-1877 readings are restored.

263

l. 1472-73: B's MS has no end-line punctuation for l. 1472; the comma was added in P1877; simultaneously, MS has a comma after *Aigisthos* in l. 1473, but the punctuation is removed in P1877. No changes were made in 1889a. Though the grammar and the rhetoric of this passage are gnarled, the MS punctuation seems slightly more logical, and is restored here.

l. 1542: The four texts collated present three different punctuation marks at the end of this line. The MS has a dash; P1877 and 1877 have an exclamation point; and 1889a has a strangely-placed period. The eight-line lament of ll. 1537-44 is repeated at ll. 1563-70, with l. 1568 (identical to 1542) retaining the exclamation point found in P1877-1877. The punctuation mark in the copy-text appears to be damaged, and the P1877-1877 reading is restored.

l. 1553: B's MS clearly reads *ones'* in this line, reflecting the plural form in the Greek original; all printed texts erroneously read *one's*. The MS reading is restored.

l. 1723: MS-1877 read *o'er-bloom*, while the copy-text omits the hyphen. The hyphen is restored in conformity with B's other uses of compound forms in the poem.

Composition and publication

B's special interest in the *Agamemnon* can be traced back to *Pauline* (March 1833), where the play exemplified the speaker's "old lore," i.e., his knowledge of ancient Greek literature:

> that king
> Treading the purple calmly to his death,
> While round him, like the clouds of eve, all dusk,
> The giant shades of fate, silently flitting,
> Pile the dim outline of the coming doom;
> (ll. 567-71, 1833 text; this edition, 1.32)

In a manuscript note on page 40 of J. S. Mill's review-copy of the poem (*Reconstruction*, B20), now in the Victoria and Albert Museum, London, B quoted the Greek behind his allusion:

> ἐπεὶ δ' ἀκούειν σοῦ κατέστραμμαι τάδε
> εἶμ' ἐς δόμων μέλαθρα πορφύρας πάτων
> Agamemnon 957

The Greek words (if the last is given its correct accent, πατῶν) mean literally: "and since I have been forced to listen to/ obey you on this point, I will go into the halls of my house treading on purples."

They are spoken by Agamemnon when he finally does what Clytaem-
nestra has been urging him to do: starts walking from his chariot
across purple cloths (normally reserved for the worship of the gods)
into his palace, where she will murder him (AP 929-30, AL 956-7).

By 1877 Aeschylus had become closely associated with B's memo-
ries of his dead wife EBB, whose interest in that poet had antedated his
own. Though in 1827 she only knew "Aeschyelus [*sic*] by his reputation,"
by March 1828 her "head and heart" were evidently "full of
Prometheus," i.e., in Aeschylus' *Prometheus Bound*, which she then knew
well enough in the original Greek to "suspect an inadvertency" in what
her Greek tutor, H. S. Boyd had said about it in a note to his translation
of the *Agamemnon* (*Correspondence*, 2.40, 107; see also *Reconstruction*,
A19). She went on to publish a verse translation of the *Prometheus* her-
self, in the same year as B's *Pauline*. But long before that she had turned
her attention to the *Agamemnon*. "I hope," she wrote to Boyd (March
1828) "that we may have a great deal of personal intercourse this sum-
mer, and that the Agamemnon may be a party concerned." It certainly
was, and according to a memorandum by Boyd, she got to the end of the
Greek text of the *Agamemnon* on 29 September 1830, having read to him
more than 1000 lines in six days (*Correspondence*, 2.120, 258n. 2).

The famous love-letters of 1845-46 were full of Aeschylean quota-
tions and allusions which came to serve as a private language between
the two poets. By February 1845 EBB had come to regard her translation
of the *Prometheus* as "the 'Blot on my escutcheon'" (a flattering allusion
to the title of B's play), but said she was thinking of writing a monologue
"of Aeschylus as he sate a blind exile on the flats of Sicily and recounted
the past to his own soul, just before the eagle cracked his great massy
skull with a stone" (*Correspondence*, 10.102). In March B's reply discussed
the τυφλὰς ... ἐλπίδας (= blind hopes) by which Prometheus claimed to
have saved mortals from being too conscious of their mortality (*Corre-
spondence*, 10.107; *Prometheus Bound*, 250-53). Continuing that discussion,
EBB asked: "Tell me . . . if Aeschylus is not the divinest of all the divine
Greek souls?" (*Correspondence*, 10.111); to which B's answer implied, yes
he is, and *you* are his modern equivalent: "Restore the Prometheus
πυρφόρος [= fire-bringing] as Shelley did the Λυόμενος [= being loosed
or unbound, as in the title of Shelley's *Prometheus Unbound* of 1820]" i.e.,
write from your own divine soul the first of the two lost plays of the
Aeschylean trilogy to which the surviving play (the Prometheus
Δεσμώτης [= Bound] belongs (*Correspondence*, 10.119).

By May 1845 both correspondents were becoming frustrated by
the language of literary allusion, the "sphinxine idiom in our talk," as
EBB called it (*Correspondence*, 10.188). B then suggested the reason for
it: when writing to a person one had never met, one was inevitably wary

of saying plainly what one meant. "So the thought of what I should find in my heart to say, and the contrast with what I suppose I ought to say . . . all these things are against me" (*Correspondence*, 10.199). Not yet daring to speak his mind, he appealed to her intuition—still using the language of classical literary allusion: "you are *you*, and know something about me, if not much, and have read Bos on the art of supplying Ellipses, and . . . will *subaudire* [= understand, supply a word omitted]" (*Correspondence*, 10.200). B's reference to the *Ellipses Graecae* of Lambertus Bos gave EBB an opening for a punning allusion to the Greek text of the *Agamemnon*: "*What do you mean about your manuscripts . . . about 'Saul' & the portfolio?* for I am afraid of hazardously supplying ellipses—and your 'Bos' comes to βοῦς ἐπὶ γλώσσῃ [= ox on tongue]" (*Correspondence*, 10.203). "Bos," the surname of the Dutch author of *Ellipses Graecae* (= Greek ellipses; 1713), is also the Latin equivalent of βοῦς (= ox); and the Watchman who speaks first in the *Agamemnon*, after one dark hint at Clytaemnestra's behaviour in her husband's absence, adds hastily: τὰ δ' ἄλλα σιγῶ· βοῦς ἐπὶ γλώσσῃ μέγας βέβηκεν (= but about the other things I'm silent—a great ox has trodden on my tongue—a proverbial phrase meaning I dare not speak freely; AP, AL 36-37; see ll. 35-36). Thus EBB's plea for plain-speaking, which led that same month to the the lovers' first meeting, was unforgettably associated in B's mind with the *Agamemnon*.

Some more recent events may have helped to make B decide to "transcribe" the *Agamemnon*. One was the publication in 1876 of Edward Fitzgerald's *Agamemnon: A Tragedy, Taken from Aeschylus*. Fitzgerald never seems to have been one of B's favorite contemporary poets. Park Honan has plausibly suggested that "Rabbi Ben Ezra" (1864; this edition, 6.226) was B's answer to the "atheism, pessimism, and rampant hedonism" of Fitzgerald's *Omar Khayyám* (Irvine and Honan, 398-89); and in 1889 B would attack Fitzgerald in a savage epigram for his reported comment on EBB's death: "no more Aurora Leighs, thank God!" (Irvine and Honan, 513-14). But now in 1876, without any such personal reason for anger, B probably found an implicit challenge in the shameless inaccuracy of Fitzgerald's version (or "Per-version" as Fitzgerald himself described it) of the Aeschylean text, and especially in the cheerful defeatism of his Preface: "I suppose that a literal version of this play, if possible, would scarce be intelligible. Even were the dialogue always clear, the lyric Choruses, which make up so large a part, are so dark and abrupt in themselves, and therefore so much the more mangled and tormented by copyist and commentator, that the most conscientious translator must not only jump at a meaning, but must bridge over a chasm . . ." (*Fitzgerald Selected Works*, Joanna Richardson, ed., [London, 1962], 387). Surely, B must have told himself, he could do better than that!

Another recent event that apparently encouraged B to transcribe the *Agamemnon* was Heinrich Schliemann's excavation of Mycenae in 1876. In September of that year *The Times* published a letter from Schliemann describing what he had found so far. The report began with a sketch of the whole area which formed the backdrop to Aeschylus' tragedy:

> In the north corner of the Plain of Argos, at the foot of two steep mountains, one of which is 2,500 ft. high and crowned by a chapel of the Prophet Elias, on a 132 ft. high and 1,200 ft. long and broad triangular rock, which falls off precipitately to the north and south and forms to the east and west six natural or artificial terraces, is situated the famous Acropolis of Mycenae.
>
> (*Times*, 27 September 1876, 10)

Schliemann, who wished to prove that Mycenae was indeed the city of Agamemnon, (wrongly) believed that he had discovered Agamemnon's grave, and is (also wrongly) reputed to have telegraphed the King of Greece: "I have gazed on the face of Agamemnon" (*The Oxford Companion to Classical Literature*, M. C. Howatson, ed., 2nd ed. [Oxford, 1989], 175; David A. Traill, *Schliemann of Troy: Treasure and Deceit* [London, 1995], 2, 162-64). In this letter he described, among artefacts he was finding, a bas relief on a tombstone of a "warrior standing in a chariot," which might well have reminded B of Agamemnon's first appearance in the play (AL 782). Schliemann's last paragraph typified his ambition to confirm by his digs the statements of ancient Greek texts: "Homer repeatedly calls Mycenae πολύχρυσος (rich in gold), and the great wealth of the city is certainly confirmed by its numerous Treasuries and the costly style of their architecture." B was similarly anxious to take those texts literally, and the opportunity was not to be missed. On 22 December 1876 he wrote to his publisher, George Smith:

> I was reading the wonderful letter of Schliemann, this morning. It strikes me that you, the famous for enterprise, might fancy something of this kind—Bring our an edition of the finest of all Greek plays—the "Agamemnon" of Aeschylus—which, in default of a better translator, I would try my hand & heart at—and illustrate it by photographs of all the "find" at Mycenae—including the remains of the City itself. Jowett pressed on me, years ago, to make such a translation, and Carlyle did the same thing a fortnight since: I could manage it, I think: but there want,—I go back to

say,—the man of enterprise,—so, turn the matter over in your mind, and if nothing is gained by my suggestion, no harm is done at least . . . If you *did* incline to the adventure, I suppose you would announce the fact—and so keep others out of the field.

(Quarterly Review No 629, July 1961, 330)

Presumably Smith's reply was encouraging, for B seems to have started work on his translation right away. According to the MS in Balliol College Library, it was finished by 23 April 1877. B's introduction was apparently written last, for that MS is dated "London, May, '77." When publishing the "transcript" (Monday, 15 October 1877), Smith showed rather less "enterprise" than B had hoped of him: though doubtless happy to cash in on the publicity for Agamemnon generated by Schliemann, he added no illustrations.

Sources

B seems to have worked mainly from the Greek text and English notes of *The Tragedies of Aeschylus: Re-edited by F. A. Paley,* 3rd Edition (London, 1870) (for B's copy, see *Reconstruction,* A24). But he was freely eclectic in his choice of individual readings, taking some, for instance, from C. H. Weise's edition of the *Tragoediae Aeschyli* (Leipsig, 1843) (*Reconstruction,* A13). As he put it in his introduction: "following no editor exclusively, I keep to the earlier readings so long as sense can be made out of them, but disregard, I hope, little of importance in recent criticism so far as I have fallen in with it" (*Introductory Note,* ll. 45-47). He made occasional use of the *Scholia in Aeschylum* (n.p., 1820), which he had inscribed and given to EBB (*Reconstruction,* A22), and evidently took a few hints from F. A. Paley's *Aeschylus Translated into English Prose* (Cambridge, 1864), of which he owned the second edition of 1871 (*Reconstruction,* A16).

Reception and After-history

Two of the work's first readers might have been expected to respond generously to B's translation: Paley, on whose Greek text and English notes it was largely based, and Carlyle, who had suggested it, and to whom it was gracefully dedicated. Sure enough, the most favorable as well as the best-informed review was Paley's in the *Athenaeum* (27 October 1877, 525-27; reprinted in *Browning: the Critical Heritage,* B. Litzinger and D. Smalley, eds. [London, 1970], 433-39). Explaining the huge difficulty of the undertaking, " *poetical* translation of the most rigid literality," Paley emphasized B's remarkable success in carrying it out:

> How can I turn, let him say, what this Greek sang above two thousand years ago into exactly correlative English, giving my version a metrical drapery, and *when possible* beauty of English phrase? And because Mr. B has nobly and unfalteringly acted up to these precepts, his transcript is most unequal in its excellence. Had he been less conscientious, he could, no man better, have given us not one bald or common-place line from the exordium of the watchman, sleeping the wakeful sleep of a house-dog, to the final strut of Aegisthus beside Clytemnestra. But Mr B *has* splendidly denied himself, and is unflinchingly crude, pointless, even clumsy, where the Greek pushes and compels him. Yet in the most rugged passages he never once flings his literality over board. To such crisis and ἀπορία [= lack of resource] Mr B is happily not reduced above some half-dozen times within the compass of the present transcript. His verbal resource is amazing. But, here and again, when, under his masterly touch, the Greek has rendered itself for a page without to us apparent effort, word for word, and phrase by phrase, into English, eloquent and sonorous, all at once, some single line crops up, which cannot be rendered both beautifully and exactly; so Mr. B leaves it unbeautiful and bald, and careers on as finely as before . . . Yet has Mr. B his compensative reward: some of his most charming touches in this play arise from the fearless audacity with which he will track our a word's root-meaning; which grasped, down he sets it, homely or not, so only that Aeschylus so meant and spoke it (op. cit., 435).

For the Greek original was not necessarily perfect; and Paley made the extremely important point that Aeschylus' conception of style was different from a modern critic's:

> Indeed, in those days bards had no canons of self-criticism; they wrote to be recited, not to be read. The ear is more lenient to repetitions than is the eye. There was then less rule and more spontaneity, and most poetry of the impulsive and impassioned order abounds in iterations. But the poets of today submit their more spontaneous outbursts to sedulous revision; hence, these little samenesses seldom reach the printing-press.

In contrast, Carlyle's private comments on B's effort to William Allingham were both ungrateful and obtuse:

> Oh yes, he called down some months ago to ask if he might dedicate it to me. I told him I should feel highly honoured. But—O bless me! *Can you understand it at all?* I went carefully into some parts of it and for my soul's salvation (laughs) couldn't make out the meaning . . . If any one tells me this is because the thing is so remote from us—I say things far remoter from our minds and experiences have been well translated into English. The book of Job, for instance. It's bad Hebrew, I understand, the original of it, and a very strange thing to us. But the translator said to himself, "the first thing I have to do is to make this as intelligible as possible to the English reader; if I do not do this I shall be—in fact *damned.*" But he succeeded most admirably, and there are very few books so well worth reading as our Book of Job.
>
> Yes, B says I ordered him to do this translation—he winds up his preface (highly to his own satisfaction, in a neat epigrammatic manner) by saying so,—summing it all up in a last word; and I did often enough tell him he might do a most excellent book, by far the best he had ever done, by translating the Greek dramatists— but O dear! He's a very foolish fellow. He picks you out the English for the Greek word by word, and now and again sticks two or three words together with hyphens; then again he snips up the sense and jingles it into rhyme! I could have told him he could do no good whatever under such conditions.
>
> (*William Allingham: A Diary,* H. Allingham and D. Radford, eds.
> [London, 1907], 257-58)

Carlyle's remarks imply that one can judge whether a work has been "well translated" without reference to the original; and they ignore the stated purpose of the Transcript. This was not to popularize Aeschylus' already famous tragedy (nor should we credit B, as some recent critics have done, with any ulterior motives for transcribing it). He was simply doing what he said he was doing: trying to give the Greekless reader some idea what the original work was actually like:

> If, because of the immense fame of the following Tragedy, I wished to acquaint myself with it, *and could only do so by the help of a translator* (my italics), I should require him to be literal at every cost save that of absolute violence to our language.
>
> (*Introductory Note,* ll. 3-6).

Except for Paley, and for J. A. Symonds, who pointed out the contradiction or "compromise" inherent in the attempt to translate literally in verse, and even in rhymed verse (*Academy*, 3 December 1877, xii, 419-20; reprinted in *Browning: the Critical Heritage*, B. Litzinger and D. Smalley, eds. [London, 1970], 440) the published reviewers were no more perceptive than Carlyle. A facetious notice in the *London Quarterly Review* (April 1878, i, 232-34; reprinted in *Browning: the Critical Heritage*, B. Litzinger and D. Smalley, eds. [London, 1970], 443-44) dismissed the whole enterprise as pointless:

> Any attempt to reproduce "the reputed magniloquence and sonority of the Greek" Mr. B wholly disclaims; he will give us "the ideas of the poet—a strict bald version of word pregnant with thing." But we contend that in such a form the ideas (supposing them there) are worthless. To the unlearned they say little or nothing; to the scholar they suggest a painful reminiscence of school-boy flounderings through passages at most a quarter understood.

Despite the critical irrelevance of the last remark, it was just such a "reminiscence" that indirectly helped to publicize B's book later. Though sales failed to justify a second edition, the memory of "schoolboy flounderings" under a classics master at Harrow prompted Terence Rattigan to write *The Browning Version* (1948). Behind the action of this play, revived on the London stage and filmed for the second time in 1994, the husband-murder of the *Agamemnon* is dimly discernible; and at a critical point the plot turns on some Greek words quoted from the tragedy: τὸν κρατοῦντα μαλθακῶς θεὸς πρόσωθεν εὐμενῶς προσδέρκεται.

> ANDREW. That means—in a rough translation: "God from afar looks graciously upon a gentle master." It comes from a speech of Agamemnon's to Clytaemnestra.
> (Terence Rattigan, *Playbill*, introd. Dan Rebellato [London, 1994], 32-35; AL 951-52; see ll. 957-58.)

In *The Browning Version* these words are written by a schoolboy in a second-hand copy of B's transcript that he is presenting to his classics master. But even the donor comments: "It's not much good," and even the recipient, though deeply grateful for the graceful gesture, seems not much more reluctant than Carlyle to look this particular gift-horse in the mouth: "It has its faults, I agree, but I think you will enjoy it more when you get used to the metre he employs."

Introductory Note]

13-14]   *to gape* . . . *Theognis*   In Aristophanes' *Acharnians* 9-11 the Athenian farmer Dicaeopolis describes his "tragic pain" when he was "gaping in expectation [ἐκεχήνη προσδοκῶν, i.e., waiting open-mouthed]" for a play by Aeschylus, and they announced one by a boring poet called Theognis instead (not the famous Theognis, the Megarian elegiac poet of the 6ᵗʰ century B.C.).

15-16]   *the employment . . . old one*   I.e., the replacement of a word by a synonym to avoid repetition in English, when the same word is is repeated in the original.

πόνος (= toil or grief), μέγας (= great), τέλος (= end), i.e., simple words which Aeschylus is content to use repeatedly in the same passage, without any effort at what H. W. Fowler terms "elegant variation."

with its congeners   With other words of the same kind.

29]   ξυμβαλεῖν οὐ ῥάδιος, *"not easy to understand,"*   Not quoted verbatim but adapted from Aristophanes' *Frogs* 929-30, where Euripides criticizes Aeschylus ῥήμαθ' ἱππόκρημνα ἃ ξυμβαλεῖν οὐ ῥᾴδι' ἦν (= horse-cliff [i.e., tremendously steep] expressions, which were not easy to understand).

30]   *his stoutest advocate among the ancients*   I.e., Aristophanes, presumably so described because at the end of his *Frogs* (l. 1473) he makes Dionysus judge Aeschylus to have won the contest for the greatest tragic poet.

32]   *Salmasius*   the eminent French scholar, Claude de Saumaise (1588-1653), best known in England for his Latin *Defensio Regia* (= Royal Defence) on behalf of Charles I, to which Milton replied for the Commonwealth with his *Pro Populo Anglicano Defensio* (= Defence for the English People; 1649).

34-36]   *he protested that . . . bag and baggage*   Paraphrased from the Latin quoted in B's footnote: *Quis Aeschylum possit . . . supellectili vel farragine* (= Who could assert that Aeschylus is now any clearer or more explicable to the modern Greek scholar than the Gospels or the Apostolic Epistles? His Agamemnon alone exceeds in obscurity all of the sacred books, with their Hebraisms and Syriasms and the whole stuff or mishmash of the Hellenistic language?; *Claudii Salmasii De Hellenistica Commentarius*, 1643, *Epistula Dedicatoria*, 37).

40-41]   *effectually clearing . . . in it*   A satirical comment on non-literal translations, possibly aimed at Fitzgerald's recent *Agamemnon: A Tragedy, Taken from Aeschylus* (1876).

51]   *an eloquent friend*   Matthew Arnold. "What are the eternal objects of poetry, among all nations, and at all times? They are actions . . . the action itself, its selection and construction, this is what is all-important. This the Greeks understood far more clearly than we do" (Preface to *Poems* 1853; *The Complete Prose Works of Matthew Arnold*, R. H. Super ed. [Ann Arbor, 1960-77], 1.3-5).

52-58] *The Greeks are . . . on stroke* Quoted from the same passage of Arnold's preface cited in 51n.

62-63] *began this practice . . . some six-and-thirty years ago* In "Artemis Prologizes," written December 1840-January 1841, and published 1842 (DeVane, *Hbk.*, 116; this edition, 3.224).

Leigh Hunt James Henry Leigh Hunt (1784-1859). For B's friendship with him, especially as a living link with Shelley, see Irvine and Honan, 130-31.

67] *hapalunetai galené* ἀπαλύνεται γαλήνη (= grows gentle with calm), Quoted from a poem attributed to Anacreon (c.570 B.C.): "See how, when Spring appears, the Graces are full of roses; see how the wave of the sea grows gentle with calm" (*Anacreontea*, M. L. West, ed. [Leipsig, 1984], 33, No. 46 [44B]).

75] *Eyripides* The Greek vowel υ has traditionally become *y* in English, as in *Thucydides* for Θουκυδίδης.

75-77] *a sturdy Briton . . . Antony Pie* A curious fact mentioned by Jonson to William Drummond: "A translation of the Emperours lyves [i.e., Suetonius' *De Vita* Caesarum] translated Antonius Pius, Antonie Pye" (*Conversations with Ben Jonson made by William Drummond of Hawthornden January 1619*, 22, reprinted in Ben Jonson's *Timber*, ed. G. B. Harrison [London, 1923]).

77-78] *with time . . . becomes satin* I.e., it is a very long, slow process by which the the leaf of the white mulberry tree (originally grown to feed silkworms) is converted into silk fabric. The proverb was first cited in 1659, in the form: "With Time, and Art, the Mulberry leafs grow to be sattin" (*Oxford Dictionary of English Proverbs*, 3rd ed. [Oxford, 1970], 822). B's joke implies that the sturdy Britons who still resist his more authentic transliteration, preferring such absurdities as "Anthonie Pie" for Antoninus Pius, will eventually learn better. He may well be proved right. Certainly the assertions of DeVane in 1955 (*Hbk.*, 416, 117) that Browning's "fad . . . has been abandoned in spite of him" and that his "strange spelling," "his practice of transliterating Greek names . . . failed of acceptance, and scholars have gone back to the traditional English spelling," have come to look rather rash in the light of such notably scholarly works as Oliver Taplin's *Homeric Soundings: The Shaping of the Iliad* (Oxford, 1992), which is full of such "strange spellings" as "Achaians, Achilleus, Hektor, Patroklos, Kronos, Menelaos," and even "Aineias."

what Keats called "vowelled Greek" See *Lamia* 2.200: "Soft went the music the soft air along / While fluent Greek a vowel'd undersong / Kept up among the guests, discoursing low."

80] *in a criticism* Apparently a reference to a review of "Mr Jebb's Translations" in the *Fortnightly Review*, 1873, Vol.20., 646-49.

80-81] *a late . . . my own* A Greek version of "Abt Vogler," the first piece in R. C. Jebb's *Translations into Greek and Latin Verse* (Cambridge, 1873), 2-15.

82-83] *the fourteenth of the sixth Pythian Ode* Apparently a mistake for "the sixth [antistrophe] of the fourth Pythian Ode," where the four Greek words quoted occur (l. 124). In his Preface (viii) Jebb stated: "The metres into which I have tried to do 'Abt Vogler' are those of the fourth Pythian."

83-85] *neither Professor Jebb . . . musical* Not a verbatim quotation, but a parody of the reviewer's flowery wording: "But alas for mortal men! When we recall the Pindaric lines on which these are moulded,—the cannon-ball ictus and thundering close of . . . the wild and wandering melody of . . . the triumphant glory of γόνον ἰδὼν κάλλιστον ἀνδρῶν [= seeing child most beautiful of men; Pindar, *Pythian Odes*, 4.124], then Mr Jebb and Mr B seem to recede together into the shades; and the Theban eagle [i.e., Pindar] is alone again in his unapproachable heaven" (*Fortnightly Review*, 1873, xx, 649). It appears from *The Life and Letters of Sir Richard Jebb* (171) that the reviewer was F. W. H. Myers, whose sympathetic interest in spiritualism might not have endeared him to the author of "Mr Sludge, the Medium" (this edition, 6.285ff.).

85] *her* Apparently a slip of the pen for "his." The participle ἰδὼν (= seeing) is masculine, and Pindar is referring to Jason's father: "as he came in, his father's eyes recognized him, and tears gushed from his aged eyelids as he rejoiced at seeing his child."

87] *Rimirando . . . uomini* Gazing at the son most beautiful of men.

88-89] τριακτῆρος οἴχεται τυχών Goes off having met his conqueror, i.e., goes off beaten. The words are quoted from the *Agamemnon* (AL 171-72; AP 165-66; ll. 184-85).

90] *It is recorded* The story is taken from Carl Gustaf Tessin's *Lettres à un jeune Prince par un ministre d'état Chargé d'Elever et l'Instruire, Traduit de Suedois* (= Letters to a young prince by a minister of state charged with his upbringing and education, translated from Swedish) (London, 1755), 129. Tessin was the art-collector largely responsible for assembling the French and Dutch collections in the National Museum of Stockholm.

92] *less unhappy son* Tessin: *"un des meilleurs peintres en mignatures que fût jamais"* (= one of the best miniature-painters that ever was).

93-94]   *profound* . . . *conceit*   He called him *"le vieux barbouilleur"* (= the old dauber).

conceit . . . *with*   Tessin: *"voulant avoir la gloire de retoucher"* (= wishing to have the glory of touching up).

98-100]   *who must* . . . *enlarged mouth*   B's elaboration of Tessin's *"avoit ridiculement élargé les bouches et les yeux"* (= had ridiculously enlarged the mouths and the eyes).

102-3]   ἀκέλευστος ἄμισθος ἀοιδά   (= uncommanded unrewarded song), a quotation from the *Agamemnon* (AL 979; l. 982), where the phrase refers to the chorus's premonitions of disaster.

104]   *commanded* . . . *Carlyle*   Allingham wrote on 5 November 1875: "C. praised B.'s translation from Euripides (*Alcestis*). 'The very best translation I ever read,' and recommended him to do more" (*William Allingham: A Diary*, H. Allingham and D. Radford, eds. [London, 1907], 240).   See also *The Diary of Alfred Domett 1872-1885*, E. A. Horsman, ed. (Oxford, 1953), 181: "Next to Shakespeare's Carlyle seemed to think the Greek plays the finest works of the human intellect. He said to B while on that subject, 'Ye won't mind me, though it's the last advice I may give ye; but you ought to translate the whole of the Greek tragedies—that is your vocation.' I said for one I would rather have him write original poems. He confessed it was much more agreeable work; but said he had a good mind to translate one play at least to gratify the old man, and dedicate it to him." That was in February 1877, and the transcript was probably written in March and April of that year (DeVane, *Hbk.*, 414).

1]   *labours*   Traditionally, English blank verse allows an unstressed extra syllable at the end of the iambic pentameter, as an occasional variation; but in this transcript B makes it the norm, whenever translating the iambic trimeter (the usual metre for spoken dialogue in Greek tragedy).

The gods . . . *labours*   an almost word-for-word equivalent of the Greek (Θεοὺς μὲν αἰτῶ τῶνδ' ἀπαλλαγὴν πόνων) in almost the same word-order; but on the principle of "in as Greek a fashion as English will bear," the reader is spared any equivalent of the particle μὲν (= something like "on the one hand").

3]   *Atreidai*   An exact transliteration of the Greek Ἀτρεῖδαι (= sons of Atreus, i.e., Agamemnon and Menelaus), in preference to the conventional Latinized spelling, *Atridae*.

4]   *I know of*   I.e., I have got to know well.

6]   *dynasts*   A near-transliteration of δυνάστας (AL 6).

    as they pride them   AL 6: ἐμπρέποντας (= conspicuous); but B cannot resist elaborating the anthropomorphic image.

    aether   B breaks his own rule in Latinizing the spelling of αἰθήρ (= upper air, sky; AL 6).

7]   *wither*   One dictionary-meaning of the original verb φθίνω (= decline, decay, waste away), though *wane* would have been a more obvious translation here (AL 7).

8]   *on ward*   B tries by alliteration to bring out two meanings of φυλάσσω (= be on guard, watch out for; AL 8).

9]   *shall bring*   Which shall bring.

    Troia   The exact spelling of Τροία (= Troy; AL 9).

10]   *audacious* Interpolated, perhaps for metrical purposes (AL 10).

11]   *man's-way-planning hoping heart of woman*   A replica of the four-word line γυναικός ἀνδρόβουλον ἐλπίζον κέαρ (AL 11). The first word, without definite article, implies "*a* woman," i.e., Clytaemnestra.

12-13]   *when I . . . of mine*   AP 12-13: "when I hold a night-wandering and dewy couch." The first adjective (νυκτίπλαγκτον) can have a causative meaning (= making wander, i.e., restless). For the second (ἔνδροσον) B follows the translation in Paley's note, "drenched with dew" (AP 12).

13]   *visions*   AP 13: ὀνείροις (= dreams), which makes more sense in the context. So why the change? B's metre required a disyllable (see 1. 1n.); and perhaps Paley's "by dreams unvisited" (AP 12) initially suggested the more alliterative "unvisited by visions"—until it seemed preferable to transcribe the participle ἐπισκοπουμένην (= looked on) more literally.

15]   *So as . . . eyelids*   The contorted word-order possibly resulted from an attempt to represent (by an f-alliteration) the quadruple β-alliteration in the Greek line: τὸ μὴ βεβαίως βλέφαρα συμβαλεῖν ὕπνῳ(= so as not to put eyelids firmly together in sleep; AP 15).

16]   *chirp*   An attempt to catch the primary meaning of μινύρεσθαι (AP 16), used by Sophocles (*Oedipus at Colonus* 671) of the nightingale's song, but by Aristophanes (*Ecclesiazusae* 880) of an old woman humming to herself, while waiting for a young lover.

17]   *infusing*   AP 17: "cutting in" (ἐντέμνων), in the sense of shredding herbs to make a medicine; but Paley's note refers to his later one (on AP 1232) where he says of a different verb (ἐντίθημι = put in): "Translate, 'And like one mixing a potion, . . . she will add to the cup of wrath . . . '" That "potion" may have suggested B's *infusing*, used in its Latin sense of "pouring in."

20]   *lucky be deliverance*   B retains the precise word-order of AP 20, but slightly alters the probable meaning, though Paley gives it in AEP 131: "may there come a happy release."

21] *dusky fire* The adjective ὀρφναίου (= dark) is a Homeric epithet of "night," but Paley explains it here (AP 21) as "because it was early morning," apparently implying that the beginnings of daylight made the distant fire look less bright; hence, probably, B's "*dusky.*" But the word may well be used to mean "in the dark," and that is how Paley seems to take it in AEP 132: "through this gloom."

22] *day-long lightness* The obvious meaning is that the fire in the night is as bright as daylight; but Paley notes that ἡμερήσιος "properly . . . means 'a day's length,' " and is "improperly used here for ἡμερινός" [= of the day]. He goes on: "In φάος [= light] there is also an allusion to the metaphorical sense, the light of joy and safety." (AP 22-23). B evidently tries to eliminate the "impropriety" by stressing that metaphorical sense and making *lightness* imply *daylong* joy.

23] *of dances the ordainment* An exact equivalent for χορῶν κατάστασιν (AP 23), i.e., a joy that sets people dancing. But B omits, presumably by mistake, the whole of line AP 24: "of many [i.e., many dances] in Argos on account of this event."

25] *show, by shouting,* An alliterative phrase to translate one word, σημαίνω (= signal, give a sign, i.e., for someone to do something;

26-28] *i' the household . . . aloft* I.e., she send up good-omened joyous cries in the household in response to this torch-blaze. B imitates the inverted word-order of the original (AP 27-29), though it was far more natural in that inflected language than it seems in non-inflected English.

28] *if haply* AP 29: "if indeed [εἴπερ]" i.e., if it really has been.

29] *boasts* An alliterative interpolation. AP 30: "is clearly seen announcing."

31] *dice* Not in the Greek, which has only "the masters' things," i.e., affairs, circumstances. But the reference to dice is made clear by Paley's note (AP 32), which may also have suggested the word *reckon*: "I shall reckon, I shall assume, to have turned up well."

32] *thrice-six* τρὶς ἓξ (AP 33). Paley explains: "i.e., each of the three dice falling with the sice [= the six marked on dice] uppermost, which was the best throw."

34] *sustain* B sticks to the primary meaning of the verb βαστάζω (= lift, raise, carry), though here, according to Liddell and Scott, 1996, it means no more than "touch" (AP 35).

35-36] *on tongue . . . trodden* Paley notes: This proverb was used of those on whom compulsory and unwilling silence was imposed (AP 36).

36] *if voice it take should* The strange order of the last two words seems to have been determined by B's chosen metre. Otherwise he retains the original word-order, quite natural in Greek: εἰ φθογγὴν λάβοι (AP 37).

38] *I'm blankness* Apparently an attempt to suggest the look of wide-eyed innocence on the face of someone denying all knowledge of a secret that he refuses to talk about. AP 38: "I forget [λήθομαι]."

39] *The tenth . . . match* As with the *Heracles*-transcript in *Aristophanes' Apology* (1875; this edition, 12.1), B does not attempt the impossible task of imitating the quantitative lyric metres used for tragic choruses. This chorus begins in anapaests, and the change from the iambics of the opening speech is marked by a change from the eleven-syllable line that B uses for dialogue to the normal ten-syllable line of English blank verse. The complicated stanzaic forms of the original chorus are simulated by an improvised scheme of irregular line-lengths and rhymes.

Priamos Πρίαμος (= Priam, king of Troy; AP 40).

match Used in the obsolete sense of opponent, antagonist, to translate ἀντίδικος (= opponent in a lawsuit; AP 41). In his metrical need for a monosyllable B sacrifices the legal metaphor, though it figures prominently in the *Oresteia*.

40] *Menelaos, Agamemnon* AP 42: Menelaus and [ἠδὲ] Agamemnon. The omission further obscures the legal metaphor, since Menelaus, as the injured husband, was the plaintiff: his brother Agamemnon merely his ally.

41] *Atreidai* Ἀτρεῖδαι (= sons of Atreus; AP 440), i.e., Menelaus and Agamemnon.

44] *thousand-sailored* Though ναύτης (from ναῦς = ship) = sailor, χιλιοναύτης, here a feminine adjective, = with a thousand ships (AP 45; Liddell and Scott, 1871).

45] *Ares* The god of war.

indignant breast AP 45: "soul [θυμοῦ]."

45-46] *as fling . . . vultures* AP 49: "like vultures [τρόπον αἰγυπιῶν]."

47] *Away . . . the thief* A barely intelligible line apparently suggested by Paley's note (AP 49): "The Atridae cry *war!* and call for vengeance for the rape of Helen, as vultures fly screaming round their eyrie when their young have been taken away . . . The poet seems merely to describe the haunts of vultures in the wild and solitary places, far away from man." The Greek text (AP 49-50) reads simply: "who, in out-of-the-way [ἐκπατίοις] pains for their children . . . ," without saying what has happened to them.

50] *Lament . . . love* AP 53-54: δεμνιοτήρη πόνον ὀρταλίχων ὀλέσαντες (= having lost the bed-watching labor of chicks). Paley quotes a Latin paraphrase: "the labour which the parents have undergone in incubating (*incubando*) their chicks." Alliteration and *Love's Labour's Lost* seem to have suggested the rest of B's "transcript."

51-52] *which hearing . . . that wail* I.e., hearing which wail. The slovenly syntax is interpolated. AP 55-7: "and hearing the wail."

53-54] *guests . . . in air* Expanded from two words; "these Metics [μετοίκων = resident aliens; AP 57]." As Paley explains, vultures are Metics to the gods, "as residents in the same aerial region"; and like Metics at Athens they have no rights to legal redress, unless some Athenian citizen (or here some god) is prepared to take up their cause (AP 55). Again B ignores the legal allusion.

55] *against who these assail* Against those who attack these. AP 59: "to transgressors [παραβᾶσιν]."

57] *Erinus* Ἐρινύς (= a Fury, or avenging deity; AP 59).

Here as there A rhyme-dictated version of AP 60: "And thus."

58] *the excelling one* AP 60: "the stronger one [ὁ κρείσσων]."

59] *Alexandros* The usual name of Paris in the *Iliad* (AP 61 and 363).

either son I i.e., both sons. AP 60 has simply "sons [παῖδας]."

61] *appointing* AP 66 has a future participle: "meaning to appoint."

62] *plays the prop* I.e., knocked off balance, the warrior has to support himself on one knee; but though "propping itself" is a possible sense of ἐρειδομένου, it probably means no more here (AP 64) than "pressing hard" into the dust, when forced to one's knees.

63-64] *in those . . . wed* A mysterious expansion of two words, ἐν προτελείοις (= in preliminary sacrifices; AP 65). Paley explains that the second word "properly" refers to rites before marriage. The general idea is that the marriage of Paris and Helen causes a war, and B seems to suggest a parallel between joining in sexual intercourse and joining in battle; *grim* and *wed* are needed for the rhyme, the latter presumably intended either as a kind of indefinite subjunctive: "when their Fury shall wed them," or as an abbreviation of the past tense "wedded" (analogous to the abbreviated past participle passive recorded in *OED*).

65] *Danaoi and Troes* Δαναοί (= Danaans, subjects of Danaus, a mythical king of Argos, so Argives; but in Homer the word is used for the Greeks in general. *Troes* (two syllables) = Τρῶες (= Trojans). In AP 66-67) both names occur in the dative: Δαναοῖσιν and Τρωσί, but B naturally transliterates their nominative cases.

All's said Interpolated.

66] *where things are* AP 67: "where they now [νῦν] are."

68-69] *Not gently . . . distilled* AW, AP 69-70: οὔθ᾽ ὑποκλαίων οὔθ᾽ ὑπολείβων οὔτε δακρύων (= neither by wailing secretly/ a little nor by

279

pouring libations secretly/ a little, nor by weeping). The text is probably corrupt, and Paley brackets "nor by weeping" as "probably spurious"; but B sticks to his policy ("I keep to the earlier readings so long as sense can be made of them") and elaborates on Weise's text. Taking λείβων in its primary sense of pouring in drops (like Latin *stillo*) he arrives at *doling out drops* and his rhyme-word, *distilled*.

70] *he we know of* No subject of the following Greek verb (third person singular) is specified in AP 71, but the scholiast comments: "he leaves out the 'anyone[τὶς]'"; and the implied subject is clearly Agamemnon.

bring the hard about to soft I.e., soften (the first meaning given in Liddell and Scott, 1871 for the verb παραθέλγω (AP 71).

72] *mock rites unsanctified by fire* AP 70: ἀπύρων ἱερῶν (= fireless rites/sacrifices). The precise meaning is disputed, but B evidently follows Paley's note (AP 70), which suggests an allusion to Agamemnon's "irregular and impious sacrifice of Iphigenia" at Aulis, in order to change the winds that were holding up the Greek fleet on its way to Troy. The *ire* (= anger) would then be her mother Clytaemnestra's.

73] *But we pay nought* AP 72: ἡμεῖς δ᾽ ἀτίται. B follows Paley's initial translation of the last word: "lit. 'non-paying,' 'qui non solvit vel poenas vel multam [= one who does not pay either penalty or fine].' This would also imply exemption from military service. But Paley goes on to suggest another translation: "but we, who take no part in the vengeance [τίσις]."

age-weighed Weighed down by age—a rhyme-word replacing the simple adjective "ancient" (AP 72).

74] *from who* From those who. The awkward phrase translates the simple noun, ἀρωγή (= help, in the sense of the expeditionary force that was sent to help Menelaus; AP 73).

76-77] *staying . . . at length* The alliteration is achieved without deviation from the original; but nothing in AP 74-75 justifies the rhyme-phrase *at length*, though it makes good sense in context, since they are describing their physical condition at least ten years after being judged too old for military service.

78] *For* Explaining the resemblance between extreme age and extreme youth for war-purposes.

79] *That's the old man's match* That's exactly like the old man's position.

83] *gone wild* A misleading insertion, apparently for the rhyme. AP 82: "wanders a dream appearing by day." Though ἀλαίνει could mean "wander in mind," it would tend to imply ineffectual absent-mindedness rather than raving madness; but the emphasis here is surely on purposeless activity, whether mental or physical. As Paley's note puts it:

"he has no energy nor consistency of mind or body; his actions and ideas are as vague as if he were dreaming, though wide awake."

85] *But thou* It is not clear from the text when Clytaemnestra comes on stage. Paley quotes a Latin note: "The chorus-leader addresses Clytaemnestra, who has meanwhile come out of the royal palace, and is busy making sacrifices on stage" (AP 83).

87] *tidings* B follows Paley's reading (πευθοῖ; AP 87), though most MSS read πειθοῖ (= persuasion), which is retained in AL 87.

87-88] *everywhere . . . aflare* B seems to picture her setting fire to the circumference of one large offering, or to a number of smaller ones. But περίπεμπτα θυοσκινεῖς (= move sent-round sacrifice) seems to imply something more complicated. Paley questions whether the second word ("of uncertain etymology and meaning") is genuine, but suggests that Clytaemnestra may be may be starting off, as if by remote control, sacrifices for which she has sent round orders to in advance.

91] *those of the mart's obeying* Those obeyed by the markets (ἀγοραίων = belonging to the market-place; AP 90). The inverted word-order (*of all gods . . . the altars*) is copied from the original.

94] *medicated with persuasions mild* So too is this strange image. The flames rise φαρμασσομένη (= medicated/drugged by, i.e., under the persuasion or influence of, olive oil.

95] *unbeguiled* AP 95: ἀδόλοισι (= guileless, here in the sense of unadulterated).

96] *clotted chrism* The noun aptly suggests the consecrated oil implied by the whole context, and almost transliterates the χρῖμα (translated *unguent*) of AP 94. The adjective less happily translates the πέλανος of AP 96 (= any half-liquid substance, but especially a mixture of meal, honey, and oil offered to the gods).

97] *abysm* A rhyme-word forced out of μυχόθεν (= from the inmost part of; AP 96].

99] *concede* I.e., to grant by way of reply. AP 98: αἰνεῖν (= speak of, as translated in Paley's note, but B apparently tries to bring out the word's other possible senses, including "praise, approve, allow."

101-2] *now . . . then* At one time . . . at another.

102] *And then . . . but from* B rejects Paley's emendation, and translates the MSS reading (as in AW 101-2), indicating by three dots that it involves a change of grammatical construction.

103] *wards away* Wards off.

106] *empowered* I.e., by having been an eye-witness.

107-8] *which . . . potentates* Which rejoiced them on their journey, i.e., when starting their journey. The adjective ὅδιον (= of a road or journey), is explained by the scholiast: "seen on the journey" (*Scholia*

354). Paley's note on the difficult passage (AP 104) admits: "The word ἐκτελέων [= mature, perfect] must be considered as altogether uncertain," but in AEP 134 translates it as "the heroes." B settles for *potentates*.

109-10] *inflates . . . song-suasion* AP 105-6: "the persuasion of songs breathes down [on me]."

110-11] *age . . . wage* A slangy version of ἀλκᾳ ξύμφυτος αἰών (= a lifetime born with/grown up with battle), as taken by Paley "to imply that the old age of the chorus has yet strength and energy enough to sing of the fight, if not to engage in it" (AP 105).

112-13] *bird . . . Despatched* I.e., the bird was an omen which encouraged the leaders of the expedition.

Teukris (Τευκρίς is an adjective of Teucer, legendary ancestor of the kings of Troy, so = Trojan (AP 112).

118] *spear-throw side* The right side was the lucky one for omens.

122] *Ah, Linos* AP 120: αἴλινον, the refrain of a mournful song, said to have originated as a dirge for Linus, whose story is variously told. In one version he was a music-teacher killed with his own lyre by Heracles.

125] *the Atreidai* B omits the stock epithet, "warlike" (AP 122).

128] *explaining signs in view* A rhyme-led expansion of one word, τεράζων (= portent-interpreting; AP 124).

131] *booty-sharing* AP 128: μοῖρα, a word generally used for "fate." But Paley translates it here as "the fortune of war," since in Homer it often means the portion of the spoil that falls to one; and B tries to bring out this more specific sense.

132] *Drain to the dregs away* Though hardly appropriate to cattle-rustling, B's image follows one of the meanings given by Liddell and Scott, 1871 for the verb ἀλαπάζω: "empty, drain, make poor."

133-34] *disturb . . . shine of* Another rhyme-led expansion of a single word, κνεφάσῃ (= darken) possibly suggested by Paley's alternative translation, "tarnish" (AP 130).

135-36] *struck . . . camp* Again the rhyme seems to dictate the metaphor, in which *damp* must carry the early sense of "check, discouragement" (*OED*). AP 131-2: προτυπέν ... στρατωθέν (= before-struck . . . assembled as an army), explained by Paley: "struck by a premature blow in the camp," i.e., before the fighting started, because of the "slaughter of . . . Iphigenia" (AP 130).

137] *envyingly is* An extraordinary use of an adverb unparalleled in AP 132, which has the simple adjective ἐπίφθονος (= envious, bearing a grudge against).

139] *her father's flying hounds* The eagles, interpreted as representing the house of Atreus, i.e., Agamemnon and Menelaus. In *Prometheus Bound* line 1022, (a play confidently attributed to Aeschylus until doubts were first raised in 1857) the eagle is also called "the winged hound of Zeus."

142] *Brood . . . birth* As Paley's note explains (AP 135), Artemis was the goddess of childbirth, and also the protectress of virgins (being one herself); so her anger at the treatment of the hare hints at Agamemnon's sacrifice of his own young, the virgin Iphigenia.

143] *Ah, Linos* See l. 122n.

146] *small dewdrop-things* AP 139: δρόσοισι (= dews). B seems charmed by this image for "the tender young," as Paley translates it, (which ADP calls "an unparalleled usage" of the word); but he rejects the MS adjective ἀέπτοις (AW 141) though as charmingly explained by the scholiast: "unable to follow their parents" (*Scholia* 355), and accepts the emendation adopted by Paley: λεπτοῖς (= small; AP 139). Thus he goes against his stated policy ("I keep to the earlier readings so long as sense can be made out of them").

147] *brute* After the sympathy shown for lion's cubs, the pejorative connotations of this rhyme-word seem inappropriate. AP 141: θηρῶν (= wild beasts).

148] *makes she suit* I.e., to Zeus. AP 142: αἰτεῖ (= asks).

151] *partly smile but partly scowl* AP 143: δεξιὰ μέν κατάμομφα δὲ (= on the right hand i.e., auspicious but open to criticism, faulty),

152] *phantasms of the fowl* I.e., the portent of the eagles. The first noun in B's almost comic phrase partly transliterates φάσματα (= appearances, apparitions). The second is an alliterative replacement for the MSS reading, στρουθῶν (= sparrows; AW 145). Paley's text brackets the word as "little applicable to the omen of the eagles" (AP 143), and firmly translates it "eagles" (AEP 135). B plays safe with *fowl* (= bird unspecified). Liddell and Scott, 1996 assumes that the word is a scribe's interpolation.

153] *Ieïos* Ἰήιος a title of Apollo, derived from the cry ἰή, with which he was invoked (associated with the verb ἰάομαι (= heal).

Paian Παιάν a title of Apollo, when invoked as the Healer (AP 144).

153-54] *to avert . . . hurt* B follows Paley's explanation of AP 144-50: "I invoke the saving aid of Apollo to divert his sister [Artemis] from fulfilling the evil part of the omen . . . by causing a long detention of the ships at Aulis, and so bringing about for herself a second and more terrible sacrifice, namely, that of a daughter, the cause of an estrangement that shows no reverence on the part of a wife for a husband; for if such sacrifice is accomplished, a fearful retributive anger is in store for the author of it, some day to rise against him, i.e., in the murder of a husband by the hand of a wife" (AP 144).

155] *waftures*   "Propulsions by air" (*OED*). The word was presumably suggested by alliteration with *work* and *thwarting*, by memories of Shakespeare (*Julius Caesar*, 2.1.246: "an angry wafture of your hand"); and by a wish to imitate the oddness of the Aeschylean wording: ἀντιπνόους ... ἐχενῇδας ἀπλοίας (= blowing-against ship-holding non-sailings; AP 145).

159]   *feast for no man's lips*   AP 146: ἄδαιτον (= not to be feasted on). Paley explains: "The sacrifice of Iphigenia, whose flesh could not be eaten like that of ordinary victims. The bloody worship of Artemis . . . was originally a kind of she-devil worship requiring human victims" (AEP 135n.).

160]   *cognate*   Used almost in the Latin sense of the word (= born with) to translate σύμφυτον (= planted-with, congenital, inborn; AP 146).

162]   *backward-darting in the path*   A literal translation of παλίνορτος (= darting back, recurrent; AP 149), plus three words added for the rhyme.

163]   *chronicler of wrath*   AP 150 has simply μῆνις (= wrath), an abstract noun which in context invites personification as Clytaemnestra.

164]   *That has . . . fate*   A line translating one Greek word, τεκνόποινος (= child-avenging; AP 150). B tries partly to explain the cryptic reference to the murder of Thyestes' children by Atreus, and the dinner-party at which he made their father eat them. See ll. 1649-59; AL 1590-96.

165-66]   *abundant . . . well*   AP 151: ξὺν μεγάλοῖς ἀγαθοῖς (= together with great good-things), i.e., along with predictions of a successful campaign.

167]   *in journeying*   AP 152: ὁδίων (= on the road; see l. 107n.).

168]   *abode of either king*   This ought to mean each king's home, as if the eagles appeared in both places. But the plural in "royal palaces" (AP 152) is probably just an example of the common use of a plural for a singular in Greek (and Latin) verse, and the reference is to the place from which the two kings started off together.

169]   *these*   I.e., the bad prediction.

    symphonious   In harmony with. AP 153: ὁμόφωνον (= with same voice).

172-73]   *if that . . . I call*   An almost word-for-word translation which nevertheless (by not taking *that* [τόδε] closely enough with *called* [κεκλημένῳ] obscures the meaning: "if it is dear to him to be called that," i.e., if that's what he likes to be called (AP 155-56, AL 160-61).

175]   *liken out*   Compare.

176]   *admeasurement*   "Applying a measure in order to ascertain or compare dimensions" (*OED*). The archaic word seems a needlessly distracting translation of ἐπισταθμώμενος (= literally: measuring by a carpenter's rule, so here metaphorically: weighing well, pondering; AP 159). But the English word is a precise equivalent of the Greek one, and may also have had sentimental value for B, since EBB had used it in 1842: "Too low for admeasurement with Spenser" (*The Greek Christian Poets and the English Poets* [London, 1863], 134).

176-77] *of powers . . . such hours* Interpolated for the rhyme.

179] *vague* AP 160: μάταν (= vain, fruitless) but paraphrased in Paley's note (AP 158): "the vague and ill-defined anxiety I feel for Agamemnon."

180] *not* AP 162, AW, AL 167: οὐδ' (= and not, nor).

whosoever . . . yore AP 162: "who was formerly great," i.e., Zeus's grandfather Uranus (the personification of οὐρανος = sky), who was castrated and supplanted by his son Cronus. B's *whosoever* accepts the force of Paley's note: "There is still a difficulty in ὅστις [normally = whoever] used for ὅς [= who]" (AP 164).

181] *Bursting . . . round* A remarkably accurate alliterative version of AP 163, The last three words representing παμμάχῳ θράσει (= all-fighting i.e., all-conquering boldness/courage).

182] *Is in our mouths* An extreme case of keeping "to the earlier readings so long as sense can be made out of them." According to Paley's note, "The old reading, οὐδὲν λέξαι [= to say nothing], is obviously corrupt"(AP 164). But B is apparently trying to make it mean something like: "he is not to be mentioned," or "we say nothing about him," because he is a thing of the past. So he is not "in our mouths." Fraenkel regards the emended reading οὐδὲ λέξεται (taking the middle verb in a passive sense = "nor will he be spoken of") as "certain" (AF 170).

183] *And who . . . to be* Zeus's father Cronus, defeated by his son in the war of the Titans against the Olympian gods.

184] *thrice throwing wrestler* τριακτήρ (= a wrestler who wins by throwing his opponent three times, so a winner; AP 165).

185] *gone to ground* AP 166: οἴχεται (= has gone away, is departed). B adapts the hunting phrase to mean "is dead and buried."

190] *Appoints . . . teach* Evidently based on Paley's reading: πάθη μάθος ... κυρίως ἔχειν (= sufferings to own learning like masters) as explained in his note (AP 170): "sufferings . . . contain in themselves, as a peculiar property, a moral and an instruction." The preferred reading now seems to be that of AW 177-78: πάθει μάθος ... κυρίως ἔχειν(= Learning by Suffering to be valid [as a law]; AL 177-78).

191] *of each* Inserted for the rhyme.

192] *sheds in dew* AP 172: στάζει (= lets fall in drops, distills. There is no *dew* in the Greek. Paley's note translates "instils," and describes

285

the verb as "very appropriately used of the slow and imperceptible process of inspiring moral views and sentiments."

195] *enforced no less* Although it is enforced.

196-77] *As they . . . awful seat* AP 176: "sitting on the awful [i.e., authoritative] bench." Paley explains (AP 175, 1596) the reference to the steersman's bench in a ship.

198] *old* The normal meaning of πρέσβυς; but here, as the Scholiast and Paley both explain, it means "older," i.e., Agamemnon (AP 177; *Scholia* 357).

199] *Disparaging no seer* I.e., not daring to question the authority of any seer (AP 179).

200] *With bated breath* B seizes the familiar phrase, though its meaning is inappropriate here. AP 180: ἐμπαίοις τύχαισι συμπνέων (= breathing-with in-striking misfortunes), explained by Paley: "not blowing an adverse gale to," i.e., "submitting to the circumstances which befell him," and obediently taking the seer's advice to sacrifice his daughter.

202-3] *every pulse . . . strength* A translation of one Greek word, κεναγγεῖ (= emptying vessels), explained by Paley as "emptying the stores of wine" (AP 181), or "the delay in sailing that was exhausting their stores" (AEP 136). But B apparently jumped from the word *vessel* to the thought of blood-vessels and a kind of psychosomatic exhaustion.

205] *In Aulis station* While standing at anchor at Aulis.

206] *Strumon* A river in Thrace, to the north-east.

207] *Tempters . . . naught* The line represents three Greek words, δύσορμοι βροτῶν ἄλαι (= with-bad-anchorage wanderings of men). Paley explains: "which cause mariners to lose their course and drift into harbourless seas" (AP 185).

209] *carded* AP 190: κατέξαινον (= carded or combed away like wool, i.e., wore out).

211] *Argeians* Ἀργεῖοι (= inhabitants of Argos, Argives; AP 190).

212] *more grave and grand* The alliterating phrase translates βριθύτερον (= heavier).

213] *Than aught before* B follows Paley's interpretation: "It is implied that some remedies had been recommended, tried, and found to fail, before this last and terrible resource was enjoined" (AP 192). But it may be better to take the genitive translated *for the storm* (χείματος) as a genitive of comparison: = heavier than the storm (ADP, AL 199-200).

yea, for the storm and dearth Expanded from πικροῦ χείματος (= the bitter storm).

215] *Shrieked forth* An accurate translation of ἔκλαγξεν (AP 195), which suggests the emotional delivery of a prophet in a state of divine possession.

216] *Adducing Artemis* Paley explains: "It was understood that she demanded virgin blood" (AP 194).

217] *striking staves on earth* According to Paley "a gesture of impatience" (AP 195); but it is used by Telemachus, when complaining to the Ithacan assembly about the suitors, before bursting into tears (Homer, *Odyssey* 2.80), and seems here more expressive of distress.

222] *tide* a rhyme-word translating the more natural ῥειθροις (= streams; AP 203).

226] *fleet-fugitive* λιπόναυς (= ship-leaver, i.e., deserter; AP 205).

227] *Failing of duty to allies* a translation of ξυμμαχίας ἁμαρτών (= missing/failing alliance; AP 206, AL 214), which makes sense in context, but would be an unparalleled use of the verb. The meaning might possibly be: "losing my allies," since they would desert him if he kept them hanging around much longer.

229-30] *strive . . . desire* AP 209: ὀργᾳ περιόργως ἐπιθυμεῖν (= desire with passion very passionately; or as Paley put it, "with an eager longing," though the Greek noun and its verb ὀργάω have sexual connotations).

231] *Well . . . require* i.e., a favorable wind. The line translates εὖ γὰρ εἴη (= may it be well; AP 208).

232-36] *But when . . . wildest range* B follows Paley's paraphrase (AP 211): "But when he had put on the harness of necessity (i.e., when he found there was no help for it), blowing a changed gale of heart that was impious, unblest, unholy, from which he conceived a new resolve to entertain all-daring sentiments."

Yoke-trace the rope or strap attaching a draught-horse's neck to the yoke, a precise translation of λέπαδνον (AP 211).

240] *strange* Interpolated for the rhyme (AP 217).

242-43] *anchors . . . rite* AP 219: προτέλεια ναῶν (= preliminary sacrifice of ships, i.e., before setting sail.

244-46] *Prayings . . . wage* B reproduces the inverted word-order of the original (AP 222). The *captains* are the subject.

247] *vows done* Prayers having been made; an imitation of a Greek or Latin absolute construction, and of the Latin use of *votum* (= vow) to mean "prayer"—both gratuitously unEnglish, since the Greek original is simply μετ᾽ εὐχὰν (= after prayer; AP 223).

248] *Kid-like* AP 224: δίκαν χιμαίρας (= in the manner of a she-goat) i.e., as if she were an animal being sacrificed. Paley explains: "It was the custom to kill the victim held aloft in this position, that the life-blood might sprinkle the altar" (AP 224).

swathed in pall AP 225: πέπλοισι περιπετῆ (= falling-round with robes), a phrase of disputed meaning translated by Paley: "wrapped round in her robes" (AEP 136-7).

249] *have no fear at all* AP 225: παντὶ θυμῷ (= with all courage).
250-51] *fair mouth's guard / And frontage* AP 226-27: στόματος ...
καλλιπρῴρου φυλακὰν (= guard of beautiful-prowed mouth), another
disputed phrase. B rejects Paley's solution (to make "guard" the sub-
ject, not the object, of the infinitive: "And that a guard over her fair
mouth should stop"); and tries by *frontage* to parallel the comparison
of the girl's mouth to a ship's prow, possibly implying that it might be
seen as the advance-*guard* of the whole ship.
253] *By dint . . . speech* A resourceful equivalent for Aeschylus' ex-
traordinary expression: "by force and voiceless strength of bridles"
(βίᾳ χαλινῶν τ᾽ ἀναύδῳ μένει). Paley's own prose translation was far
from faithful: "by the forcibly imposed silence of a gag" (AEP 137).
254] *saffron-vest* I.e., yellow dress. AP 230: "dyes of saffron."
   shed A precise translation of the verb χέω (= pour, shed, let fall;
AP 230). In her horizontal position, he clothing hangs down from her
(ADP 239; for a different interpretation, see AF 239).
262] *unpolluted* ἀταύρωτος (= unbulled, unmated, virgin; AP 236).
263] *third libation* Paley explains (AP 237) that banquets ended with
three libations, the third to Zeus Savior. The libations were accompa-
nied or preceded by the singing of a religious hymn called a *paian*.
267] *it is fate* Inserted for the rhyme (AP 240).
268-69] *justice . . . preponderate* The text, punctuation, and meaning
here have been much disputed. Paley reads: Δίκα δὲ τοῖς μὲν παθοῦσιν
μαθεῖν ἐπιρρέπει (= But justice makes learning to fall on those on-the-
one-hand who have suffered), and paraphrases: "But justice on these
indeed (who have been the guilty authors of the sacrifice (i.e.,
Agamemnon) causes knowledge to fall by sad experience" (AP 241). B
interpolates the notion of *desire* to learn, and extracts *preponderate* from
another possible sense of ἐπιρρέπει (= tip the scales in a certain direc-
tion); cf. ADP 249ff., AL 250-1)
270-71] *But . . . welcome* Again the text is doubtful. B seems to be
following Weise's reading: τὸ προκλύειν δ᾽ ἥλυσιν προχαιρέτω (= but
to hear in advance the coming, i.e., the future, farewell in advance [to
that]; AW 251).
271] *and welcome* B's puzzling addition, perhaps to mean: "and
I'm only too glad to say goodbye to such knowledge"; or conceivably
alluding to Pope's "Welcome the coming, speed the going guest" (*Imi-
tations of Horace, Satires* II, 2.157), so as to mean: "welcome the future
when it comes, but say goodbye to the knowledge of the future, and
hurry it off."
272-74] *part for part . . . event* Another textual crux. B disdains
Paley's emended text (with αὐγαῖς = sunbeams, for αὐταῖς= them; AP

245; cf. AL 254), and tries to make sense of another emended version of the MS reading: τορὸν γὰρ ἥξει σύναρθρον αὐταῖς (= clear it will come jointed to them-feminine). Assuming that "them" means Calchas's predictive skills (perhaps understanding τεχναῖς = skills), he translates: *conformably to Kalchas' art*; while *part for part* seems to mean "bit by bit, each bit of the future corresponding to a bit of the prediction." *Kalchas* was the *army-prophet* first mentioned in l. 124.

275-76] *But . . . betide* Generally in line with Paley's note: "We might correctly enough translate 'So let us say, in reference to what is next to come, May all be well!' " (AP 246).

What is to do I.e., how we shall fare in future. B obscures the meaning by insisting on the inherent ambiguity of the Greek verb πράσσω (= 1. do in the sense of act, 2. do in the sense of fare, as in the modern idiom, "How are you doing?" So the Greek text here (AP 246), πέλοιτο ...εὖ πρᾶξις means "may there be good doing in sense 2."

277] *as we* B follows Paley in assuming that the Chorus are referring to themselves (not, as some think, to Clytaemnestra, who has just come on stage), when they say ὡς θέλει τοδ᾽ ἄγχιστον ...ἕρκος (= as wishes this nearest . . . bulwark; AP 247; cf. AF 256f., AL 256-7).

the next allied In the sense of Paley's alternative translation of ἄγχιστον: "most nearly related" (AEP 137n.).

278] *Apian* Argive (from Apis, a mythical king of Argos).

281] *the male-seat man-bereaved* B translates ἄρσενος (= male) twice, both as an adjective with *seat* (θρόνου = seat, throne), as Paley suggests, and also as a noun with *bereaved* (ἐρημωθέντος; AP 251, ADP 260).

283] *for good news' hope* In the hope of good news; the slightly odd use of *for* was possibly suggested by Paley's paraphrase (AP 252): "Tell me whether you are sacrificing to thank the gods for favors received, or only begging them to confirm your hopes"—i.e., *for* confirmation of your hopes

thus wide All over the place like this (see ll. 87-88n.).

284] *art thou mute,—no grudge* I.e., if you'd rather not say anything, I shan't blame you. AP 254: οὐδὲ σιγώσῃ φθόνος (= nor is there grudge against you being silent).

285-86] *Good-news-announcer . . . become* I.e., may morning become an announcer of good news. The optative γένοιτο (= become) expresses a wish; but B's word-order, which seems to imply a possibility, is merely modelled on that of the Greek (AP 255-56).

285] *by-word* AP 255: παροιμία (= proverb); but no such proverb is found elsewhere (ADP 264).

286] *Night* I.e., from the beacon seen last night, as Paley explains (AP 252).

287] *past all hope of hearing* B's wording adequately covers the other meaning that Paley sees in μεῖζον ἐλπίδος κλύειν (= greater than hope to hear; AP 257): "You shall learn what will delight you beyond the mere *hope* of hearing" (AP 252; cf. ADP 266).

288] *Priamos* See l. 39n.

    Argeioi Ἀργεῖοι (= inhabitants of Argos, Argives (AP 258).

289] *want of faith* a needlessly misleading translation of ἀπιστίας (= disbelief; AP 259; AL 268), i.e., I don't understand such an incredible statement.

290] *Troia* See l. 9n.

    Achaioi Achaeans, a name used in Homer for the Greeks generally, as here (AP 260).

291] *the tear-drop* an expansion of "a tear" (δάκρυον; AP 261) required for B's metre. See l. 1n.

292] *glad . . . convicts* B accepts Paley's interpretation of εὖ φρονοῦντος and of κατηγορεῖ "convicts you of being glad" (AP 262), though the first phrase would normally imply being well disposed, or loyal to someone, and the verb, as Paley admits, ought to mean "give evidence against you" (cf. AL 271). Perhaps Clytaemnestra's private meaning is that loyalty to Agamemnon is disloyalty to herself.

293] *For . . . token* I.e., what's your evidence for all this? The line translates the Greek almost word for word, including the common elliptical use of γάρ (= for) in questions, to give the reason for asking (I ask because I'd like to know; AP 263). Such stichomythia (στιχομυθία = dialogue in alternate lines) in Greek tragedy is often compressed to the point of obscurity.

294] *What's here* What you can see for yourself. AP 264, AW 273: ἔστιν (= there is evidence). Presumably B's translation implies an impatient gesture indicating the whole situation created by the beacon.

    how else AP 264, AW 273: τί δ' οὐχί (= and what/why not?), a common expression to mean "how could it be otherwise?" so "of course."

    the god There is no definite article in the Greek, and there is no reason to think that any particular god was in Clytaemnestra's mind; but Paley inserts a *the* both in his note (AP 263) and in his prose translation (AEP 138, where a footnote suggests: "By a false blaze, or accidental fire in the woods &c." The best translation of θεοῦ here (AL 273) is probably "a god" or "some god."

296] *take* accept.

    sleep-burthened AP 266: βριζούσης (= sleepy, sleeping); but B tries to bring out an assumed connection with βρίθω (= be weighed down).

297] *puffed . . . up* AP 267: ἐπίανεν = fattened—but translated by Paley: "inflated" (AEP 138).

unwinged omen AP 267: "unwinged [ἄπτερος] saying." Paley takes the obscure adjective to mean not derived from birds (a common source of omens).

298] *mockest grossly* AP 268: ἐμωμήσω (= you have found fault with.

299] *even* One of the meanings of καί (= and, also, even etc.), but one which makes no sense here, where the modern equivalent would be "actually"—or as Paley suggested, "*was* it captured?" (AP 269).

300] *this same . . . dawn* AP 270: τῆς νῦν τεκούσης φῶς τόδ' εὐφρόνης (= during the night that gave birth to this light).

301] *And . . . swiftness* A literal translation of AP 271; i.e., what messenger could bring the news so quickly?

302] *Hephaistos* ῞Ηφαιστος, the god of fire. Some geographical details of the beacon-journey from Troy to Argos are "obscure to us" (ADP 281f.).

Ide ῎Ιδη, a mountain near Troy (the name implies a wooded hill).

303] *Beacon did beacon send* Beacon sent to beacon.

the poster OED quotes a use of this word for "a messenger, a carrier of news," but B was possibly thinking of the witches in *Macbeth* 1.3.33: "Posters of the sea and land." AP 273 uses ἄγγαρος, a Persian word for a courier on horseback in a rapid-communication system described by Herodotus (8.98).

304] *rock Hermaian* The rock of Hermes on the island of Lemnos.

305] *a third . . . island* A misleading version of AP 275: "and from the island, third, [ἐκ νήσου τρίτον, i.e., as the third leg of the journey] a great torch." The *torch* is the object of the verb *received*.

306] *Zeus's . . . summit* The subject of the verb *received*. AP 276: "the Athoan steep of Zeus," glossed by Paley: "The summit of Athos sacred to Zeus."

307] *upsoaring as to stride sea over* The alliterative striding-image is B's addition to Paley's translation of AP 277: "rising high so as to cross the back of [νωτίσαι = to back] the sea" (AEP 138).

308] *strong lamp-voyager* AP 278: "strength of travelling torch [λαμπάδος]." B transliterates the first four letters of the Greek word.

all for joyance Paley takes the vague phrase πρὸς ἡδονὴν (= to, for, at pleasure) rather prosaically to mean "bearing the good tidings," "with its welcome message" (AP 277, AEP 138); but B's more imaginative version lets the reader ascribe the pleasure, not just to the recipients of the message, but to the beacon-light itself.

309]   *gold-glorious*   An accurate as well as resonant version of χρυσοφεγγὲς (= with golden light/splendour; AP 279).

any sun like   Like any sun. Where other translators would have ignored the indefinite τις (= some, any), or reduced it to a mere "a," B succeeds in giving it almost idiomatic significance.

310]   *Pass on—the pine-tree*   The syntactical incoherence of this sentence faithfully copies that of the Greek, which has no main verb ("Perhaps," says Paley, "suppressed,—in fact, forgotten-in the length of the sentence" (AP 277).

pine-tree   The beacon made of pine-wood.

Makistos   Μάκιστος (= greatest, highest), said to mean a mountain in Euboea "more than ninety miles," as Paley points out (AP 276), from Athos.

311-12]   *Who . . . missive*   A much disputed passage, which Paley interpreted: "he then, not delaying nor heedlessly overcome by sleep, passed on [παρῆκεν] his share [μέρος] of the messenger-fire" (AP 277). But B, like modern editors, preferred to give the first Greek word its common sense of "pass over, neglect," though he did not, like them, take the second to mean the messenger's part, role, or duty (cf. ADP 291, AL 291).

313]   *stream Euripos*   The strait between Euboea and Boeotia.

314]   *Messapios*   Identified by a scholiast as "a mountain between Euboea and Boeotia" (*Scholia* 359).

warders   φύλαξι (= guards; AP 284), i.e., those set to watch for the beacon-signal.

315]   *played herald*   AP 285: παρήγγειλαν (= passed on the message).

316]   *grey old*   There is no specific mention of color in the Greek; but B gets as close as he can to the spelling of the original word, γραίας (= old; AP 286), possibly encouraged by the inclusion of "gray" (along with "old" and "aged") among the meanings given for this shortened form of γεραίας(= old) in Liddell and Scott, 1871.

317]   *strengthening still*   The idea of a *crescendo* is B's improvement on AP 287: σθένουσα (= being strong).

lamp   A near-transliteration of λαμπάς (AP 287), though at that period the word did not mean "lamp" but "torch," i.e., the beacon-bonfire.

decaying nowise   AP 287: "not yet being darkened."

318]   *Plain Asopos*   AP 288: "plain of Asopus," a river in Boeotia.

318-19]   *full-moon-fashion / Effulgent*   AP 288-89: "in the manner of a bright [φαιδρᾶς] moon." Was it a wish to mimic the repeated π-sounds in AP 287-90 (οὐδέπω ...πέδιον Ἀσωποῦ...πρὸς λέπας...πομποῦ πυρός) by an *f*-alliteration that made the moon a *full* one?.

319]   *Kithairon*   The westerly part of a mountain-range between Attica and Boeotia.

320]   *Roused . . . escort*   An *r*-alliterating version of a line translated by Paley: "waked up a fresh relay of the messenger-fire" (AP 290, AEP 139). The word πομπός can mean *escort*, but it can also mean "messenger," the sense needed here.

321]   *far escort*   An awkard repetition apparently meant to emphasize that πομπός (= escort, messenger) and τηλέπομπος (= far-sent) are both derived from πέμπω (= send).

322]   *burning . . . you*   AP 292: "burning more than the things that have been said."

323]   *Lake Gorgopis*   an inlet in the NE corner of the Corinthian gulf (*Aeschylus: Agamemnon*, A. Sidgwick, ed., 6ᵗʰ ed. [Oxford, 1925] 302).

324]   *Aigiplanktos*   Ἀιγίπλαγκτος(= wandered over by goats), a mountain near Megara.

   safe   B's anthropomorphic interpolation (AP 294).

325]   *never stint the fire-stuff*   Most MSS read: μὴ χαρίζεσθαι πυρός (= not to give freely of fire), which makes no sense. Paley adopts the emendation χρονίζεσθαι, to mean "it urged on the succession of the fire not to linger in its course" (AP 295); but B's *stint* apparently follows the emended reading of AW 294: χατίζεσθαι πυρός (= not to be wanting in fire), adding the *stuff*, i.e., fuel, to match his metre.

326]   *ungrudged*   The literal meaning of ἀφθόνῳ, though "ungrudging" might have been clearer.

327]   *of flame a huge beard*   The inverted word-order of the original (AP 297).

   ay, the very foreland   B struggles to bring out Paley's interpretation of καί here: "*even* the promontory implies that the flame was so bright that it could be seen beyond the point farthest removed in that direction from Aegiplanctus" (AP 298).

328]   *strike above*   I.e., strike beyond. The prefix ὑπερ can mean "above" as well as "beyond"; but here in ὑπερβάλλειν (AP 298) the latter sense seems to suit the context better.

329]   *look-out . . . Saronic*   Apparently adapted from Paley's gloss: "the distant headland which commands a view of the Saronic Gulf" (AP 298); which involves the emendation of the MS reading κάτοπτρον (= mirror) to κάτοπτον (= within sight of). The Saronic Gulf is a bay of the Aegean between Attica and Argolis.

330]   *outpost*   I.e., of Argos itself. AP 300: ἀστυγείτονας σκοπάς (= city-neighbouring look-out places.

331]   *Arachnaios*   Ἀρχναῖος (= spider-mountain), north of the road from Argos to Epidaurus.

332] *Atreidai* See l. 3n.
333] *Ide* See l. 302n.
  unforefathered AP 302: ἄπαππον (= with no grandfather, un-grandfathered). But after the seven beacon-stages just listed, B understandably implies a few more generations.
334] *the flambeau-bearers* AP 303: λαμπαδηφόρων (= torch-bearers). B's *flambeau-bearers* suits his metre better, and possibly seemed more appropriate as a name for the Athenian Lampadephoria (Λαμπαδηφορία) or Torch-Race, to which Paley's note referred: "The phraseology seems borrowed from the Lampadephoria" (AP 303). He also quoted extracts from Herodotus (8.98) and Pausanias (1.30:2) which explained the rules for this ritual relay race, in which fire was taken from one altar to another. B omits, presumably by mistake, the next line (AP 304, AW 313, AL 313), which Paley translates: "and so were they regularly transmitted one from another" (AEP 139).
335] *He beats* He wins. The rest of B's line "transcribes," without trying to interpret, AP 305: νικᾷ δ᾽ ὁ πρῶτος καὶ τελευταῖος δραμών (= and wins the first and/also/though last having run/running). The meaning is much disputed. Paley gives several suggested interpretations, including one of his own in "a former edition": "'And the first is the conqueror, though he took up the race the last;' i.e., the first who reached the goal was the beacon on the Arachnaean hill, though it was the last lighted . . . The reader must choose which of the above interpretations he prefers, it being hard to arrive at a conclusion altogether satisfactory." B's seems to take the same line. The general meaning is: "my system of beacons is like the Lampadephoria, except that everybody wins, so long as the last look-out gets the message." But Paley's quotation from Pausanias (i.30.2) adds point to the simile: τὸ δὲ ἀγώνισμα, ὁμοῦ τῷ δρόμῳ φυλάξαι τὴν δᾷδα ἔτι καιομένην ἐστίν (= the contest [in the Lampadephoria] is to keep the torch still burning while running). So if you arrive first but your torch has gone out, the prize goes to the next finisher whose torch is still burning; Here the last beacon to be seen alight at the end of the journey is as much the winner as the first to be lighted.
336] *Such . . . token* in answer to the Chorus's question in AP 263; l. 293. Aeschylus used the same word for *token* in both question and answer: τέκμαρ (= sure sign or token), and B does so too.
337] *Troia* See l. 9n.
338] *anon* AP 308: αὖθις (normally = again); but B follows Paley's note, which quotes an alternative meaning given in Hesychius' lexicon: "after this," and translates "hereafter."

woman a correct translation of γύναι which, despite the male chauvinism already implied by the chorus, is not so rude as it sounds in English, though Paley feels it necessary to translate it "Queen"(AEP 139).

339-40] *But now . . . them* AP 309-10: "But I would wish to hear these words all through again, and wonder at them again, as you say [ὡς λέγεις] them." However, B's *if thou tell* suggests that he is translating AW 319 which, like two of the three MSS, reads ὡς λέγοις (optative ? = as you would say). Optatives are used in remote conditional clauses and polite requests; so B may intend *if thou tell* as a blend of the two constructions, with *tell* as an English subjunctive.

342] *I think a noise* She tries to imagine the scene in the captured city.

no mixture AP 312: ἄμικτον(= unmixed, unmixable), explained by Paley: "A cry discordant, not blending one with the other, viz. the cry of wailing on the part of the conquered, and of shouting and contending for food and lodging on that of the conquerors."

343] *Sour wine and unguent* oil and vinegar. But B chooses the less familiar definitions of ὄξος and ἄλειφα (= vinegar and oil) given e.g. in Liddell and Scott, 1871 (AP 313).

344] *Standers-apart, not lovers* διχοστατοῦντα ... οὐ φίλως (= standing apart not lovingly); see AP 314, where Paley defends and keeps the MS reading, which "most editors" wished to emend.

345] *partwise* Apparently meant to mean "apart, separately," to translate δίχα (AP 315), already used as a prefix in the participle translated *Standers-apart* (AP 314).

347, 351] *those . . . these* The former (*captives*) . . . *these* The latter (*conquerors*). B imitates the Greek convention by which ἐκεῖνοι (= those) would mean the further away of two words just mentioned in a sentence, and οὗτοι (= these) would mean the nearer—rather perversely, since in the original (AP 317-21) a quite different idiom is used: οἱ μὲν (= the former), and τοὺς δ' (= the latter).

347] *upon the bodies prostrate* Prostrate upon the bodies. AP 317: "having fallen around the bodies," i.e., in a last embrace.

348-49] *parents— / The old men . . . longer* AP 318-19: "aged parents," where γερόντων is used as an adjective, not a noun, as B seems to assume.

free no longer Prisoners of war were normally made slaves.

351-52] *after-battle . . . night-faring* A literal translation of AP 321-22: νυκτίπλαγτος ἐκ μάχης πόνος νῆστις. Paley explains: "The hungry toil of keeping watch during the night after the fight" (AP 321).

352] *marshals* B brings out the ironical use of a verb (τάσσει = draws up in order; AP 323) suggesting military discipline, where instinctive needs are actually dominant.

353-54] *billet / Of sharing* AP 323: ἐν μέρει τεκμήριον (= token in share/turn, i.e., no billeting order or voucher).

355] *Troic* Trojan. B partly transliterates the Greek word here (Τρωικοῖς; AP 325). *OED* quotes two uses of *Troic*, one in a classical study of 1831, and the other in Gladstone's *Homer* (1878), the year after B's *Agamemnon* was published.

356] *upæthral* Again B partly transliterates the original Greek word (ὑπαιθρίων = under the sky, in the open air; AP 326); but this time he coined a new English word for the purpose. Surprisingly, he ignored the rough breathing on the first vowel, which he normally transcribed as an *h* (e.g. *Hellas* for Ἑλλάς in l. 114). He did not, however, break his own rule of transliterating αι as *ai*. In the MS he clearly wrote, "upaithral," but the habit of Latinized spelling was too strong for the printer of the first edition, who turned it into "upæthral," and the 1889 text preserved the mistake.

357] *luckless creatures* The text is disputed, but B follows Paley, who retains the MS reading: ὡς δυσδαίμονες, "which almost every editor has altered," explaining the sentence: "Now at length delivered from the frosts and dews of the clear, open sky, since (or when) the poor wearied men will be able to repose the whole night without having to keep guard" (AP 326). A widely accepted emendation is: ὡς δ᾽ εὐδαίμονες(= and like happy men; ADP 336, AL 336).

360] *structures* I.e., buildings, temples etc., (ἱδρύματα = things founded, built; AP 330).

362] *But see no* "But let them beware lest any" (AEP 140).

prior AP 331: πρότερον (= before, sooner, earlier), which Paley takes to mean: "before they leave Troy" (AP 332) or "too soon" (AEP 140).

365] *double race-course* AP 334: διαύλου (of the diaulos = where one ran round round the end-post and back to the start.

366-68] *guilty to the gods . . . be* A close translation of AP 336-68, even to the inverted participial construction (ἐγρηγορὸς ... γένοιτ᾽ ἂν = awakened would become). Paley paraphrased: "But if the army should come home guilty of sins against the gods (i.e., sacrilege), the calamity due to them from those who have perished may not be suffered to sleep, even if no sudden and startling calamity . . . should befall them" (AP 336). For Clytaemnestra *those slaughtered* presumably includes her daughter Iphigenia.

368] *outbursting* AP 338: πρόσπαια (= striking-upon, sudden).

369]   *beat*   prevail, get the upper hand (κρατοίη, AP 340).

no turn . . . balance   I.e., decisively. B brings out the full meaning of μὴ διχορρόπως ἰδεῖν (= not waveringly to see: the ῥοπ-stem regularly refers to the "turn of the scales" (Liddell and Scott, 1871).

370]   *For . . . gain of*   AP 341: "For of many good things I have taken-for-myself [or] chosen the benefit." B seems to understand the verb (εἱλόμην) in the second of these senses, to give both a public meaning (my moral choice is to want good to prevail), and also a very private one (my chosen objective is a satisfying revenge on Agamemnon and a happy union with Aegisthus). This interpretation brings out the ambiguity that Aeschylus doubtless intended, far better than Paley's translation of εἱλόμην ("I have got"), and his paraphrase: "Since I have been blessed in so many and such great advantages, may no envy of the gods bring evil upon me" (AP 341)

371]   *kindly*   AP 342: εὐφρόνως, which may well mean "sensibly" here; but B follows Paley's note: "it more probably means 'obligingly,' i.e., in reply to my request" (see ll. 339-40).

374]   *For . . . labours*   AP 345: χάρις γὰρ οὐκ ἄτιμος εἴργασται πόνων (= for a not valueless return for labors has been made). Paley paraphrased: "no inadequate return for all our trouble." B struggles to suggest the multiple meanings of χάρις (= grace, favor, sense of favor received, gratitude, favor in return).

375]   *friendly*   Because Troy was captured under cover of darkness (ADP 357).

376]   *boons*   AP 347: κόσμων (= ornaments); but the meaning here is disputed. B follows Paley's translation ("prizes") while indulging his own taste for alliteration.

378]   *snare*   AP 349: δίκτυον (= net), a key-image in this play.

380]   *Captivity's great sweep-net*   AP 351-52: μέγα δουλείας γάγγαμον (= great net of slavery).

381]   *Ate*   Two syllables: ῎Ατη (= infatuation or delusion sent by the gods, and consequent ruin or disaster), an important concept, often personified, in Aeschylus' theory of divine retribution.

382]   *fear*   AP 353: αἰδοῦμαι (= reverence, stand in awe of).

guest's friend   Ξένιον (a title of Zeus in his capacity of god of guests and hospitality, relevant because Paris was a guest of Menelaus and seduced his host's wife).

384]   *Alexandros*   See l. 59n.

385]   *the white*   The circular bands of white on an archery-target. AP 356: "Neither before the mark nor above the stars," explained by Paley: "[neither] falling short of the mark [nor] going above the stars (too high)"—which makes B's alliterative *wide* inappropriate.

386] *foolish* One meaning of ἠλίθιον, but the more relevant one here is "vain, ineffectual," as in Paley's note: "might not light in vain" (AP 355).

387] *they have it, as men say* B follows Paley's suggestion that πληγὰν ἔχουσιν (= they have a blow) was "a familiar phrase borrowed from single-handed combatants, like *habet* [= he has] of the Roman gladiators" (AP 358). But here the words are: Διὸς πλαγὰν ἔχουσιν εἰπεῖν (= they have a blow from/of Zeus to say), which Paley explains: "Yes, 'tis from Zeus Xenius that they have received their blow, so to say it."

389] *has he done* B translates the MS reading ἔπραξεν (AW 370), rejecting the emendation adopted by Paley: ἔπραξαν (= they have fared; AP 360).

393] *the good and fair* AP 362: χάρις (= grace, beauty).

394] *Of . . . touch* AP 362: the literal meaning of ἀθίκτων (= not to be touched, i.e., holy things).

395] *profane* AP 364: οὐκ εὐσεβής (= not pious).

396] *That they do care* Not in the Greek text, but in Paley's note: ...τὸ μέλειν θεούς βροτῶν (= i.e., that gods care about mortals; AP 365).

398] *Outbreathing "Ares"* I.e., in a warlike spirit, or as Paley puts it, "of rebellion against the gods" (AP 365).

399] *spill* Abound so as to overflow (the literal sense of the Latin verb *abundo*).

400-401] *Be man's . . . harm off* Let man possess enough to keep harm off. AP 369-70: ἔστω ... ἀπήμαντον (= let it be without harm), but the "it" is unspecified. B slightly improves on one of the meanings suggested by Paley for this cryptic phrase: "that moderate wealth which, while it brings no harm to the possessor . . ." (AP 369).

401-2] *in himself . . . mind* The notion of *self*-sufficiency is not necessarily implied by the verb ἀπαρκεῖν, which might mean either that he has enough, or that he is content with what he has. The general sense is clear: "so that he has enough to satisfy a sensible person."

404-5] *kicks . . . disappearing* AP 375: "kicks into invisibility [ἀφάνειαν]."

405] *Right* AP 375: δίκας (which in this play usually means justice, but Paley translates it here as "Righteousness").

Yes interpolated, apparently for the rhyme.

406] *the sad persuasiveness* AP 476: ἁ τάλαινα πειθώ, where the definite article seems to be used as a Homeric demonstrative (translated "that" by Paley, AEP 141), and the adjective, derived from a verb signifying patient endurance, probably means "persistent" (ADP 385), though Paley glosses the whole phrase as "a wretched and fatal impulse" (AP 376).

407]   *Ate*   See l. 381n.

insufferable   A literal translation of ἄφερτος (AP 377)—though B, who had deliberately used current slang in the *Inn Album,* must have realized the comic effect of the adjective here, while ignoring Paley's paraphrase for it: "in an irresistible manner" (AP 376f.).

407-8]   *that . . . beforehand*   AP 376: προβουλόπαις (= foreplanning-child), the puzzling MS reading which Paley says, "seems fairly capable of two meanings,— 'the fore-counselling child of infatuation,' or 'devising beforehand calamity for posterity' (παισίν προβουλεύουσα [= before-planning for children])." B's *Treason* must have come from Paley's "calamity," which has no apparent basis in the Greek. Recent editors adopt an emendation to mean "child of fore-planning Ate" (ADP, AL 386).

410]   *A light dread-lamping-mischief*   AP 380: φῶς αἰνολαμπὲς σίνος (= light terrible-shining mischief), which Paley annotates: "φῶς is the nominative in apposition, 'shines as a balefully-gleaming light.' " B just transcribes the three words, rather unscrupulously allowing the reader to take the noun *light* for an adjective, but exploiting the resemblance of -λαμπὲς to English *lamp.*

410-11]   *just . . . bronze*   AP 381: κακοῦ δὲ χαλκοῦ τρόπον (= and in the manner of bad bronze). Paley explains the simile: "Bronze, when composed of a due proportion of copper and tin, has a green rust . . . and becomes bright by friction, whereas if unskilfully mixed it turns quite black externally, and is liable to become dim and speckled after being polished" (AP 383).

412]   *puttings to the touch*   Applications of a touchstone, the meaning given for προσβολαῖς here as recently as Liddell and Scott, 1996 (cf. AL 391); but some editors doubt if a touchstone was ever used on bronze, as Paley himself seems to have doubted: "But perhaps we should read χρυσοῦ [= gold], in allusion to the use of the touchstone (βάσανος)." The meaning of προσβολαῖς may be simply "incidental knocks" (ADP 390f.).

413]   *Black-clotted*   The precise meaning of μελαμπαγής (AP 383), a word used by Aeschylus elsewhere for clotted blood.

is he   Paley notes: "The man himself is said to turn black when put to the test by . . . a confusion between the image and the thing compared" (AP 383).

judged at once   As soon as he is tested.

414]   *He seeks—the boy*   As often in B's *Agamemnon,* the parenthetical incoherence results from B's anxiety to replicate the Greek word-order: διώκει παῖς (= chases boy, i.e., boy chases). The verb-ending shows that the subject is an unspecified "he, she, or it," but once it is specified as "boy" no "he" is needed in English. But in this particular case the *boy* will turn out later to be Paris, in an implied simile, as Paley explains: "he is as a boy in pursuit of a bird" (AP 384).

　　seeks . . . clutch　AP 385: "chases a flying bird."

415]　*brand*　AP 386: πρόστριμμα (= something rubbed on, inflicted, so a brand, disgrace). Here it may be particularly apt in the sense of something "rubbed off on" his city by Paris, the "contagion of his crime," a suggestion noted by Paley: "i.e., he makes the city share in his crime" (AP 384).

416]　*of his land*　Interpolated for the rhyme.

418]　*him who brought about*　B follows the first interpretation of ἐπίστροφον quoted by Paley: "him who brings on such sufferings" (AP 388).

419]　*in grapple throws*　AP 389: καθαιρεῖ (= takes down, demolishes, destroys); but B elaborates the suggestion in Paley's note: "a metaphor from wrestling, perhaps" (AP 388).

422]　*Shamed*　Treated shamefully, dishonored (ᾔσχυνε, AP 392).

423-24]　*townsmen*　I.e., fellow-citizens

　　a-spread / With shields　A rhyme-led version of AP 393: ἀσπίστορας (= armed with shields, shield-bearing).

　　spear-thrusts of sea-armament　AP 394: λογχίμους ναυβάτας ὁπλισμοὺς (= with-spears seagoing armings). Paley explains: "Helen, on leaving her home, bequeathed to her fellow-citizens nothing but the turmoil of war, and brought to her new abode only destruction in place of a dowry" (AP 395).

430-31]　*dints . . . imprints*　That a husband's love imprints. AP 401: στίβοι φιλάνορες (= man-love beaten-tracks/footsteps/traces).

432]　*There she stands silent*　The text is much disputed. Paley's reading, which he thinks "affords the most plausible sense," refers the whole passage to the deserted husband, Menelaus; but B follows Weise's text (AW 412-13), which makes Helen the initial subject, and is closer to the MSS: πάρεστι σιγᾶσ᾽ (= is there silent).

432-3]　*meets no honour—no / Shame*　AW 412: ἄτιμος, ἀλοίδορος (= unhonored, unreproached).

433]　*gone long ago*　AW 413: ἀφεμένων (= sent/let go away).

437]　*statues*　I.e., of Helen, as Paley assumes (AP 406).

437-38]　*in place of eyes / Those blanks*　AP 408: ὀμμάτων ... ἐν ἀχηνίαις (= in wants of eyes), paraphrased in Liddell and Scott, 1871: "the eyes' blank gaze."

438]　*all Aphrodite*　I.e., all the beauty and charm.

439-40]　*But . . . vain*　A word-for-word translation of AP 410-11, except that πάρεισι (= are there) contains no idea of *stand*ing; that χάρις (= grace, beauty) would more aptly be given the second sense here;

and that the simple adjective "vain" has been changed for emphasis, rhyme and metre into *that's vain*.

439-44] *"But . . . sleep!"* B follows Paley in continuing the quotation-marks started at l. 429 (AP 400). There are no such marks in Weise.

441] *seems* B tidies up the anacoluthon in the Greek, where a masculine participle attached to the husband ("seeming to see") is left hanging as the subject of the verb changes to the disappearing "vision."

442] *hands through* A rhyme-led inversion of διὰ χερῶν (= through [his] hands/arms; AP 413).

443-44] *Gone . . . sleep* AP 413-14: βέβακεν ὄψις οὐ μεθύστερον πτεροῖς ὀπαδοῖς ὕπνου κελεύθοις (? = the vision has gone not later on wings attendant-on / attendants [ὀπαδοῖς] paths of sleep). Paley follows the MSS, taking "not later" to mean, "as soon as it has appeared," and explaining the image as "a poetical way of saying, 'it slips away as a winged dream'" (AP 412, 415). Recent editors accept the emendation rejected by Paley: ὀπαδοῦσ' (= attending on), to produce the sense: "no longer accompanying on wings the paths of sleep" (ADP 425). B accepts with Paley the MSS reading ὀπαδοῖς, but translates it "servants" and interpolates *left to creep* for the rhyme.

446] *by much* A rhyming insertion justifiable by the original tautology: "more surpassingly" (ὑπερβατώτερα; AP 417).

447] *But . . . everywhere* AP 418: τὸ πᾶν δ' (= but the all), explained by Paley: "Such are the regrets at home . . . and . . . surpassing these; but generally (τὸ πᾶν) there are griefs which the friends of the absent Argive army have to endure, in the deaths of so many brave men."

450] *the heart must bear* That the heart must bear. AP 419: τλησικάρδιος (= of enduring heart), an adjective normally attached to a person, but here to *sorrow*. B follows the first of two meanings suggested by Paley: "endured in the heart."

451] *Sits* B's pictorial improvement on πρέπει (= is conspicuous; AP 419).

452] *Many a circumstance* AP 421: πολλὰ (= many things).

   at least A common meaning of γοῦν, but one which makes more rhyme than reason here (AP 421), where its sense seems simply emphatic (Yes indeed), or perhaps confirmative, i.e., giving "part proof" of what has just been said (J. D. Denniston, *The Greek Particles*, 2nd ed. [London, 1950], 451).

453] *the very breast* AP 421: πρὸς ἧπαρ (= to the liver, as the seat of emotion).

455] *any sent away* I.e., any relative or friend sent off to the war.

456] *And* "But" would have been a better equivalent for δὲ here, since the preceding μὲν (= on the one hand) marks the bitter contrast between the live men that their families sent off to Troy, and what they get sent back to them in exchange (AP 423-25).

457] *Armour* Paley's note (AP 425) offers two possible meanings for τεύχη here: urns or arms). This was B's choice, presumably because "urns" seemed to duplicate "ashes."

459] *for the dead* AP 426: σωμάτων (= of bodies). Paley explains: "who barters bodies for gold . . . because in the heroic ages both corpses and captives were ransomed for gold" (AP 426-30).

461] *Due-weight* B's ironical interpretation of the adjective βαρὺ (= heavy; AP 428), which Paley translates metaphorically as "sore" or "grievous," but calls the reading "suspicious because . . . we should have looked for a qualifying adjective like κοῦφον [= light]."

462] *What move the tear on tear* AP 429: δυσδάκρυτον (= much-wept).

463] *A charred scrap* A beautifully apt equivalent for πυροθὲν ... ψῆγμα (burnt scraping).

465] *For . . . return* A defensible explansion of a single adjective attached to "ashes": ἀντήνορος (= instead of a man; AP 429-30)

468] *a slaughtered pile* B's rephrasing of Paley's translation ("among heaps of slain") for ἐν φοναῖς (= on slaughters; AP 433).

469] *not his own* interpolated to emphasize the point (AP 434-35).

470] *But things there be* In AP 436 τὰ δὲ (= but other things) is merely the object of the verb of speaking (someone makes other complaints), but B's instinct for drama turns the phrase into direct speech. As Paley explains, these "*secret* murmurs of dissatisfaction are contrasted with the . . . open expression of feeling" just described. The verb βαύζω does indeed mean "bark," being derived from a dog's βαύ βαύ (= bow wow). But Aeschylus seems to use it here (as in his *Persae* 13) of quieter grumbling, so "growl" or "snarl" might fit the context better.

471] *When no man harks* A resourceful rhyme to translate σῖγα (quietly) .

472] *grief that's grudge* An alliterative rendering of φθονερὸν ἄλγος (= resentful pain). B overlooks the verb ἕρπει (= creeps, i.e., "stealthily spreads," as Paley translates it; AP 437, AEP 142).

473] *who first sought the judge* I.e., who sought legal redress. For the metaphor, see l. 39n. Here B's four English words represent one Greek one: προδίκοις (a compound of προ = before and δικ = judgment/lawsuit; AP 438). B stresses the two elements, while following Paley's note on the word: "'the principals in the suit' against Priam."

476] *as at birth* Interpolated, not merely for the rhyme, but in response to Paley's note on εὔμορφοι (= fair-formed): "'in their (natural) beauty,' i.e., unburnt, and therefore contrasted with the ghastly forms on the pyre" (AP 441).

477] *It . . . earth* AP 441: ἐχθρὰ δ᾽ ἔχοντας ἔκρυψεν (And hostile [earth] has hidden [them] having/holding). B attempts to reproduce the compressed play on words: The dead young men "occupy" (κατέχουσι = hold-down), a verb implying the success of an invading army in acquiring enemy land) graves in Trojan land, and that enemy land has covered them, the occupiers (ἔχοντας, participle of the simple verb included in the previous compound one.

478] *big with anger* The pregnancy-image is B's. AP 442: "heavy is the talk of citizens together-with [ξὺν] anger."

479] *pays . . . incurred* Paley paraphrases: "performs the part (pays the debt) of an imprecation solemnly ratified by the people . . . The meaning is, that the just indignation of the people calls forth the anger of the gods against the Atridae as much as a formal curse would have done" (AP 444).

480-81] *And . . . fear* AP 445-46: "And my anxiety waits to hear something night-covered [νυκτηρεφές]."

484] *Erinues* plural of *Erinus* See l. 57n.

at due periods AP 448: "in time [χρόνῳ]."

485-86] *Whoever . . . right* AP 459: "him who is lucky without justice."

487-88] *strain . . . success* Reasonably close to the untranslatable original: παλιντυχεῖ τριβᾷ (= with-back-again-luck rubbing-away; AP 450).

489] *blind* A possible meaning of ἀμαυρὸν, which covers many forms of feebleness, visual and physical (e.g. dim, dark, obscure, weak); but Paley, like most editors, stresses the notion of obscurity: "brought low and reduced . . . to nothingness from his high estate" (AP 451). B independently stresses the blindness, thinking of the infatuation involved in the concept of Ate, and perhaps the blindness-image in Sophocles' treatment of Oedipus.

489-90] *and among . . . might* No power avails to help a man who has come to be among the not-seen (ἀίστοις, a word closely connected with Ἁίδης (= Hades, the world of the dead; AP 451). B preserves the inverted word-order of the original: ἐν δ᾽ ἀίστοις τελέθοντος οὔτις ἀλκά (= among the unseens a man being [there is] no might).

491] *The being praised* Here B gives the meaning, but not a literal translation, of the strange Greek idiom: τὸ...κλύειν εὖ (= the hearing well, i.e., hearing nice things said about one, being well spoken of (AP 453).

outrageously Despite his prejudice against emendations, B seems to translate Paley's reading, ὑπερκόπως (= excessively), though the MSS read ὑπερκότως (= with excessive anger). Perhaps he felt less compunction because *outrageously* seemed to include *rage?*

492]   *at the eyes of such a one*   AP 454 has simply ὅσσοις (= at eyes), but Paley's note explains: "Lightning is hurled against their eyes so as to blind them."

493]   *thunder-stone*   A synonym for a thunderbolt used by Shakespeare (*Julius Caesar* (1.3.49) and Shelley (*Prometheus Unbound* (4.341); presumably used here to suggest "archaic workmanship" (see *Introductory Note*, l. 8).

494]   *Therefore*   AP 456: κρίνω δ᾽ (= but I choose).

495-96]   *so much . . . unespied*   Expanded from one word, ἄφθονον (= provoking no envy, i.e., moderate; AP 456).

498]   *Nor . . . see*   An almost word-for-word translation of AP 458: μήτ᾽ οὖν αὐτός ἁλούς ὑπ᾽ ἄλλων βίον κατίδοιμι (= nor indeed myself captured by others life see), i.e., nor live the life of a slave.

502-6]   *Who is . . . the same*   B seems to follow Paley's paraphrase (AP 463): "Who is so childish or so bereft of sense (as) after having had his heart inflamed by the new tidings of the beacon-light, afterwards by a change of the account to give way to grief?" But Paley's "or" is correct, not B's *and* (AP 463: ἤ). In making νέοις (= new) refer to the *novel* form of communication B was conceivably right. His *evidence* is further from λόγου (= word, story) than Paley's "account"; and though *Be worsted* is among the lexicon definitions of καμεῖν (otherwise = be weary, feel distress), it makes little sense where there is no question of any contest. However, it does point vaguely towards the real meaning, which is: one should not be too quick to believe good news, because one feels even worse if it is later disproved.

507]   *nature*   B seems to accept Paley's interpretation of the doubtful MS reading αἰχμᾷ (= spear) as "disposition" (AP 467), or "impulsive character" (AEP 143). ADP 483 calls the reading "unintelligible, and therefore perhaps to be marked as corrupt."

508]   *Before its view*   Before you can see it. AP 468: πρὸ τοῦ φανέντος (= before it appears).

   take a grace for granted   A neat alliteration to cover another phrase of disputed meaning: χάριν ξυναινέσαι (= consent/assent to a grace). Paley explains: "It is consistent with a woman's temperament to acquiesce in what is pleasing to her in preference to what is certain" (AP 467), cf. AEP 143: "in preference to what is certainly known."

509]   *Too . . . made*   AP 469-70: πιθανὸς ἄγαν ὁ θῆλυς ὅρος ἐπινέμεται (= Too trustful/credulous, the female boundary is grazed across quick-passing. Paley explains that the verb was a technical term for trespassing on a neighbor's land or letting one's cattle trespass,— and paraphrases: "Too credulous, the boundary of the female mind is encroached upon by rapid inroads" (AP 467).

512]   *glory*   A common meaning of κλέος, though here it is probably used in its other sense of "report, rumour." Nor does γυναικογήρυτον (= spoken by women; AP 471) imply any *vaunt*ing. Paley paraphrases: "a report spread by a woman perishes by a quick extinction" (AP 468).

512-13]   *Klutaimnestra*   B follows the MSS in ascribing this speech to Clytaemnestra, as does Weise (AW 489), though Paley and most editors give it to the chorus. Paley explains the emendation: "Clytaemnestra has not been present on the stage while the preceding remarks about female credulity were made, and therefore she cannot be supposed to reply to them" (AP 432).

514]   *exchanges, fire with fire*   I.e., one fire is replaced by another, or the fire is transferred from one beacon to another. AP 473: πυρός παραλλαγάς (= exchanges/ transfers of fire).

517-18]   *o'ershadowed . . . olive*   Normally a sign of good news.

518]   *dust, mud's thirsty brother*   AP 477: κάσις πηλοῦ ...διψία κόνις an expression hilariously parodied by the poet and classical scholar, A. E. Housman: "Mud's sister, not himself, adorns my shoes" ("Fragment of a Greek Tragedy," 13), where κόνις (= dust) is more correctly made feminine.

519]   *Close neighbours*   AP 478: ξύνουρος (= sharing a border with); *on his garb* is interpolated to suit Paley's note: "The meaning is that the dust and the mud at the top and bottom of the garment show by their combination that the wearer has come from a distance, and so can tell the news *in propria persona* [in his own person]" (AP 477).

521]   *by fire-smoke*   AP 480: καπνῷ πυρός (= by smoke of fire), which Paley annotates: "i.e., now that it is day; for the *flame* was only fit for the night" (AP 477).

522]   *But . . . speaking*   Either explicitly confirm and amplify the good news.

523]   *Word contrary to which*   AP 481: "but the opposite word to these things" i.e., the expected alternative, "or refute it."

  I ought but love it   AP 482: ἀποστέργω (= I love no more, loathe, reject), i.e., "perish the thought." He superstitiously avoids even mentioning it.

524]   *For . . . appendage*   AP 483: εὖ γὰρ πρὸς εὖ φανεῖσι προσθήκη πέλοι (= may there be a well addition to what has well appeared), explained by Paley: "For I pray that an addition may happily be made to what has already happily appeared (or, been realized)."

525]   *Whoever prays*   Paley's note quotes an editorial comment: "The chorus says this thinking of Clytaemnestra" (AP 284).

527]   *Ha*   It is hard to guess why B chose to use this exclamation, which must even then have sounded like a caricature of melodrama—

unless because it resembled the original ἰώ in expressing a variety of emotions, including joy, as presumably here (AP 486).

Argeian See l. 211n.

529] *chancing* AP 488: τυχών (= happening, in the most fortuitous sense, but also hitting a mark deliberately aimed at, gaining one's end).

530] *never prayed I* Not quite the right verb. He probably did *pray* for it, but never thought he'd get it. The original verb αὐχέω implies an element of boasting, and here (AP 489) implies confident assertion. Can B have absent-mindedly confused αὐχέω with εὔχομαι (= pray)?

531] *share my part* B retains the slight tautology of the Greek idiom μετέχω μέρος (= share a share; AP 490).

533] *Puthian* (= adjective of Πυθώ, the old name for the oracle at Delphi). The *king* is Apollo, who in *Iliad* 1.48 shoots arrows of plague at the Greeks attacking Troy.

534] *urging* Used in the Latin and earlier English sense of driving or impelling a weapon (e.g. a spear in Cowper's 1791 translation of the *Iliad*, 5.70).

535] *Skamandros* Σκάμανδρος, a river at Troy.

cam'st B seems to follow Paley in keeping the meaning of the non-scanning MS reading ἦλθες (= you came) by accepting the emendation ἦσθα (= you came; AP 494).

adverse AP 511: ἀνάρσιος (= hostile).

536] *healer* B rejects the MS reading in Weise's text and translates the emendation παιώνιος in Paley's (AW, AP 512).

537] *conquest-granting* B follows Paley's explanation of the variously interpreted adjective ἀγωνίους (related to ἀγών= contest, assembly): "all who have had any share in obtaining the victory for the Greeks" (AP 496)

538] *my tutelary* τὸν ... ἐμὸν τιμάορον (= my helper), paraphrased by Paley: "my own special patron" (AP 497), since Hermes was the herald of the gods.

539] *veneration* object of veneration. B imitates the use of σέβας (= reverence, object of reverence; AP 498).

540] *Heroes* beings intermediate between gods and men, often with one divine and one human parent; here as often local deities.

our forthsenders B coins a noun to translate the common Greek use of definite article + participle as noun-equivalent, in this case to τοὺς πέμψαντας (= those who sent, i.e., sent us to Troy. Paley explains: "who allowed the army to go out, or who did not oppose the expedition" (AP 499).

540-41] *friendly . . . receive* Kindly to receive the army back again. The infinitive follows *invoke*, in the sense of pray, beseech.

542] *Ha* Again translating ἰώ (see l. 527.).

mansions of my monarchs AP 501: μέλαθρα βασιλέων (= houses of kings), but the alliterating possessive proved irresistible.

543] *awful seats* Identified by Paley as "The seats of the king and queen in front of the palace, according to the custom of heroic times" (AP 502).

deities sun-fronting Paley: "The statues of gods placed so as to face the east."

544] *long time absent* AP 504: πολλῷ χρόνῳ (= in/after much time). B glosses over the puzzling MS reading ἦπου πάλαι (= ? in truth long ago) and ignores the emendation read by Weise and Paley: εἴ που πάλαι (= if anywhere long ago, i.e., now, if ever in the past; AW 520, AP 503).

546] *king Agamemnon* B preserves the fine rhetorical effect of the delayed subject, but only by prior insertion of a *he*, and of a dash (AP 506).

547] *clear shows your duty* AP 507: καὶ γὰρ οὖν πρέπει (= for indeed it is fitting); but B's *shows* ingeniously works in another meaning of πρέπει (= it is conspicuous).

548] *dug under* Almost the literal meaning of the verb κατασκάπτω (= dig down), though here and elsewhere it comes to mean "destroy utterly, raze to the ground."

Troia See l. 9n.

549] *the Avenger* AP 508: δικηφόρος (= justice-bringing—as B might have been expected to translate it here, since δίκη/justice is a central theme and key-word of the play).

plains are outploughed AP 509: κατείργασται πέδον ([the] plain has been thoroughly worked i.e., brought under cultivation). B's coinage *outploughed* seems to mean "ploughed up."

550] *unrecognizable* AP 510: ἄϊστοι (= unseen, invisible, i.e., destroyed.

551] *seed* It is not clear whether B takes this word literally, or metaphorically like Paley: "and the rising generation is utterly perished out of the whole land" (AEP 144).

552] *yoke-strap* AP 512: ζευκτήριον (= yoke); but B correctly implies that the word was originally an adjective (= for yoking), and thinks of the strap that bound the yoke to the harness.

553-54] *happy man . . . worthiest* AP 514: "he comes a happy man and (δ') worthiest." B's dash marks his difficulty in retaining the inverted word-order.

554-55] *of what mortals / Now are* AP 514-15: βροτῶν τῶν νῦν (= of present-day mortals); but B's hint of inferiority to their predecessors comes, not from this context, but from *Iliad* 1.271-72: "but with them no man could fight of those who are now mortals upon the earth."

555] *accomplice* AP 515: συντελὴς (= joint payer of taxes, fines etc.); Paley suggests: "Probably the idea is, that the city, as equally involved in the guilt (by not returning Helen and her stolen wealth), was also involved in the payment for the injury."

556] *Outvaunts . . . done-by* I.e., can boast that their "suffering has been less than the heinousness of their deed, or perhaps than what they gained by their deed" (AP 513). B adapts Chesterfield's phrase, "Do as you would be done by" (*Letter to his Son*, 16 October 1747), or perhaps Kingsley's "Mrs Doasyouwouldbedoneby" (*The Water Babies*, ch. 5).

557] *rape* Used in the early sense of a carrying away by force, to translate ἁρπαγῆς (= a snatching away; AP 517).

559] *mowed* AP 519: ἔθρισεν (= mowed, harvested, reaped, possibly in the metaphorical sense: "got that return for what he had sowed"; ADP 536). But B seems to take the verb more in the physical sense of mowing down, i.e., destroying, or in Paley's phrase, "razing to the ground" (AP 520).

to atoms a slight anachronism: Democritus, who first thought of atoms (ἄτομα = things uncuttable, indivisible) was born in 460 B.C., Aeschylus died in 456. B was translating πανώλεθρον (= all-destroyed; AP 518). Did the unsuitable phrase pop into his head from an association of ideas between *mow*ing and a lexicon definition of the adjective ἄτομος: *unmown*, as with λείμων (= meadow) in Sophocles, *Trachiniae*, 200?

560] *Debts . . . over* AP 520: "And the sons of Priam have paid double θαμάρτια [glossed by the scholiast as 'the wages of the sin']." Paley explains: "in that they have been compelled to give up Helen, and have had their city razed to the ground" (*Scholia* 362, AP 520).

561] *Achaians* See l. 290n.

562] *I hail* I.e., I return your greeting. Surprisingly, B has obscured the point of the repeated verb, imprecisely translated *hail*. In fact χαῖρε, though commonly used as a greeting or farewell, is an imperative meaning "rejoice!" (AP 521); to which the herald replies χαίρω, "I do rejoice." Paley's note makes the train of thought clear: "'I bid you joy, herald of the Grecian army . . . My joy is such that I am content to die'" (AP 521-33).

to die . . . longer The text is uncertain, but both Weise and Paley (AW 539, AP 522) read: τεθνᾶναι δ' οὐκ ἔτ' ἀντερῶ θεοῖς (= and I shall not any longer gainsay, i.e., speak against, object to, refuse the gods to be dead).

563] *exercise* An exact translation of ἐγύμνασεν (= trained in gymnastic exercise; AP 523). The sense is: were you terribly homesick?

564] *at least* A common meaning of the particle γε, but quite irrelevant here, where there is no sense of limitation, and it merely emphasizes the preceding word ἐνδακρύειν (= weep; AP 524).

565] *What . . . gainers* B follows Weise (AW 542) in making the line a question: τερπνῆς ἄρ᾽ ἦτε τῆσδ᾽ ἐπήβολοι νόσου (= Then you were having-gained this pleasant disease?). Paley reads the same words as a statement, makes the ἐπήβολοι (= having gained) passive in meaning, i.e., "having been gained by, possessed by." He then translates: "A pleasing affection truly this which you had upon you" (AP 521-33). Recent editors tend to agree with Paley (AF, ADP, AL 542).

566] *How . . . master* A literal translation of AP 526, implying: How do you mean? I shan't understand unless you explain.

567] *For . . . stricken* Because your love was returned: you longed for those who longed for you.

569] *from dark mind* Paley explains: "A mind which darkly broods over thoughts which it dare not express" (AP 529) or "a darkly-boding heart" (AEP 145).

570] *Whence . . . army* B translates the much disputed MS reading (AW 547: πόθεν τὸ δύσφρον τοῦτ᾽ ἐπῆν, στύγος στρατῷ [= whence this gloomy-thought was-on hatred to/for army?]). Paley's text (AP 530) inserts a comma before "hatred," and he translates: "Whence came this uneasy feeling over you, so distasteful to the army" (AEP 145), explaining, "so unsuitable to its present joyful return," and "To receive the returning army with joyful face was regarded as an important omen; the gloomy looks and anxious feelings now alluded to caused apprehension to the herald" (AP 530).

571] *Of . . . silence* I.e., when things are bad I always find it best to say nothing.

572] *And . . . any* AP 532: "And how, kings being absent, did you fear any people?" i.e., while the king was away, why were you afraid to speak freely?

573] *So . . . dying* I was (and am) so frightened of some people that, to quote your own remark just now, I'd be glad to die. He is thinking of Clytaemnestra and Aegisthus.

574] *For . . . out* The herald is either being obtuse, in assuming that the chorus is as pleased about everything as he is himself; or perhaps being clever enough to take the hint, and prudently changing the subject.

in much time AP 534: ἐν πολλῷ χρόνῳ. Paley paraphrases: "during the lapse of a long time" (AP 535).

575] *had luck in falling* Turned out fortunately. B translates εὐπετῶς (= falling well), a metaphor from dicing).

576] *faulty* AP 536: ἐπίμομφα (= things you can find fault with, open to criticism).

578] *should I tell of* If I were to tell of (syntactically a remote condition, implying that I'm not going to. The apodosis is left unstated, something like "you'd understand what I mean."

lodgments Lodgings, living accommodation.

579] *ill-strewn* AP 539: κακοστρώτους—a word in which the *strew*-component commonly referred to bedding. They had to sleep in the narrow gangways on the ships.

579-80] *what . . . portion* B retains the incoherent sentence-construction of the Greek (AP 538-40).

581] *As . . . hatred* AP 541: "As for the things on land, there was in addition more hatred/objects of hatred," i.e., conditions on land were even more hateful.

582] *beds were ours* A stranger phrase than the elliptical original: εὐναὶ ... ἦσαν (= beds were / there were beds; AP 542).

584] *Dews kept a-sprinkle* No more incongruous than the original: δρόσοι κατεψέκαζον (= dews drizzled down), which Paley ascribes to Aeschylus' "ignorance of the real origin of dew" (AP 543).

584-85] *abiding . . . vestures* A literal translation of ἔμπεδον σίνος ἐσθημάτων (AP 544-5) i.e., which constantly spoilt our clothes.

585] *making . . . matting* B's pleasant realization of ἔνθηρον τρίχα (= wild-beast hair), which reminded Paley "of the care the Greeks have always taken in combing their locks" (AP 343), though some recent editors take the adjective to mean "full of wildlife" (i.e., verminous), or take the noun to mean the hair/wool of the clothes (AF 562, ADP 561-62, AL 561-62).

586] *Winter . . . bird-slaying* B closely follows the Greek word-order (AP 546).

587] *Idaian* AP 547: Ἰδαία (= of Mount Ida; see l. 302n.).

588] *couches* Paley annotated: "Literally, "whenever the sea slept tranquilly, having fallen on its mid-day couch unstirred by wind" (AP 548). But Fraenkel (AF 565) takes κοίταις in an abstract sense to mean the condition of lying or resting, i.e., the sea's siesta.

590] *these* AP 550: ταῦτα (= these things).

592] *mind uprising* Care about coming to life again (ἀναστῆναι μέλειν = care to stand up i.e., be resurrected). Paley explains: "Our trials are past; and they are passed, to those who have perished, so that they will never hereafter care even to rise from their graves to life again" (AP 550).

593]   *tell in numbers* AP 553: ἐν ψήφῳ λέγειν (= tell in pebble; pebbles were used as counters).

   deprived I.e., deprived of life, though the original word ἀναλωθέντας actually means "spent, squandered, so killed" (AP 553).

594]   *fate's fresh outbreak* A much more accurate translation of τύχης παλιγκότου (= again-spiteful chance) than Paley's conventional "the frowns of fortune," since the adjective is properly used of wounds breaking out afresh (Liddell and Scott, 1871).

595]   *I . . . misfortunes* Possibly based on the translation given in Liddell and Scott, 1871 for πολλὰ χαίρειν ξυμφοραῖς καταξιῶ, "I bid a long farewell to calamities." But Paley's tentative interpretation seems closer to the normal meaning of καταξιῶ (= think fit) and makes good sense in the context: "I think we ought (not only not to grieve, but) *even* to rejoice greatly at the events which have happened" (AP 555.

596]   *the left* Those who are left, a literal rendering of τοῖς λοιποῖσιν (AP 556).

   Argeian See l. 211n.

597]   *beats* νικᾳ (= wins/defeats, i.e., is the most important; AP 557).

598]   *'tis . . . sunlight,* B obscures the most obvious sense of AP 558: "so that it is reasonable to boast, in this light of the sun" [i.e., on this day, or "to this light of the sun," as Paley translates it in AEP 146: "Troy has been taken . . ."].

599]   *the aery flyers* AP 559: ποτωμένοις (= flying). Paley paraphrased: "The Argives, as they joyfully speed on their way, may boast . . ." (AP 559), though the reference may be to their fame rather than their joy (ADP 576)

601]   *trophies* Paley suggests: "Trojan arms."

602]   *domes* I.e., temples, but B habitually transcribes δόμος, the noun used in AP 562, like this, to emphasize its resemblance to the English one, without implying anything like a cupola.

   new glory to grow ancient An explanatory expansion of ἀρχαῖον γάνος (= ancient joy/pride), translated by Paley: "a glory of olden times" (AEP 146).

604]   *army-leaders* The etymolological sense of στρατηγούς (AP 564) though the word is normally translated "generals."

   grace AP 564: χάρις (= grace, favor), here used in the second sense, and with the the implication that gratitude is required.

605]   *Thou hast my whole word* The literal meaning of the Greek (except for the interpolation of *my*), i.e., that's all I have to tell you.

311

606] *O'ercome . . . gainsay* AP 566: νικώμενος λόγοισιν οὐκ ἀναίνομαι (= defeated by words I do not refuse, i.e., you've convinced me, and I accept what you say).

607] *For . . . well"* AP 567: ἀεὶ γὰρ ἡβᾷ τοῖς γέρουσιν εὖ μαθεῖν (= for it is always young for old men to learn well). B's quotation-marks are apparently meant to indicate the pun detected by Paley: "'to learn well,' i.e., good news, a sort of play on the proverb 'never too old to learn'" (AP 566). Cf. Fraenkel's hardly realistic comment: "It is a powerful and striking thought that whereas a man grows older, his capacity for learning does not do the same, but keeps itself continually young" (AF 584).

609] *make me rich too* Paley explains: "Though it is reasonable that these matters should be especially a care to Clytemnestra . . . yet at the same time (it is equally reasonable) to enrich, i.e., inform, me" (AP 569). But if Fraenkel is right in assuming that the chorus has just "caught sight of the queen, who is coming out of the house" (AF 585), the remark is a hasty imitation of a loyal servant, who rejoices in every good thing that happens to his employers.

612] *dispersion* B's strange translation of ἀνάστασιν (= making to stand up, i.e., depopulation, desolation; AP 572) was possibly suggested by a note to Paley's translation (AEP 147): "Removal of the people as slaves."

613] *girding* Jeering at. AP 573: ἐνίπτων (= reproving, reproaching).

613-14] *Through . . . thinkest* B reproduces the exact word-order of AP 573-4, drawing the line only at the placing of the preposition διὰ (= through) after its noun. His *fire-bearers* is the precise equivalent of the Greek word πυρφόροι, though that is not actually used here. The original word is φρυκτωρῶν (= beacons or beacon-watchers; AP 573). Paley translates: "Do you give credence to bon-fires . . . ?" (AEP 147).

615] *high to lift heart up* I.e., to rejoice too soon.

616] *wit-bewildered* AP 576: πλαγτὸς (= wandering in mind).

617] *female-song with* Though Greek prepositions are often placed after their nouns (see ll. 613-14n.), that is no excuse for the unEnglish order here, where there is no preposition in the Greek, only a dative of the noun νόμῳ = with song). Paley translates: "in a feminine strain" and explains as a refererence to the ὀλολυγμός (= cry of joy, B's *shout*) "inasmuch as it was the shout raised at a sacrifice peculiarly by the women. Clytaemnestra had commenced it . . . and others, even males, had taken it up at her bidding" (AP 577). Clytaemnestra is replying, of course, to the previous charge: "How like a woman!"

619] *congratulating* Used in the old (intransitive) sense of "rejoicing," to translate εὐφημοῦντες (= saying words of good omen, shouting in triumph (AP 579).

gods' seats The literal meaning of θεῶν ἕδραις (AP 579), i.e., temples.

620] *Soothing . . . fragrant* An almost literal translation of a puzzling line (AP 580), with *soothing* to represent κοιμῶντες (= lulling to sleep). Paley annotates: "'As they put out the fragrant . . . incense-fed flame,' probably by pouring wine upon it"; but the meaning may be: "they heap incense . . . on the fire, thus 'putting to sleep' the *flame* (and creating *smoke* instead)" (ADP 598).

621] *what's more* AP 581: τὰ μάσσω (= the longer/larger things), i.e., why need you tell me any more?. B keeps close to the original word-order.

622] *word* the primary meaning of λόγον, though it commonly means "story," as here (AP 582). As often, B seems to opt for the oddest rendering.

624-27] *for . . . gates* B retains the syntactical incoherence of the Greek (AP 584-87)—which is possibly meant to suggest Clytaemnestra's uneasiness at the approaching confrontation with her husband.

629] *A faithful . . . coming* A word-for-word translation of AP 589, a line variously interpreted. Paley takes it as a "wish which the herald is instructed to convey, transferred, of necessity, to the third person, from the nature of the narrative," though his explanation is unconvincing: "With great truth to nature the poet makes this wish to be dictated by Clytaemnestra, conscious as she is that she has *not* been faithful to her lord. She avoids, as in itself suspicious, the direct assertion, 'he will find'" (AP 581). What she says seems suspicious enough, even if one makes the super-subtle distinction: "Not 'may he find a faithful wife at home' (as if the matter was open to doubt in anyone's mind), but 'let him discover that the wife in his house is a faithful one'" (ADP 606; cf. AF 606).

632-33] *no signet-impress . . . harm to* AP 592-93: "having destroyed no seal [σημαντήριον = mark or seal put on something by its owner]," in this case, according to a scholiast, on the husband's bed (*Scholia* 363).

635] *bronze-dippings* B translates, without attempting to explain, χαλκοῦ βαφὰς (= dippings/dyeings/temperings of bronze; AP 595). Paley mentions various interpretations, e.g. "'any more than I know how to imbrue a sword in blood' . . . she here disclaims any knowledge of the murder she all the while intends to perpetrate"; and adds, "Perhaps the simplest way is to take it as a saying or proverb to express any thing inconceivable or unlikely." The scholiast refers it to the tempering of iron by dipping it into cold water (*Scholia* 363).

637] *not bad* AP 597: οὐκ αἰσχρὸς (= not disgraceful). B follows AW 613 and the MSS in assigning this speech to the herald, though Paley (like recent editors) assigns it to Clytaemnestra, translating: "Such is my boast, and every word of it is true; a boast which no high-born lady need be ashamed to utter" (AP 596; cf. AF, ADP 613f.). As in *Hamlet* 3.2.230, "The lady doth protest too much."

638-39] *Ay . . . seemly* AP 598-99: "Thus this woman spoke a word fair-seemingly to thee learning [μανθάνοντι] by clear interpreters"— apparently a guarded hint to the herald of Clytaemnestra's insincerity. Paley notes: "Divested of the ambiguity arising from the irony of the speaker, these verses mean, 'So much for her fine speech, which must be unintelligible to you (the herald) without clear interpreters to expound it'" (AP 599). B's *that hast a knowledge from clear interpreters* is possibly meant as a heavily sarcastic version of Paley's "must be unintelligible to you," in the form: "now you're a lot wiser!"

640] *Meneleos* The Attic spelling of Menelaos is used by Aeschylus here (AP 600), and B faithfully transliterates it.

ask of Ask about.

643] *false and pleasant* AP 603: τὰ ψευδῆ καλὰ (= lies as beautiful/good, i.e., to please you; or perhaps false good news). Paley paraphrases: "It is impossible that I should tell good news which is false, for friends to enjoy for a length of time."

644] *to reap the fruits of* A more accurate translation of καρποῦσθαι than Paley's "enjoy."

through a long time I.e., I can't tell you false good news that you'll enjoy for any length of time, for you'll learn the truth very soon.

645] *How . . . on* An almost word-for-word translation of AP 605, but one which misses the meaning: "if only you could manage to tell good new that's true!" πῶς ἄν + optative commonly expresses a wish.

646] *For . . . sundered* Again B obscures the meaning, this time by leaving out τάδε (= these things). Paley explains the line: "for (as you say) when these two (good tidings and truth) are separated, they do not easily escape detection" (AP 605). The MSS and all editors attribute this line (AL 623) to the Chorus; but B gives it to the Herald, apparently as a response to the Chorus's idea of combining *good* with *true*.

647] *Achaic* Achaian (see l. 290n.). B tried to keep the Greek spelling at AP 607, Ἀχαιϊκοῦ, but in the process overlooked the second *iota* with its diaeresis (i.e., the second *i*), and wrote in the MS "Achaic," making the word look disyllabic, though the scansion required a trisyllable (*Achaiïc*).

648] *I announce no falsehood* AP 608: οὐ ψευδῆ λέγω (= I do not tell lies).

649] *forth-putting* AP 609: ἀναχθεὶς (= putting out to sea).

650]   *wide woe*   I.e., a widespread and common disaster. AP 610: κοινὸν ἄχθος (shared-in-common grief).

651]   *topping*   ἄκρος (= at the top, so first-rate). Was B amused to find a parallel in Aeschylus for the slang of his day, or merely indifferent to his readers' probable reactions?

652]   *a long . . . spoken*   A neat replica of the original line: μακρὸν δὲ πῆμα συντόμως ἐφημίσω (AP 612).

653-54]   *Whether . . . bruited*   Equally faithful to the Greek (AP 613-14), though more remote from normal English. Paley annotated: '"Was it about him as alive or dead that a report was mentioned by the other sailors?" i.e., what do *they* say about him?' (AP 613).

656]   *Helios*   AP 616: ῞Ηλιος ((= the sun-god, called "all-seeing" in *Prometheus Bound* 91, traditionally attributed to Aeschylus).

658]   *Attack . . . anger*   AP 618: 'come and end, by the anger of the gods [δαιμόνων].'

659]   *It suits not*   It is not fitting.

660]   *distinct each god's due*   AP 620: χωρὶς ἡ τιμὴ θεῶν (= apart [is] the honor of gods'). Paley explains: "'The honours paid to the gods in thanksgiving and in deprecating evil are quite distinct.' The Greeks greatly disliked the mixing up good news with bad" (AP 620).

662]   *fall'n host's*   AP 622: "of a fallen army."

      God ward off   I.e., which may God forbid. B is translating the adjective attached to the *woes*, ἄπευκτα (= to be deprecated, literally "such as one prays may not come to pass," AF 638; AP 621).

663]   *One popular wound*   AP 623: ἕλκος ἕν τὸ δήμιον (= one wound of-the-people). "The Herald's Greek becomes incoherent here, if the MSS are to be believed. It may be mistaken in theory, as it is impossible in practice, to treat it according to the rules of normal grammar" (ADP 640f.). B has to make what he can of a passage where both text and meaning are much disputed.

664]   *sacrificed*   AW 641, AP 624, AL 641: ἐξαγισθέντας, of which "the meaning can only be guessed; perhaps 'sacrificed' [or 'taken as victims'] from many homes" (ADP 640f.). B follows Paley's suggestion: "many who have fallen victims from many a home" (AP 624).

665]   *two-thonged whip*   διπλῇ μάστιγι (= double whip), explained by Paley: "A *double* calamity of war is here described, in its relation both to the state and to private families"(AP 623).

667]   *Of . . . weighted*   B keeps the inverted word-order of the Greek, translated by Paley: "When, I say, a messenger comes loaded with calamities like these, it is fitting and in place to recite this paean of the Furies" (AP 627), i.e., to dwell on the bad news of Menelaus' disappearance.

669] *matters saved* AP 629: σωτηρίων ... πραγμάτων (= things to do with saving/safety/salvation).

672] *urged by gods' wrath* AP 632: οὐκ ἀμήνιτον θεῶν (= not wrathless of the gods).

675] *Argeian* See l. 211n.

676] *bad-wave* AP 636: δυσκύμαντα (an adjective combining the stem of κῦμα = wave with the prefix δυσ- = hard, bad, ill etc. The *outbreak* has no separate equivalent in the Greek.

677] *ships ... breezes* B keeps the original word-order, and comes as close as he can to the spelling of Θρῄκιαι (= Thracian, i.e., from Thrace in the north.

678] *these* I.e., the *ships*. *butted at* the precise metaphor implied by κεροτυπούμεναι (= horn-struck; AP 638); though *fury* replaces βίᾳ (= force, violence) possibly for metrical reasons.

679] *typhoon* AP 639: τυφῶ. B suspends his usual rule of transcribing Greek υ as English *u*.

680] *a bad herd's whirling* B ignores Paley's prosaic paraphrase: "the unsteady guidance of the unskilled helmsman," and translates ποιμένος κακοῦ (= bad shepherd; AP 640) more literally and imaginatively, presumably taking it to mean the storm-wind whirling the ships round like a flock of frightened sheep. That interpretation parallels the previous butting-image (AP 638), on which the scholiast had commented: "the metaphor is drawn from bulls" (*Scholia* 363).

682] *on flower with corpses* A fine rendering of ἀνθοῦν ... νεκροῖς (AP 642).

683] *naval ravage* AP 643: "naval wrecks," i.e., wrecks of ships.

684] *But ... too* Almost a versification of Paley's note: "Us however and our ship, uninjured in its hull" (AP 644).

685] *outstole ... outprayed* B translates the prefixes of the two verbs (ἐκ = out) without bothering to explain what the two compounds mean (ἐξέκλεψεν = stole away, i.e., from the general destruction) and ἐξητήσατο (= begged off; AP 645).

686] *tiller touching* The happy alliteration was invited by the original words: οἴακος θιγών (= touching the handle of the rudder; AP 646).

687] *willing* I.e., willingly, i.e., she chose to sit. But B replicates the original participle θέλουσα; AP 647.

688] *So as* So that. B retains the original ὡς (= as), and so does Paley's note: "'So as neither when at her moorings to feel the force of the breakers, nor to be stranded upon the iron-bound shore,' i.e., by dragging the anchor" (AP 648).

690] *the water-Haides* AP 650: ᾅδην πόντιον (= ocean Hades; AP 650).

692] *We chewed the cud* AP 652: ἐβουκολοῦμεν, a strange use of a verb which in the active form, as here, should mean "we tended cattle" but in the passive could be put into the mouth of the cattle themselves to mean, "we grazed." In Aeschylus' *Eumenides* 79, however, it is given the sense of ruminating or brooding on. Here in the *Agamemnon* its meaning is disputed, but B follows Paley's "brooded over," while retaining the bucolic metaphor (AP 652; see ll. 678, 680).

698] *Foremost . . . thou* I.e., the one thing you can be sure of is that he will come.

699] *sun reports him* See l. 656n.

702] *Some hope is* There is some hope that. AP 662: ἐλπίς τις (= some hope, with ἐστί = is, understood).

703] *such things* AP 663: τοσαῦτα (= so many things, i.e., so much.

704] *Who . . . named* AP 664: "Who ever named . . . ?" The Chorus goes on to play on the etymological suggestions of Helen's name, Ἑλένη. As usual, B marks the change in the original to lyric verse by switching into irregular rhymed verse.

705] *the future* AP 666: τοῦ πεπρωμένου (= what is fated).

706] *in happy mood* ἐν τυχᾳ (= in luck, i.e., luckily).

707] *Her . . . bridegroom* AP 669: τὰν δορίγαμβρον (= the spear-bride, i.e., either causing war by marriage or wooed by battle). Paley translates: "Bringing war by her marriage" (AP 669) and "spear-wooed" (AEP 150).

on all sides contention-wooed AP 669: ἀμφινεικῆ (= all-round-quarrel, i.e., object of contention.

708] *Helena* The name itself does not appear in the text, but B's interrogative interpolation neatly explains to the English reader what is going on.

mark the suture Notice the connection of sounds with ideas—a rather expensive rhyme to translate one Greek word, πρεπόντως (= fittingly, appropriately; AP 670).

709] *Ship's-Hell . . . City's-Hell* The original words are ἑλέναυς (= destroyer of ships), ἕλανδρος (= destroyer of men), ἑλέπτολις (= destroyer of cities). The idea of translating the pun by using the ἑλ- prefix (= catch, conquer, kill, destroy) in the sense of its English sound was suggested by Paley: "The play on the word may be rendered by 'a hell to ships' &c." (AP 671).

710] *delicately-pompous* A reasonably literal translation of the compound adjective ἁβροτίμων (delicate-honor), though the the τιμ-component may be used in its common sense of "value, price" to produce "delicate and costly" (ADP 690). Paley assumes so in his note: "the dainty and precious curtains by which she was hid from vulgar gaze . . . like some beauty in an Eastern harem" (AP 672).

that pavilion well Interpolated for the rhyme.

712] *earth-born* Though Paley quotes Hesychius' definition of the word γίγαντος as "great, strong"(AP 672), B gives its literal meaning. He probably remembered that the Titan Zephyrus, god of the West Wind, while generally thought gentle, was classed by Hesiod among winds that may suddenly become a "bane to mortals" by "scattering ships and destroying sailors" (*Theogony* 868-76). In that character of ἑλέναυς it might well take Ἑλένη to Troy.

713] *leaders of the pack* I.e., of hounds. AP 675: κυναγοὶ (= dog-leaders, huntsmen).

716] *visible no more* AP 676: ἄφαντον (= invisible), explained by Paley: "the pursuers sailed in vain, since the bark had reached Troy before they got even a sight of it" (AP 675).

717] *Simois* A river near Troy.

718] *For . . . gore* AP 680: "bloody because of strife," a phrase variously explained. Paley suggests: "The poet seems to call Helen herself . . . a cause or subject of strife. They sailed *on account* of one who was destined to . . . bring about the ordained war."

720] *marriage-care* B tries to bring out the original pun on κῆδος (= 1. care, sorrow, 2. connection by marriage; AP 681).

721] *tables' abuse* I.e., abuse of hospitality, since Paris was Menelaus' guest. The placing of the apostrophe was a mistake in B's MS. He should have written *table's*, since τραπέζας (= of table; AP 683) is a genitive *singular*, not a plural. Yet his apostrophe, rather high up, is certainly to the right of *tables* (though I wonder if his flying pen could have landed too far to the right, simply to avoid the long tail of the *y* in *rightly*, hanging down from the line above).

722] *hearth-partaker* The literal meaning of ξυνεστίου (AP 684), a synonym for "guest"; but here used as an adjective with Zeus to indicate his function as the god of hospitality.

724] *with noisy throat* AP 686: ἐκφάτως (= outspokenly), a word not found elsewhere and variously interpreted; but by Paley as "'with loud voice' . . . i.e., sharing openly, and as abettors in the crime, in the festivities which Paris instituted on his return with his bride to Troy" (AP 685).

725] *the hymenaeal note* The marriage-hymn.

731] *The . . . marries* AP 692: τὸν αἰνόλεκτρον (= the terrible-marriage-bed).

732]   *She*   The city of Troy.

734]   *slaughter*   AP 695: αἷμα (= blood), translated "slaughter" in Paley's note (AP 694).

735]   *And thus a man*   The words imply a kind of simile. Neither Paris nor Helen is directly compared to the lion cub, but the disaster that naturally follows the introduction of the charming young animal is compared to the equally predictable one that followed the charming young pair's marriage, at first a cause of general rejoicing.

  by no milk's help   AP 697: ἀγάλακτον (= milkless, i.e., getting no milk, for the cub has been taken away from its mother unweaned). But B seems to follow Paley's translation, which slightly misses the point: "not fed on milk" (AP 698).

738]   *life's first festal stage*   AP 699: ἐν βιότου προτελείοις (= in the beginning of [its] life). B's *festal* cleverly adapts the literal meaning of προτελείοις, "preliminary religious rites" (often before a wedding), to suggest a young animal's *joie de vivre*.

741]   *A thing . . . warms*   AP 701: γεραροῖς ἐπίχαρτον (= something for elders to rejoice over). B's *pride,* suggestive of the modern tendency to keep dangerous pets as status-symbols, has some etymological justification, since the related verb ἐπιχαίρω commonly means "exult over enemies." But Paley seems right to call this "bad sense of the verb . . . only an accidental one," and to paraphrase the words here as "the delight of the old men."

743]   *to hand*   I.e., when stroked.

744]   *Wagging its tail*   That is the normal meaning of σαίνων (AP 704) when used of dogs; but did Aeschylus or B realize what the gesture expressed in felines?

  at belly's strict command   I.e., because it was hungry. AP 704: γαστρὸς ἀνάγκαις (= by necessities of stomach).

750]   *was watered*   AP 711: ἐφύρθη (= was defiled; but the primary meaning of the verb was to mix with something *wet*, so B's odd translation had more than the rhyme to justify it.

753]   *some priest*   I.e., like some priest. AP 715: ἱερεύς τις, where the first word carries its more relevant meaning of "sacrificer," and the second (= some, any, a certain) implies in this context, "a kind of."

754]   *Até*   See l. 381n.

  by nurture thus increased   AP 715: προσεθρέφθη (= was reared in addition, i.e., to the human residents, so that the total number of inmates was *increased* .

756]   *soul*   AP 717: φρόνημα (= spirit). Paley explains: "a spirit of unruffled calm" (i.e., the Trojans felt no anxiety about the arrival of Helen).

759] *spirit-biting* The literal meaning of δηξίθυμον (AP 720), odder in English than in Greek, where δάκνω (= bite) is a common metaphor for intense emotional impact.

760] *from . . . bending* Paley: "The metaphor is from the race-course" (AP 721).

762] *Ill-resident* AP 724: δύσεδρος (= bringing evil by sitting or staying).

ill-mate AP 724: δυσόμιλος (= bringing evil in one's company, bad to associate or live with).

762-63] *in power . . . Priamidai* A rhyme-led, alliterative version of συμένα Πριαμίδαισιν (= rushing upon the sons of Priam; AP 724).

764] *Hospitable* I.e., the god of hospitality.

765] *Erinus* See l. 57n.

for a . . . dower Expanded from one word, νυμφόκλαυτος (= bride-weeping; AP 726). Paley explains: "she brought shame and reproach, not to say suffering, on other wives."

774] *Of my own mind I am* I have my own opinion. AP 732: μονόφρων εἰμί (= I am alone in my opinion).

775] *many* AP 735: πλείονα (= more i.e., such deeds).

777] *that correctly estimate* I.e., that judge rightly (εὐθυδίκων = right-judging; AP 736).

779, 780] *Arrogance* AP 738-40: Ὕβρις ... Ὕβριν (Hubris, almost a technical term in Aeschylus' doctrine of retribution).

781] *Or now, or then,* Sooner or later.

appointed morrow AP 740: τὸ κύριον (= the appointed i.e., time).

782] *And she . . . Satiety* Here the text of the MSS is corrupt, and B seems generally to follow Paley's emended reading(AP 743): νέα δ᾽ ἔφυσεν Κόρον (= and young [Hubris] gives birth to Satiety), which Paley himself translates: "and this young Insolence gives birth to Pride of Satiety" (AEP 151). But it is not clear why B transferred the *young* from the mother to the child.

783] *with whom . . . can be* The literal meaning of the adjectives ἄμαχον ... ἀπόλεμον (AP 744), i.e., irresistible.

787] *well-omened* Though the basic meaning of ἐναίσιμον is connected with fate, and with omens that predict what is fated, it seems to be used here in its common sense of "righteous," as Paley translates it (AP 749, AEP 151; cf. AL 775).

788] *stations* Apparently used in the obsolete sense of standing-places, extended to imply mansions (from Latin *mansiones* = staying-places). The original word is ἔδεθλα, a form of ἐδάφη (= floors, pavements). Paley translates "palace," as the context requires (AEP 151). B's *stations* is the object of *leaving*, of which the subject is *Justice* personified.

793] *Stamped . . . stealth* AP 754: παράσημον αἴνῳ (= wrongly stamped, like counterfeit coinage, with praise), interpreted by Paley: "undeservedly esteemed, or praised, as riches are praised, for their influence, however much they may be abused by the possessor."

795] *Approach then . . . the son* B imitates the rhythm of the original metre (AP 756-82, AL 782-809), prompted perhaps by the footnote to Paley's translation: "With these anapaestics the Chorus go to meet their returning king" (AEP 151.

Troia See l. 9n.

796] *overhitting* Overshooting.

797] *underbending* The literal meaning of ὑποκάμψας, explained by Paley as a change of metaphor "from *shooting* to *turning short* of the terminal pillar in the stadium" (AP 759), an explanation called "highly improbable" by Fraenkel, who thinks the word need not always "denote a swerve in a sideways direction" but "rather a swerve in general from the direction that leads to the goal" (AF 786).

798-815] *Many of mortals . . . the city conducted* The original of this passage was probably designed to be ambiguous: a veiled warning to Agamemnon. The chorus-leader's generalizations about insincere praise and sympathy are primarily aimed at Clytaemnestra, but his words have been variously interpreted.

798] *hasten to honour* AP 762: προτίουσι (= honor in preference, prefer).

799] *Passing by justice* AP 762: δίκην παραβάντες (= 1. having transgressed justice, or 2. transgressing justice). Paley takes the aorist participle the first way, and applies it to Agamemnon: "Now many men, when they have acted wrongly, prefer mere appearance to reality . . . . That is, they prefer insincere praise to honest blame, when they are conscious of having deserved the latter . . . . The general sense seems to be: 'Many men like to be thought what they are not, and many flatterers are to be found who are willing to profess their sympathy in the joys and sorrows of others'" (AP 761). B appears to take the participle in the second sense, applying it to the flatterers.

free I.e., they feel free to groan. The original adjective is ἕτοιμος (= ready, prepared to).

800] *bite* The literal meaning of δῆγμα (AP 764). See l. 759n.

liver The literal meaning of ἧπαρ. The liver was thought the seat of the emotions.

801] *They joy with the joyful* καὶ ξυγχαίρουσιν ὁμοιοπρεπεῖς ἀγέλαστα πρόσωπα βιαζόμενοι, is explained by Paley: "And in like manner men rejoice with others, assuming the same appearance of joy by doing violence to their unsmiling countenances" (AP 766).

801] *one outside on each, too* Each of them with the same external expression (*outside*), or each with a *smile* (802) on his face.

803-4] *good . . . his flock* Expanded from two Greek words: ἀγαθός προβατογνώμων (= a good judge of sheep; AP 768). A stock Homeric epithet for Agamemnon is "shepherd of the people" (e.g. *Iliad* 2.243), so the implication here is that he is too good a judge of character to be taken in by insincere praise.

804] *it is not* A too literal translation of οὐκ ἔστι (AP 769), where the words have their common meaning of "it is not possible."

805] *surprise* A noun used (for the rhyme) in an old sense of the verb: "to detect" (*OED*, sense 3). AP 769: λαθεῖν (= to escape his notice).

806-7] *As they . . . be kind* I.e., to escape his detection in their seeming friendliness but actual fawning. Paley noted "a little confusion" in the Greek wording (which B has faithfully reproduced), and explained that ὑδαρεῖ (= *watery*) was properly used of wine with "an undue admixture of water" (AP 770).

808] *Helena* Inconsistently, B uses the Latin form of the Greek name, Ἑλένη (AP 773).

809] *oh, by no help of the Muses* AP 774: κάρτ᾽ ἀπομούσως (= far away from the Muses, most inartistically); i.e., I had an ugly picture of you in my mind).

810] *Not well . . . directing* An almost humorously literal version of AP 775, where πραπίδων (= *midriff*, diaphragm) refers to the supposed seat of the understanding.

811] *bringing . . . at stake* The textual crux at this point has been called by Fraenkel "one of the most awkward" in the play (AF 803f.). Among several suggested readings, B rejects Paley's, and paraphrases Weise's: θράσος ἀκούσιον ἀνδράσι θνῄσκουσι κομίζων (= "bringing unwilling courage to dying men"; AW 803-4). "Most editors" according to Paley (AP 776) took "unwilling" to mean "that kind of forced or reluctant valor which soldiers are supposed to feel when engaged in a cause which they have little at heart." Paley's preferred an emendation replacing ἀκούσιον (= unwilling) by ἐκ θυσιῶν (= from/by sacrifices). Either way, the allusion must be to Agamemnon's sacrifice of his daughter to encourage the Greek army when held up by winds at Aulis.

812] *from no outside of mind* οὐκ ἀπ᾽ ἄκρας φρενός (= not from the top or surface of the mind, i.e., with deep feeling.

812-13] *gracious thou . . . their part* Expanded from four Greek words of uncertain meaning: εὔφρων πόνος εὖ τελέσασι (= toil [is] cheering/gracious/kindly to those having ended [it] well). Paley explains: "the work done brings to us a kindly feeling towards (or perhaps, 'is cheering to') those who have accomplished it well." "This, of course," Paley continues, "is intentionally guarded and equivocal" (AP 778). B tries to leave it equally so; but the context requires the general sense: "I thought badly of you about Iphigenia, but now I sympathize with your natural satisfaction at having got the job well done—if you really have."

815] *conducted* B's verb misses the full implication of οἰκουροῦντα (= keeping or guarding the *house*, like a watchdog or a *wife*; AP 782), which points to Clytaemnestra, and also to Aegisthus, a *citizen* who is later called an οἰκουρός (= stay-at-home; AP 1196; AL 1225).

816] *the gods, the local* Such an unEnglish repetition of the definite article is common in Greek; but there is no excuse for it here (AP 783), where no definite article occurs, but simply a noun followed by an adjective: θεοὺς ἐγχωρίους (= gods of-the-country).

817] *'Tis right addressing* Here again, the use of the participle could be paralleled in Greek, but is not in the original, which uses a normal infinitive: δίκη προσειπεῖν (= it is right [for me] to address; AP 784).

with me the partners AP 784: ἐμοὶ μεταιτίους (= jointly responsible with me), the first of several hubristic remarks by Agamemnon.

817, 818] *right . . . right things* B preserves the significant repetition of the stem in δίκη (= justice, right) and δικαίων (= right things, i.e., justice, punishment, retribution).

818] *done the city* Done to the city—though Agamemnon's original wording is more self-congratulatory: ὧν ἐπραξάμην (= which I have done; AP 785)

819] *Priamos* See l. 39n.

from no tongue I.e., not from any spoken arguments, as in a human law-suit, but from infallible, divine knowledge.

820] *the rights o' the cause* In thus translating the single word δίκας (AP 786, here = law-suit) B continues to reproduce the repetition of the δικ-/right/justice stem.

Ilion The name for Troy used here in the original (AP 787).

821] *the bloody vase* In Athenian lawcourts each juror gave his verdict by putting a pebble (ψῆφος, hence *psephology*) into one of two κάδοι (= pails, jars, urns). Aeschylus' adjective αἱματηρόν (= bloody) refers to the so-called κάδος θανάτου (= urn of death, i.e., condemnation-urn; but he uses uses a different noun, τεῦχος which, among many other lexicon definitions, can mean "a balloting urn" as here (AP 788) or (in Aeschylus' *Choephori* 99) "a vase for libations." In opting for *vase* after *bloody*, B can hardly have been serious. The slang sense of *bloody* was "in general colloquial use from the Restoration . . . now constantly in the mouths of the lowest classes, but by respectable people considered 'a horrid word'" (*OED*).

not oscillating Without hesitation. AP 788: οὐ διχορρόπως (= not with scales going down on either side, not equally balanced, wavering.

822] *the rival vessel* The opposite urn, for acquittal, known as the κάδος ἐλέου (= urn of mercy; ADP 815).

823] *lip-edge* Despite his policy of keeping "to the earlier readings so long as sense can be made out of them," B evidently agrees with Paley that "no intelligible sense can be extracted" from the χειρός (= hand) given by the the MSS and translates the emendation χεῖλος (= lip), as an allusion to the story of Pandora's box in Hesiod: "only Hope remained there . . . under the lips (χείλεσιν of the box, and did not fly outside" (AP 790; *Works and Days* 96-8); i.e., Troy was left with nothing but hope of acquttal. Later editors, however, have extracted adequate sense from "the hope of a hand" carrying a pebble (AF, ADP 816f., AL 817).

825] *Ate* See l. 381n.

burnt offerings B translates θυηλαί, which Paley calls an "almost irresistible emendation for θύελλαι [= storms]" in the MSS. But modern editors have resisted the temptation (AF, ADP, AL 819).

826] *fulsome* AP 793: πίονας (= fat, fertile, rich). There may, as Paley suggests, be an allusion to expensive oriental perfumes (AP 792, AEP 152, footnote).

827] *grace* AP 794: χάριν, here used in the sense of gratitude, thanks.

many mindful Unnecessarily odd English for πολύμνηστον (= much remembering or remembered; AP 794), since the stem πολυ means much or many, according to context.

828] *outrageous* AP 795: ὑπερκότους (= exceedingly angry, cruel). The word poses a problem to any translator, since the prefix ὑπερ implies excess, but self-criticism is out of character for Agamemnon. Paley's solution was to stress the κότος (= anger, resentment) component, interpret as "vindictive," and translate: "the stake-nets of our vengeance" (AEP 152-3). B's solution was to use an English word which began with an equivalent of ὑπερ (French *outre*, from Latin *ultra*) but which could also carry the obsolete, not necessarily pejorative meaning of "enormous, extraordinary, unusual" (*OED*, sense 1).

829] *built them round with* B translates an emendation "made independently by Hermann and Paley" (AF 822ff.): ἐφραξάμεσθα (= we fenced [them] round, or, as in Paley's note, "we constructed round them"; AP 795).

830] *It did . . . monster* In trying to keep some of the original word-order B interpolates both the *It* and the dash. AP 797: πόλιν διημάθυνεν Ἀργεῖον δάκος (= the Argive bite/biting animal reduced the city to dust).

831] *horse's nestling* A neatly accurate translation of AP 798: ἵππου νεοσσός, since νεοσσός (= animal's young) is most often used of birds, and the armed men nestled inside the wooden horse.

832] *at setting of the Pleiads* Editors have argued about the point of this information (which contradicts the usual tradition about the season when Troy fell: AF, ADP 826); but B was probably content to accept the explanation quoted by Paley, that "the time is mentioned which would best account for the storm before described" (AP799).

833] *tower* The commonest sense of πύργος; but here (AP 800) it seems more likely to mean, as often, the city-wall or rampart.

raw-flesh-feeding The precise meaning of ὠμηστής (AP 800).

834] *Lion* With one *leap*, the horse-chick has now become the lion-symbol of the Atridae (AP 800).

836] *I remember hearing—* AP 803: μέμνημαι κλύων (= I remember hearing). B's dash was possibly in deference to Paley's note that these words were best taken "as parenthetical . . . . He means, that the *long* . . . address . . . to the gods has not driven out of his mind the words he had just heard . . . . But, if . . . taken . . . to signify, 'but as for your sentiments, I remember hearing them and I say the same,' too much prominence is given to the fact of remembering what in truth he could not possibly have forgotten" (AP 803). Even as a parenthesis, however, the remark seems faintly absurd, and it may be better to take the participle κλύων not as *what* he remembers, but simply to mean: "Hearing, I remember them . . . ," or as Fraenkel puts it, "I have heard, and so remember them" (AF 830), i.e., (more colloquially) I haven't forgotten what you just said to me.

837] *thou co-pleader hast me* You have me as a co-pleader in a law-court, an advocate. But ξυνήγορον (= speaking-with, agreeing) need not be a legal metaphor here (AP 804), Though Paley translates it: "you have in me an advocate of your views" (AEP 153), Fraenkel takes it more literally: "one who will speak on thy side" (AF 831).

839] *without grudge* Though the MS reading is φθόνων (plural), B seems to translate the emendation to the singular read by Weise and Paley (AW 833, AP 806).

successful When he is successful. AP 806: τὸν εὐτυχοῦντα (= who is successful).

840] *For . . . seated* AP 806: δύσφρων γάρ ἰὸς καρδίαν προσήμενος (= for a malignant poison seated close to the heart). B's *moody* translates a less relevant meaning of δύσφρων, "heavy in heart, sorrowful."

841] *to who gained the sickness* AP 808: τῷ πεπαμένῳ νόσον (= for the man who has got the disease [i.e., of jealousy]). The ironical hint of profit in *gained* is not necessarily implied by the perfect participle of πάομαι (= get, acquire).

842] *made heavy* AP 809: βαρύνεται (= weighed down) i.e., by that half of his double *burthen*, a point slightly obscured by B's anxiety to stress that the verb is derived from βαρύς (= heavy).

843] *And . . . groans at* A replica of the original word-order.

out-of-door The literal meaning of θυραῖον, though it here means simply "other people's" (AP 810).

844-46] *Knowing . . . to me* These lines have been variously interpreted. B generally follows Paley: "I can declare, from my own knowledge, that men who seemed to be very well disposed to me were but the mirror (the unreal semblance) of friendship, the shadow of a shade" (AP 811).

844] *I'd call* The direct object of this verb is *those seeming . . . The names* he calls them come, as in the original, first.

846] *mighty* B's private linguistic joke? The word κάρτα (= very; AP 813) derives from the stem κράτος (= power, strength, *might*). But, unlike the colloquial adverb *mighty*, it is a regular part of tragic diction.

847] *just* Only (μόνος, AP 814).

who sailed not willing Who was at first reluctant to join the expedition.

848] *When joined on* AP 815: ζευχθεὶς (= having been yoked).

the ready trace-horse I.e., the willing helper. Trace-horses were often used to help pull up-hill.

850] *For . . . concernment* The hyphenation suggests some Greek compound, but all we have here is: "and as for other things, to do with city and gods" (AP 817).

851] *common courts* Though ἀγών (= contest) can mean a legal case or trial, it is probably used here in its Homeric sense of "gathering, assembly" (AP 818).

852] *what holds seemly* AP 819: τὸ μὲν καλῶς ἔχον (= what is well). The use of ἔχω (= have, hold) with an adverb to mean "be in the state of that adverb" is too common to need singling out here as an oddity, thus obscuring the simple sense: where things are all right, we must see how to keep them that way. But B spasmodically remembers that he is supposed to be giving "the very turn of each phrase in as Greek a fashion as English will bear" (*Introductory Note*, ll.10-11).

854] *Paionian* Belonging to Paian or Paion, the physician of the gods.

855] *kindly* So understood by Paley (AEP 153) and others, though Fraenkel insists that εὐφρόνως here means "judiciously" (AF 849; cf. ADP 849: "In the manner in which a sensible . . . person would act").

856]   *turn pain from sickness*   I.e., make the sickness less painful. B appears to translate literally what Paley calls "an excellent emendation": ἀποστρέψαι (= turn away), though Paley himself translated it differently: "avert the mischief of the disease" (AP 823, AEP 153).

857]   *domes and homes*   AP 824: μέλαθρα καὶ δόμους (= roofs and houses). B continues his idiosyncratic practice of semi-transliterating both δόμος and δῶμα (= house) into *dome* (see l. 602n.); and also seizes the excuse for an internal rhyme.

   by altar   AP 824: ἐφεστίους—an odd use of an adjective which means "at the hearth" to mean "having a hearth." Since ῾Εστία (= Hearth) was worhipped as a household god, Paley translated the whole phrase: "the central *altars* of the house" (AEP 153).

858]   *raise the right-hand*   AP 825: δεξιώσομαι (= shall offer the right hand, greet with the right hand). B's guess at the physical gesture described was possibly based on Paley's note, which ended "'to pledge the right hand,' as a gage of good faith, may be the more true meaning."

859]   *far sending*   AP 826: πρόσω πέμψαντες (= having sent me far away [when I started off to Troy]).

861]   *my worships*   The usual form of this respectful address would be "your worships." The only uses of "my worship" recorded in *OED* are jocular references to the speaker. Perhaps B meant to hint an element of sarcasm in Clytaemnestra's respect. AP 828: πρέσβος ᾿Αργείων τόδε (= this object-of-reverence of Argives, i.e., this reverend assembly of Argives). Since the first word is derived from πρέσβυς (= old man), Paley translates: "reverend Argive elders here present" (AEP 153).

862-63]   *I shall . . . before you*   AP 829-30: οὐκ αἰσχυνοῦμαι τοὺς φιλάνορας τρόπους λέξαι προς ὑμᾶς (= I shall not be ashamed to tell you about my man/husband-loving character), i.e., how much I love my husband; though, as Paley notes, the double meaning of ἀνήρ suggests that she may be thinking of Aegisthus (AP 832).

864]   *diffidence*   AP 831: τάρβος (= terror), but weakened into "bashfulness" by Paley, who explains: "It was not usual for Greek women to speak in public, especially on such a subject" (AEP 154).

866]   *Ilion*   See l. 820n.

869]   *back-revenging*   AP 836: παλιγκότους, a compound of πάλιν (= back) and κότος (= grudge, rancor), explained in Liddell and Scott, 1871: "properly of wounds, *breaking out afresh*," and metaphororically, "*malignant, spiteful.*" B seems to have extracted his notion of revenge from the idea of a grudge coming back at one, where Paley was content to translate it by a vague "adverse" (AEP 154). By the original word Clytaemnestra may imply that rumours of her husband's death are spread deliberately to hurt her, or simply that they are very hurtful.

870]   *now This . . . now That*   I.e., this man . . . that man. B needlessly obscures the meaning of τὸν μὲν ... τὸν δὲ (= one man . . . another man; AP 837), i.e., various messengers with various reports.

bring after   AP 837: ἐπεισφέρειν (= bring in besides or after).

871]   *in the household*   AP 838: δόμοις (= to the house, i.e., for the whole house to hear).

872-73]   *if so many . . . husband*   If my husband had chanced on i.e., actually received.

873]   *used to dribble*   AP 840: ὠχετεύετο (= were conducted or channeled by conduit or canal). The notion that the reports were pure drivel was added by B.

874]   *to speak of*   AP 841: λέγειν (= 1. to speak, say, tell; 2. to count). B seems to follow Paley, who translates "one might say" (sense 1; AEP 154). But sense 2 suits the context better (ADP 866ff.). The net-image, here almost a joke, will be repeated by Cassandra when foreseeing the murder of Agamemnon (1114-7), and by Clytaemnestra herself when describing how she did it (AL 1381-84).

875]   *dying*   AP 842: τεθνηκὼς (= dead), i.e., if he had died.

as the words abounded   A literal translation of: ὡς ἐπλήθυον λόγοι (AP 842); but the meaning is probably: if his deaths had been as numerous as the stories of his death (AF, ADP, AL 869).

876]   *Geruon*   A three-headed or three-bodied giant whose cattle were stolen by Hercules as one of his Labors. Paley's "plain English of the whole passage" is: "If he had died as often as was reported, he must have had three lives like a second triple Geryon, and been buried as many times, once for each shape" (AP 844).

877]   *Plenty . . . count not*   A line included in Weise's text (AW 871), but suspected by most editors, including Paley, of being spurious, chiefly because it seems too silly for Aeschylus to have written it (see AF, ADP 871). But B may well have accepted it as sound psychology. Like the Player Queen in *Hamlet* (3.2.177-230) Clytaemnestra "doth protest too much." By its wild exaggeration and almost hysterical humor, her dramatic monologue betrays her anxiety not to let her husband hear the truth about her before she can kill him.

878]   *Of earth . . . taking*   A metaphor for burial like Pindar's "clothing of earth" (*Nemean Odes*, 11.16).

880]   *rumours back-revenging*   See l. 869n.

881]   *Many the halters*   I.e., I often tried to hang myself.

above head   AP 848: ἄνωθεν (= from above).

882]   *main force*   A rendering of πρὸς βίαν (= by force) possibly suggested by Paley's note: "She appears to mean, that nothing but main force would make her desist from the attempt" (AP 848).

883] *From this cause* I.e., Orestes had to be sent away because his mother was liable to commit suicide at any moment (ADP 877); or as Paley explained it, to relieve her of "at least one additional source of care" in case of Agamemnon's death (AP 850).

sure Apparently B's abbreviation of "be assured" in Paley's note: "such are the true reasons, be assured, why the boy is not present here." His emphasis on truth and assurance is based on the particle τοι (= let me tell you, in truth; AP 850). Agamemnon would naturally expect to find his young son at home, and Clytaemnestra hastily tries to explain his absence. B preserves the rather illogical sequence of ideas in the original sentence, which shows that she is thinking on her feet.

884] *troth-plights* Again B abbreviates Paley: "that dear representative of our plighted faith" (AEP 154).

886] *him brings up* I.e., he is being brought up by. The un-English word-order, though common in Greek, is actually B's contribution, for the original has the verb before, not after, its object. AP 853: τρέφει ...αὐτὸν (= brings-up . . . him).

guest-captive AP 853: δορύξενος (= spear-guest-friend). Paley's note quotes Plutarch's explanation of the term to mean a prisoner of war who is taken home by his captor and treated as a friend; a meaning accepted by Liddell and Scott in earlier editions, but rejected in 1996 in favor of "war-friend, ally."

887] *that told on both sides* AP 854: ἀμφίλεκτα (= spoken all round or on both sides). Paley quoted various explanations, but preferred: "'troubles of a twofold nature,' lit. 'to be spoken on both sides of a question,' namely, the two chances enumerated, as if in direct explanation, immediately after."

889-90] *anarchy's . . . council* AP 856-57: δημόθρους ἀναρχία βουλὴν καταρρίψειεν. B follows Paley: "anarchy arising from popular discontents might overthrow the royal council" (AEP 153). But "βουλὴ in the sense 'Council' is not found elsewhere in Tragedy" (ADP 883-84), and Fraenkel translates it in an abstract sense: "lack of a ruler, asserted noisily by the people, might overthrow deliberation" (AF 883-84).

890] *born with* The literal sense of σύγγονον, though Paley explained its meaning here (AP 857) as "inborn, natural."

892] *excuse* AP 859: σκῆψις. Though the Greek word (like the English one), does not *necessarily* mean that the alleged reason for excusing is false, it so often has that meaning that Clytaemnestra might have been expected to avoid it here; so Paley translates it as "reason" (AEP 154). But B probably took her unfortunate word-choice as unconscious self-betrayal. See l. 877n.).

893-94] *of my wails . . . dried up* B seems determined to exaggerate every hint of oddness in the Greek (AP 860-61). Though κλαίω (= cry, wail, lament, of any loud expression of pain or sorrow; Liddell and Scott, 1996), was primarily a verb of sound, it became associated with the idea of tears, and the same is true of the related noun used here, κλαυμάτων (= wailings, weepings). The word πηγαὶ (= *Fountains*) implies tears too. But B insists on the gratuitously bizarre notion of dried-up wails.

895] *late-to-bed* The literal meaning of ὀψικοίτοις (AP 862), though the context suggests "sleepless far into the night."

896-97] *Bewailing . . . unattended to* I.e., bewailing the fact that the beacons to announce your victory were never lighted.

    what concerned thee AP 863: ἀμφί σοι (= concerning thee).

900] *that filled . . . fellow-sleep-time* Hardly more obscure than the original: πλείω τοῦ ξυνεύδοντος χρόνου (= more than the sleeping-with time), explained by Paley: "more in number than could have happened in the space of time coincident with sleep" (AP 867).

902] *the dog* I.e., the watchdog.

904] *ground-prop* B's coinage, apparently suggested by Paley's translation of στῦλον ποδήρη (= pillar reaching down to the feet): "ground-pillar" (AEP 155), and his note: "a pillar based on the ground; the main pillar of a roof,—any upright prop . . ."(AP 871).

908] *The joy . . . fatal* AP 875: τερπνὸν δὲ τἀναγκαῖον ἐκφυγεῖν ἅπαν (= and [it is] delightful to escape all the necessary/ constraining/ fated/fatal). Paley translated: "to have escaped from all constraint" (AEP 155). What did B mean by the dash before his *fatal*? A private thought of Clytaemnestra's that nobody could escape his fate, nor could Agamemnon escape his fated punishment?

910] *Envy* I.e., the jealousy of the gods (φθόνος, AP 877) which might well be excited by her unqualified praise. In fact, she is intent on exciting it, notably by making him walk on purple.

    for I.e., I have suffered so much up to now that I can surely be pardoned for speaking in such strong terms now.

    old evils AP 877: τὰ πρὶν κακὰ (= the former evils).

911] *to me* A literal translation of μοι (AP 878), which does not here mean motion "towards me," but is an "ethic dative" implying "for my sake, to please me, I beg you."

    dear headship AP 878: φίλον κάρα (= dear head, a common periphrasis in Greek tragedy for a person, i.e., "dear one."

912] *this car* I.e., the chariot in which he has arrived.

    earthward An unfortunate translation of χαμαὶ (= on the ground, to the ground; AP 889), since he can hardly avoid putting his foot *towards* the earth.

914]   *why tarry*   AP 881: τί μέλλετε (= why are you delaying, hesitating).

whose the task allotted   Whose allotted task it is.

carpet-spreadings   The cumbrous compound translates a single Greek word for carpets (πετάσμασιν; AP 882), but B seems anxious to show that the noun is derived from a verb meaning "spread."

917]   *So . . . Justice*   An imitation of the original word-order (AP 884). The dash before *Justice* was possibly meant to signal the double meaning of the line. For Agamemnon it is to mean that justice has been done on Paris and the Trojans, and his own safe homecoming is beyond his wildest hopes. For Clytaemnestra it means that justice is about to be done on Agamemnon for his sacrifice of Iphigenia, and his homecoming will prove (in the other sense of ἄελπτον) "unexpected."

918]   *by no sleep conquered*   I.e., vigilant.

919]   *justly*   Again the preliminary dash may be meant to emphasize the double meaning.

(*gods to aid!*) *appointed*   AP 886: ξὺν θεοῖς εἱμαρμένα (= with the help of gods fated). B seems to follow Paley's paraphrase: "as the justice of the gods and the decrees of fate combine to bring about."

920]   *Leda*   A Queen of Sparta who, when seduced by Zeus in the form of a swan, gave birth to both Helen and Clytaemnestra.

of my household warder   Guardian (φύλαξ = guard; AP 887) of my household. *OED* lists no use of *warder* = jailer before 1855.

921]   *suitably*   I.e., in proportion to. The hint of "pleasantry, not to say ironical bantering" that Paley detects here is not confirmed by anything else in Agamemnon's pompous speeches.

923]   *from others . . . favour*   Paley explains: "to praise me according to my just deserts, some other person than a wife should be the speaker" (AP 889). B's choice of *go* to translate ἔρχεσθαι (= come or go) in this context seems rather perverse, since normal English would surely use "come": "just praise should come from someone not my wife."

924-25]   *not me . . . Mollify*   Do not mollify me. The awkward word-order does not this time imitate the original, but is an attempt to emphasize the *me*, as in Paley's note: "ἐμέ, emphatic, '*me* of all people,' who am a warrior" (AP 891).

Mollify   Used not in its modern but in its Latin sense (= make soft), to translate ἄβρυνε (= make delicate, treat delicately, i.e., pamper, mollycoddle).

925]   *barbarous*   Used not in its modern sense of "uncivilized" but in its original contemptuous one of "non-Greek." In Aeschylus' *Persians* the Persians were made to call themselves βάρβαροι (= barbarians), and implicitly satirized for their grovelling obedience to kings and tyrants, and their addiction to fine clothes. Here Agamemnon, with the oriental Trojans in mind, is making the same two points: Clytaemnestra's gross flattery (*groundward-falling clamour*), like her *strewing it* [the ground] *with garments* is unworthy of a Greek.

926]   *gape forth*   AP 894: προσχάνῃς, an insulting word (= gape, stare open-mouthed at me).

928]   *Envied*   See l. 910n.

behoves we   It behoves us to.

929, 932]   *varied*   B carefully preserves the literal meaning of ποικίλοις, ποικίλων, though the related verb and noun developed a reference to embroidery or tapestry.

931]   *I say*   the basic meaning of λέγω; but here, with the infinitive σέβειν (= to worship, honor), it probably means "I tell you, I command you" (AP 898).

932-33]   *apart from . . . is loud*   Paley's note explains: "his fame is sufficiently great without . . . foot-mats (a contemptuous phrase) or purple garments strewn in his way" (AP 899-902).

foot-mats   AP 899 ποδοψήστρων (= foot-cloths, foot-wipers, as commonly used to wipe the feet after washing them; *Scholia* 366).

933]   *not to lose one's senses*   AP 900: τὸ μὴ κακῶς φρονεῖν (= not to think badly), i.e., to have a little common sense.

934]   *behoves we*   See l. 928n.

934-35]   *him call happy*   A common saying, first attributed to Solon in Herodotus (i, 32) and rephrased in the (probably spurious) final chorus of Sophocles' *Oedipus Tyrannus* (1528f.).

935]   *loved well-being*   AP 902: εὐεστοῖ φίλῃ (= dear well-being, i.e., welcome prosperity.

936]   *If al . . . I*   The text and meaning are disputed, but B seems to follow Paley's interpretation: "if in all things I shall act as discreetly as in this, I have no fear for the result . . . since I shall not excite the φθόνος [= jealousy] of the gods by my pride" (AP 903).

brave man, I   εὐθαρσὴς ἐγώ (= of good courage I), i.e., I am confident, I'm not worrying.

937]   *this say . . . to me*   AP 904: τόδ᾽ εἶπε μὴ παρὰ γνώμην ἐμοί (= tell this not against judgement/ purpose/ will/ opinion to me). An "extremely controversial" passage (AF 931-4). B seems to reject Paley's translation ("do speak on this matter not contrary to my will") in favor of one attributed in Paley's note to "an eminent scholar . . . : '*C*. Now answer me this question without disguising your real opinion. *A*. My real opinion, be assured, I shall not misrepresent'" (AP 904).

938]   *do not tamper*   AP 905: διαφθεροῦντ᾽ (future participle = that I shall not destroy/corrupt).

939] *Vowed'st . . . thus* I.e., Is it because of some vow you made to the gods in a moment of fear that you're refusing to do this? In Paley's text (AP 906) this a statement, but B follows Weise's (AW 933) in making it a question. In this interpretation Clytaemnestra suggests that he is taking this line now because, in a moment of fear during the war, he vowed that he would do so, if saved from that particular peril.

940] *If any . . . outspoke* I.e., If I did make any such vow, I well knew this resolution that I expressed—I knew exactly what I was vowing to do. AP 907: εἴπερ τις, εἰδώς γ᾽ εὖ τόδ᾽ ἐξεῖπον τέλος (= if any [understanding, ὅρκος = vow], knowing well I spoke out this end [or, as in Paley's note "this decision, this final determination"]). B's italicization of *I* presumably implied Agamemnon's indignant rejection of Clytaemnestra's suggestion that his present line was the result of a moment of panic in the past: "I'm not the man to behave like that!" Alternatively, the italicization may indicate that B took εἴπερ τις (*If any*) to mean not "if any vow was made" but "if any man ever did, *I* knew (or should have known) exactly what I was committing myself to."

941] *Priamos* See l. 39n.

   thus victor If he had won, as you have. AP 908: εἰ τάδ᾽ ἤνυσεν (= if he had accomplished these things).

942] *varied vests* Multi-colored garments. See l. 929, 932n.

   passaged The curious verb translates the very common βῆναι (= gone, stepped, walked). Was it preferred to "passed" for purely metrical reasons?

943] *struck with awe* B translates Weise's participle αἰδεσθείς (= reverencing), as in one manuscript, and retains his three dots to indicate an interruption (AW 937). Paley reads αἰδεσθῇς (aorist subjunctive = [don't] reverence; AP 910).

945] *Ay . . . valued* AP 912: ὁ δ᾽ ἀφθόνητός γ᾽ οὐκ ἐπίζηλος πέλει (= but the unenvied man is not enviable). B does not quite bring out the distinction between the two Greek adjectives: the first refers to envy as a cause of bad feeling, a grudge; the second to envy simply as an indication of success or happiness. Paley paraphrases: "'Well, but he who is unenvied is not admired'—is not to be reckoned a prosperous and happy man."

946] *battle* AP 913: μάχης (= battle, but here a battle of words). He means: "A woman shouldn't be so argumentative," though his words recall Hector's, when he tells his wife to get on with her own work at the loom and the distaff, but "war [πόλεμος] shall be for men" (*Iliad* 6.490-93).

947] *to the . . . beating* AP 914: τοῖς δ᾽ ὀλβίοις γε καὶ τὸ νικᾶσθαι πρέπει (= to the prosperous, even to be be conquered is becoming), i.e., a real conqueror like you should gracefully accept defeat in a mere battle of words.

948] *What . . . too* Paley paraphrases: "'What! do *you* show your regard for that sort of victory,' viz. which consists in defeat? In other words, apply your own rule to yourself, and see if you are inclined to follow it" (AP 915).

949] *Persuade thee* I.e., persuade yourself. AP 916: πιθοῦ (aorist imperative middle of πείθω = obey). Though the middle voice in Greek often has a reflexive meaning, the middle of this particular verb normally means "be persuaded, obey, comply." B's unusual rendering serves here to emphasize the voluntary transfer of *power*.

willing Willingly. The adverbial use of the adjective *willing* mimics that of the original adjective (ἑκών; AP 916) but *for once* is an imaginative interpolation.

950] *if this seems so to thee* I.e., if that's what you want me to do. AP 917: εἰ δοκεῖ σοι ταυθ᾽ (= if these things seem [good] to thee—a common extension of the meaning of the verb δοκεῖ (= it seems).

950-51] *shoes, let someone / Loose* B retains the inverted word-order of the original (AP 917-18).

951] *under* Not yet symbolic of a hubristic feeling in Agamemnon that such things are beneath him, but a literal translation of ὑπαί, explained by the fact that ὑπολύειν (= loose under) was the "normal term for undoing footwear" (ADP 944).

foot's serviceable carriage This time B does reproduce the grotesque hubris of the Greek: πρόδουλον ἔμβασιν ποδός (= slave-substitute step-on of the foot; AP 918)

952] *sea-products* AP 919: ἀλουργέσιν (= sea-worked), an adjective applied to textiles dyed with genuine purple, i.e., with juice from the purple-fish (i.e., *Murex* shellfish), as opposed to any imitations).

953] *the god's eye* A misprint from the first edition. The *gods* are plural, and in the MS B correctly wrote "gods' eye." According to Paley the θεῶν (= of gods; AP 920) "virtually belongs both to ἀλουργέσιν and to ὄμματος [= *sea-products* and *eye*]," i.e., the gods might *grudge* his walking on things more appropriate to them. ADP 946 takes θεῶν only in this latter sense ("these vestments belong to the worship of the gods"), but cf. AL 946 ("Heaven's jealous eye").

954] *strewment-spoiling* B translates an early French emendation adopted by Paley (στρωματοφθορεῖν; AP 921).

956] *of these things, thus then* I.e., so much for that.

this female-stranger Cassandra, the prophetic daughter of Priam, awarded by the Greeks to Agamemnon after the sack of Troy, as a slave-concubine.

962-63]   *So, since . . . purples treading*   Here B translates the climactic lines (AP 929-30, AL 956-57) alluded to in his *Pauline* (567-71).

hear   The basic meaning of ἀκούειν, here used in its common sense of "obey" (AP 929).

I am brought about   AP 929: κατέστραμμαι (= I have been bent or twisted down , i.e., overborne, subdued, compelled).

964]   *There is the sea*   She is simply saying that there are plenty more *purples* where those came from; but her grandiose language expresses her triumph that the victim has finally walked into the trap.

exhaust   AP 931: κατασβέσει (= dry up). B's English verb is well chosen, since it combines the meaning of Latin *exhaurio* (= drain up liquid) with the consumer-connotation of "using up."

965]   *worth-its-weight-in-silver*   The lexicon-definition of ἰσάργυρον (literally = equal-silver; AP 932).

966]   *dye*   AP 933: κηκῖδα (= ooze, exudate).

ever fresh and fresh   AP 933: παγκαίνιστον (= all-renewable).

tincture   Used in the sense of Latin *tinctura* (= dyeing, dye).

967]   *At home*   B translates οἴκοις (= in the houses), an emendation adopted by both Weise and Paley (AW 961, AP 934).

967-68]   *we begin . . . with having*   AP 934-35: ὑπάρχει ... ἔχειν, which Paley translates (with οἴκοις): "To our house . . . it belongs to have"(AEP 157). But B tries to bring out the primary sense of the verb ὑπάρχω (= begin).

968]   *to lack, the household knows not*   AP 935: πένεσθαι δ᾿ οὐκ ἐπίσταται δόμος (= and the house doesn't know how to be poor, i.e., to run short of anything).

969-70]   *Of many . . . scheming*   I.e., I would have vowed to trample on any number of garments, if an oracle had told me to do so, when I was trying to bring about my husband's safe return.

971]   *dear*   Interpolated on the precedent of Paley's "thy dear life" (AEP 157). AP 938: ψυχῆς ... τῆσδε (= this soul, i.e., life).

972]   *root existing*   So long as the root survives. B translates the genitive absolute literally.

goes up houses   An imaginative explanation of AP 939: ἵκετ᾿ ἐς δόμους (= arrives at houses).

973]   *Seirius dog-star*   Its rising around July proverbially brought the season of greatest heat. Clytaemnestra's mixed metaphors imply that Agamemnon's return brings warmth in winter and coolness in summer.

978-80]   *perfect man . . . Zeus Perfecter . . . perfect thou . . . make perfect*   B struggles to reproduce the original pun (AP 945-47) on the adjective τέλειος (= 1. brought to completion, 2. able to bring to completion).

In sense 2 the *man* is the lord and master of the house, with full authority to control it; and *Zeus* has the power to grant *prayers,* and otherwise accomplish anything. Such an association of Agamemnon with Zeus may be seen as the climax of her efforts to bring down the punishment of hubris on her husband.

980] *of things . . . perfect* AP 947: τῶνπερ ἂν μέλλῃς τελεῖν (= of whatever things you are going/intending to accomplish—a private reference to her own plans of murder).

981] *fear* B translates the reading of most MSS, δεῖμα, though both Weise and Paley prefer the reading of one MS, δεῖγμα, dubiously interpreted to mean a "phantom, image, or portent, presented to the mind and conjured up by an excited brain" (AW 976, AP 949).

982] *groundedly* B stresses the derivation of ἐμπέδως (= in-groundly), though the word's common meaning, "abidingly, continually," would here avoid the apparent contradiction between *groundedly stationed* and *flits.* But

983] *fronting* AP 949: προστατήριον (= standing before).

portent-watcher A literal translation of τερασκόπου (AP 950), i.e., divining, prophetic.

984] *prophet-play* I.e., play the prophet—a hyphenated verb apparently coined to imitate the compound verb μαντιπολεῖ (= prophesies; AP 951), on the assumption that is was a compound of μάντις (= prophet) and πολέω (= go about). The delayed subject of the verb is *lay* (= song, translating ἀοιδὰ): why should my song be prophetic, i.e., full of foreboding?

985] *uncalled unpaid* AP 951: ἀκέλευστος ἄμισθος (= unordered unpaid; see *Introductory Note,* 1.102-3). The typical bard sang to order and was paid for it; but the chorus-leader's song is and involuntary response to his persistent fears.

986] *having spat forth* B translates the emendation ἀποπτύσαν, adopted by Weise (AW 980) but not by Paley (AP 952).

bad AP 953: δυσκρίτων (= hard to interpret).

she Interpolated for the rhyme, and to anticipate the delayed subject of the participle (*having spat forth*). In the Greek this subject is not actually feminine, but the neuter noun θάρσος (= boldness; AP 954).

987] *beloved* AP 955: φίλον (= dear), an adjective often attached in Homer to knees, heart, and other parts of the body as a kind of possessive adjective (= my own, his own etc.). B's stronger adjective *beloved* gratuitously stresses the oddness of this Homeric usage.

well-suasive A literal rendering of εὐπιθὲς (= well-persuasive; AP 954), used here perhaps in the sense of "reassuring."

988-91] *For time . . . bands* The Greek text at this point has been described as "hopelessly corrupt," but the general sense may be: "Why am I so frightened? A long time has passed since the army went to Troy, and now they are safely home again, and nothing disastrous has occurred" (ADP 984-7).

988] *by a throw of all the hands* B is trying to to translate either the MS reading, ξυνεμβόλοις, (AW 984), a word not found elsewhere, but compounded of stems signifying "together," "in," and "throw"; or perhaps the emendation adopted by Paley (AP 956), ξυνεμβολαῖς (= throwings-in together). Presumably the rhyme-word *hands* has the sense of "members of the crew."

990] *Has past from youth to oldness* AW 985-86, AP 957-58: παρήβησεν (= has passed its youth).

995] *Itself its teacher too* Four words to "transcribe" one: αὐτοδίδακτος (= self-taught; AP 963).

996] *Erinus* See l. 57n.

the whole a literal translation of τὸ πᾶν, though here (AP 964), as Paley points out in his note, it is used adverbially to mean "at all" (AEP 158).

997] *nor my inwards sin* I.e., nor does my gut-feeling deceive me. AP 966: σπλάγχνα δ᾿ οὔτι ματᾷζει (= and my viscera are not talking at all foolishly).

998] *rolled in whirls* AP 968: δίναις κυκλούμενον (= circling in eddies).
against Up against, close to.

999] *behind* Used in the old sense of "later, hereafter." B was possibly remembering that the Greek word, ὄπισθεν (= behind), though not used here, can also refer to the future.

1000] *from my hope* A misleadingly literal translation of ἀπ᾿ ἐμᾶς ... ἐλπίδος, since the meaning is "contrary to my expectation," as Paley's note points out (AP 969, cf. AEP 158). B seems to expect his Greekless reader to know that ἐλπίς (= hope) can also mean "expectation either of good or evil" (Liddell and Scott, 1871).

1002] *Especially at least* Faced with a passage agreed to be "incurably corrupt" (ADP 1001-6; cf. AF 1001f.), B translates Paley's text (AP 972f.) without trying to make it intelligible; but the underlying train of thought may be that excessive health and wealth both lead to disaster.

1003] *the term's insatiable* A literal rendering of ἀκόρεστον τέρμα (AP 973), where the noun probably means "a boundary," i.e., the point where health turns into disease; and the adjective implies, "no one can ever have enough of health."

1003-4] *its weight . . . lean* The *weight* is interpolated for the rhyme, in an attempt to express the sense of Paley's paraphrase: "Men never think they have prosperity enough (regardless of the danger they incur); for disease (calamity) is ever at hand like a neighbour leaning against a party wall, and ready to throw it down and overwhelm them" (AP 972).

1007-16] *Has struck . . . has not sunk . . . has not . . . overwhelmed . . . Has done away* B translates literally the Greek "gnomic" aorists, where a past tense ia used without any implication of time to express a general truth.

1008-12] *Now, when . . . hull* I.e., in such a nautical crisis, total disaster can be averted by jettisoning part of the cargo.

1008] *than the treasure* Than the whole treasure.

1009] *Fear casts* AP 979: ὄκνος βαλὼν (= Fear throwing), i.e., the seaman throws, in fear of complete shipwreck.

   sling AP 980: σφενδόνας (= sling), but here used, not of the war-weapon, but either metaphorically (= an act of throwing), or perhaps, since the word is used elsewhere for a dockyard crane, to suggest some sort of rope-tackle improvised for the emergency (ADP 1008ff., cf. AF 1005).

   in right measure AP 980: εὐμέτρου (= well-measured, i.e., well-judged, well-aimed); but B has transferred the adjective from the *sling*, where it belongs, to the *peril.*

1010] *It has . . . freight* AP 981: οὐκ ἔδυ πρόπας δόμος (= the whole house has not sunk). The ship symbolizes the house of Atreus, and the Chorus is hoping that it too may be saved from ultimate calamity.

1011] *freighted* An accurate translation of γέμων (AP 982); but the rhetorical repetition of the rhyme-word *freight* has no equivalent in the Greek.

1012] *hull* The literal meaning of σκάφος (AP 983), though the word is commonly used, as here, in the general sense of "ship."

1013-19] *Then too . . . call back* The Chorus is now considering how far the dangers of excess can be reduced. The shipwreck that threatens great wealth, can be averted by judicious jettisoning; the famine that may follow a good harvest can be counteracted by another good one; but once blood is shed (e.g. the sacrifice of Iphigenia, a case of excess in which Agamemnon "went too far" to obtain a good wind for his fleet), disaster is irrevocable.

1013] *Zeus* The weather-god as well as the god of justice.

1014] *Two-handedly profuse* AP 985: ἀμφιλαφής (= taking on both or all sides, far-spreading, extensive, abundant). Was B hinting at Zeus's justice-aspect as well as his weather-aspect—a generous dispenser of corn with both hands, but also "that two-handed engine at the door" which "Stands ready to strike once, and smite no more," as in Milton's, *Lycidas,* 130-31?

1015] *for yearly use* I.e., "sufficient for the year," as Paley translates ἐπεταιᾶν (AP 985, AEP 158).

1016] *famine, the disease* AP 986: νῆστιν ... νόσον (= not-eating disease), The disease-image concludes a passage which began with the Hippocratic notion of excessive *health* (ὑγείας, AP 972; l.1002; see Hippocrates, *Aphorisms,* i. 3: "good condition at its peak is dangerous, if it has gone to extremes"; ADP 1004).

1017] *falling* AP 987: πεσὸν (= having fallen, i.e., once it has fallen).

deadly, black B's linking of the two adjectives obscures their original function. The first, θανάσιμον (= to do with death, deadly) immediately follows πεσὸν ἅπαξ (= once having fallen, i.e., once it has fallen; AP 987) and is clearly predicative (= in death); but the second, μέλαν (= black) immediately precedes the noun αἷμα (= blood; AP 988), and is attributive: "black blood," a stock phrase in the *Iliad.*

1018] *In times ere these* A possible translation of προπάροιθε (= before, in either space or time). But in his note here (AP 987) Paley takes it with ἀνδρὸς to mean "at a man's feet." B's interpretation can be supported by Fraenkel's "aforetime" (AF 151).

1019] *call back* AP 989: ἀγκαλέσαιτ' (= call up or back). The first suits the context better, but the perhaps the rhyme decided B's choice.

1020] *had not else stopped* Would not otherwise have stopped. Here B follows Weise (AW 1023) in ignoring the phrase ἐπ' εὐλαβείᾳ (= ? as a precaution) or ἐπ' ἀβλαβείᾳ (= ? in a harmless manner) which follows in the MSS. Paley, though including the first phrase in his text, thinks it "by no means improbable" that it was merely "a gloss . . . wrongly transposed to this place" (AP 990n.).

one who rightly knew Asclepius, the Homeric hero (later worshipped as the god of medicine) who was blasted by a thunderbolt from Zeus for bringing Hippolytus back to life.

1021] *bring . . . again* AP 991: ἀνάγειν (= bring up or back). Was it for the sake of consistency that B again chose the slightly less appropriate sense of the prefix ἀνα-? See l. 1019n.

1022-23] *did not . . . than due* AP 993-95: εἰ δὲ μὴ τεταγμένα μοῖρα μοῖραν ἐκ θεῶν εἶργε μὴ πλέον φέρειν (= and if fate appointed from/by gods did not prevent fate from carrying-off more). The meaning is obscure and disputed, but may possibly be something like: "and if one lot, appointed by the gods, did not prevent another from getting more than its share," i.e., were it not the case that nothing I can say can possibly affect Agamemnon's fate . . . .

1025] *Would have all out* Would come out with all my fears. AP 997: ἂν τάδ' ἐξέχει (= would be pouring these things out).

1026] *Moodily grieved* AP 999: θυμαλγής (= grieving in soul).

1027] *unwind* An image not dictated by the rhyme, but exactly translating ἐκτολοπεύσειν (= wind off carded wool for spinning), i.e., unravel from my confused thoughts.

1028] *enkindling* AP 1001: ζωπυρουμένας (= kindled into flame, set on fire (passive).

1030] *not angrily* The literal meaning of ἀμηνίτως (AP 1003), i.e., kindly. Clytaemnestra implies that Cassandra is lucky to be made a slave in such a good home.

1031] *Partaker of hand-sprinklings* I.e., sharer of the holy water for washing the hands before meals and sacrifices. B stresses the derivation of χερνίβων (= hand-wash; AP 1004). It was normal for slaves to take part in household religious rites, not, as Clytaemnestra implies, a special favor.

the many With pretended kindness. Clytaemnestra seizes every opportunity to humiliate the princess.

1032] *his the Owner's altar close to* AP 1005: κτησίου βωμοῦ πέλας (= near the of-ownership altar). The late positioning of *close to* imitates the Greek word-order; but the *his* is interpolated, apparently to mean "Agamemnon's" and to stress that he is now Cassandra's owner. However, the adjective κτησίου is generally taken to be short for Διός Κτησίου (= Zeus Ktesios, i.e., Zeus the protector of household property), so emphasizing that Cassandra is no more than a κτῆμα, a chattel.

1033] *car* The chariot from which Agamemnon has already stepped down.

be high-minded A literal translation of ὑπερφρόνει (= think-above), i.e., consider it beneath your dignity to step down

1034] *Alkmené's child* Heracles, who was sentenced by the Delphic oracle to a year's slavery for a murder. Sold to Omphale, Queen of Lydia, he was made to dress as a woman and do woman's work.

1035] *slave's barley-bread his living* The text is very doubtful; but B seems to translate a phrase of which Paley guessed one MS reading to be "probably a corruption" (AP 1007): δουλίας μάζης βίον (= a life of slavish barley-bread).

1036] *If, then . . . o'erbalance* A rather too literal equivalent of a line explained by Paley: "Supplying an ellipse ('the lot of slavery is indeed always hard'), we may accurately render the rest, 'but if the necessity of this lot *should* befall anyone, there is much advantage in having masters of ancient family property'" (AP 1009).

1038] *never hoping* AP 1011: οὔποτ' ἐλπίσαντες (= never having expected [it]). See l. 1000n.

1039] *beyond measure* The translation of παρὰ στάθμην given in Paley's note (AP 1012).

1040]   *with us*   I.e., at our house.

   as law warrants   AP 1013: οἷάπερ νομίζεται (= as is customary),
though B stresses the later meaning of the related word νόμος (= law).
1041]   *To thee . . . speaking*   It was to you that she has just been speak-
ing. The Greek is only slightly clearer than the English: σοί τοι
λέγουσα παύεται σαφῆ λόγον (= to you in truth she stops speaking a
clear speech; AP 1014). Since Cassandra makes no reply, the Chorus is
simply making sure that she realizes that Clytaemnestra was addressing
her; but B makes the wording even stranger by insisting on the etymo-
logical connection between παύεται and *pause*.
   the fatal nets   See ll. 378, 380, 877 and nn.
1042-43]   *obeying . . . disobey too*   AP 1016: πείθοι᾽ ἄν, εἰ πείθοι᾽·
ἀπειθοίης δ᾽ ἴσως (= obey, if you're going to obey; or perhaps disobey;
cf. ADP 1049: "The optative with ἄν in place of the imperative [often
used for the sake of courtesy])." But B seems to follow Paley's para-
phrase: "Whether you obey or not, you are within her toils, you cannot
help yourself"(AP 1014).
1044]   *in the swallow's fashion*   The twittering of swallows was a
proverbial simile among the Greeks for the absurd noises made by bar-
barians (i.e., non Greeks) speaking their own languages.
1046]   *I . . . persuade her*   A literal translation of πείθω νιν. But the sense
of the whole irritable remark must be: "unless she doesn't understand
Greek, she knows perfectly well what I'm saying and will do what I say."
   speaking within mind's scope   AP 1019: ἔσω φρενῶν λέγουσα (=
speaking within minds), interpreted by Paley: "speaking within her
comprehension."
1047]   *The best . . . speaks of*   I.e., as Paley puts it, "She says what is best
for you under the present circumstances" (AP 1020).
1048]   *this thy car-enthronement*   AP 1021: τόνδ᾽ ἁμαξήρη θρόνον (=
this attached-to-a-chariot throne).
1049]   *this thing at door*   Though it suits the context to make
Clytaemnestra call Cassandra a *thing*, there is nothing in the Greek to
justify it. The text and meaning are disputed, as Paley's note explains,
but whether B is translating the MSS reading θυραίαν τήνδ᾽ (AW
1055), or Paley's θυραίᾳ τῇδ᾽ (AP 1022), both adjectives are feminine,
not neuter. Conceivably, though, B takes τήνδ᾽ (= this) to go, not with
Cassandra, but with a feminine noun τριβὴν (= time-waste), under-
stood as a cognate accusative from the verb τρίβειν (= to waste time). If
so, *this thing at door* could mean "this wasting time at the door."
   for me no leisure   There is no leisure to me (the verb "to be" omit-
ted, as often in Greek), I have no leisure. i.e., I'm too busy to waste
time with her.

1050] *as concerns the hearth mid-navelled* A word-for-word version of AP 1023: τὰ μὲν γὰρ ἑστίας μεσομφάλου, as explained in Paley's note: "as regards the family altar" or "the things belonging to the family altar." But the τὰ (= the) may go with the μῆλα (= *sheep*) in the next line, possibly in the Homeric sense of a demonstrative: "they, the sheep" or "the sheep there" (ADP 1056-57).

1051] *fireside slaying* AP 1024: πρὸς σφαγὰς πυρὸς (= for slaughters of fire), paraphrased by Paley: "to be sacrificed for the fire," i.e., for burnt offerings. But Fraenkel detects textual corruption in the phrase (AF 1.154n.), and ADP comments: "all is darkness here" (ADP 1056-57).

1052] *By those . . . favour* I.e., Clytaemnestra. But there is probably a double meaning: publicly, she never expected the divine *favour* (χάριν) of being allowed to celebrate her husband's return. Privately, she is thinking of a different form of *fireside slaying*. But Fraenkel and others delete the whole line (AP 1025).

1054] *being witless* AP 1027: ἀξυνήμων οὖσα (= being not-understanding). B makes it more insulting than the original, which simply means: "if you don't understand what I say because you don't know Greek. . . ." But Clytaemnestra is by now too angry at having her orders apparently ignored, to realize the absurdity of her next remark, delightfully parodied by A. E. Housman: "But if you . . . do not understand a word I say, Then wave your hand, to signify as much" ("Fragment of a Greek Tragedy," 6-8).

1055] *as Kars do* AP 1028: καρβάνῳ χερί (= with barbarian hand). B appears to derive κάρβανος, a variant of Βάρβαρος (= barbarian) from Κάρ (= a Carian, transliterated as Kar), remembering that the hero of Aristophanes' *Plutus* was a slave called Καρίων (= a little Kar). Carians were generally despised, as slaves and mercenaries.

1057] *her way* The way she is behaving. AP 1030: τρόπος (= manner, character, temperament).

1058] *hears* The most literal sense of κλύει (AP 1031), though here used in its common meaning of "listens to, obeys."

senses AP 1031: φρενῶν (= mind).

1061] *Before* Until.

1062] *Not I . . . be* I'm not going to throw away i.e., waste any more words, only to be treated with contempt. B imitates the Greek word-order, somewhat obscuring the meaning of the verb ἀτιμωθήσομαι (= will be dishonored; AP 1035).

1063] *compassionate* Have pity on [her]—though the reader seems almost invited to mistake the archaic verb for the familiar adjective. The original word is ἐποικτείρω (= I have pity/compassion on).

will chafe not   AP 1036: οὐ θυμώσομαι (= shall not be angry [with her].

1065]   *prove yoke's use*   Experience for the first time the use of the yoke. AP 1038: καίνισον ζυγόν (= have new the yoke, i.e., bear your new yoke).

1066]   *Otototoi*   B transliterates the original exlamation of pain or grief, ὀτοτοτοῖ (AP 1039). Cassandra begins singing in a lyrical metre, with the Chorus-leader responding in iambics, the normal metre of dialogue.

Gods   B clings to a long-exploded theory that πόποι, an exclamation of pain or surprise, was a plural noun in the vocative, meaning "gods" (Liddell and Scott, 1996; cf. AEP 160 footnote).

Earth   AP 1039: δᾶ, explained by a scholiast as Doric for γῆ (= earth; *Scholia* 367); but the word is now thought to be an exclamation of horror (AF, ADP 1072).

Apollon   B transliterates the MS reading: Ἄπολλον (= vocative of Apollo, the god of prophecy; AW 1078).

1068]   *Why didst thou "ototoi"*   AP 1041: τί ταῦτ᾽ ἀντότυξας (Why did you make this cry of ototoi). B imitates the Greek in turning the exclamation into a verb (ὀτοτύζω = cry ototoi).

Loxias   A title of Apollo as god of prophecy.

1069]   *Since he . . . a mourner*   "Mournful songs were inappropriate to the cult of Apollo" (ADP 1075), since he was also the god of the sun, so of "joy and brightness" (AP 1042).

1072]   *Ill-boding*   AP 1045: δυσφημοῦσα (= uttering words of ill-omen). Getting no reply to his question from Cassandra, the chorus-leader is talking about her to the others.

1073]   *Nowise . . . helpful*   I.e., a god who is nowise empowered. But *empowered* slightly obscures the meaning of προσήκοντα (= concerned or suited) here, i.e., Apollo is not concerned with assisting one in sorrows'(Liddell and Scott, 1996).

1075]   *Guard of the ways*   AP 1048: ἀγυιᾶτ᾽ (= guardian of the streets). "Cassandra sees and addresses the symbol of Apollo standing at the palace gates . . . a block of stone, cone-shaped or with a rounded top," part of the scenery of Athenian tragedy (ADP 1080).

destroyer   AP 1048: ἀπόλλων, a pun on the name Ἀπόλλων, as if ἀπολλύων, present participle of the verb ἀπόλλυμι (= destroy).

1076]   *quite*   AP 1049: οὐ μόλις (= not hardly, scarcely, with difficulty). Liddell and Scott, 1996 takes this to imply "completely, quite," but it may mean "easily" (ADP 1082).

1078]   *Remains . . . present*   An almost word for word translation of AP 1051: (μένει τὸ θεῖον δουλίᾳ φρενί), i.e., slave though she is, she can still prophesy.

1081]   *Ha*   AP 1054: ἆ (an unaspirated exclamation expressive of various strong emotions. Perhaps B thought the aspirated form of the same vowel-sound, as used by Shakespeare and the Elizabethans, "appropriate to archaic workmanship" (*Introductory Note*, 1. 8). See 1. 527n.

  what roof   AP 1054: ποίαν στέγην (= what sort of roof). "Cassandra knows perfectly well where she is: the question conveys her feeling of horror and foreboding" (ADP 1087). But the chorus-leader takes her question literally.

1084]   *How! How!*   In Paley's text and in one MS Cassandra merely repeats her previous exclamation: ἆ ἆ (AP 1057). But that would spoil B's rhyme. (A literal translation in rhyming verse is of course a contradiction in terms).

1085]   *then*   Though οὖν by itself could mean *then* (inferential), μὲν οὖν regularly means, as here, "nay rather," as Paley takes it: "Nay, rather, to a house detested of the gods" (AP 1058).

1086]   *Self-slaying evils*   The literal meaning of αὐτοφόνα κακὰ (AP 1059), though the sense here is probably killings of kindred, family murders. (cf. AEP 160).

  halters too   The text is uncertain, but B seems to follow Paley's καὶ ἀρτάναι (= and nooses, i.e., hangings; AP 1059).

1087]   *Man's-shambles*   AP 1060: ἀνδροσφαγεῖον (= slaughterhouse of men).

  blood-besprinkler of the ground   The text is uncertain, but B translates Paley's reading: πέδου ῥαντήριον (sprinkler of the ground; AP 1060), making the implicit *blood-* explicit.

1089]   *snuffs*   B's improvement on ματεύει (= searches for; AP 1062).

1090]   *How! How!*   AP 1063: ἆ ἆ (see 1. 1084n.).

1091]   *By . . . now*   AP 1064, AW 1095: μαρτυρίοισι γὰρ τοῖσδ᾽ ἐπιπείθομαι (= [Yes] for I trust these testimonies).

1092]   *dressed in the fire*   Expanded for the rhyme from one word, ὀπτάς (= roasted; AP 1066).

1095]   *are we in scent of*   AP 1068, AW 1099: μαστεύομεν (= are we looking for, i.e., do we need); but B prefers to repeat the hound-metaphor from AP 1061 (see 1. 1088-89), where the related verb ματεύει (= is looking for) was used.

1096]   *Ah, gods*   AP 1069: ἰὼ, πόποι, an exclamation of horror; but B takes the second word in its obsolete interpretation to mean "gods." See 1. 1066n.

  she meditate   AP 1069: μήδεται (= does he, she, or it plot?)—a dramatic ambiguity impossible to reproduce in English. So B supplies a subject for the verb, of the gender that Cassandra is dimly envisaging, i.e., Clytaemnestra: "What ever is the woman plotting to do?" The verb itself (μήδεται) has even been seen as a punning reference to Clytaemnestra's name, spelt without the ν (= *n*), as Κλυταιμήστρα, and taken to imply "famous for plotting" (from κλυτός [= famous], and μήδεται [= plot], the verb used in AP 1069, and 1071).

1098] *Great . . . ill* AP 1071: μέγ᾿ ἐν δόμοισι τοῖσδε μήδεται κακόν (= great in houses these [she] plots [an] evil). In trying to reproduce the original word-order (and also to use *ill* as a rhyme-word), B inevitably obscures the fact that the neuter adjective μέγα (= great) qualifies the neuter noun κακόν (= evil, *ill*).

1100] *Resistance* The original word is ἀλκά (AP 1072), of which the most relevant meaning is probably "help" or "defence"; but B's translation implies that there is nothing to stop her doing whatever she likes.

1102] *Of these I witless am* I.e., I know nothing of the murder that she seems to be predicting

1103] *those* The allusion to how Atreus made Thyestes eat the flesh of his sons for dinner.

bruits them Spreads the story of them about. AP 1075: βοᾷ (= shouts them).

1104] *consummatest* AP 1076: τελεῖς (= you accomplish or will accomplish). B's choice of verb stresses the irony of consummating a marriage by murdering your husband

1105] *thy bed's common guest* A rhyme-led expansion of the adjective ὁμοδέμνιον (= sharing one's bed; AP 1077).

1106] *having brightened* The literal meaning of φαιδρύνασα, though here (AP 1078), as in some other contexts, it implies washing clean. B imitates the Greek in leaving the main verb to be understood: "will you murder your husband and bedmate, after giving him a bath?"

1107] *Consummation* AP 1078: τέλος (= end, accomplishment), the noun of the verb just translated *consummatest*. See l. 1104n.

1109] *at life* B's explanatory interpolation slightly spoils the dramatic effect. He seems to be translating, not the emendation adopted by Paley (ὀρέγματα [= stretchings out; AP 1080]), but the MS reading, ὀρεγομένα (= [she] stretching out; AW 1111). In either case Cassandra sees shadowy hands moving, but cannot yet see what they are doing (cf. ADP 1110f.).

1110] *Nor yet . . . thee* Apparently B's equivalent for the modern slang: "I'm not with you" (= I don't understand). AP 1081, AW 1112: οὔπω ξυνῆκα (aorist of συνίημι [= I did not yet understand]). Can B have mistaken the second word for an aorist of σύνειμι (= go or come together)?

1110-11] *for—after . . . resourceless* AP 1081-82: νῦν γὰρ ἐξ αἰνιγμάτων ἐπαργέμοισι θεσφάτοις ἀμηχανῶ (= for now out of riddles

I am baffled by obscure oracles). The words are variously interpreted, but Paley paraphrased: "Now, instead of being enlightened after all your enigmas, I am only perplexed by equally obscure prophecies" (AP 1081).

1112-13]   *Eh, eh . . . espy*   B partly transliterates, partly reproduces the sound-effects of AP 1083: ἒἒ παπαῖ, παπαῖ,τί τόδε φαίνεται (= oh! oh! alas! alas! what is this that appears?). The first three Greek words are an exclamation of surprise and horror, with which the last word happens to rhyme (happens, because rhyme is not a normal feature of Greek versification), and B seizes the opportunity to rhyme on the same vowel-sound.

1114]   *net of Haides*   AP 1084: δίκτυον ... Ἅιδου. See l. 378n. B retains the Greek spelling of Hades (Ἅιδης).

1117]   *who takes part in the murder*   AP 1085: ἡ ξυναιτία φόνου (= who shares in the guilt of murder). The meaning has been much discussed (e.g. in AF 1116). See also ADP 1116: "it is not clear whether ξυναιτία means 'sharing the guilt' *with the net* or *with Aegisthus*." B seems to be following Paley's note: "'No! 'tis the sharer of his bed who is the snare, she who takes part in the murder,' i.e., with Justice and the Furies"(AP 1085).

1118-23]   *But may . . . atoning*   I.e., may the people of Argos rise in revolt against the house of Atreus and shout for the murderess to be punished by stoning. B is elaborating two lines (AP 1086-87): στάσις δ᾽ ἀκόρετος γένει κατολολυξάτω θύματος λευσίμου (?= let revolt, insatiable against the race/family, shriek over a stoning sacrifice/victim). But the words have been understood in various ways, and the στάσις here may mean not "revolt" but either "a spirit of discord" (ADP 1117), or a pack of Furies, as Paley takes it (AEP 161).

1125]   *Not me . . . enlightens*   AP 1089: οὔ με φαιδρύνει. B seems to prefer the Scholiast's interpretation, οὐ σεσαφήνισται (= has not made clear, or as Paley quotes it, "does not enlighten me"), to Paley's own interpretation, "does not cheer me" (*Scholia* 369, AP 1089, AEP 161).

1126-27]   *To my heart . . . crocus-dye*   A literal translation of the Greek (AP 1090-1). Yellow was the proverbial color of the complexion at moments of terror, when blood was believed to run towards the heart (ADP 1121-22).

1128-31]   *Which makes . . . sun*   I.e., blood which, pouring out on the battlefield, causes death. The text is obscure and corrupt, but B seems to reject an emendation adopted by Paley (καιρία = fatal wound), and adopt another mentioned in Paley's note, δορὶ πτωσίμοις (= those fallen by the spear, AP 1090). Hence *On earth by the spear that lie.*

1133]   *How! How!*   AP 1094: ἇ ἇ exclamations of horror (see also l. 1084n.).

1134] *quick* Interpolated for the rhyme and to suggest the urgency of the next command.

1135] *Keep the bull from the cow* The warning would naturally suggest concern for the cow's safety, so here it stresses the unnatural situation of a wife more dangerous than her husband. Cf. ADP 1125-26.

1136] *In the vesture catching him* I.e., entangling him in the garment metaphorically described as the hunting-net.

1137] *With . . . trick* Here there is a textual crux, much discussed (e.g. AF 1127, ADP 1126-28). B literally translates Paley's reading: μελαγκέρῳ μηχανήματι (AP 1096). The *horn* is the murder-weapon (continuing the cow-metaphor for Clytaemnestra), the *trick* is her treachery and the *black* implies her malice.

1138] *the watery vase* I.e., the bath. AP 1097: ἐν ἐνύδρῳ τεύχει (= in the watery vessel). Though Liddell and Scott included "vase" among possible meanings of the noun, B's only apparent excuse for using it here is the eye-rhyme.

1139] *craft-killing cauldron* An accurate though pleasantly alliterative rendering of δολοφόνου λέβητος (AP 1098). Was B also pleased to think that *cauldron* was ultimately derived from Latin *caldarium* (= hot bath)?

case AP 1098: τύχαν (= happening, fatal event.

1140] *a topping critic* AP 1099: γνώμων ἄκρος (= topmost/highest/supreme judge). The faint whiff of Gilbert and Sullivan in the the previous line (AP 1098) seems to have switched B momentarily into a parody mode, doubtless amused by the similarity between fifth-century Greek idiom and Victorian slang.

1141-42] *to some . . . these* I.e., this sounds to me like bad news.

1143] *beside* besides (AP 1101: δὲ = and/but)

1144] *that sing the event* B translates an emendation mentioned in Paley's note (AP 1103) but not adopted by him: θεσπιῳδοί (= singing-prophecies).

1147] *Of me . . . fortunes* The original word-order (AP 1105).

1148] *I bewail* B rejects an emendation adopted by Paley (θροεῖς = you cry aloud; AP 1106), and translates the MS reading: θροῶ (= I cry aloud; AW 1137).

my proper my own.

1149] *As . . . throw* Expanded from one participle: ἐπεγχέασ' (= pouring in besides; AW 1137), i.e., adding her own imminent murder to Agamemnon's.

1150] *Why* AP 1107: ποῖ (= whither, to what end or purpose).

thou Presumably Apollo.

1151-52] *for nought . . . was sought* Interpolated for the rhyme. AW 1139, AP 1108: τί γὰρ (= for why [else]?).

347

1153]   *mind-mazed*   An alliterative but accurate rendering of φρενομανής (AP 1109).

1155]   *A lay—no lay*   AP 1111: νόμον ἄνομον (= a not-songlike song, a tuneless tune). B tries to bring out the original relationship between noun and adjective.

1156]   *nightingale*   One might have expected B, with his passion for etymology, to emphasize that the noun here (ἀήδων; AP 1114), though traditionally used of the nightingale, simply means "singer."

1157]   *noise*   AP 1112: βοᾶς (= crying, shouting, whether in joy or, as here, in grief).

well-away   a Chaucerian exclamation of sorrow. There seems no good reason but the rhyme and the alliteration for using the archaism here to represent the familiar interjection φεῦ (= alas; AP 1112); but B's introduction sanctioned the "use of certain allowable constructions which, happening to be out of daily favour, are all the more appropriate to archaic workmanship" (*Introductory Note*, 1 l. 6-8).

1158]   *From her unhappy breast*   AP 1112: ταλαίναις φρεσίν (in her unhappy mind).

1159]   *Itus, Itus*   In this version of the myth, Procne was changed into a nightingale after she had killed her son Itys and served him up for dinner to his father Tereus, in revenge for Tereus' rape of her sister Philomela.

1160]   *With evils . . . each side*   The literal meaning of the adjective attached to βίον (= life), ἀμφιθαλῆ (AP 1114). The adjective was normally used of a child who had both parents living. Here, combined with κακοῖς (= evils) it seems to imply that both Itys's parents have suffered or committed crimes. But the rhyme-word *rife* suggests that B took the prefix ἀμφι (= on both sides, or on all sides, around) in the second sense, so that the adjective came to mean "abounding in."

1162]   *nightingale, the clear resounder*   AP 1115: λιγείας ... ἀηδόνος (= clear-toned nightingale). B's *resounder* was possibly added, not just for the rhyme, but to stress the connection between ἀηδών and singing (see l. 1156n.).

1164]   *misfortunes*   Paley's note (AP 1117 lists various ways of resolving the apparent contradiction between the nightingale's ceaseless laments and her living κλαυμάτων ἄτερ (= without weepings). He concludes: "Or lastly . . . κλαύματα may be understood 'non de cantu lusciniae, sed de malis quae lugenda sunt'" (= not about the song of the nightingale, but about evils that must be lamented). Hence B's *misfortunes.*

1166]   *spear, the two-edged thing*   AP 1118: ἀμφήκει δορί (= two-edged spear. A hard-earned rhyme for the unstressed last syllable of *sundering!*

1167]   *pain*   AP 1120: δύας (= pains); but the plural, though fitting the context better, would have spoiled the rhyme.

1168]   *And spasms*   Interpolated.

in vain   AP 1120: ματαίους (= vain, idle, pointless; not an adverb but an adjective attached to the *pains*. Paley explains as "'groundless,' without any visible cause or motive."

1169]   *things that terrify*   The object of *strikest up*. AP 1121: τὰ ...ἐπίφοβα (= these terrifying things; for the τὰ is here a demonstrative, not a definite article).

1170]   *changing*   Not in the Greek; but B was possibly thinking of Paley's note (AP 1122): "Mixed up with shrill cries and intonations as if you were singing the kind of music called the orthian strain."

unintelligible   AP 1121: δυσφάτῳ (= hard/bad to say, so perhaps ill-omened). But B follows the interpretation of the scholiast quoted by Paley: ἀσαφεῖ, αἰνιγματῶδει (= unclear, riddling; *Scholia* 371).

cry   Intent on his rhyme, B has to sacrifice the connotations of the Greek κλαγγᾷ, normally used of sounds made by birds or animals.

1171]   *Orthian style*   A traditional melody of very high pitch (ὄρθιος = straight up, shrill).

1173-74]   *Whence . . . evils bode*   The literal meaning of AP 1123-24 (πόθεν ὅρους ἔχεις θεσπεσίας ὁδοῦ), i.e., "who marked out for you the ill-omened path which your prophecy follows?" (ADP 1154-55).

1176]   *Skamandros*   A precise transliteration of Σκάμανδρος, traditionally anglicized as Scamander, a river of Troy.

1176-77]   *the draught / Paternal*   AP 1127: πάτριον ποτόν (= paternal drink), i.e., from which my fathers drank.

1177-78]   *to these . . . I brought*   AP 1128-29: τότε μὲν ἀμφὶ σὰς ἀϊόνας ... ἠνυτόμαν τροφαῖς (= then around thy banks I was being finished/perfected with feedings/ bringings-up), i.e., was brought up as a child. From the notion of finishing in the Greek verb B extracts his rhyme-word *ends*, interpolating *these* to stress the contrast between Cassandra's past and her present.

1179]   *Kokutos and Acheron*   Κωκυτός and Ἀχέρων, the rivers of Wailing and of Pain in Hades. Unlike Cocytus, the usual spelling of the first in English, B's exact transliteration brings out the first name's derivation from κωκύω (= I wail). The second comes from ἄχος (= pain, grief), cognate with the English *ache*.

1180]   *these*   Unaccountably interpolated—for why should she go on predicting what will by then have taken place? AP 1131: θεσπιωδήσειν (= shall be singing prophecies).

1182]   *babe*   AP 1133: νεογνὸς (= new-born child).

1183]   *bite*   See l. 759n.

here under I.e., under my heart (with a gesture). B accepts an adverbial interpretation of ὑπαὶ (= under, by) mentioned but rejected in a note by Paley, who paraphrased: "'I have received a blow through (*or* from) a bloody bite'—a bite to the quick, a sting to the heart" (AP 1134).

1184] *woe-wreaking* AP 1135: δυσαλγεῖ (= very painful).

1185] *shrill-shrieking* A type of utterance certainly suggested before (see l. 1172n.). But here (AP 1135) μινυρὰ θρεομένας probably means "complaining in a low tone, whining, whimpering" (Liddell and Scott, 1996).

1188-89] *ah, pity / Of* A rhyme-led variation on the repeated exclamation of sorrow, ἰώ (AP 1137, 1138).

1190] *In the ramparts' aid* Paley's interpretation of πρόπυργοι (= for *or* in front of the walls): "'offered in defence of the walls,' viz. that they might hold out" (AP 1139).

1192] *the burthen endure* Expanded from one word: παθεῖν (= suffer; AP 1142).

1193] *with the soul on fire* B's characteristic version of the possibly corrupt MS reading θερμόνους (= with warm mind; AP 1143. AW 1172).

1194] *me* myself. There is no object for *cast* (βαλῶ) in the MS text, but B follows Paley's qualified defence of the "harsh . . . ellipse" of ἐμαυτὴν (= myself; AP 1143).

and expire Interpolated for the rhyme.

1195] *on the former consequent* I.e., that follow from what you have just said.

1197] *fiend* AP 1146: δαίμων, a neutral term at this period for a god or a spirit, which only with Christianity developed the sense of a demon or *fiend*.

1198] *melodize* AP 1147: μελίζειν (= sing of). but B emphasizes the connection with μέλος (= song, melody).

thy sorrows AP 1147: πάθη (= sufferings). B interpolates *thy*.

else, in singing Interpolated for the rhyme.

1200] *Calamitous* AP 1147: γοερὰ (= to be groaned at, lamentable).

1203] *Well then* B adopts Paley's interpretation of καὶ μὴν (AP 1149), to imply: "if, as you say, you're baffled about the *the end*, here it is." Her new clarity is marked by a change from lyric verses to the normal metre for dialogue, iambic trimeters; so B goes into his regular equivalent, iambic pentameters with an extra final syllable (see l. 1n.).

1205] *But bright* Paley explains: "the metaphor is entirely changed, and borrowed from a clear and brisk wind, which, while it sweeps away the clouds from the sky, at the same time makes the waves heave and roll like dark mountain masses against the bright horizon."

it seems The primary meaning of ἔοικεν (AP 1151). But when followed, as here, by a future infinitive, it would normally mean "seems likely to," or "it seems that it will."

1206] *Breathing* AP 1152: πνέων (= breathing or blowing). Since the verb is often used of winds, it does not necessarily imply the gentleness that it does in English, and is quite compatible with Paley's "brisk wind."

to penetrate thee AP 1152, AW 1181: ἐσήξειν (= to be about to come in). Although in his translation (AEP 163) Paley recognizes the future tense ("methinks it will"), he ignores it when paraphrasing the word in his note (AP 1149): "to reach your inmost soul." Hence presumably B's present infinitive, and interpolated *thee.* Fraenkel adopts an emendation: ἐσάιξειν (= rush/dash in; AF 1181, cf. AL 1181).

1207-8] *a woe . . . this* I.e., according to Paley, than "the griefs of myself and my native city" (AP 1049).

1209] *witness* AP 1155: μαρτυρεῖτε (an imperative plural to the chorus). Paley paraphrases: "Bear witness, while you run along with me in the chase, that I am scenting the footsteps of evils long ago perpetrated in the family."

1211] *never quits a Choros* B reproduces the inverted word-order of the Greek, and precisely transliterates the subject of the verb, χορός (= chorus; AP 1157), thus emphasizing the implicit comparison of the Furies to the singing and dancing tragic Chorus. They will actually be the Chorus in the last play of the *Oresteia* trilogy, the *Eumenides*, (Εὐμενίδες = Kindly Females, a euphemism for the Furies).

1212] *One-voiced* AP 1158: ξύμφθογγος (= voicing together) as a well-trained Chorus should.

not well-tuned . . . utters B tries to replicate the original word-play: οὐκ εὔφωνος· οὐ γὰρ εὖ λέγει (= not well-voiced, for it does not speak well; AP 1158).

1213] *to get more courage* A fair translation of ὡς θρασύνεσθαι πλέον (AP 1159), though it cannot convey the fact that θράσος (= daring, courage) can be used pejoratively (= impudence, audacity).

1214] *Komos* AP 1160: κῶμος (= band of revellers, drinking-party).
keeps stays.

1215] *sister* AP 1161: Paley's suggested translation of ξυγγόνων (= born-with, blood-related, kindred, brother, sister; AP 1161). But the point here is the Furies' relationship, not with each other, but with the House of Atreus. They are hereditary forces demanding vengeance for the murders of family-members. See AF 1190, 2.544-45, ADP 1190, and l. 57n.

1216] *within . . . sitting* B seems to miss the implication of δώμασιν προσήμεναι (= sitting close to the house, i.e., besieging it (AF, ADP 1191).
1217] *The first beginning curse* AP 1163: πρώταρχον ἄτην, i.e., that is the subject of their *hymn*; *curse* is a necessarily vague translation of the complicated concept *Ate* (see l. 381n.).

spit forth at I.e., express their disgust at by spitting. But B has very slightly changed the metaphor of ἀπέπτυσαν (= spit out, i.e., reject with disgust).
1218] *The Brother's . . . hostile* AP 1164: εὐνὰς ἀδελφοῦ τῷ πατοῦντι δυσμενεῖς (= brother's bed hostile to him who trampled it). The reference is to Thyestes' adultery with his brother Atreus' wife, and Atreus' murder of Thyestes' children in revenge. But the wording is ambiguous: *hostile* could be accusative, qualifying *bed*, or nominative, qualifying the *Furies*; and the trampling could be literal (getting on to) or metaphorical (despising and so violating its sanctity). Paley's note mentions these possibilities (AP 1163), but concludes that the hostility is shown by the bed, not the Furies: "What the Furies loathe is not the adultery itself, but the vengeance taken for it." B seems to follow Paley. If so, *spurned it* means "scorned and so violated its sanctity." For recent interpretations, contrast AF 1193 with ADP 1193.
1219] *Have I . . . bowman* I.e., am I right or wrong? Archery, like sailing, is among the commonest sources of imagery in Greek tragedy.
1220] *knock at doors* the literal meaning of θυροκόπος (AP 1166). Like Gipsies in England, Greek oracle-mongers (χρησμόλογοι) went from door to door, offering to tell fortunes.
1221] *Henceforward* Interpolated to represent "when I am gone" in Paley's note explaining the significance of λόγῳ (= in/by word) in AP 1168: "'Bear witness for me when I am gone, by swearing beforehand that I know *not merely by hearsay* the ancient crimes of this house.' That is, Swear to me *now*, when I am present to hear the testimony, that I have a supernatural knowledge, in order that, when the predicted events have come to pass, you may remember it was no vain trifler who told you" (AP 1167). For other interpretations of the disputed passage see AF 1196f.
1223-24] *And how . . . thy cure* I.e., how would an oath help?
1226] *Shouldst hit in speaking* A literal translation of κυρεῖν λέγουσαν (AP 1172), paraphrased by Paley: "should rightly speak." See l. 1219n.
1227] *office* B's translation of τέλει (AP 1173), though among the many lexicon-definitions of the word, it was possibly suggested by Paley's note: "It was Apollo who appointed me to the office of a prophetess."
1228] *longing* AP 1174: ἱμέρῳ (= longing, love, desire).

1229]   *At first*   AP 1175: προτοῦ (= before this, formerly); B ignores Paley's more accurate translation: "hitherto."

1230]   *more relaxed*   AP 1176: ἁβρύνεται ... πλέον (= is more delicate). B seems slightly to miss the point, though correctly explained in Paley's note: "The word signifies to be nice or particular, to pride or pique oneself on any subject." The Chorus-leader means that such delicate feelings are a luxury Cassandra can no longer afford; her "present position leaves no room for coy reticence" (ADP 1205).

1231]   *athlete*   AP 1177: παλαιστὴς (= wrestler). The general sense is simply that Apollo was an irresistible lover; but B may have feared that a literal translation would shock his Victorian readers, where Paley thought it wiser to paraphrase: "Well, he *was* a lover who inspired me with great affection" (AEP 164). Even Liddell and Scott, 1996 bowdlerizes the word here into "suitor." How much should be read into the original image is disputable. In the Lucianic short story Λούκιος ἢ Ὄνος (= "Lucius or The Ass" sexual intercourse is lengthily described in the technical terms of wrestling, and the girl involved is called Palaestra (Παλαίστρα = wrestling-school); but here in Aeschylus Fraenkel's comment seems almost too literal-minded: "Modern prudishness has been busy weakening the force of this magnificent line . . . . Apollo did not in a metaphorical sense contend for her heart or her favour, but actually wrestled with her . . . . For all that she withdraws before the consummation. How that could be the poet does not reveal" (AF 1206; 3.555).

1232]   *the work of children*   I.e., of producing children.

        ye   By using this archaic plural, B marks the fact that the verb ἤλθετον (= *went*; AP 1178) is in the dual (= did the two of you go?).

        law's way   B appears to accept Paley's interpretation of the MS reading: νόμῳ (= by custom/law): "By regular and legitimate marriage . . . as a wife" (AP 1178). But the Chorus-leader's question is less absurd if the noun is understood in its other sense of "custom," i.e., "did you go on to have children by him, as usually happens in such circumstances?" (cf. ADP 1207).

1233]   *Loxias*   An epithet of Apollo.

1234]   *Already . . . possessed of*   When already possessed of the inspired wits, i.e., when you had already got possession of the gift of prophecy? But the meaning of AP 1180 is slightly different: ἤδη τέχναισιν ἐνθέοις ᾑρημένη (= having already been taken captive/possessed by inspired arts). B seems to have parsed the participle as a middle, though the dative noun (τέχναισιν) proves it a passive.

1235]   *Already . . . foretold*   An almost word-for-words version of AP 1181: ἤδη πολίταις πάντ᾽ ἐθέσπιζον πάθη (= I was already prophesying all sufferings to the citizens/townsmen). But B has made the line almost unintelligible in English by giving no sign that *townsmen* is in the dative, that in verse a definite article can be understood when not included, and that the verb is imperfect (= was foretelling). He had, however, the general excuse that such passages of stichomythia (dialogue in alternate lines of verse) are often expressed too concisely to be both literally and intelligibly translated.

1236]   *unhurt*   B translates ἄνατος, an emendation of the MS reading ἄνακτος (= of the lord), adopted by Weise and in 1950 described by Fraenkel as "a certain restoration"). Paley adopted in his text a different emendation, but in his later prose translation rendered the word as "unharmed" (AP 1182, AEP 164, AW, AF 1211).

1237]   *when I sinned*   I.e., after I had sinned.

1238]   *sooth*   Truth—a mistranslation of πιστά (= trustworthy, credible things; AP 1184), possibly inspired by the alliteration.

1239]   *Halloo, halloo*   AP 1185: ἰού, ἰού a non-specific cry of joy or grief. Was B trying to continue the hunting-hound image of 1088-89?

1241]   *prelusive last-lays*   The last word of the Greek line (AP 1187, AW, AL 1216) seems to have been inadvertently transferred by a scribe from the following line. Paley comments: "As the true reading cannot be ascertained, it is better to mark a lacuna than to supply a conjectural word"; so that is what he does, giving φροιμίοις (= with foresongs, preludes) as the final authentic word. B prefers to have a guess at what is missing, and comes up with an oxymoron: songs that are a prelude to something else (the murder) but are themselves the last of a series. The only textual basis for *last-lays* is that the prefix of the word mistakenly inserted by the scribe (ἐφ = ἐπί) can sometimes mean "after" or "in addition" (as in ἐπίλογος = epilogue). Presumably B meant to imply that Cassandra's prelude to the murder is her own swan-song.

1242]   *household*   The last syllable seems to have been added simply for the versification (AP 1288: δόμοις houses; poetic plural for singular)

   seated   AP 1288: ἐφημένους (= sitting at, by, or close to the house; the misplaced word mentioned in the previous note).

1243]   *of dreams . . . figures*   I.e., like figures in dreams. B imitates the original wording and word-order: ὀνείρων προσφερεῖς μορφώμασιν (= of dreams brought-near/approaching/resembling shapes; AP 1189).

1244]   *Children . . . beloveds*   A literal translation of AP 1190: παῖδες θανόντες ὡσπερεὶ πρὸς τῶν φίλων —except that "dear ones" is inappropriately replaced by *beloveds* to suit B's metre. Editors have been puzzled by the apparent suggestion that murderers can be identified from the appearance of their victims, and Paley explains: "The words are out of their natural order, ὡσπερεὶ παῖδες as it were children, 'forms like children.' "

1245] *Hands they have filled* B slightly increases the horror of χεῖρας ... πλήθοντες (= being full as to their hands; AP 1191), by making the intransitive present participle a transitive past one.

    meal domestic AP 1191: οἰκείας βορᾶς (= of their own food, i.e., "of their own flesh served as food," Liddell and Scott, 1996). Though οἰκεῖος, an adjective derived from οἶκος (= house), can indeed mean *domestic,* one of its commonest senses is "one's own." See l. 164n., and ll. 1652f.

1248] *plans punishment a certain* B imitates the inverted word-order of AP 1194.

    Lion I.e., Aegisthus, Thyestes' son and Clytaemnestra's lover. See l. 834n.

1249] *wallows* A happy rendering of στρωφώμενον (= turning constantly; AP 1195), which both expresses the physical meaning of the Greek word and adds the relevant connotations of sensual indulgence attached to the English one (while supplying the trochaic ending required for B's line).

1250] *(ah, me!)* If the parenthetical οἴμοι (= ah me!) is the right reading, rather than an ironical οἶμαι (= I think), as Paley suggests (AP 1196), it may either express dismay at the kind of watch-dog that Aegisthus has proved himself, or sorrow at the *master*'s return in triumph over Cassandra's home city, or (looking forward to *mine*) at the thought that he is now her *master* too. Fraenkel regards the whole of that line (AF, AL 1226) as "indubitably interpolated" (AF 3.562).

1253] *lewd* B follows Paley (AP 1199, AEP 165) in translating μισήτης (= lewd) rather than the differently accented μισητῆς (= hated, hateful).

1254] *Speaking, outspreading* AP 1200: λέξασα κἀκτείνασα (= having spoken and stretched out, i.e., having spoken at length).

    shiny-souled In translating φαιδρόνους (= with a bright mind) B seems to choose the least appropriate sense possible for the first component, φαιδρός (= bright, shining, radiant, so metaphorically: beaming with joy, cheerful). The hint of a polished, reflecting surface is hardly relevant here (AP 1200). Cassandra surely implies that Clytaemnestra seemed pleased to welcome her husband home. Paley paraphrased: "with so blithe a heart" (AEP 165); Fraenkel, "with radiant friendliness" (AF 1229).

1255] *Atè* See l. 381n.

    will reach to AP 1201: τεύξεται (= will hit the mark of, reach as her aim). See l. 1219n.

1256] *the female, the male's slayer* AP 1202-3 makes the simple statement: "the female is the male's slayer," but B follows Weise's punctuation, which makes the ἔστι (= is or she is) begin the next sentence (AW 1232).

1257] *hateful* B omits a form of litotes characteristic of Greek tragic diction: δυσφιλὲς (= hard to love, unlovable; AP 1203).

bite-beast A fair translation of δάκος, a neuter noun from δάκνω (= I bite), i.e., an animal whose bite is dangerous (Liddell and Scott, 1871).

1258] *amphisbaina* AP 1204: ἀμφίσβαινα (= both-go), a kind of serpent supposed to be able to move both forwards and backwards, and to have a second head on its tail.

Skulla AP 1203: Σκύλλαν, Scylla, a monster with six heads and three rows of teeth, who lived in a cave opposite the whirlpool Charybdis in Homer, *Odyssey*, 12.85-100.

1259] *Revelling* An eccentric translation of θύουσαν (= raging; AP 1206), possibly suggested by the fact that θύω (= sacrifice) , generally treated as a different verb from θύω (= rage), can mean "celebrate with sacrifices."

Haides' mother The meaning of this phrase "has been vigorously discussed for a century and a half" (AF 1235). Paley's note translates it "mother of Death" (AP 1206), but AEP 165 offers the more picturesque "hag of hell." The main point at issue is whether Clytaemnestra is seen as a cause of death or as a hellish mother (i.e., of Iphigenia, whose sacrifice she avenges).

1260-61] *curse . . . at friends* Has B got bored with the problems of translating, and momentarily stopped trying? In fact, the Greek is not gibberish, as these English words suggest, but perfectly coherent: ἄσπονδόν τ᾽ ἀρὰν φίλοις πνέουσαν (= and breathing truceless curse/ruin/mischief against dear-ones). The "and" simply links the two participles (= raging and breathing); truceless, i.e., admitting no truce = implacable; and the metaphor of breathing slaughter etc. is common in both languages.

1261] *How piously she shouted* AP 1207: ὡς δ᾽ ἐπωλολύξατο (= and how she raised a cry of triumph).

1262] *all-courageous* A misleading translation of παντότολμος (= all-daring; AP 1208), where the daring (τόλμα) is pejorative (i.e., there's nothing she wouldn't dare to do, she'd stick at nothing).

turn of battle I.e., when the enemy is routed.

1263] *the back-bringing safety* I.e., at her husband's safe return. AP 1209: νόστιμῳ σωτηρίᾳ (= at the to-do-with-return safety).

1264] *Of this . . . persuade* And if I cannot persuade you of the truth of this.

all's one   B adopts Paley's translation of ὅμοιον (= [it is] like, similar): "It is all one whether you believe me or not" (AP 1210).

1265]   *present*   I.e., as an eye-witness, when you see my murdered corpse.

1268]   *I went with*   AP 1214: ξυνῆκα (= I understood). Again B *seems* to mistake the verb from which the second part of this compound comes. It is an aorist of ἵημι (= send), not of εἶμι (= go). See l. 1110n.

1269]   *Listing*   Listening to, hearing.

what's true . . . out-imaged   AP 1215: ἀληθῶς οὐδὲν ἐξῃκασμένα (= things truly [spoken], in no way [just] portrayed in likenesses), i.e., literally, not metaphorically described. B's *as life* was interpolated, and his puzzling *out-imaged* translated the prefix of the compound verb (ἐξ= out), while suggesting the linguistic connection of the rest with εἰκών (= likeness, image).

1270]   *I say, thou*   Cassandra becomes more explicit, in response to a line which B has (doubtless inadvertently) omitted: AP 1216: τὰ δ᾽ ἀλλ᾽ ἀκούσας ἐκ δρόμου πεσὼν τρέχω (= but on hearing the other things I am running after falling out of the track), i.e., I've lost track of what you mean, I don't understand what you're saying. Cf. AL 1245.

fate   The primary meaning of μόρον (AP 1216), but the word commonly implies, as here, "death."

1272]   *But Paian . . . here*   AP 1219: ἀλλ᾽ οὔτι Παίων τῷδ᾽ ἐπιστατεῖ λόγῳ (= But Paean [the god of healing] does not at all stand-by-as-helper or preside over this word/saying). The general sense is that the situation is irremediable, and the prophecy must be fulfilled; but there is also some complicated word-play. "Paean" means both the god of healing, and a hymn to Apollo in that capacity. According to Fraenkel (AF 1248), such a hymn "could be regarded as a particular kind of εὐφημεῖν [= speaking *good words*, as the Chorus-leader has just urged Cassandra to do]." She retorts, punningly, that she is not singing that kind of hymn; and also that the imminent murder is not describable in "good words." B complicates the passage further by mixing in the archaic idiom, "serve one in no stead," that is, be of no advantage or profit to one (*OED, Stead*, sb., iv, 13b).

1273]   *the thing*   I.e., *Agamemnon's fate*, which the Chorus-leader assumes to be death from natural causes.

be near   AP 1220: παρέσται (= will be near).

never be it   B seems to ignore Paley's emendation πω (= not yet), and translate the MS reading retained by Weise: πως (= not any way, not in any circumstances (AW 1249).

1274]   *to kill are busy*   I.e., they are concentrating on murder. AP 1221: τοῖς δ᾽ ἀποκτείνειν μέλει (= but to them it is a care to kill). The actual moment of the murder will be marked by a cry off stage.

1275] *Of what man* By what man. The original noun ἀνδρός (= of a man as opposed to a woman) provokes Cassandra's next remark.

is it ministered Is it being prepared.

sorrow AP 1222: ἄχος (= pain, distress); but as Paley notes, it "often means 'a cause of grief,' and indirectly 'a crime'" He translates it here, "this horrid crime" (AEP 165).

1276] *wide . . . foretellings* You are looking wide of the mark that my predictions point to (i.e., murder by a woman, Clytaemnestra). The Greek text is disputed. B seems to be rejecting an emendation adopted by Paley, and translating a MS reading retained by Weise: ἦ κάρτ᾽ ἄρ᾽ ἂν παρεσκόπεις χρησμῶν ἐμῶν (= then you would very much be looking aside from i.e., missing the sense of my oracles). For the textual problem see AF, ADP 1252.

1277] *For* I.e., Yes, I fail to understand them because. The elliptical use of γάρ (= for) to mean "Yes, for" or "No, for" is common in Greek.

the fulfiller's AP 1224: τοῦ τελοῦντος (= of the one who will accomplish / execute / fulfil). B takes it to mean "fulfil the *foretellings*," though it is more often understood as "execute the murder."

scheme I.e., how he will contrive to do it, to "get the better of Agamemnon in his own house surrounded by his own people" (ADP 1253).

I have not gone with I have not understood. Again B seems to have mistaken the literal meaning of ξυνῆκα (= I have put together, I have understood; AP 1224). See l. 1110n.

1278] *too well* Because she has been taken prisoner by the Greeks.

1279] *For Puthian . . . too* B obscures the simple sense of AP 1226, AW 1255: καὶ γὰρ τὰ πυθόκραντα, δυσμαθῆ δ᾽ ὅμως (= For Pythian oracles also [know Greek], but [are] nevertheless hard to learn/understand); or as Paley put it, "So are Pythian oracles (couched in Greek), but they are still hard to understand (AEP 165)."

1280] *Papai* See l. 1112-13n.

this interpolated into AP 1227, possibly from Paley's "this prophetic fire!" (AEP 166).

what fire AP 1227: οἷον τό πῦρ (= of what kind the fire!).

1281] *Ototoi* See ll. 1168n., 1170n.

Lukeion So spelled in the MS, but evidently a slip of the pen for *Lukeian.* AP 1228: Λύκει᾽, an elided form of Λύκειε, vocative of Λύκειος, an epithet of Apollo variously interpreted: either as the wolf-killer (λύκος = wolf), or as born in Lycia, or as the god of light (λύκη = light, cf. Latin *lux*). In a context where Aegisthus is called *the wolf* (l. 1283), the first interpretation seems most relevant (see AF 1257). B's replacement of *an* by *on* in *Lukeion Apollon* may be explained by what

Paley elsewhere called "the common error [among scribes] of assimilating terminations" (AP 1270).

Apollon AP 1228: ῎Απολλον, vocative of ᾿Απόλλων (= Apollo).

1282]   *She, the* AP 1229: αὕτη (= this [woman]).

lioness I.e., Clytaemnestra. See l. 834n.

1283]   *The wolf* I.e., Aegisthus.

generous To translate εὐγενοῦς (= both high-born and noble in character; AP 1230), B chooses an English adjective which in its Latin origin similarly combines those two meanings.

1284]   *Kills* AP 1231, AW 1260: κτενεῖ (= will kill). Cassandra is foreseeing her own death. Did B mistake the contracting future for a historic present, which would have been κτείνει?

1284-85]   *as a poison / Brewing* As if brewing a poison. The original participle is simply τεύχουσα (= making; AP 1232).

1285]   *put my . . . anger* Paley paraphrases: "add to the cup of wrath (that already in store for her husband for the death of Iphigenia) a requital for me also" (AP 1232). B's *price* for μισθὸν (= pay/ reward/retribution) needlessly obscures the meaning.

1287]   *the bringing me* For bringing me i.e., as his concubine

1289]   *wands* σκῆπτρα (= staffs; plural for singular as often in poetry), i.e., her prophet's staff.

fillets Woollen bands worn round the neck (ADP 1264ff.).

1291]   *Go, to perdition falling* She tears off and throws down her badges of office

Boons exchange we The Greek text is corrupt. B abandons Paley, and translates Weise's: ἀγαθῶ δ᾿ ἀμείψομαι (= and I will exchange two good things.

1292]   *Some other Até* B returns to Paley's text: ἄλλην τιν᾿ ἄτην, which Paley translates: "enrich some other author of woe instead of me" (AP 1239). See l. 381n.

1294]   *having looked upon me* Paley paraphrases: "after he has coldly looked on while I have been made a laughing stock" (AP 1240). The two participles (*stripping, having looked*) are not followed in the Greek by any main verb, and there may be corruption in the MS text.

1295-96]   *laughed . . . weighed* I.e., laughed at by friends who were equivalent to foes, if you weighed them against one another. The meaning of AP 1242 is disputed: καταγελωμένην μετὰ φίλων ὑπ᾿ ἐχθρῶν οὐ διχορρόπως (= laughed at with friends by foes not with-a-two-way-fall-of-the-scale). B follows Paley's explanation: "by one just as much as the other, by all alike, without distinction or difference."

1296-97]   *and vainly— / For* AP 1243-44: μάτην. ... δὲ (= vainly, but/and). It is not clear in the Greek whether the *vainly* looks forward or backwards. Paley follows it with a full stop, Weise (AW 1272) with a colon. B understands the word to look forward, and by interpolating *and* before it, and *for* after it extracts a tolerable meaning: "their ridicule was in vain, for I just put up with it." But the word might equally mean that the ridicule was foolish, or unfair.

1297]   *stroller*   Used in its early sense of "vagrant, vagabond, itinerant beggar," to translate φοιτᾶς (= roaming about; AP 1244).

   as I   As if I.

   gipsy   AP 1244: ἀγύρτρια (= collector, beggar). But see l. 1220n.

1298]   *Beggar, unhappy*   As Paley's note points out, "It was not what she *was*, but what she was *called*, that these words were intended to express" (AP 1244).

1299]   *prophet me undoing*   AP 1246: μάντιν ἐκπράξας ἐμὲ (= having finished me off, prophet). Paley's note offers the translation: "After wreaking his vengeance on me as a prophetess"; but it also mentions other interpretations: "having *unmade* me," (i.e., presumably, made me no longer a prophetess), and "having undone me." In AEP 166 Paley seems to translate ἐκπράξας in two different senses simultaneously: "to wreak vengeance on me whom he had made a prophetess," where *wreak vengeance* takes the verb ἐκπράσσω (= do out) to mean "exact his due," and *made a prophetess* takes it to mean "make into." Amid such confusion B had every excuse for offering an ambiguous equivalent of the three Greek words, an equivalent which might equally well mean "undoing/destroying me who am a prophetess" or "unmaking me as a prophetess." The doubt about Aeschylus' meaning has continued (see AF, ADP 1275).

1301]   *hack-block*   An aptly brutal-sounding translation of ἐπίξηνον (= a butcher's chopping-block AP 1248 (ADP 1277).

1302]   *She struck*   I.e., she, *prophet me*, having been struck. AP 1249: κοπείσης (= explained in Paley's note as a"genitive absolute, by a common Aeschylean usage." It needed explaining, since no subject of the participle is grammatically specified, except as being feminine).

   with . . . sacrificing   B translates AP 1249, AW 1278: θερμῷ ... φοινίῳ προσφάγματι (= with a warm bloody preliminary-sacrifice).

1303]   *will death be*   AP 1250: τεθνήξομεν (= shall we die, i.e., she and Agamemnon).

1304]   *another*   I.e., Orestes.

1305]   *doomsman*   Judge. AP 1252: ποινάτωρ (= avenger, punisher.

1306]   *an exile*   AP 1253: ἀπόξενος (= a stranger to, far away from).

1307]   *for friends*   AP 1254: φίλοις (= dear ones). Though the word can mean *friends*, its meaning here is clearly "members of his family."

copestone these curses I.e., to put the coping stone on these curses—a powerfully alliterative yet almost literal translation (AP 1254). B imitates the Greek in making a verb from the noun "coping-stone" (θριγκόω from θριγκός), but fails to reproduce the effect of the future participle θριγκώσων (= being about to, in order to). Orestes' murder of his mother is seen as the climax of the series of crimes committed by members of the House of Atreus; B's *curses* translates ἄτας (= *Atēs*). See l. 381n.

1309] *Him shall . . . prostration* B copies the inverted word-order of AP 1256.

prostration used in its original Latin sense of "overthrow" to translate (ὑπτίασμα = supine position, or act of making supine).

fallen AP 1256: κειμένου (= lying i.e., dead). Paley paraphrases "the death of the father shall bring back the son from exile to avenge him" (AP 1255).

1310] *like an indweller* B rejects the emendation adopted by Paley and most subsequent editors: κάτοικτος (= piteous, i.e., piteously; AP 1257), and translates the MS reading retained by Weise: κάτοικος (= inhabitant thus; AW 1286). B's *like* must have been either a forced interpretation of "inhabitant thus," or a silent emendation of the Greek text to read ὥς (= like an inhabitant). Presumably B understood Cassandra to mean: "If I were a local resident, I might bewail the murder of Agamemnon; but as I'm a Trojan, and always knew what would happen to Troy and the Trojans, I accept my own fate, as a small price to pay for Agamemnon's punishment by the gods."

1311] *foresaw* AP 1258: εἶδον (= saw).

1312] *Suffering as it has suffered* More specific than the original. AP 1259: πράξασαν ὡς ἔπραξεν (= faring as it has fared).

and who And those who (i.e., Agamemnon).

took B translates an emendation not adopted in Paley's text, but mentioned in his notes as "very ingenious and probable": εἶλον (= took, captured), rather than the MS reading εἶχον (= used to hold, occupy) retained by Weise (AW 1288), which would refer to the Trojans. Recent editors have made the same decision as B, e.g. AF, ADP, AL 1287).

1313] *are faring* AP 1260: ἀπαλλάσσουσιν (= are getting off, coming off).

1314] *will suffer* AP 1261: πράξω (= I will fare), which Paley convincingly explains as alluding to the previous use of the same verb in AP 1259 (see l. 1312n.); i.e., Cassandra says she will meet the same fate as Troy has met. So B repeats his own verb, *suffer*.

1315] *I call, I speak to* In the original (AP 1262) there is only one verb, προσεννέπω (= I speak to).

1316] *on an opportune blow chancing* Having the luck to be struck a mortal blow. The adjective καίριος means at exactly the right time (i.e., *opportune*) or place, which is the relevant meaning here (AP 1263).

1317-18] *blood . . . outflow* AP 1264-5: αἱμάτων εὐθνησίμων ἀπορρυέντων (= blood having flowed away with easy death).

1318] *close up* An awkward expansion of *close* apparently dictated by B's chosen metre.

1319] *learned* For the same reason, perhaps, Cassandra has become *learned* (two syllables). The natural translation of σοφὴ here (AP 1266) would surely have been "wise," though the same Greek adjective could indeed refer to her acquired skill in prophecy.

1320] *long hast thou outstretched* A literal translation of μακρὰν ἔτεινας (AP 1267), i.e., you have spoken at length.

1321] *comes that* Interpolated for greater clarity.

1322] *god-led* AP 1268: θεηλάτου (= god-driven), but perhaps B wished to avoid the idea of compulsion suggested by "driven," since Paley had explained: "A favourable omen, or the contrary, was derived from the manner in which the victim approached the altar."

treadest B carefully preserves the primary sense of the verb πατέω (= bringing the foot down on to the ground), possibly to suggest Cassandra's firm, deliberate gait—though Paley's note (AP 1268) took the verb as a mere synonym for στείχω (= walk, go, come).

1323] *no! Some time more* Here the reading of the Greek MSS is unintelligible: οὔ ... χρόνῳ πλέω (= not/no . . . time [dative singular] more [accusative singular/nominative/ accusative neuter plural]). Fraenkel comments (1950): "A satisfactory explanation or restoration has so far not been put forward . . . . I do not know what to do with the passage except to recognize a corruption" (AF 1299). B seems to ignore the emendations adopted by Weise and Paley (AW 1299, AP 1270), and make his own guess at the meaning, presumably implying: "There's no way of escaping death, but there is just a little time left before it comes."

1324] *He last* He who is last. AP 1271: ὁ δ' ὕστατος (= but the last). In the MS the word printed as *He* might possibly (by comparison with the writing of *There's* in the previous line) be deciphered as a hurriedly scribbled *The*.

anyhow Perhaps not the most appropriate translation of γε, which normally just emphasizes the word immediately before it, here ὕστατος (= last).

is . . . advantaged   I.e., has the advantage of the extra time. B seems to be extracting his own sense from AP 1271: τοῦ χρόνου πρεσβεύεται (= has the advantage of time), while ignoring the interpretation supported in Paley's note: "Yes, but he who comes last is first in point of time." Recent editors have rejected this paradoxical race-image in favor of an interpretation which takes ὁ ὕστατος τοῦ χρόνου together, to mean "the last of the time," i.e., "Yes, but the last of one's time is valued most" (AF 1300), or "but it is just the last remnant of one's time (such as you now have) that is held most precious" (ADP 1299-1300). The uncertainty about the line's meaning results partly from the many possible senses of πρεσβεύεται (= is given the rights of seniority, so, is chiefly honored, so, has the advantage, has the best of it).

1325]   *It comes, the day*   AP 1272: ἥκει τόδ᾽ ἦμαρ (= this day has come). Though present in form, ἥκει comes from a verb which is perfect in sense (= it has come, is already here).

1326]   *know*   AP 1273: ἴσθι (= 2ⁿᵈ person singular imperative; a common Greek idiom meaning "you may be assured that" or "let me tell you that." Here it almost implies "you can have the satisfaction of knowing that you're a very brave woman."

patient   Not the most appropriate translation of τλήμων (= enduring), which in this context seems to imply something more active and positive, like "steadfast" or "stout-hearted" (Liddell and Scott, 1871). But B was doubtless influenced by the paraphrase in Paley's note: "Well, you are at least a patient sufferer of courageous heart" (AP 1274-75).

1327]   *Such . . . happy-fortuned*   A sadly realistic comment: "you have to be pretty miserable to get compliments like that!"

1328]   *gloriously*   Rather too strong for εὐκλεῶς (= with a good fame or reputation; AP 1275), especially as Cassandra "is to be cut down like a cow at the altar" (ADP 1304; l. 1322).

for man   Not a sexist remark: the original noun is not ἀνδρί (= a male) but βροτῷ (= a mortal; AP 1275).

grace   One of the many meanings of the original noun, χάρις (= grace, favor, sense of favor received, gratitude, gratification). Here (AP 1275) it may perhaps mean, "something to be thankful for, some satisfaction, something on the plus side."

1329]   *Ah, sire . . . children*   The idea of a noble death makes her think of her brothers who died fighting for Troy.

1330]   *turns thee backwards*   Cassandra has suddenly stopped walking towards the palace, and shied away from it.

1332] *if 'tis no spirit's loathing* Unless it's some spiritual revulsion? AP 1279: φρενῶν στύγος (= hatred of mind).

1333, 1337] *household* Apparently used by B for "house" (AP 1280: δόμοι, 1284: δόμοισι) simply to suit his metre.

1334] *How else* AP 1281: καί πῶς (= and how?), which is generally taken, as by Paley in his note, to mean "Surely not!" (cf. Fraenkel's "Nay, nay" (AF 1310). But B takes it in the common elliptical sense of πῶς γάρ οὔ (= for how not?), i.e., how could it fail to be so, How can you ask?, or What do you expect? Since φόνον can mean "slaughter" just as well as "murder," he may well be right, and the literal-minded Chorus-leader replies to her horrified intuition: "Yes, of course you can smell blood—they've just been slaughtering an animal for sacrifice."

1335] *steam* AP 1282: ἀτμός (= steam, vapor, though often used of smells); but B seems to go for the English word that in the steam age will sound most incongruous.

is proper AP 1282: πρέπει (= suits, fits i.e., the sort of smell that you would expect to come from a tomb). But again B seems to enjoy evoking the irrelevant connotations of an important Victorian concept, propriety.

1336] *No Surian . . . of* I.e., what you say hardly suggests that the house is perfumed with Syrian incense—an ironical understatement typical of tragic chorus-leaders. However, a scholiast quoted by Fraenkel (AF 1312; 3.609) sees no irony here: "What you describe, he means, is no incense, but now [i.e., in fact] the house is full of incense." The word translated *honour* is ἀγλάισμα (= ornament, decoration; AP 1283). B's capitalization of *House* was presumably meant to indicate the House of Atreus, though there is no such special significance in the original word, δώμασιν (= houses, i.e., house, palace).

1337] *even in* AP 1284: κἄν (= καὶ ἐν = also in), i.e., she will bewail her fate and Agamemnon's inside the house as well as outside it.

1338] *Life suffice me* AP 1285: ἀρκείτω βίος (= let life suffice), i.e., let me be satisfied with this much life.

1339] *Ah, strangers* "A cry of appeal to the bystanders to bear witness . . . to her ill-treatment" (ADP 1315). Under the Attic legal system, "Only if the . . . cry of distress has been raised, can evidence of the deed of violence be later laid before a court of law" (AF 1317; 3.614). The word translated *strangers* is ξένοι (also = foreigners, guests, hosts). See l. 1344n.

1340] *I cry not "ah"* Paley's note (AP 1287) compared the formation of δυσοίζω with that of φεύξειν (= cry φεῦ = alas!), so B assumed that δυσοίζω meant to cry οἴ, an exclamation of grief like *ah* in English (although Cassandra has not recently used that exclamation). But Paley may have been wrong (see ADP 1316), and Liddell and Scott, 1996 glosses the verb here "fear, tremble at."

1341]   *Idly*   B translates the emendation adopted by Paley, ἄλλως (= without reason; AP 1288).

to me, the dead   I.e., who will by then be dead. AP 1288: θανούση...μοι (= to me, having died).

1342]   *a woman*   I.e., Clytaemnestra.

1343]   *a man ill-wived*   I.e., Agamemnon.

a man   I.e., Aegisthus.

perish   AP 1290: πέση (= fall).

1344]   *This hospitality I ask*   AP 1291: ἐπιξενοῦμαι ταῦτα (?= I claim these things as a stranger). The meaning of the verb is uncertain (see AF 1320), but B follows Paley's note: "The proper meaning must have been 'to get another to stand to you in the relation of ξένος, or host,' and thence to appeal to him as a witness in your favor. For in the heroic ages, the relation of a host to a guest . . . was more than a mere matter of friendship,—it involved religious and legal obligations of the highest kind, which were especially binding when claimed as a last request" (AP 1291).

as dying   AP 1291: ὡς θανουμένη (= as being about to die), but B ignores the significant future tense of the participle.

1345]   *sufferer*   AP 1292: τλῆμον (= suffering, unhappy). B produces a needlessly odd effect by turning the adjective (O suffering one!) into a noun.

thee . . . pity   The incoherence is not in the Greek. AP 1292: οἰκτείρω σε θεσφάτου μόρου (= I pity you for your foretold fate).

1346]   *I fain am*   AP 1293: θέλω (= I wish), but such a natural translation would not have fitted B's metre.

1347]   *No dirge*   B translates the emendation adopted by Paley for "the tame and unmeaning ῥῆσιν ἢ θρῆνον᾽ (= speech or dirge; AP 1293)."

1348-49]   *to my own . . . too*   "The words are incurably corrupt" (ADP 1324-25). B seems to be translating a suggested emendation mentioned in Paley's note: τίνειν φόνον (= to pay for the murder (AP 1294).

1350]   *slave*   AP 1297: δούλης (= slave-girl), i.e., Cassandra.

easy-managed hand's work   A literal translation of εὐμαροῦς χειρώματος (AP 1298), i.e., an easy murder to commit, or perhaps an easy victim to overcome (ADP 1326); though the adjective was too loosely paraphrased by Paley: "unheeded," "a matter of indifference" (AP 1297).

1352]   *Why*   Interpolated   (AP 1299).

any shade would turn them B ignores Paley's emended text and interpretation ("one may liken them to a sketch"; AP 1299) and translates the MS reading: σκιά τις ἂν τρέψειεν (AW 1328), presumably giving the verb its the common meaning of "change, alter" (AF 1328).

1353] *By throws . . . picture* An almost word for word reproduction of Βολαῖς ὑγρώσσων σπόγγος ὤλεσεν γραφὴν (AP 1300), where the word for *throws* is used in the sense of "strokes," and the verb is in the gnomic aorist, i.e., a past tense implying a present general truth. But B's exclamation mark was possible meant to explain the past tense differently: as something that has already happened before one is aware of it.

1354] *And more . . . pity* AP 1301, AW 1330: καὶ ταῦτ᾽ ἐκείνων μᾶλλον οἰκτείρω πολύ (= and I pity these things [i.e., the latter] much more than those things [i.e., the former]). B leaves out the second half of the comparison, and interpolates *in mortals,* possibly for the alliteration. What exactly Aeschylus meant by the "latter" and the "former" remains very uncertain. See AF 1328-30; 3.620-22.

1359] *aroints* "Drives off with an execration" (*OED*); a word of unknown origin, used by Shakespeare as an imperative exclamation meaning "Avaunt! Begone!" (*Macbeth* 1.3.6), and by EBB as a transitive verb: "Whiskered cats arointed flee" (*To Flush,* l. 18). That was perhaps why B used the word here.

1360] *whereat a finger points* AP 1303: δακτυλοδείκτων, "i.e., already enviable enough" (ADP 1331-42).

1362] *Priamos* See l. 39n.

celestials AP 1306: μάκαρες (= happy, blessed ones, i.e., immortal gods).

1364] *the former* AP 1309: προτέρων, which Paley explains: "And if for those who are already dead (viz. Iphigenia and the children of Thyestes) he himself by dying ordains the retribution of yet another death . . ." (AP 1311).

1365-66] *for those . . . Dying* The original word-play is simpler: τοῖσι θανοῦσι θανὼν (= dying for those who had died; AP 1310).

1367] *would not pray* There is no *not* in the MSS, but B translates the οὐκ (= not) in an emendation mentioned in Paley's note as necessary to those who take εὔξαιτο (= would pray or would boast) in the former sense (AP 1312).

1368-69] *unmischievous / Daimon* AP 1312-13: ἀσινεῖ δαίμονι (= unharmful genius or guardian spirit, i.e., destiny).

who would not Not repeated in the Greek.

hearing thus AP 1313: τάδ᾽ ἀκούων (= hearing these things).

1370] *Ah me* Agamemnon yells offstage from inside the palace.

within me   AP 1314: ἔσω (= within, inside). Paley's (unintentionally comic?) note points out that the adverb should strictly imply motion (= *into* inside), but that in this context "it is not difficult to see that motion is in some way involved in the act." Fraenkel defends the use of the word here against a charge of being feeble and superfluous: "the Tragedians inserted ἔσω where they wanted to emphasize that a wound went deep and penetrated the vitals" (AF 1343).

1371]   *a wounded one*   Someone wounded; AP 1315: οὐτασμένος (= having been wounded), a participle attached to τίς (= who?).

1372]   *struck by*   I.e., struck by a second stroke. B's English is more incoherent than the Greek: δευτέραν πεπληγμένος (= struck a second i.e., stroke), with the noun of the verb, πληγὴν (= stroke) easily understood from its use two lines before (AP 1316, 1314).

1373]   *This work*   AP 1317: τοὔργον (= the work).

   by   To judge by.

1374]   *But we . . . share*   B tries to make sense of the MS reading κοινωσώμεθ' ἄν πως, rejecting the emendation adopted by Paley (κοινωσώμεθ' ἄν [i.e., ἃ ἂν] πως), which would with some difficulty have given the sense: "Let us impart to each other whatever safe counsels may chance to occur to us" (AP 1318). Recent editors have adopted a different emendation (ἤν πως = let us discuss with one another if somehow there is some safe plan, or our plans are safe; AF, ADP, AL 1347).

   solid   AP: ἀσφαλῆ (= firm, fast, safe); but perhaps B wanted to stress the derivation (= not liable to fall or cause to fall).

1375]   *I, in the first place*   The chorus set up a committee to discuss the situation—an episode made slightly less farcical by the initial emphasis on their age and decrepitude (ll. 73-84; AL 72-82).

   opinion   AP 1319: γνώμην, a word also used for a "motion" or "proposal" in a formal debate.

1376]   *help-cry*   AP 1320: βοήν (= cry), but Paley's note explains that the word is used for βοήθειαν (= running-to-a-cry, i.e., help).

   to house here   the actual words of the proposed shout (πρὸς δῶμα δεῦρο).

1377]   *to fall upon them*   There is no *them* in the Greek; and though ἐμπεσεῖν could well mean "fall upon, attack" in a different context, here (AP 1321) it probably means "break in" to the palace.

1380]   *the main point*   B seizes on the physical meaning of ἀκμή (= sharp edge, point) to employ a familiar English metaphor; but the Greek word is evidently used here (AP 1324) in its common sense of "the fitting time, high time to do something": τὸ μὴ μέλλειν δ' ἀκμή (= and it's high time not to delay, i.e., this is no moment to hesitate).

1381-82]   *they prelude . . . city*   I.e., this looks like the prelude to the establishment of a tyranny.

1383]   *For we waste time*   An elliptical use of γάρ (= for) implying: "yes, and they'll probably get away with it, since we're doing nothing to stop them." See l. 1277n.

1383-84]   *this waiting's . . . ground*   Spurning such dignified delay as ours. But there is no *this* in the Greek, and both the text and its meaning are disputed.

1384]   *allow the hand no slumber*   AP 1328: οὐ καθεύδουσιν χερί (= do not sleep with the hand, i.e., are ceaselessly active).

1385]   *some plan*   AP 1329, AW 1358: βουλῆς ἧς τινος (= what plan). B seems to have overlooked the second word, which when followed by the third (τινος = some, any) indicates an indirect question: "I know not chancing on what plan I should speak," i.e., I don't know what plan to suggest.

1386]   *'Tis . . . also*   I.e., There's no point in being a back-seat driver.

1387]   *I'm schemeless*   A good equivalent for δυσμηχανῶ (= I can't think of any μηχανή (= scheme) for doing something; AP 1331).

1388]   *a dead man*   AP 1332: τὸν θανόντα (= the man who has died), i.e., Agamemnon.

1389]   *protracting*   B translates τείνοντες (= stretching out), an emendation adopted by Paley for the MS reading κτείνοντες (= killing). This speaker awkwardly exposes what the others are trying to hide—that they're *afraid* to do anything.

1390]   *these rulers*   But the meaning is probably, as Paley's note suggests, "give way to these disgracers *as* our rulers" (AP 1334).

1392]   *the riper finish*   AP 1336: πεπαιτέρα ... μοῖρα (= the riper, i.e., softer, *milder* fate). Was B also thinking of *King Lear* (5.2.9-11)? "Men must endure / Their going hence even as their coming hither, / Ripeness is all."

1393]   *by . . . of him*   On the evidence of his two cries (ll. 1370, 1372).

1395]   *these things concerning*   B imitates the placing of the preposition after its noun at the end of the line (πέρι = about, so accented instead of the usual περί; AP 1339).

1397]   *This same . . . abound in*   A word-for-word translation (apart from the interpolated *same*) of AP 1341: ταύτην ἐπαινεῖν πάντοθεν πληθύνομαι. The words have been variously understood, but Paley translates the verb as a technical term in voting: "I am in a majority," and explains: "The Coryphaeus [= chorus-leader] speaks last, and in a manner sums up the votes, which are 'to know for certain that Atrides is, as he is, i.e., alive or dead, and not to go on guessing' . . . . There can be no doubt that πάντοθεν [= from all sides] means 'the votes from all sides having been taken' "(AP 1339).

this I.e., the last speaker's opinion.

1398] *what he's doing* An amusing mistranslation of AP 1342: κυροῦνθ᾽ ὅπως (= more like "how he's doing"; literally "happening to be how").

1398-99] *KLUTAIMNESTRA* Clytaemnestra appears, standing over the dead bodies of Agamemnon and Cassandra.

1399-1400] *Much having . . . shamed be* B retains almost exactly the original word-order (AP 1343-3).

to suit the purpose καιρίως (= to suit the καιρός or right moment).

spoken I.e., by me.

1401] *how* How else, i.e., without a little lying.

1401-2] *in semblance, / Friends* AP 1345-46: φίλοις δοκοῦσιν εἶναι (= seeming, i.e., pretending to be friends).

1402] *proposing* Used in sense of Latin *proponens* (= purposing, designing), to translate πορσύνων (= preparing; AP 1345).

1402-3] *sorrow's . . . outleaping* Raise the enclosing net of sorrow to a height too great to overleap. The translation is fairly literal, though the *frame* seems to have been added to suit B's metre.

1405] *an old victory* Paley explains: "i.e., of the time when Agamemnon carried his point in slaying Iphigenia. Thus νίκη παλαιὰ [= old victory] is distinguished from the recent victory over Troy" (AP 1348). Recent editors emend νίκης (= victory) to νείκης(= quarrel, feud; see AF, ADP, AL 1378).

with time, I grant you AP 1349: σὺν χρόνῳ γε μήν, glossed by Paley: "'yet after a long time,' i.e., though long thought of, it has not been executed till late."

1408] *As that . . . ward off* AP 1352: ὡς μήτε φεύγειν μήτ᾽ ἀμύνασθαι μόρον (= so that he could neither escape nor ward off his fate).

1409] *wrap-round* B tries to reproduce the compound ἀμφίβλη–στρον (= throw-around; AP 1353). But it had been used as early as Hesiod (*Shield of Heracles*, 215) to mean a fisherman's casting-net.

with no outlet ἄπειρον (= endless), but B seems to follow Paley's note: "giving no exit to the head and hands."

1410] *the rich woe* AP 1354: πλοῦτον ... κακόν (= the evil wealth).

1412] *there! And* B's dash, italics, and exclamation-mark add an extra dimension of sadistic triumph to the simple meaning of αὐτοῦ (= at the very place, on the spot; AP 1356).

1414] *Zeus* B translates Διὸς, an emendation of the MS reading Ἅιδου (= of Hades), adopted by Paley and most subsequent editors. This allows Clytaemnestra her little joke. See next note.

guardian of the dead νεκρῶν σωτῆρος (= savior of corpses). The third libation was normally made to Zeus Soter (Σωτήρ = savior, preserver, who might reasonably be expected to keep people *alive*.

favour I.e., offering (AP 1358: χάριν. See l. 374n.

1415] *of him* B carefully retains the reflexive pronoun αὑτοῦ (= of himself, i.e., his own; AP 1359).

rages AP 1359: ὁρμαίνει, the MS reading, which Paley explains to mean: "his soul, as it were in suspense between life and death, is indignant at the treacherous deed." More to modern taste, of course, is the emendation ὀρυγάνει (= "he belches out his life"; AF 1388).

1416] *a brisk blood-spatter* B's robust rendering of Aeschylus' surprising ὀξεῖαν αἵματος σφαγὴν (= a sharp slaughter of blood; AP 1360; see ADP 1387).

1417] *drop of slaughterous dew* AP 1361: ψακάδι φοινίας δρόσου (= drop/shower of bloody dew).

1418] *god-given* AP 1362: διοσδότῳ (= Zeus-sent; Zeus was the god of the weather). B accepts this emendation adopted by Paley.

dewy-comfort B's resourceful translation of the hardly-translatable word γάνει (= brightness, joy) applied to water and wine "from their quickening and refreshing qualities" (Liddell and Scott, 1996), so here meaning "rain."

1419] *The sown-stuff* This must be the seed itself, though the original word, σπορητὸς (= sown) is, as Paley's note explains, an adjective implying some noun like "field" or "earth" that is sown with seed.

at I.e., than the *sown-stuff* rejoices.

in its birth-throes from the calyx AP 1363-64: κάλυκος ἐν λοχεύμασιν (= in the childbirth of the calyx).

1420] *Argives, my revered here* AP 1364: πρέσβος Ἀργείων τόδε (= this revered-object of Argives), i.e., since the noun is connected with old age, revered Argive elders, a courtesy-title sarcastically intended.

1421] *Ye may . . . rejoice* I.e., rejoice or not as you please.

1423] *right over and above, too* Not right over and above the corpse, as one might think. B is translating ὑπερδίκως μὲν οὖν (= or rather, hyper-rightly).

1424-25] *The cup . . . drinks of* AP 1368-69: τοσῶνδε κρατῆρ' ἐν δόμοις κακῶν ὅδε πλήσας ἀραίων αὐτὸς ἐκπίνει μολών. B seems to follow Paley's translation: "A bowl of so many evils in the house has this man filled with curses, and now drains it himself on his return." But the interpretation of the passage has been endlessly debated (see especially AF 1395f.; 3.657).

1427] *Is she . . . boasts* She who delivers such a boasting speech. In the original the criticism is more direct: "are you who boast" (AP 1371).

1428] *Ye test me* I.e., you are trying it on with me, seeing how far you can go.

1429] *to you knowers* AP 1373: πρὸς εἰδότας (= to [you] knowing, i.e., I'm telling you what you already know.

1432] *the right hand here* AP 1376: τῆσδε δεξιᾶς χερὸς (= of this right hand); but B's deictic interpretation of the demonstrative adjective (i.e., as implying a pointing gesture) is entirely in line with the conventions of Greek stage-diction.

1433] *Ay* Interpolated.

1434] *What . . . drink* The Chorus-leader suggests that she must have been sent mad by some poison. B continues his system of translating lyric metres (as opposed to iambics) into irregular rhymed verse.

1437] *set on thee* AP 1381: ἐπέθου (= set or take on yourself, undertake).

1438] *This sacrifice* AP 1381: τόδε ... θύος, which Paley translates as "this incense," i.e., she had placed "the incense of the people's wrath on her devoted head." More plausibly, the word has been taken as a euphemism for the murder (ADP 1409-10).

1439-40] *And popular . . . thy head* Expanded from δημοθρόους τ' ἀράς (= and people-shouted curses). B rejects Paley's punctuation in favor of Weise's (AW 1409).

1442] *The man from the city* Interpolated to bring out the original word-play: two compound verbs with the prefix ἄπο (= off, away) followed by an adjective with the same prefix, ἀπόπολις (= off from the city). B follows Paley and Weise in accepting that word as an emendation (for reasons of metre as well as meaning) of the MS reading, ἄπολις (= cityless, stateless).

1445] *A hate immense* I.e., an object of hate, an alternative meaning of the abstract noun μῖσος (= hatred). The rhyme-word (for *citizens*) only roughly translates ὄβριμον (= strong, mighty; AP 1411). Had B lined it up as a possible rhyme for Paley's translation of θύος—"incense"?

1448] *Nothing of this* B translates the MS reading, οὐδὲν τόδ' (= nothing this; AW 1414), though Paley adopted the emendation οὐδὲν τοτ' (= nothing then, i.e., when Agamemnon sacrificed Iphigenia), which makes a significant antithesis against the preceding νῦν μὲν (= now on the one hand); cf. AF, ADP, AL 1414. Presumably B's version was intended to mean: "You brought no such charges"; but the sense is probably "you did nothing to oppose him."

the man here AP: ἀνδρί τῳδε (= this man); see l. 1432n.

1449] *no more awe-checked* An explanation rather than a translation of οὐ προτιμῶν (= not honoring-before), i.e., paying more attention to, thinking more of it; AP 1388).

1450] *graze-flocks* The literal meaning of νομεύμασιν is "things put out to graze" (AP 1389).

1451] *his* The italics have a slightly confusing effect, as if Clytaemnestra were denying that it was her child too; but they were simply meant to translate the reflexive pronoun αὑτοῦ (= of himself, i.e., his own; AP 1390).

fruit of travail Again, an explanation rather than a translation of ὠδῖν᾽ (= travail, labor, child-birth; AP 1391).

1452] *song-spell* B's hyphenated coinage brings out both the primary and secondary meanings of the single word ἐπῳδὸν (AP 1391)

Threkian B imitates the Ionic spelling of "Thracian" used here by Aeschylus (Θρηκίων for Θρᾳκίων; AP 1391).

blowings The literal meaning of ἀημάτων, i.e., winds (AP 1391).

1453] *Not him . . . banish* Shouldn't you have banished *him?*

1454] *Pollution's penalty* As a punishment for that polluting crime of his.

hearing The original word, ἐπήκοος (AP 1403) may have been used in a "semi-judicial" sense of hearing a case in court, or "taking cognizance" (AF 1420).

1455] *Justicer* Dispenser of justice, judge; an archaic word probably chosen because the original word, δικαστὴς (= judge; AP 1404) is similarly derived from a noun that means "justice" (δίκη).

1455-59] *Now, this . . . be modest* B seems to follow the interpretation in Paley's note: "But I tell you to threaten me thus, with the understanding that I am prepared on the same terms to submit to *your* rule, if you should have conquered me by force (as I claim your obedience if the victory should be mine)"; "Conquer before you presume to use threats" (AP 1394).

1459] *certes* Certainly. AP 1398: γοῦν (= at least, at any rate).

taught . . . be modest I.e., taught discretion.

1460-61] *Greatly-intending . . . cried* Could B have been trying to imitate, however distantly, the rhythm of these first words (μεγαλόμητις εἶ, περίφρονα δ᾽ ἔλακες)? An English reader who had learned to scan Greek quantitative verse, but had not unlearned English habits of accentuation might well read the two phrases aloud in the rhythm: tum-ti-ti-tum-ti-tum, tum-ti-ti-tum-ti-ti-tum, although the first, fourth and fifth of these tums were actually short syllables, not long ones.

Greatly-intending AP 1399: μεγαλόμητις (= with great schemes or plans, ambitious.

Much-mindful AP 1400: περίφρονα (= very thoughtful or proud, haughty, overweening things); here the latter sense is suggested in Paley's note, and assumed by later editors (e.g . AW, ADP, AL 1426).

1462-65] *(Since . . . a pride* B seems not to be following any particular version of the much-disputed text, but simply versifying Paley's account of the general sense: "You have proudly boasted, as indeed your mind is maddened by a sense of your condition as a murderess, that a blood-spot yet unavenged is conspicuous on your brow" (AP 1400).

with its slaughter-outpouring part   AP 1400-1401: φονολιβεῖ τύχᾳ (= at a blood-dripping chance).

a patch . . . to match   Possibly suggested by Paley's note that the λίπος ἐπ᾽ ὀμμάτων αἵματος (= grease of blood on the eyes; AP 1402) alludes to the "drop of bloody dew" that splashed on to Clytaemnestra during the murder (AP 1361; l. 1417). However, the allusion may be to her bloodshot eyes, rather than her bloodstained brow (ADP 1426). Cf. *Aeschylus: Oresteia,* H. Lloyd-Jones, tr. (London, 1979) 1427: "Bloodshot eyes were thought to be a symptom of madness. The idea that Clytaemnestra's eyes were actually stained with blood is wholly foreign to the conventions of Greek tragedy, which disdained this kind of realism."

for a pride   Perhaps an abbreviation of "for you to be proud of," though no Greek text seems to contain any basis for it. Presumably it was dictated by the rhyme, combined with the wording of Paley's note ("you have proudly boasted"; AP 1400).

1467]   *blow with blow to expiate*   Paley translated it "to repay blow" (AEP 171).

1468]   *And this . . . warrant*   AP 1406: καὶ τήνδ᾽ ἀκούεις ὁρκίων ἐμῶν θέμιν (= and thou hearest also this *themis* of my oaths). But the precise meaning here of θέμις (= established or divine law or right) is disputed (see ADP 1431). B's *just warrant* seems to be based on Paley's note (AP 1406): "a periphrasis . . . giving the notion of a divine sanction to the oath on the part of the powers invoked."

1469]   *By who . . . Justice*   AP 1407: "By the fulfilling Justice of my daughter," explained by Paley: "the accomplished or satisfied vengeance for Iphigenia."

1470]   *Ate, Erinus*   See ll. 381n., 57n.

by whose help   AP 1408: αἶσι (= to, for, or by whom).

1471]   *Not mine . . . palace*   I do not imagine that Fear will ever haunt my palace. B's reliance on dashes for punctuation has increased the obscurity of a sentence already capable of several interpretations: οὔ μοι φόβου μέλαθρον ἐλπὶς ἐμπατεῖ (= for me expectation of fear does no tread in palace). B translates the MS reading for the last word, mentioned in Paley's note (AP 1409), but emended in his text). For recent interpretations see AF, ADP 1434. The general sense, though, is clear: threatened by the Chorus with punishment, Clytaemnestra replies that she is not afraid of anything, so long as Aegisthus is around the house to protect her.

1472-73] *there burns a fire,* / *Aigisthos* I.e., Aigisthos burns/kindles a fire. AP 1410-11: αἴθη πῦρ ... Αἴγισθος, ὡς τὸ πρόσθεν εὖ φρονῶν (= Aegisthus kindles a fire, well-disposed to me as before. B retains the inverted word-order of the original.

1474] *Since . . . boldness* An almost word-for-word replica of AP 1412, except that *Since he to me* should be "For he to us" (regal plural for singular).

1475] *he* Agamemnon.

this female γυναικὸς τῆσδε (= this woman/wife); but B strangely suppresses the most relevant second meaning.

1476] *Dainty* AP 1414: μείλιγμα (= a thing to soothe or gladden), usually translated here as "darling," though the emphasis may be more on his womanizing than his sex-appeal (see AF, ADP 1439). But what possessed B to call Agamemnon a *Dainty?* Was it the thought that μείλιγμα comes from something edible, μέλι (= honey)—or a subconscious association with other "soothing things" in Keats (*Isabella,* 374): "Those dainties made to still an infant's cries"?

all the Chruseids under Ilion I.e., all the slave-girls attached to the army before Troy. Chryseis (stem Chryseid-) was a prisoner of war allotted to Agamemnon in the *Iliad.* He strongly objected to her being returned to her father, the priest of Apollo, in order to stop the plague, and publicly declared: "I very much want to keep her in my home, for I prefer her to Clytaemnestra, my wedded wife, since she's not at all inferior to her, physically or mentally or in technical skills" (1.112-115). When he agreed to let Chryseis go, he took off Achilles' slave-girl Briseis, as a replacement.

1477] *she* Cassandra.

1479-80] *the sailors'... common* B translates Weise's text, which accepts the emendation ἰσοτρίβης (= equal-rubbing) for the MS reading ἱστοτρίβης (= mast-rubbing); but retains, unlike Paley, the MS reading ναυτίλων σελμάτων (= sailors' benches; AW 1442-43, AP 1417-18). The general meaning of what Paley calls a "somewhat coarse expression" is clear enough, but not the nature of the equality (ἰσο-): did she rub the benches equally with the sailors, or, as B seems to take it, with Agamemnon? See AF 1442f., ADP 1443.

unpunished A definition of ἄτιμα given in Liddell and Scott, 1871; but here it probably means "undeservedly," i.e., they have met their deserts (AF, ADP, AL 1443).

1481] *is—thus* AP 1419 has simply οὕτως (= thus); and though the verb "to be" can always be understood in a verbless Greek sentence, this adverb seems to qualify the verb κεῖται (= lies), understood from a few lines later (AP 1421; l. 1483), i.e., he lies thus, and she lies.

swan-fashion "This is the earliest allusion to the belief that swans sing before they are to die" (ALG 1444). For B the latest would probably have been Tennyson's "The Dying Swan" (1830).

1482] *dying wailing* Not two participles but a participle and a verbal noun, if B is being true to his transcript-principles. AP 1420: τὸν ὕστατον μέλψασα θανάσιμον γόον (= having sung its last deathly lament).

1483] *to him, a sweetheart* AP 1421: φιλήτωρ τῷδε (= lover to this man). But B's *sweetheart* follows naturally from Paley's note that φιλήτωρ "is not a substantive from φιλεῖν [= to love], but an adjective compounded of φίλος [= dear] and ἦτωρ [= heart]"—a derivation which Fraenkel calls "nonsense" (AF 1446; cf. ADP 446).

me she brought to To me she brought. B imitates the compound verb ἐπήγαγεν (= brought-to).

1484] *by-nicety* Extra-delicacy. AP 1422: παροψώνημα (= a side-dainty, i.e., an addition to the regular diet).

the whet of dalliance I.e., something to stimulate sexual appetite. The whole line reads: εὐνῆς παροψώνημα τῆς ἐμῆς χλιδῆς (= a side-dainty of the luxury/voluptuousness of my bed; AP 1422, AW 1447). Paley paraphrases the antithesis: "dear to him in death, while to me she has brought a new relish to the enjoyment of my union (with Aegisthus)." Fraenkel thinks such kinkiness out of character for Clytaemnestra ("Even in her taunts . . . she remains a queen"); and therefore assumes some textual corruption. Lloyd-Jones comments: "This seems to be an insufficient reason for refusing to accept the meaning that the words appear to bear" (ALG 1446). B evidently thought the same.

1485-86] *Alas . . . come* A "transcriber" ought surely to have shown that this wish was actually expressed as a question: φεῦ, τίς ἄν ... μόλοι ... μοῖρα (= Alas, what fate might come); but B simply follows Paley's note (AP 1423-30): "Would that some death would come . . . ."

1487] *in quickness* A literal translation of ἐν τάχει (i.e., quickly), happily rhyming with *sickness*, which has no closer equivalent in the Greek than μὴ περιώδυνος (= not very painful; an adjective attached to μοῖρα (= fate, death).

1488, 1489] *Neither . . . Neither* Not in the Greek, which has only "not very painful and not (μηδέ) confining-to-bed" (δεμνιοτήρης).

1490] *And bear* Grammatically parallel to *come*, i.e., would come . . . and bear. Aeschylus' syntax is clearer: "fate might come, bearing" (φέρουσα; present participle).

sleeping A verbal noun (to suit B's rhyme and rhythm) to translate the simple noun ὕπνον (= sleep).

1492]   *keeper*   I.e., protector (with punning assonance to link it with *bed-keeping?*). AP 1426: φύλακος (= guard, guardian).

   kindest of mood   A rhyme-word almost justified by etymology, since εὐμενεστάτου (AP 1427) is the superlative of εὐμενής (= with a good μένος = spirit, temper, disposition, i.e., well-disposed, kind).

1493]   *much strife*   I.e., the Trojan War, for the sake of Helen; but the Greek text has only πολλά (= many things; AP 1428).

1494]   *By . . . life*   AP 1429: πρὸς γυναικὸς δ' ἀπέφθισεν βίον (= and at the hands of a woman he made life waste away)—a strange verb to describe such a violent death, but at least it gives B a chance to alliterate.

1496]   *Law-breaking*   B rejects the emendation παράνους (= out of her mind, mad) adopted by Paley and modern editors, and translates παράνομος, which was apparently his own emendation (regardless of metre) of the MS reading παρανόμους (AP, AF, ADP, AL 1455).

1498-1503]   *and now . . . of a spouse*   Paley comments: "The text here is so corrupt, that it seems quite a vain attempt to explain or restore it" (AP 1434); but he offers a possible paraphrase, which B seems to adapt: "Now you (Helen) have caused to blossom a bloody murder accomplished, indelible; for there already (i.e., before) existed in the house a heavy woe in store for a husband."

1500-1501]   *red . . . disperse*   AP 1435: δι' αἶμ' ἄνιπτον (= because of unwashable-out blood).

1502]   *the House*   See l. 1336n.

1503]   *all-subduing*   B slightly strengthens one of the two meanings suggested for ἐρίδματος (strongly built, strongly subduing; AP 1437; cf. ADP 1458-61).

   woe of a spouse   AP 1437: ἀνδρὸς οἰζύς (= woe of a man/husband). The choice of a common-gender noun was possibly made not just for the rhyme, but to allow of two interpretations: "woe in store for a husband," as Paley took it, or woe of a wife for her sacrificed daughter, which motivated Clytaemnestra.

1510]   *Danaoi*   See l. 65n.

1511]   *immense*   AP 1443: ἀξύστατον translated by Paley, "beyond compare," but other interpretations include "irresistible," "incurable," and "a wound that does not close up" (see AF 1467, 3.693; ADP 1467).

   annoy   used in the Spenserian sense of "grief, pain" to translate ἄλγος (= pain, grief).

1512]   *Daimon*   See ll. 1368-69n.

1513]   *this household*   AP 1444: δώμασι (= [the] houses, i.e., the house). See l. 1333, 1337n.

double-raced AP 1444: διφυίοισι (= of two natures, races, or families; though here, according to Liddell and Scott, 1996, it is a mere synonym for "two."

1514] *Tantalidai* Sons of Tantalus. A scholiast takes this to refer to "Atreus and Thyestes, or Agamemnon and Menelaus" (*Scholia* 373), but the last two seem more relevant to the context (ADP 1468f.). After Tantalus' son, Pelops, the line divided into two families, going down through Atreus to Agamemnon, and through Thyestes to Aegisthus.

Tantalidai is B's transliteration of Ταντάλιδαι, (sons, descendants of Tantalus), nominative of the dative used in AP 1444).

1514-15] *a rule . . . now* You now rule me with a rule that is like-minded with that of the displaced rulers. AP 1446-47: κράτος τ' ἰσόψυχον ἐκ γυναικῶν καρδιόδηκτον ἐμοὶ κρατύνεις (= and you rule over-me a rule equal-in-spirit from women heart-biting). Fraenkel leaves a gap in his translation, with the note: "I cannot understand this passage"(AF 1470-71; but see 3.695). B appears to follow Paley's explanatory note (AP 1447): "The chorus merely means that the . . . usurped female authority over them is intolerable to bear. The legitimate power of Agamemnon and Menelaus has been allowed to fall into the hands of their wives, who themselves exercise . . . a like-minded (i.e., equally imperious) authority; but as they are influenced by the demon of the house, he is said to hold sway in and through the women."

1519] *Something* There is no such word in the Greek; but B may be having a private joke. As a dramatist he uses the capitalized word to give an eerie feeling of an invisible presence, to suit Paley's note: "The Chorus fancies the demon is actually there in the form of a crow or raven uttering its dismal strain" (AP 1448). As a baffled translator B may also mean that there is a word missing in the Greek text, and that the subject of the verb ἐπεύχεται (= *doth . . . vaunt*; AP 1450) is uncertain. The masculine participle read by the MSS, σταθείς (= *Stationed*) implies that the subject is the *Daimon*—who has just been addressed in the second person singular, but must now have mysteriously switched to the third. A suggested emendation, the elided feminine participle, σταθεῖσ', implies that the subject of the verb is Clytaemnestra, who is indeed standing over the dead body. Yet though editors disagree about its identity, *Something* must be the subject of the verb.

1520-21] *hast thou . . . opinion* You have corrected your previous statement i.e., that Clytaemnestra was solely to blame. A perversely literal translation of AP 1451: ὤρθωσας στόματος γνώμην, since the Greek verb = make ὀρθός (= straight, upright, but constantly used metaphorically = right).

1522]   *the Sprite*   A rhyme-led alias for the *Daimon*.

1523]   *triply gross*   AP 1152: τριπάχυιον (= thrice-fat, thrice-gorged), possibly with a reference to the daimon's activity "through three generations" (ADP 1476, Liddell and Scott, 1996), though Fraenkel condemns this interpretation (AF 1476).

1524]   *O'er . . . dominion*   That has dominion over the family (expanded for the rhyme from AP 1453: γέννης τῆσδε (= of this race/family).

1525-26]   *Eros / The carnage-licker*   AP 1454: ἔρως αἱματολοιχὸς (= blood-licking desire, i.e., a lust for blood-licking).

1528]   *the elder throe*   AP 1456: τὸ πάλαιον ἄχος (= the ancient pain/grief).

   ichor   B simply transliterates ἰχώρ (AW 1480) printed without explanation as ἴχωρ in AP 1487, and translated in Paley's note as "gore"). In Homer the word is used for the immortal blood that "flows in the blessed gods" (*Iliad* 5.340), but here Fraenkel translates it "pus," implying a wound that will not heal (AF 1480, cf. ADP 1480).

1529]   *of might*   interpolated. AP 1458: μέγαν (= great).

1534]   *By Ate's malice*   Expanded for the rhyme from ἀτηρᾶς (adjective = to do with, caused by Ate; AP 1460). See l. 381n.

1536]   *Oh, oh*   Here B's eye must have jumped from ἰώ, ἰή (= oh, oh) in AP 1461 to ἰώ, ἰώ (= Oh, oh) in AP 1466, overlooking the lines between, which he failed to translate: ἰώ, ἰή, διαὶ Διὸς παναιτίου, πανεργέτα· τί γὰρ βροτοῖς ἄνευ Διὸς τελεῖται; τί τῶνδ' οὐ θεόκραντόν ἐστιν (= Oh, oh, through Zeus, all-causing, all-effecting; for without Zeus what is brought about for mortals? which of these things is not god-ordained? [AP 1461-64, AW, AF, ADP, AL 1485-88]). As Paley's note explains, though the immediate cause is the family *Daimon*, the ultimate cause is Zeus, "the real author of every event" (AP 1458).

1539]   *where webs . . . thee*   AP 1469: ἀράχνης ἐν ὑφάσματι τῷδε (= in this spider's web), i.e., the robe used by Clytaemnestra to entangle him.

1540]   *life breathing away*   The original word-order for "breathing away life" (AP 1470).

1542]   *This couch*   I.e., thou liest on this couch. But *couch* is probably not the best translation of κοίταν, the noun of the verb κεῖμαι (= lie), which can mean the act or state, as well as the physical place, of lying. So here (AP 1471) it is probably a cognate object: "you are lying this sort of lying," i.e., lying like this.

   not free   A literal translation of ἀνελεύθερον (AP 1472), but the normal implication of the word is "unworthy of a free man, illiberal, slavish, ignoble."

1543] *slavish* B translates δουλίῳ (= slavish), an emendation for the MS reading δολίῳ (= guileful, treacherous) which Paley's note called "tempting," i.e., to avoid the duplication of thought with *not* free, but did not adopt (AP 1471).

1544] *two-edged dart* AP 1473: ἀμφιτόμῳ βελέμνῳ. Rather inconsistently, B does not give the literal meaning of the adjective (= cutting on both sides) but brings out the inappropriateness of the noun (= a thrown or shot weapon, not a hand-held one, as presumably used by Clytaemnnestra).

1545] *boastest* The traditionally assumed meaning of the verb αὐχέω, but unsuitable here (AP 1474), since one can hardly boast of what someone else has done. Paley translates it as "you insist" (AEP 173), and Liddell and Scott, 1996 gives the verb an additional meaning of "declare loudly"; but Fraenkel cites evidence to show that Aeschylus used αὐχέω in a special sense of his own: "to utter or hold a confident belief," and translates it "Thou are confident that" (AF 1497, 3.707-8).

1546-47] *But . . . Wife* But stop calling me the wife of Agamemnon. AP 1475-6: μὴ δ' ἐπιλεχθῆς ᾿Αγαμεμνονίαν εἶναι μ' ἄλοχον (? = and/but do not consider me to be the Agamemnonian wife). The unparalleled use of an aorist passive of ἐπιλέγω in this sense is described by Fraenkel as a "notorious difficulty," and he finds another in the "unique" use of μηδέ (= and/but not) "without a preceding negative clause"; so he assumes textual corruption. B follows Paley, who translates: "do not reckon," "do not assume," which is in line with a scholiast's gloss: "μὴ νόμιζε [= do not think]" (AP 1474; AF 1498, 3.708-10).

1548-49] *showing . . . corpse* AP 1477-78: φανταζόμενος δὲ γυναικί νεκροῦ (= appearing to the wife of the corpse; cf. ALG 1500, misprinted 1600). But Paley and most editors have taken the words to mean: "likening himself to the wife," "taking on the semblance of the wife." This might amount to "a remarkable abuse of language" (ADP 1498-1500), but B followed Paley, and his rhyme (*showing himself in sign*) was possibly based on Paley's note: "Usually, φαντάζεσθαι is simply 'to appear'; but it properly means 'to present oneself so as to be recognized by semblance,' whence it easily passes into the meaning in the text" (AP 1477). Thus taking semblance/resemblance as a recognition-*sign*, the transcriber may have arrived at his weird use of *sign* for "resemblance." He may also have been thinking of Latin *signum* (= sign, symbol, image, effigy, statue, picture). Thus Clytaemnestra's visible appearance as the murderess was merely a picture of her, adopted by the *Daimon* as a disguise.

1549] *corpse thou dost see* AP 1477-78: "this corpse." See l. 1432n.

1550]   *avenging-ghost*   Avenging spirit. AP 1478: Ἀλάστωρ, Alastor (= non-forgetter, Avenger). The *ghost* was possibly added, not just for the rhyme, but because the Liddell and Scott entry included "with or without δαίμων [= spirit]," and B wished to bring out the identity between this "Alastor" and the *Daimon* of l. 1512. The word had been borrowed and given a psychological meaning by his favorite poet Shelley in *Alastor; or The Spirit of Solitude* (1816).

1551]   *host*   AP 1479: θοινατῆρος (= feaster), i.e., when he made Thyestes eat his own sons. See l. 164n.

1553]   *ones'*   The reference is to Thyestes' children. AP 1481: νεαροῖς (plural).

1557]   *the sire's*   I.e., Atreus'.

1558-60]   *He . . . Ares*   AP 1485-87: βιάζεται ... μέλας Ἄρης (= black Ares forces/is forced). B employs his slightly misleading device for retaining the Greek word-order when the verb comes some way ahead of its subject: first extracting an extra "he, she, or it" from the verb, and then inserting a dash before the real subject.

   is forced   βιάζεται is commonly taken as a middle (= forces his way or acts with violence), but B follows Paley in taking it as passive: "is forced onwards by fresh showers of kindred blood" (AEP 173; cf. AF, ADP, ALG 1509).

   Black Ares   Black perhaps, because the god of war should not operate off the battlefield.

1560-62]   *to where . . . food*   B denies himself the simplest way out of a great textual difficulty, the emendation (adopted by Paley and subsequent editors) of the MS reading δὲ καὶ (= but and) to δίκαν (= justice, punishment, atonement). Paley says of the MS reading: "it appears utterly hopeless to extort any plausible meaning out of it" (AP 1488; AF, ADP, AL 1511). Rising to that challenge, B makes what he can of Weise's text: ὅποι δὲ καὶ προβαίνων πάχνᾳ κουροβόρῳ παρέξει (= ? to where but and advancing he will provide to/for/by boy-feeding frost). The "frost" is explained by Liddell and Scott, 1871 as "clotted blood," and by Paley as "congealed blood (because 'not yet washed out of the family')"; AEP 173. But B's own transcript of the passage must have been based on the method used by the poet in Shelley's *Alastor* (125-7) for deciphering ancient "memorials . . . [He] gazed / And gazed, till meaning on his vacant mind / Flashed like strong inspiration."

1563-70]   See ll. 1536-44nn.

1571-72]   *No death . . . to be*   B translates two lines bracketed by Paley as textually corrupt, but accepted by Weise (AP 1498-99, AW 1521-22). There is also probably a line or two missing (ADP 1521-29).

1571] *"unfit for the free"* The quotation marks imply that Clytaemnestra is quoting the Chorus-leader's English words; but in fact she is only referring to the implication of the Greek word ἀνελεύθερον (= not free; AP 1471, 1496) which was translated literally in ll. 1542, 1568.

1573] *slavish* For this emendation, B seems to rely on Paley's note (AP 1499): "If the two verses are genuine, we can hardly help reading δούλιον [= slavish, instead of δολίαν = guileful, treacherous] . . . 'Not so, for it was not the death of a slave, but of his own child, that he caused to the house.'" To extract that sense, however, the Greek words must form a negative statement (as they do in AW 1523-24) not a question expecting the answer "Yes," as they do in B's version.

1577f.] *Having done well by . . .* Another textual crux. The MSS read Ἰφιγένειαν ἀνάξια δράσας ἄξια πάσχων (= having done unworthy things to Iphigenia suffering worthy things himself)—on which one modern editor comments (ADP 1521-29): "The sense requires what the MSS have . . . 'suffering what he deserves, having done to Iphigeneia what she did not deserve.'" But Paley suspected corruption, finding "the sense weak and the metre intolerable" (AP 1503), though in AEP 173 he made adequate sense of it: "Iphigenia . . . he treated with undeserved cruelty, and now, when he is himself treated as he deserves . . . ." B seems to be translating an emendation tentatively included in Paley's text: ἄξια (= worthy things) for ἀνάξια (= unworthy things; AP 1504); but only by making the phrase heavily sarcastic can Agamemnon be said by Clytaemnestra to have *done well by* his daughter.

1578-79] *loudly / Bear himself proudly* I.e., boast that he is a victim of injustice. B's two rhyme-words are extracted from one Greek word μεγαλαυχείτω (= let him boast greatly; AP 1505).

1580] *amerced* Punished.

1581] *that sword's . . . first* Rhetorically expanded from AP 1507: ἅπερ ἦρξεν (= what he started).

1583] *feasible* Not quite the sense of εὐπάλαμον (= well-contrived; AP 1509), which stresses ingenuity rather than practicability.

1586] *That ruins the roof* AP 1511: δομοσφαλῆ (= ruining the house), but the triple alliteration was apparently irresistible, and B could argue that elsewhere in Greek, as in Latin, the word for "roof" is often used for "house" (στέγη, *tectum*) and that rain makes every house-owner worry about his roof.

1587] *warning-drop* The first part of this compound is interpolated into ψεκάς (= a small drop); but B was probably thinking of Paley's note: "It no longer rains in *mere* drops, but with a full stream of blood" (AP 1512).

1591]   *Woe*   An interjection used to translate ἰώ, an exclamation of joy, pain, or grief.

1594]   *bath-vase*   Why such a weird compound to translate the simple word δροίτας (= bathing-tub, bath; AP 1518)? If the verse required an extra syllable, surely "bathtub" would have been better, since the point was the indignity of the great king's laying-out. But perhaps B thought that would clash with the implications of *silver-sided*, an adjective recalling the δύ᾽ ἀργυρέας ἀσαμίνθους (= two silver baths), which figured among the expensive presents collected by Menelaus in Homer, *Odyssey*, 4.128. See l. 1138n.

1600-1601]   *in place / Of*   A possible sense of ἀντί, but here in AP 1523 it seems to mean "in return for."

1602]   *wickedly*   AP 1524: ἀδίκως (= unjustly, improperly), where the word probably refers less to her immorality than to her defiance of normal custom.

1603]   *tale of praise*   B gives two possible meanings of one Greek word αἶνον (= 1. tale, story, 2. praise); accepting the emendation adopted by Paley, but unaccountably omitting the phrase "with tears," which appears in both Paley's and Weise's texts, though in slightly different forms (AP 1526: ξὺν δακρύοις, AW 1549: οὺν δάκρυσιν).

1604]   *At . . . sent*   AP 1525-26: ἐπ᾽ ἀνδρὶ θείῳ ... ἰάπτων (= sending forth over the god-like man); but as the verb ἰάπτων can be used of hurling a weapon, and as Paley's note (AP 1525) mentions that "it may be used intransitively" of "aiming or pointing at him," B seems to play with the notion of Clytaemnestra's firing off a funeral oration at her dead husband as a kind of final attack (though that would probably have required a different case after the preposition ἐπί).

1605]   *From . . . intent*   Though expressed in the masculine gender, this refers to Clytaemnestra, perhaps implying: how can any murderer be sincere in delivering a funeral oration over his victim?

1606-7]   *It . . . care*   A literal translation of AP 1528-29; i.e., that's no business of yours.

1608-9]   *down there . . . down there*   Expanded from the repeated prefix (κατά = down) in the compound verbs κάππεσεν (= he fell down) and καταθάψομεν (= we shall down-bury; AP 1530).

1612]   *with kindliness*   AP 1532: ἀσπασίως (= with a glad welcome). As Paley comments, "All this, of course, is ironically said."

1613]   *as the case requires*   B cleverly combines his own need for a rhyme with the sarcastic implications of ὡς χρή (= as is right and proper; AP 1533).

1615]   *Passage of Groans*   AP 1535: πόρθμευμ᾽ ἀχέων (= ferry-crossing of pains/sorrows), i.e., Acheron, the river of pains across which the dead had to be ferried before arriving in Hades.

hands AP 1536: χεῖρε (= hands or arms). B chooses the meaning less appropriate to the context.

1616] *that kindest of sires* A thought implied but (more effectively) left unstated by Aeschylus (AP 1536).

1617] *This . . . of blame* I.e., "Reproach thus meets reproach (our attack on Clytaemnestra answered by hers on Agamemnon)" (ADP 1560-66).

1618] *Hard battle* The literal meaning of δύσμαχα, but here (AP 1538) it may mean no more than: "it's a hard struggle, it's difficult."

each claim Interpolated for the rhyme, and to clarify the meaning.

1619-20] *"He is . . . to pay"* The quotation-marks seem to come from Paley's translation, where the statements are explained, without supporting evidence, as "Proverbs expressing the just law of retaliation" (AEP 174n.). AP 1539: φέρει φέροντ᾽, ἐκτίνει δ᾽ ὁ καίνων (= he carries away the carrying one, i.e., the plunderer is plundered, and the killing one pays in full, i.e., the full penalty).

1622] *in time* Both Weise and Paley (AW 1563, AP 1540) retain the MS reading: μίμνοντος ἐν χρόνῳ Διός (= while Zeus remains in time), which Paley explains as "A short expression for 'while time remains and Zeus is lord of all.'" Rejecting that admittedly questionable interpretation, B resourcefully shifts the ἐν χρόνῳ (= in time) to the next line. Recent editors emend it to ἐν θρόνῳ (= on throne); while Zeus remains on his throne (AF, AL 1563).

1623] *House* See l. 1336n.

cursed brood A literal translation of γονὰν ἀραῖον (AP 1542); but as Paley's note suggests, the meaning here is probably: "'No one can now eject from the family a brood of curses,' i.e., the calamities in store for it from the imprecation of Thyestes."

1624] *The . . . glued* Not, as one might suspect, a desperate expedient to find a rhyme, but a precise equivalent of the original: κεκόλληται γένος πρὸς ἄτᾳ (AP 1543). For *Até* see l. 381n.

1625] *Thou . . . oracle* Paley explains: "You have rightly entered into this topic of the divine law of retribution . . . . There is no difficulty in interpreting χρησμός [= oracle] of a divine declaration, especially as the earliest use of oracles was to guide men in a just course of action" (AP 1544).

1626] *With a true result* AP 1544: ξὺν ἀληθείᾳ (= with truth).

I will not a future tense, but a translation of ἐθέλω (= I am willing to; AP 1546).

1627]   *the Daimon*   I.e., the avenging spirit. See ll. 1369-70 and n..

   Pleisthenidai   The sons of Pleisthenes, i.e., the House of Atreus, though "the place of this shadowy person, Pleisthenes, in the line of Atreus is wholly uncertain" (ADP 1569; cf. AF 3.740).

1628]   *Making an oath*   A reasonable translation of ὅρκους θεμένη (= putting oaths in place; AP 1547); but it now appears that the phrase came to mean "making a sworn compact" (ADP 1569-73) or "making a covenant" (AF 1570). Her bargain with the *Daimon* is to accept the present situation, on condition that he causes no more trouble in future.

1629]   *For the rest*   A literal translation of λοιπὸν (= left over, remaining; AP 1348), which ignores the probably implied noun χρόνον (= time), giving the meaning: "for the rest of time," i.e., henceforth, in future. But B follows Paley's interpretation: "'for what remains,' i.e., as the other side or condition of the compact" (AP 1548).

1630]   *House*   See l. 1336n.

   a guest   Interpolated for the rhyme.

1636-37]   *These . . . mutually-murderous*   AP 1553-54: ἀλληλοφόνους μανίας (= each-other-murdering madnesses).

1641]   *spun*   AP 1558: ὑφαντοῖς (= woven).

   Erinues   See l. 57n., 484n.

1643]   *repaying*   I.e., paying the penalty for.

1645]   *Thuestes*   The object of *drove.* B retains the original word-order, but does nothing to indicate the accusative case (Θυέστην, AP 1562), which in the inflected Greek makes the meaning perfectly clear. Nor do the interpolated dashes give much help to the English reader.

1646]   *contested*   I.e., Thyestes had challenged Atreus' right to the throne.

1647]   *household*   AP 1564: δόμων (= houses, i.e., house). See ll. 1333, 1337n.

1648]   *to the hearth turned, a suppliant*   AP 1565: προστρόπαιος ἑστίας. B translates the phrase literally, and then adds *a suppliant* to explain it; i.e., Thyestes begged for mercy from his brother. The hearth was the traditional place for a suppliant to make his supplication, e.g. Odysseus in Homer, *Odyssey,* 7.153-4).

1649]   *the fate assured him*   AP 1566: μοῖραν ... ἀσφαλῆ (= a safe fate), interpreted by Paley and later editors as "a promise of safety, that he should not die" (AEP 175; cf. AF 1588: "a safe lot, safe from dying"). B's independent interpretation was presumably based on another lexicon-definition of the adjective ἀσφαλής: "sure, certain." But the context suggests that Atreus explicitly promised to let Thyestes live in safety, and kept that promise—only to get his revenge another way.

1650]   *paternal threshold*   The threshold of his father's home.

1651]   *Just there*   I.e., at the moment he entered the house.

host-wise   AP 1568: ξένια (= by way of hospitality).

this man's   Agamemnon's.

1652]   *soul-keenly more than kindly*   B tries, by alliteration and an echo of Shakespeare's "A little more than kin, and less than kind" (*Hamlet* 1.2.65), to give some force to the ironical phrase: προθύμως μᾶλλον ἢ φίλως (= soul-forwardly, i.e., eagerly rather than kindly; AP 1569). It was doubtless meant to contrast Atreus' apparent efforts to be a good host with the cruelty of what he actually did; but "it is hard to believe that Aeschylus wrote" this "remarkably insipid expression" (ADP 1591).

seeming   I.e., pretending.

1653]   *joyous*   AP 1570: εὐθύμως (= cheerfully), i.e., to celebrate his brother's home-coming.

a flesh-day   AP 1570: κρεουργὸν ἦμαρ (= meat-working day), annotated by Paley: "'a festive day,'—a day on which meat was distributed after a solemn sacrifice."

1654]   *a meal . . . children*   AP: δαῖτα παιδείων κρεῶν (= a feast of child-meat). Surprisingly, B avoids the obvious feast-flesh alliteration, perhaps to increase the horror by placing it in the context of an ordinary family-*meal.*

1655]   *the hands' top divisions*   AP 1572: χερῶν ἄκρους κτένας (= top/endmost combs of the hands). B tries to come nearer to the original metaphor than Paley's "fingers at the tips of the hands" or "top joints of the hands" (AP 1573, AEP 175).

1656]   *He hid*   B translates ἔκρυπτ', the emendation adopted by Paley, for the MS reading retained by Weise, ἔθρυπτ' (= crushed, minced; AP 1573, AW 1595).

1657]   *unshowing*   I.e., not clearly showing their human origin; an inadequate translation of AP 1574: ἄσημα (= without sign), i.e., unrecognizable.

1658]   *perdition*   AP 1575: ἄσωτον (= not saved or, as here, not saving), i.e., fatal to, disastrous for. B's replacement of the adjective by a noun with Christian connotations of non-salvation tends to obscure the sense.

1659]   *'ware of*   AP 1576: ἐπιγνοὺς (= having realized). B's wording was possibly over-abbreviated from Paley's "when he was made aware" (AEP 175), explained by his note: "Subsequently discovering the deed, viz. on the hands and feet being shown to him" (AP 1576).

ill-omened   AP 1576: οὐ καταίσιον (= not righteous).

1660]   *He . . . carnage*   The *shriek*, to translate the less dramatic ὤμωξεν (= he said οἴμοι = oh me! or woe is me!) seems to have come from Paley's note: "'He shrieked, and fell back (recoiled) vomiting from the slaughter,' i.e., slain flesh" (AP 1577).

1661-62] *And fate . . . down* AP 1578: μόρον δ᾽ ἄφερτον Πελοπίδαις ἐπεύχεται (= and prays an unbearable fate on the sons of Pelops. See l. 1514n.

1662-63] *putting in . . . the feast* Rejecting Paley's emended text, B tries to translate the MS reading as in Weise 1601: λάκτισμα δείπνου ξυνδίκως τιθεὶς ἀρᾷ (= putting kick of meal together-with / curse). The sense is apparently that Thyestes kicks over the table at which he has been eating, to symbolize his curse: may the whole *race of Pleisthenes* be similarly overthrown. See l. 1627n.

1664] *and thence is* And that's why.

1665] *it is given thee* AP 1581: σοι ...πάρα (= it is possible for you).

prostrate AP 1581: πεσόντα (= having fallen), i.e., struck down.

1666] *rightly . . . stitch-man* AP 1582: δίκαιος ... ῥαφεύς (= the just stitcher, i.e., planner).

1667] *third from ten* The MS reading, retained by Weise (AW 1605) and thought probably corrupt by Paley (AP 1583), is τρίτον ...ἐπὶ δέκ᾽ (= third on ten, i.e., thirteenth). B seems to have hazarded an emendation of his own, reading ἀπὸ (= from) for ἐπὶ (= on); but Fraenkel comments: "For more than a hundred years it has been thought necessary to correct not an error of a copyist but the thought of the poet . . . does it not heighten the horror of the bloody deed to say that twelve children were butchered and the thirteenth alone, a babe still in swaddling-clothes, escaped with its bare life?" (AF 1605; 3.758-59; contrast ADP 1605: "a ludicrous multitude in this context δέκ᾽ [= ten] is almost certainly corrupt").

1668] *swathe-bands* Swaddling clothes.

1670] *being without-doors* Paley explained: "though not present at the time in the house, yet I reached him . . . by the plot that I laid" (AP 1586).

1671] *ill-will* AP 1587: δυσβουλίας, a noun that usually means an ill-advised plan, but seems here to mean a wicked or destructive one (ADP 1608-9; cf. AF 1609, 3.760). Presumably B thought any such hint of self-criticism out of character for Aegisthus in this context, so chose to derive the word from βούλομαι (= wish, will) rather than βουλεύω (= take counsel).

1674] *arrogance . . . not* AP 1590: ὑβρίζειν ἐν κακοῖσιν οὐ σέβω (= ? I do not honour to-exult in evils). Paley interprets: "'I approve not insolence in misfortunes,' i.e., in a crisis like the present," but it is doubtful whether the words can carry that meaning. Fraenkel translates: "triumph in misfortune is a thing I care not to practise" (AF 1612); but the MS text may be "impossible" and require emendation (ADP 1612).

1675]   *Dost thou . . . here*   I.e., do you admit that you deliberately killed this man? In AP 1591 ἑκὼν (= willing) is similarly placed between *say* and *killed*. B's dash was evidently intended both to detach the willingness from the saying, and also to mark the antithesis between φῇς (= thou sayest) and φημ' (= I say).

1676]   *lamentable*   AP 1592: ἔποικτον (= pitiable, piteous).

1677]   *in justice*   A literal translation of ἐν δίκῃ (AP 1593), which here probably means: "in the hour of Justice (or Judgement)" (AF, ADP 1615).

1678]   *The people's . . . curses*   AP 1594: δημορριφεὶς ... λευσίμους ἀράς (= thrown-by-the-people to-do-with-stoning curses).

1679]   *soundest*   AP 1595: φωνεῖς (= you voice, speak, utter, say); but B insists on the irrelevant primary meaning of the verb, which is to make any sort of sound.

1680]   *Oarage*   AP 1596: κώπη (= oar), but B's metre required another syllable.

   mid-bench   AP 1596: ζυγῷ (= cross-plank, bench), here "used for the little deck at the stern of the ship . . . on which the helmsman had his seat" (AF 1617f.).

1681]   *know*   AP 1597: γνώσει (= will get to know, learn, find out); but this time B ignores the more relevant primary meaning of the verb.

   how heavy is teaching   AP 1596: ὡς διδάσκεσθαι βαρὺ (= how heavy/grievous it is to be taught).

1682]   *of the like age*   AP 1598: τηλικούτῳ (= of such an age), i.e., at your time of life.

   bidden be modest   AP 1598: σωφρονεῖν εἰρημένον (= when told to be sensible).

1683]   *and old age*   The most obvious translation of καὶ τὸ γῆρας, but one which makes no sense in the context, where the three words must be the object, not subject, of the verb διδάσκειν (= to teach) and mean "even old age," as Paley's note made clear enough: " 'But imprisonment and the pangs of hunger are first-rate trainers of the mind for teaching even old age,' which under ordinary circumstances is slow to be instructed" (AP 1599).

1684-85]   *prophets / At souls'-cure*   AP 1600-1601: φρενῶν ἰατρομάντεις (= doctor-prophets of minds).

   aught   Interpolated to explain the pregnant participle ὁρῶν (= seeing; AP 1601), i.e., if you can see anything, can't you see this?

1686]   *Against goads kick not*   A literal translation of AP 1602: πρὸς κέντρα μὴ λάκτιζε. For the proverbial image cf. Aeschylus *Prometheus Bound* 325, and Acts 9:5, 26:14.

tript-up   B rejects the emendation (for the meaningless MS reading πήσας) adopted by Paley and recent editors: παισάς (= having struck [i.e., them]), and translates the emendation adopted by Weise, πταίσας (= having stumbled; AP 1602, AF, ADP, AL, ALG, AW 1624).

1687-89]   *Woman, thou . . . too*   Except for interpolating *thy* before *husband,* and the final *too,* B translates almost word for word the MS reading retained by Weise and (doubtfully) by Paley: γύναι, σὺ τοῦδ᾽ ἥκοντος ἐκ μάχης νέον οἰκουρὸς εὐνὴν ἀνδρὸς αἰσχύνουσ᾽ ἅμα ἀνδρὶ στρατηγῷ τονδ᾽ ἐβούλευσας μόρον (= woman, you, staying at home [and] at the same time shaming the bed of this man/husband newly returned from battle, did you plan this fate /death for a man/husband general?; AW 1625-27, AP 1603-5). Here the feminine participle αἰσχύνουσ᾽ (= shaming, *disgracing*) implies that the speech is addressed to Clytaemnestra, though apparently spoken to Aegisthus, in response to his claim of having planned the murder. The final *too* was presumably inserted as a belated answer to that claim, perhaps implying that Aegisthus is being insultingly lumped together with Clytaemnestra as a kind of composite female, rather as Hamlet addressed his murderous step-father as "Mother," explaining: "father and mother is man and wife; man and wife is one flesh, and so, my mother" (*Hamlet,* 4.3.51-52). Recent editors assume that the speech is indeed addressed to Aegisthus, insultingly called a woman, and that the feminine particiciple, which they emend to the masculine form, was inserted by a puzzled scribe (AF 1625 ff., 3.768-70; ADP, AL 1625-27).

1690]   *These . . . prime-begetters*   I.e., you'll suffer for that last insult as well.

1691]   *opposed to Orpheus*   I.e., the opposite of Orpheus' tongue (of the legendary poet, singer, and musician). B translates the Greek words, but obscures their obvious meaning: Ὀρφεῖ δὲ γλῶσσαν τὴν ἐναντίαν ἔχεις (= but you have a tongue opposite to Orpheus; AP 1607). In putting no apostrophe after *Orpheus* in his MS, B imitated the slight illogicality of the Greek grammar.

1692]   *grace-charm*   AP 1608: χαρᾷ (= delight); but B was possibly remembering that this noun, like χάρις (= grace) comes from χαίρω (= rejoice).

1693]   *upstirring*   AP 1609: ἐξορίνας (= out-stirring, i.e., exasperating).

these wild yelpings   AP 1609: νηπίοις ὑλάγμασιν (= foolish barkings).

Notes to Page 89

1694]   *Wilt lead them*   AP 1610: ἄξει. B follows Paley's note in taking this verb to be in the middle voice: "You forsooth, after irritating people by your senseless barkings, think to lead them to your own purposes." Recent editors interpret the verb as passive: "Orpheus *led on* all that heard him, you will be *led off* to execution" (ADP 1629-32; cf. AF, AL 1632).

1696]   *not when*   Unlike Paley (AP 1612), B follows the MS reading, οὐκ ἐπειδὴ, but ignores the redundant second οὐκ (= not) before ἔτλης (= *daredst*; AW 1634-35).

1698]   *For*   I.e., no, didn't kill him myself, for—a common elliptical use of γὰρ (= for) in Greek (AP 1614).

   certes   AP 1614: σαφῶς (= clearly). There is no obvious reason for the substituted archaism.

1699]   *looked after*   AP 1615: ὕποπτον (= looked-at-from-under, i.e., viewed with suspicion, suspected). Searching for an exact equivalent of the Greek word, B may have recalled Shakespeare's *Measure for Measure* 1.2.144: "Is lechery so look'd after?" i.e., kept such a close watch on (see *OED*, s.v. *Look after*).

   old-begotten   a rather perverse translation of παλαιογενής (= ancient-born; AP 1615), since it introduces the irrelevant idea of paternity.

1701]   *the no-man-minder*   The man who pays no attention to anyone—a precise rendering of AP 1617: τὸν ... μὴ πειθάνορα (= the not man-obeying, from πείθομαι = obey and νρ = man).

1702]   *trace-horse*   "The trace-horse bore no collar, and was harnessed by the side of the pair under the yoke" (AL 1640).

1703]   *corned-up colt*   An alliterative version of κριθῶντα πῶλον (= barley-fed foal). Trace-horses were particularly well fed, because they had to "exert great strength in taking the chariot round the bend" (ADP 1640, cf. AF 1641).

   that   The translation of ὁ (commonly = the) as a demonstrative was probably suggested by Paley's note (AP 1619) finding a "direct allusion" to Aegisthus' previous threat of hunger-pangs (AP 1599; l. 1683).

   bad friend   AP 1619: δυσφιλής (= hard to love, unlovable, so hateful; derived from δυσ prefix [= hard-, bad-, ill-] and φιλέω [= I love]); but B's imaginative metaphor was extracted from another derivative of the same verb, φίλος (= friend).

1704]   *shall behold him gentle*   A literal translation of AP 1620: μαλθακόν σφ᾽ ἐπόψεται, i.e., will soon tame him.

1705]   *this man here*   The object of *slay*. B follows the Greek word-order (AP 1621).

1706]   *But,—helped,—a woman*   AP 1622-4: ἀλλὰ σὺν γυνὴ ... ἔκτεινε (= but with [you] a woman killed). B's dashes were presumably intended to make the Greek word-order more intelligible in uninflected English. "Aegisthus has claimed the full credit for the deed: it is therefore only to be expected that the Chorus will retort 'then why did you let a woman *associate herself* with you?' even though they may think that Clytaemnestra's part was much the more important" (ADP 1644).

1707]   *pest*   AP 1623: μίασμα (= pollution, someone that pollutes).

1708]   *Orestes*   Son of Agamemnon and Clytaemnestra.

   where may he see light now   AP 1624, AW 1646: Ὀρέστης ἆρά που βλέπει φάος (= does Orestes [Agamemnon's son] see light anywhere, i.e., is he alive anywhere?). B strangely rejects the MS reading adopted by Weise, Paley, and recent editors: που (= somewhere, anywhere), and tries to make sense of a another MS reading: ποῦ (= where?), though that interrogative adverb is inconsistent with the preceding interrogative particle ἆρα, which implies a different form of question (AF 1646; 1.192n.).

1711]   *But since . . . shalt know*   Here B changes his metre to imitate the trochaic tetrameters catalectic used by Aeschylus at this point (AP 1627, AL 1649), where Fraenkel draws attention to "the jerk with which the rhythm changes to greater excitement, just as in some of Mozart's operas we are affected by the change of measure in the finale of an act" (AF 1649ff.). The metre had been famously anglicized by Tennyson in *Locksley Hall* (1842).

   and not talk   And not only talk about doing it. B translates the emendation adopted by Paley: κοὐ (= and not) for the MS reading: καὶ (= and).

   thou soon shalt know   Paley explains: "a formula of threatening" (AP 1627).

1712]   *Up then, comrades dear*   Weise follows the MSS in giving this line to the chorus-leader (AW 1650); but B translates Paley's text, which gives it to Aegisthus, addressing his bodyguard (AP 1628). For the arguments on both sides, see AF 1650, 3.781-84.

   the proper . . . this   AP 1628: τοὔργον οὐχ ἑκὰς τόδε (= this job is not far away), i.e., get ready to do what I've told you.

1713]   *hilt in hold*   An alliterative rendering of πρόκωπον (= held by the hilt; AP 1629).

1714]   *hilt in hold*   AP 1630: πρόκωπος (= with my hand on my sword-hilt; AP 1630).

   do not refuse to   I.e., am prepared to.

1715]   *to who accept it*   I.e., who accept the omen of such a pronouncement. AP 1631: δεχομένοις (= to those who accept). Paley's note explains: "We accept your words, when you say you are ready to die; and we take our chance in the conflict."

demand AP 1631: αἱρούμεθα (= take-for-ourselves, choose). B presumably thought a stronger verb more appropriate to the dramatic situation.

1716] *may we do* AP 1632: δράσωμεν (= let us do). The subjunctive is clearly hortative.

1717] *To have . . . to me* AP 1633: ἀλλὰ καὶ τάδ᾽ ἐξαμῆσαι πολλὰ δύστηνον θέρος (= but to reap off even these many [evils] is a miserable harvest). B follows Paley's note: "To have reaped even these evils, so many in number, is an unhappy harvest"; but strangely fails to translate the important adjective δύστηνον (= miserable, unhappy).

1717-18] Here, for no obvious reason (impatience to get the transcript finished?) B fails to translate a line of Greek: πημονῆς δ᾽ ἅλις γ᾽ ὑπάρχει· μηδὲν αἱματώμεθα (= and there is enough of suffering—let us make ourselves no [more] bloodstained; AP 1634, AW 1656).

1718] *Go . . . old men* B translates the emendation adopted by Paley: στεῖχε καὶ σὺ χοἰ γέροντες (AP 1635). The MSS read: στείχετε δ᾽ οἱ γέροντες (= and go the old men).

1719] *It behoved . . . did* Here the MS text has been described as "incurably corrupt" (ADP 1657-58; cf. AF 1657-58, 3.792-95). B tries to extract some sense from Weise's minimal emendation: ἐρξάντα καιρὸν χρῆν τάδ᾽ ὡς ἐπράξαμεν (= [for someone] having acted right-time it was necessary [to do] these things as we did; AW 1658).

1720] *And if . . . assent* B translates Paley's emended text, as explained in his note: "The sense appears to be, 'Should there have been enough of these troubles (i.e., if it is the will of the gods that they should henceforth cease . . .) we will take it'" (AP 1637).

1721] *heel* AP 1637: χηλῇ (= hoof or claw). B seems more interested in the sound of the Greek word (*chele*) than its meaning.

ones Interpolated, perhaps to show that the participle *stricken* (AP 1637) goes with the previous *we*.

1723] *o'er-bloom* AP 1640: ἀπανθίσαι (= pick flowers). Paley's note explains: "But to think that these men should thus gather the flowers of their vain tongue against me."

1724] *the Daimon's power experimenting on* AP 1641: δαίμονος πειρωμένους (= trying/ testing the daimon). Paley's note compares with the English phrase "tempting fortune."

1725] *of modest knowledge missing* AP 1642: σώφρονος γνώμης δ᾽ ἁμαρτεῖν (= and miss sensible judgement). B's *of*, not required in English after the verb *miss*, marks the genitive case required in Greek after ἁμαρτάνω.

the ruler Here some words are missing in the MSS after τὸν κρατοῦντα (= the man ruling) as marked by three asterisks in Weise's text (AW 1664). B inserts *me*, but does not translate the words conjecturally inserted by Paley: θ᾽ ὑβρίσαι (= and insult; AP 1642), i.e., the ruler.

1726] *Ne'er may this befall Argeians* Not a wish in the original: οὐκ ἂν Ἀργεῖων τόδ᾽ εἴη (= this would not be of Argives, i.e., characteristic of them, like them; AP 1643, AW, AL 1665).

1727] *Anyhow . . . yes, I* AP 1644: ἀλλ᾽ ἐγώ (= but I). In Greek, however, a personal pronoun is always emphatic, since the person is already expressed in the verb.

1728] *make Orestes straightway come* AP 1645: Ὀρέστην δεῦρ᾽ ἀπευθύνῃ μολεῖν (= direct Orestes to come hither). But the verb for *direct* (ἀπευθύνω), though derived from εὐθύς (= straight), really means "guide by a straight or direct route"; not, as B's *straightway* suggests, "make him come immediately."

1729] *myself* I.e., from my own experience of exile.

fugitives AP 1646: φεύγοντας ἄνδρας (= fleeing men); but the verb φεύγω (= flee) often implies being an exile, and that is the meaning here.

on hopes are pasture-fed The Greek is simpler: ἐλπίδας σιτουμένους (= feed on hopes; AP 1646).

1730] *Do thy deed* AP 1647: πρᾶσσε (= go on doing, i.e., as you are doing now. But since the Greek verb, like the English one, can mean faring as well as acting, the implication may well be: go on acting wickedly but faring well.

since the power is thine Since you can. AP 1647: ἐπεὶ πάρα (= since it is possible).

1732] *bearing thee audacious* Elaborated from one word, θαρσῶν (= being bold, cheerful, confident; AP 1649).

his females by AP 1649: θηλείας πέλας (= close to the female). B's plural suggests a hasty misreading of the genitive singular required by πέλας for an accusative plural.

1733] *Have not thou respect for* Pay no attention to.

these . . . yelpings AP 1650: τῶνδ᾽ ὑλαγμάτων (= these . . . barkings).

1734] *it* Interpolated. The textual problems of the Greek text which greatly increased the difficulty of B's undertaking, continued to the last line. AP 1651: θήσομεν (= will arrange). The absence of an object for this verb, unparalleled in Aeschylus, made Fraenkel believe that the missing object had been wrongly replaced in the MS by τῶνδε (= these = B's *this*). See AF 1672ff., 3.800-803.

excellently well   AP 1651: καλῶς (= beautifully, or well). B's more resonant final phrase may have been suggested by Shakespeare's Orestes, Hamlet, when contemptuously dismissing Polonius: "Do you know me, my lord?" "Excellent well; you are a fishmonger" (*Hamlet* 2.2.173-74). Was the verbal echo even meant to remind the English reader that Clytaemnestra's triumph would soon be ended, in the second play of the trilogy, by her son?

LA SAISIAZ: THE TWO POETS OF CROISIC

Emendations to the Text

The following emendations have been made to the 1889a copy-text:

La Saisiaz, l. 477: The MS-1878 comma after *incalculable* became a period in 1889a. Had this change been deliberate, *every* would have been capitalized. The MS-1878 comma has been restored.
La Saisiaz, l. 490: The 1889a edition omits the exclamation point though leaving a space before the quotation marks. The MS-1878 exclamation point has been restored.
La Saisiaz, l. 604: The MS, 1878, and 1889a editions all omit the quotation mark at the end of the line. The required quotation mark has been added.
The Two Poets of Croisic, l. 488: The 1889a edition has no punctuation at the end of the sentence. The MS-1878 period has been restored.
The Two Poets of Croisic, l. 592: The 1889a edition has no punctuation at the end of the sentence. The MS-1878 exclamation point has been restored.
The Two Poets of Croisic, l. 664: The 1889a edition omits the quotation marks at the end of the sentence. The MS-1878 quotation marks have been restored.
The Two Poets of Croisic, l. 1175: The 1889a edition omits the comma between the second and third *quack* in the series. The MS-1878 comma has been restored.

Texts

The manuscripts of "La Saisiaz" and "The Two Poets of Croisic" are in the Library of Balliol College, Oxford (Balliol MS. 390), bound with the manuscript of *Pacchiarotto and How He Worked in Distemper: with Other Poems*. Ashby Bland Crowder has described these manuscripts in this edition, 13.318-19.
The author's proofs for the two poems were sent to B by Spottiswoode in two batches, the first on 23 March 1878 and the second on 1 April. B made forty corrections, only twenty-three of which are substantive, the remaining seventeen involving such things as inserting missing page numbers and deleting ink smudges. Otherwise, the proofs are identical to the 1878 first edition. The proofs were bound by

Zaehnsdorf in 8vo, full brown levant morocco. Four autographed signed letters from B to Barnett Smith of Highgate Hill, written between 1873 and 1889, have been pasted in the blank leaves in the front of the volume. The volume, with the letters, was auctioned by Emmett for the Anderson Galleries of New York as Lot 107 on 19 October 1918 and was bought by Carl Pforzheimer for $181.50. It is now in the Pforzheimer Collection of the New York Public Library (Misc. 721; *Reconstruction*, E222).

The first edition was published by Smith, Elder, & Co. on 15 May 1878, just seven months after *The Agamemnon of Aeschylus* and eleven months before *Dramatic Idyls*. Bound in forest-green cloth boards, post octavo, and selling for seven shillings, it contained 201 pages, not counting the title page, a dedication (to Mrs. Sutherland Orr), table of contents, and advertisements. For a full bibliographical description, see Broughton, 20. There was no subsequent edition until the poems were published in Volume 14 of the 1888-89a edition along with *Pacchiarotto and How He Worked in Distemper: with Other Poems*. This volume, bound in brown cloth boards, has 279 pages in addition to unnumbered title and contents pages.

The dedication to Mrs. Sutherland Orr in the 1878 edition was omitted, perhaps as an oversight, in the *Poetical Works* of 1888-89. Mrs. Orr, born Alexandra Leighton in St. Petersburg in 1828, was a sister of the painter, Frederick Leighton. Her grandfather was court physician to the czar, and she was named for her godmother, the Empress Alexandra. In 1857, two years after meeting B in Paris, she married Colonel Sutherland Orr, whom she accompanied to India during the Mutiny and who died in 1858, little more than a year after their marriage. In 1869 she settled in London, where she lived with her father in Kensington Park Gardens, not far from B's house in Warwick Crescent. From this time on Mrs. Orr and B were close friends, he visiting her two afternoons a week and once saying, just a few years before his death, that she was his dearest woman friend. Mrs. Orr was an active member of the Browning Society and the author of two books on B, *A Handbook to the Works of Robert Browning* (1886) and *Life and Letters of Robert Browning* (1891). She died in 1903.

Reception

Despite DeVane's statement that *La Saisiaz: The Two Poets of Croisic* "was widely, and generally favorably, noticed" (*Hbk.*, 420), there were only five reviews before the publication in the next year of *Dramatic*

Idyls, which received much more attention. The first of these, an unsigned review by Theodore Watts[-Dunton], appeared in *The Athenaeum* only ten days after publication. The review begins with warm praise for the epilogue ("What a pretty tale you told me"), B never having "written anything so lovely" (25 May 1878, 661). There is praise, too, for "La Saisiaz," described as "a vigorous and eloquent protest against the scientific materialism of the day" and as "full of beautiful thoughts, beautifully expressed" (662, 663). On the other hand, "the action of the poem is merely used as an occasion for ratiocinative writing" (662), more appropriate for a sermon than a poem, and the trochaic tetrameter catalectics are too "sprightly" for the subject (662). As for "The Two Poets of Croisic," Watts summarizes the story of Paul Desforges-Maillard and quibbles about there being no double or triple rhymes in the ottava rima stanzas. Of the volume as a whole, he concludes that "Mr. Browning has lost none of his marvellous vigour of intellect, and there are passages here and there which can compare with his very best work" (664).

G. A. Simcox's review in *The Academy* on 1 June 1878 is more descriptive than evaluative. Like Watts, Simcox finds passages here and there to praise, but in "La Saisiaz" B "has made out a stronger case for what he believes in than for what he is sure of" (479), and "The Two Poets of Croisic" falls off abruptly with the concluding reflections on fame (480). The anonymous review in *Public Opinion* one week later (8 June 1878) finds little to praise in either poem and laments that B's obscurity spoils his undeniable poetic gift.

One week after this unfavorable review, *The Saturday Review* published a longer and much harsher criticism of the obscurity of the volume. B is a poet of "unquestioned rank," but he does not "condescend to be lucid," writing "in a shorthand of crabbed and condensed phrases" and taking "pleasure in irritating admiring readers by harsh constructions in grammar and in prosody" (15 June 1878, 759). Few readers "will trouble themselves to understand the metaphysical portion" of "La Saisiaz" (759). "The Two Poets of Croisic" is a "diffuse narrative of wholly uninteresting events, and of abstruse disquisitions prosecuted in obscure and enigmatic language" (760).

Following these early reviews, criticism has focused almost exclusively on "La Saisiaz," a poem valued more as an important statement of B's religious views than as an example of his best poetry. "The Two Poets of Croisic," unredeemed in critics' eyes by the intellectual substance of the other poem, has faded into relative obscurity, almost as forgotten as the two poets themselves.

LA SAISIAZ

PROLOGUE TO *LA SAISIAZ*

1-5] *Good . . . free* In a letter of 30 January 1880, B explained these five lines to J. D. Williams: "Oh,—'good to forgive—best to forget'— only means the feeling on a review of a life's 'fret,' as it dwindles into insignificancy before an opening prospect of a new and—so far as the old is concerned—a 'fretless' existence" (T. J. Collins and W. J. Pickering, "Letters from Robert Browning to the Rev. J. D. Williams, 1874-1889," *Browning Institute Studies*, 4 [1976], 14).

LA SAISIAZ

Date and Composition] B finished the poem on 9 November 1877, the date of the Balliol manuscript and the "London's mid-November" he refers to in l. 606. He probably began writing it in late September or early October, soon after his return to England from the continent. Miss Smith died on 14 September, the date beneath the title, and six days later B left La Saisiaz to return home by way of Paris.

The twenty-one page manuscript is exceptionally clean, evidently a fair copy and not the original. There are occasional notes to begin new paragraphs, a few transpositions of words, and changes in spelling from Collonges to Collonge. The manuscript thus gives little evidence of B's method of composition. There are about 230 textual variants between the manuscript and the 1878 edition, of which about 170 are minor—chiefly punctuation—and the remaining 60 or so are verbal, usually a matter of substituting one word for another. Only about 35 textual changes were made for the 1889a edition, just one of them a verbal substitution.

Sources] In a letter of 30 January 1880 to J. D. Williams, B wrote that "La Saisiaz" was the only poem "relating to a personal experience (at least, *directly*) in all my books." He then added that he "could not tell the incidents of that memorable week more faithfully in prose and as an accurate account of what happened: and they impressed me so much that I could proceed to nothing else till I had in some way put it all on paper. There was much more to say,—but what *is* said is strictly true" (T. J. Collins and W. J. Pickering, "Letters from Robert Browning to the Rev. J. D. Williams, 1874-1889," *Browning Institute Studies*, 4 [1976], 14).

La Saisiaz

The personal experience was the sudden death of B's old friend Miss Annie Egerton Smith on 14 September 1877. A well-to-do spinster and part owner of the Liverpool *Mercury*, she and B had known each other for twenty-five years, sharing a love for music and sharing as well occasional holidays. She had joined B and his sister, Sarianna, in Le Croisic in 1866 and 1867 and had vacationed with them on the Isle of Arran in 1876. In early August of 1877 the three of them rented a chalet owned by a Dr. Roussel and known as La Saisiaz, in France just five miles south of Geneva. Well up the slopes of Mt. Salève above the village of Collonges-sous-Salève, the house is at the end of the Route de la Saisiaz in an area known as Les Terrasses de Geneve. The house today is almost exactly the same as it was when B was there.

Disappointed at first with the countryside, B came to appreciate its beauties and to enjoy visiting the literary sites associated with Rousseau, Gibbon, Voltaire, and Byron. On the evening of 13 September, B and Miss Smith had climbed part way up Mt. Salève, just behind the chalet, anticipating their excursion all the way to the top by carriage on the following day. But the next morning B returned to the house after his morning swim to discover Miss Smith dead, collapsed upon the floor of her dressing room. The day after her death, 15 September, B wrote Mrs. Charles Skirrow a letter describing what had happened. The letter, now in the Armstrong Browning Library, was incorrectly dated by B as 15 November instead of 15 September:

Dear Friend, I got your gay and kind letter yesterday. How did it find me, can you suppose? Poor Miss Smith, who had been the evening before in exceptionally good health and spirits, and, after taking a pleasant walk with me, had arranged for an excursion the next day, was found dead in her dressing-room—where, a short time before, her maid had left her full of hopes about the weather, and the little events of the journey which was to begin at 10; perhaps half-an-hour after, or less, I returned from my usual walk to breakfast at 9: and, failing to see Miss Smith about the house or grounds, I spoke to her maid, who was at the breakfast-table, and heard that Miss Smith had not left her room yet. "Quite right," I said, "she reserves her strength for our expedition": and made the same remark to my sister who was in the balcony above, as I went up to her. I then walked to the windows of Miss Smith on the other side,—was surprised at not having a recognition and good-morning; and observed thro' the thin curtains that no figure was dimly visible in the bed-room,—as, when the outside shutters were open, must needs be the case. I stepped to the next window,—and was struck by the same still more remarkable absence of a figure—for *there*, in the dressing-room, she was sure to be. I looked through an opening in the curtain, and saw her kneeling on the ground—which her poor head touched. I called my sister, who ran in—cried to me—and brought me to her side. She was quite warm—but dead. The servants tried the common remedies, in vain. I sent for a Doctor to Geneva—failing to find one at the next two villages—and he arrived after some delay—but no sort of assistance would have been of any avail: it was a case of the most thorough "apoplexie foudroyante": she must have died *standing*, and fallen as we found her. So, have I lost one of the most devoted friends I ever had in my life—a friend of some five-and-twenty years standing: I have been much favoured in friendships—especially from women: no one ever was more disinterestedly devoted to me who grieve to remember how little I was ever able to do in return for so much.

(DeVane and Knickerbocker, 240-41)

As B said in his letter to Williams, the poem is a very faithful rendering of this tragic experience. But it is even more his reflections on the experience when he was back in London. The poem involves an often deeply uneasy or agonized, but nonetheless honest and even ruthless intellectual questioning of his own attitudes to religious faith, life's purposes, the functions of suffering, and the nature of good and evil. Five days after Miss Smith's death, B climbed to the top of Mt. Salève, and it is this moment that is the present time of the poem. B was quite shaken by her death and never returned to La Saisiaz. Four years later he wrote Mrs. Thomas FitzGerald from France: "I can assure you, however, that if unfortunately Geneva had been quite in the way, I should have never turned more than—perhaps—my head in the direction of that ill-omened "La Saziaz" [sic]: it, and all connected with it, are painful to me, and I have fitter ways of affectionately bringing poor Miss S. to mind than by visiting her grave" (Letter of 6 September 1881; McAleer, 124).

One source for B's discussion of the existence of God and the immortality of the soul is a series of articles that appeared in the *Nineteenth Century* as "A Modern Symposium, upon The Soul and Future Life." Especially relevant is Frederic Harrison's two-part article, "The Soul and Future Life," in the June and July issues of 1877. In the poem B says that he and Miss Smith discussed the series, citing the title in l. 164. W. H. Griffin and H. C. Minchin (*The Life of Robert Browning*, 3rd ed. [London, 1938], 264) and DeVane (*Hbk.*, 422) regard "La Saisiaz" as B's contribution to the debate. H. N. Fairchild, on the other hand, discounts the importance of these articles to the poem, saying that it "could easily have been written just as it stands if the *Nineteenth century* [sic] had never existed" (*"La Saisiaz* and *The Nineteenth Century,"* *Modern Philology* 48 [1950]: 110).

Title] Mrs. Sutherland Orr says that "La Saisiaz" is "Savoyard for 'The Sun'" (*Hbk.*, 188). It seems likely that Mrs. Orr, a close friend of B and the person to whom *La Saisiaz: The Two Poets of Croisic* was dedicated, would have learned the meaning from the poet himself. It is just as likely that B, who heard "the history of his little estate [La Saisiaz] from its owner [Dr. Roussel]" (Letter of 30 August 1877; McAleer, 46), would have learned the meaning from the man who built the chalet and gave it its name. Despite these probabilities, convincing evidence indicates that Mrs. Orr was wrong. For one thing, Savoyard dictionaries cite "solâ" as the equivalent of "soleil" ("sun"). "Saisiaz" does not appear in these dictionaries. For another, Park Honan has produced evidence that the meaning is "rock-cleft" ("The Meaning of the Term 'La Saisiaz,'" *Browning Newsletter* 5 [Fall 1970]: 29), and indeed in the same letter to Mrs. FitzGerald cited above, B refers to "the notch in the mountain-wall behind it [La Saisiaz]" (47). Finally, Robert Jeantet,

Professor of French at the University of Akron, informs me that "saisiaz" probably derives from the Latin word "saxea," meaning "rock," and that "saisiaz" is a variation of "saisies," as in Plateau des Saisies, near Albertville, France. The Plateau des Saisies has prominent rock outcroppings as does Mt. Salève just behind La Saisiaz. The conclusion, then, is that "La Saisiaz" means "the rock," or possibly as Honan has said, "the rock-cleft." "Saisiaz" is pronounced [se'zjɑ].

1] *Dared and done* J. C. Maxwell ("Browning and Christopher Smart," *Notes and Queries* [December 1959]: 449) has attributed the source to Christopher Smart's "A Song to David": "And now the matchless deed's achieved, / DETERMINED, DARED, AND DONE" (ll. 515-16). B's "How you have dared and done all this, under my very eyes, for my only sake?" (letter to EBB, 13 September 1846; *Correspondence*, 13.360), refers not only to EBB's marrying him the day before, but to those elaborate plans and arrangements (involving some subterfuge on her part) that preceded the difficult elopement from her father's house at Wimpole Street. B's biographers explore the implications, as does J. Markus in *Dared and Done: The Marriage of Elizabeth Barrett and Robert Browning* (New York, 1995). B repeats the words in ll. 2, 25-27, 32, 132, and 138, as well as in a number of other poems.
7] *outspread* An expanse or expansion (*OED*, sense 2, where this line is cited).
16] *cyclamen* Plant with white, pink (as here), or red flowers, also known as sowbread because swine relish its roots.
17] *sloe-tree's* Sloe-tree is another name for the blackthorn.
18] *wilding apple* A wild apple tree, that is, a crab apple.
   redden ripe the mountain-ash The mountain ash has bright scarlet berries.
24] *Collonge* About a mile from La Saisiaz, Collonges-sous-Salève is the French town where Annie Egerton Smith was buried.
29] *mountain* Mount Salève, rising just behind La Saiziaz to an elevation of 3300 feet above Lake Geneva and, because of the view, a popular place for day outings.
37] *Jura* The mountain range of eastern France and western Switzerland.
40] *magnific* Magnificent (literary and archaic).
44] *lake* Lake Geneva
45] *Geneva* In a letter to Mrs. Thomas FitzGerald B described the view from the chalet: "Geneva lying under us, with the lake and the whole plain bounded by the Jura and our own Salève" (17 August 1877; DeVane and Knickerbocker, 45).

53] *pair* B's sister, Sarianna, and their French friend, Gustave Dourlans, whom they had met through Joseph Milsand.

56] *lamping* Shining (*OED* cites l. 5345 of *Aristophanes' Apology*: "Fire—with smoke—All night went lamping on!").

prepotency of Mars Prepotent because bright, but particularly bright every seventy-nine years, one of these cycles occurring in 1877, the year of the poem.

62] *travelled friend* Gustave Dourlans, who was to accompany them the next day.

75] *Blanc* Mont Blanc, about fifty miles to the southeast.

77] *some three weeks since* I.e., 28 August. B described this occasion to Mrs. Thomas FitzGerald in a letter of 30 August 1877: "We had a pleasant excursion two days ago: took our meal, after a morning's journey, on the top of a mountain in the full view of Mont Blanc and its brethren" (McAleer, 47).

80] *What . . . counter-play* During B's stay at La Saisiaz in August and September of 1877, the French were preparing to elect the chamber of deputies. Marie Edmé Patrice Maurice de MacMahon (1808-93), Marshall of France and second president of the third republic, had dissolved the chamber of deputies with its republican majority in June and called for new elections in October, hoping to return a majority of monarchists. Léon Gambetta (1838-82) led the republican opposition, which retained its majority in the October election. In January 1879 the republicans gained control of the senate as well, and MacMahon resigned as president.

83] *forth I fared* Journeyed or made my way (archaic or poetical). Cf. "Numpholeptos," ll. 66-67, 75-76, and 149-50.

84] *bath-pool* B described the setting of La Saisiaz to Mrs. Thomas FitzGerald: "How lovely is this place in its solitude and seclusion, with its trees and shrubs and flowers, and above all its live mountain stream which supplies three fountains, and two delightful baths, a marvel of delicate delight framed in with trees—I bathe there twice a day" (17 August 1877; McAleer, 44-45).

88] *ardours* Fires or flames, in this case the light of the morning sun.

92] *terrace* The verandah on to which Miss Smith's bedroom opened.

96] *blue lake's* Lake Geneva's.

97] *Mazy Arve* The Arve River flows down from Mont Blanc and empties into Lake Geneva. Cf. Coleridge's description of the Alph: "Five miles meandering in a mazy motion" ("Kubla Khan," l. 25).

99] *city's* Geneva's

102] *money-making* The aptitude of the Swiss for making and keeping money is legendary. Ll. 99-104 are humorous and partly self-mocking, as B is one of the tourists he deprecates.

104] *the texts whence Calvin* The Bible, for Calvin the only source of God's law. John Calvin (1509-64) had settled permanently in Geneva in 1541.

116] *the first* Even one.

provocation The act of calling or summoning (*OED* labels this sense obsolete and cites this line).

130] *Alpine-rose . . . Edelweiss* The alpine rose is a rhododendron, growing to five or six feet high and having a dark pink or red flower. The edelweiss is small and has a white flower (its name translates as "noble white"). B is using the difference in size and color to contrast his impression of Miss Smith with that of others.

154] *lisp . . . sphere-song out of reach* B contrasts inadequate human speech ("lisp") and divine truth. The music of the celestial spheres was beyond human hearing. Cf. Milton's "the heavenly tune, which none can hear / Of human mold with gross unpurged ear" ("Arcades," ll. 72-73) and Shakespeare's *The Merchant of Venice* 5.1.60-65.

163-64] *What . . . Life* The articles in *The Nineteenth Century*, described above in the source notes.

212] *Tuscan* Dante (1265-1321) was born in Florence, in Tuscany.

213-15] *I believe . . . soul* B is translating the last sentence of Ch. 8, Bk. 2 of Dante's *Il Convivio* (*The Banquet*). On 11 May 1876 B quoted the passage in a letter, explaining that fourteen years earlier he had inscribed it in EBB's Bible (Hood, 172).

318] *fineless* Boundless, infinite, unlimited (*OED* labels the word "rare" and cites this line).

327] *glassing* Reflecting, mirroring

342] *creature of an hour* Creature of a short or limited space of time (*OED* cites l. 76 of "Abt Vogler": "When eternity affirms the conception of an hour"). Cf. Keats's "fair creature of an hour" ("When I have fears," l. 9).

353] *Job-like . . . blains* Cf. Job 2:7-8: "So went Satan forth from the presence of the Lord, and smote Job with sore boils from the sole of his foot unto his crown. And he took him a postsherd to scrape himself withal; and he sat down among the ashes."

354] *whirlwind . . . explains* Cf. Job 38:1: "Then the Lord answered Job out of the whirlwind . . . ."

355-56] *vindicate . . . candid* Cf. Pope's "Laugh where we must, be candid where we can; / But vindicate the ways of God to man" (*An Essay on Man*, 1:15-16).

369]   *balsam*   An aromatic resinous product of trees, used as a balm.
372]   *alembic*   An apparatus formerly used in distilling.
    elixir   The essence extracted by distillation in the alembic, figuratively her soul (*OED* cites this line).
381-84]   *vast . . . chase*   The musical references may be general or specific. As regular companions at musical concerts in London, B and Miss Smith shared tastes in music and many musical experiences. Beethoven, because of both his romantic genius and his deafness in later life, was known as a giant, a Titan of symphonic sound. The fourth movement of the sixth symphony, the Pastoral (1809), in which a walk in the country is interrupted by a storm, may be the allusion here. In Mozart's *The Magic Flute* (1791) thunder and lightning accompany the Queen of the Night's aria in Act 2, but are calmed by the priestly Sarastro. But B's references may invoke more generally the stylistic difference between romantic extremes and classical order as represented by the two composers. B's fullest statement of his sense of music as the most universal art, inclusive of nature, spirit, and human emotion, is given in his "Parleying With Charles Avison" (this edition, 16.112-30 and nn.).
403]   *in thy behoof*   For thy use, benefit, or advantage, that is, the prize in the next line. B used the word similarly in l. 14 of "A Forgiveness" (this edition, 13.412)
419]   *grudge . . . Greek*   The vengefulness of Greek gods. Cf. The chorus's warning about Artemis's resentment against Agamemnon and Menelaus in B's *The Agamemnon of Æschylus*, also completed in 1877:

> Only, have care lest grudge of any god disturb
> With cloud the unsullied shine of that great force, the curb
> Of Troia, struck with damp
> Beforehand in the camp!
>   (ll. 133-36; this edition, 14.17-18)

421]   *blindworms*   Limbless European lizards with snakelike bodies, also called slowworms.
422]   *python*   In Greek mythology the dragon or serpent killed by Apollo at Delphi, and thus a monster or scourge.
430]   *mingled measure*   Cf. Coleridge's "Kubla Khan": "Where was heard the mingled measure / From the fountain and the caves" (ll. 33-34).
434]   *seventy years*   Ps. 90:10: "The days of our years are threescore years and ten . . . ."
444]   *drop*   A medicinal potion, in this context for sleeping, but in "The Laboratory" (this edition, 4.200) a poison: "What a drop!" (l. 29) and "delicate droplet" (l. 43).

446] *provided room* Cf. John 14:2: "In my Father's house are many mansions . . . . I go to prepare a place for you."

478] *gain or loss* A favorite phrase of B's, taken from "But what things were gain to me, those I counted loss for Christ" (Phil. 3:7). See also ll. 360-61 and 389.

525] The dialogue between Fancy and Reason (beginning with l. 405) ends with l. 524, and in this line B returns to his own voice.

546] *Athanasius contra mundum* Athanasius against the world, from Richard Hooker's *Of the Laws of Ecclesiastical Polity (1594-1662)*: "So this was the plain condition of those times: the whole world against Athanasius, and Athanasius against it" (5.XLII.5). Athanasius, Bishop of Alexandria, defended the doctrine of the Trinity at the Council of Nicaea in 325.

553] *Bossex* Bossey, a village near Geneva and residence of Jean Jacques Rousseau (1712-78) during two years of his boyhood (1719-21).

554] *a fiery flying serpent* Isa. 14:29: "out of the serpent's root shall come forth a cockatrice, and his fruit shall be a fiery flying serpent." See also Isa. 30:6. The image of the "fiery flying serpent" was possibly inspired by the "dung-heap" in l. 552 since the cockatrice's egg was reputedly hatched by a toad on a dunghill.

555-56] *Diodati . . . Byron's sake* Lord Byron (1788-1824) rented the Villa Diodati on the shores of Lake Geneva in 1816. There he worked on *Childe Harold's Pilgrimage*, the source of the quotations below in ll. 564-70.

561-63] *All . . . it* Rousseau's belief that humans were much happier in a state of nature than they are in civilized society.

564] *Dying . . . dolphin-hues* A reference to Byron's *Childe Harold's Pilgrimage*, 4.29:

> parting day
> Dies like the dolphin, whom each pang imbues
> With a new colour as it gasps away . . . .

565] *Storm . . . eye* A reference to Byron's *Childe Harold's Pilgrimage*, 3.92:

> Oh night,
> And storm, and darkness, ye are wondrous strong,
> Yet lovely in your strength, as is the light
> Of a dark eye in woman!

565-66] *Ye . . . fellow* A sentiment pervading Canto 3 of Byron's *Childe Harold's Pilgrimage*, one expression of which appears in stanza 72:

> to me
> High mountains are a feeling, but the hum
> Of human cities torture . . . .

566-70] *thou . . . gods* A reference to Byron's *Childe Harold's Pilgrimage*, 4.180:

> the vile strength he [man] wields
> For earth's destruction thou [the ocean] dost all despise
> Spurning him from thy bosom to the skies,
> And send'st him, shivering in thy playful spray
> And howling, to his Gods . . . .

In a letter written to Miss Smith on 16 August 1873 B denied a newspaper report that he had called Byron a flatfish, explaining,

I never said nor wrote a word against or about Byron's poetry or power in my life; but I did say, that, if he were in earnest and preferred being with the sea to associating with mankind, he would do well to stay with the sea's population; thereby simply taking him at his word, had it been honest—whereas it was altogether dishonest, seeing that nobody cared so much about the opinions of mankind, and deferred to them, as he who was thus posturing and pretending to despise them.

(Hood, 159)

569-70] *Man . . . dog* Byron compares the dog favorably to man in "Inscription on the Monument of a Newfoundland Dog."
573] *Fame* The referent of the opening line of "The Two Poets of Croisic": "'Fame!' Yes, I said it and you read it."
579] *pine-tree of Makistos* On the island of Euboea, one of a series of bonfires that announced to Argos the Greek victory over Troy. Cf. B's *The Agamemnon of Aeschylus,*:

> And,—so upsoaring as to stride sea over,
> The strong lamp-voyager, and all for joyance—
> Did the gold-glorious splendor, any sun like,
> Pass on—the pine-tree—to Makistos' watch-place . . . .
>
> (ll. 307-10; this edition, 14.25)

580-604] In the summary conclusion of the poem, B calls to witness a gallery of types and viewpoints, all resistant in one way or another to traditional Christian faith. Gibbon, Rousseau, Byron, and Voltaire are assembled by virtue of their connections with the region of Switzerland near where Miss Smith died (see nn. below on Lausanne, Bossex, Diodati, and Ferney). Gibbon, who admired the virtues of ancient Rome, showed the role of the early church in the decline of Roman civilization. Byron's immoral life earned him the epithet of poet of the Satanic school. Rousseau's advocacy of the role of nature over institutional Christianity in childhood education scandalized his generation. Voltaire mocked many abuses of religious practice and belief, elevating rational power over providential faith in changing society. The tree/snake images of the passage evoke variations on Genesis. Crowning and usurping the different viewpoints, B offers his own witness and affirmation of faith in ll. 599-604.

582] *Lausanne* City on the northern shore of Lake Geneva and residence of Edward Gibbon (1737-94) for two periods of his life, 1753-58 and 1783 till his death. During the second of these he completed his *Decline and Fall of the Roman Empire.*

583] *aspic* Poetical form of *asp* (see *Antony and Cleopatra*, 5.2.293).

586] *Ferney* Village near Geneva and residence of Voltaire (1694-1778), now known as Ferney-Voltaire.

588-89] *Bossex . . . Jean-Jacques* Rousseau, see note to l. 553.

590] *Diodati* Byron, see note to ll. 555-56.

602] *flamboyant* Like a flame, either by being wavy or by having color, but the French sense of *flaming* or *blazing* seems to fit best.

603] *bauble* "A baton or stick, surmounted by a fantastically carved head with asses' ears, carried by the Court Fool or jester of former days as a mock emblem of office" (*OED*, sense 4). "Wit's bauble" refers to "witty as wit's self Voltaire" in l. 596.

rod A staff carried as a symbol of office or authority. "Learning's rod" refers to "Learned for the nonce as Gibbon" in l. 596.

606] *London's mid-November* The poem was written in London and dated 9 November.

613] *root* The bulb of a perennial plant, dug up in the fall for replanting in the spring.

614] *re-interment* Interring again, in the sense of planting again (*OED* cites this line).

THE TWO POETS OF CROISIC

PROLOGUE TO *THE TWO POETS OF CROISIC*

Source]   B evidently wrote the prologue with EBB in mind, only she having such an influence on his life.
2]   *May-morn* B first met EBB in May of 1845.

THE TWO POETS OF CROISIC

Date and Composition]   At the end of his manuscript B wrote that he began the poem on Saturday, 10 November (the day after completing "La Saisiaz") and finished it on 8 December 1877, exactly four weeks later. He must have worked very quickly and steadily to complete the forty-nine-page manuscript with its 160 ottava rima stanzas in so short a time. One sign of haste is his misnumbering of the stanzas by having skipped number 31, going from 30 to 32. He apparently did not catch the mistake until he reached the eighth stanza from the end inasmuch as the number of this stanza and the numbers of the remaining stanzas are unchanged. He then went back and wrote over the stanza numbers beginning with stanza 31, but in correcting them he again skipped a number, this time stanza 150, so that stanzas 150 through 160 are misnumbered in the manuscript as stanzas 151 through 161. The mistake was corrected in the 1878 edition, and the 1889a edition changed the Arabic numerals of the manuscript and the 1878 edition to Roman numerals.

Another sign of rapid composition is a manuscript filled with changes, some no doubt made afterwards but many obviously made at the time B was writing the poem. Not a single stanza of the 160 is without a correction of some sort, and many are so heavily marked and changed as to be almost illegible.

There are about 550 textual variants between the manuscript and the 1878 edition, the majority of changes (ca. 350) involving punctuation, along with a few in capitalization and spelling. The remaining 200 or so changes are mainly word substitutions. With the 1878 and 1889a editions there are only about 85 variants, of which around 20 are verbal.

Sources]   The description of Le Croisic in stanzas 10-16 is based upon B's holidays there during August and September of 1866 and 1867. Le Croisic had a population of about 6,000 in the seventeenth century, but less than half that in B's time. It was a popular place for holidays in the mid nineteenth century, attracting some 800 visitors each summer. B wrote to Isabella Blagden that "usually it is fashionable and full, but this season reports of the cholera and other causes have kept people away, and we have it nearly to ourselves: we are in the most delicious and peculiar old house I ever occupied, the oldest in the town,— plenty of great rooms . . . the little town, and surrounding country are wild and primitive, even a trifle beyond Pornic perhaps" (7 August 1866; Hood, 100). Though not the oldest in Le Croisic, the house does date from the seventeenth century. Long known as the Hôtel d'Aiguillon after the Duke of Aiguillon, governor of Brittany, who resided there in the eighteenth century, it was bought by the city government in 1907 and is now the Hôtel de Ville.

The stories of the two poets come from volume 3 of *Promenade au Croisic* (Paris, 1828) by Gustave Grandpré, the pen name of Auguste

Browning's lodgings in Le Croisic

Julien Marie Lorieux (1797-1842). A native of Croisic, Lorieux was a lawyer and judge in Nantes, as well as author of books on law, history, and travel. B apparently worked from Sarianna's handwritten transcripts of the relevant passages from the book, the chapter on Gentilhomme appearing in 3:81-87 and the one on Desforges-Maillard in 3:45-55. Sarianna's transcripts are now in the Armstrong Browning Library. In the poem B says that the story of Gentilhomme is "true to the least word" (l. 190), and he does indeed follow his source very closely, although not quite "to the least word." B identifies René Gentilhomme as a page to the Prince of Condé (l. 200), but Grandpré, quoting the inscription around Dupré's portrait of Gentilhomme, identifies him as a page to *"Monseigneur frère du roi,"* Gaston, Duke of Orleans. B may have committed this error through the mistaken belief that Condé was the brother of King Louis XIII, for in l. 202 of the manuscript he wrongly identified Condé as the brother of the King, an error corrected by the substitution of "cousin" for "brother" in the proofs of the 1878 edition. Perhaps, too, B was looking for a way to explain why Gentilhomme was at Condé's pleasure house when lightning struck the ducal crown.

However, the fact is that the latter event occurred at Gaston's chateau at Blois and not, as Grandpré said, at Condé's pleasure house. The significance of the location is that it was Gaston, not Condé, whose hopes for succession were dashed by the prophesy of the King's having a son. The truth makes more sense than the error because only Gaston was known as the Duke and only he would have cause to lament that he would always be Duke and never King. Henry II of Bourbon (1588-1646), third Prince of Condé, was never called Duke because he was from birth a prince, his father having predeceased him. Henry's son, Louis, Duke of Enghien, was popularly known as *Monsieur le Duc* until his father's death in 1646, when he became fourth Prince of Condé. Later called the Great Condé, Louis could not be the one in question, however, because he was not next to Gaston in line of inheritance, because he fully expected to succeed his father as prince and not remain a duke all his life, and because when the event occurred he was in his teens, at school and without an established household, much less a pleasure house.

Grandpré was wrong in placing Gentilhomme at the Prince of Condé's estate and in thus making Condé the disappointed heir because his source for the story was wrong. Although Grandpré cites no source, he clearly copied his story from a letter written by Paul Desforges-Maillard, the other poet of Croisic, and published in the *Mercure de France* for June 1745 (pp. 113-22). In this letter Desforges-Maillard tells of seeing in someone's house a portrait of René Gentilhomme, which he describes in detail. His curiosity piqued, he searched fruit-lessly for information about the earlier poet until he wrote his friend, René de Chevaye, who responded with an account of Gentilhomme, which Desforges-Maillard quotes in the letter printed in the *Mercure*. De Chevaye, then, is the ultimate and erroneous source of the story of Gentilhomme's predicting the birth of the dauphin. Desforges-Mail-lard quoted de Chevaye's story, Grandpré copied it from Desforges-Maillard, Sarianna transcribed it from Grandpré, and B based his poem on the transcript, believing it to be "true to the least word" but not knowing that de Chevaye had it wrong in the first place.

There remains the final question of why de Chevaye got Gaston and Condé mixed up. The answer is probably that he misremembered. In response to Desforges-Maillard's inquiry, he wrote that his copy of Gentilhomme's poems had been lost when his house in Nantes burned down and that he was recounting the story from memory. In admitting that the story of the prophecy was the only thing he remembered about Gentilhomme, de Chevaye allows for the possibility that he may not have remembered even this quite correctly.

The most accurate account of what actually happened is by Stéphane Halgan in his *Anthologie des Poètes Bretons du XVIIᵉ Siècle* (Nantes, 1884). According to Halgan, Gentilhomme was a page to Gas-ton at his chateau at Blois in 1635 when a dolphin (*un dauphin*) caught in the Loire inspired Gentilhomme to predict the birth of a dauphin to Louis XIII. Two years later lightning struck the roof of the chateau, damaging an ornamental royal crown but leaving untouched a ducal crown. Gentilhomme interpreted this event to mean that Gaston was destined to wear only the crown of a duke, never that of a king, in con-firmation of his earlier prediction that a dauphin would be born to in-herit the throne. This prophecy is the one he cast in poetry:

Là, le foudre frappant la couronne royale,
Sans briser ni brusler la couronne ducale,
A mon esprit de feu fait voir très clairement,
MONSIEUR, que vous serez un grand duc seulement;
Qu'en jouant vous perdrez un royal héritage.

("There, the lightning striking the royal crown without breaking or burn-ing the ducal crown made my inflamed spirit see very clearly, Sir, that you will be only a grand duke and that you will lose a royal inheritance.")

The rest of the story about the prophecy is as de Chevaye and, later, Grandpré, report it: the prophecy was true, Gentilhomme had his portrait painted by Dupré and engraved by Daret, and he enjoyed short-lived fame as Royal Poet. The substitution of Condé for Gaston in B's poem does not affect the essential subject of a prophecy resulting in brief fame, followed in turn by obscurity. Except for B's assertion that his account is historically true, the case of mistaken identity is of no more consequence here than in the sonnet where Keats mistakes Cortes for Balboa. De Chevaye, Desforges-Maillard, and Grandpré do not report Gentilhomme's later misadventures. After the prophecy, he had an affair with Gaston's mistress, Louyson Roger, and fled to Holland, Richelieu having interceded for his life. There he became embroiled in another amorous scrape by seducing Princess Louise of Bohemia and surviving an attempted assassination by her brother. He returned to France, where he died in 1671.

For the story of Paul Desforges-Maillard, B again followed Grandpré closely, and in this case Grandpré's information was more accurate, based as it was on an episode both more recent and more celebrated than the one involving Gentilhomme. B does enlarge the role of Paul's sister and varies from his source in attributing to her the deceitful plan to use her name, and he does invent many details, but otherwise he follows the basic outline of Grandpré's account.

1] *Fame . . . it* See "La Saisiaz" ll. 573 and 595.

7] *splendidest* One of B's idiosyncratic formations of the superlative.

11] *pandemonium* The palace built by the fallen angels in *Paradise Lost.*

27] *bore away the bell* Carried off the prize, referring to a golden or silver bell awarded to the winner of a contest.

30] *Octogenarian Keats* Keats died at the age of twenty-five.

32] *span-long* The short time of a human life.

39] *tonguelet* A little tongue (*OED* cites this line).

40] *copperas* The protosulphate of iron or ferrous sulphate, also called green vitriol.

46-7] *Son . . . spark* The likely source is Job 5:7: "Yet man is born unto trouble, as the sparks fly upward." The literal translation of the dependent clause is "as sure as Resheph's sons soar afloat." Resheph was a Canaanite plague-god, associated with fire, whose name is used seven times in the Old Testament to denote flames or lightning. Thus "Resheph's sons" are "sons of the flame," or "sons of the coal," that is, sparks.

49] *lesser lights* Horace's *minora sidera* (*Epode* 15. 2). Fainter stars or planets, figuratively people of lesser fame. Cf. "Epilogue" to *Dramatis Personae* (l. 46), *Red Cotton Night-Cap Country* (1:506), and this passage from Shakespeare's *Pericles* (2.3.39-42):

Had princes sit like stars about his throne,
And he the sun for them to reverence;
None that beheld him but, like lesser lights,
Did vail their crowns to his supremacy . . . .

53] *Constellate* Cluster together like stars in a constellation

swords, scrolls, harps The sword could be the sword of Orion or of Perseus, and the harp the constellation Lyra (Orpheus's lyre), but the scroll appears only in the phrase "the scroll of heaven," referring to all the legendary figures immortalized as stars. These three probably represent the hero (sword), sage (scroll), and bard (harp) mentioned in l. 23.

59] *columnar* In the form of a column.

61] *bicker* Flash, glean, quiver, or glisten (poetical).

61-2] *blue . . . zinc's* Zinc is a bluish-white metal, its residue on the firewood thus producing a blue-tinted flame.

74] *land-strip* The peninsula of Le Croisic, on the southern coast of Brittany, which B and his sister visited in 1866 and 1867.

79] *town* The town is also called Le Croisic.

83] *Guérande* A town about six miles northeast of Le Croisic, described by B as "the delicious old city of Guerande, intact with its moat, wall, towers and gates: it is the old seat of all the genuine Bretagne noblesse, who live on in the old way and with the old ideas" (letter of 19 February 1867 to Baron Seymour Kirkup, in Hood, 107). B had read Balzac's *Béatrix*, which is set in Guérande and which emphasizes the old-fashioned ways of its inhabitants. This town, as well as Batz nearby (see below), was also known for the traditional and picturesque ways in which some of the inhabitants worked in collecting salt.

84-86] *Batz . . . salt* A town of about 1100 inhabitants in B's time, reputedly founded by Saxons, whose principal industry was making salt from sea water. Just two miles from Le Croisic, it was described by B as "the strange, solitary Bourg de Batz—a Saxon colony of stalwart men who retain exactly the dress of their forefathers, three hundred years ago—white tunic, baggy breeches, stockings, even shoes, all white, but a great black flap-hat with red fringes. These are the *paludiers* who collect the salt from the *salines*, which forms the staple produce of the place" (letter of 19 February 1867 to Baron Seymour Kirkup; Hood, 106-7).

90-120] *Druids' . . . fisticuffs* Of the Druidical rites described in these stanzas, B wrote, "Croisic is the old head-seat of Druidism in France, probably mentioned by Strabo: the people were still Pagan a couple of hundred years ago, despite the priests' teaching and preaching, and the women used to dance round a phallic stone still upright there with obscene circumstances enough,—till the general civilization got too strong for this" (letter of 19 February 1867 to Baron Seymour Kirkup; Hood, 106).

107-8]   *Menhir . . . church-spire*   Le Menhir de la Pierre Longue is a monumental, obelisk-like stone eight-feet high, standing only a short distance from the church at Le Croisic. It is like the far more numerous and famous stones at Carnac. The spire is 168 feet high and belongs to l'Èglise Notre-Dame de Pitié, built in the sixteenth century.

116]   *shent*   Reproached or reproved, but the *OED* says that in later use the passive often means to be punished. Either meaning fits.

152]   *beasts or gods*   Cf. Pope's "In doubt to deem himself a god, or beast" (*An Essay on Man*, 2:8). B transposes the words in l. 168.

155-56]   *turn/Cedar from hyssop-on-the-wall*   Make the great out of the small. Cf. 1 Kings 4:33: "And he [Solomon] spake of trees, from the cedar tree that is in Lebanon even unto the hyssop that springeth out of the wall . . . ." The cedar and the hyssop refer back to the tree and shrub in the preceding stanza.

160]   *Hervé Riel*   The Croisickese hero who rescued the French fleet in 1692 and about whom B wrote a poem in 1867 (published in *Pacchiarotto* [1876], this edition, 13.205). A statue of him was erected in Le Croisic in 1913.

162]   *billet's*   A thick piece of firewood. Cf. "Ivàn Ivànovitch" (*Dramatic Idyls, First Series*, this edition, 14.233), where Ivàn with his axe "Changed bole to billets" (l. 38).

165-66]   *gules . . . you*   In heraldic terms, *gules* is *red* and *vert* is *green*.

168]   *gods or beasts*   See l. 152.

185-6]   *Assist,/Clio*   An invocation to Clio, the muse of history.

191]   *sixteen hundred years and ten*   The year of Gentilhomme's birth.

193]   *René Gentilhomme*   René Gentilhomme, Sieur de Lespine, was born in Le Croisic in July of 1610 and died 12 November 1671.

196]   *Better do than say*   Grandpré reports that the engraving of Gentilhomme's portrait has the poet's coat of arms with the motto "*Mieux faire que dire.*" It is at the bottom center of the picture on p. 418.

199]   *proper age*   At the age of twenty-five.

200]   *Prince of Condé's*   Henry II of Bourbon, third prince of Condé (1588-1646), father of the Great Condé, and cousin of Louis XIII. Condé is the family name of a cadet branch of the French royal house of Bourbon. However, as explained in the source notes, Gentilhomme was in the service of Gaston, the King's brother, not of Condé.

201]   *"The Duke"*   De Chevaye, whose letter Grandpré quotes, confuses father and son in referring to "*M. Le Prince de Condé, qu'on appelait alors M. le Duc"* ("Monsieur the Prince of Condé who was then called Monsieur the Duke"). See the source notes for an explanation of how it was the son, Louis, who was known as the Duke, and not the father.

204] *Anne of Austria* Queen of France (1601-66), daughter of Philip III of Spain, and wife (from 1615) of Louis XIII. She assumed the regency of her son Louis XIV in 1643 and figures as an important character in Dumas's *The Three Musketeers* (1844).

208] *Next King . . . wince* In B's "At the 'Mermaid,'" Shakespeare does wince when called "Next Poet" (this edition, 13.166-71 and nn.).

212] *Gaston* Jean Baptiste Gaston (1608-60), Duke of Orleans and younger brother of Louis XIII.

223] *spleen-fits* Ill-humor (*OED* cites this line).

225-28] *his . . . decease* B wrote this note at the end of Sarianna's transcript of Grandpré: "Lespine (René Thimothée) Gentilhomme du Croisic, mort dit on—en 1610: auteur d'un petit poème de la *Parure des Dames*. Père de René—" ("Lespine [René Thimothée] Gentleman of Croisic, died they say–in 1610: author of a little poem, 'The Ornament of Ladies.' Father of René"). Although René was commonly believed to be the son of René-Thimothée, he was in fact the son of Jean Gentilhomme, a keeper of salt rather than a poet.

229] *sacred fire* Poetic inspiration.

240] *"love"—not "dove."* Besides "dove," rhyming dictionaries list only four rhymes for "love": "above," "glove," "of," and "shove."

241-42] *silence. . . Muse* Cf. John Stuart Mill's "Poetry . . . is the natural fruit of solitude and meditation" ("What is Poetry?").

243] *our new picturesque* New because the picturesque was not established as an aesthetic category until the latter part of the eighteenth century.

248] *Araminte* Gentilhomme's "Ode to Araminte." See l. 288.

249-56] *When . . . base* In de Chevaye's letter, quoted by Grandpré, Gentilhomme is said to have written his poem prophesying the birth of a dauphin "*à l'occasion du tonnerre qui venait d'écraser une couronne ducale, placée sur le pilier de l'escalier du jardin de cette maison, duquel accident il tirait dans ses vers un augure, qu'il regardait comme certain, de la naissance d'un dauphin.*" ("on the occasion of a thunderbolt that had just shattered a ducal crown placed on a pillar of the steps in a garden of this house, which event he interpreted in his verse as an augury, which he regarded as certain, of the birth of a dauphin.")

258] *wrappage* A wrap or outer covering.

269-70] *Pebble . . . giant* An allusion to David and Goliath (I Sam.17).

272] *peacock-prince* The peacock is traditionally associated with pride.

285] *for better or for worse* From the marriage vow in the Book of Common Prayer.

289] *crowquill calligraph* The most common pen was made from the quill of a goose, but crow quills were used for fine lines.

294] *earth's break-up, amid the falling rocks* Cf. Luke 21:5-6, 11: "And as some spoke of the temple, how it was adorned with noble stones and offerings, he [Jesus] said, 'As for these things which you see, the days will come when there shall not be left here one stone upon another that will not be thrown down. . . . there will be great earthquakes . . . .'"

297] *so terribly he pens* According to B's source, "*la fureur poétique le possédât bien pour faire dans le lieu où il était, une prédiction*" ("the poetic fury possessed him to make in the place where he was a prediction").

299] *divinior mens* Inspired thought or genius, literally *diviner thought* (Horace, *Satires*, 1.4.43).

302] *Rhadamanthine* Inflexibly rigorous or severe (*OED* cites this line). Rhadamanthus, son of Zeus and Europa, was one of the judges in the lower world.

305-6] Grandpré quotes de Chavaye's remark that Gentilhomme's prediction was "*contraire aux intérêts du prince de Condé qui l'avait reçu chez lui, et qui par la mort de Louis 13 et de Gaston d'Orléans son frère, était héritier présomptif de la couronne, car il y dit positivement qu'il doit se contenter d'être toute sa vie M. le Duc, tout court.*" ("contrary to the interests of the Prince of Condé, who had received him into his house and who, upon the death of Louis XIII and of Gaston of Orleans, his brother, was heir apparent of the crown, because he said emphatically that he must be contented with being his whole life simply Monsieur the Duke.") Stanzas XXXIX and XL are B's invention, not a translation of Gentilhomme's poem.

311] *Sol's self* The "Next King" will be Louis XIV, styled the Sun King.

320] *Dauphin* The title of the eldest son of the king of France used from 1349 to 1830.

     glads gladdens (archaic).

321] *some forty lines* Grandpré's source states that Gentilhomme wrote "*une pièce d'environ quarante vers.*"

335-36] *cony-kind . . . folk* Prov. 30:26: "The conies are but a feeble folk . . . ." The biblical cony is not a rabbit but a rock-badger (*Hyrax Syriacus*).

344] *sun* See note to l. 311.

345-50] *And . . . agape* Quoting de Chavaye's letter, Grandpré writes that Gentilhomme received more than twenty compliments in verse, besides "*autres de plusieurs officiers et ecclésiastiques de Nantes, et de quelques autres de Tours."* ("others from several officials and clergymen from Nantes, and from some others from Tours.")

360]   *Simeon*   In the temple Simeon held the infant Jesus and proclaimed him the salvation sent by God (Luke 2:25-35). This event is commemorated in the church on 2 February as the feast of the Presentation of Our Lord Jesus Christ in the Temple.

360-61]   *God's . . . boy*   The child was baptized Louis-Dieudonné.

363]   *Royal Poet*   De Chevaye's letter, quoted by Grandpré, concludes, *"Une autre circonstance dont je me souviens, c'est qu'il parait que cette prédiction avait procuré à l'auteur le nom de poëte royal, mais je ne me rappelle pas qu'il en ait reçu d'autre récompense."* (Another thing I remember is that this prediction procured for the author the title of royal poet, but I do not recall that he received any other compensation.")

377]   *Du Pré*   Guillaume Dupré (ca. 1574-1647), painter, sculptor and engraver of medals.

378]   *Daret*   Pierre Daret (1604-78), drawer and engraver. Daret's engraved portrait of Gentilhomme, reproduced on p. 418, is in the Musée Dobrée, Nantes.

381-84]   *And . . . trump*   The Latin epigram beneath Gentilhomme's portrait says nothing of Parnassus with its two peaks, only that "You see the picture of a poet blowing through bronze, / Who joined the Getic trumpet with the Delphic quill (*"Aspicis effigiem vatis spirantis in aere, / Qui junxit Geticae Delphica plectra tubae. . ."*). The lines probably refer to Gentilhomme's being both a prophet (the trumpet) and a poet (the quill) and also perhaps to his prophecy being Christian (i.e. Getic, or Gothic) since it forecast God's gift of a child to Louis, while his poetry was Greek (Delphic) in its neoclassic manner. Grandpré reports that the epigram was written by *"J. Leochens, Scotus eloquentiae et philo. professor."* This is John Leech, an early seventeenth-century Scottish epigrammist. B's addition of Gentilhomme's being between "the biforked hill" of Parnassus reinforces the idea of combining prophecy and poetry because the mountain, with its two dominant peaks of Tithorea and Lycoreia, was sacred to both the Muses and Apollo, whose oracle resided at Delphi, on the slope of the mountain.

397-98]   *Red . . . both*   B here returns to the opening image of the flames, the red representing René Gentilhomme and the green Paul Desforges-Maillard (see l. 165).

401]   *Somebody*   Gustave Grandpré. In stanzas LI-LVII B repeats Grandpré's story of how he came to learn about Gentilhomme. During a visit to Le Croisic Grandpré saw the portrait of Gentilhomme described in stanza XLVIII and asked the unnamed owner of the portrait about the subject. The owner knew nothing, but Grandpré's inquiries

Daret's engraved portrait of René Gentilhomme (Musée Dobrée, Nantes).

led him to discover that a hundred years earlier Paul Desforges-Maillard, the other poet of Le Croisic, had also been curious about the subject of the portrait and had written to René de Chavaye, auditor in the accounting office of Brittany. De Chavaye responded by letter to Desforges-Maillard's inquiry that he had in fact once owned a book of Gentilhomme's poetry but that it had been destroyed when his house in Nantes burned down. De Chavaye did, however, remember the story of Gentilhomme's prediction and recounted it in the letter to Desforges-Maillard. This letter is the source for Grandpré, who is the source for B. See the source notes.

404]   *owner*   Grandpré leaves blank the name of the owner.

422]   *perks*   Pranks or trims, as a bird its plumage.

423]   *eyed wing*   Of the butterfly (l. 420), perhaps the peacock butterfly (*Vanessa Io*), "conspicuous from the 'eyes' on the upper surface of its wings" (*Encyclopaedia Britannica*, 9th ed., 4:595). B mentions this type of butterfly in *Red Cotton Night-Cap Country* (4:970).

   imperial   Majestic, lofty.

434]   *somebody*   Unknown to Grandpré, who reports that "*Desforges fit de vains efforts pour se procurer ses oeuvres; on lui dit pourtant que M. de Chavaye, auditeur à la chambre des comptes de Bretagne, en possédait un exemplaire.*" ("Deforges made futile attempts to procure these works; he was told, however, that Monsieur de Chevaye, auditor of the accounting office of Brittany, possessed a copy.")

444]   *in duodecimo*   The size of a book or page, one-twelfth of a whole sheet and measuring about 5 inches by 7¾ inches. De Chevaye described the book as "*un petit recueil d'environ cinquante feuillets in. 12 . . . .*"

461-62]   *nowhere . . . Croisic*   The portrait must have disappeared between when Grandpré saw it about 1828 and when B was in Croisic in 1866 and 1867, if Grandpré did indeed see it, as he claims to have done. His description of the portrait is so much like the one of Desforges-Maillard published in the *Mercury* as to arouse suspicions of plagiarism.

488]   *fortalice*   A small fort or the small outwork of a fortification.

546-49]   *Paul . . . René*   Paul Desforges-Maillard (the hyphen is usually added) was born in Le Croisic on 24 April 1699 at the end of the seventeenth century; René Gentilhomme was born at its beginning in 1610. Desforges-Maillard was a lawyer who held various jobs as a government bureaucrat. He died of dropsy on 10 December 1772.

549-50]   *Cease . . . Providence*   Echoing Pope's "presume not God to scan" (*An Essay on Man*, 2:1).

555-56]   *In . . . chiefly*   Grandpré says that he made for himself "*une sort de réputation dans sa jeunesse, en composant des couplets de circonstance*

DESFORGES-MAILLARD
1699 - 1772

Ad Lalauze sc.

Imp A Quantin

Frontispiece to Poésies Diverse de Desforges-Maillard, avec une notice bio-bibliographique par Honoré Bonhomme. Paris: A. Quantin, 1880.

et de petits vers de société." ("a kind of reputation in his youth by composing occasional verse and little poems about society.")

561-62] *inch . . . ell* An ell is 45 inches. *Inch* and *ell* appear together in the proverb "Give him an inch and he'll take an ell."

567] *Guérande as Batz* See notes to lines 83 and 84-86. Both towns are very close to Le Croisic, and so his fame was not widespread.

577] *prize* According to Grandpré, Desforges-Maillard's limited local success "*suffit longtemps à ses désirs, mais enfin, donnant à son ambition un nouvel essor, il se mit sur les rangs pour disputer le prix de poésie, lorsqu'en 1730, l'académie proposa au concours* les progrès de l'art de la navigation sous Louis XIV." ("satisfied him for a long time, but finally he more ambitiously decided to compete for the poetry prize, proposed by the Academy in 1730, on the subject of the progress of the art of navigation during the reign of Louis XIV.")

Academy's The French Academy, officially organized by Cardinal Richelieu in 1635 to study literature and language.

581] *last king's reign* The reign of Louis XIV (1643-1715).

585] *Neptune and Amphitrité* The god of the sea and his wife.

Thetis A sister of Amphitrité and the mother of Achilles, Homer's "silver-footed Thetis, daughter of the Old Man of the Sea."

586] *Tethys* Grandmother of Amphitrité and Thetis, one of the Titans and wife of Oceanus.

tag Serve as a tag, that is, the rhyme at the end of a poetical line (*OED* cites the line, its only example of the intransitive in this sense).

587-88] *Triton . . . Virgil* In the first book of *The Aeneid*, Triton, the son of Neptune, pulls Aeneas's ships off a reef.

588] *winds* The four winds are represented by the four people in the following line.

589] *De Maille* Armand de Maillé (1619-46), Marquis of Brézé and Duke of Fronsac. He was nominal commander of the Mediterranean fleet from 1639 to 1645 and was killed in the victory over the Spanish fleet at Orbitello.

Vendôme Probably François de Vendôme (1616-69), Duke of Beaufort. Superintendent of navigation, he fought a Turkish fleet off the coast of North Africa in 1665. But the reference may possibly be to his father, César de Bourbon (1594-1665), Duke of Vendôme and natural son of Henry IV. He also was a superintendent of navigation, who, in 1655, fought a Spanish fleet off the coast of Barcelona.

Vermandois Louis de Bourbon (1667-83), Count of Vermandois, natural son of Louis XIV and of Louise de La Vallière. Although given the honorary title of admiral at the age of two, he was, as the French say, *un amiral suisse*, and died as a soldier at the battle of Courtrai.

Toulouse Louis-Alexandre de Bourbon (1678-1737), Count of Toulouse, legitimate son of Louis XIV. An admiral during the War of Spanish Succession, he commanded the fleet against the British at the battle of Malaga in 1704.

592] *Regent* See l. 204n. Anne was Regent of France during Louis XIV's minority.

lymph Water (poetical).

593] *irritabilis gens* Horace's *genus irritable vatum* (*Epistles*, 2.2.102), translated by Coleridge as "the touchy race of poets" in chapter two of his *Biographia Literaria*, where he describes the phrase as "the old sarcasm of Horace upon the scribblers of his time."

597] *divinior mens* See l. 299n.

602] *Forty's* The French Academy has forty members.

611] *Phoebus . . . train* The muses were followers of Phoebus Apollo, god of lyric poetry.

613] *high-throned . . . Seine* The Institut de France, which houses the French Academy, is in the heart of Paris on the left bank of the Seine beside the Pont des Arts. The impressive site was very familiar to B from his sojourns and walks in Paris.

620] *clink* Rhyme or jingle (*OED* cites this line).

626] *Brain-vibrios* The vibrio is a worm-like microorganism, here apparently a variation on *worm in the brain*, defined by the *OED* as "whim . . . a perverse fancy or desire; a streak of madness or insanity" (sense 11b, obsolete). These vibrios describe Paul's fury at the rejection of his poem, but in "Martin Relph" the "worm inside which bores at the brain" (l. 72) is a guilty conscience, and in "Caliban upon Setebos" "maggots scamper through my brain" (l. 72) when Caliban is drunk.

642] *Chevalier La Roque* Antoine De La Roque (1672-1744), editor of the Paris *Mercury*. *Chevalier* is a title signifying leadership or eminence; it is not a title of nobility.

643] *pride of place* In falconry, the highest point of the bird's flight before diving at its prey.

646] *literators* Literary men, from the French *littérateurs* (*OED* cites this line).

648] *Mercury* *Mercure de France*, newspaper founded in 1672.

649-50] *By . . . poem* The friend was l'abbé Maurinay, whom Grandpré does not identify, writing only that "*par l'entremise d'un ami, il fit présenter son poëme au chevalier de La Roque, alors rédacteur du* Mercure, *avec prière de l'insérer dans un des numéros de son journal.*" ("through the intervention of a friend his poem was submitted to the Chevalier de la Roque, at that time the editor of the *Mercury*, with a request to print it in one of the issues of his journal.")

650-51] *appeal . . . Jews* Possibly a reference to St. Paul's appeal to Caesar (Acts 25-26).

659] *Pierian rill* Water sacred to the Muses, reputedly born in Pieria, and thus a source of poetical inspiration.

660] *clodpoles* Blockheads. Sometimes spelled *clotpole*, as B does in "Pacchiarotto," l. 266 (this edition, 13.149); *OED* cites this line.

669] *crambo* Doggerel, from a rhyming game of the same name. B says that his "Pambo" is "crambo" in line 2 of the poem bearing that title (in *Jocoseria* [1883]).

673] *poltroon* "A coward; a nidgit; a scoundrel" (Johnson's *Dictionary*).

696] *cock / O' the roost* Variation on *cock of the walk*, that is, leader or chief person.

721] *Talent should minister to genius* A commonplace among those who believed that although natural genius was most important to an artist, learning and skill (i.e. talent) were necessary as well. Cf. Coleridge's "Genius must have talent as its complement and implement. . ." (*Table Talk*, 20 August 1833). See the quotation from B's letter in the note to l. 797.

727] *mounted Roland's crest* Worn the helmet of Roland, Charlemagne's knight and the hero of *The Song of Roland*.

731] *swans or geese* Excellent poets, as opposed to bad ones. Cf. Virgil's *Eclogue* 9: "Harsh are the sweetest lays that I can bring, / So screams a goose where swans melodious sing" (Beattie's translation).

734-35] *bared . . . image* A reference to "You entered lists with visor up" in l. 726.

742] *velvet-compliment three-pile* Three-pile velvet is woven with three threads to the loop of the pile and thus is especially thick.

743-44] *nor . . . Nor* Poetical version of *neither . . . nor*, a favorite of B.

   stock . . . stone Proverbial for insensible, unfeeling.

748] *went to wall* Gave way, succumbed in a conflict or struggle.

751] *found out what's o'clock* Discovered the real state of things (*OED* cites this line). Comparable to "know what time it is."

761] *Deïdamia . . . Achilles* Daughter of Lycomedes, King of Skyros, Deïdamia was seduced by Achilles while he was disguised as a woman to avoid sailing to Troy. The story is apt because Paul's masculine poem will be "femininely frocked" to win over La Roque.

767] *lady's-smock* The cuckooflower, playing on "femininely frock" in l. 759.

776] *Phoebus and the tuneful choir* Phoebus Apollo and the muses.

777-92] *Who . . . Malcrais* Grandpré writes that "*Desforges Maillard avait une soeur, femme de beaucoup d'esprit, d'un extérieur et de manières agréables, qui dans le monde se faisait appeler mademoiselle Malcrais de La Vigne. Par une manie fort commune à cette époque, où chacun semblait crain-*

dre de porter son nom, mademoiselle Desforges avait pris celui d'une pièce de vigne dépendante de la terre de Brederac, propriété de famille qu'habitait souvent M. Desforges, et qu'il a chantée dans des vers aussi durs que son nom. C'est elle que Desforges choisit pour secrétaire." ("Desforges-Maillard had a sister, a high-spirited woman, with attractive features and manners, who referred to herself in society as Mademoiselle Malcrais de la Vigne. Because of a very common habit of this time, when people seemed to be afraid of using their own names, Mademoiselle Desforges had taken her name from a vineyard attached to the estate of Brederac, a family property where Monsieur Desforges frequently stayed and where he had sung in verses as hard as his name [the iron forge in Desforges]. It is she whom Desforges chooses as his secretary.")

In B's poem she not merely copies the poems but concocts the stratagem.

783]   *Arouet*   Françoise Marie Arouet, whose pen name was Voltaire. The name "Desforges" had itself been assumed by the poet, who was born simply "Maillard."

786]   *Brederac*   Mentioned by Grandpré in the note to ll. 777-92. Desforges-Maillard wrote a poem about the place, titled simply "Bredérac," and described in the subtitle as a "*petite maison de campagne de l'auteur*" ("a little country house of the author's").

787]   *vineyard*   The English equivalent of *vigne* in l. 785.

797]   *Oh angel and yet ape*   The highest and lowest. In a letter to Mrs. Thomas FitzGerald (19 September 1880), B. made the point that an artist must first master technique by citing the example of a young friend, who "had great imagination, and at once tried to draw things much above angels when he was unable really to properly draw apes" (McAleer, 94).

809]   *Turk*   The Turk was popularly reputed to be cruel and unfeeling, the "terrible Turk."

811]   *Pen-driver*   One who drives a pen, a writer (*OED* cites this line).

824]   *Deshoulières*   Antoinette du Ligier de la Garde Deshoulières (1638-94), who was known especially for her pastoral poetry (see l. 838), published in the *Mercury* and thus left her chair at that journal vacant for Malcrais, one of whose nicknames was "*la moderne Deshoulières.*" Her poetry was much admired by Voltaire.

830]   *blade*   synecdoche for *oar*, B shifting the flight image to that of a boat race.

831]   *Sappho* Another of Malcrais's nicknames was "*la Sapho bretonne.*"

833]   *well a-foot, advanced the game*   A pun on *game*, as in a favorite expression of Sherlock Holmes, "the game's afoot." Cf. "Before the game is afoot thou still let'st slip" (*I Henry IV*, 1.3.278) and "The game's afoot!" (*Henry V*, 3.1.32).

834-47]   *More. . . . rapture*   According to Grandpré, "*Bientôt il ne fut plus question dans Paris que des poésies de mademoiselle Malcrais, sans cesse des épîtres galantes lui arrivaient par la voie du* Mercure, *les petits vers, les couplets pleuvaient de toutes parts, et les épithètes de nouvelle Deshoulières, de Sapho moderne, de dixième muse, d'ornement du Parnasse français n'étaient point épargnées. L'on formerait un volume des vers adressés à mademoiselle Malcrais ou publiés à sa louange.*" ("Soon the poems of Mademoiselle Malcrais were the talk of all Paris, flirtatious letters constantly arrived for her in care of the *Mercury*, little verses and couplets rained down from all directions, and in them she was called by such epithets as the new Deshoulières, the modern Sappho, the tenth muse, and the jewel of the French Parnassus. The poems addressed to Mademoiselle Malcrais were collected in a volume published in her honor.")

842]   *Noodledom*   The world of noodles, stupid or silly persons (*OED* cites this line). Cf. "Bishop Blougram's Apology," 426 (this edition, 5.308).

853]   *pride shall have a fall*   Cf. "Pride goeth before destruction, and a haughty spirit before a fall" (Prov. 16:18).

854]   *aroints*   In Shakespeare, an imperative verb meaning *begone*. "Used by Mr. and Mrs. Browning as a vb: To drive away with an execration" (*OED*, which cites this line).

855]   *cross-buttock*   To throw an opponent over the hip in wrestling (*OED* cites this line). Cf. *The Ring and the Book* (4.756; this edition, 7.207 and n.).

857-58]   *epistle . . . prose*   Voltaire's epic poem, *La Henriade* (1728), and his *Histoire de Charles XII* (1731). The epistle is dated 15 August 1732.

859]   *suit and service*   Attendance at court and personal service due from a tenant to his feudal lord. Cf. Herbert's "He that forbears / To suit and serve his need, / Deserves his load" ("The Collar," ll. 30-32).

865-86]   *Oh . . . pleasure*   B translates the part of Voltaire's verse epistle (the beginning and the end, ll. 1-11, 69-79) transcribed by Grandpré:

Toi dont la voix brillante a volé sur nos rives,
Toi qui tiens dans Paris nos muses attentives,
　　　Qui sait si bien associer,
　　　Et la science et l'art de plaire,
　　　Et les talens de Deshoulière
　　　Et les études de Dacier,

J'ose envoyer aux pieds de ta muse divine
Quelques faibles écrits, enfan[t]s de mon repos:
Charles fut seulement l'objet de mes travaux,
     Henri quatre fut mon héros,
     Et tu seras mon héroïne.

. . . .

Il est donc vrai, grand Dieu! il ne faut plus que j'aime.
La foule des beaux-arts, dont je veux tour à tour
     Remplir le vide de moi-même,
N'est point encore assez pour remplacer l'amour.
Je fais ce que je puis, hélas! pour être sage,
     Pour amuser ma liberté;
     Mais si quelque jeune beauté,
     Empruntant ta vivacité,
     Me parlait ton charmant langage,
Je rentrerais bientôt dans ma captivité.

870] *Dacier* Anne Lefèvre Dacier (1654?-1720), classical scholar who translated Homer, Sappho, Aristophanes, and Plautus.

871] *Weak . . . crabs* B's translation echoes Byron's *Hours of Idleness*, the poems of which are described in the preface as "the fruits of the lighter hours." *Crabs* are the fruit of the wild apple tree.

886] *Reach* Hold out, give.

887] *wash-hand basin* A basin for washing the hands, but because of the "stomach-moving tribute," apparently to be used for another purpose (*OED* cites this line).

891-92] *Fathers of Trévoux . . . Dictionary* A dictionary compiled by the Jesuits of Trévoux between 1704 and 1771. Grandpré writes that *"Les révérens pères de Trévoux eux-mêmes se crurent obligés de lui payer leur tribut d'éloges. . ."* and then he quotes the entry: "'*Mlle Malcrais de la Vigne du Croisic est auteur de plusieurs belles pièces de vers'* (Dictionnaire de Trévoux, *au mot* Auteur.)." ("The reverend fathers of Trévoux deemed themselvers obliged to pay tribute to her with a eulogy . . . Mademoiselle Malcrais de la Vigne from Le Croisic is the author of several beautiful pieces of verse [*Dictionary of Trévoux*, under *Author*].")

895] *Jean Baptiste Rousseau* Lyric poet (1670-1741), who lived in Brussels in exile from 1712 and who later feuded with Voltaire. Not to be confused with Jean Jacques Rousseau.

897-904] *At . . . loose* Grandpré writes that *"La Roque trouva les vers charman[t]s, et leur accorda sans difficulté une place dans le* Mercure; *bien plus, il se prit d'une belle passion pour la muse bretonne, et entama avec elle un commerce de galanterie épistolaire. L'on prétend même que dans un moment d'abandon, il s'émancipa jusqu'à lui écrire: 'Je vous aime, ma chère Bretonne; pardonnez cet aveu, mais le mot est lâché.'"* ("La Roque found the verses charming and easily made a place for them in the *Mercury*; furthermore, he was overcome with a beautiful passion for the Breton muse and began to exchange with her flirtatious letters. In a moment of abandon, he allowed himself to write to her: 'I love you, my dear Breton; pardon the confession, but the word has been spoken.'")

899]   *hilt and heft*   Tautological, both words referring to the handle of a sword. *Heft* is a variant of *haft* (*OED* cites this line).

901]   *reft*   Took away forcibly.

905-12]   *He's . . . Donne*   B is quoting ll. 338-40 of John Donne's "Metempsychosis" ("The Progresse of the Soul"):

'Tis greatest now, and to destruction
Nearest; There's no pause at perfection.
Greatnesse a period hath, but hath no station.

Donne's "-ion" is two syllables.

913-1000]   The conversation between Paul and his sister in stanzas CXV-CXXV is B's invention. Grandpré says only, *"En voulant jouir de son triomphe, Desforges gâta tout."*

914]   *dexter*   Heraldic term for *right*, continuing the mock heroic language of *gules* and *vert* (ll. 165-66) and *suit and service* (l. 859).

927]   *famine at Fame's feast*   Cf. Edward Young's "Poor in abundance, famish'd at a feast" (*Night Thoughts*, Night 7. 44).

934-36]   *He . . . so*   Paul has confused the legend of Hercules with an episode in Virgil's *Aeneid*. In his last labor Hercules throttles Cerberus, the three-headed dog of Hades, and drags him back to earth. In Book 6 of *The Aeneid* the sibyl calms Cerberus with a sop of honey and drugged meal, allowing Aeneas to pass. This is the passage Dante has in mind when, in Canto 6 of *The Inferno*, Virgil forces dirt down the dog's throat. "A sop to Cerberus" has become proverbial.

941-42]   *Phoebus . . . Diana*   Phoebus Apollo and Diana were brother and sister (and both archers), thus substituting here for Paul and his sister.

949]   *earnest into sport*   Cf. Plautus's "If anything is spoken in jest, it is not fair to turn it to earnest (*Amphitruo* 3.2.39). See also the last line of Chaucer's "Miller's Prologue": "And eek men shal nat maken ernest of game." Variations of the expression appear in at least five other poems by B.

966-67]   *Phoebé . . . Python*   A reference to ll. 941-42, Phoebé being another name for Diana. Phoebus Apollo killed the monstrous python of Parnassus with an arrow, thus earning the nickname *Pythian*.

973] *Rousseau's* Jean Baptiste rather than Jean Jacques. Grandpré says that Jean Baptiste composed this quatrain for Desforges-Maillard's portrait:

> Si sous un nom d'emprunt autrefois si charmant,
> Maillard brilla sur le Parnasse,
> Aujourd'hui sous le sien, encor plus dignement,
> Il sait y conserver sa place.

("If at one time under an assumed name so charming Maillard shone on Parnassus, now under his own name, yet more worthy, he knows how to maintain his position.")

For his part, Desforges-Maillard wrote an epitaph for Rousseau, whom he calls in the subtitle "*le plus grand poète lyrique depuis Pindare et Horace*" ("the greatest lyric poet since Pindar and Horace").

977-79] *Somebody . . . natural* Unidentified. A *natural* is a simpleton, a dim-wit.

984] *quack* Talk pretentiously and ignorantly, like a quack.

1008] *Idalian* From Idalium (now Dali), a town in Venus's birthplace of Cyprus, where there was a well-known temple dedicated to the goddess.

1009-1104] *Soon . . . cash* In describing Desforges-Maillard's meeting with La Roque and Voltaire, B elaborates on Grandpré's account:

> *Il se rendit à Paris et se découvrit d'abord à M. de la Roque. Fort surpris de la métamorphose, La Roque eut cependant le bon esprit d'en rire, et se promit aussitôt d'en tirer parti, pour faire pièce à Voltaire qu'il n'aimait pas. Il se chargea donc volontiers d'introduire M. Desforges auprès de son adorateur; il se rendit avec lui chez Voltaire, et fit annoncer mademoiselle Malcrais de la Vigne.* Le grand homme *se fit attendre un moment, il était à sa toilette et prenait soin de se parer, afin de paraître avec plus d'avantage devant la belle Bretonne. Enfin la porte s'ouvrit, et Voltaire entra; mais, lorsque, au lieu de la* muse divine *dont son imagination avait tracé le portrait, il n'aperçut qu'un petit homme fort laid, et d'assez mince apparence, il devint furieux, et sortit brusquement pour ne plus reparaître. Jamais il ne pardonna à La Roque cette mystification.*

("He traveled to Paris and revealed himself first to Monsieur de la Roque. Very surprised by the metamorphosis, La Roque nevertheless had the good humor to laugh about it and promised also to help play a prank on Voltaire, whom he did not like. He voluntarily took it upon himself, then, to bring Monsieur Desforges together with his admirer; he went with him to Voltaire's house and had Mademoiselle Malcrais de la Vigne announced. *The great man* caused a brief delay; he was at this toilet and took pains to prepare himself so as to show himself to best advantage to the beautiful Breton. Finally the door opened and Voltaire entered, but when instead of the *divine muse* whose portrait his imagination had painted he perceived a little man, quite ugly and unprepossessing, he grew furious and brusquely left, never to reappear. Never did he forgive La Roque for the deception.")

1010]   *tic-toc*   Variant of *tick-tock*, the sound of a double knock (*OED* cites this line).

1014]   *brock*   A badger.

1016]   *inched out*   Eked out by inches or small amounts (*OED* cites this line).

1034]   *yield the pas*   From the French *céder le pas*, to give the right of going first.

1039-40]   *Comic sock / For tragic buskin*   The low shoe worn by actors in Greek comedy and the high boot worn by those in tragedy, thus changing from the tragic attitude to the comic one.

1041-43]   *wren-like . . . eagle*   One of the smallest and one of the largest of birds. Cf. "An eagle's the game her pride prefers, / Though she snaps at a wren instead!" ("A Light Woman," ll. 15-16; this edition, 5.258).

1043]   *acquist*   Acquisition (obsolete).

1062]   *haut-de-chausses*   Knee breeches, attire for a man, as opposed to the petticoats of the previous line.

1076]   *killing*   Overpoweringly beautiful or attractive.

1079]   *pomatum*   Pomade, a scented ointment for skin or hair.

1081]   *barbered ten times o'er*   "[Antony] Being barbered ten times o'er, goes to the feast" (*Antony and Cleopatra*, 2.2.224).

1089]   *fierce*   Inflame (obsolete as a verb).

1091]   *carte-and-tierce*   Practice between fencers who thrust and parry in the carte (or "quart") and tierce positions alternately. Figuratively, not real combat.

1120]   *unicorn*   The unicorn was the only animal feared by the lion.

1122-24]   *In . . . Macchiavelli*   The quotation has not been found in any of Machiavelli's writings, but similar ideas appear in his works and those of classical writers, Seneca's *De Ira*, for example: "Fear always recoils upon those who inspire it" (2.11.3).

1135]   *knocking-under*   Acknowledging defeat, knuckling under.

1149]   *House of Fame*   The temple of fame (see l. 647). In Chaucer's "The House of Fame" the poet dreams of visiting such a house, adorned with statues of famous historians and poets.

1152]   *chaps*   Fellows, formerly contemptuously, as here. Also jaws, a pun suggested by the context.

1161]   *Bergerac*   Grandpré makes no mention of this town in southwestern France. B probably meant Brederac, the country house of the Maillard family, and thus Paul's "rude heritage" (see note to l. 786). B repeats the error in l. 1176 and l. 1184.

1165]   *angle*   Ingle-nook.

1173]   *this badger, and that fox*   Paul calls La Roque a brock (badger) in l. 1014. Voltaire would be the fox.

1175]   *Fiddlepin's end*   Not listed in the *OED*, but as two words a *fiddle pin* is the tuning-peg of a fiddle. The meaning of the phrase seems to be the same as *fiddlestick's end*, which B originally wrote in the manuscript and which is defined by the *OED* as *nonsense, fiddle-de-dee*. The phrase also appears in *The Ring and the Book*, 2.229 (this edition, 7.66).

   quack, quack, quack   See l. 984.

1191-92]   *After . . . alive*   A translation of two lines from Jean Baptiste Rousseau's *Épigrammes XXII*: "*Après sa morte il crut vivre, / Et mourut dès son vivant*." Grandpré used the lines as an epigraph for his chapter on René Gentilhomme. Sarianna omitted them in her transcript, but B added them at the end of it.

1197-98]   *rat who belled / The cat*   From a fable first appearing in the twelfth century and retold by Langland in ll. 146-81 of the prologue to *Piers Plowman*. In the story rats propose putting a bell around the cat's neck to warn them of danger, but none is brave enough to do so. To bell the cat is thus a brave and daring deed. Cf. B's "Too Late," ll. 75-76 (this edition, 6.216 and n.).

1202]   *Piron's "Métromanie"*   Alexis Piron (1689-1773) wrote about the episode in *La Métromanie ou le Poète*, first performed in 1738. Voltaire referred to the play as *La Piromanie*.

1204]   *Demoiselle No-end-of-names-behind*   The name in Piron's play is Mériadec de Kersic de Quimper Corentin.

1208]   *see his epitaph*   Piron proposed as his own epitaph "Ci-gît Piron, qui ne fut rien, pas même académicien" ("Here lies Piron, who was nothing, not even an academician"). Piron had been refused membership in the French Academy when his enemies resurrected an obscene poem written in his youth, titled "Ode to Priapus."

1209-16]   *But . . . alone*   The gold image of this stanza is like that of the gold ring in *The Ring and the Book*. Truth and fancy refer back to fact and fancy in stanza XXIV, and *sparkle* in the last line leads into the poem's primary image of the log fire, reintroduced in the next stanza.

1223]   *chowse*   Variant of *chouse*, to dupe, cheat, trick (colloquial).

1225]   *Agamemnons*   An allusion to Horace, *Odes*, 4.9.25-28:

vixere forte ante Agamemnona
multi; sed omnes illacrimabiles
urgentur ignotique longa
nocte, carent quia vate sacro.

("Many heroes lived before Agamemnon, but they are all unmourned and consigned to oblivion because they had no bard to sing their praises.")

1226]   *later bards*   Many of B's contemporaries, Matthew Arnold among them, argued for historical subjects in poetry partly on the basis that the modern age had few suitable heroes.

1230]   *First-rate*   The largest of British warships, in contrast to the "slight bark" in the preceding line.

1232]   *Beddoes*   Thomas Lovell Beddoes (1803-49), physician and poet, committed suicide in 1849, disappointed by fortune. B inherited his papers in 1872.

1245]   *acquist*   See note to l. 1043.

1248]   *slave-sorrows to his chariot linked*   Amulets hung beneath the triumpher's chariot in a Roman triumph as antidotes to the envious eye of fortune. See lines 139-51 of B's "'Imperante Augusto Natus Est—'" where the "instrument of shame" attached to the chariot is a cross (in *Asolando* [1889], this edition, volume 17).

1264]   *glad*   Beautiful

1267]   *vivid*   Vigorous and lively (*OED* cites this line).

1267-68]   *horse . . . thunder*   Cf. Job 39:19: "Hast thou given the horse strength? Hast thou clothed his neck with thunder?"

1274]   *save my breath for better purpose*   Possibly an allusion to the proverbial "Save your breath to cool your porridge."

1275]   *blink*   A gleam of light from the fire.

EPILOGUE TO *THE TWO POETS OF CROISIC*

Date and Composition]   The manuscript is dated 15 January 1878, five and a half weeks after the completion date of "The Two Poets of Croisic." The eighteen six-line stanzas occupy four and a half pages of the manuscript (pp. 71-75) and have far fewer corrections than "The Two Poets," only about twenty in the total of 108 lines. B made some twenty-five changes, mainly in punctuation, for the 1878 edition. There are only two textual variants in the 1878 and 1889a editions, one in punctuation and one in capitalization. In the manuscript B titled the poem "Eunomos of Locri," after the lyre player in his source, but he struck through this title and published the poem untitled in both the 1878 and 1889a editions.

Source]   The poem is based on a story attributed to Paulus Silentiarius in *The Greek Anthology* (Book 6, Item 54; a slightly different version by an anonymous author appears in Book 9, Item 584). W. R. Paton's translation in the *Loeb Classical Library* is as follows:

To Lycorean Apollo doth Locrian Eunomus dedicate the brazen cicada, in memory of his contest for the crown. The contest was in lyre-playing, and opposite him stood his competitor, Parthis. But when the Locrian shell rang to the stroke of the plectrum, the string cracked with a hoarse cry. But before the running melody could go lame, a cicada lighted on the lyre chirping tenderly and caught up the vanishing note of the chord, adapting to the fashion of our playing its wild music that used to echo in the woods. Therefore, divine Son of Leto, doth he honour thee with the gift of thy cicada, perching the brazen songster upon thy lyre.

(Book 6, #54 of *The Greek Anthology*, trans. W. R. Paton, *The Loeb Classical Library* [London and New York, 1920]: 1:327).

J. G. Winter in "Browning's Epilogue to 'The Two Poets of Croisic,'" (*Modern Language Notes* 24 [1909]: 210-14) gives a full account of the source and argues that EBB introduced it to B. The theme of poetic fame links the epilogue to both "La Saisiaz" and "The Two Poets of Croisic."

65]   *Lotte's power*   Charlotte or "Lotte" is adored by the hero in Goethe's tragic short novel, *Die Leiden des jungen Werthers* (*The Sorrows of Young Werther*) of 1774. She helps the "soul-development" of Werther, as B implies, although the young man's obsessive, self-indulgent love for the married Lotte is fatal.

104]   *casting pearls*   Cf. Matt. 7:6: "neither cast ye your pearls before swine."

DRAMATIC IDYLS, FIRST SERIES

Emendations to the Text

The following emendations have been made to the 1889a copy-text:

Pheidippides, ll. 61-63: The present l. 62 was inserted posthumously in the 1895 Cambridge edition of B's works: *The Complete Poetic and Dramatic Works of Robert Browning*. B did not catch and correct the omitted line for either the 1882 or the 1888-89 editions, although the omission had been pointed out to him. In a letter to B the Reverend J. D. Williams observed that "you, or the printer owe us a line on p. 37, to rhyme with 'bar'" (T. J. Collins and W. J. Pickering, "Letters from Robert Browning to the Rev. J. D. Williams, 1874-1889," *Browning Institute Studies*, 4 [1976], 18). In a footnote, Collins and Pickering correctly remark that "Williams was mistaken in his line reference, for it is the following line that demanded a rhyming line—'Jutted, a stoppage of stone against me, blocking the way' (l. 59)." In a letter of 21 April, 1880, B informed Williams that "I really profit by your notice of the want of rhyme in 'Pheidippides' which somehow never struck me. I change the last line's 'too' into 'rare,'—and the matter is mended as well as the case admits,—now that the poem has stiffened in the mold" (17). Though the error Williams pointed out concerns the missing l. 62 in stanza 8, the mistake B actually corrected for the 1882 second edition, the correction he mentioned in his response to Williams, is an error in stanza 11, l. 88. Stanza 11 is also missing a line in the 1879 edition, but B noticed this omission and inserted l. 86 in the edition of 1882. The omission of a line in stanza 8 noticed by Reverend Williams was, however, not corrected in any edition during B's lifetime.

The line added to the Cambridge edition of 1895 scans well enough and certainly sounds like B, but all we know about its origin comes from DeVane: "after B's death line 62 was inserted in the text *according to his instructions*" (*Hbk.*, 433; emphasis added). DeVane's phrasing suggests that he either saw or had been told of some document with B's authority behind the line as added. We are unable to locate such evidence, but our editorial judgment is that it would improperly withhold information from the reader of this edition were we to omit l. 62. Since this emendation is not supported by our usual expectation of documentary evidence, we have enclosed the line in brackets. See also "Pheidippides," *Sources and Influences* below.

Halbert and Hob, l. 13: MS-1879 read *son lay curled*; 1882 erroneously dropped the first letter of *lay*, creating nonsense. The 1889a compositors compounded the error by setting the word as *aye*, a slightly different kind of nonsense. The MS-1879 reading *son lay curled* is restored.

Ivàn Ivànovitch, l. 168: The copy-text omits the third point of a three-point ellipsis; the MS-1882 reading is restored.

Ivàn Ivànovitch, l. 169: A necessary comma at the end of this line, present in MS-1882, is omitted in 1889a; the comma is restored.

Ivàn Ivànovitch, l. 227: The copy-text reads *Besides* where MS-1882 have *Beside*, though the 1889a reading is idiomatically acceptable, B's habit throughout his career was to use *beside* to mean "also" or "beyond that," and the change to *Besides* is probably a compositor's blunder. The MS-1882 reading is thus restored.

Ivàn Ivànovitch, l. 282: The copy-text lacks an accent over the first *a* in the word *Stàrosta*; the MS-1882 reading is restored.

Ivàn Ivànovitch, l. 349: In 1879 and 1882, a colon appears at the end of the line; 1889a has no punctuation. The 1879-1882 reading is restored.

Tray, l. 9: The copy-text lacks the first point of a three-point ellipsis, though a space for it remains; the MS-1882 punctuation is restored. 1889a also lacks necessary closing quotation marks at the end of the line; the MS-1882 punctuation is restored.

Ned Bratts, l. 134: The copy-text has no punctuation at the end of this line; the comma present in MS-1882 is restored.

Composition

B's manuscript for *Dramatic Idyls* reveals no composition dates, but B wrote at least two of the poems at the Splügen Pass in Switzerland in August 1878. Nearly four years later, on 11 March 1982, he informed Furnivall: "The story of 'Old Tod,' as told in Bunyan's 'Life & Death of Mr Badman,' was distinctly in my mind when I wrote 'Ned Bratts'—at the Splügen, without reference to what I had read when quite a boy. I wrote 'Ivan Ivanovitch' at the same place and altitude." (*Browning's Trumpeter: The Correspondence of Robert Browning and Frederick Furnivall, 1872-89*, ed. W. E. Peterson, [Washington D.C., 1979], 50). It seems probable that more than two of the idyls were written during this sojourn in Switzerland. Mrs. Sutherland Orr reveals that during this period, B was remarkably prolific: "He was preparing the first series of *Dramatic Idylls* [*sic*]; and several of these, including Iván Ivánovitch, were produced with such rapidity that Miss Browning refused to countenance a prolonged stay on the mountain, unless he worked at a more reasonable rate" (*Life*, 323).

The neatly-written manuscript has few major alterations. Most of B's changes involve wording, punctuation, or clarity and consistency in the use of quotation marks. He obviously wrote the idyls with decision and fluency. Very few alterations are "on-line" ones made when he was composing. Most of his changes involve the canceling a word, phrase, or short passage, and adding a new version above or below the line. The first edition of *Dramatic Idyls* appeared in 1879. Three years later, for the work's second edition, B made a few minor changes, and he did so again for the *Poetical Wortks* of 1888-89. A notable mistake that escaped his notice involves the missing line in "Pheidippides" (see *Emendations to the Text* above).

In a letter to Wilfred Meynell, published in an article in the *Athenaeum* on 4 January 1890, B discusses his choice of title:

> An idyl, as you know, is a succinct little story complete in itself; not necessarily concerning pastoral matters, by any means, though from the prevalency of such topics in the Idyls of Theocritus, such is the general notion. These of mine are called 'Dramatic' because the story is told by some actor in it, not by the poet himself. The subjects are somber enough, with the exception of the Greek one; and are all in rhymed verse; this last in a metre of my own." (Quoted in DeVane, *Hbk.*, 430.)

The word *dramatic* was a favorite with B, one that occurs with notable frequency in his titles. It does not necessarily mean that the stories involve vivid incidents and gripping adventures; B's letter to Meynell reveals that he used the term in a more technical sense to indicate the presence of a narrator. B's use of dramatic narrators in his idyls is, of course, part of his life-long custom of speaking through poetic characters. However, in his study of B's later poetry, Clyde de L. Ryals notes that "the poet did not accurately describe what he had accomplished" because only one of the idyls, "Ned Bratts," is told by a character in the story (*Browning's Later Poetry, 1871-1889* [Ithaca, NY, 1975], 168). Several other tales are told by narrators who are not actors in the idyl.

There is some evidence that B thought of his idyls as conforming to Greek models. In a letter of 15 March 1885 to Edmund Gosse, B picked "Clive" as one of the four or five poems that he would "not object to be judged by," specifying that "Clive" is idyllic "in the Greek sense" (Hood, 235-36). Since "Clive" is not idyllic in the pastoral sense, it appears that B permitted himself wide latitude in his definition of *idyl.* For him the term seems to be more evocative and suggestive than rigorously meaningful. The idea that he was capitalizing on the cachet given the term by Tennyson's *Idylls of the King* seems plausible.

Texts

At Balliol College, Oxford, the three manuscripts of *Dramatic Idyls, Dramatic Idyls: Second Series* and *Jocoseria* are bound together in brown morocco. The volume number is 391. On the front cover, stamped in gold, is the poet's family coat of arms.

The six poems of *Dramatic Idyls* were written on lined 8-inch by 10-inch paper. All pages, except for the first page which contains the title and the table of contents, are numbered, 1 through 51, in red ink in the upper right-hand corner. Each poem has a separate title page, and each poem is numbered, 1 through 6, in B's hand.

Centered in the top third of the first unnumbered page are the words "Dramatic Idyls. / by Robert Browning." Centered in the bottom two-thirds of the first page is the word "Contents," and underneath that is a list of the titles of the six dramatic idyls. This first page has an unusual feature: a horizontal fold, about of third of the way down the page, has been mended on the verso side with postage tape. In block letters on the tape is the word *POSTAGE* and on the tape there are indications of stamp perforations. This feature was described and interpreted by DeVane as follows: "The manuscript has the word 'Postage' written upon it, and bears also the signs of some rough usage. It is possible that Browning mailed the poems to Smith, Elder and Co. from Venice in November, 1878. But if this was the case it is not clear why the volume did not appear until 28 April 1879. Perhaps the package was mailed from somewhere in England during the first months of 1879. Perhaps the publishers, receiving the manuscript from Venice, thought that immediate publication of the volume would follow too closely upon *La Saisiaz,* which had appeared in May, 1878" (*Hbk.,* 428-29). In fact, the word *POSTAGE* is not written on the manuscript; it is printed on the tape, which appears to have the sole function of mending a fold, or perhaps a tear, in the paper. Whether or not B used the tape, there is no evidence that the manuscript was ever mailed. Nor apparently was it a victim of rough usage except for the first page.

The first edition of *Dramatic Idyls* was published by Smith, Elder, and Co. on 28 April 1879. The volume, 143 numbered pages, bound in yellow-brown cloth boards, sold for five shillings. For a full bibliographical description of the edition see Broughton, 20-21. In 1882 a second edition was printed by Smith, Elder and Co. This second edition is entitled *Dramatic Idyls, First Series* on the spine and title-page, because in 1880 *Dramatic Idyls: Second Series* had appeared. For the second edition, B made several corrections; *Dramatic Idyls, First Series* appeared in Volume 15 of the 1888-89 *Poetical Works,* and B made still further corrections for that edition.

Reception

Dramatic Idyls has given rise to a wide range of critical opinion. In his study of B, G. K. Chesterton refers to "Pheidippides" and "Ivàn Ivànovitch" as "masterpieces" (*Robert Browning* [New York, 1903], 127). At the other extreme, J. M. Cohen considers *Dramatic Idyls: First Series* together with *Dramatic Idyls: Second Series* and *Jocoseria* and pronounces that "the contents of these three books are on a lower level of inspiration than any other group of Browning's poems" (*Robert Browning* [London, 1952], 156). Contemporary reviewers also displayed a remarkable diversity of opinion; if they have anything in common, it may be in what they do not say, namely, that B's poetry is overly-intellectual, arcane, and obscure. That had been a prevailing note in B criticism ever since *Sordello,* and some of B's other volumes of the seventies, such as *Balaustion's Adventure* and *Aristophanes' Apology,* had not improved his reputation in this regard. Readers realized that, by employing the short narrative in *Dramatic Idyls,* B had returned to a more accessible, popular form.

In 1886, three years before B's death, Arthur Symonds published one of the first general overviews of B as a poet—*An Introduction to Study of Browning* ([London, 1886]). Symonds finds that the controlling theme of *Dramatic Idyls* is the "idea of a turning-point or testing-time in the lives of men" which is "more or less expressed or implied in very much of Mr. Browning's poetry, but nowhere is it expressed so completely, so concisely, so consecutively, as here"(185). To this conception of the book's thematic unity many other critics have assented. Symonds also discerns a wholly new preoccupation in the idyls:

> "His idyls are short poems of passionate action, presenting in the most graphic and concentrated way a single episode or tragic crisis. Not only by their concreteness and popular effectiveness, their extraordinary vigour of conception and expression, are they distinguished from much of Mr. Browning's later writing: they

have in addition this significant novelty of interest, that here for the first time Mr. Browning has found subjects for his poetry among the poor, that here for the first time he has painted, with all his graphic realism, the human comedy of the lower classes" (184).

In the study of B's later poetry cited above, Clyde Ryals explores a more contemporary interest in the formal departures of *Dramatic Idyls* from B's earlier practice, arguing that the idyls are not dramatic monologues in the traditional Browning sense at all. Their exterior narrators and methods, and their strong emphasis on ethical content, says Ryals, fundamentally revise the indirect methods of the classic monologues of B's earlier work.

The idyl which has attracted more critical attention than any other—no doubt because of its sensational subject matter—is "Ivàn Ivànovitch." The numerous readers who have commented on the poem are in marked disagreement on the issue of the mother's guilt, and, indeed, about the question of whether or not there is an authorial endorsement of the Pope's verdict. Edward Dowden believes that B is outraged by the mother's actions. "It is the absence of human virtue which appalls him . . . . This it is which condemns to a swift, and what the poem represents as a just, abolishment from earth the mother who . . . has given her children to the wolves, and has thereby proved the complete nullity of her womanhood" (*Robert Browning* [London, 1904], 352-53). Tennyson, however, staunchly defended the mother: "I think the woman was right. The wolves would have eaten them all. She might have saved part by what she did" (*William Allingham: A Diary*, H. Allingham and D. Radford, eds. [London, 1907], 314). Modern critics are far less certain that one can judge the mother by a simple, dichotomous criterion, and they do not, for the most part, believe that B necessarily implies his approval of such a judgement. E. Warwick Slinn, for example, argues that B intentionally designed his poem to produce an effect of moral ambiguity: "I am not suggesting that Browning intends us to condemn Ivàn; nor am I suggesting that he intends to exonerate Loùscha. I am explaining what I regard as a deliberate enigma in the poem" ("The Judgement of Instinct in Ivàn Ivànovitch," *BSN* vol. 1, no. 1 [March, 1974]: 8). In *The Focusing Artifice* [Athens, OH, 1968], Roma King also stresses the enigmatic element in the poem:

The poem treats a moral paradox, emphasizing the complexity of good and evil and the irrationality of human conduct. The woman is damned by her violence; Ivàn is saved by his. The difference lies not in the acts themselves but in the motives that prompted them. Morality is subjective rather than external. Why the impulsive action of two people should proceed form such diverse motives and produce such different ends remains inscrutable" (221-22).

MARTIN RELPH

Sources and Influences]   In explaining the provenance of "Martin Relph" in a letter to Herbert Gilchrist, on 4 December 1885, B denied that any part of the poem had "historical foundation." But he admitted to Gilchrist:

> I read, perhaps fifty years ago, a little tale, in a publication of that time, in which was the incident of a woman being executed, after the military fashion, for some treasonable act, real or supposed, during the War of Independence in America,—her lover, furnished with a pardon, arriving just too late, and dying at the sound of the musketry. This incident I used, transferring it to England: all the part played by 'Martin Relph' is of my own fancying, and indeed constitutes the 'motive' of the poem: its only reason for existence (ABL).

The publication to which B refers has not been identified.

The incident appears to have been transferred to the mid-eighteenth century—to the time of the failed Jacobite rebellion of 1845-46. On the basis of internal evidence, it is difficult to specify an exact date for the events related in the poem, but several indications point to the rebellion of 1745. The British Captain speaks of a "quarrel that sets the land on fire, between King George and his foes" (l. 29). The King referred to is most probably George II, and his foes, Charles Edward Stuart and his supporters. The Mayor who detains Vincent Parkes does so because his name "sounds French" (l. 134). The French, of course, supported Bonnie Prince Charlie. However, placing the events of the poem in 1745 is problematic. The Young Pretender invaded England in November of 1745. His army, having penetrated England as far south as Derby, was ordered to retreat to the north, and by December the Jacobite forces were once again back in Scotland, where, in 1846, they were finally to be decisively defeated at Culloden. The events dramatized in B's poem take place in England and concern a rebel success in outwitting the king's army. On the occasion of Rosamund Page's execution, the Captain tells the assembled witnesses that the army marched in less than a month previously and that within a week of their arrival the rebels were in possession of vital intelligence (ll. 35-6). If the quarrel referred to by the Captain is the Jacobite rebellion of 1745-46, the successful spying incident must have occurred during the early days of the invasion, in November or December, when the rebels were still in England. But the events described in B's poem must take place in springtime: details in Rosamund's confiscated letter indicate spring, and Vincent Parkes is delayed in delivering his pardon partly because "the floods were out" (l. 126). Flooding is more probable in the spring than in November. Indeed, if we assume that Martin Relph makes his first-of-May public confession on the anniversary of the execution of Rosamund Page, her arrest and week-long detention occurred at the end of April. It is conceivable, though unlikely, that the events of the poem transpire in the spring of 1746, sometime before the battle of Culloden on 16 April. However, Culloden Moor is in the far north of Scotland, and in the spring 1746 most of the English army was in Scotland, not in England, where the poem is set.

Either B is mistaken about the season in which the Jacobites invaded England, or perhaps he is referring to another King George and to other foes. In 1715, during the reign of George I, there was another, smaller rebellion in support of the Old Jacobite Pretender, James Francis Stuart; however, the suppression of that insurrection also took place in November. The most plausible conclusion is that B transferred his story from the American War of Independence to the Jacobite Rebellion of 1745, and in the act of transference was less than rigorously accurate about exact dates.

The names of the characters are B's invention.

5] *Methuselah* The most long-lived of the Biblical patriarchs, he lived nine hundred and sixty-nine years (Gen. 6:25-27).

8] *Get you behind . . . used to be* An allusion to the Devil's temptation of Christ, who spurns the tempter with the words "Get thee behind me, Satan": see Luke 4:8 and Matt. 4:10. Christ also addresses this remark to Peter: see Matt. 16:23 and Mark 8:33.

12] *the cap which fits* The remark that is appropriate. If a cap fits, "the description or remark suits or is felt to suit (a particular person)" (*OED*).

14] *worm* "A grief or passion that preys stealthily on a man's heart or torments his conscience" (*OED*). See e.g., Chaucer's "The Physician's Tale," l. 280.

17] *first of May* May Day, an ancient holiday observed on the first day of May, celebrates the return of spring and fruitfulness. It has no traditional associations with remorse or confession of sins. Martin

Relph may make public confession then because it is the anniversary of Rosamund Page's execution.

29] *King George* See *Sources and Influences.*

46] *no nook we may call our own* The lodging of military troops in the homes of civilians was a common practice, and frequently a source of grievance.

49] *The murder, you see, was out* See Chaucer: "Mordre wol out, certeyn, it wol nat faille" ("The Prioress's Tale," 96); "Mordre wol out, that se we day by day" ("The Nun's Priest's Tale," 232). "Murder will out" became a proverbial expression. Here the Captain refers, not literally to murder, but to treason.

67] *in the noose* In view of the fact that Rosamund Page is shot, not hanged, this reference to the noose is either a mistake or a metaphor for any form of capital punishment.

91] *serpent's twine* The serpent that holds Relph rigid and prevents him from calling out is, apparently, the devil. Satan appeared in the form of a serpent when he tempted Eve Gen. 3:1-6.

92] *gibbet's rigid corpse* The bodies of hung criminals were often bound with chains and left hanging on the gibbet as an example to potential lawbreakers.

111] *Till death us do part* This phrase occurs in "The Form of Solemnization of Matrimony" from *The Book of Common Prayer.*

120] *lamb in the lions' den* The account of Daniel's being cast into the lion's den is given in Dan. 6.

140] *Judas the Damned* The disciple who betrayed Christ. In *The Inferno* Dante places Judas, along with Brutus and Cassius, in the lowest circle of hell, reserved for traitors to their lords, where they are punished by being devoured by Satan.

PHEIDIPPIDES

Sources and Influences] The Greek defeat of the Persian forces of Darius at Marathon (490 B.C.) is one of the climacterics of Greek history, and indeed of Western civilization. Under the generalship of Miltiades the greatly outnumbered Greek army won a surprising and decisive victory over their Persian adversaries at Marathon, a plain about twenty-five miles northeast of Athens. Both B and EBB were inspired to write poems about this battle. Robert used it as historical background for two of the Dramatic Idyls—"Pheidippides" and "Echetlos." At the age of fourteen Elizabeth produced a four-book epic entitled *Battle of Marathon.* One of the episodes in this work, written in heroic couplets in imitation of Pope's translations of Homer, deals with Pheidippides' encounter with the god Pan.

Accounts of the Pheidippides' role in the battle of Marathon are many. The first and most complete version is that of Herodotus:

And first, before they left the city [Athens], the generals sent off to Sparta a herald, one Pheidippides, who was by birth an Athenian, and by profession and practice a trained runner. This man, according to the account which he gave to the Athenians on his return, when he was near Mount Parthenium, above Tegea, fell in with the god Pan, who called him by his name, and bade him ask the Athenians "wherefore they neglected him so entirely, when he was kindly disposed towards them, and had often helped them in times past, and would do so again in time to come?" The Athenians, entirely believing in the truth of this report, as soon as their affairs were once more in good order, set up a temple to Pan under the Acropolis, and in return for the message which I have recorded, established in his honour yearly sacrifices and a torch-race.

On the occasion of which we speak, when Pheidippides was sent by the Athenian generals, and according to his own account, saw Pan on his journey, he reached Sparta on the very next day after quitting the city of Athens. Upon his arrival he went before the rulers, and said to them—

"Men of Lacedæmon, the Athenians beseech you to hasten to their aid, and not allow that state, which is the most ancient in all Greece, to be enslaved by the barbarians. Eretria, look you, is already carried away captive, and Greece weakened by the loss of no mean city."

Thus did Pheidippides deliver the message committed to him. And the Spartans wished to help the Athenians, but were unable to give them any present succour, as they did not like to break their established law. It was the ninth day of the first decade, and they could not march out of Sparta on the ninth, when the moon had not reached the full. So they waited for the full of the moon (*The History of Herodotus*, tr. George Rawlinson [New York, 1860], 6.105-6).

A shortened version of this story is also given by Pausanius, who alters the spelling of the runner's name to Philippides:

. . . when the Persians had landed in Attica Philippides was sent to carry the tidings to Lacedaemon. On his return he said that the

Lacedaemonians had postponed their departure, because it was their custom not to go out to fight before the moon was full. Philippides went on to say that near Mount Parthenius he had been met by Pan, who told him that he was friendly to the Athenians and would come to Marathon to fight for them.

(*Description of Greece,* tr. W. H. S. Jones [London, 1931], 1.28.4).

Neither Herodotus nor Pausanius speaks of a runner who died after reaching Athens and delivering to his fellow citizens news of their victory over the Persians at Marathon. This story appears in Plutarch's "Bellone an pace clariores fuerint Athenienses" where there is some doubt about the identity of the messenger:

Thersippus of Eroeadae brought the first news of the victory at Marathon, as Heraclides of Pontus relates. But most report that Eucles, running armed with his wounds reeking from the fight, and falling through the door into the first house he met, expired with only these words in his mouth, "God save ye, we are well" (*Plutarch's Essays and Miscellanies,* tr. R. Smith [Boston and New York, 1909], 5.403).

In his "A Slip of the Tongue in Salutation," Lucian gives Philippides credit for this exploit. Discussing the Greek salutation for "Joy," or "Rejoice," Lucian comments that "the modern use of the word dates back to Philippides the dispatch-runner. Bringing the news of Marathon, he found the archons seated, in suspense regarding the issue of the battle. 'Joy, we win!' he said, and died upon his message, breathing his last in the word Joy" (*The Works of Lucian of Samosata,* tr. H.W. Fowler and F.G. Fowler [Oxford, 1905], 1.36). B uses these dying words as the epigram for his poem.

A comprehensive and useful overview of the classical sources employed by B in his poem is provided by J. W. Cunliffe in his article "Browning and the Marathon Race" (*PMLA* 24 [1909]: 154-63). Cunliffe casts doubt on the historical authenticity of Pheidippides' race to Athens after the Greek victory at Marathon. Referring to Plutarch's citation of Heraclides of Pontus as one source for the story, Cunliffe observes that Heraclides "flourished about 150 years after Marathon, and . . . was notoriously inclined to myth; his works have almost entirely perished, and those now extant, so far as I have been able to discover, contain no reference to Marathon" (157).

Cunliffe also discusses a "mistake" which B made in geography. Herodotus asserts that Pheidippides met Pan on Mount Parthenium.

B, however, places the meeting at "Parnes ridge." Cunliffe argues that this location is "out of the way, as a glance at the map will show; no runner who knew his business, whether amateur or professional, would have left the straight road from Eleusis to Athens, close by the coast, to stray ten miles off into the hills." However, Cunliffe quotes a colleague, John McNaughton, who believes that B deliberately deviated from his source "because Parnes is in Attica, while Parthenium is in Arcadia. He [McNaughton] writes that Browning 'must have an Attic hill at all costs, when what he wants to say is that it is the spirit of her own mountains, her own autochthonous vigor, which is going to save Athens. He consciously sacrifices, in a small and obvious point, literal accuracy to the larger truth'" (159).

B did make two unequivocal mistakes in his composition of the poem—mistakes which he later rectified. B employs an eight line stanza with a complicated rhyme scheme: abcddcab. In the first edition, however, stanzas eight and eleven have only seven lines. DeVane plausibly argues that these omissions were caused by "Browning's inability to keep the complicated rhyme-scheme in mind as he wrote" (*Hbk.*, 433). For the second edition of 1882, B added a line to the eleventh stanza and made other alterations to make this stanza conform to the others. The line omission in the eighth stanza, however, was not detected and corrected until after the publication of the complete works of 1889-90. For a complete discussion of this issue, see *Emendations to the Text* above.

4]   *Zeus the Defender*   A common epithet for Zeus, the chief god in the Olympian pantheon.

Her of the ægis and spear   Athena, the daughter of Zeus, was the eponymous patroness of Athens. A warrior goddess, she is traditionally associated with an aegis, or shield, and spear.

5]   *ye of the bow and the buskin*   Artemis, the goddess of the hunt and of the moon, is traditionally associated with a bow and arrow, and with buskins, heavy leather boots.

8]   *Pan*   Half human and half goat, Pan is the god of woods, fields, and shepherds. E.B.B. was attracted to Pan as a subject of poetry. See her "The Dead Pan," "Flush or Faunus," and "A Musical Instrument."

9]   *Archons*   One of nine chief magistrates of Athens.

tettix   An "ornament worn in the hair by Athenians before Solon's time, as an emblem of their being aboriginal" (*OED*). Solon died c. 560 B.C. If the *OED* is correct, B's reference to the wearing of the tettix in the fifth century is anachronistic. (See also *Aristophanes' Apology*, 451n.; this edition 12.311.)

11]　*myrtle*　A shrub with tiny evergreen leaves. Greek heroes were honored with crowns of myrtle.

12]　*Sparta*　A Greek city-state in the Peloponnese. See *Sources and Influences.*

13]　*Persia*　An empire ruled, at the time of the action of this poem, by Darius I. Persian armies invaded Greece and were defeated at the battle of Marathon. See *Sources and Influences.*

15]　*two days, two nights*　Herodotus states that it took Pheidippides only one day to run the approximately one hundred and thirty-five miles from Athens to Sparta. In "Browning and the Marathon Race," Cunliffe argues that B's estimate of the time required is more probable (*PMLA* 24 [1909]: 161).

18]　*slaves'-tribute*　As a symbolic act, indicating their submission to Persian rule, Darius demanded that Greek city states offer him earth and water. Athens refused to give him this slaves' tribute. See Herodotus 6.48-49.

19]　*Eretria*　This city on the southern coast of Euboea was destroyed by the Persians.

20]　*Hellas*　The Greek word for Greece.

31]　*Thunder, thou Zeus*　Zeus is the god of thunder.

32]　*Phoibos and Artemis*　Phœbus Apollo was the Greek god of archery, prophecy and music. Artemis, his twin sister, was the goddess of chastity and of the hunt. She presided over childbirth and was associated with the moon.

33]　*Olumpos*　The Greek gods resided on Mount Olympus in Thessaly.

47]　*filleted victim*　The heads of animals sacrificed to the gods were adorned with fillets, or headbands.

　　fulsome libation　The Greeks poured out wine as an offering to the gods. A fulsome libation is a generous, or abundant, offering.

49]　*Oak and olive and bay*　Wreathes made from the leaves of these trees were used to crown heroes.

52]　*Parnes*　See *Sources and Influences.*

62]　*Erebos*　Erebus is a place of darkness in the underworld.

80]　*greaved-thigh*　Greaves are armor designed to cover the lower leg and sometimes the knee. Greaves that protect the thigh, though unusual, are not unknown. In *Greece and Rome at War* Peter Connolly writes that "although thigh guards are shown in sculptures, only one Greek example survives at Olympia. This is really just an extension of the greave and covers only the lower thigh. In art they are shown covering the middle of the thigh" ([Englewood Cliffs, NJ, 1981], 59).

83] *Fennel* The Greek word for Marathon means fennel-field. E. Berdoe observes in his *Browning Cyclopaedia* (2ⁿᵈ ed. [London, 1892], 337) that "when Pan gave the handful of fennel to the courier he gave him Μαραθρον—that is to say, the fennel field where the battle was to be."

89] *Miltiades* The general who led the Greek army at Marathon.

106] *Akropolis* The fortified citadel in Athens.

111] *Rejoice, we conquer* See *Sources and Influences*.

HALBERT AND HOB

Sources and Influences] In his *Nicomachaen Ethics* Aristotle attempts to show that "incontinence with respect to temper is less disgraceful than incontinence with respect to desires." This comparative mitigation of disgracefulness is explicable in part because "anger and harsh temper are more natural than desires." To illustrate his argument Aristotle provides two examples. The first is the case of "the man who defended himself for beating his father by saying 'he too beat his father, and his father beat his,' and, pointing to his child he said, 'and he will beat me when he becomes a man, for it runs in the family.'" The second case concerns a man "who, when being dragged out of the house by his son, ordered him to stop at the doorway, for he too dragged his own father as far as the doorway" (tr. Hippocrates G. Apostle [Grinnell, IA, 1975] 125-26). In "Halbert and Hob" B uses Aristotle's example of the man who drags his father only to the doorway, but he changes its moral. Instead of arguing that anger is excusable on the grounds of its "natural-ness," B states that only a "reason out of nature" (l. 66) can soften hard hearts. In Hob's abrupt change of heart and his subsequent mild behavior, B sees the operation of a supernatural agency. Thus B "corrects" Aristotle's naturalistic ethic by applying to the story the doctrine of Christian grace.

In his manuscript and in the first edition of 1879 B confused the names of father and son. In lines 45 and 52 the father refers to his son by using his own name, Halbert. This mistake was caught and corrected in the 1882 edition.

1] *whelped* Born.

2] *North England* Speculating about why B set the action of his poem in northern England, DeVane suggests that, among other possible reasons, B "needed a sparsely settled and backward country for his scene" (*Hbk.*, 437).

15] *Christmas night* B may set the action of his poem on Christmas night because it is a notable instance of supernatural intervention in the affairs of men. See *Sources and Influences*.

24]   *save the sexton . . . parish shell*   Save the church officer in charge of digging graves the cost of a coffin purchased with public money.

29]   *mammoth*   "Something huge of size" (*OED*).

34]   *eld*   Old man.

35]   *Trundle*   Roll.

59]   *new-yeaned.*   Newly born.

65]   *Is there . . . O Lear*   Referring to his daughters Goneril and Regan, King Lear asks, "Is there any cause in nature that makes these hard hearts?" (3.6.81-2). Lear implies that the answer to his rhetorical question is that such wickedness is unnatural. B implies that the softening of such hard hearts requires supernatural intervention. See *Sources and Influences.*

IVÀN IVÀNOVITCH

Sources and Influences]   The unusual, even sensational, subject matter of B's "Ivàn Ivànovitch" is no doubt in part responsible for the fact that it is one of the best known of his poems. He wrote it in 1878, in Switzerland, where he and his sister had paused on their way to Italy (See *Composition*). Mrs. Orr reports that, after arriving in Venice, B met a Russian lady whom he consulted "on the names he was introducing" in the poem (Orr, *Life*, 312). For details of setting and characterization, B must have drawn on his own personal experiences in and impressions of Russia. In 1834, when he was twenty-two, B accompanied the Chevalier de Benkhausen to St. Petersburg, serving in the capacity of secretary. His stay in Russia was brief, less than three months, but he retained vivid memories of the trip throughout his life (See Irvine and Honan, 42-44).

Mrs. Orr claims that "Ivàn Ivànovitch" is based upon "a popular Russian story, known as 'The Judgement of God'" (*Hbk.*, 311), but the Russian scholar M. Alekseev claims that the source is a French book published in Paris in 1845, F. Lacroix's *Les mystères de la Russie, Tableau politique et moral de l'empire russe* (Pagnere, Editeur). Lacroix's version of the story concerns only the devouring of the children by the wolves and contains no mention of the mother's punishment by Ivàn Ivànovitch. Though there is no direct evidence that B read Lacroix, the book was a popular success that was translated into several different languages, including Italian, and Alekseev believes that it is probable that B was aware of it ("Die Quellen zum Idyll 'Ivàn Ivànovitch' von Rob. Browning," *Jahrbuch für Kultur und Geschichte der Slaven* 9 [1933]: 417-27).

In his book Lacroix presents a far from flattering picture of Russia; the ignorance of the peasantry and the barbaric brutality of the governing classes are emphasized throughout. The story of the mother beset by wolves is related in a brief, summary fashion:

> On raconte qu'une femme russe revenant, avec ses trois enfants, d'un village voisin de sa demeure, au milieu de l'hiver et par un froid rigoureux, fut assaillie par des loups affamés. Pour échapper à la poursuite de ces redoutables animaux, elle excita la cheval attelé à son traîneau et chercha, mais vainement, à épouvanter les loups par ses cris. Le traîneau avançait rapidement sur la neige, mais la troupe acharnée ailait aussi vite, et la paysanne vit qu'il ne lui restait aucune chance de salut. En ce moment supréme, elle va sans doute, croyez-vous, placer ses enfants sur le traîneau, fouetter vigoureusement le coursier, dans l'espoir qu'il les ramènera tout seul au village, puis se livrer elle-mème , mère courageuse et devouée, à la voracité des loups? Pointé Ce sont ses enfants qu'elle abandonne.
>
> Elle en jette d'abord un, puis, cette proie n'ayant fait qu'aiguiser l'appétit des bêtes féroces, elle laisse tomber le second. Enfin, le troisième suit bientôt ses deux frères; et la mère triomphante rentre, saine et sauve, sous le toit conjugal (323-24)

(It is told that a Russian woman returning with her three children from a village far from home, in the middle of winter and through a harsh cold, was assailed by famished wolves. To escape these formidable animals, she urged on her horse, which was harnessed to a sleigh, and tried in vain to scare the wolves with her cries. The sleigh advanced quickly over the snow, but the fierce troop was going just as quickly, and the peasant woman saw that she had no chance for salvation. At this supreme moment she will as a matter of course, you may think, place her children on the sleigh, vigorously whip the steed in the hope that he will take them back to the village alone, and surrender herself, courageous and devoted mother, to the voracity of the wolves? Not at all. It is her children whom she abandons.

She first throws off one, then, this prey having only whetted the appetite of these ferocious beasts, she lets the second fall. Lastly, the third quickly follows his two brothers; and the triumphant mother returns, safe and sound, to the shelter of her conjugal roof.)

Lacroix's judgment of the unfortunate mother is as severe and moralistic as Ivan's: "Voilà ce que l'esclavage fait d'une femme, d'une mère. De pareils faits sont possibles partout où une cause puissante de per-version agit incessamment sur l'esprit et le moral d'un peuple" (324). (This is what slavery does to a woman, to a mother. Similar acts are possible anywhere a powerful, perverse cause acts incessantly on the spirit and morals of a people.)

The source which B almost certainly used—one which includes an account of the mother's punishment—is a book published anonymously in England in 1855, *An Englishwoman in Russia*. The unknown authoress spent ten years in Russia, and her book is an anecdotal account of the customs and manners of the Russian people. Without ever naming him, she appears to have been aware of Lacroix and to have read his book, but her assessments are somewhat less harsh than Lacroix's: "I trust that I have done full justice to all the amiable and *social* excellences of the Russians. Of their other qualities I beg the reader to form his own judgment. 'Une nation de barbares polis,' said a French gentleman, in speaking of them; but one cannot deny that they possess the *good* qualities of savages, as well as their *bad* ones" ("Preface" [New York, 1970], viii). Her account, which is more detailed than Lacroix's, describes a peasant woman with her three children driving a sledge through the forest:

A dreadful anecdote was told me of a peasant woman and her children, who were crossing the forest that stretched for many miles between her isba and the neighboring village. They were in one of those small country sledges, in shape something like a boat, drawn by a single horse. Suddenly they heard a rustling sound among the trees; it was but faint at first, but it rapidly approached; the instinct of the affrighted steed told him that danger was near at hand, he rushed on with redoubled speed. Presently the short yelp of a wolf aroused the mother; she started up and gazed around; to her terror she beheld a mighty pack of wolves sweeping across the frozen snow, in full cry upon their traces. She seized the whip, and endeavoured by repeated blows to urge on the fear-stricken horse to even greater swiftness. The poor animal needed no incentive to hasten his steps, but his force was well-nigh spent; his convulsive gasping showed how painfully his utmost energies were exerted. "But courage! There is hope! The village is in sight! Far off it is true, but we shall gain it yet!" So thought the unhappy mother as she cast a look of horror on the hungry savage beasts that were following in the rear, and saw that they were rapidly gaining upon her. Now they are near enough for her to see their open mouths and hanging tongues, their fiery eyes and bristling hair, as they rush on with unrelenting speed, turning neither to the right nor to the left, but steadily pursuing their horrible chace [*sic.*]. At last they came near enough for their eager breathing to be heard, and the foremost was within a few yards of the sledge; the overspent horse flagged in his speed; all hope seemed lost, when the wretched woman, frantic with despair, caught up one of her three children and threw him into the midst of the pack, trusting by this means to gain a little time by which the others might be saved. He was devoured in an instant; and the famished wolves, whose appetite it had only served to whet, again rushed after the retreating family. The second and the third infant were sacrificed in the same dreadful manner; but now the village was gained. A peasant came out of an isba, at the sight of whom the wolves fell back. The almost insensible women threw herself out of the sledge, and, when she could find sufficient strength to speak, she related the fearful danger in which she had been, and the horrible means she had employed to escape from it.

"And did you *throw them all* to the wolves, even the little baby you held in your arms?" exclaimed the horror-stricken peasant.

"Yes, all!" was the reply.

The words had scarcely escaped from the white lips of the miserable mother, when the man laid her dead at his feet with a single blow of the axe with which he was cleaving wood when she arrived. He was arrested for the murder, and the case was decided by the Emperor, *who pardoned* him, wisely making allowance for his agitation and the sudden impulse with which horror and indignation at the unnatural act had inspired him (164-5).

B's poem significantly differs from this source. First, B's Russian narrator characterizes his story as a traditional children's tale which is "possibly quite as true" (l. 16) as the story of Adam and Eve. Furthermore, it would be a simplification to assert that B's mother throws her children to the wolves. She says of her first child that perhaps her "hands relaxed their grasp, got tangled in the wraps" (l. 148). Of the second child, Terentiï, she says, "No fear, this time, your mother flings . . . / Flings? I flung? Never!" (ll.168-9). The defensive tone of her self-questioning suggests that perhaps she did fling her first child; however, it is only by dent of "ripping, tooth and claw" (l. 184) through her crossed arms that the wolf manages to snatch Terentiï. The third child is surrendered to the wolf only after the mother's strenuous efforts to save him. Finally, in the original there is only one judgment on the issue of Ivan's guilt: the Emperor declares that the mother's executioner is innocent. By having the Pomeschik and the Pope arrive at diametrically different conclusions about Ivan, the secular authority concluding that he is guilty and the religious authority pronouncing him to be innocent, B introduces a note of moral ambiguity into his idyl.

Another version of B's wolf story is told by Willa Cather in her novel *My Ántonia*. Two of her characters, Pavel and Peter, are Russian immigrants who find work as farm hands in Nebraska. As young men in Russia, they travel to a neighboring village to attend a wedding, after which they drive the bride and groom home in a sledge. Pavel and Peter are in the lead; five more sledges follow them. Wolves attack and, one by one, eat all of the occupants in the rear sledges. In order to delay the wolves, Pavel pushes the bride and groom out of the sledge and, in the nick of time, he and Peter reach the safety of their own village. Their deed becomes well-known, and everyone considers it to be so heinous that the two men are expelled from their village ([Boston, 1977], 38-40).

1] *quoth I* As in "Martin Relph" B employs a first person character in a framing narration. This character may or may not be B.

Russ Russian.

11] *tale told children, time out of mind* DeVane reports that B believed the source of his story to be a folk tale. This belief is, apparently, an error. See *Sources and Influences*.

14] *Peter's time* Peter the Great, tsar of Russia from 1682-1725.

15] *Germanized, Frenchified* The narrator's friend, the Russ, is obviously a Slavophile. It was precisely Peter the Great who opened up Russia to Western influences. There was a heated debate in Peter's time between the Slavophiles, who wished to isolate Russia from European influences, and the Westernizers.

19] *verst* A Russian measure of distance; approximately one third of a mile.

28] *Neva's mouth* The Neva is a navigable Russian river that empties into the Gulf of Finland.

38] *billets* Thick pieces of firewood.

44] *sledge* A vehicle with runners, a sleigh.

53] *Droug* A Russian word for *friend.*

55] *motherkin* Little mother.

72] *Loukèria, Loùscha!* Loùscha is the diminutive form of the name Loukèria.

100] *chirrup* "To make a sharp thin sound (by suction) with the lips compressed by way of encouragement or greeting (to a horse, an infant, etc.)" (*OED*).

101]   *glib*   Smooth.

133]   *Satan-faced*   The idea that a wolf is the instrument of Satan, or even Satan in disguise, was a widespread folk belief.

137]   *Stiòpka*   The diminutive form of the name Stepàn.

156]   *brats*   A derogatory term for a child. "In the 16th and 17th c. sometimes used without contempt, though nearly always implying insignificance" (*OED*).

166]   *Teriòscha*   The diminutive form of the name Terentiì.

181]   *Pope*   A priest of the Russian Orthodox church.

189-91]   *bad Màrpha . . . sisterhood*   The idea that wolves could transform themselves into werewolves and witches was a common superstition.

282]   *Starosta*   The head man of a village.

   style   Title.

284]   *Pomeschik*   Pomeshchiks were "holders of grants of land on which they paid no taxes, but for which they were required to perform service, usually military in nature . . . [;] late in the seventeenth century, the influence of the pomeshchiks reached such heights that the term 'pomeshchick' was generally used to designate a noble landowner" (Basil Dmytryshyn, *A History of Russia* [Englewood Cliffs, NJ, 1977], 218-19).

286]   *thorpe's*   A thorpe is a village.

317-19]   *Your young men . . . dream dreams*   "your sons and your daughters shall prophesy, your old men shall dream dreams, your young men shall see visions" Joel 2:28. See also Acts 2:17.

324]   *Shall the dead praise thee*   "Wilt thou show wonders to the dead? Shall the dead arise and praise thee?" Ps. 88:10.

324-25]   *The whole . . . thy glory*   "Holy, holy, holy is the Lord of hosts: the whole earth is full of his glory," Isa. 6:3. See also, e.g., Ps. 57:5 and 11; Ps. 72:19; Ps. 108:5; Isa. 6:3; Ezek. 43:2.

333]   *complexed*   Made complex, complicated.

343]   *discrowned*   Deprived of a crown.

359]   *trow*   Believe.

380-81]   *Moses . . . twain-tables*   "And I made an ark of shittim wood, and hewed two tables of stone like unto the first, and went up into the mount, having the two tables in mine hand. And he wrote on the tables, according to the first writing, the ten commandments, which the Lord spake unto you in the mount out of the midst of fire in the day of the assembly: and the Lord gave them unto me," Deut. 10:3-4.

412]   *Kremlin*   A citadel in Moscow, the center of the Russian government.

421]   *Kolokol*   A large Kremlin bell.

TRAY

Sources and Influences] Though "Tray" is the shortest and arguably the slightest of the six idyls, B expresses in this poem two of his most serious convictions: his hatred of vivisection and his rejection of materialism. Throughout his life B was an enthusiastic lover of and advocate for animals. Mrs. Orr relates that in his youth B "kept owls and monkeys, magpies and hedgehogs, an eagle, and even a couple of large snakes" (*Life*, 27). In addition to these undomesticated creatures, there were also dogs in the Browning household, one of whom, B tells us in "Development" (l. 11), was named Tray. In poems such as "The Lady and the Painter" and "Donald" B reprehends cruelty to animals, the most extreme form of which is vivisection, a practice which horrified him and of which he was a committed, life-long opponent. He was a Vice-President of the Victoria Street Society, an anti-vivisection group. One of the founders of this organization, Frances Power Cobbe, wrote an autobiography in which she details her involvement with the anti-vivisection movement in England. In this book Cobbe includes a letter written by B in which he forcefully condemns a practice that he considered to be cruel and barbaric: "I would rather submit to the worst of the deaths, so far as pain goes, than have a single dog or cat tortured on the pretense of sparing me a twinge or two" (quoted in *Life of Frances Power Cobbe* [Boston and New York, 1894], 345). In *Browning's Message to His Time* Edward Berdoe devotes a chapter to B's opposition to vivisection and provides a further example of his willingness to support measures against it. In 1889 Berdoe had asked him to become a patron of a hospital "intended for the treatment of patients on principles which exclude vivisection." In his reply B writes that he would be "delighted if the association of my name with those of the patrons of the proposed scheme for an Anti-Vivisection Hospital be of the least service in so holy a cause" ([London, 1906], 176). And in a poem written after "Tray" he again explicitly addresses the issue of vivisection. One of the speakers in "Arcades Ambo," from *Asolondo,* is a cruel, censorious character who blandly proclaims that he "would have no end of brutes/ Cut up alive to guess what suits/ My case and saves my toe from shoots" (ll. 12-4).

The bystander whose remarks conclude "Tray" is a person who, in supposing that soul is a secretion, adopts an extreme materialist position. B means for his reader to understand that the bystander's attitude is self-evidently preposterous. The issue of the validity or invalidity of materialistic conceptions of the soul is one which drew considerable attention in 1877. In the summer of that year the positivist philosopher

Frederic Harrison published in *The Nineteenth Century* two articles on "The Soul and Future Life" ([June, 1877]: 623-36, and [July, 1877]: 832-42). Harrison argues against the notion that the soul is a distinct entity which is separate from the body and which lives on after the death of the body, but at the same time he argues against the doctrine of materialism which seeks to explain all of man's capacities and activities in reductive, physiological terms. The September and October issues of *The Nineteenth Century* printed retorts to Harrison's articles—retorts, largely critical, that were written by nine different authors, among them Professor Thomas Huxley, Lord Selborne, W. R. Greg, and Rev. Baldwin Brown. The series concluded with a final essay by Harrison in which he restates without modification his original position.

It is almost certain that B read these articles. In *La Saisiaz*, published in 1878, he refers to "a certain fence-play,—strife/ Sundry minds of mark engaged in 'On the Soul and Future Life'" (ll. 163-4; this edition, 14.105). These lines seem clearly to refer to the essays in *The Nineteenth Century*. In "The Source and Meaning of Browning's *Tray*," C. R. Tracy argues that certain passages in Harrison's original essay "state exactly the position Browning took in 'Tray,' and suggested it to him. Even the notion of illustrating it from the soul of a dog came from Harrison's articles" (*PMLA* 55 [1940]: 616). If the concept of suggestion implies that the articles were so critically instrumental in the conception and composition of the poem that it would not have been written without their influence, then to assert such a causal relationship is to conjecture. There is no direct evidence to show when, or under what conditions, B wrote the poem. It is certain, however, that B was opposed to materialism long before Harrison attacked it. Still, B in all probability read not only Harrison's original essays but also the numerous rejoinders which they provoked, and it is safe to assert that the entire series was on B's mind when he wrote "Tray."

In his poem B contrasts three kinds of poets. The first is a "medievalizer" employing obscure, archaic diction. Contemporary examples of poetry written in a style that seemed to B to be an affectation are Tennyson's *Idylls of the King*, Morris' *The Defense of Guinevere, and Other Poems* and *Sigurd the Volsung*, and numerous poems by Dante Gabriel Rossetti. Indeed, even the deliberately antique effects contrived by Edmund Spenser are conceivably relevant, although one need not stray from B's own period to discover numerous examples of poetry in the manner of "Bard the first." Byron is the obvious real incarnation of the fictional "Bard the second." The parody here seems specifically to refer to *Manfred*. Byron's Satanic hero is restrained from leaping from the Jungfrau mountain in the Alps by a passing chamois hunter. Byron was a poet admired by B from youth, as well as satirized. *Fifine at the Fair* employs Byronic forms, themes, and characters. Instead of fake histrionics, the third Bard provides a tale of unassuming, contemporary—albeit canine—heroism.

     Mrs. Orr writes that the poem is based on an actual incident witnessed in Paris by "a friend of Mr. Browning's" (*Hbk.*, 313).

2]   *Bard the first*   See *Sources and Influences.*

4]   *helm and eke his habergeon*   Helmet and also his jacket of scale armor.

6]   *sin-scathed brow*   Mark of Cain.

     Bard the second   See *Sources and Influences.*

32]   *prime*   First-rate.

38]   *prerogatived*   Endowed with a prerogative.

NED BRATTS

Sources and Influences]   In "Ned Bratts" B pays homage to John Bunyan, an author he deeply admired. The poet takes his tale from Bunyan and alters its setting to include Bunyan as a character. The original exemplum is in the latter's *The Life and Death of Mr. Badman,* his own sequel in 1680 to *The Pilgrim's Progress* which had appeared two years earlier. In "Author to the Reader" in the sequel, Bunyan discusses the relationship between the two works: "As I was considering with my self, what I had written concerning the Progress of the Pilgrim from this World to Glory; and how it had been acceptable to many in this Nation: It came again into my mind to write, as then, of him that was going to Heaven, so now, of the Life and Death of the Ungodly, and of their travel from this world to Hell" (ed. J. Forrest and R. Sharrock [Oxford, 1988], 1). The book is in the form of a dialogue in which Mr. Wiseman tells the tale of Old Tod, the original of Ned Bratts. The story itself is as follows:

> At a Summer Assizes holden at *Hartfort,* while the Judge was sitting upon the Bench, comes this old *Tod* into the Court, cloathed in a green suit, with his Leathern Girdle in his hand, his Bosom open, and all on a dung sweat, as if he had run for his Life; and being come in, he spake aloud as follows: **My lord,* said he, *Here is the varyest Rogue that breaths upon the face of the earth. I have been a thief from a Child: When I was but a little one, I gave my self to rob Orchards, and to do other such like wicked things, and I have continued a*

thief ever since. My Lord, there has not been a Robbery committed thus many years within so many miles of this place, but I have either been at it, or privy to it.

The Judge thought the fellow was mad, but after some conference with some of the Justices, they agreed to Indict him; and so they did of several felonious Actions; to all which he heartily confessed Guilty, and so was hanged with his Wife at the same time (23).

Mr. Wiseman explains that this story of old Tod is relevant to Mr. Badman because, just as the former began a life of vice by stealing, so did the former. Both cases are intended to exemplify the moral that a life begun in sin, ends in sin.

B remembered reading this story as a boy, and decades later on his Swiss journey in 1878 he wrote the incident without consulting his source. Probably he had already thought of "Ned Bratts" before leaving for the Alps since in a letter to Mrs. Thomas FitzGerald, dated 3 August 1878, from his London residence, he remarks that there had been "no complete Bunyan found among your books or your goodness would have apprised me" (*Learned Lady*, ed. E. C. McAleer [Cambridge, 1966], 52-3). He no doubt wanted the complete works of Bunyan so that he could reread not only *The Life and Death of Mr. Badman*, but also *The Pilgrim's Progress*, which also plays a significant part in B's idyl. *The Browning Collections* lists a Bunyan volume, *Works, being Several Discourses on Various Divine Subjects*, which B inscribed with his name and the date Nov. 6, '78 (*Reconstruction*, A529). He probably acquired this book after returning from his vacation so that he could consult Bunyan's works. The many parallels drawn between Ned's career and similar incidents in *The Pilgrim's Progress* demonstrate an accurate knowledge of Bunyan's allegory. B had remarkable powers of retention, and perhaps he correctly remembered all of these incidents, but it seems likely that he availed himself of the opportunity to check his work against Bunyan's originals before submitting his idyl to the printers.

B not only changes the name of old Tod to Ned Bratts, but he also alters the locale of Ned's self-incriminating confession from Hartford to Bedford, the town where Bunyan was imprisoned. This change is made so that B might introduce Bunyan as a character and make him the instrument of Ned's abrupt conversion to Christianity. However, B was misinformed about the date of publication of *The Pilgrim's Progress*. The idyl is set in 1672, twelve years after the restoration of Charles II (see ll. 315-16). The Book which Bunyan's daughter gives to Ned's wife Tab (see ll. 188-89) is *The Pilgrim's Progress*; however, it was not published until 1678. What was B's source for biographical information about Bunyan? DeVane suggests that he may have relied upon Southey's biography (*Hbk.*, 443-44); however, this work, *The Pilgrim's Progress with a life of John Bunyan by Robert Southey*, published in 1830, is not listed in *The Browning Collections*. A book which is listed there is Bunyan's *The Pilgrim's Progress, with Explanatory Notes by T. Scott, and a Life of the Author by J. Condor*, published in 1845 (*Reconstruction*, A528). If B read either of these books he would not have gotten correct information about the publication date of *The Pilgrim's Progress*. Both Southey and Condor believed that there were no existing copies of the first edition of Bunyan's allegory. After they wrote their biographical sketches, copies of the first edition of 1678 were discovered. For an account of the establishment of correct publication date, see John Brown's *John Bunyan: His Life, Times and Work* (London, 1885), 453-54.

B's rendering of Ned Bratt's experience is much longer and far more complex than Bunyan's exemplum about old Tod. Whatever the "moral" of B's idyl may be, it is not the simple, straightforward one which Mr. Wiseman draws in Bunyan's allegory, namely, that a life begun in sin will end in sin. The jocular tone which B adopts suggests that he is far from recommending the behavior of a convert to Christianity who insures against the temptation of a relapse by requesting that he be executed. For a perceptive analysis of Ned's misunderstanding of Bunyan's book see Roy. E. Gridley's "'Ned Bratts': A Commentary" (*BSN* vol. 6, no. 1 [March 1976]: 10-16).

For the 1882 edition of *Dramatic Idyls: First Series* B increased the length of "Ned Bratts" by two lines—325 and 326. For the collected works of 1889 he dropped the footnote to line 180 (see 180n.).

1] *Bedford* The municipal borough of Bedfordshire, where Bunyan was a member of the Baptist church and where he was imprisoned.

Special Assize A trial, usually presided over by visiting judges acting "under certain special commissions"(*OED*).

4] *flat* A tract of farmland.

5] *bibbing* Drinking.

12] *tag-rag and bobtail* "A contemptuous term for a number of persons of various sorts and conditions, all and sundry, esp. of the lower classes" (*OED*).

a-bowsing Drinking.

13] *Quality* People of good social position.

15] *Chief Justice Jukes . . . Brother Small* Fictional names.

18] *forbye* Besides.

32] *frizzles* Curls on a wig.

33] *fleered* To *fleer* is "to smile or grin contemptuously" (*OED*).

35] *puritans . . . prayer* Bunyan, a Nonconformist, was intermittently imprisoned from 1661 to 1672, and again from December 1676 to June 1677. Nonconformists were actively persecuted after the Restoration of Charles II in 1660. The offense for which Bunyan was originally imprisoned was preaching. He refused to promise that, if released, he would cease preaching Nonconformist doctrines.

36] *laid by the heels* "put in irons or the stocks" (*OED*).

38] *slit of the nose* An ancient form of legal enforcement going back to tenth century Danish law in Ireland.

42] *spirituous* Reeking of alcohol.
　　musk Odor.
　　mesh Network.

43] *Entoiled* Entrapped, ensnared.
　　Serjeant "A member of the superior order of barristers (abolished in 1880) from which, until 1873, the Common Law judges were always chosen" (*OED*).

53] *muck-sweat* Profuse sweat.

64] *javelineers* "One of a body of men in the retinue of a sheriff who carried spears or pikes . . . and escorted the judges at the assizes" (*OED*). B's is the only recorded use of the word.

67] *tithesman* B's coinage. A man who pays tithes to his church.

78] *quean* An impudent woman, a hussy.

79] *noggin* A small mug of liquor.

82] *midden* Refuse-heap.

83] *billet* A thick piece of firewood.

86] *baulked a d——* Perhaps this cryptic phrase means "I baulked at using a stronger word than *lily-livered*, namely *damned*, to refer to the knaves."

92] *Od's curse* God's curse.

96] *danced . . . no floor* Was hanged.

97] *houghed* Hamstrung.

98] *scripture-trees called bays* "I have seen the wicked in great power, and spreading himself like a green bay tree": Ps. 37:35.

100] *Zounds* God's wounds.

102] *Book* Bunyan's *The Pilgrim's Progress*. There are two parts of *The Pilgrim's Progress*. The first part, published in 1678, concerns the journey of Christian from this world to heaven. The second part, published in 1684, concerns a similar journey taken by Christian's wife, Christiana, and their children. Ned has, or course, read only the first part.

104] *'Sdeath* God's death.

106] *to keep my whistle wet* To have a drink.

108] *strawy* Light, worthless.

112] *I'll be bail* I can guarantee you.

114] *Gammer* B uses the popular working-class term for a woman, as he does with "Gaffer" in line 119 for an old man.

    crab Crab-apple.

117] *Bagman* Commercial traveler.

    fuddling-cap Drinking cap.

119] *Gaffer* Title for an old man.

124] *knobstick* A stick or club with a rounded head.

126] *pad on my prate-apace* Trudge along my chatterbox.

129] *Tinker* A craftsman who mends household utensils.

    cage Jail.

130] *twelve years* Bunyan was first imprisoned in 1661, a year after the restoration of Charles II to the throne.

133] *tagged* Tipped at their ends with metal.

135] *His girl* One of Bunyan's daughters, Mary (b. 1650), was blind.

141] *Patmore* There is some uncertainty about where Bunyan was imprisoned. The traditional belief that he was incarcerated in the town jail that stood on the Bedford bridge has been put into question. Because Bunyan's offense was not committed in the borough of Bedford, it is probable that he was imprisoned in the county jail. In any case, Bunyan can not have spent the last days of his imprisonment in the Bedford town jail because it was destroyed by a flood in 1671. For a full account of this matter, see John Brown's *John Bunyan: His Life, Times and Work* (London, 1885), 160-62.

    turnkey Jailer.

144] *Lawks* Lord.

    troth Good faith.

156] *Dives* "The Latin word for 'rich (man),' occurring in the Vulgate, Luke 16; whence commonly taken as the proper name of the rich man in that parable; and used generically for 'rich man'" (*OED*). The parable in Luke 16:19-31 compares the fates of a beggar, Lazarus, who is carried by angels into Abraham's bosom, and a rich man, who dies and goes to hell. The parable is the subject of one of Bunyan's sermons, *A Few Sights from Hell or the Groans of a Damned Soul.*

156-57] *wain . . . of Charles* Charles's Wain is the constellation of stars known as Ursa Major. Ned has made the rich man of the Biblical story a contemporary. As such, he might live in the reign of Charles II, and he might even be a royal retainer in the train of Charles II. However, he could not be in a constellation. Ned imperfectly remembers Bunyan's language which, as he observes, is quite different from his own.

161] *marrow-bones* Knees.

165]   *Champed*   Pounded, mashed.

166]   *dreriment*   The *OED* defines "dreariment" as "dreary or dismal condition, or the expression of it." Spenser, who invented the word, spelled it "dreeriment." In the context of B's idyl, "dreriment" apparently refers to the dead bark which encases the living cells of a tree.

168]   *cleave the cloister*   To penetrate the enclosed place.

170]   *cumbers it the ground*   "Behold, these three years I come seeking fruit on this fig tree and find none: cut it down; why cumbereth it the ground?" (Luke 13:7).

171]   *sloughed about with scurf*   Covered with, or sheathed in, incrustations.

172]   *stag-horns*   "The bare upper branches of a tree" (*OED*). B's is the only recorded use of the word.

174]   *marle*   Soil. "*Burning marle*: used symbolically, after Milton, for the torments of Hell" (*OED*).

178]   *Tophet*   Hell.

179]   *Look unto me and be ye saved*   Isa. 45:22.

180]   *I strike . . . my rod*   The Lord speaks these words to Moses: "Behold, I will stand before thee there upon the rock in Horeb; and thou shalt smite the rock, and there shall come water out of it, that the people may drink" Exod. 17:6. See also Num. 20:11.

    outstreats   Flows. In the editions of 1879 and 1882, B footnotes this line as follows: "'They did not eat / His flesh, nor suck those oils which thence outstreat.' Donne's *Progress of the Soul*, line 344." The footnote was cut for 1888-89. The *OED* gives only two citations for the word *outstreat*—Donne's and B's. B was an enthusiastic admirer of Donne; he also quotes "The Progresse of the Soul" in "The Two Poets of Croisic," ll. 905-12 (this edition, 14.182).

181]   *Be your sins scarlet*   "Come now, and let us reason together, saith the Lord: though your sins be as scarlet, they shall be as white as snow; though they be red like crimson, they shall be as wool" Isa. 1:18.

195]   *slough*   An enclosing layer, or sheath.

201]   *just-lugged bear*   Just-baited. Bearbaiting was a spectator sport which involved setting dogs upon a tethered bear.

203-4]   *A burden . . . Christmas*   Christian carries a burden of sin upon his back. Ned mistakes Christian's name and seems to confuse Christian's burden with Father Christmas's sack.

204-5]   *Joseph's sack . . . was*   The sack which holds the cup belongs to Benjamin, not Joseph. Joseph has a silver cup put in his brother's sack in order to make it appear that Benjamin is a thief (Gen. 44). Since Benjamin is actually innocent, the point of Ned's comparison is that his sins, unlike Benjamin's, are real.

206] *chine* Spine.

207] *pitched me as I flung* "Threw pitch at me as black as the pitch I threw at her." Tab's defense against the accusation of adultery is that the pot should not call the kettle black.

211] *I must off, my burden* Christian loses his burden of sin at the foot of a cross, symbolizing that "there is no deliverance from the guilt and burden of sin, but by the death and blood of Christ" (Bunyan, 27)

213] *a mountain's sure to fall* Mount Sinai. Having strayed from the straight and narrow path to salvation, Christian arrives at the foot of a mountain. He is afraid to venture further "lest the Hill should fall on his head" (Bunyan, 20).

214] *Destruction* Christian lives in the City of Destruction. Because it will "sink lower than the grave, into a place that burns with fire and brimstone" he leaves the city and journeys toward heaven (Bunyan, 13).

215] *'scape the wrath in time* The Evangelist, who assists Christian with good advice, gives him a parchment roll on which is written *"Fly from the wrath to come"* (Bunyan, 12).

216] *wicket-gate* To reach the straight and narrow path to salvation, Christian must pass through a Wicket Gate. Compare Matt. 7:13: "Enter ye at the strait gate: for wide is the gate, and broad is the way, that leadeth to destruction, and many there be which go in thereat."

217] *Despond the slough* This swamp into which Christian falls is "the descent whither the scum and filth that attends conviction for sin doth continually run, and therefore is it called the Slough of Despond: for still as the sinner is awakened about his lost condition, there ariseth in his soul many fears, and doubts, and discouraging apprehensions" (Bunyan, 17).

218] *House Beautiful* No house in the first part of *The Pilgrim's Progress* is specifically referred to as the House Beautiful, but Christian in the House of the Interpreter is shown "a stately palace, beautiful to behold" that appears to be symbolic of heaven: a man of stout countenance who fights his way into it hears to his satisfaction that "Eternal Glory" lies within (Bunyan, 31-2). However, Ned may be referring to the House of the Lord of the Hill. The Lord of the Hill is Christ. The porter of the house explains to Christian "this house was built by the Lord of the Hill, and he built it for the relief and security of pilgrims" (Bunyan, 42). Christian spends time in this house and receives improving guidance from Prudence, Piety and Charity.

222] *enemy horned and winged* Christian fights and vanquishes the monster Apollyon: "he had wings like a dragon, feet like a bear, and out of his belly came fire and smoke, and his mouth was as the mouth of a lion" (Bunyan, 51). Compare Rev. 9:11: "And they had a king over them, which is the angel of the bottomless pit, whose name in the Hebrew tongue is Abaddon, but in the Greek tongue hath his name Apollyon."

227] *Hopeful* One of Christian's companions. Like Christian, he succeeds in entering the Celestial City.

   ding "To speak with wearying reiteration" (*OED*).

229] *thrid the windings* Make one's way through a meandering path.

231] *Master Faithful* One of Christian's companions. He meets a martyr's death in the town of Vanity.

   Delightful Mounts From the top of the House of the Lord of the Hill Christian is able to make out the Delectable Mountains—beautiful, fertile country close to the Gate of the Celestial City.

232] *Vanity Fair* A fair held in the town of Vanity. The fair features many snares and temptations. In Vanity Christian is imprisoned, and his companion Faithful is tortured and killed.

243] *nearest way to Heaven-gate* After Faithful is tortured and burned at the stake, a chariot appears and he is "carried up through the clouds, with sound of trumpet, the nearest way to the Celestial Gate" (Bunyan, 86).

   Odds my life God's my life. An oath.

246] *Master Worldly-Wiseman* He "prefers Morality before the Strait Gate," that is, he believes that he may be saved by good deeds alone (Bunyan, 20).

   Master Interpreter In the House of the Interpreter, the master of the house interprets for Christian various allegorical scenes. Ned makes the mistake of calling his judge by the name of one of the bad characters in *The Pilgrim's Progress*, but he immediately corrects himself.

263] *peach* Inform.

270] *Sackerson* In Shakespeare's *The Merry Wives of Windsor* (1.1.307) Slender refers to Sackerson, a bear used for baiting.

271] *Brawl* A dance.

273-74] *Iron Cage . . . Lost Man inside* In the House of the Interpreter Christian speaks with a man so far gone in sin that he is unable to repent. His iron cage symbolizes despair.

278] *old Mote House* A *mote-hill* is a variation of *moot-hill*, "a hill on which 'moots' or assemblies were held." To *moot* an issue is "to argue, to plead, to discuss, dispute, esp. in a law case" (*OED*). The court house in which Ned is tried is, apparently, on an eminence.

288] *I wis* I know.

289-90] *fox/ Convicting geese* Proverbial: A fox should not be on the jury at a goose's trial.

292] *Reynard's* Reynard is a fox.

  i' feggs Variation if *i'fegs*. By my faith.

303] *dog-days* Days of hot weather.

  Amicus Curiæ Friend of the court. A friend of the court is a person who advises the court, but is not involved in litigation. Ned is a friend of the court in the special sense that he incriminates himself.

310] *Freeholder* Landowner.

316] *Astræa Redux* Justice returned. Astræa is the goddess of justice. John Dryden celebrates the Restoration of Charles II in his famous poem *Astræa Redux*.

323] *jail-distemper* Illness induced by incarceration.

328] *Bunyan's Statue* A statue of Bunyan was presented to the town of Bedford in 1872. Sculpted by Sir J. Edgar Boehm, it stands in St. Peters Green.